14 33/7

N. A. DOBROLYUBOV

SELECTED
PHILOSOPHICAL
ESSAYS

N. A. DOBROLYUBOV

SELECTED PHILOSOPHICAL ESSAYS

TRANSLATED
BY
J. FINEBERG

FOREIGN LANGUAGES PUBLISHING HOUSE

Moscow 1948

The essays of N. A. Dobrolyubov in this volume have been selected from the latest, 1946, Russian two-volume edition of the *Selected Philosophical Essays of N. A. Dobrolyubov*, compiled by the Institute of Philosophy of the Academy of Sciences of the U.S.S.R. and published by State Publishers of Political Literature, Moscow.

The Publishers

Printed in the Union of Soviet Socialist Republics

CONTENTS

Page

THE PHILOSOPHICAL AND SOCIO-POLITICAL VIEWS
OF N. A. DOBROLYUBOV VII

A LETTER TO V. V. LAVRSKY *August 3 (15), 1856* . . 3

THE IMPORTANCE OF AUTHORITY IN EDUCATION
Reflections on Mr. Pirogov's *Problems of Life* 6

PROVINCIAL SKETCHES by M. E. Saltykov 30

A COMPARATIVE PHYSIOLOGICO-PSYCHOLOGICAL
VIEW ON THE BEGINNING AND END OF LIFE by
Prof. W. Bervi 62

THE ORGANIC DEVELOPMENT OF MAN IN CON-
NECTION WITH HIS MENTAL AND SPIRITUAL
ACTIVITIES 72

THE FIRST YEARS OF THE REIGN OF PETER THE
GREAT. *The History of the Reign of Peter the Great*
by N. Ustryalov 104

THE WORKS OF V. BELINSKY 172

WHAT IS OBLOMOVSHCHINA? *Oblomov,* A Novel by
I. A. Goncharov 174

REALM OF DARKNESS. The Works of A. Ostrovsky . . 218

CHENSKY'S COURTSHIP OR MATERIALISM AND IDE-
ALISM. THE INEVITABILITY OF IDEALISM IN
MATERIALISM by Y. Savich 373

CONTENTS

Page

WHEN WILL THE DAY COME? *On the Eve*, a novel by
I. S. Turgenev 388

GOOD INTENTIONS AND ACTION. *Tales and Short
Stories* by A. Pleshcheyev 439

FEATURES FOR THE CHARACTERIZATION OF THE
RUSSIAN COMMON PEOPLE. *Stories of the Life of
the Russian Common People by* Marco Vovchok . . . 463

A RAY OF LIGHT IN THE REALM OF DARKNESS.
The Thunderstorm. A drama in five acts by A. N. Ostrovsky 543

RUSSIAN CIVILIZATION AS CONCOCTED BY MR.
ZHEREBTSOV 1858 (*Essays*) 629

EXPLANATORY NOTES 637

NAME INDEX 647

THE PHILOSOPHICAL AND
SOCIO-POLITICAL VIEWS OF
N. A. DOBROLYUBOV

The life and work of Nikolai Alexandrovich Dobrolyubov constitute one of the most vivid and remarkable pages in the history of Russian culture and Russian philosophy.

Dobrolyubov's socio-political and literary activities deservedly won the high appreciation of the classics of Marxism.

Appraising the different trends of Russian public thought, Engels, in his well-known letter to E. Papritz, wrote:

"Although some schools were mostly distinguished for their revolutionary ardour rather than for their scientific researches, and although there was, and is today, some groping in different directions, on the other hand there was also critical thought and devoted search for pure theory worthy of a people from whose ranks Dobrolyubov and Chernyshevsky sprang. I am speaking not only of active revolutionary socialists, but also of the historical and critical school in Russian literature, which stands infinitely higher than all that official historical science produced in Germany and France."*

V. I. Lenin, in speaking of Dobrolyubov, emphasized that to all educated and thinking Russia was dear the memory of a writer "who passionately hated tyranny, and passionately looked forward to a people's uprising against the 'Turks at home,' *i.e.*, against the autocratic government."**

The Soviet people profoundly honour the memory of Dobrolyubov, the ardent fighter against the system of autocracy and serfdom, the true patriot who fought for the liberation of the peoples

---

* Marx and Engels, *Collected Works*, Russ. ed., Vol. XXVII. p. 389.
** Lenin, *Collected Works*, Eng. ed., Vol. IV, Book II, p. 73.

of Russia from social and national oppression, the great revolutionary thinker and democrat, a classic of Russian materialist philosophy and distinguished literary critic and publicist.

Dobrolyubov—eminent and versatile thinker, author of remarkable works on philosophy and sociology, aesthetics and literary criticism, ethics and pedagogics—was and remains the pride of the Russian people and of all the peoples of the U.S.S.R.

* * *

Nikolai Alexandrovich Dobrolyubov was born in Nizhni Novgorod in 1836, in the family of a priest. In 1848 he graduated from an ecclesiastical school and in 1853 from an ecclesiastical seminary. Already in his early years he betrayed extraordinary interest in history and literature, philosophy and the natural sciences. The ecclesiastical seminary could not satisfy his enquiring mind and his varied interests, and so he turned to books and magazines.

While at the seminary, Dobrolyubov's attention was particularly drawn to the magazines *Otechestvenniye Zapiski* and *Sovremennik* that were then published in Russia. It was in these magazines that he first became acquainted with the philosophical and political views of Herzen and Belinsky, which left indelible traces upon his mind and played an extremely important role in the moulding of his world outlook. In 1850 he read Herzen's "Letters on the Study of Nature," and was enraptured by them; somewhat later he studied the works of Belinsky, in particular his essays on Pushkin and his reviews of Russian literature. Dobrolyubov's diaries show that while, during his first years at the seminary, the Slavophile magazine *Moskvityanin* made a considerable impression upon him, towards the end of his studies at the seminary, the influence of Belinsky's essays had obliterated all traces of Slavophile illusions from his mind.

Already at that time Dobrolyubov began to hate the system of autocracy and serfdom, police tyranny and violence.

His first literary essays in the field of philosophy—the philosophical "assignments" on which he worked while at the ecclesiastical seminary, in particular, his "Reflections on the Resurrection of Bodies," evidently written in 1852—indicate that already in his early youth he was inclined towards materialism, shared the views of Bacon and Herzen on the role of experience in man's cognition of the outside world, and preferred materialism in philosophy and materialistic natural science to the religious world outlook.

In 1853 Dobrolyubov went to St. Petersburg, where he took up history and philology at the Central Pedagogical Institute. In this Institute he lived in the stifling atmosphere of official "science" and religio-scholastic ideology; but in spite of the trend that predominated at this Institute, it was during his stay there that he became a definitely moulded revolutionary democrat and materialist.

It was during these years that, in addition to studying the works of Belinsky and Herzen, he made a critical study of the theories of the French enlighteners and utopian socialists, the works of Hegel, of the Young Hegelians, Bruno Bauer and Strauss, and the materialist philosophy of Feuerbach. His study of philosophical and socio-political doctrines finally convinced him of the correctness of the materialist and democratic convictions of Belinsky and Herzen. In his letter to Lavrsky of August 3, 1856, he himself, in a roundabout way, names the thinkers, whose works helped him to formulate his own world outlook. "... I console myself with the hope," he wrote, "that you are strong in your beliefs, that your head has long been tightly closed to pernicious convictions, and that neither Strauss nor Bruno Bauer, nor Feuerbach himself, not to speak of a Herzen or Belinsky, can turn you from your path."

In the Pedagogical Institute there was formed around Dobrolyubov a students' philosophical and political circle, which, in 1855-56, issued an illegal magazine in manuscript form entitled *Slukhi*. In this circle Dobrolyubov played the leading role; at its meetings he criticized the feudal conditions that prevailed in Russia at that time and the rottenness of the tsarist regime which became most strikingly revealed during the Crimean War. In an article on the secret societies that existed in Russia in 1817-25, he referred with sympathy to the more revolutionary section of the "true sons of the fatherland," namely, the Decembrists headed by Pestel, and was critical of the moderate Decembrists who were afraid to draw the common soldiers and the people into the movement for emancipation.

Already in his first literary production, written while he was at the Central Pedagogical Institute ("The Russian Historical Novel," "A Few Biographical and Bibliographical Notes on Pushkin," "Some Comments on Didacticism in Stories and Novels," etc.) Dobrolyubov showed that he possessed uncommon talent as a publicist, a critical mind in which democratic convictions were taking shape. It was at this time that he also wrote a number of poems of a political character which were circulated secretly. In the poem "Thoughts beside Olenin's Coffin," which he wrote in 1855, he calls upon the best people of Russia to enter the fight against tsarism:

> ... Rise then Rūs, for deeds of glory—
> For the struggle great and holy!...
> Seize your sacred rights
> From those infamous knights
> Whose symbol is the knout....
> She will go!... She will rise,
> By holy consciousness inspired,
> And all the world will gaze enthralled
> At freedom's banner of glory.

In 1856, a year before he graduated from the Pedagogical Institute, Dobrolyubov met Chernyshevsky, whose articles in *Sovremennik* had already produced a profound impression upon him. From that time onwards he became Chernyshevsky's follower and colleague and a most active contributor to *Sovremennik*, organ of the revolutionary-democratic movement of the 1850's. In August 1856 *Sovremennik* published Dobrolyubov's first essay, "A Conversation With Lovers of Russian Literature," which at once attracted the attention of literary circles of that time.

After graduating from the Institute in 1857, Dobrolyubov took charge of the department of literary criticism of *Sovremennik* and, together with Chernyshevsky and Nekrasov, played a leading role on the magazine. For four years after that, scarcely an issue of *Sovremennik* appeared which did not contain essays and reviews by Dobrolyubov. Every one of these attracted the attention of the educated section of Russian society and exercised enormous influence upon the progressive strata of the Russian non-aristocrat intelligentsia. Many of Dobrolyubov's critical essays on literature— in particular "What Is Oblomovshchina?" "Realm of Darkness,"

"A Ray of Light in the Realm of Darkness," "When Will the Day Come?" "From Moscow to Leipzig," "Features for the Characterization of the Russian Common People," "The Organic Development of Man in Connection with His Mental and Spiritual Activities," "Russian Civilization as Concocted by Mr. Zherebtsov"— were valuable contributions to the treasury of Russian and world culture.

In 1859 *Sovremennik* began to publish a companion satirical magazine entitled *Svistok,* of which Dobrolyubov was in charge. This magazine played an important part in the struggle waged by revolutionary democracy against the ideologists of landlord and bourgeois liberalism who fawned upon tsarism.

In *Sovremennik*, Dobrolyubov, no less resolutely than Chernyshevsky, pursued a line towards a rupture with that section of the liberal elements who feared the approaching peasant revolution and were inclining towards a compromise with tsarism. Chernyshevsky and Dobrolyubov prevented Turgenev and his friends of the liberal trend (Kavelin, Druzhinin and Botkin) who were frightened by the growing revolutionary movement in Russia, from converting *Sovremennik* into an organ of moderate liberalism. Towards the end of the 1850's the magazine definitely became a militant organ of revolutionary democracy.

Using *Sovremennik* as his rostrum from which to address the whole of Russia, Dobrolyubov, to the end of his days, denounced the champions of serfdom and the liberals, propagated the ideas of revolutionary democracy and utopian socialism, disseminated among the Russian public the ideas of philosophical materialism and the "algebra of revolution," *i.e.,* dialectics, ideologically inspired the non-aristocrat democratic intelligentsia and prepared it for the people's democratic revolution, which, in Dobrolyubov's opinion, was to be brought about by the masses of the people themselves, and primarily by the peasantry.

Excessive toil, persecution by the censor, and material want sapped Dobrolyubov's health, and in 1860 he fell seriously ill. He went abroad to take a cure and stayed there for nearly a year, but he derived no benefit from it. In 1861 Nikolai Alexandrovich Dobrolyubov died at the early age of twenty-five.

It can be confidently asserted that not a single Russian or West-European thinker of the period before Marx produced, at so early an age, such first-class works as those that came from the pen of Dobrolyubov. Not one of them succeeded in so short a period in working out such a profound, integrated and many-sided world outlook as Dobrolyubov did during the four years of his literary activity.

Like Belinsky and Chernyshevsky, Dobrolyubov could not, under the conditions prevailing in tsarist Russia, expound his philosophical ideas and political convictions in the straight and open form in which West-European thinkers were able to do. It was no accident that Dobrolyubov chose the field of aesthetics and literary criticism as well as the fields of ethics and pedagogics. Through these channels he was able, in the censored press, to prop-agate his philosophical and socio-political views, the ideas of a revolutionary democratic transformation of society.

Dobrolyubov's philosophical and literary-critical talent was able to blossom forth thanks to the preceding development of Russian classical materialist philosophy.

Dobrolyubov was spared the necessity of traversing the painful road of philosophical and political exploration covered by Belin-sky and Herzen. In developing his philosophical and political doc-trine he took as his starting point the materialist and democratic convictions which he had already arrived at in his youth as a dis-ciple and follower of Belinsky, Herzen and Chernyshevsky.

Dobrolyubov conducted his activities in the spheres of philos-ophy and literary criticism in close collaboration with N. G. Cher-nyshevsky. With his characteristic modesty, he always admitted that in this intellectual collaboration, Chernyshevsky played the lead-ing role; Chernyshevsky, in his turn, laid stress on Dobrolyubov's extraordinary talent and on the enormous importance his work had for the Russian people. Shortly after Dobrolyubov's death Chernyshevsky wrote: "For two and a half months already, scarce-ly a day passes but what I weep. . . . I too am a useful man, but better that I had died than he. In him the Russian people have lost their best champion." "O, how he loved you, people! His words did not reach you, but when you become what he wanted you to be, you will learn how much this young genius, the best of your sons, did for you."

The works of Dobrolyubov served to educate the Russian rev-olutionary democrats of the latter half of the 19th century.

Dobrolyubov—the outstanding thinker, the passionate accuser of and fighter against the system of autocracy and serfdom, the champion of realism and democracy in literature and public life, and a true Russian patriot—will forever be cherished and remembered by the Russian people.

*   *   *

Dobrolyubov's theoretical work, all his activities as a publicist and literary critic, were prompted by the desire to prove the necessity of a democratic revolution in Russia and of rebuilding society on new, and as he thought, on socialist lines. The philosophical basis of his revolutionary-democratic views was provided by the materialist theory and the dialectical principle of universal development, which he propagated in the censored press from the beginning of his literary activities.

In order that the ideas of philosophical materialism and dialectics could capture the minds of progressive people in Russia and lead them to the struggle for the transformation of society, it was necessary to liberate the public mind from the influence of idealistic philosophical systems and the metaphysical method of thinking.

Dobrolyubov actively entered the ideological struggle that was being waged in his day.

He combated all the forms of idealism and mysticism that were then current in Russia from the standpoint of materialism. In saying that many philosophical systems had outlived their time and were meaningless, Dobrolyubov had in mind primarily those avowed idealists who "beginning with Plato, are up in arms... against realism and, although not yet understanding it properly, confuse its doctrine," and also against the eclectics who "insist on having dualism, who want to divide the world into *noumena* and *phenomena*, asserting that only pure ideas possess actual reality, while all phenomena, *i.e.*, all that is visible, is only the reflection of these higher ideas."[*]

Dobrolyubov also regarded the teleological conception of the world as obsolete and meaningless.

---

[*] N. A. Dobrolyubov, *Collected Works*, Vol. I, 206, (Russ. ed. as are all references to his *Collected Works*).

"It is high time," he wrote, "to abandon also the abstract ideas according to which life is said to be formed, in the same way as we have at last abandoned the teleological dreams which were so much in vogue at the time of the Schoolmen."[*]

He urged the necessity of freeing literature and life from the influence of the religious "allegories" which appeared at the time "when mankind, not yet conscious of its inner strength, was entirely under the influence of the external world and, influenced by an inexperienced imagination, saw some mysterious power in all things."[**]

In all his works of literary criticism he attacked mysticism in literature and philosophy and ridiculed the fruitless dreaming of the mystics and their isolation from real life.

Thus, in his review of Polonsky's poems (1859), he wrote concerning that poet:

"In all things he sees some special, mysterious meaning: to him, the world is inhabited by strange visions, which carry him far beyond the borders of reality. It cannot be denied that such a mood ... is very unfavourable and even perilous for the poet's success. This mood may easily pass into meaningless mysticism, or may dissipate itself in far-fetched comparisons and allegories."[***]

Dobrolyubov sharply criticized German idealism for its unsoundness and contempt for the study of nature. "All our efforts," he wrote, "to picture to ourselves an abstract spirit bereft of all material qualities, or positively to determine its nature, have always been, and always will be, absolutely fruitless."[****]

During the whole of his short life Dobrolyubov fought passionately against reactionary idealistic theories, being of the opinion that "the whole meaning of art and philosophy lies in rousing the slumbering forces of the people."

There are not two elements—the material and the spiritual—in the world, asserted Dobrolyubov. All that exists represents different states of the one moving and developing matter. Matter is

---

[*] N. A. Dobrolyubov, *Collected Works*, Vol. I, p. 206.
[**] Ibid., p. 207.
[***] N. A. Dobrolyubov, *Collected Works*, Vol. II, p. 489.
[****] *See* p. 79 of this volume.

eternal, it is neither created nor destroyed, it merely changes its form.

"Nothing disappears in substance," said Dobrolyubov; "only forms and personalities change."*

There are no forces in the world existing separately and apart from matter. Dobrolyubov regarded force as a fundamental quality of matter, a mode of motion inseparable from it. "In the material world," he wrote, "we do not know of a single object in which some force peculiar to it does not manifest itself. Similarly, we cannot conceive of force independent of matter. Force is a fundamental, inalienable quality of matter, and cannot exist separately. It cannot be communicated to matter, it can only be roused in it."**

Man, asserted Dobrolyubov, is a part of nature, the most perfect of its creatures, the highest stage of development achieved by the universe.

In arguing that the world is material, he entered into battle with the reactionary idealistic theories of his time.

In reviewing the book by Professor Wilhelm Bervi of the Kazan University, *A Comparative Physiologico-Psychological View on the Beginning and End of Life,* Dobrolyubov ridiculed the idealistic legend that the sciences must seek for a non-material element in nature.

"Mixing up the natural sciences with the moral sciences," he wrote, "Mr. Bervi imposes obligations on naturalists which have never entered anybody's head except that of a mediaeval alchemist. He wants physical research to pursue not a knowledge of the changes in and the actions of matter, but to search in matter for the spirit, for archeus, ether, vital force, in short, for anything, as long as this 'something' is not positive, material, but 'inaccessible to the senses.' "*** While it was natural that the existence of such elements should have been assumed in the Middle Ages, asserted Dobrolyubov, it is absolutely out of place in our age of the development of the natural sciences, when man has worked out and mastered a new method of cognition based on experience,

---

* N. A. Dobrolyubov, *Collected Works,* Vol. I, p. 343.
** N. A. Dobrolyubov, *Collected Works,* Vol. IV, p. 309.
*** See p. 65 of this volume.

when all theoretical deductions are based on factual knowledge and not on dreamy theories and hazy guessing.

In his review of Savich's book *The Inevitability of Idealism in Materialism*, Dobrolyubov shows that it is undignified for an educated man in our age to occupy himself with the question of the antagonism between the two opposite elements in the world and in man, because science has already provided sufficient proof that there are no such two elements. "Since the now commonly known truth became widespread, namely, that force is an inevitable quality of matter, and that matter exists for our minds only to the extent that some kind of force is revealed in it—since that time, we have been of the opinion that all these Ormuzds and Arimans were totally superfluous."*

The whole course of human life and the entire development of science has proved that there are no *a priori* truths. All the ideas that arise in man's mind are engendered by existing reality and are the reflection in man's mind of material objects which exist independently of man's mind and which affect his sense organs. All that the human mind has produced has been acquired by the experience of human life and taken from life.

While advocating the materialistic view that matter is primary and mind is secondary, Dobrolyubov was remote from the crude vulgar materialism which identified thought with matter and belittled the role and importance of ideas in the life of society.

"We regard as ridiculous and pitiful the ignorant claims of crude materialism which degrades the lofty mission of the spiritual side of man by arguing that a man's soul consists of some kind of very fine matter. The absurdity of this argument has been proved so long ago, and so irrefutably, they so thoroughly contradict the findings of the natural sciences, that at the present time only the most backward and ignorant can still withhold their contempt for this crudely materialistic argument. We do not wish to say that bodily activity is more important than spiritual, nor do we wish to present physical pleasure as our sole object in life."**

While, however, thought is non-material and non-substantial, it does not in the least mean that the thoughts, ideas and views of

---

* *See* p. 374 of this volume.
** *See* p. 74 of this volume.

men arose spontaneously of themselves, or that they were inspired by some mystical, supernatural power. The material for thought is taken exclusively from our knowledge of external material objects.

Dobrolyubov repudiated the idealistic assertion that thinking is possible without reality, that thoughts are possible without matter. "What, then," he asked, "constitutes the material for thought if not our knowledge of external objects? Is thought possible without an object? Would it not then be something inconceivable, devoid of all form and content? To urge the possibility of such an objectless and formless thought is positively like asserting that it is possible to make something out of nothing!. . ."*

The object of philosophical analysis, according to Dobrolyubov, is to find the material causes, the material elements of all the ideas and thoughts of men in order to transform these material elements in conformity with the demands of human nature and reason.

In his review of the work of the learned divine, the Archimandrite Gavriil (Kikodze) *The Foundations of Experimental Psychology*, Dobrolyubov ardently defended the materialist thesis that laws must be deduced from facts and that facts must not be adjusted to preconceived laws. He repudiated Gavriil's assertion that a non-material substance is the basis of thought, and that the brain cannot be regarded as the basis of sensation because its composition and form are too simple. Basing himself on the data of the science of physiology of his day, he showed that the human brain is of complex construction, and that it is precisely in the brain that changes take place which engender the process of consciousness and which reflect reality as a result of the influence external objects exercise upon the sense organs.

"In the organic kingdom," he wrote, "we know of nothing that has a more peculiar appearance, a more complex structure and, finally, a more remarkable chemical composition than the brain. . . . There is not a single organ in animals which comes anywhere near to the brain in fineness and complexity of its structure. . . . That the brain is closely connected with mental activity is proved to us

---

* N. A. Dobrolyubov, *Collected Works*, Vol. III, p. 241.

by very many impressive facts.... They are known to everybody who is in the least familiar with physiology."*

In his essay on "The Organic Development of Man in Connection with His Mental and Spiritual Activities," Dobrolyubov, summing up the data of the science of psychology of his day, drew the conclusion that "man does not develop conceptions within himself but obtains them from the outside world."**

Dobrolyubov tried to give not only a materialistic explanation of the process by which concepts are formed in the mind of an individual, but also a scientific interpretation of the entire history of human knowledge.

In his essay "Realm of Darkness," he showed that man's first act of consciousness is to distinguish himself from the other objects that exist in the world, he becomes conscious of the *difference* between himself and those other objects. Subsequently, in the course of his life and struggle against the forces of nature which oppose him, man enters into hostile relationships with the external, material objects and realizes that he is their *antithesis*. Then man begins to discover in the material world that surrounds him a "conflict," *a struggle of opposite forces*, and thus is formed the conception of the struggle between light and darkness, heat and cold, land and sea, etc. "Finally, man turns from the external world to himself, and gradually becomes conscious of a conflict between certain antagonistic impulses within his own nature. Unable as yet to grasp the idea of universal unity and harmony, he also assumes the existence within himself, as well as in nature, of different, mutually hostile principles.... Hence the conclusion that there are two hostile beings in man—one, the inner and higher, springing from the element of good, and the other external, coarse and dark, created by the power of evil."

Lately, said Dobrolyubov, science has presented the human organism, as well as all the phenomena of nature, as the *unity of opposite forces*, and has elevated "apparent contradictions to natural unity."

Dobrolyubov's utterances still contain many elements of anthropologism which seeks to reduce the antagonisms in

---

* N. A. Dobrolyubov, *Collected Works*, Vol. IV, pp. 309-11.
** *See* p. 94 of this volume.

society to the contradictions in human nature, in the human organism.

But here, too, the main point is that he proves that the world is material and that matter is primary in relation to mind.

Dobrolyubov also gave a materialistic answer to the second aspect of the fundamental philosophical question, by asserting that man is capable of knowing the surrounding world and of forming a correct conception of all the objects that exist in the world.

In opposition to the preachings of religion that the powers of human reason are limited, and to agnostic disbelief in the possibility of knowing the world, Dobrolyubov showed that man is capable of correctly knowing nature, and that human knowledge, notwithstanding its relative and transient character, to an increasing degree represents objective truths.

In his review of Kusakov's book *The Verity of Concepts, or the Authenticity of Human Knowledge*, Dobrolyubov refuted the author's agnosticism and asserted that with agnostics who doubt the reality of the objects around us, the reality of all that people have verified in life over and over again, it is impossible to argue with the aid of philosophical proofs.

"Indeed," he said, "what philosophical proof can I bring forward to show that my hand is my hand and not Mr. Kusakov's? How can this be proved to a man who does not believe? Whatever you say to him he will have only one answer: how can you prove it? And then will follow an endless discussion for the discovery of the beginning of all beginnings. ..."*

Dobrolyubov's criterion of the truth of human knowledge was that it should coincide with reality, and he believed that man's life provides sufficient confirmation of the correctness of our knowledge.

Dobrolyubov no less sharply rebuffed the mystics who asserted that truth is reached intuitively, independently of man's cognition of the material world. Thus, he ridiculed the philosophical researches of the writer Zherebtsov, who stood close to the Slavophiles, and who, in his *History of Russian Civilization*, asserted that the Russian people, because of their very nature, are capable

---

* N. A. Dobrolyubov, *Collected Works*, Vol. III, p. 361.

of correctly understanding reality directly, intuitively, without any learning, even without acquiring information about surrounding objects. Criticizing the idealistic theory which separates *thinking* from *knowing*, Dobrolyubov showed that the wider and the more comprehensive the people's knowledge about the objects of the material world, the more capable are they of correct logical thinking.

Hence, concluded Dobrolyubov, the Russian people must create such social conditions in Russia as will facilitate the dissemination of scientific knowledge and correct logical thinking. "National distinctions," he explained, "in general, depend most of all upon the historical circumstances of a nation's development. This can be said especially of purely intellectual development. All distinctions in this respect must be regarded as the result of civilization, and not its root cause."*

Truth, according to Dobrolyubov, is the living truth of reality, its meaning, its substance; man is capable of penetrating this substance of reality, of knowing its living truth.

Living truth, the true essence of the phenomena that surround man, can be reached if men take real facts as the point of departure for their judgments, without binding themselves beforehand with abstract theories and excogitated ideals.

The objective method of cognizing truth, the method based on experience, does not, however, preclude but, on the contrary, presupposes the possession by the researcher and the person active in the field of politics of a firm and definite system of views and convictions. But these views and convictions will facilitate the cognition of truth only if they are not thrust upon reality, but conform to it.

Dobrolyubov's philosophical materialism, like Chernyshevsky's materialism, was not free from anthropologism. Often he regarded man not as a social being, but merely as a biological organism.

This happened most often when he attacked the dualistic distinction between soul and body. In opposition to dualism, he urged the oneness of the physical and psychological processes, the oneness of "body" and "soul" in the human organism. According to Dobrolyubov, anthropology is the science that refutes the scholastic doctrine of the antagonism between soul and body. It regards

---

* N. A. Dobrolyubov, *Collected Works*, Vol. III, p. 242.

man as a single, indivisible organism, and reveals the inseparable connection that exists between physiological functions and spiritual acts.

"Anthropology," wrote Dobrolyubov, "has clearly proved to us, first of all, that all our efforts to picture to ourselves an abstract spirit bereft of all material qualities, or positively to determine its nature, have always been, and always will be, absolutely fruitless.... Modern science alone refuted the scholastic dualist conception of man and began to study him as a complete, undivided whole, corporal and spiritual, without attempting to separate the two. It discerned in the soul the force which permeates and inspires the whole of man's body."*

The principal condition for fruitful spiritual activity, according to Dobrolyubov, is the sound and proper development of the human organs, primarily the sense organs. But even while sharing the anthropological view of the nature of man, he, unlike Feuerbach, had a historical approach to man and his requirements.

He showed that the healthy development of the human organism, fruitful intellectual activity, will become possible only when man obtains the necessary social conditions for his development, and primarily, the opportunity to enjoy material wealth and the benefits of education, freedom from tyranny and the right to employ his strength and capabilities in any field of social life.

Thus, although Dobrolyubov utilized the "anthropological principle" in criticizing dualism and substantiating his democratic program, he did not confine himself to "anthropologism," but went beyond it.

In order that man may be able to reach truth and arrange his life and activities in conformity with his natural strivings, it is necessary to change the organization of social relationships—such was the deduction which Dobrolyubov drew from the materialistic views on man and nature.

True science, like true art, cannot stand aloof from the sufferings and needs of the people, asserted Dobrolyubov. The principles of this true, humanistic science are the antithesis of those of so-called "pure science," the object of which is to give pleasure to

---

* See pp. 79-80 of this volume.

the mind. He described the so-called "pure science" trend as the "gastronomic" trend, and considered it unworthy of respect.

In his review of Nikitin's poetry, he wrote:

"Man's disharmony with his whole environment has long been noted, and it has long been depicted in poetry. But formerly, the causes of this disharmony were sought either in the mysterious forces of nature, or in the dualistic structure of the human being; and poetry depicted external nature and man's psychological conflict accordingly. Today a simpler view is gaining ground in the public mind: attention is being turned to the distribution of the gifts of nature among men, to the organization of social relationships. All sciences are therefore working out a concept of society; poetry (in the broad sense of the term) also set about doing this long ago; the novel, a product of modern times, today the most widespread of all the forms of poetic production, sprang directly from the modern view that the arrangement of social relationships is the cause of the universal discord which is now causing uneasiness to every man who has at least once pondered over the meaning of his existence."*

Thus, the anthropological element in Dobrolyubov's materialism is not identical with Feuerbach's anthropological materialism.

Unlike Feuerbach, Dobrolyubov did not divorce man from his social-historical environment, and materialism from the revolutionary struggle.

Unlike Feuerbach, Dobrolyubov was remote from passive contemplation, from the theory of non-intervention in practical social life. He called upon man to change the world, and asserted that cognition of life takes place in the process of lively activity and eternal struggle, and should serve the object of changing social life.

Feuerbach always spoke of man in general and disregarded the class division of society. Dobrolyubov, like Chernyshevsky, emphasized that society is divided into conflicting classes, imbued with different strivings and pursuing antagonistic interests.

Unlike Feuerbach's materialism, that of Dobrolyubov was free from all streaks of religion and mysticism. The desire to create a new religion based on the deification of human sentiments and

---

* N. A. Dobrolyubov, *Collected Works*, Vol. II, pp. 585-86.

passions was alien to him. His revolutionary-democratic convictions precluded Feuerbach's abstract morals, the preaching of "universal love," which Engels called the "universal orgy of reconciliation."

All the more reason is there for not identifying Dobrolyubov's materialism with the Feuerbach type of materialism because, contrary to the metaphysical method of thinking which predominates in Feuerbach's system, Dobrolyubov sought to combine his materialistic theory with the dialectical idea of evolution, with the dialectical method.

* * *

It was from the works of Belinsky and Herzen that Dobrolyubov first made his acquaintance with dialectics.

His profound and comprehensive study of real life, nature and society, his active participation in the ideological and political struggle against aristocratic reaction and landlord and bourgeois liberalism, finally convinced Dobrolyubov that dialectics does not mean scholastic speculations, not abstract principles imposed upon the world, but that dialectics is inherent in reality itself, that it is the universal principle of life itself.

Unlike Hegel and his disciples, Dobrolyubov, in speaking of the subject of dialectical logic, showed that its categories and concepts reflected the real processes that take place in nature and in social life.

"The men of that generation," wrote Dobrolyubov concerning the Russian idealist dialecticians of the 1830's and the 1840's, "were imbued with lofty but somewhat abstract strivings. They strove towards the truth, wanted good to prevail, they were charmed by everything that was beautiful; but for them the *principle* was supreme. By *principle* they meant the universal philosophical idea, which they regarded as the basis of all their logic and morality. They purchased their principle at the price of the frightful torment of doubt and negation, and could never free themselves from its oppressive, deadening influence. There was something pantheistic in their recognition of the principle: for them life meant serving the principle, man was the slave of the principle; every deed that was not in conformity with the principle was regarded as a crime.... Thorough masters of abstract logic, they were totally ignorant of the logic of life and, therefore, regarded as frightfully easy everything that was easily arrived at by means of syllogisms, and at the same time they frightfully emasculated the whole of life in their efforts to compress it into their logical moulds."*

Dobrolyubov noted that even among the generation of the 1830's and 1840's there were people who succeeded in linking the philosophical principle with real vitality, and who rose up to fight "circumstances." These were Belinsky and those who thought like him.

The logic of the men of the new generation rejected the formulae, taken on trust, which doomed mankind to quietism, to resignation to the circumstances of its life which, in fact, were only transient. This logic considered that it was not only possible but necessary to wage a struggle for the transformation of reality, a struggle based on a knowledge of the laws of reality itself.

"Recognizing the immutable laws of historical development," said Dobrolyubov, "the men of the present generation do not place unreal hopes upon themselves, do not think that they can alter history at their own will, do not think that they are immune to the influence of circumstances.... But at the same time they do not in the least sink into apathy and indifference, for they are also aware of their own worth. They look upon themselves as one of the wheels of a machine, as one of the circumstances which govern the course of world events. As all world circumstances are interconnected and to some extent subordinated to each other, they too are subordinated to necessity, to the force of things; but beyond this subordination, they do not bow down to any idols whatsoever, they uphold the independence and sovereignty of all their actions against all casually arising claims."**

Like Herzen, Belinsky and Chernyshevsky, Dobrolyubov regarded dialectics as the logical foundation of the revolutionary world outlook, as the "algebra of revolution."

Dobrolyubov's dialectical method revealed itself not in the shape of abstract logical formulae and categories, but in his

---

* N. A. Dobrolyubov, *Collected Works*, Vol. IV, pp. 58-59.
** *Ibid.*, p. 62.

analysis of the social phenomena of his time, and also in his philosophical and aesthetical analysis of the literature of his period.

In examining the character of a nation's art, he found the connection between that art and surrounding reality, the environment in which it arose and developed. He strongly opposed the metaphysical method of thinking in literature and art which is satisfied with a simple description of casual facts and phenomena divorced from the whole of surrounding circumstances. "To tear a fact out of living reality," he wrote, "and to put it on a shelf side by side with dusty folios, or to classify a few fragmentary, casual facts on the basis of schoolbook logical divisions, means destroying that vitality which lies in this very fact when put in connection with surrounding reality."*

Thus, he regarded popular legends as a reflection, expressed in the thoughts and sentiments of the people, of the circumstances under which the people live.

In his essay "What is Oblomovshchina?" Dobrolyubov revealed the inseverable connection that existed between the slave-serf system that prevailed in Russia, the life of the gentry, and the intellectual and moral stagnation among the landlord class. Examining "Oblomovshchina" in connection and in interaction with the environment in which it arose, he started out from the premise that truth is always concrete, and that everything depends upon conditions, time and place.

Dobrolyubov vividly depicted the interdependence of social phenomena, and of how people's actions are conditioned by their environment in his essays "Realm of Darkness" and "A Ray of Light in the Realm of Darkness," in which he critically analyzed the works of Ostrovsky.

Dobrolyubov taught that it was wrong to confine oneself to expressing indignation at this or that act of lawlessness on the part of individual landlords and government officials, that it was necessary to discern the direct connection between these acts of lawlessness and the entire autocratic-landlord machinery of state.

According to Dobrolyubov, the primary condition of dialectical thinking is to take all the phenomena of nature, society and

---

* N. A. Dobrolyubov, *Collected Works*, Vol. I, p. 432.

the human mind in their interconnection and interaction. He wrote: "Help me to understand the character of a phenomenon, its place among the rest, its meaning and importance in the general course of life, and I assure you that in this way you will help me to form a far more correct opinion about the matter in hand than you will with all the syllogisms you may choose to prove your case."*

The dialectical analysis of a great variety of phenomena of reality in their interconnection enabled Dobrolyubov to arrive at the conclusion that real life is governed by the universal principle of motion and development.

There is nothing absolute and immobile in the world, everything is relative and transient. Only matter—the foundation of all the phenomena of nature—is eternal and uncreatable. "In nature everything advances gradually from the simple to the more complex, from the imperfect to the more perfect; but everywhere there is the one and the same matter, only at different stages of development."**

Inorganic bodies undergo changes in volume and internal composition, undergo mechanical and chemical processes, but they do not betray the characteristics of life; plants, which represent matter at a higher stage of development than inorganic bodies, already betray symptoms of the processes of life; in the animal world, life is revealed still more palpably, the ability to change location, and high nervous activity, appear. "Man, the most perfect of animals," wrote Dobrolyubov, "constitutes the last stage of the development of beings inhabiting the visible universe; why, for that very reason alone, should we not assume that men possess that which we do not observe among less developed beings? And if the most developed part of a man's body is his brain, why not assume that the brain is capable of an activity that we do not observe in a stone or a tree."***

The principle of motion and development governs also social life. The laws of social life, Dobrolyubov asserted, "are in themselves neither eternal nor absolute. In accepting them as condi-

---

* See p. 558 of this volume.
** N. A. Dobrolyubov, *Collected Works*, Vol. IV, p. 310.
*** *Ibid.*, p. 311.

tions which have evolved from the experience of the past we do not by any means pledge ourselves to regard them as perfect and to reject all other conditions. On the contrary, by its very nature, my contract with society includes the obligation to try to find the best possible laws.... The very respect for law eliminates stagnation and immobility in social organization; it gives scope and work for the mind and will; this very respect for law often calls for the violation of the formal status...."*

The dialectical principle of motion and development reveals itself to a no lesser degree in the sphere of human thought, according to Dobrolyubov. The life and practical activity of men extend the boundaries of their knowledge, make once fruitful views obsolete and generate new ideas and systems of views. Ideologists who cling to obsolete and antiquated ideas which have become dead dogmas long ago and have been refuted by the whole course of life, look ridiculous.

The fact that ideas and beliefs formerly prevalent are superseded by new ones in the course of time does not, however, mean that they vanish without leaving a trace. According to Dobrolyubov, everything new, including a new system of ideas, retains much of the old that has been superseded by subsequent development.

Dobrolyubov's essay "The Degree to Which the People Have Participated in the Development of Russian Literature," is a model of the historical, dialectical approach to poetry. When mankind, he says, was entirely under the influence of the external world and was not yet conscious of its strength, its poetry, or rather the monstrous images of mythology, reflected man's oppression by the frightful forces of nature. Subsequently, as man began to become conscious of his importance and to utilize the forces of nature in his own interests, poetry began to assume anthropomorphic forms. When war brought gains and trophies for some and slavery and oppression for others, poetry began to laud the victors and extol the obedience of slaves and vassals. What at one time was the product of its age, subsequently contradicts the truth of life and becomes monstrous and meaningless. "What has outlived its time," concluded Dobrolyubov, "no longer has any meaning.... The

---

* See pp. 331-32 of this volume.

Greek gods may have been beautiful in ancient Greece, but they are revolting in the French tragedies and in our odes of the last century. The appeals of the knights of the Middle Ages may have roused hundreds of thousands of men to go and fight the heathens, to liberate the Holy Places, but the same appeals, repeated in Europe in the 19th century, would rouse nothing but laughter."*

Dobrolyubov not only upheld the dialectical method as a theoretical principle; with the aid of dialectics he smote the enemies of revolutionary democracy who urged that Russia must preserve the "immutable foundations" of her life, which have existed from the days of antiquity, and reject all innovations.

Criticizing Shevyrev's metaphysical propositions, Dobrolyubov wrote that "resting content with the *immutable truth,* which he discovered in ancient Rūs, leads to the most gloomy stagnation and death.... Mr. Shevyrev's *one and lofty* truth, eternally characteristic of ancient Rūs, is totally alien to all the vital interests of modern Russia."**

Dobrolyubov called upon Russian society to rise up and fight conservatism and routine; he contrasted movement and life to the "stagnation of the marsh": "it is as easy to perish in a marsh as at sea; but while the sea is attractively dangerous, the marsh is dangerously repulsive. Better to suffer shipwreck than sink in the mire."***

Running through all Dobrolyubov's works is the idea that the new social relationships will triumph, because the need for them springs from the very development of life, and is recognized by the progressive forces of society which are capable of setting society in motion.

Dobrolyubov availed himself of every opportunity to show that political struggle is a social law and that social development is impossible without such a struggle. He repeatedly emphasized that the main content of the history of society at the different stages of its development has been the struggle of the aristocracy

---

* N. A. Dobrolyubov, *Collected Works,* Vol. I, p. 206.
** N. A. Dobrolyubov, *Collected Works,* Vol. II, p. 450.
*** N. A. Dobrolyubov, *Collected Works,* Vol. I, p. 278.

against democracy, and that, at bottom, this was a struggle between parasitism and labour.

In laying new paths in literature and art, Dobrolyubov tried
with the aid of the dialectical method to prove the necessity of
active art, and he advocated the creation of works of art that would
not only truthfully portray actual reality, but also inspire progressive people to change this reality.

"An artist," he wrote, "is not a photographic plate which
reflects only the present moment: if he were, there would be neither
life nor meaning in works of art. The artist supplements the fragmentary impression of the moment with his creative sense, gener-
alizes in his soul particular phenomena, creates one harmonious
whole out of separate features, finds a living connection and
consistency in the apparently unconnected phenomena, and merges
and works up in his whole world outlook the varied and contradictory sides of living reality."[*]

Dobrolyubov, however, like Chernyshevsky, was not thoroughly
consistent in applying the dialectical method to all the phenomena
of reality. The interpretation of natural phenomena given in his
writings reveal remnants of the old metaphysical materialism:
qualitative changes are often attributed exclusively to quantitative
changes, the influence of elements of anthropologism is often to
be seen, particularly when he discusses the origin of the human
mind, or the behaviour of men.

Dobrolyubov's limited world outlook is most clearly revealed
in his interpretation of social phenomena, since, in the main, he
regarded social development from the idealist standpoint. The features of anthropologism visible in his approach to man and to
human society also show that Dobrolyubov did not completely discard the metaphysical mode of thinking. In his works we meet
with the assertion that the ideological life of society and the material conditions of its existence are equally important sides of
the social process. When, however, he regards the ideological life
of man as being independent of the material conditions of existence of society, he often gives it an "anthropological" explanation, he ascribes it to the physiological conditions of the life of
the individual, and thereby obliterates the borderline which serves

---

[*] N. A. Dobrolyubov, *Collected Works*, Vol. II, p. 373.

as the basis of the dialectical transition from nature to society. This shows once again that it is impossible to be a consistent adherent of the dialectical method unless one applies materialism to the interpretation of the laws of social development.

* * *

In the activities of Chernyshevsky and Dobrolyubov "democracy and socialism were merged into one inseparable and indissoluble whole" (Lenin).

In all his works Dobrolyubov tried ideologically to prove the necessity of a people's revolution and of establishing democratic government with the object of bringing about the socialist transformation of society.

In his diary on January 15, 1857, he wrote:

"I am a desperate socialist, ready at this moment to enter a society that is not wealthy, with equal rights and common property for all members; while he [Shcheglov, an acquaintaince of Dobrolyubov's—M.Y.]—a revolutionary, filled with hatred for all authority over him, recognizes the necessity of inequality of rights and property even in mankind's highest ideal, and rebels against authority only because, I think, he sees the absurdity of the *status quo* and regards himself as being superior to it.... The North American States are his ideal. My ideal does not yet exist on earth, except, perhaps, the democratic society, a meeting of which has been described by Herzen."*

From this it is evident that Dobrolyubov was not satisfied with bourgeois democracy even in the form in which it existed in the United States in his time. Nor was he satisfied with the bourgeois-democratic system in England, or, as he put it, "the examples of English brutality."**

Dobrolyubov, the revolutionary democrat, dreamed of a different social system. He longed for a social system in which there would be no parasites, in which everybody would work. He was

---

* N. A. Dobrolyubov, *Collected Works*, Vol. VI, p. 453. Dobrolyubov had read the pamphlet *February 27, 1855. The People's Meeting to Commemorate the Revolution of 1848*, which Herzen published through his Free Press.

** N. A. Dobrolyubov, *Collected Works*, Vol. VI, p. 232.

not yet clear in his mind as to the form this society would take, but he was convinced that mankind would create such a new society on socialist lines.

He became convinced that the new society could not triumph without a revolution, and he firmly took his stand as a revolutionary fighter for the interests of the people.

Dobrolyubov himself, in one of his letters to Slavutinsky, revealed the ideological-political meaning of his activities in the following words:

"We know [and you know too] that the confusion which prevails today cannot be cleared up without the spontaneous action of popular life, [*i.e.*, revolution—*M.Y.*]. To rouse this action in at least that section of society which is open to our influence, we must act not in a way that will lull, but in the very opposite way. We must group the facts of Russian life which need correction and improvement, we must draw the attention of readers to what is going on around them, we must taunt them with all the abominations that go on, pursue them, torment them, give them no rest until all this mass of filth becomes abhorrent to the reader, until at last it touches him on the raw and makes him jump up and cry out in passion: 'Why this is as bad as penal servitude! Better let my miserable soul perish; I have no wish to live in this slough any longer!' This is what we must achieve, and this explains the tone of my criticism and of the political articles in *Sovremennik* and *Svistok*."*

Like Chernyshevsky, Dobrolyubov was of the opinion that the principal task that confronted the progressive forces in Russia was to abolish serfdom and all that it gave rise to, since they contradicted natural law and human nature.

Influenced by the Russian and French enlighteners, Dobrolyubov, in the first period of his activities, sometimes expressed the hope that "selfish calculation and habitual indolence must be silenced by the greatness of the general movement that has commenced for the good of mankind"; but soon these hopes were finally and irretrievably superseded by the conviction that without an "axe," without a peasant revolution, it would be impossible to abolish serfdom and to reform Russia.

---

* *Ogni*, Petrograd, 1916, pp. 67-68.

In all his works Dobrolyubov sowed in Russian society hatred for serfdom, he appraised all social phenomena from the democratic standpoint and, like Chernyshevsky, "was able to influence all the political events of his time in the revolutionary spirit by propagating, in spite of the impediments and obstacles raised by the censorship, the idea of a peasant revolution, the idea of a mass struggle to overthrow all the old authorities."*

Dobrolyubov called for an expansion of the struggle of the peasantry against serfdom. In his essay "When Will the Day Come?" he wrote: "We ourselves said ... that we do not need hero liberators, that we were a nation of rulers, not of slaves. ...

"Yes, we are safeguarded against outside dangers; even if we were obliged to wage an external struggle we can be calm about it. ... But have we not many internal enemies? Is it not necessary to wage a struggle against them? And is not heroism needed for such a struggle?"**

Contrary to the liberals, and unlike the West-European utopian socialists, Dobrolyubov asserted that without a violent revolution, the abolition of society based on exploitation and the transition to a new system of society was impossible.

"All the means of education, all the advantages of the latest discoveries and inventions," he wrote in his essay "The People's Cause," "are owned by the non-working classes of society, [which have nothing whatever to gain from handing over the weapons against themselves to those whose labour they have up to now utilized gratis]. Consequently, unless exceptional, extraordinary circumstances intervene, it is no use expecting the beneficial dissemination of education and sound tendencies among the masses of the people."***

To bring about these "exceptional, extraordinary circumstances," progressive people in society must rouse the masses of the people for a struggle, rouse them for historic action.

Dobrolyubov placed great hopes upon the great forces latent among the people; he listened to the mighty "murmur of popular life," sensing in it the approaching people's revolution.

---

* Lenin, *Collected Works*, Russ. ed., Vol. XV, p. 144.
** *See* p. 436 of this volume.
*** N. A. Dobrolyubov, *Collected Works*, Vol. IV, p. 107.

The people's revolution was to lead to the establishment of democratic government, government by the working classes. Dobrolyubov did not single out the industrial workers from among the general mass of the oppressed—the peasants, the artisans and the non-aristocrat intelligentsia; all were to take part in the administration of the state.

In his opinion the best form of state was a democratic republic.

While emphasizing the superiority of the democratic system over the absolutist system, he did not in the least idealize bourgeois democracy, for he understood perfectly well that formal equality before the law did not yet mean actual equality among men. He clearly realized that capitalism had not ushered in that universal prosperity which the enlighteners of the 18th century dreamed of, that it had not brought the masses of the people real freedom, material well-being and a cultured life. He was extremely critical of bourgeois economic and political theories which glorified capitalism and represented that system as a "Golden Age" for the people.

"Political economy," he said, "proudly proclaims itself a science which deals with the wealth of *nations*; but in substance, it concerns itself only with the most profitable employment and the speediest accumulation of capital, consequently, it serves only the capitalist class, and pays very little attention to the masses of the people who own no capital, who own nothing but their own labour."*

In a number of his works Dobrolyubov subjected bourgeois liberalism to withering criticism. The liberals, he asserted, were afraid of the masses of the people and of genuine, fundamental changes.

"As soon as the question is put in a broader way they begin to fear anarchy, barbarism, plunder, and so forth, and anathemize the subversive theories which foster respect for *suffrage universel*.... Once they enter the groove of the routine liberals who flaunt phrases about order and peace, freedom within the limits of the law, peaceful and slow progress worked out in parliamentary debates, etc., they can no longer be excused on the grounds of reason or law."**

* N. A. Dobrolyubov, *Collected Works*, Vol. I, p. 211.
** N. A. Dobrolyubov, *Collected Works*, Vol. III, pp. 288-89.

Dobrolyubov dreamed of the erection on the ruins of serfdom and capitalism of a new social system, under which there would be no exploitation of man by man, and all would receive not only the right, but the actual opportunity to enjoy material wealth and the benefits of education.

The social system under which "all will live well" would be created when the principal means of production became public property. Material wealth must belong to those who create it and be distributed according to the quantity and quality of the labour men spend in creating it.

"A man's importance in society," said Dobrolyubov, "must be determined by his personal qualities, and each should receive material wealth in strict proportion to the quantity and quality of the work he performs: and then everybody will study hard in order to do his work in the best possible way, and there will be no room for parasites."*

In urging that it was possible and necessary to pass to the socialist system, Dobrolyubov, unlike the apologists for the capitalist system, argued that mankind, when freed from exploitation, would work with enthusiasm.

"Many even reach such a stage," he wrote, "that they cannot conceive of man working willingly, with enthusiasm. Read the argument in *Ekonomicheski Ukazatel* to the effect that everybody would die of starvation resulting from idleness if by the equal distribution of wealth people were robbed of the incentive to accumulate capital...."**

Properly understood personal interest presupposes a struggle for such a just social system under which individual capabilities, inclinations and strivings can find wide scope for their development.

"A man needs happiness," wrote Dobrolyubov, "he has a right to it, and must strive to achieve it at all costs. Happiness—whatever it may mean for each individual—is possible only if a man's primary material requirements are satisfied, if his present position is secure. ... If existing social relationships are out of harmony with the demands of supreme justice and fail to satisfy

---

* N. A. Dobrolyubov, *Collected Works*, Vol. II, p. 187.

** See p. 208 of this volume.

the striving for happiness as we understand it, it is obvious, we think, that a fundamental change of these relationships is needed."*

Like Robert Owen, Saint-Simon, and the other ideologists of utopian socialism whose theories Dobrolyubov critically assimilated, he took as his premise that a man is neither good nor bad at birth, but only potentially one or the other. A man is born with the ability to receive impressions from the outside world. Owing to this, a man who lives in a definite environment yields to its influences and effects. To enable men to abandon bad actions and habits, it is necessary to change the social environment in which they live and develop, to change the character of social relationships.

These premises make Dobrolyubov akin to the ideologists of utopian socialism, but his utopian socialism differed fundamentally from West-European utopian socialism. He stood for the class struggle and, like Herzen and Chernyshevsky, inseparably combined the ideas of socialism with the ideas of revolutionary democracy. He believed that it was impossible to establish socialism unless power passed into the hands of the masses of the people.

Following Herzen and Chernyshevsky, Dobrolyubov assumed that under definite conditions Russia could avoid the capitalist stage of development and go straight on to the road to socialism. In his opinion the principal condition that would enable Russia to develop on socialist lines was a people's, peasant revolution. As a result of the victory of such a revolution, he believed, democratic government would be established in Russia, and this government would set out to transform society on socialist lines on the basis of rural peasant communities. Like Chernyshevsky, Dobrolyubov, who dreamed of passing to socialism through the old peasant communities, "did not, and could not, in the sixties of the last century, see that the development of capitalism and of the proletariat alone could create the material conditions and the social force necessary for the achievement of socialism."** Nevertheless, faith in the communal system that prevailed in the Russian countryside did not lead Dobrolyubov to idle admiration of the old, anti-

---

* N. A. Dobrolyubov, *Collected Works*, Vol. IV, p. 103.
** Lenin, *Collected Works*, Russ. ed., Vol. XV, p. 144.

quated forms of social life, as it did the Slavophiles; it enabled him to understand the need for a peasant revolution and led him to urge the need for a heroic struggle by the people against tsarism and serfdom.

Unlike Herzen, and in some degree Chernyshevsky, Dobrolyubov did not think that Russia would inevitably take the non-capitalist path of development towards socialism, although he preferred that path. In his essay "From Moscow to Leipzig," he wrote:

"Yes, fortunately for us, we entered the field of historical life later than other nations. Tracing the course of development of the nations of Western Europe, and picturing to ourselves what it has now reached, we may foster the gratifying hope that ours will be a better path. That we must traverse the same path, there can be no doubt, and it does not even sadden us in the least. . . . Nor can there be any doubt that we, too, will not altogether avoid errors and digressions on our future path of development. Still, our path will be an easier one; still, our civic development may somewhat more rapidly pass through the phases through which it passed so slowly in Western Europe. But the main thing is that we can and must proceed more resolutely and firmly, because we are already armed with experience and knowledge."*

In assuming that socialism could be established in Russia only as the result of a people's revolution, Dobrolyubov went beyond the limits of utopian socialism, but he did not free himself from the utopian hope that the peasant revolution in Russia would bear a socialist character; actually, however, it had to give free reign to commodity-capitalist relationships.

Dobrolyubov's revolutionary democratic world outlook lent peculiar features to his utopian socialism. While the Western utopian socialists—Saint-Simon, Fourier and Robert Owen—appealed to the ruling classes and governing circles and counted on their generosity and common sense to achieve their socialist ideals, Dobrolyubov regarded the revolutionary people as the only force that was capable of creating the new society.

Unlike the ideologists of utopian socialism in Western Europe who stood aloof from the mass political struggle, from the revolu-

---

* N. A. Dobrolyubov, *Collected Works*, Vol. IV, p. 402.

tionary movement of their time, Dobrolyubov, like Chernyshevsky, was an ideologist of the peasant revolution.

The founders of utopian socialism looked upon the working classes merely as the *object* of social changes. Dobrolyubov, however, looked upon the "working people" not only as the object but also as the *subject* of socialist changes, as the only force capable of creating the new social system. "The proletarian," he asserted, "understands his position far better than many noble-minded scholars who place their hopes in the generosity of elder brothers towards younger brothers."*

Dobrolyubov tried to work out a theoretical basis for his program of democratic and socialist changes, but in formulating the sociological grounds for his political program he did not succeed in liberating himself from the idealistic conception of history, and in taking the stand of materialism, although we can find materialistic tendencies in his explanations of social phenomena in nearly all his works.

He often regarded men's ideas and the material conditions of life as being equal factors in the development of society, as having equal importance. Thus, in his essay "Russian Civilization as Concocted by Mr. Zherebtsov," we find the idealistic statement that "in the development of nations and of the whole of mankind—the very principles which are recognized as the principal motive forces of history undoubtedly depend upon the state of man's knowledge of the world in this or that epoch,"** and also the idealistic thesis in which Dobrolyubov tries to show that the principal obstacle to the development of world history is "failure to understand wherein lies real good and the effort to find it where it does not nor cannot exist."*** Nevertheless, in that very same essay Dobrolyubov shows that the difference in the intellectual development of nations depends most of all upon historical circumstances, that there is no such thing as a national ideology, for nations are divided into classes, that the struggle between aristocracy and democracy constitutes the main content of history.

---

* *Ibid.*, p. 393.
** N. A. Dobrolyubov, *Collected Works*, Vol. III, p. 241
*** *Ibid.*, p. 244.

But Dobrolyubov gave an idealistic explanation of the rise of exploitation, of the rule of the exploiting classes in society. He asserted that "parasitism" was due to the fact that the amount of knowledge in society was insignificant and was unevenly distributed among men. The people were deficient in education and, therefore, had not learned properly to appraise the place and role of labour in the life of society, and this, according to Dobrolyubov, explains why "parasitism" could maintain its rule.

The anthropological motives which were characteristic of Dobrolyubov's materialism sometimes led him to erroneous conclusions in sociological questions. Thus, proceeding from the anthropological principle, he arrived at the incorrect conclusion that all the contradictions inherent in social life spring from the eternal contradiction that is said to be inherent in human nature. "Everywhere," he wrote, "in all things, the existence is revealed of two parties, a conservative and a progressive, eternal parties corresponding to the two sides of human nature: force of habit and desire for improvements." While appealing to human nature, he abstracted himself from the material conditions of life of society: anthropological abstractions, "force of habit" and "desire for improvements," came to the forefront, and this led Dobrolyubov to give an idealistic interpretation of the struggle in and progress of society.

But it was not the features of anthropologism that were decisive in Dobrolyubov's sociological views. His "man" was not a naturalistic abstraction, but a social, historical man, who lived under definite social conditions.

Like Chernyshevsky, Dobrolyubov began to regard the material life of men as an extremely important aspect of their lives and activities. By material life he meant the material conditions of life and the means with which these conditions are achieved and maintained. The material side of social life, according to Dobrolyubov, determines man's relation to nature.

But Dobrolyubov did not lose sight of the other side of man's "material life"—the human relationships that are established in the process of production and distribution of wealth. He held that "the distribution of the gifts of nature among men" is of great importance in the life of society.

Criticizing the liberals, Dobrolyubov said that they reveal an abstract understanding of the question, they emphasize the *rights* of man and ignore the question of the actual *opportunity* to exercise these rights. And yet, "in all everyday relationships this material side predominates over the abstract side . . . people who lack material security attach little importance to abstract rights and even lose a clear conception of what they are."*

In spite of his own assertion that people are poor because they do not understand the wise and natural principles upon which social life should be based, Dobrolyubov often regarded the history of society as a process which takes place for reasons that are independent of the mind and will of man. "Human relationships," he wrote, "are rarely based on rational calculation; for the most part they arise fortuitously, and moreover, the behaviour of some towards others is in most cases quite unconscious, as it were, it is dictated by routine, by one's disposition at the given moment, by the influence of numerous extraneous causes."**

Dobrolyubov believed that the laws which govern the organization and life of society are not eternal but transient, because the material requirements and needs of men imperatively call for a change of the old and obsolete economic laws.

Realizing that the existing mode of production and distribution of material wealth fails to satisfy the constantly growing needs of the bulk of the people, a section of society begins to fight the old order of things and tries to bring about social changes.

Unlike the idealist enlighteners, Dobrolyubov understood that no ideology by itself can change the structure of society. The fact that progressive people in society have become aware of the needs that have matured in society can lead to the satisfaction of these needs only as the result of the practical activities of men; but this will take place only if the activities of the men who have become aware of society's needs go beyond the limits of the purely ideological sphere.

Dobrolyubov sharply criticized the idealists who are of the opinion that "literature directs history, that it [changes states, rouses or tames people], even alters national customs and charac-

---

* *See* p. 577 of this volume.
** *See* p. 562 of this volume.

ter, especially poetry—oh, poetry, in their opinion, introduces new elements into life, creates everything out of nothing."* Actually, literature is not the legislator but the mouthpiece of social interests.

The dissemination of positive knowledge in society cannot by itself abolish social injustice. History, according to Dobrolyubov, shows that "with the progress of education among the exploiting classes only the form of exploitation changes and becomes more refined and subtle: in substance, however, everything remains as before as long as the opportunity to exploit remains,"**

Dobrolyubov attached enormous importance to the task of making the masses of the people aware of their "natural needs," and he rightly believed that once they became aware of their true needs the "common people" would no longer tolerate the old order of things. He, therefore, held that it was the function of literature and education to awaken among the masses of the people the consciousness of their historical tasks and thereby set this great force into motion.

Dobrolyubov came close to a correct understanding of the role of the individual and of the masses of the people in the history of society.

In his essay on Stankevich, he stated that it was as wrong to worship the so-called "men chosen by destiny," to forget the activities of the masses of people, as to "abolish the individual," to refuse to recognize the important role the individual plays in the history of society, to assert that the individual by himself is of no importance.

Truly outstanding men act in conformity with the laws that govern the historical development of society and can play an important role in accelerating or retarding the historical process.

"No doubt," said Dobrolyubov, "great historical reformers exercise considerable influence on the development and course of the historical events of their time and among their people; but it must not be forgotten that before their influence begins to tell, they themselves are influenced by the ideas and customs of the time and of the society which they later begin to influence by

---

* N. A. Dobrolyubov, *Collected Works*, Vol. I, p. 205.
** N. A. Dobrolyubov, *Collected Works*, Vol. IV, p. 394.

the power of their genius.... History concerns itself with men,
even with great men, only because they were important for the
nation, or for mankind. Consequently, the main task of the biographer of a great man is to show how the latter succeeded in
utilizing the means at his disposal in his time, how he gave expression to the elements of living development that he could find
in his nation.... The importance of great historical figures can
be compared with the importance of rain, which beneficiently re-
freshes the earth, but which, after all, consists of the vapour
which rose from that same earth."*

From this point of view, Dobrolyubov's polemic with the Slavophiles on the question of the reforms introduced by Peter I is
of considerable interest.

In Dobrolyubov's opinion Peter became the great reformer of
Russia because he understood, and satisfied, the real needs of his
time and his people; Peter's reforms must not be regarded as a
sudden leap in Russia's history, having no connection with the
preceding development of the people. Peter's activities as a really
great man expressed the requirements of national life.

The principal force which determines the trend of all historical events, in Dobrolyubov's opinion, is the people. Over and over
again he refuted the erroneous view that the people are an inert,
immobile mass.

"Granted," he wrote, "that our people really suffer from being disunited; granted that they are overburdened with manual
labour which robs them of all desire to think of common interests; granted that in this country the very achievements of civilization are often transformed into a means for the more skilful
exploitation of the people. But even taking all these facts for
granted, we hope ... to arrive not at despair about the vital forces
of the people, not at the conviction that they are absolutely apathetic and incapable of engaging in public affairs, but at conclusions the very opposite of this."**

The masses of the people, said Dobrolyubov, feel at every
step the effects of hunger and cold, tyranny and violence, and
these real facts of life can give rise to such a mass movement of

---

* N. A. Dobrolyubov, *Collected Works*, Vol. III, pp. 120-21.
** N. A. Dobrolyubov, *Collected Works*, Vol. IV, p. 108.

the people as will upset all the book theories and assumptions of educated pessimists.

The whole inner meaning of history, its substance, its trend, according to Dobrolyubov, consists in the struggle the masses of the people wage to abolish parasitism and to elevate labour.

Dobrolyubov was a true Russian patriot, a lover of the Russian people, who strove to create in his motherland, Russia, a material and spiritual civilization that would be superior to West-European bourgeois civilization. He, like Belinsky, strongly attacked the bourgeois cosmopolitans who treated their country, the Russian people, with disdain and tried to subordinate the Russian nation to some West-European influence; and he trounced the Pan-Slavists who extolled the former patriarchal backwardness of Russia and tried to isolate her from the rest of mankind.

"The distinguishing feature of virile, active patriotism," wrote Dobrolyubov, "is precisely the fact that it precludes all international enmity, and a man who is inspired by such patriotism is ready to work for the whole of mankind, if only he can be useful to it. If he confines his activities to his own country, it is because he feels that this is his proper place, that this is where he can be most useful. . . . Genuine patriotism, being a specific manifestation of love for mankind, is incompatible with dislike for individual nations. . . . If we interpret patriotism in this way we will understand why it is developing with exceptional power in those countries where every individual is given considerable opportunity consciously to work for the benefit of society."*

Although Dobrolyubov did not reach an understanding of the objective, historical laws which guide society from capitalism to socialism he, nevertheless, was profoundly convinced that the ideals of socialism could be put into practice.

Dobrolyubov dreamed of a new, socialist society, in which the needs of the people would be the determining stimulus to development. But, remaining on the ground of reality from which his protest against the old order had sprung, he was unable, under the conditions prevailing in backward, feudal Russia, to perceive the proletariat as the force which history had vested with the task of leading the transition "from the kingdom of necessity to the

---

* N. A. Dobrolyubov, *Collected Works*, Vol. III, pp. 227-28.

kingdom of freedom." The ground of reality from which Dobrolyubov's revolutionary-democratic ideas had sprung was the serf
system, under which the masses had been downtrodden by centuries of slavery and were only just getting into motion. In his opinion, the peasantry and the revolutionary intelligentsia constituted
the force that was capable, under the conditions of that system, of
rising for a struggle against tsarism and serfdom. Dobrolyubov's
revolutionary-democratic ideas did not, and could not at that time,
reach the minds of the broad masses of the peasantry and rouse
them for the revolutionary struggle, but they did rouse and inspire
the progressive people among the non-aristocrat intelligentsia for
the struggle against the autocratic and landlord system, a struggle
for the great cause of the people.

In the endeavour to awaken the democratic consciousness of
the masses of the people and to rouse them for a struggle against
tsarism and serfdom, Dobrolyubov turned his gaze and hopes to
literature and literary criticism. Following V. G. Belinsky and
N. G. Chernyshevsky, he strove to blaze new paths in the development of Russian literature and art; he tirelessly and passionately
fought for the creation of a truly popular literature. As he conceived it, this literature was to reflect surrounding reality truthfully and comprehensively, sign the death warrant of the old, feudal order and ideas, and inspire all the virile and progressive
forces of the Russian people to wage a struggle for the freedom
and happiness of the toiling masses, for the progress of popular
culture.

To Dobrolyubov and Chernyshevsky fell the great honour in
the 1850's of fighting for a Russian literature that would deal
with the people and pursue definite aims, in opposition to the
efforts of the liberal writers, headed by I. S. Turgenev, to isolate
literature from the revolutionary struggle and become dispassionate
"servants of the muses."

Dobrolyubov became the champion of the realistic works of
A. N. Ostrovsky, Goncharov, Koltsov, Nikitin, Shevchenko and
Saltykov-Shchedrin; he denounced works that were imbued with
the idealistic and mystical world outlook and drew people away
from creative activities directed towards the transformation of
society into the sphere of "sentimental dreaming." We have in
mind the works of Count Sollogub, Yazikov, Podolinsky, Polon-

sky and other writers who were remote from and alien to the people.

In Dobrolyubov's literary essays the aesthetical principles of Russian revolutionary democracy found vivid expression.

To him, *realism* was the first and chief principle of aesthetics. He fought tirelessly for the realistic trend in literature and art, and demanded that works of art should truthfully reflect all sides and all the contradictions of actual reality. Life does not proceed according to literary theories; on the contrary, literature changes in accordance with the trend of life, he argued.

"At the present time," he wrote, "life is asserting its rights on every side; to spite mystificators of every kind, realism is invading every sphere. Virile realism must also penetrate poetry, and if a remarkable poet appears among us soon, it will be in this field and not in the field of aesthetic subtleties."*

Dobrolyubov understood the subject of art realistically, in the spirit of philosophical materialism. In his opinion, art is a complete picture of life in its active development; it is strictly subordinated to all "material conditions" and at the same time free in the choice of the "most interesting points .of view." Art, while reproducing life in artistic forms, is, of course, inferior to the beautiful in real life, it is less perfect than the beautiful in real life; but it can give mankind a true picture of the character and substance of the phenomena of life it depicts.

In his essay "A. S. Pushkin" he revealed the road to realism for Russian literature. Formerly, he said, Russian poets wrote odes to court festivals and similar events with which the people were not concerned; later they turned to humanistic ideas, but understanding them in an extremely abstract manner, they dropped into sentimentality; ignoring real distress, they lamented over imaginary sorrow, paying homage to prevailing vice, they denounced non-existent vice and extolled ideal virtue. Becoming convinced that the real world was not so good, Russian poetry found consolation in some ephemeral, nebulous world, in the sphere of shades, apparitions and other phantoms. Dropping into mysticism, our poetry of that time strove towards the transcendental and the unknown, and regarded the sinful world as being unworthy of their

---

* N. A. Dobrolyubov, *Collected Works*, Vol. II, p. 578.

attention. Pushkin had succeeded in freeing Russian literature from the rule of these trends, and in his works the real Russian world was revealed for the first time. ". . . When, after the events of the Patriotic War,* Russians began to acquire self-consciousness, having had opportunities to come into contact with all classes of Russian society, Pushkin was able to comprehend the true needs and the true character of the life of the people."**

Pushkin, discovering the real but as yet unexplored world, was unable to see all its imperfections, and did not make a strict analysis of reality; but his poetry paved the way for a new, realistic trend in literature.

In our time, too, said Dobrolyubov, there are still poets who strive to distract society's attention from its real needs and interests, who seek "rest from the vanities of the world" in a world of sweet dreams, in the mystical contemplation of the "transcendental." Although the appearance of such works seems absurd and unnatural in the present epoch, it is to be explained by the desire of the oppressing classes which rule society to distract the attention of the oppressed classes from all social injustices and the imperfections of the social system.

In Dobrolyubov's opinion, art can be fruitful only if it constantly pushes forward, if those engaged in art regard it as a powerful instrument for knowing and changing the world.

In his essay "Realm of Darkness" Dobrolyubov wrote: "In recognizing faithfulness to life as the chief merit of an artistic production, we thereby point to the criterion by which we gauge the *merit* and importance of every phenomenon in literature. The degree to which an author's eye penetrates the very substance of phenomena, and the extent to which he embraces the different sides of life in his work, determine the degree of his talent."***

Dobrolyubov's most important principle in aesthetics was purposefulness in art. *The pursuit of a lofty ideal in art* is a guarantee that art will develop and, at the same time, a condition for its social utility.

---

* The Napoleonic invasion in 1812.—*Tr.*
** N. A. Dobrolyubov, *Collected Works*, Vol. I, p. 114.
*** *See* p. 242 of this volume.

Dobrolyubov worked out his revolutionary-democratic theory of art in the course of his struggle against the bourgeois-aristocratic idealistic theory of "art for art's sake."

Concerning the champions of "art for art's sake" he wrote: "They want nothing more nor less than that the author and artist should stand aloof from all vital problems, that he should have no rational convictions, that he should avoid philosophy like the plague, and that he should at all costs—*sing like a bird on a bough*, to use Goethe's expression, which has always been their motto."* Regarding the theory of "art for art's sake" as the production of idle and well-fed gourmands who are alien to the people, he argued that the interests of art were severely damaged by this wrong interpretation of its mission.

"And what exalts art most," he exclaims, "the description of a babbling brook and the contrast of hill and dale, or the presentation of the course of human life and the conflicts of different principles and social interests?"**

He expressed the hope that literature would become imbued with the lofty ideal of liberating toiling humanity and thus become one of the motive forces of social development.

"We are convinced," he wrote, "that, given a certain degree of development of the people, literature will become one of the motive forces of society; and we cling to the hope that here, in Russia, too, literature will one day acquire this significance. It is not the case so far, no more than it is at present hardly anywhere on the continent of Europe, and it would be useless to deceive oneself with dreams of self-delusion. . . . But we want to believe that it will be so one day."***

At the very beginning of his activities as a literary critic, Dobrolyubov called upon authors and critics to utter a new, democratic word in science and art, "to spread in society a bright outlook, truly noble convictions." The pursuit of an ideal is the indispensable and determining factor in the contents of every work of literature and art, he argued; and he strongly urged the necessity for a close alliance between art, science and philosophy. This

---

* N. A. Dobrolyubov, *Collected Works*, Vol. II, p. 421.
** (See p. 56 of this volume.
*** N. A. Dobrolyubov, *Collected Works*, Vol. IV, p. 89.

idea he brought out in exceptionally strong relief in his essay "Realm of Darkness."

". . . Thinking power and creative ability are both character-istic of and equally necessary for the philosopher and the poet," he wrote. "The greatness of a philosophical mind and the greatness of poetic genius equally consist in the ability at a glance to grasp the essential features of an object, distingush them from the casual ones and organize them properly in one's mind, to master them in such a way as to be able freely to call them forth for every possible combination. . . . Each fashions his world outlook on the basis of the facts that succeeded in reaching his mind."*

A vitally important principle of Dobrolyubov's aesthetics was his effort *to make literature and art play an active role in the transformation of society.* In his opinion, the object of works of art should be not only to depict in artistic images the most im-portant aspects of reality, but also to reveal their interconnection in the present, determine their trend of development in the future, and inspire men to wage a conscious struggle for the realization of that future.

Dobrolyubov entertained the hope that a *people's party* in literature would be formed in Russia, *i.e.,* that a democratic lit-erature would spring up that would inspire the people and rouse them for a struggle for the transformation of society. It is the mission of this democratic literature, he wrote, "to open their [the people's—*M. Y.*] eyes to the actual state of affairs, to awaken the spiritual forces latent among them, to imbue them with an under-standing of the dignity of man, of truth and goodness, of natural rights and duties, in short—to enlighten them; and as soon as the Russian wakes and turns over, the enemies who have beset him will turn in headlong flight."**

Dobrolyubov's aesthetics were based on the consistent pursuit of the principle of *popular art.* In his opinion, art is one of the forms of the spiritual life of the people. Genuine works of art express the life, the world outlook of the people.

Truly popular works of art are not only those which depict the lives of the lower estates and classes of society. All works of

---

* *See* p. 235 of this volume.
** *Literary Heritage,* No. 25-26, 1936, p. 308.

art which depict the lives of the different classes of society are truly popular, provided, however, they are imbued with humanistic ideas, with sympathy and respect for the people.

Dobrolyubov did not reach a correct understanding of partisanship in literature, but he clearly saw that in the society of his day, "even poetry has been constantly affected by the spirit of parties and classes."

The principles of revolutionary-democratic aesthetics which Dobrolyubov advocated, his struggle for realism in art, for art that pursued definite ideals, that was popular and played an active role in transforming society, were of enormous importance in the development of Russian democratic literature.

Following Belinsky, Herzen and Chernyshevsky, Dobrolyubov carried among the progressive strata of Russian society the ideas of materialism and dialectics, utopian socialism and revolutionary democracy; he fought for the overthrow of the obsolete feudal order and thereby objectively prepared the ideological ground for the dissemination of Marxism in Russia. Nikolai Alexandrovich Dobrolyubov is dear to the hearts of the Soviet people, and of progressive people everywhere, as a great revolutionary democrat, an outstanding figure in Russian democratic culture and a brilliant forerunner of Marxism in Russia.

M. YOVCHUK

N. A. DOBROLYUBOV

SELECTED
PHILOSOPHICAL
ESSAYS

A LETTER TO V. V. LAVRSKY[1]*

August 3 (15), 1856

Valerian Victorovich,

I VENTURE to recall the long-forgotten time of our cordial, comradely conversations and to redeem the sin of my long silence. It was wrong of me, of course, not to have written to you all this time, but still, I have a very good excuse. After our last meeting a great deal happened to me that completely turned my thoughts from friendly correspondence. Recall our last conversation during which, owing to some strange and insatiable thirst for activity, I expressed the wish "to enter into life" as soon as possible, whereas you expressed your disgust at such a speedy entry.... On the day after this conversation my wish was granted in the most horrible and most unforeseen manner.... The house and the orphans were left on my hands.... Well—this bitter experience did not induce me to repent of my wish. It was hard and unusual at first, I felt bitter for a long time, even now everything is still sad, and even now the new joys of thought and freedom cannot compensate for the joyous recollections of childhood, like that soul in Lermontov's poem for whom

> The songs of heaven could not be stilled
> By the tedious songs of earth.[2]

But I long for my peaceful childhood only in the way that Schiller longed for the Greek gods, as the poets long for the Golden Age. I found the strength within me to resign myself to my personal lot: the pleasure of work served to compensate me for the former pleasure of indolence, acquisitions of the mind for the infatuations of the heart, love for mankind for love for kin.... I wonder whether you will not think that "I am speaking in an involved and unintelligible way"; perhaps my simple words

---

* Superior numbers indicate the explanatory note given in the appendix under the title of each essay.—*Tr.*

contradict your metaphysical phraseology. But I ask you to remember that in orthodox philosophy I did not go further than
what I had the displeasure of hearing from Andrei Yegorovich;[3]
and in all that I read after that I found the diametrically opposite of what was taught by him and, probably, by all the other
academic philosophers; therefore, leave my terminology alone
and understand my words in their simple meaning without attributing any lofty pretensions and views to them. I hope, however,
that you do not do that, because you too have probably changed
during these two years.... How I would like to see some of my
comrades and speak with them!... What has become of those
meek lambs from Christ's flock? What have these outcast goats
been transformed into? The Kazan Academy must have done
something to you too, probably put you in chains, only not, of
course, the golden ones you wrote me about on the occasion of
my entering the institute (I am really sorry I have such a good
memory). Have you become still more entrenched in virtue and
thoroughly imbued with the sacred motto of orthodoxy, autocracy
and nationality,[4] have you imbued your soul sufficiently with
pious reflections about this[5]—and similar[5]—subjects important
for the good of the world? Are you dozing peacefully in the shade
of an all-reconciling faith, or has the corrupting breath of the
turbulent West penetrated also the Kazan refuge of orthodoxy
and, eluding the hundred-eyed Arguses in the shape of *Pravoslavny Sobesednik*[6] and others, disturbed your calm and dreamless
sleep? If so, I regret it with all my heart; but I console myself
with the hope that you are strong in your beliefs, that your head
has long been tightly closed to pernicious convictions, and that
neither Strauss nor Bruno Bauer, nor Feuerbach himself, not to
speak of a Herzen or Belinsky, can turn you from your path.
It is only in this conviction, assuming that you, as always, are
ready with Christian meekness to forgive your neighbour, that
I venture to write these lines.[7]

As for me, I am satisfied with my new life—without hopes,
without dreams, without illusions, but also without craven fear,
without the contradiction between natural inspirations and supernatural inhibitions. I live and work for myself in the hope that
my labours will benefit others. For two years I have been fighting
my old enemies, internal and external. I went out to fight without

arrogance, but also without cowardice—proud and calm. I looked this mysterious life straight in the face and found that it was nothing like what Father Paissi and the Most Reverend Jeremiah[8] had described it. It was necessary to go against my old ideas and against those from whom I had imbibed them. At first I proceeded timidly and cautiously, then more boldly, and finally, both ardent dreams and fervid foes yielded to my cool perseverance. Now I am resting on my laurels, knowing that I have nothing to reproach myself for, and that those whose opinion and love I cherish will also not reproach me for anything. They say that the road of bold truth that I have taken will one day lead me to a bad end. This is quite likely, but I know that I shall not die in vain. Consequently, even in the last extreme I shall have the inalienable consolation I have always had, namely, that I have lived and worked not without some use. . . .

But this is a matter of the distant future. At present I want, for a little time, to recall the past, and I hope that you will help me in this by writing to me. I liked the talks we had, notwithstanding the fact that we often thumped each other and I, perhaps, even got the worst of it. Shall we now turn our backs on each other only because our roads have diverged somewhat? I, at all events, would not like this to happen. I hope you too do not want it. Write to me, then, Valerian Victorovich, and tell me how you are living, about your studies, your successes, the Academy, the ideas now prevalent in it, and so forth; about our comrades, of whom I have heard nothing for three years already. I would have written V.I.S., but I do not know where to address the letter. I am afraid to address it to the Academy: you are all probably so busy there that you will have no time even to read my letter, let alone answer it. Even (to write) to you I have deliberately chosen the vacation period, when you will not be oppressed by the burden of exalted reflection and have a spare moment to devote to Seminary recollections which you (who knows?) may be ashamed of. But it gives me pleasure to think that you are not ashamed of me as a man who was also, at one time, ashamed of the Seminary, and who only recently has realized its true significance—negative, of course. At all events I am waiting, waiting impatiently, for a letter from you.

N. DOBROLYUBOV

THE IMPORTANCE OF AUTHORITY
IN EDUCATION[9]

REFLECTIONS ON Mr. PIROGOV'S *PROBLEMS OF LIFE*

THE INTELLECTUAL movement in our society to which the events of the past few years have given rise, has recently turned its attention also to the problems of education. Two magazines devoted to education are now being published, and articles on education appear from time to time in other publications too. But the first to draw attention to this important subject was *Morskoi Sbornik* (*Naval Magazine*), which at the beginning of last year published an article on education by Mr. Böhm. This was followed by other articles that expressed views, more or less new and correct, on this subject. Many of these articles were favourably received by their readers, but none enjoyed such complete and brilliant success as Mr. Pirogov's "Problems of Life." He astonished everybody by the clarity of his views, the noble trend of his thoughts, the ardour and vivacity of his dialectics, and his artistic presentation of the subject under discussion. Everybody who read Mr. Pirogov's article expressed admiration for it; everybody talked about it, discussed it, formed his own opinions and drew his own conclusions. In this case, the public even anticipated the literary critics, who merely endorsed the favourable opinion that was generally expressed, without making a detailed analysis of the article or drawing any conclusions of their own. This fact speaks very strongly in favour of Russian public opinion, and it is all the more remarkable for the reason that Mr. Pirogov's article is not by any means conspicuous for sentimental slush or pompous pronouncements calculated to soothe negligent parents and educators; it does not try to adjust itself to the existing order of things, but, on the contrary, hurls the bitter truth straight in the face of society; not hesitating to say that there is evil in our midst, it boldly and passionately, for the sake of supreme, eternal truth, attacks the petty interests of the age, the narrow-mindedness and the selfish strivings that prevail in modern society. The favour with which the public received this article has a profound and sacred significance. It shows that with all its imperfections, with all its aberrations in practical life, our society wants, and is able, at least to understand what is good and just and what it should strive for. It already possesses so much inner strength that it is no longer scared by the consciousness of its defects; and consciousness of past and present evil is the surest pledge that good is possible in the future. Welcoming this noble impulse of the Russian people with profound joy and sincere sympathy, we take the liberty to express a few thoughts concerning Mr. Pirogov's article, thoughts that will arise in the mind of every thinking reader. We are particularly encouraged to do this by the fact that we have not yet met anywhere a more honest exposition of the ideas contained in Mr. Pirogov's general, aphoristic propositions.

The substance of the ideas expounded in "Problems of Life" is the following. The main and highest principles of our education are [totally] out of harmony with the prevailing trend in society. The result is that, on completing a course of education and on entering society, we find ourselves obliged *either* to renounce all that which we were taught in order to adjust ourselves to society, *or else* follow our own rules and convictions, and thus set ourselves in opposition to the social trend. To sacrifice sacred, higher convictions for the sake of mundane advantage, however, is too immoral and repugnant a step; but where shall we find the strength to go against falsehood? Education does not in the least prepare us for this struggle against the false trend of society. It does not even take the slightest trouble to imbue us with loftier, human convictions; all it is concerned with is to train us to become scientists, lawyers, physicians, soldiers, and so on and so forth. And yet, on entering life, a man wants to have certain convictions, he wants to define what he is, what his goal and mission are. Examining himself, he finds ready-made solutions for these problems as given by his education; but on examining society he perceives in it strivings which run counter to these solutions. He wants to combat evil and falsehood, but here the utter unsoundness of his previous education comes to light: he is unfit for the struggle; he must first re-educate himself [in order to enter the arena of the struggle].... Meanwhile, the years fly, life goes on, it is necessary to act ... and the man acts, at random, often falling under the burden of difficult problems, and he is swept by the swift current of the crowd, first to one side and then to another, because he cannot act independently; the inner man in him has not been developed; he lacks convictions; and convic-' tions are not easily acquired:

"Only those can have convictions, who *from their earliest years have been trained to look penetratingly into themselves,* who from their earliest years have been trained *to love truth sincerely, staunchly to stand up for it, and to be unconstrainedly frank*—both with *their teachers* as well as with their fellows."

This is what Mr. Pirogov dwells on. He points to the evil in education and proves his propositions with relentless and irresistible logic. He helps us to understand and to discern the cause of the evil: the predominance of externals in education itself, neglect of the inner man. But how is the inner man killed in children? How is it that externals are more developed? What particular influences cause them to cross life's threshold unprepared and helpless? Mr. Pirogov does not analyze these questions in detail, he leaves the answers to be conjectured. We shall take the liberty here of expressing a few thoughts that arose in our mind on reading "Problems of Life."

[In treating of the problems of education from the lofty heights of present-day pedagogics, we have up till now behaved in a way that is strongly reminiscent of the fable in which wolves are appointed to supervise sheep. In that fable every circumstance was fully taken into consideration, every opinion was canvassed, but one thing was forgotten—the sheep were not consulted. Similarly,] most of our ideas on pedagogics, while fully taking into consideration the problems of higher philosophy and laying down true and useful rules from the religious, political, moral, general psychological, and so forth, aspect, lose sight of one very important circumstance, *viz.,* the actual life and nature of children and, in general, of all those who are being educated.... That is why the child is often sacrificed to pedagogical considerations. Mounted on his moral hobbyhorse, the teacher regards his pupil as his property, as a thing, to do with as he pleases. "The child must not have a will of its own," the wise pedagogues say. "It must blindly obey its parents, teachers, and seniors generally. Its teacher's commands must be the supreme law, and those commands must be obeyed without the slightest argument. Absolute obedience—this is the main and sole condition of education. The ultimate object of education is to substitute the *rational* will of the teacher for the *irrational* will of the child."

All this sounds very logical and correct, does it not? But recalling the description of this *rational* education given in "Problems of Life," and with the impressions of our own upbringing and education still fresh in our minds, we cannot listen to logical arguments of this kind without a sceptical smile. All of them clearly reveal only one thing—the frightfully pedantic pride of the worthy pedagogues combined with contempt for the dignity of human nature in general. When saying that to the child the teacher is the personification of the moral law and rational conviction, they obviously place the teacher on an inaccessibly lofty pedestal as a model of infallible morality and wisdom. One would readily agree, of course, that if such an ideal teacher existed, absolute, blind obedience to his authority would not cause the child any particular harm (except the real harm of retarding the independent development of its individuality). But, firstly, the ideal teacher would not demand such *absolute* obedience: he would try to develop rational strivings and convictions in his pupil as quickly as possible. And secondly, to set out to find infallible and ideal teachers and educators in our times would be an exceedingly brave but utterly wasted effort. Too many conditions are needed for this. First of all, the moral rules of the educator must be absolutely correct, and they must be strictly applied in every contingency in life, however particular and petty. For him no question can be obscure and no situation doubtful, for what will the teacher do if such a situation arises and he must order the child to do something? The child must implicitly obey every command, and consequently, must never provoke argument or discussion. Moreover, it is assumed that the teacher is absolutely dispassionate: he must never be moved by anger or by love, he must never feel indolent or tired, good moods and bad must not exist for him, he cannot be an ordinary man, he must be a special type of machine, the strict embodiment of the moral law. As far as we know, however, no such machine has been invented yet, and if some announce that they have discovered the secret of such an invention, it is only another expression of their contempt for human nature and of their desire at all costs to be as unlike a human being as possible. If, however, it is assumed that the teacher may be governed by passion, who can guarantee the absolute infallibility of his actions towards the child? Would it not be better to train the child to reason rationally from its earliest years [so that it may, as soon as possible, acquire the ability and strength to disobey our commands when we order it to do something wrong]?

As regards his intellect, the ideal teacher must possess clear, firm and infallible convictions, and extremely high and all-sided development, an extensive and versatile knowledge, all in complete harmony with general principles. His very nature must be much superior to that of the child in every respect. If this is not the case, what will happen when the teacher, for example, will express admiration for Derzhavin and compel his pupil to learn the ode "God," while the child has already become fond of Pushkin and regards the ode "God" as a [totally] unintelligible jumble of words? Suppose a child is compelled to go on practising the musical scales for a whole year when its fingers have long been freely running up and down the keyboard and it is just longing to play, and to go on playing? Suppose a child admires a picture, a statue, a song, flowers and insects, examines with curiosity some apparatus used in physics or chemistry and puts a question to the teacher which the latter is unable to answer?... [Here it is useless insisting on absolute obedience!] Are there many teachers and educators who are capable of answering *all* questions children ask? Many, of course, have on more than one occasion seen a perky seven or eight-year-old child floor a worthy greybeard and leave him baffled. And yet, this worthy greybeard has a pupil who must obey him implicitly!... He, of course, will not baffle anybody!

Thus, the ideal teacher who does not wish the child to argue and develop convictions [but demands nothing but obedience] must be prepared for everything, must know everything, must have ready-made solutions for *all* the problems that might arise in the mind of his pupil, and anticipate all the opinions, arguments and conclusions that might sometime take shape in the child's mind. Only if he is thus prepared will he be able, at least to some extent, to perform his functions as an educator without violating the child's nature. Moreover, he must have the strength to guide his pupil along the true and best path in every field. If he discovers in the child an inclination for music or painting, a passion for botanics, a facile mathematical mind, poetic sensitiveness, ability to learn languages, etc., etc., he must be fully capable of developing all these inclinations in his pupil. If, however, he is incapable of undertaking this task, it shows that he himself is not yet sufficiently trained, not yet sufficiently developed to guide others. [And if that is the case, he has no right to demand implicit obedience.]

But even if we assume that the teacher can always rise above the individuality of the pupil (which happens, although, of course, not always, not by any means) he, at all events, cannot rise above an entire generation. The child is preparing to live in new surroundings, his environment will not be that of twenty or thirty years ago, when his teacher received his education. And usually, a teacher not only fails to foresee, but he simply fails to understand the requirements of the new times and thinks they are absurd. He tries to keep his pupil to the concepts and rules to which he himself adheres: quite a natural and comprehensible striving, but, nevertheless, one that becomes exceedingly harmful as soon as it begins to restrict the child's will and mind. The result is that the development of the pupil's natural reasoning faculties is retarded, and his receptiveness to the phenomena and requirements of the life of the society in which he will have to act is sometimes entirely deadened by the old prejudices and opinions he accepted on faith from his teacher in his childhood. Such an education is undoubtedly the foe of all improvement and progress, and it leads to lifeless immobility and stagnation.... Its influence affects not only separate individuals, but the whole of society.

If the prejudices and errors of the old generation are forcibly implanted into the child's impressionable soul from its earliest years, then the enlightenment and improvement of an entire nation is long delayed by this unfortunate circumstance. True, the bitter experience of life convinces an entire generation that what it was told in childhood was false, and a man loses part of his childish enthusiasm for what he had been taught in the past and had been refuted by life; nevertheless, by force of habit, he clings to what he had been taught in the past and imparts it to his children, only with less enthusiasm than it was imparted to him. The new generation loses a particle of the awe it felt for inculcated ideas; but, on the other hand, inborn habit is strengthened, and as time goes on the people cling more unconsciously and, for that very reason, the more tenaciously, to the traditions of their fathers. Life must make it impossible for these long moribund traditions to continue; a powerful thinker, a genius must arise to compel society to feel the need for and the possibility of change in the accepted, irrational principles. And after this discovery, how slowly and feebly the new idea takes root; how long it takes to penetrate the depths of men's souls and spread among the masses! Centuries have passed since it was proved that the earth moves, but to this day our common people, constantly hearing that the sun has risen and the sun has set, look upon it as an enormous lantern moving across the sky from east to west. The divine doctrines of Christianity have been preached in Russia for nine centuries already, but among the people belief in hobgoblins, water sprites and wood sprites is still strong. Even those who subsequently abandon the beliefs of their childhood in theory, long yield to them in practice. There are many educated people who are familiar with the phenomena of electricity and yet hide in horror in a dark room during a thunderstorm; similarly, there are many others who have acquired the ability to discuss true human virtues, and still, when appraising their friends, they attach most importance to a refined French accent and to a fashionable waistcoat. What is this due to if not the influence of the irrational impressions of childhood, imparted to the child, unfortunately, by those whom it loves or respects? But you will say: "It is inevitable that the older generations should influence the younger, and it is impossible to destroy this influence, the more so that, although it has some bad sides, it also has many good sides: all the treasures of knowledge accumulated in past centuries are imparted to the child precisely through this influence, and without it, it would be impossible to bring a man up to the line from which he must, in life, continue all that which mankind had done before him." This argument is quite just, and we would be unwise if we were to demand the destruction of that which naturally arises of itself, exists, and cannot be destroyed. But, on the other hand, we see no reason why we should advocate that which is of itself inevitable. The younger generation must necessarily be influenced by the older generation, and this is extremely beneficial for the development and perfection of a man, and of mankind. Nobody will contest this obvious truth. All we say is: why make the past the ideal for the future? Why demand from new generations *absolute, blind* submission to the *opinions* of preceding generations? Why destroy the independent development of a child by violating its nature, killing its belief in itself, and compelling it to do only what *I wish it to do,* and only *in the way I want it done,* and only *because I want it?*... By demanding such *absolute* obedience you are preventing the rational, proper and free development of the child. How harmfully this affects the entire moral being of a child can be seen from innumerable facts, and can be proved also on theoretical grounds. We shall present some of these.

First of all we shall define more clearly what is meant by *absolute* obedience. *Absolute* means not conditioned by any circumstances, unaffected by any contingency, not springing from any external or internal cause, but self-existent and containing its own justification. This is the kind of obedience that we demand from children, and the necessity for which was only recently very strongly urged by Pastor Sederholm in *Morskoi Sbornik* (1856, No. 14).[10] This means that the child must obey without question, that it must blindly believe its teacher, regard his commands alone as infallible and everything else as wrong, and lastly, that it must do all this not because it is good and just, but because it is so ordered and, therefore, must be good and just.

Let us see what psychological effect such a renunciation of will must have upon the child.

First let us suppose that the teachers and educators are ideal. Their admonitions are always just, always consistent, always commensurate with the degree of the child's spiritual development; they themselves are loved and respected by the children. Let us suppose that teachers of this type demand *absolute* and not *rational* obedience from children. What is the result?

A command is given; the child obeys without question; for this it is praised and rewarded. But there is nothing worthy of reward in the act itself; the child obeys the command forthwith because the thing it is ordered to do seems quite natural, because it coincides with its own wishes. Why then is it praised? Obviously because it obeys.

Another command is given; the pupil does not like it, he

thinks it is unjust and uncalled for, and voices objection. He is told that he must obey and not argue. His teacher is angry with him. Unwillingly he obeys, but the thought that his objection was just remains strongly embedded in his mind. Why then was he rebuked? Obviously for his disobedience.

Similar incidents occur often, and gradually the sense of truth and respect for rational conviction dies out in the child's soul, and their place is taken by blind obedience to authority.

You will say that later, when the pupil grows wiser, he will realize how rational were the commands of his teacher. This, of course, does happen, and it is very good, but only for the teacher, who thereby wins more respect for himself; but it is not good for the pupil, upon whom such discoveries have quite the opposite effect. Realizing a year, a month, a week, a day, and even an hour later, at all events too late (because the thing has been done, and done not from conviction [but by command]), realizing that his objection was foolish and groundless, the child loses confidence in his own powers of reasoning, his own arguments lose courage and vigour, he becomes afraid to form an opinion of his own and dares not follow the dictates of his own convictions even when they appear to him to be as clear as daylight.... He will think to himself: perhaps something is wrong.... Perhaps, a little later on, it will turn out that I was wrong.... Hence, irresoluteness, procrastination, listlessness, inclination to wait and see rather than to act—features which are retained for the rest of one's life, and which we are often astonished to see in people who are gifted with remarkable ability to reason theoretically [but who lack the courage to put their thoughts into practice].

But what if the child was right in the absolute sense, if his objection to the command was sound from the point of view of higher principles and contradicted only the circumstances of everyday life? The circumstances of everyday life justify the teacher; the child is aware of this; but as he had not yet been consciously convinced of the principle, the higher truth, being out of harmony with life, gradually passes into the category of abstract, useless ideas, mere fantasy.

Here are some examples. In conversation at home a boy says that his playmate is a thief. The boy's father rebukes him and tells him not to say anything like that again. The boy feels hurt and thinks the rebuke is unjust. But one evening, a week later, another playmate of his accuses the little thief of stealing. This causes an uproar. The two families quarrel, the candid chatterbox is punished. . . . The father says to the boy: There! You see what comes of this sort of thing!

A boy becomes very friendly with an old manservant. The boy's arrogant tutor rebukes him for this and forbids him to talk to the old man. But the boy disobeys. One day the boy misbehaves so badly in the servants' hall that the old manservant unceremoniously takes him by the arm and puts him out, respectfully admonishing him the while. The boy feels offended at this. The tutor is horrified on witnessing this incident and to stir up the boy's pride he says: There! You see what comes of being disobedient!. . . Wait, he will thrash you one of these days, if you keep chummy with him!. . . The boy repents of having been friendly with the old man, as if it were a crime.

A governess orders a girl to behave properly—stand straight, walk steadily, keep your head up, speak only when you are spoken to, etc. With rules like these inculcated in her mind she goes to a party. There are many children at the hostess' house and they are all very merry. They romp and play, laugh and chatter, make a lot of noise and have lots of fun. The girl would like to join them, but the governess says that this is improper, and so she sits alone and gazes enviously at the other girls having a merry time, especially at one who seemed to be enjoying herself more than the rest. . . . But suddenly this girl falls and breaks her leg. . . . The triumphant governess says to her humble ward: There! You see what comes from misbehaving!. . .

And so on and so forth. Judge then, impartially, to what extent absolute obedience serves here to develop the moral sense. Does not such upbringing, on the contrary, kill the good and holy elements that are innate in a child? Is it not natural, under these circumstances, that it should take the exception for the rule, and a distorted system for a natural one? And who will be to blame for this? Will it be the child?

And yet, how richly a man's mind could develop, and what strength of conviction would grow in him and merge with his whole being if he were taught in his earliest years to *think* about what he was doing, if every act the child performed was performed with the conviction that it was necessary and just, if it grew accustomed to ponder over its actions and did what others told it to do not out of respect for the person who commands, but out of conviction that what was done was right!... [True, in that case, many educators would have to resign their posts, because their pupils would prove to them that they did not know how to command!]

By killing boldness and independence of mind in the child, *absolute* obedience also harmfully affects the emotions. Consciousness of its individuality and of certain human rights begins to arise very early in the minds of children (if it only *begins* and is not born with them). This consciousness [necessarily] demands [satisfaction in the shape of] the opportunity to pursue *its own* desires [and not serve as an unconscious tool for the achievement of the unknown objects of others]. As soon as a child's strivings are satisfied, *i.e.*, as soon as it is given scope for thinking and acting independently (to some degree at least), the child is happy and cheerful, is imbued with the most charming feelings, it is gentle, betrays no sign of irritability, and displays the most amiable and rational obedience to what it considers just. On the other hand, when a child's activity is restricted and its strivings are suppressed, finding neither the desired satisfaction nor even a rational explanation, when instead of a conscious individual life the child must, like a corpse or an automaton, serve merely as an obedient tool [of another's will] then, naturally, the child's soul becomes weighted down by gloom; it becomes morose, listless, lifeless, shows dislike for others and becomes the victim of the basest emotions and inclinations. In his attitude towards his teacher, until he acquires the *absolute* virtue of a machine, the pupil is very irritable and distrustful. And subsequently, even after he has succeeded in effacing himself to some extent, he nevertheless retains a dislike for his teacher who demands only *absolute* obedience to his commands [justly, although only by a vague instinct, regarding his teacher as a tyrant and an enemy of his individuality, which a man can never entirely renounce, no matter how much he may try].

Is it necessary to speak of the fatal influence the habit of *absolute* obedience exerts upon the development of the will?

It would seem to be quite superfluous, and we would gladly have skipped this point in silence if we had not before our eyes the strange contentions of Mr. Sederholm (*Morskoi Sbornik*, No. 14), who affirms that "the efforts a child makes to overcome its own will and subordinate it to that of another develops its *moral strength* (!). This alone rouses in the child's soul the first manifestation of morality, the first moral struggle, and only with it does *human* life proper commence. And as a result of ceaseless exercise in this struggle, his will becomes so fortified that later, when his education is finished, he is capable of obeying *himself* and of doing what his reason and conscience dictate to him." The whole of this argument reminds us of a clever parent who, wishing his son to develop a supple body, compelled him to balance himself on his back across a narrow plank raised about three feet from the ground. The child waved its arms and legs, trying to find some support, failed to find it and, worn out by its efforts, slipped from the plank with a frightful shriek. As a result of these wise methods its development was stunted, and, in addition, it could never afterwards cross a bridge without a shudder. Generally speaking, this system of knocking out a wedge with the aid of another wedge has been in vogue [among us] for a long time [and we have long witnessed its frightful results]. A child is afraid of the dark, so it is locked in a dark room; a child dislikes a certain kind of food, so it is deliberately compelled to eat that food every day for a whole week; a child is fond of reading, but it is sent out to play; it wants to romp about, but it is ordered to keep still—and often all this is done not because it is thought necessary and useful for the child, but because of the pure and altruistic pedagogical motive of training the child to be obedient.... Incidentally, our practical educators are somewhat more consistent than Mr. Sederholm; they bluntly say: "The child must be trained to be obedient; if it is not broken in now, it will be too late to attempt to break it in later." Thus, they frankly admit that their object is to present society with future Molchalins.[11] Mr. Sederholm says that obedience cultivates a strong will! But this is the same as if I, in suppressing every mental impulse in my pupil, were to say to him every time I did so [(as teachers who demand *absolute* obedience usually do)]: "Don't argue!" and drew from this the following deduction:

"This develops the pupil's mental faculties, for it compels him to think and compare the correctness of my opinion with the incorrectness of his objections." Is this not as logical an assumption as Mr. Sederholm's? And is it not easy to bring up children in this way?

Mr. Sederholm's reference to *struggle* is beside the point. Actually, there is no struggle here, but surrender without a fight, which, if repeated often, will produce not a strong will, but moral flabbiness. And even if there is a struggle, it is a most irrational one: on the one hand, there is the inner strength, the natural inclinations, which the child regards as correct; on the other hand, there is the external, incomprehensible pressure of another's tyranny, or what the child regards as tyranny.... [With *absolute* obedience] victory is usually achieved by the *external* force, and this must inevitably kill internal vigour [and kill all desire to resist external influences]. Furthermore, we must not lose sight of one other circumstance: many of the commands that are given to a child are often of a kind about which it has not yet formed any definite opinion, and so it makes no difference to it whether it obeys them or not. Without understanding why, it does what it is told only because it is told to do so. There is no [struggle] here, there is only unthinking obedience, and this, subsequently, grows into a habit. A man brought up in this way remains for the rest of his life an object of different influences, which are determined not by rational necessity, not by deliberate choice, but by sheer accident. Such a man will follow the lead of the first person into whose hands he falls.

The influence which *absolute* obedience exercises on the *conscience* (to which Mr. Sederholm also refers), may be seen from all that has been said above. Growing accustomed to doing everything without thinking, doing it not because he is convinced that it is right and good, but only because he is ordered to do so, a man becomes indifferent to good and evil and does things repugnant to the moral sense without any qualms of conscience, and justifies himself with the plea that "*I obeyed orders.*"

These are the inevitable consequences of the absolute obedience method. But think how many more inconveniences this causes when orders are obeyed. The teacher's commands may be wrong and inconsistent and, therefore, will distort the child's natural logic. If the child has several teachers, their commands may contradict each other and the child, obliged to obey them all, finds itself in a dark labyrinth, from which it can find escape only by losing its sense of moral duty (if it has not before that worked out its *own* rules and, therefore, has developed a contempt for its teachers). All the teacher's defects, moral and intellectual, may be easily imparted to the pupil who has been trained to harmonize his actions not with the moral law, not with the dictates of reason, but exclusively with the absolute will of the teacher.

Thus, lack of independent judgment and opinions, a constant feeling of dissatisfaction deep down in the heart, listlessness and irresoluteness in action, lack of will to resist outside influences, loss of personality in general and, as a consequence, frivolousness and baseness, a weak and vague sense of duty and inability to introduce into life something new, more perfect, different from previously established standards—such are the gifts which [*absolute* obedience during upbringing] bestows upon the man in sending him out into the battle of life!... And it is with qualities such as these that a man must fight for his convictions [against the whole of society] and, accustomed to live under the guidance of another's mind, to act at the dictates of another's will, he must suddenly make *himself* the criterion of the whole of society, he must say: you are wrong, I am right; you are doing evil, this is the way to do good! But where will he acquire the strength to do this? What will he fight for? Will he fight for the authority of his teachers, who had guided his life and his concepts up to now? And besides, who gave him the right to do this? [Properly speaking, his relationships have not changed in the least: up to now they had been relations of subordination in upbringing and education; from now on his relations with his fellows at work and in social intercourse will be the same. What mind can assimilate such a conclusion: here is a line—fifteen or twenty years—to which you are led while being compelled implicitly and *absolutely to obey* others; this was done so that you may, after crossing this line, be able to *fight* others. It would be far more natural] to conclude that in his subsequent life too a man must behave exactly as he had been compelled to up to now.

2*

All these arguments are, of course, based on the assumption that the system [of *absolute* obedience] is a perfect success. But there are natures with which this system cannot possibly succeed. These are the proud, strong and energetic natures. Receiving normal, free development, they rise high above the crowd and astonish the world by the richness and immensity of their spiritual strength. These men perform great deeds and become the benefactors of mankind. But if their natural development is retarded, if they are hedged in by commonplace routine, by the narrow concepts of some very narrow-minded teacher, having no room in which to spread their wings, and compelled to plod along the narrow track which the teacher regards as quite convenient and proper, such people either drop into apathetic idleness, become superfluous in the world, or become blind and violent opponents of the very principles upon which they had been brought up. Then they become a misery to themselves and a terror to society, which is obliged to banish them. The most striking example of such a turn of affairs is presented by *Voltaire*, who was brought up according to the [pious] and stern rules of the Jesuit schools, which are based on lifeless obedience. Once he has become convinced that his teacher is wrong, such a pupil does not stop.... And what can stop him? Good and evil, falsity and truth, are all mixed up in his mind in imperative commands, and he sees them only through the prism of his frustrated individuality. His moral sense is stunted, his mind is not trained to ponder calmly and unhurriedly over his actions; all he knows and believes has been hammered into his head without his own will and emotions playing any part in this. Hence, his whole inner world, not developed by him independently, but thrust upon him from outside, seems to him to be alien, external, is easily upset at one stroke, especially if some influence, the very opposite of his teacher's, intervenes. Embittered, [against his oppressors] he develops within himself the spirit of contradiction and becomes the opponent not only of abuses, but of the very principles that are accepted by society. It goes without saying that an early death awaits him, or else a life of suffering and discontent with himself and others, a life wasted in fruitless search, because he is unable to settle down to any particular thing. How many noble and gifted natures, the victims of teachers' commands, have perished in this way, sometimes with loud complaints, but most often simply in sullen anger against the world, perishing without any fuss, and leaving no trace?

But what would you have?—we shall be asked. Would you give the child complete liberty, put no curb upon him, and yield to his caprices?

Not at all. All we say is that a child must not be trained, as dogs are trained, by being compelled to perform tricks at the sign of its trainer. We want education to be guided by reason, and this reason should not only be understood by the teacher, but should also be clear to the child. We affirm that all the measures the teacher takes should be so applied as to find full and clear justification in the child's mind. We demand that teachers should show more respect for human nature and try to develop and not suppress the *inner man* in their pupils; that the object of education should be to make a man moral not by habit, but by consciousness and conviction.

"But this is a ridiculous and absurd claim," the profound pedagogues will answer with a contemptuous smile. "Is it possible to demand that a little child should be able to reason correctly about problems of high morality? Is it possible to *convince* it when it is not yet developed enough to be convinced by argument? On sending a boy out for a walk it would be absurd to read him a course of lectures on physiology to prove to him why walking is beneficial; and it would be equally absurd, when giving him the multiplication tables, to enumerate all the mathematical calculations in which they are needed in order to prove how useful it is to learn them. . . . [The main task of education is to achieve at all costs the absolute obedience of the pupil to his superiors, and if this cannot be achieved by persuasion it must be achieved by fear."]

There is one flaw in all these arguments—the acceptance of [the present] *status quo* as the normal state of affairs. I agree with you when you say that children have not yet developed to the stage of clearly understanding their duties; but it is precisely your duty to develop this understanding in them. That is why they are educated. But instead of imbuing them with conscious convictions you suppress those which develop in the child spon-

taneously; and your only aim is to make children the unconscious and obedient tools of your commands. Realizing that the
child does not understand you, you calmly fold your arms and
imagine that all you can do is sit on the seashore and wait for
favourable weather, as much as to say: perhaps the child will
reveal ability when it grows up, and then it will be possible to
talk to it; but for the time being it must do what I tell it to
do. If that is the case, what is your function, O most learned
pedagogues? And what is the use of education?... Is it not your
bounden duty to get the child to understand you?... You exist
for the child, not the child for you; you must adjust yourselves
to its nature, to its spiritual condition, in the same way as a
physician adjusts himself to his patient, and a tailor to his customer. "The child is not yet developed"—but how can it develop if you make no effort to develop it, but, on the contrary,
retard its natural development? From your logic it follows that
it is impossible to learn a foreign language in a rational way
because you don't understand it when you start learning—and
therefore, the pupil must be compelled simply to repeat unfamiliar sounds until he has learnt them by heart, without understanding their meaning, as much as to say: when he has mem-
orized a lot of words, the meaning of them will somehow
gradually dawn upon him!... There is scarcely anything that
stands out so vividly in all these arguments as the desire to
disguise one's indolence and various selfish motives under the
cloak of the most sacred principles of virtue. But by degrading
rational convictions, by compelling the pupil to act without
thinking, one may undermine them far more quickly than by
allowing the child the widest [possible] freedom of development. All these shortsighted arguments about the undeveloped
state of the child's nature are strongly reminiscent of those gentlemen who protest against Gogol and his followers on the ground
that these writers are merely beating the air, that their methods
are ineffective, and that the type of people they attack can be
impressed only by a cudgel, not by persuasion.... As if anybody
can be taught anything with a cudgel! As if thrashing a man can
make him morally better and imbue him with any conviction
except the one, perhaps, that you are stronger than he!... In
training animals, of course, the *argumentum baculinum* is extreme-

ly effective; with its aid horses are broken in, bears are taught to dance, and even human beings are trained to perform all sorts of special tricks. But with all their skill and agility, neither horses nor bears, nor many of the human beings thus trained, become the least bit wiser!

"But how," the learned pedagogues also ask, "is the child to be protected from the pernicious influences that surround it? Should it be allowed to learn that these influences are pernicious by its own experience? If it were, not a single child would survive. Having experienced, for example, what poison is, or what it means to fall out of a fourth floor window, the child will scarcely be grateful to the pedagogue who, out of his profound respect for human nature, had tried persuasion at the critical moment, and had not dared simply to take the poison away from the child, or to drag it away from the window. . . ." Leaving aside the [ludicrous] absurd aspect of this argument, according to which, for example, a subordinate cannot save a drowning superior (because he cannot demand absolute obedience from him, and without this it is impossible to save him), we shall observe one thing. Children often fall from windows and take arsenic instead of sugar precisely because the system of absolute obedience compels them only to obey, but gives them no real understanding of things, it awakens no rational convictions in them.

If the complaints about the unreasonableness of children at least had some foundation! Actually, they are downright calumny, invented by the idle fancies of incompetent pedagogues for their own ends. First of all we must observe that education does not give us reason any more than, say, logic teaches us to think, grammar to speak, poetry to be a poet, etc. The object of education, like that of every other theoretical science which deals with man's internal world, is to stimulate and to clear up in the mind that which has long lived in the soul, but has lived spontaneously, unconsciously and unaccountably. Impart reason to a monkey with your system [of *absolute* obedience] and the whole world will bow in reverence to this system and bring up its children in accordance with its rules. But you cannot do that and, therefore, you must humbly recognize the rights of reason in the very nature of the child; you must not neglect it, but wisely utilize the advantages it offers you.

Children possess far more reason than is supposed. They are very clever and perspicacious, although, as a rule, they are unable to shape or express their thoughts clearly and definitely. A child's logic is very clearly revealed in the earliest period of its life, and the best proof of this is its language. It may be positively stated that a three or four-year-old child never heard half the words it gives utterance to; it composes and utters them on the models of those it has heard, and nearly always composes them correctly. The same may be said about forms: a child that has no conception of grammar will use all the cases, tenses, declensions, etc., of unfamiliar words no less correctly than you do yourself when, already an adult, you learn a foreign language. From this it follows that at least the power of induction and analogy, the ability to classify, develops in a child very early.

The same must be said about understanding the connection between cause and effect. Once having burned its finger at a candle, a child will never grasp a candle with its bare hand again; noting that snow comes in winter and there is no snow in the summer, a child, seeing the snow melt in the spring, guesses that summer is coming, etc., etc. Every child fondles those who fondle it, and shrinks from those who treat it unkindly, etc.

More than that: children very early form conceptions. After learning what a house, a book, a table, etc., is, a child will infallibly recognize all other houses, books and tables, although the new ones it sees do not resemble those it had previously seen. This shows that concepts already form in its mind, and, as is well known, to form concepts one must be able to form judgments and draw deductions.

Why have the learned pedagogues taken it into their heads that children are incapable of understanding rational persuasion and can be ruled only by fear, deception, and so forth? I cannot imagine why a false conviction should take root in a child's soul more readily than a true one. A child must not be soothed in a reasonable way when it is crying, but it is permissible to say to it "Don't cry; if you do the bogeyman will take you"; or "Stop crying; if you don't I shall thrash you." I should like to know what connection there is between a child crying and a bogeyman or the birch, and what logic the child is supposed to possess when it is admonished in this way?

"But," it is said, "a child cannot yet reason correctly about concrete cases because it still lacks experience: it has seen and knows so little as yet." This is quite true, and it is precisely the teacher's duty as quickly as possible to impart to the child the largest possible amount of knowledge about all sorts of things, taking care, particularly, that the child understands them fully and correctly. The very fact that the child contradicts, provides opportunities for imparting this knowledge, and the teacher's failure to answer this contradiction can be due only to his indolence or cowardice, but not to rational conviction. You order your pupil to do something; he says it cannot be done—well, show him *how* to do it. The child wants to do something, but you say that it cannot be done and you ask it how it intends to achieve its object. It tells you about the plans it has in its mind; prove to him consistently, and in detail, that his object cannot be achieved. And this will provide you with many splendid opportunities to impart to the child an enormous amount of true and interesting knowledge about the laws of nature, about the spiritual life of man, and the organization of society! Believe me, the child will understand your explanations and take note of them.

In general it may be said that in most cases the adults are to blame when children fail to understand. As a rule, the casual events in life somewhat shake the firmness of pure logic; *de jure* and *de facto* are inextricably interwoven; and we, accustomed to digressions, often permit an application of fundamental principles, or draw general conclusions from isolated facts, which pure logic cannot possibly tolerate. The pure, virginal logic of the infant mind does not accept this and, therefore, the child obstinately refuses to understand all the illogical things we unconsciously do, or say, out of our polite regard for the *status quo*. If you fill the child's mind with true knowledge, it will be difficult for you to hammer into its head a false conclusion drawn from this knowledge; if you have first compelled the child to accept a false premise, it will take you a long time to induce it to accept the conclusion you have drawn, which, although correct in itself, logically contradicts the original premise. Firm insistence

upon these illogical conclusions without a detailed and frank
explanation of the circumstances which called them forth will
inevitably lead to the distortion of the child's natural common
sense, and, unfortunately, we are guilty of such distortion far too
often.

Equally harmful for a child's intelligence is the unnatural
system of education in vogue among us. Knowledge can be acquired only by the analytical method; science itself developed
in this way; and yet, even the most elementary subjects are introduced with the synthesis! This is a totally perverse method,
which causes lessons to be unclear, confused and lifeless. For
example, every subject is begun with an introduction in which
the nature, importance, the benefits, sub-divisions, etc., of the
subject are stressed. I ask you, how do you expect a boy to understand all this before he has studied the subject itself? History
is divided into ancient, mediaeval and modern; every part is divided into the following periods, and so forth. What is this
division based on? What will it cling to in the mind of a boy
who has no idea of what history is? Geography is a science
which shows, etc.; it consists of three parts: mathematical, physical and political. The first deals with such and such, the second with such and such, and so forth. Can we expect a child
to make head or tail of this sort of geography if it is introduced
to him in this way?

And yet, see how much curiosity, what an eager desire to investigate the truth children display! The instinct of truth speaks
in them very loudly, louder perhaps than in adults. They are not
interested in the phantoms which people have created for themselves and to which they attach extreme importance. They do
not study heraldry, they do not go into all the niceties of philology or metaphysics, they do not strive for rank and honour (that
is, of course, if this is not dinned into them from the day they
are born). But how eagerly they turn to nature, how joyfully
they study all that is real and not shadowy, how interested they
are in every phenomenon of life! They dislike the abstract, and
this saves their souls from the forcible invasion of sophistries
which even those who are doing their utmost to force them into
the souls of their pupils cannot prove and explain. Yes, children are still fortunate in that nature does not at once lose its hold

over them, does not at once allow them to fall victims to perverse, biased and one-sided human theory!

"But," we shall be told, "children have a great propensity for evil; the child's innate propensity for evil must be actively combated." Without going into a detailed analysis of this opinion we shall take the liberty of answering it in the words of Mr. Pirogov who, of course, is fully to be trusted in a matter dealing with the characteristics of human nature. This is what he says:

"Good and evil are fairly well balanced within us. Hence, there is no reason to think that our innate inclinations, even if little developed by education, attract us more to evil than to good. But the laws of a well-organized society, imbuing us with confidence in justice and in the vigilance of our rulers, could eliminate even the last traces of propensity for evil."

But even if it is true that we have an innate propensity for evil, can you undertake to eliminate it? Can you, who constantly contradict yourselves, who by your actions refute your own rules, who condemn your own actions by theoretical principles and stumble at every step, who sacrifice the commands of supreme nature to the selfish demands of crude egoism—can you afford to throw stones at an innocent child and with pharisaical haughtiness protest against that little which you have found in it? No! First re-educate yourselves and then set to work to rectify the human nature of the children under your care.

If children cannot be regarded as the ideal of moral perfection, at all events, one must agree that they are far more moral than adults. They do not tell lies (until they are reduced to that by fear); they are ashamed of everything that is evil, they preserve within themselves the sacred sentiment of love for human beings free from all mundane prejudices. They become intimate with their fellows without inquiring whether they are rich, or their equals by birth; they even show a special propensity to become intimate with those who have been wronged by fate, with servants, and so forth. And their feelings are always expressed by deeds, they do not remain on their lips as they do with adults; a child will never eat an apple that has been given to it without sharing it with its brother, or sister, whom it loves; when it goes to a party it will always bring home a sweetmeat for its beloved nurse; it cries at the sight of its mother's tears out of pity for her. And in general, the opinion that the predominating sentiment in children is animal egoism is totally without foundation. If they show no sign of a strongly developed love for country and for humanity, it is, of course, because the scope of their ideas has not yet expanded enough to contain entire humanity. They do not know these things, and you cannot love what you do not know.

No, it is not for nothing that children have been set up as an example to us even by Him, before Whom peoples bow in reverence and Whose doctrines the world has proclaimed for so many centuries. Yes, we must learn from children, we ourselves must be reborn, *become like children,* to acquire a knowledge of real good and truth. And if we want to turn our attention to education, we must start by ceasing to despise the nature of children, and by ceasing to regard them as being incapable of understanding the dictates of reason. On the contrary, we must make use of the inner treasures which the nature of children offers us. Many of these natural treasures are still unexplored, many, in the words of the Bible, are hid from the wise and prudent and revealed unto babes!...

The object of this plea for the rights of infant nature against pedagogical tyranny, which checks natural development, was to point to one of the most important defects in our educational methods. We have not gone into details, we have merely advanced general propositions in the hope that wise educators, if they agree with us, will themselves realize what they must do, and how and what they must not do. The art of handling children cannot be imparted didactically; we can only indicate the principles upon which it should be based and the object which it should pursue. And we think that the main thing the educator should have in mind is respect for the human nature in children, to give it scope for free normal development, to try, first and foremost, to give it a correct understanding of things, to imbue it with living and firm convictions—to induce it to act consciously, out of respect for good and truth, and not out of fear and selfish expectation of praise and reward.

This is a difficult task, but not an impossible one. A beginning in turning to the child's innate reason was already made over a half a century ago by that noble and unselfish philanthropist and educationalist Pestallozzi. It was with reference to his school that Mme. de Staël made the significant observation that "childrens' failure to understand always comes more from obscure exposition than from the difficulty of the subjects" (*De l'Allemagne*). Thousands of experiments have confirmed the truth of this observation since it was made, and we must regretfully confess that it remains true to this day. Not only the mental but —and this is even more deplorable—also the moral education of children suffers, among us, from the same dogmatism, superficiality and lifelessness. To free ourselves from this miserable state, to pay attention not to the lifeless letter but to the living spirit, not to the achievement of external form but to the development of the inner man—such is the task which modern Russian education has to perform.

PROVINCIAL SKETCHES

FROM THE MEMOIRS OF
AULIC COUNCILLOR RETIRED, SHCHEDRIN
Compiled and Published by M. E. Saltykov
Vol. III, Moscow, 1857

A LITTLE over a year has passed since Mr. Shchedrin's first "Sketches" appeared in *Russki Vestnik*[13] (*Russian Herald*) and met with the enthusiastic approval of the entire Russian public. Mr. Shchedrin has remained in his arena to this day, continuing his noble fight without showing the slightest sign of fatigue. He has published story after story, constantly revealing in them how large is his stock of weapons and how inexhaustible his fund of observation. Nor is this all. More and more fighters keep joining him. Fired by his example, and "burning with superior ardour," even those who had been silent hitherto and had hidden in the crowd of indifferent spectators have gallantly rushed into the bloodless battlefield, armed with the mighty weapon of the pen. The public is still curiously watching this scene of heroic endeavour, and stories in the *Shchedrin style* are the first to be read in the magazines. But one cannot help observing that both the public and literature have lost their former zest, their former ardour; and the interest in social problems that a good many people now display has an air about it of old-fashioned clothes which they are about to discard. Those who began to read the Russian magazines only this year and have no idea of what they contained two years ago, have missed a few of the best moments of their lives. It sounds strange to speak of that period as of the long and distant past; nevertheless, there can be no doubt that it has passed away, and it will be a long time before Russian literature sees another period like it. In general, we seem to grow up very quickly and suddenly; we become sated and disillusioned before we have really been charmed. We do indeed grow quickly, like giants, not daily but hourly,

so to speak; but having grown up, we do not know what to do with
our stature. We suddenly find ourselves cramped and struggling
for air, because our natures have greatly expanded, while the
world is narrow and low-ceilinged—we have no room to turn
around, or to stand upright, to our full height. We sit huddled
and crouching, "borne down by the burden of knowledge and
doubt,"[14] absolutely inactive, until something very extraordinary
rouses us. In studying Russian popular literature, one of our
learned professors compared with amazing insight the Russian
people with Ilya of Murom,[15] who sat motionless for thirty years
and then, suddenly, after quaffing a cup of strong beer which
some pilgrims had given him, became imbued with giant strength
and went forth to perform amazing deeds. Indeed, our entire
history is distinguished for a peculiar impulsiveness: our state
came into being at one stroke; at one stroke Christianity was
introduced; we suddenly turned all our old habits and customs
upside down and caught up with Europe at a bound, and even
outstripped her; now, however, we are beginning to revile
Europe a little, and to invent a Russian outlook. . . . So it was
in big things, and so it was in small: we suddenly make a dash
for something and then sit down again and, like Ilya of Murom,
sit motionless, completely indifferent to what goes on in the
world. Two years ago we were stirred by the war, which revealed
to us the potency of European education and our own weakness.
It seemed as though we had awakened after heavy slumber, had
opened our eyes to our domestic and social life, and had guessed
that there was something that we lacked. No sooner did this dawn
upon us than we, with rare conscientiousness and sincerity,
began to expose "our social sores." Now, however, many are
beginning to laugh at this; and the sceptics who, from the very
beginning, had asserted that all this was

> The lurid raving of a morbid soul,
> Or the stimulation of a captive mind,[16]

are now expressing malicious glee as they glance ironically at
the grown-up children who always allow their enthusiasm to run
away with them and who see everything in rosy colours. But
whatever you may think, there is nothing to laugh at about
them: there was so much that was beautiful and noble, so much

youthfulness and freshness in their enthusiasm. Indeed, it was
a pleasure to see the universal animation: seeing how everybody
was unanimously and tirelessly striving to expose "our social
sores," to expose our shortcomings in every possible field, even
the most shy and reticent seemed unable to resist the general enthusiasm. What questions were raised then! What remote corners
were reached! One loud, energetic call swept the country "from
Perm to Taurida": [17] "Go forth all ye who can save Rūs from
the internal evil!" And everybody rose, everybody spoke up—
firmly, strongly and wisely. The old folks appeared to throw
off their habitual indolence; young men rose and set to work
for the common cause with fresh vigour. Literature, as always,
served as the first mouthpiece of the public aspirations, clarify-
ing them, and moderating them by a strict and thoughtful discussion of all the questions raised. Literature appeared to have
acquired social significance: it devoted itself almost exclusively
to the questions which engaged the mind of the public. The public began to speak about means of communication—and the
magazines published scores of articles about railways and other
means of communication, frankly admitting that we have lacked
good roads hitherto and have lost no little because of it. The
question of tariffs arose—and at once a number of articles appeared about free trade and protection. Attention was drawn to
the economic conditions of the people—and literature began to
talk about the conditions of the agricultural class, about free
labour, and other economic problems, giving prominence mainly
to what we lacked and to what we ought to do. Voices were
heard among the public stressing the importance of education
and the unsatisfactory system that had existed among us up till
then—and at once sternly critical articles on education were
written, the publication of pedagogical journals was undertaken,
and the more bitter the truth expressed in any article, the louder
was the applause with which it was rewarded. A protest was
raised against the abuses of bureaucracy—and "Provincial Sketches" appeared in a series of brilliant articles which ruthlessly
denounced all the dark deeds performed by the minor officials
and dragged them into the light of day. Bitter reproaches were
heard everywhere and nobody thought of contradicting them.
Poets and prose writers, scholars and amateurs, theoreticians and

practical men—all self-sacrificingly plunged into the gloomy bog of ignorance and abuse with the torch of exposure. In their souls seethed a mighty strength, their speeches breathed the fire of inspiration, which burnt up the tares in our native fields. Poet, arise!—each poet called encouragingly to himself, pondering over his mission:

> Let your challenging verse,
> The tocsin of truth divine, ring out
> To awaken slumbering thought
> To punish those of evil ways,
> That all untruth may perish.[18]

Fight in the name of supreme truth against the petty interests of the times!—exclaimed the highly educated critics. "Training for this fight, which faces every decent individual in our society, must commence in the very first years of a child's life, at the very beginning of its education!" "Science must boldly enter the fight against ignorance and prejudice," said the best of our scholars. "We must be grateful to the war for having revealed to us many of the dark sides of our life, against which we must now unitedly set out to fight, in order to uphold the honour of our country!" These powerful, noble and unselfish appeals could not fail to find an echo in the hearts of those who were concerned with the welfare of their country; and, indeed, many hearts throbbed more strongly in response to these inspired appeals. Many listened to this Russian, nation-wide confession with a sad smile, and even with tears in their eyes, and then proudly raised their heads and solemnly vowed to devote themselves to honest, tireless and fearless activity. There were also such who—owing to circumstances and to their own weakness—had been absorbed in the banalities of life and looked with horror upon their own lives and bitterly admitted that they were revolting. What did all these people have in view? What induced them to subject themselves to this solemn self-accusation? Nothing exceptional. They merely repeated the words of one of their heralds:

> To new brave deeds a mighty voice will call us,
> Tears of repentance will bring us relief

and they, in the goodness of their hearts, believed that the deed would soon follow the word. Even tub-thumping had an earnest

and accusatory ring about it at that time. That hollowest of
windbags, Mr. Nadimov,[19] boldly declaimed from the stage of
the Alexandrinsky Theatre:[20] "Let us shout for the whole of Rūs
to hear that the time has come to tear evil out by the roots!"
and the audience burst into frenzied enthusiasm and applauded
Mr. Nadimov as if he had really set to work to tear evil out
by the roots. "What are you laughing at? You are laughing at
yourselves!" said a sceptic at a performance of *The Government Official*, recalling aloud the words of Gogol. But nobody
was embarrassed by these words: the sceptic's neighbours in the
theatre proudly looked him straight in the face as if they wanted to answer him in the words of the same comedian: "Yes, we
are laughing at ourselves, because we hear the voice of our
noble Russian nature, because we hear the command from on
high to be better than others."[21]

Thus, everybody came to life, everybody became inspired
with a desire to march forward along the path of enlightenment
and moral improvement. A stranger, on hearing these appeals,
on witnessing this movement two years ago, must undoubtedly
have thought that a giant was awakening, stretching his limbs
after prolonged slumber, putting his thoughts in order and preparing to redeem his long inactivity by deeds of amazing magnitude. Such an assumption would have been quite natural: the
pure and lofty strivings of the men who were active in public
affairs and in literature looked so powerful, swift and swirling
that it seemed as though nothing could resist them in their on-
ward rush and that they would sweep away all the barriers that
had been erected by ignorance, wash away all the impurities
that had been created in Russian life by egoism, selfishness and
social indolence. Hearts then throbbed strongly and joyfully,
filled with the conviction that realization of defects is already
half way to rectification, and that the Russian never likes to do
anything by halves. If anybody had dared to assert that Ilya of
Murom, who had sat motionless for so many years, had now
got up only to mark time, it would have been regarded as
blasphemy. On the contrary, once he had got up, he had to keep
going forward without stopping, enjoying life, and performing
glorious deeds. And everybody expected these deeds to be performed, everybody waited with bated breath for something great

and extraordinary. Everything assumed an air of solemn preparation, as on the eve of some great festival:

> And then in winding procession
> Wended the light-winged friends:
> Airy youth so filled with *dreams*
> And a host of living *hopes*.[22]

It was a joyous time, a time of universal enthusiasm and ardour.... It seemed, somehow, that everybody's soul was more widely open to all that is good; everything around looked brighter. It was as though the warm breath of spring had blown upon the stiff frozen earth, and every living creature joyously began to inhale this spring air; every breast expanded, and all speech flowed sonorous and smooth, like a river freed from the ice. It was a glorious time! And it was not so long ago!

But two years passed, and although nothing exceptionally important happened during this period, public aspirations seem to be far different today from what they were then. We have already suffered much disillusionment on the new road: many of our hopes have turned out to be idle dreams; we have seen many things that are capable of misleading the most simple of optimists, who, in general, are distinguished for their simplicity. The former enthusiasm, the former tone of sincerity and pride is lacking too....

> O lofty speech,
> O proud strength,
> Whither have you gone?[23]

Talk goes on today too, of course; we do not say that public opinion has entirely forgotten the questions which so greatly excited it recently. All we say is that this enthusiastic talk is having little effect upon the life and activities of society; and this proves that up till now the majority of our home-grown progressives have played "not with their innards, but with their skins," as Mr. Shchedrin puts it.

Literature is conscientiously continuing its work: it regards service to the cause of social betterment as its most sacred mission. It has already cast off its swaddling clothes forever and, whatever happens, neither footmen's congratulations on highly solemn festivals, nor valets' odes to gentlemen on their promo-

3*

tion to high rank, nor tavern dithyrambs in honour of some
festival celebrated with fireworks and illuminations will now
acquire rights of citizenship in it. Literature is still actively
exposing social wrongs, still issuing its call for everything that
is good and noble; it is still urging upon society the need for
honest and useful activity, it is singing the old song:

> Get up, awake, arise,
> Upon thyself cast thine eyes.[24]

But the former enthusiastic response from the public is lacking.
The public is already weary, it regards its function almost at an
end, it almost regards itself as worthy of a laurel crown for the
interest it has shown in social problems and in the new writers
who are engaged in exposing our evils. Only from time to time
are flashes, uneven and sporadic, seen here and there of the
fire of enthusiasm that had raged before. But even these flashes
vanish without leaving a trace, without exerting any influence
upon public activity. It appears, then, that the enthusiasm and
hopes were premature, and that many of those who so heartily
welcomed the dawn of the new era were suddenly overcome by
the desire to wait for noon and decided to go to sleep till then;
that a still larger number, who had blessed heroic deeds, suddenly fell silent and ran into hiding when they realized that
brave deeds must be performed not by words alone, that real
action and sacrifice were needed. Everybody impatiently expected, wished and prayed for improvements, cried out angrily
against abuses and denounced the indolence and apathy of others
—but few, very few, got down to real work. Scared by imaginary difficulties and obstacles, many of those who could have
done much that was truly useful

> Wilted on the threshold without a struggle.[25]

Things happened that were far from lofty and were even
rather unforeseen: in a way, the Russian public played the part
of the talented nature. Our readers have, of course, already read
"Provincial Sketches" and are therefore probably familiar with
some of the talented natures that Mr. Shchedrin depicts. But,
perhaps, not all our readers have pondered over the essence of
this type of man and over his significance in our society. We
therefore take the liberty to examine these natures in greater

detail, for, in our opinion, they rather vividly express the predominant character of society. The types of talented natures are extremely varied, but they all have something in common, namely, their *talent*, which sometimes evokes sincere regret and gives one cause for very sad reflection. Their position is, of course, ridiculous, even revolting, but the ridicule which the position of these gentlemen evokes must not be applied to their natures as such, which are by no means lacking in good qualities. Mr. Shchedrin describes their occupations and characteristics as follows:

"Some occupy themselves with walking up and down the room in a dressing gown and whistling for the want of something better to do; others become jaundiced and develop into provincial Mephistopheles; a third type become horsedealers or cardsharpers; a fourth type consume enormous quantities of vodka; a fifth, at their leisure, chew the cud over their past and protest bitterly against the present. ... What is common to all these gentlemen is, firstly, the 'worm,' secondly, that they have found no place 'at life's festive board,' thirdly, their extraordinarily expansive natures. But the main thing is—the worm. This silly worm is the cause of the fact that our Pechorins[26] shuffle from one end of the room to the other, not knowing where to lay their heads; it has already introduced them to the neighbouring squires: Polezhayev, Sopikov and Khrapovitsky.* I regret to say that the Pechorins are to be found only among the young folk. The old and hoary government official or squire cannot become a Pechorin; he looks at life with a practical eye and regards its thorns and inconveniences as inevitable and irremediable. These are fleas and bedbugs, which have bitten him so often that they have ceased to be enemies, in fact, if anything, they are his good friends. He does not probe into the causes of things, but accepts them as they are without racking his brain over what they might have been if... etc. The young man, on the contrary, is beginning vaguely to understand that there is something wrong around him; something disjointed, something that fails to hang together; he finds himself in strange contradiction with his entire environment; he wants to protest against this, but lacking the necessary vitality, all he can do is scoff, or adopt the pseudo-tragic pose of indignation." ("Provincial Sketches," Vol. III, p. 69, et sup.)

You see, therefore, that in spite of the irony with which Mr. Shchedrin treats the talented natures, he himself cannot but reveal that there is something good at the bottom of them. There is nothing reprehensible in their strivings; on the contrary, they place them on a considerably higher level than the apathetic

---

* The Russian equivalent of: Lazybones, Snuffles and Snorer.—*Tr.*

mediocrities who look at life with a practical eye and find blissful relief from all doubts and problems in the behests of teachers, or in the signatures of their superiors. The misfortune of
the wasted talented natures is that they lack vitality. If vitality
were infused into them in time, something positively good may
come of them. Long ago somebody observed that there are no
incapable people in the world, there are only people in the
wrong place; the clumsy coachman who upset his sleigh and
threw the government official into the snow, and the government
official who was dismissed from the service for incompetence,
may both have proved competent if they had changed places.
Perhaps the government official has a natural bent for handling
horses, and the coachman may well be able to handle legal
affairs.... The whole trouble arises from the fact that they are
both in the wrong place, and for this, neither the government
official nor the coachman is to blame; their fate, that "stupid
turkey hen," as the devil-may-care Russian saying has it, is to
blame. The same is the case with all the talented natures: their
development is one-sided, out of harmony with their needs, and
yielding to the force of hostile circumstances, they find themselves on the wrong road. They are not so brutish, weak-spirited
or blind as to yield without resistance, in the simplehearted belief
that this is as it should be; this is their virtue. But they lack
sufficient inner strength, wisdom and nobility of spirit to hold
out to the end, to persevere in their virtuous strivings and not
drop into apathy, phrasemongering, and even into rascality;
this is their greatest, most frightful vice. But obviously it is not
an innate vice. It springs from weakness of character combined
with ardent strivings. Ardent strivings in themselves are extremely
praiseworthy and are simply a symptom of a man's youthfulness; and, as everybody agrees, character is not born with a
man, it is acquired during his education, and becomes definitely moulded in the subsequent tribulations of life. Consequently,
strictly speaking, the individual retains only a lively impressionable nature—a symptom by no means bad; for all the rest,
the environment of that nature is to blame. We shall be asked:
why does not this environment exercise the same influence on
others; why has it this fatal effect only upon the talented natures? The answer to this is simple. These natures, being so impres-

sionable, run ahead of others, often take upon themselves more than they can carry, and more often than others meet with opposition which they are not strong enough to resist. While good and well-behaved children enjoy the calm of blissful ignorance, bearing in mind that they are children and, therefore, must build their own little world without interfering in the affairs of grownups, impressionable and impetuous children are constantly intruding into places into which they are not invited, become familiar with life's squabbles at an early age, and receive from the grownups practical refutation of their childish thoughts. In some, innate logic and the habit of being active gain the upper hand: they examine practical views from all sides and appraise them very correctly; they do not yield to force of circumstances, do not sink to angry phrasemongering and cynical indolence, vexed because they are unable to do anything great, but contend against the hostile forces to the end, and if they do not succeed in vanquishing them and fall, the very noise of their fall summons new self-sacrificing fighters to the spot where their corpses lie. But there are few strong men of this type. The majority fail to withstand the onslaught of the foe and die morally without benefiting others, and often even causing them harm. From the social standpoint, of course, they do not deserve praise; in society they are always either parasites or rascals. It is not our intention to justify them, nor do we wish to exalt their idleness over the unostentatious activities of humble toilers. We only want to say that the talented natures give more promise of good development than the well-behaved, good, obedient, etc. children, and that, given favourable circumstances, their development would produce good fruit. We may perhaps compare them with fertile soil. Sow maize, rye and nettles in good soil somewhere in the environs of St. Petersburg [if such soil can be found there]. The maize, of course, will not come up at all, because of the diverse charms of the St. Petersburg climate, and the rye will be swamped by the nettles. You have a field, but it is of no earthly use. How can you compare it by its fruits with another field, of rather poor soil, it is true, but which has produced rye, even if in a meagre quantity. It canno: be denied, however, that the soil in the first field was better than in the second. Abandoned and neglected, and, in addition, hidden from the sun by fences and

buildings and cluttered up with all sorts of garbage, it could produce nothing but nettles. If it had fallen into the hands of a good
farmer, the latter would not only have cleared it of the garbage
and have weeded out the nettles, but would also have reaped a
good harvest and, in addition, would have built himself a fine
hothouse and would have raised the most tender plants by protecting them from the various unfavourable influences of St. Petersburg.

If what we have said above needs proof, we need not go far
to find it. Mr. Shchedrin has depicted for us three types of talented natures: the Mephistophelean, the drunken wastrel, and
the rascal. One must admit that the choice of these three types
is very apt. The failure of talented natures usually ends in one
of these ways. All are revolting and harmful, or at all events
useless; but go back to the time when these gentlemen were on
the threshold of life, probe deeply into their natures, and you
will see that all their passions originated from good intentions;
their fall was due simply to their inability to resist external influences. What this inability is due to we have already partly
explained. We shall merely add that, being dependent upon inertia which is characteristic of everything in the world, this quality grows from the constant habit of passively imbibing other
people's ideas, and the more this passive nature is possessed of
intellect and fresh strength, the more revolting does this become. If
a man who is incapable of putting half a dozen words together
spends all his life as a copyist there is nothing disappointing
about it. He is inconspicuous: he is pleased with his fate, he is
not ambitious; for he knows that it is dangerous to leap into the
air if you have no wings. . . . But a man who grasps things easily
and quickly, who has live and lofty strivings and is fully conscious
of his own strength—if such a man is suddenly overcome by indolence, he drops out of all activity and employs his talents only
in beating the air, or in diverse activities of an unpraiseworthy
kind: now that is disappointing and bitter to behold. Such a man
immediately becomes conspicuous, because he wearies everybody
with his complaints about the injustice of his fate, annoys everybody with his sarcastic remarks about his neighbours, and ar-
rests everybody's attention by his deliberate and premeditated
idleness. Take Mr. Korepanov for example. He is not conspicu-

ous in the society of Krutogorsk because of his idleness, or because he spends his life in trivialities. He is not shallower than others: like others he is in government service; like others he attends the children's balls given by Princess Anna Lvovna, and like others he has no particular interests. In short, there is nothing remarkable about him, and you pass him by with an absent-minded glance and think to yourself: "Here is another of the vast number who are vegetating in Krutogorsk, busily doing nothing, and having no idea that there are better fields of activity...." But Mr. Korepanov suddenly stops you with the exclamation:

"Please don't confuse me with this crowd; I am much better than any of them, I assure you. Never mind the fact that I mingle with them and, like them, do nothing.... Believe me, I could do more, very much more if I wanted to.... But I don't want to...." "That makes it worse," you answer. "It shows, Monsieur Korepanov, that you yourself are to blame for being a nonentity. You can't expect anything from these people; they are doing what they can. Is it their fault that they lack the ability to do more? But you are much worse than they, because you are not even doing what you can. You are simply a waster, Monsieur Korepanov."

And would you believe it? Korepanov at once agrees with you and begins to revile himself.

"Yes," he says, not without a touch of subtle irony. "I am stupid, I am weak, I have a tiny, insignificant soul. I even envy the smug satisfaction and tranquility that is written on the faces of my fellow officials; it shows that, after all, they have not wasted their lives.... But I was always filled with doubt, and senselessly rushed from one thing to another.... But what did I gain by it?... I would have had a much easier time if I had gotten myself a soft job, as Nikolai Fyodorovich did; if I had married Anfisa Ivanovna, who can make shawls out of old pantaloons, I would be counting my money now, as Semyon Semyonovich is doing...."

You agree that this would have been much easier than riving and striving all one's life, but Korepanov reveals his utter disgust for the activities of Nikolai Fyodorovich, Semyon Semyonovich, and their ilk. He even tries to imbue the children of Semyon Semyonovich and Nikolai Fyodorovich with disgust for the thieving propensities and parsimonious lives of their parents, and he is proud of the services he has rendered in this matter. He calls Krutogorsk a cesspool, and is very displeased with the fact that here everybody must forever wear the livery he has once put on. From Korepanov's sallies you judge that he has been to a good school, can distinguish between good and evil, and knows what real morality is. He himself admits that in his youth he had sat at the feet of the learned, but that he had made no good use of his learning. You see, he did not want to swot over books and pick up knowledge a grain at a time, but waited for somebody to "pour it [knowledge] into his head out of a pitcher and thus make him as wise as Minerva." This, then, was the first fall in the face of difficulties, the first triumph of indolence. Later, Korepanov would not go into government service, where he could have found more scope for his talents, because "he wanted to eat, and this could not be found in St. Petersburg or Moscow all at once." You see, he was too lazy to procure things for himself gradually, by working for it: he wanted to have everything at once. And so he went to Krutogorsk, where he had relations "who, of course, had a nice soft job ready for him...." Here he performed his duties in the perfunctory manner that everybody did, but mainly he fumed with anger against everybody, trying to prove his own superiority and the injustice of fate. To tell the truth, fate was indeed unkind to him, but it was unkind in giving him relations who had managed to prepare a soft job for the idler, and had thereby relieved him of the necessity of trying to obtain a situation and bread for himself. Had that not been the case, Korepanov would have been a capable official and would not have been lost for honest and useful activity by sinking to the level of a mediocre Mephistopheles.

Let us now examine Luzgin, also a talented nature, but of another type. There is nothing positively bad about this type. Recalling Luzgin's past, Mr. Shchedrin says that he had been rashly kind and generous, that the blood coursed swiftly through his veins, and that this life-giving stream of youth was abundant and inexhaustible. Luzgin himself, in candid conversation, says that much love, ardour and passion has remained in his heart even in middle age. He regrets that he wasted so much time in his youth, not so much at lectures, but in playing the dashing fellow. There are some splendid spots in his life. He married a poor governess who was employed by his neighbour and suffered from the persecution of her libidinous master and from the caprices of her mistress. He did not want to go into government service in St. Petersburg because of the "frosted people there, sort of cold and clammy," who ran about all day long seeking the good fortune to be able to twist their mouths into a smile at the sight of a person whose favours they needed. He stopped visiting his school chum because the latter wanted to dazzle him with his acquaintances, such as Actual State Councillor Strekoza, Princess Oboldui-Tarakanova, etc. It cannot be denied that this reveals a kind and sympathetic nature with truly noble inclinations. He might be taken for a good and peaceful squire who had at last found in his family circle a peaceful haven after the trials and tribulations of life. But that would be a wrong conclusion: although Luzgin, on his own confession, did not attend lectures, nevertheless, some higher knowledge did penetrate his head, and he can no longer rest content within his narrow sphere—"The dimensions are strangling us," he said. "We are expansive by nature and we would like to take everything in our embrace, but the dimensions are too small. We still have an immense amount of ardour and passion, but we have no outlet for them: the sphere is too small, we have no room to spread ourselves in. . . ." But who, Mr. Luzgin, prevented you from taking hold of only as much as your strength could cope with? Why are you vegetating in the country and not performing public duty at least in some elected office? But you see, when Luzgin returned from college his mother said to him: "You stay near me." Moreover, he found evil neighbours, and so he stayed, the more so that he had shown a disposition for indolence from his earliest years. But in the country he is dying from ennui; his education had not been so complete as to enable him to rest content with himself and his family hearth; he longs for other diversions and, of course, finds them without great difficulty: every day he drinks until he is blind drunk, driving his wife to despair and ruining his own health. . . . But tell me, pray, is nature to blame for this? Luzgin tries to throw all the blame on nature, although, strictly speaking, he is not trying to justify himself. On the contrary, like all talented natures, he fearlessly and shamelessly dilates on his own vices at great length and assures you that he is a pig, that he has sunk very low, and that he is despicable from head to toe. But all this self-accusation is of little use. He no longer has the strength to rise: "I have become so accustomed to idleness that it has become part of me, so that I have no wish even to think of anything," he says. But he does not wish to take the blame for everything. Realizing that he lacks the strength to rise, he tries to assure himself that this was the edict of fate and it cannot be otherwise; so it is evident that "this fire is destined to burn out in my breast without expressing itself in any way." And convinced of this, he despairingly takes up the glass to drown his vexatious impulses in drink. And then he complains about nature in the following extremely comical manner:

"Why," he asks, "did she not make me a Zeno, but bestow upon me the inclinations of a Sybarite? Why did she not harden my heart for the struggle against the thorns of stern reality, instead of softening it and making it capable of responding only to the good and beautiful?... It looks very much as though nature is a ninny...."

But why blame nature, Mr. Luzgin? Nature sends all men into God's world weak and helpless: she does not deliberately harden or soften anybody in the expectation that this gentleman will fight and this one will not, and therefore, as a measure of precaution, endow each one with such and such qualities. To justify your indolence you conjure up the idea that nature is ill-disposed towards you and has softened you because of certain intrigues. Nothing of the kind: men are hardened not in the lap of nature, but in the crucible of worldly experience. And you lack this hardening because it was not necessary for you, from the very beginning, to combat your laziness, because you permitted others to think and act for you. As a result, although you have a kind heart and it responds to all that is beautiful, you yourself have turned out to be not only a bad man, but also a vulgar and even a sordid one. That is what we shall tell Luzgin, not wishing to encourage him in laziness and cynicism. But addressing our readers, we cannot, of course, refrain from adding that fate has really been rather hard on Luzgin. He was taken out of the simple, direct, patriarchal relations of the countryside and given a smattering of higher matters, but he was not given firm and sound principles; his interest in the sciences was not even roused to a degree to make him prefer them to the diversions of the dashing beau. At the very first attempts to do something he encountered obstacles: his mother and his home kept him away from government service; then *evil* neighbours enticed him into the hunting field and into orgies of pleasure; and then, proud upstarts and spineless lickspittles roused in him a revulsion for St. Petersburg life. For him this was too much: his propensity for laziness, his habit of submitting to the demands of another's will, and his too superficial education rendered him incapable of withstanding constant temptation. And then fate took the trouble to prepare for him a home, where he could live at the expense of others. ... And thus perished a man who under other circumstances might have been somebody.

There is yet another type of talented nature which seems to be quite different from the two we have already examined, but in substance resembles them very closely. An example of this type is provided by Gorekhvastov, whom Mr. Shchedrin describes. At first sight this individual appears to be very active. He is a schemer, a rascal, a cardsharper; he disguises himself in an official uniform, embezzles government money, compels somebody to jump out of a window, jumps out of windows himself, and succeeds in amassing a fortune and in losing it again. What greater activity can you have than this—energetic, sustained, but directed in a bad channel? This, one would think, is not a weak character, containing the seeds of good but doomed because of its indolence and weakness; it is a strong, wicked soul, gifted only for every kind of villainy. It is totally unlike the two pusillanimous characters depicted by Mr. Shchedrin which we have just examined. So it appears at first sight. But if we look more closely we shall find that, in substance, Gorekhvastov is exactly like Korepanov and Luzgin. The only difference between them is that the two latter had, at least, learnt something, and in spite of the superficiality of their education they assimilated some of the simplest rules of honesty such as, for example, that it is shameful to steal, abhorrent to cheat at cards, etc. Gorekhvastov was not even taught this; instead, he was taught only good manners and to be able to *causer* about all things. As a talented nature he yielded to this instruction and his manners did, indeed, seem to be good, and he became a splendid *causeur*. His chums visited Frenchwomen on Sundays and he went too, because he lacked the will to resist temptation; for, like Luzgin and Korepanov, he lacked an internal sheet anchor. Pyotr Burkov introduced him to men whose career and mission in life were limited to not altogether honest deeds on the green baize field, and he associated with them; these men started an affair *en grand* with the object of swindling a merchant, and he became the zealous executor of this scheme; Pyotr Burkov told him about life *en artiste*, and he agreed to live *en artiste*; he was invited to visit fairs—and he was ready for that. Sometimes his good instincts seemed to awaken within him: for example, he felt ashamed to sell himself to an ugly old squiress who had designs upon his athletic figure. But Burkov told him that this was all nonsense and *ordered* him to consent for the sake of the rights of friendship —and Gorekhvastov consented. Tell me, can a more weak-spirited man be imagined? He is much weaker than Luzgin and Korepanov because he has even fewer internal convictions than they: he positively cannot resist surrounding influences, he cannot even escape them through idleness, but directly yields to them.... And then he goes on further, by inertia, and often even gives outward signs of firmness and courage, befitting the circumstances. The only thing is that this energy and firmness resembles the courage displayed by the footman who shouts loudly from the doorstep to the coachman: "Bring her up!" and immediately afterwards obsequiously helps his master into the carriage, and stands meekly in front of him if the latter takes it into his head to slap his face. Gorekhvastov's courage vanishes in an instant: he trembles and turns pale as soon as he sees a *Chevalier* or other police official anywhere near him, or even when somebody, in strange company, calls him "cad" and amiably threatens to throw him out of the window. He reveals inability to resist outside influences at every step, and reveals it more than Korepanov and Luzgin.

Indolence, abhorrence of work, is also an important feature of his character, notwithstanding his apparent tireless activity. He refused to go into government service and became a swindler precisely because he "did not wish to sit in some stuffy cubbyhole seven hours a day, every day, longing for the place of Assistant Head Clerk." He feels that he is "above the common level," that he could be a poet, an author, a promoter and a capitalist. But he wants to get the utmost without working for it, and so he chose the career of a cardsharper as the easiest road to wealth. Ruined, he now lives on the fourth floor in the style of an actor, and what pleases him most about this is the complete abandon with which he can live. Even the sight of his neighbour Dremilov always poring over a book fills him with aversion. The mere mention of drudgery of this kind drives him into a frenzy. "What kind of a life is it, I ask you?" he exclaims. "Can a man, has a man, a right to sacrifice himself to hemorrhoids? And where will it get him anyway?" etc. Gorekhvastov is not satisfied with being a practical idler: he strives to elevate his idleness to a theory. He even positively asserts that "a genius needs no education, because everything comes to him of its own accord. For example, ask me... well, about anything you like!... I'll give you the answer on anything, because it is my Russian character, I was born like it." As you see, this gentleman too, like Luzgin, is not averse to blaming nature for his shallowness—he was born like it! But what he says clearly reveals a degree of indolence that far exceeds the natural desire for peace and quiet, which is permissible for every man.

"But he is a gambler, a cheat and a schemer," we may be told. "This, too, calls for considerable activity. To amass a fortune Gorekhvastov worked with his head, his hands and his feet, with all the members of his body. He did not sleep for whole nights, he subjected himself to danger, wandered from fair to fair, jumped from a second floor window to the street. You may think what you like, but a passive, indolent nature which finds supreme bliss in apathetic inactivity is incapable of doing that sort of thing."

All this appears to be very true at first sight. But after a little reflection it will not be difficult to perceive that even Gorekhvastov's activity is absolutely passive, it is activity enforced by purely external circumstances. On nearly every occasion his actions are prompted by others, he is led by other rascals, he nearly always steadily proceeds in the direction in which he is pushed. Perhaps he is not altogether idle; but is there a single person in the world who is absolutely idle? One spends all his days at the billiard table, a second plays chess, a third smokes cigars with an air of profundity. One may spend half the day walking for the sake of exercise and spend the other half in finding employment for his stomach, which can scarcely cope with the task given it in the twenty-four hours.... One spends all his life retailing news, another is bored to death in the theatre every night, etc., etc. All this, after all, is work, and no person can dispense with work of this kind all his life, because the law of nature itself dictates movement of some kind. But what is this movement? What is its goal? What force induces it? These are the questions that we must put to ourselves in appraising human activity. Even a stone flies in the direction in which you throw it, and if you aim it skilfully at the water it will form rings on the surface. If you boil water it will seethe so strongly that it will boil over, but it will at once spread over the floor and cool—and leave only a puddle. The activities of wasted talented natures boil over like this and nothing more. They have already lost the inner urge to activity; they lack the patience and firmness to pursue their goal consciously and steadily. They are capable of a single impulse, even a strong one, because, in general, their internal strength being low, they are inclined to be carried away by external impressions; but a single setback, a single obstacle, which cannot be removed at one stroke, and their energy deserts them, leaving their innate indolence to gain the upper hand. They are all active representatives of that conception of things which Gorekhvastov expresses in the following words:

"I am a patriot, Nikolai Ivanovich, I love the Russian because he never stops to think very long. Other people, Germans, or French, ponder over every single thing so long that it makes you sick to look at them, one would think they want to give birth to a child; but we Russians, we go up to a thing, glance at it, shrug our shoulders and say: 'What, can't do that? The power of the Cross inspires us! We can do it in the twinkle of the eye!' And it is so. As soon as we take up the axe, the chips begin to fly. Geniuses, one might say! We learned all the sciences without studying! You know, I love to watch our muzhiks at work; they lie on their backs all day long, but when they do start work, things begin to hum, and you wonder how they manage to do it!"

In addition to weakness of spirit and indolence, Gorekhvastov betrays the secondary symptoms of the talented nature. He will tell you about the feats he has performed with amazing candour while vigorously reviling himself in the telling of it, excelling in this respect Korepanov and Luzgin, in so far as his nature is more expansive than theirs.

"I am a cad!" he will exclaim, tearing his hair. "I don't deserve to be in the company of decent people! I am a cad, I wasted my youth! I must ask you to forgive me for daring to pollute your house with my presence."

What profound repentance!—you may think. But don't worry: it is simply a flash to soothe his conscience, as much as to say: "We are not as banal as others, we are conscious of our superior Russian nature and know that we could be very good if we wanted to." But these flashes do not affect Gorekhvastov's activities in the least. Just when he is declaiming against his own unworthiness he is arrested for the embezzlement of government money by a woman with whom he had had "improper relations." Having wasted his youth, this gentleman has become so lazy that he even does not want to steal himself, but compels his mistress to do so for him.

We shall now leave Mr. Shchedrin's talented friends and discuss the question more abstractly, to avoid causing offence to anyone personally. In our opinion, the members of a young society which has not yet managed thoroughly to formulate all its views and opinions, a society which, owing to unfavourable circumstances, has not cultivated the art of self-determination for actions (to use a scientific term) must inevitably come under two main categories. One is quite passive, impersonal and extremely limited both in its capabilities and in its requirements. These are the quiet ones: they never get excited, are never beset by doubts, and not only never leave their rut, but do not suspect that it is possible to leave it. At school, at work, and in life generally, they are always *well-behaved*: they do what they are told; when they are given a lesson to learn they learn it, when they are told how far to go they go so far and no further. These people are already lifeless, hopeless, you can expect nothing from them, and it is no use attempting to direct them on to the good road. However much you may try to guide them they will not cease to be nonentities, they will not develop your ideas, they will not be your assistants. They, like ship's ballast, only lend stability to the ship of society amidst stormy winds and the buffeting of heavy seas. It is difficult to rouse them, they are inert, and are blindly faithful to the one rule they have learned by rote, to the authority they have once and for all accepted. They deviate from this only in practice, and then always unconsciously. They may praise a novel by George Sand, until they learn that it was written by George Sand; they may even laugh on hearing some absurdity if you do not tell them that you had read this absurdity in some book

that they admire; they may even condemn some despicable action
if they do not know that it was performed by a general. But as
soon as the authority comes to light their consciousness is awakened, and then no argument can shake them.... These people
have neither convictions nor principles: for them only rules and
forms exist. There is something in their activities that resembles
the antics of a bear which dances for its master's profit and for
the amusement of an idle crowd; their conversation reminds one
of a parrot which in reply to all your questions utters a single
word it has learnt by heart, and often, quite out of place, calls
you "fool" when you pet it. Incidentally, some people find consolation even in this: it is interesting to hear a bird talking like
a human being, they say.

The other half of the young society consists precisely of those
who are called "modern heroes," "provincial Pechorins," "county
Hamlets," and lastly "talented natures." The last appellation
least of all, perhaps, fits the idea that we wish to convey, but it
is not a matter of appellations. There is little of nature here, of
course; more active are mundane circumstances, which consist,
firstly, of the conditions of the times. As Mr. Shchedrin has already observed, Pechorin propensities and claims to talent always
appear in a young generation which possesses a relatively larger
fund of fresh strength and a livelier impressionableness. Subjected to diverse influences, the young people find themselves at
last compelled to make their choice. An internal struggle arises,
which continues unceasingly in some exceptional personalities,
goes on actively and independently, and in which inner, organic,
natural impulses are clearly separated from external influences
that operate more or less violently. But such personalities are the
exceptions, and the lower the level of education of society as a
whole, the rarer are these personalities. The majority of the people
whose minds become active in a society which is little educated
prove to be weak and unfitted to withstand the obstacles that await
them. From the moment they come into the world, in the first,
most impressionable, years of their lives, the people of the new
generation are surrounded by an environment which does not
think, which is not guided by moral principles, which regards ideas
of any kind as the inventions of the devil, and which in practice
unconsciously bends and breaks the will of the child. This second

circumstance—the resistance offered by early education and the entire environment to the ideas of the times to which the new generation already belongs—leads to the fall of the majority of the talented natures. If any requirements arise which the former environment and the former life do not satisfy, they must seek satisfaction in another place; but this calls for great and sustained effort, it is necessary for a long time to go against the current. But the ship ran aground long ago and the ballast is weighting it down. Seeing that everything around them is in motion—waves roll on and ships sail past—the talented natures are also eager to go somewhere, but· they lack the strength to refloat the ship and steer her in the direction they want to go; and they are afraid to leave the ship and depart from their friends: the sea holds unknown dangers and they are poor swimmers. The more skilful and intrepid swimmers leave the ship and make for the shore, and from there they call to their fellows and show them the way to safety. But in vain; the poor swimmers are afraid to plunge into the waves, and they confine themselves to cursing their own cowardice and their predicament. Now and again, glancing at a streak of foam speeding by, or encouraged by a shout they hear through the captain's megaphone, they suddenly imagine that their ship is sailing before the winds and they exclaim enthusiastically: "She's off! She's off!" But soon they realize that they were the victims of an optical illusion, and again they begin to curse, or they sink into apathetic inaction, forgetting the simple truth that they will die in these shoals unless they set to work themselves to refloat the ship, and above all, at least help the captain and the crew to throw the ballast overboard and so lighten the vessel.

Nobody, of course, will find any difficulty in deciding which of the two categories is the best. At the present time *both are worse,* so to speak, and woe to the society which rests content with these two categories for long, and in which the number of redeeming exceptions does not increase from year to year. Lack of all self-reliance, indolent apathy and striving after externals are the fundamental characteristics of the talented natures, as well as of those who belong to the social ballast, although they do not all possess these characteristics to the same degree. Consequently, neither the one nor the other sort of people is of great value to a society which strives after conscious and independent

4*

life and activity. The best of the talented natures will do no
more than understand in theory what is needed and shout loudly
when it is not too dangerous to do so. Under unfavourable circumstances, however, they will begin to talk ambiguously, or even
entirely against their own convictions. The most valiant of them
will fall silent and will regard their silence as heroism, as much
as to say: "We are martyrs to our convictions. Everybody is talking
against their consciences and profit by it; we too could profit
by preaching other people's ideas which we ourselves do not
share; but we are not hypocrites and so we remain silent, keeping
the views which we have worked out for ourselves secret until
it is possible to express them without apprehension." And so the
profoundest silence, the most complete immobility reigns in society, disturbed perhaps only by the debauchery of the talented
natures who encroach upon the security of humble citizens.

But the young and not yet fully developed society has a future,
and for this future the second category of people, *i.e.*, the people
with the expansive natures, are, after all, far more promising than
the lifeless creatures who lack all aspirations. At all events, they
will not exercise that paralyzing influence upon the generations
that follow them because they already have a vague premonition
of the truth, they express justification, timid and feeble, but justification nevertheless, of the impulses of youth. Luzgin no longer
dares to thrash his children when they catch him telling lies;
Korepanov fearlessly inculcates in the young generation of Krutogorsk "a loathing for the abominations in which their dear parents are wallowing." Rudin[27] (another talented nature) exercised
a more beneficial influence upon the young student Bassistov than
all his professors put together. The talented natures at least betray
feeble rudiments of activity, they want at least to turn over in
their minds, this way and that, what has been imparted to them
by others; the useless, impersonal natures do not even suspect that
it is necessary, and possible, for them to act themselves; passive
submission to external influences not only fails to stimulate them
to activity, but even lulls and soothes them still more in the
process of mechanical progression which they call life and activity.... It would be wrong to blame these unhappy toilers if
only for the reason that they lack a will of their own, lack thoughts
of their own and, therefore, cannot be blamed for anything. But

one cannot avoid a feeling of regret at their condition, and wishing that the number of people of this type who wrongly bear human semblance would steadily diminish.

Reverting now to the beginning of our essay, we intend to put the following question to our readers: do not the majority of the members of our society fall into the two categories we have mentioned? Are not the people who combine truth and lofty striving with honest and tireless activity exceptions among us? We have no doubt, every one of our readers can count among his acquaintances scores of men who from the day they were born have never thought of a single question that did not concern their own skins, and scores of others who have wasted all their lives on problems and doubts without attempting to settle any one of them by their own activity, and who, in fact, act contrary to those solutions which they have found for themselves in theory. How many people do we see who humble themselves before those whom in their heart of hearts they despise, who laugh at what they fear, who do things which they know perfectly well are loathsome, who say things they do not believe, and so forth? What is this due to? To the same cause that sends the talented natures to their doom—it is due to inadequate development of the inner strength required to be able to resist external influences. Today, thank God, we all know something, because we have all received a little education. But the trouble is that so few of us take advantage of this education, so few of us dare to test by our own mental efforts the teachings of others, to throw the light of our own thoughts upon the system of others, and to take the road of ruthless negation with the object of searching for pure truth; the majority imbibe education only through their memory, and if they exercise their brains sometimes, it is not because they are induced to do so by some living internal impulse, but only because their minds were stuffed with a doctrine which commands that one should think. And so, thinking by order commences without the heart taking any part in it, and with only the subtleties of dialectics being observed. Even this is good, of course: after all, it is better than absolutely lifeless non-thinking. But life is not grasped with the aid of dialectics; and he who has failed to penetrate the diversity of its influences by his own efforts, unshackled by the theories with which his mind was stuffed in the period of his ignorance, will fail to understand its course. In society in which the forms and formulas senselessly and unreasoningly borrowed from others still strongly affect individuals, fruitful and consistent activities cannot be expected for a long time to come. Many minds may show signs of fine impulses produced by borrowed convictions, but all these —both the impulses and the convictions—perish uselessly and scatter like dust, unable to resist the pressure of the dark and heavy mass that bars their road. That is why nations pass so slowly from the state of passive acceptance to the state of independent activity. The number of people who think independently grows slowly, almost imperceptibly, from generation to generation, and opportunities for putting ideas into pratice grow even more slowly. No nation has as yet reached the ideal of independent individual activity, and there are only a few nations in which consciously developed individuals are not exceptions.

Our society is still very young compared to European civilization, and it is therefore not surprising that the vast majority of its members are so passive towards science and thought. Among this majority there are peaceful citizens who are distinguished for their amazing capacity easily to reconcile all the contradictions that arise from the mingling of the new concepts engendered by life with the old habits acquired in childhood. There are also talented natures of different kinds who declaim vociferously about their own inactivity and, at their leisure, ruminate over their past and protest against the present. It is they who usually talk about their superior Russian natures, the virtues of which they define after the manner of Gorekhvastov: "We Russians are geniuses, one might say; we learned all the sciences without studying!. . ." Indeed, let us continue Gorekhvastov's statement and picture to ourselves certain phenomena of our social life: "As soon as we take up the axe, the chips begin to fly. . . . They lie on their backs all day long, but when they do start. . . ." "In a century and a half we caught up with Europe and even outstripped her"—many of the talented natures will exclaim, echoing Gorekhvastov. "We were ahead of Europe eight centuries ago," others will answer. "We have always been different from other people; we learned all the sciences without studying long ago, because geniuses don't have to study: we Russians are all born like it."

Unfortunately, all this is mere words, words bereft of intrinsic

meaning. This talk about our extraordinarily rapid growth is merely a rhetorical flourish. Ancient Rūs has handed down to us a
large stock of naively related facts about the bribery and corruption of government officials. A hundred years ago Sumarokov earned
the gratitude of his contemporaries by his successful campaign
against the "nettleseeds."* Sixty years ago the magazines, commenting on Kapnist's comedy, foretold the eradication of bribery.[28]
Mr. Shchedrin himself buried past times only a year ago.[29] But
all these corpses have come to life again, and their shrill voices
are heard in the third part of the "Sketches" and in other recent
literary productions. Does this prove that we have grown very
much morally and intellectually? Does it not, on the contrary,
recall to our minds the picture of Gorekhvastov tragically declaiming against his own baseness and loathsomeness, tearing his
hair and uttering words of repentance, while at the same time planning a new piece of thievery?

"Now look what you have talked yourself into at last?" practical
people will say in answer to the above. "You yourself at last admit that the type
of literature you praise so much is impotent, don't you? What has the
painting of all these loathsome pictures, sordid scenes and banal and despicable characters led to? What has the exposure of our social sores, which
you have always praised so highly, led to? It turns out that there is no
sense in your literary revelations and that there can be none. You may take
it for granted that police sergeants and inspectors will not read your arguments and sketches, and even if they do they will only swear at you and
say: it's all very well for them to write all this stuff, they have nothing
else to do; but we have so much to do that God alone can help us to get
it all done. And you can take it for granted that a man's consciousness of
his duties to his stomach, to his family, to his superiors, and so forth,
will be stronger than the arguments in all your books. It is a pity that
literature is debasing itself by descending from the glorious heights of
fantasy into the dark pool of sordid reality. It should carry pure
sacrifices to the altar of the Muses; but instead of that, its priests take
to the broom. You are born for inspiration, for *sweet* music and prayers,
why then do you descend to mundane cares, why do you pursue those
goals which seem to interest you so much? Art must have no goal outside
of itself; if it has, it becomes distorted, vulgar, sinks to the level of a
trade, and all this without any benefit to society, with the sole object of
providing an outlet for some gentleman's spleen. Stop writing this sort of
stuff: it won't lead to any good. Age-long experience should convince you
of this indefeasible truth. Depict for us the lofty sentiments, noble natures

---

* Corrupt petty officials.—*Tr.*

and ideal men. Give us models of the good and beautiful that we can admire, that will provide rest and consolation for our souls after witnessing
the tribulations and heart-rending scenes of mundane life. Write about
art, write on subjects that will fill our hearts with sweet tenderness or
reverent awe, and lastly, describe the beauties of nature, of the heavens. . . .
Then your literature will be fulfilling its real mission—to serve art—and
then it will be useful, pleasant, and above all artistic."

These words of practical people ring with a note of bitterness. These people have long been looking askance at the trend
which has upset their theories and has even to some extent affected their practice too. Their objections are not new, of course, they
are simply a variation of Pushkin's poem "The Mob," with the
addition, perhaps, of some sentimental lines from Ilya of Murom:

> Oh, we cannot always bitter tears
> Be shedding as our woes we tell.
> A moment's oblivion let us find
> Under fantasy's bewitching spell.[30]

Why not seek oblivion if you want to, especially if it is only
for a moment? But, owing to their innate indolence, the talented
natures want oblivion to last very long, for ever if possible. In
their slumbers they are ready to curse the "voice of truth" with
all their heart if it suddenly disturbs their sweet dreams. Many of
the aesthetically educated talented natures strongly desire this oblivion in order to find bliss in repose. But we confess that we could
never understand the "bliss of madness," and still less can we
understand why people want to make art the servant of this madness. You do not wish to look at what is loathsome and disgusting in life; is literature a darning woman whom you want to
compel to darn the holes in your worn-out clothing? You know
that man is unable out of his own head to invent the slightest thing
that did not exist before; good or bad, everything is taken from
nature and from real life. When does an artist subordinate himself
most to his preconceived goal—when, in his productions, he expresses the true essence of the phenomena surrounding him, without
concealing or adorning anything or when he deliberately tries to
choose only the exalted and the ideal, in conformity with the fas-
tidious instincts of aesthetical theory? And what exalts art most—
the description of a babbling brook and the contrast of hill and
dale, or the presentation of the course of human life and the conflicts of different principles and social interests? It is your pleas-

ure to describe the servants of the public trend as muckrakers. So be it. We shall not protest against this. We shall even express our sincere gratitude to you and our astonishment at your aesthetical wisdom, and put you on a par with the German professor (just think—a professor! and a German professor at that!) concerning whom Heine says:

Mit seinen Nachtmützen und Schlafrockfetzen
Stopft er die Lücken des Weltenbaus.31

If literary revelations produce no practical and beneficial results, or produce extremely little results, who is to blame? Will you say it is literature? As it is, you accuse it of being too harsh, of not minding its own business, and so forth. It is making the strongest effort it is capable of, but you are dissatisfied with its activities and want to put a stop to them because they are feeble! You would be far more consistent if you said that it is necessary to sharpen the tone of literary revelations in order to achieve practical results more easily. Then there would be no dispute between us, although, even then, we would not dare to promise exceptional success in the improvement of morals by means of literature. Literature does not constitute such a predominating force in our lives as to be able to subordinate everything to itself: it serves as the mouthpiece of the concepts and strivings of the educated minority and is accessible only to this minority; its influence on the masses is only indirect, and it spreads very slowly. Besides, by its very nature, literature cannot be a coercive force that eliminates the physical or moral possibility of acting against the law. It abhors violence and coercion and prefers calm, dispassionate and unfettered discussion. It raises questions, examines them from all sides, communicates facts, stimulates the thoughts and feelings of men, but does not appropriate to itself any executive power such as you demand of it. We call to mind just now the beginning of the work of a French author, celebrated in its day, on an important question. In it the author says: "I am asked whether I am a ruler or a legislator, since I dare write about politics. To this I answer: I write precisely because I am not a ruler or a legislator. If I were one or the other I would not waste time talking about what has to be done: I would either do things or remain silent...." It is high time the mission of the writer was understood; it ought to be understood that his weapons are words, persuasion and not material force. If you admit the truth of certain convictions and fail to act up to them, you have only yourself to blame; it shows that you are spineless, that you are unable to combat difficulties, that you do not yet fully understand the necessity of honestly co-ordinating conduct with ideas. If you dislike those convictions it is another matter. In that case, publicly express your own convictions, prove that Mr. Shchedrin is not speaking the truth, that he is conjuring up things that have never happened. The public will listen to you too and decide who is right and who is wrong. Under those circumstances, literature will, of course, acquire greater importance, although even in that case it will not perform miracles and will not stop the course of history. To illustrate our point we shall take ancient history, in order not to involve modern nations in this controversy. That the Athenians were a literary people nobody can deny. Cases in court were decided by the effect the reading of a good tragedy had upon the judges; rhetoric ruled the destinies of the state. But nothing could avert the decline of Athens when the people lost their valour. The shafts of wit which Aristophanes—to whom the comedians of our day cannot hold a candle—shot at Cleon were telling indeed and delighted the indigent citizens, but after all it was Cleon, being a wealthy man, who ruled the Athenians with the assistance of a few other rich men. Demosthenes publicly preached his philippics to the whole people. Philip was aware of the orator's power; he said that he feared him more than an entire army, and realizing that the struggle must be waged with equal weapons, he bribed Aeschines, who could match his strength against Demosthenes, to take up the cudgels on his behalf. The fight was a protracted one and, at last, the course of events itself proved that Demosthenes was right: the Athenians heeded his exhortations, mustered an army at last and went against Philip. But all Demosthenes' eloquence was unable to bring back the times of Miltiades and Themistocles. The Athenians submitted to Philip. But was Demosthenes to blame for having spoken out? Can it be argued that it would have been better had he kept silent?

After careful reflection, however, we have become convinced that it is really not worth while seriously to defend Mr. Shchedrin and his trend. All Mr. Shchedrin's criticism applies to an insignificant minority of our people, which will grow more and more insignificant as education spreads. And the reproaches hurled at Mr. Shchedrin are heard only in the remote and barely perceptible circles of this minority. When, however, Mr. Shchedrin's name becomes known among the masses it will always be pronounced with respect and gratitude: he loves the people, he discerns many good and noble, although undeveloped, or wrongly directed, instincts among these humble, simplehearted toilers. It is these he defends from all sorts of talented natures and humble mediocrities, and from them he withholds all criticism. In his "Worshippers" he draws a magnificent contrast between the simplehearted faith, the fresh and virile sentiments of the common people, and the haughty vapidity of Darya Mikhailovna, the general's wife, or the nauseating bombast of the tavern licensee Khreptyugin. Is it derogatory to national dignity, or lack of patriotism, when a man of noble character relates how the pious people are driven away from the holy icons in which they sincerely believe and worship in order to make room for Darya Mikhailovna, the general's wife, who superciliously says *c'est joli*; or how a semi-illiterate clerk mocks at the simplehearted faith of an old man and says: "A common man can never understand the phenomena of nature as suggested to him by his ignorance"; or how water is snatched from the lips of the weary pilgrim women who are dying of thirst in order to fill Ivan Onufrich Khreptyugin's silver samovar? No, the shafts of criticism are directed against those who are offended by such stories and recklessly repudiate their country by putting themselves forward as the people. They are the withered parts, the dry branches of the tree which the expert marks for the gardener to lop off; and it is they who are raising a howl that the tree is being mutilated, that the tree is perishing. Yes, the tree may perish if these dry and withered branches are not lopped off. The tree will lose nothing if this is done: it is fresh and young, it can be reared and straightened; its vital force is so strong that new, sound branches will soon grow in the place of those that have been lopped off. As for the dry branches, they deserve no pity: let them be of some use to somebody, if only to heat a stove.

For the unspoiled, common class of people, and for all that is fresh and sound in Russia, Mr. Shchedrin expresses a most lively sympathy. We think that the scene he depicts of worshippers and pilgrims waiting in the cathedral square for the appearance of the holy icons will provide repose for the eyes of the most aesthetic and exalted. There is no sentimentality or false idealization in this picture; the people are depicted as they really are, with all their shortcomings, crudeness and ignorance. Grief, poverty and rags, and hunger appear on the scene; and you hear songs sung about the advent of Antichrist, for

> The hair is cut and chins are shaven,
> And Latin clothes are being worn....

But these poor, ignorant pilgrims, these superstitious peasant women rouse in us a feeling not of ridicule or disgust, but of pity and sympathy: sadness overcomes us when we hear the women talk about their forthcoming migration to the Siberian lands beyond Perm. They are loth to leave their old homes, loth to leave their parents' graves, but what can they do? Life has become hard in the old place: the land is just tundra and marsch, families are large, food is scarce, and there are no means with which to pay taxes. But in Siberia, they say, wheat grows well and cattle breed. The gossips sigh, and the conversation evidently subsides. But, continues Mr. Shchedrin:

"There is no end to this heartfelt pain, to this gnawing want, which we indifferently call the phenomena of everyday life. They are ceaselessly maturing in the hearts of the poor toilers, and find expression in complaints which are always couched in the same terms and are always fruitless, but are nevertheless repeated over and over again, because a man cannot suppress a groan when that groan, which has fully matured without effort on his part, escapes from his breast.

" 'That's how it is, brother,' says an elderly and very meek looking muzhik, on meeting a fellow villager in the square. 'That's how it is. They've taken Matyusha for the army too!'

"His coarse, tanned face twitches almost imperceptibly, his voice trembles, and the usual restrained sigh escapes from his breast.

" 'And he was such a good lad, too,' continued the muzhik. 'He wouldn't hurt a fly. Did what he was told, and he went off as quiet as a lamb. Didn't say a word when they said he was fit.'

"And suddenly the picture of this good quiet lad Matyusha rises before my eyes, not as a rollicking fellow, but rather as a timid, hardworking and honest youth. I see him behind the plough, vigorous and strong, in spite of the perspiration pouring down his tanned face; I see him at home, uncomplainingly performing all the domestic chores; I see him in church, standing humbly, and frenziedly crossing himself; I see him late at night sleeping the sleep of the just after a hard day's work, which for him knows no end. I see his old father and mother adoring their darling child; and I see the box with the little scrolls from which the lots are drawn, and I hear the words: 'fit', 'fit', 'fit'. . . .

" 'What, have you come here to pray, Uncle Ivan?' the muzhik asks his fellow villager.

" 'Yes, to the saint. . . . Perhaps our Little Father will have mercy on him!' answers the old man in a trembling voice. 'They found nothing wrong with him. My Matyusha I mean. His body was as white as snow, and so strong. . . .'

"And this entire crowd came here with pure hearts, preserving in all its purity the spiritual mite which they had promised the most holy and most exalted image of God's saint. Listening to their conversation I myself begin to realize the possibility and the legitimacy of this irresistible striving to perform a feat of spiritual heroism, which can be so simply and naturally explained by all the circumstances that encompass the simple lives of the common people" (Vol. III, pp. 152-154).

We are brought to a halt here by this moving sentiment. We shall only note in conclusion how evenly and smoothly, but how selflessly, simply and frankly, the profound sentiments, the profound faith of these people are expressed, and expressed not in exclamations, but in deeds. Nothing like the utterances of the phrase-mongers we mentioned at the beginning of this essay. We must not allow the talk of those gentlemen to mislead us; it is useless reposing our hopes in them; they are capable only of uttering phrases; within them indolence and apathy reigns. The living, fresh masses are not like that: they do not like to talk much, they do not flaunt their suffering and grief, and often they do not quite understand them. But once this sensible and businesslike "mir"* does grasp something, once it utters its simple word, the word that springs from life itself, it will be a potent word, and it will do what it promises to do. It can be fully relied on.

* World or community.—*Tr.*

A COMPARATIVE PHYSIOLOGICO-PSYCHOLOGICAL VIEW ON THE BEGINNING AND END OF LIFE

A PAPER BY MERITED PROFESSOR W. BERVI

Kazan 1858[32]

THE PROCESS of life is a subject in which Merited Professor Bervi is little interested; he even regards interest in the process of life as a materialist trend which leads to crude sensualism. To keep away from matter as far as possible and, as he expresses it, "to help as far as possible" to distract man's attention from the problems of present life, Merited Professor Bervi casts a physiologico-psychological glance at man—before his birth and after his death, *i. e.*, to put it poetically,

> Unites the end with the beginning
> And death on the living bestows....[33]

Mr. Bervi's ideas on psychology apply more to the infant in its mother's womb, and his physiological researches to the lifeless corpse in which all physiological functions have ceased. In this corpse Mr. Bervi discerns some sort of a spirit, and he subjects it to physiological investigation, having no suspicion that the spirit which is given off as the corpse decays belongs not to the realm of physiology, but to the realm of chemistry. Anybody else would have found it hard to confuse chemistry with physiology in our days, but not so Mr. Bervi, because he refuses to belong to our times and is doing his utmost to discover some means by which our times could be annihilated, killed. It was with this object that he published his physiologico-psychological view, in which he expresses, among other things, his displeasure at the fact that all the natural sciences have turned to material researches beneficial to present life. This trend of the natural sciences is like a dagger at Mr. Bervi's throat. Because of the natural sciences he denounces our times as a whole. After read-

ing the Merited Professor's pamphlet we fully understand what
rouses his indignation, and we even sympathize with him in his
sad predicament, although, unfortunately, we cannot in any way
assuage his grief. Indeed, every page of Mr. Bervi's physiologico-
psychological research shows that he studied the natural sciences
very long ago, in those remote times when Schubert and Eschenmayer reigned in the sphere of anthropology, and perhaps even
before that, in those pre-historic times before Lavoisier was born.
Judging by the fact that, in confirmation of his opinions, he
quotes passages in Latin from the works of Bacon, Seneca and
Cicero, and even (to explain his entire pamphlet, we think),
the Latin proverb: *errare humanum est,* which as is well known
means: to err is human, we think we would not be far wrong if
we dated Mr. Bervi's education in the Middle Ages. Mr. Bervi is
totally ignorant of the researches of the modern naturalists. He
bases himself most of all on the authority of Plinius; on rare
occasions he refers to Blumenbach and Bougainville. Of the mod-
erns he knows only his "scientific collaborator P. A. Pell, who
has palpably proved how illusory are all conclusions intended
to prove the transformation of oats into rye." Is it surprising
then that, with this state of his knowledge, Mr. Bervi should be
so extremely displeased with our times, in which the natural
sciences have made such enormous progress and have reconciled
philosophical reflections about the forces of nature with the results of experimental researches into the nature of matter. Today
the natural sciences have adopted the positive method; all conclusions are based on experimental, factual knowledge and not
on dreamy theories concocted at random by somebody, some time,
and not on the obscure guesswork with which ignorance and half-
knowledge was satisfied in the days of old. Today the ancient
authorities, before whom Mr. Bervi stands in awe, are no longer
recognized, and, generally speaking, authorities in scientific research are of no great importance. Today, young people not only
unhesitatingly describe Paracelsus dreaming as nonsense, but
even find that Liebig, of whom we think Mr. Bervi has never
heard, was mistaken; they read Moleschott, Du Bois-Reymond and
Vogt, and even do not take these on faith, but try to test and
even supplement them by their own investigations. When they
do take up the study of the natural sciences, young people com-

bine it with the philosophy of nature, in which, again, they follow not Plato, not Oken, nor even Schelling, but the best, bold-
est and most practical of the pupils of Hegel.[34] How can Mr.
Bervi help being angry with all this when in philosophy he stopped
at Fichte, whom, incidentally, he fails to understand and whose
doctrines "seem to be vaguely remote to him." How can he
help being angry with our times when the successes achieved
by the natural sciences completely upset his mediaeval theories
and make them look ridiculous not only in the eyes of the spe-
cialist who follows the successes of the positive sciences, but
even in the eyes of every educated man who was born somewhat
later than Lavoisier and Fichte. Mr. Bervi dislikes our times
because they have run past him. But are the times to blame for
that? Who tells Mr. Bervi to lag behind? And if he lacks the
strength to continue the journey, why remain on the road and be
an obstacle to others? The progress of time and knowledge cannot halt and wait for any adept of science, even if he is a professor.... Yes, Merited Professor Bervi has dropped behind
science, very far behind, and we are sincerely sorry for him. We
are always saddened by the sight of belated birds in the autumn
who have failed to reach warmer climes, at the sight of a waggon
which has dropped behind the rest and is forlornly wending its
way on the deserted road alone, of a chicken which, dallying
by the wayside, has not followed its mother with the rest of
the brood and is dashing about frantically looking for her
where she had been a moment ago but, alas, is no longer
there. The same sadness overcomes us at the sight of that other
belated creature, Mr. Bervi, standing at the crossroads of life, as
the poet has it,

> Like a tombstone
> Among the habitations of the living....

Out of pity for Mr. Bervi we wanted to keep silent about
him and his physiologico-psychological view, but after reading
his pamphlet, and brief reflection, we came to the conclusion
that our pity for Mr. Bervi was totally undeserved. We found
the worthy author of the "View" to be so smug as to rouse not
sympathy but sentiments of quite another kind. He does not
admit that he has dropped behind. He does not even try to un-

derstand the results of the latest researches. He does not wish
to catch up with those who have outstripped him and—what do
you think?—he tries to stop those who are passing him and
proceeding further along the road of knowledge. He says that
the natural sciences are not studying the things they ought to
study, that they are on the wrong track; in other words, he
denies the importance of the results of the positive researches of
modern times. What are the tasks which, in Mr. Bervi's opinion,
face the sciences and which the sciences are neglecting? These
tasks are extremely intricate, and had they not been accomplished
in the Middle Ages, their invention would have done honour to
the intelligence of Kifa Mokiyevich.[35] You see—psychology must
try to define the difference between the vital element and the
soul of man; physiology must investigate the vital processes in
a lifeless corpse; physics must search for a force separate from
matter, and for matter free from the influence of force; chemistry must analyze bodies and search for something supersensible in them. In general, by mixing up the natural sciences
with the moral sciences Mr. Bervi imposes obligations on naturalists which have never entered anybody's head except that
of a mediaeval alchemist. He wants physical research to pursue
not a knowledge of the changes in and the actions of matter, but
to search in matter for the spirit, for archeus, ether, vital force,
in short, for anything, as long as this "something" is not positive, material, but "inaccessible to the senses." This demand is
absurd, of course, but it suits Mr. Bervi because he thinks that
in this way he can cover up his own ignorance. "It is not because I am unaware of modern researches that I do not quote
them," he says, "but because I reject them as pernicious and
impious, and as leading to crude sensualism. I adhere to the
old concepts not because I have not grasped the new, but because the new concepts fail to strive for the supersensible." That
being the case, there is no need to extend our pity to the belated
but smug wayfarer, the more so that he mocks and jeers at those
who are pushing on ahead of him. We do not wish to shield
Mr. Bervi any further; we shall expose him so that he may amuse
the esteemed public with his mystical-alchemist views, which
may have appeared to be scholastic wisdom (*sapientia scholas-
tica*) in the Middle Ages, but today can be regarded only as

the antics of a mountebank at a fair. We shall open his book, turn the pages over at random, and on every page we will be sure to find a curiosity.

For example, at the very beginning of this investigation you will find the following comparison between birth and death: before an infant's birth its mother suffers; after his birth she rejoices. Similarly, after a man's death his relatives and friends weep and suffer. Well, what of it? Listen:

"These torments, this anguish, which agitates our breasts, leads us to the solacing conviction of immortality: in the same way the birth pangs which precede birth presage the joy at the appearance of a new man in the world."

How skilfully Mr. Bervi handles his subject, does he not? He sets out to prove a subject about which the minds of educated people have been made up long ago, but, notwithstanding the easiness of the problem, he reduces the subject to ridicule by drawing a clownish comparison. This even excels the wit who argued that the increase in the number of government officials presages the early enlightenment of the state by drawing the following comparison: dawn *appears* in the sky before the rising of the sun which lights up everything; in the same way the official *appears* in the government department before enlightenment spreads over the entire state.

The following is an example of how Mr. Bervi discredits popular exposition.

"Whoever glances at the corpse of a man, or of a rabbit that has been shot, or of a slaughtered chicken, will at once say that these bodies are dead. Why? Because they have ceased to live, they have been deprived of life. Hence, death deprives the animal of life, and the dead body is the negation of the living, or something in the nature of an antithesis of the living body."

Apparently, it seems to us, one would think, that Mr. Bervi, esteemed Mr. W. Bervi, Merited Professor W. Bervi, believes, is even convinced and quite sure, that popularity, simple exposition, making things or subjects generally intelligible, requires nothing more than the repetition, reiteration, recapitulation in different words, of simple truths, the simplest propositions, things that everybody understands, and subjects about which nobody has any doubt. Esteemed Mr. W. Bervi, the author of "A Physiologico-Psychological View," Mr. W. Bervi, evidently has not the least doubt that the constant repetition of the same things in different words is popular exposition.

Unfortunately, our esteemed author does not always adhere to this popular style; almost on every page of his book we come across long periods that are impenetrable to the human mind, even destitute of logical and sometimes of grammatical sense. Take the following, for example:

"If impressions obtained through our external senses do not lead us to a cognizance of the external world and we are unable to convince ourselves of our spiritual existence which has no significance without the assistance of its body, this essential condition for all spiritual activities in this world."

Full stop, reader. What else are you waiting for? Is not what Mr. Bervi told you in this first half of the unfinished conditional period enough for you? Since "spiritual existence with its body" has already found a place here, what else would you have found if the "if" were carried to the desired conclusion?

If you turn over two pages you will find the following period:

"Like the human spirit which is gifted with free will, the vital element manifests itself in the creative qualities by independent existence, which transform into its sphere of activity substances which arrive in conformity with its objects without being governed by the general laws of physics and chemistry, which minerals cannot evade."

We did not compose this. We honestly assure the reader that we did not. We have not even added anything to Mr. Bervi's statement, nor have we subtracted anything from it. We have not even altered the spelling.

On the other hand, Mr. Bervi can laugh very wittily at the sceptics or, as he puts it, the "nihilists."

"I take the liberty of thinking," he observes with biting irony, "that if the nihilists were bitten in the leg by a dog (do you note the subtle contempt expressed here?), or if they cut their finger, they would not regard the ensuing pain as a phantom."

5*

How witty and sarcastic! All the nihilists must feel very crushed after Mr. Bervi's mockery. The only pity is that this sort of ironic mockery has been repeated almost since the time of Socrates, and was first printed in Russian, we think, in Kurganov's *Epistolary*.[36]

Merited Professor Bervi must not take offence at our depriving him of the honour of inventing wit at the expense of sceptics. He has many other inventions to his own credit, and to please Mr. Bervi we are ready to present the more curious of them to our reader's attention.

On page 60, Mr. Bervi says that the foetus in the womb, uncognizant of the external world, is engaged in *self-cognizance*, or as our worthy professor expresses it in his customarily popular style, it is "engulfed in the subjective night of self-cognizance."

On page 36 Mr. Bervi says that "man, being a body of nature, cannot evade the laws of the latter." On page 37, however, he adds: "But, being indivisible, he pursues his own goal and *changes the general laws of nature*."

It would be interesting to know which *general laws* of nature man, being indivisible, changes at his own will? Incidentally, on page 25, we find another proposition which still more exalts above nature, not only man, but all animals. Mr. Bervi asserts that animals live outside the conditions of space, or, perhaps, we had better quote Mr. Bervi's own words: "the world spirit of their (the animals') bodies manifests itself by action in time, untrammelled by the limits of space."

In describing the maternal care which nature bestows upon animals, our worthy professor, *inter alia*, indicates the purpose for which it has endowed them with the feelings of hunger and thirst. "In order that the animal may be aware of its requirements," he says, "it is stimulated to satisfy them by the feelings of hunger, cold, thirst, etc."

Incidentally, this teleology, carried to the extreme, sometimes leads our author to conclusions which cannot be described as apt. Among these inept conclusions we include the idea he expresses on p. 24, that "the part is equal to the whole." Mr. Bervi says that "some of the productions of nature are the purest representatives of matter," and he goes on to say:

"These productions have no significance of their own below their own centre; hence, in its significance, every *part* of them is *equal to the whole*. This applies to bodies which in their totality comprise so-called inanimate nature: minerals, salts, water, etc."

We repeat: the above is word for word what is printed on pages 23-24 of the pamphlet by Merited Professor W. Bervi: "A Physiologico-Psychological View on the Beginning and End of Life." We may be told that Mr. Bervi had not dimension but something else in mind, and that the words "significance of" alter the case in his favour. But we ask you and Mr. Bervi: what determines the significance of inorganic objects of equal composition if not their dimensions? On what else if not dimension can you base your judgment of the significance of two pieces of pure silver of different weight, two blocks of the same kind of granite, marble, etc.? No. However you may try to tone it down, our thesis that Mr. Bervi regards the parts of certain bodies as being equal to their whole remains valid.

We may be told that it is impossible that Mr. Bervi should be unaware of the axiom that the part is always less than the whole. But it is possible. We have analogical proof of this, and convincing proof at that. This is what Mr. Bervi says on page 50:

"I assume that I have a heart, lungs, a liver, etc. This is a mental conclusion based on an analogy, *in exactly the same way as I assume* that Jupiter and Saturn are bodies similar to our Earth and, like the latter, are inhabited."

Well, had we told you that Mr. Bervi does not even know whether he has a heart and lungs you would not have believed us. We hope you will believe us now that we have quoted his own words. He himself says that he does not know for certain whether he has a heart or not. He says, *I assume that I have, in exactly the same way as* I assume that Saturn is inhabited.... But it may not be inhabited. It is simply an analogy.

Such is Mr. Bervi's reasoning, and we have added nothing to his ideas. If you don't believe us you can investigate the matter for yourself: that is why we have given the page numbers wherever we have quoted Mr. Bervi's views.

You will agree that all this is extremely amusing, and the opinions of Mr. Bervi which we have quoted would have been sufficient to save the critic the trouble of bothering with his pamphlet. In all probability our readers have long been wondering why we have taken so much trouble to pick out different curiosities from Mr. Bervi's pamphlet when five lines would have been enough to make a laughingstock of it. To show why we have devoted so much attention to Mr. Bervi we shall quote another excerpt, which will be the last, and of course it will prove to the reader that ridicule alone is not enough here, and that Mr. Bervi's case is not even amusing. On page 4 he says: "I am publishing what I teach my students every year," and he adds: "My students are youths and, as such, are responsive to every lofty ideal." This, then, is the grave and deplorable aspect of the question. Mr. Bervi is, of course, at liberty to dream about anything he likes, to curse the present development of the natural sciences, to doubt whether he has a heart and lungs, and at the same time to believe that the part is equal to the whole and that an animal feels hunger only in order to become aware of its requirements. But he teaches all this to his youthful students. That is the whole trouble; and in all probability he teaches them something even worse, because in publishing his lectures, every professor does his best to polish them up. Furthermore, its ostentatious style and the flaunting of totally superfluous and, to tell the truth, very cheap scholarship, shows that Mr. Bervi's lecture was composed for exhibition. Here you find reference to Scipio, to Regulus, Louis XIV, Napoleon, the constellation Taurus, the fecundity of rats, to a pike that was caught in 1497, the industry of bees, wild Siberian foxes, etc., etc. He quotes verses by Voltaire and Goethe, says that the planet Neptune should have been called Newton, that Arab steeds are splendid, that the United States of America is a frightful bane to mankind, etc. Since he took the trouble to include in his lectures extraneous reflections of this kind, Mr. Bervi might, of course, if he were able, have taken the trouble to get his scientific conceptions correct, to make his conclusions logical or, at least, to make his exposition read sensibly. Let us suppose even that Mr. Bervi, for example, knows that the part is always less than the whole (a bold assumption, and totally *a priori*, with no real foundation; but let us assume it out of respect for Mr. Bervi's professorial title): but is this any consolation to his students if he handles them in the way he has handled this pamphlet? Not at all, in our opinion. The students deserve our sincere pity in this case and not Mr. Bervi. He forfeits all right to our pity, if only for the reason that he is so imperturbably smug in spite of his ignorance of science and his incredible violation of common sense. But the "responsive youths" under his guidance fully deserve the pity of every educated man, because they are compelled to listen to Mr. W. Bervi at all costs, for he is their professor.

THE ORGANIC DEVELOPMENT OF MAN IN CONNECTION WITH HIS MENTAL AND SPIRITUAL ACTIVITIES

ORGANIC EDUCATION APPLIED TO SELF-EDUCATION
AND TO THE CULTIVATION OF HEALTH BY K. F. SCHNELL.
Translated from the German by F. Böhmer, St. Petersburg 1857

A BOOK ON THE HEALTHY AND SICK MAN BY DR. K. E. BOCK
Translated from the German by J. Poulsen and F. Böhmer
St. Petersburg 1857, in two parts[37]

BOTH the works mentioned above appeared in Russian rather long ago, but, we think, did not attract particular attention on the part of the Russian public. And yet, these two books are really remarkable, especially for us, who have been misled by the high-flown theories of learned pedagogues who say such things about the spiritual development of man as to make one's hair stand on end. Thus, Schnell, without resorting to any subtle theorizing, says bluntly that "the supreme object of education should be the cultivation of sound health." He commences his book with this definition and ends with it, and it runs consistently through all sections of his work. Dr. Bock also affirms that the most important thing in education is concern for health, the constant exercise of all the senses and their adjustment to diverse impressions.

There can be no doubt that Schnell's definition, being extremely simple, will at once be understood by every reader. But there can be no doubt also that many will hasten to interpret it in a very limited sense and, as a consequence, will hurl well-intentioned ridicule at Bock and Schnell, as well as at us, who regard this a very sensible principle. "Your idea is not new," we shall be told with biting irony. "You have the honour of sharing it with Madame Prostakova, with Mr. Skotinin[38] and, with the parents of Pan Khalyavsky[39] whom Osnovyanenko describes, and, in general, with all the mamas and papas who regard the word *education* as being synonymous with *fattening*. Unfortunately, your theory that the *object of education should be sound health* still has many advocates among the dying generation of provincial grandmothers, aunties and nurses who welcome their wards on returning home from the university with the words: 'Good Lord, how they have tortured you there! It was a pleasure to look at you when you went away. But you are as thin as a matchstick now! That's the result of your accursed education!' Your idea will gladden the hearts of all the numbskulls who learn nothing until they are fifteen, but whose faces are as ruddy as apples, because they do nothing from morning till night," and so on and so forth.

In answer to all these arguments raised by our enlightened opponents we can say that not every ailment emaciates a man, and not all stoutness is a sign of good health. We ask them to remember the poetic complaint of the corpulent old fellow who asserts that people

> From the immensity of my girth
> Get a wrong impression of my worth—

not knowing that

> Though so robust in appearance,
> With rosy cheeks and belly round,
> Against cruel fate I have a grievance,
> For my health is far from sound.

Yes, the mistake Madame Prostakova and her ilk made was not that they were concerned about the health of their children, but that they did not know what good health was. Mother stuffs her Mitrofanushka[40] with food. For example, she gives him ten slices of pork and five or six griddlecakes for supper. He goes to bed and tosses about all night and in the morning goes around in a daze. . . . Is this sound health? If sound health means that the functions of vegetable life can proceed in a man unhindered, and that his body does not know the constant feeling of acute pain, then, perhaps, one may agree that all fat idiots are absolutely healthy. But in that case a man afflicted with paralysis and also one who is suffering from delirium tremens must also be regarded as healthy. We, however, regard both as sick men, and very sick men at that. More than that, we also regard as sick, or at all events not quite healthy, a man who constantly suffers from hysteria, spasms, migraine, all sorts of nervous disorders, etc.

Afflictions of all kinds such as deafness, blindness, etc., must also be included in the category of sicknesses. And this applies also to the special, abnormal conditions, in which some people find themselves, such as, for example, insomnia, or apathy towards everything, complete loss of memory, all sorts of monomanias, general debility, incapacity for any effort of will, etc. In short, sound health must not be regarded merely as the external soundness of the body, but the natural harmonious development of the entire organism in general, and the correct performance of all its functions.

This too may be challenged, and on fairly good grounds. Reference may be made to the lower class of the people who are usually of better physical health than the upper classes; reference may be made to savages who enjoy perfect health and possess enormous physical strength; on the other hand, reference may be made to numerous great scholars, poets and statesmen who are emaciated, sick and feeble.... From this comparison a conclusion may be drawn which at first sight may seem to have some grounds: if the entire development of a man is directed towards the sole purpose of making him healthy, then we should follow the ideal of the Iroquois, who, it is said, have no knowledge of sickness in any form, and deny all importance to great men who are famous for their mental and spiritual activities.

If this objection is closely examined, however, it will be rejected as absolutely unsound and for many reasons. First of all we must repeat that by a healthy organism we do not mean only the physical fitness of the body. We regard as ridiculous and pitiful the ignorant claims of crude materialism which degrades the lofty mission of the spiritual side of man by arguing that a man's soul consists of some kind of very fine matter. The absurdity of this argument has been proved so long ago, and so irrefutably, they so thoroughly contradict the findings of the natural sciences, that at the present time only the most backward and ignorant can still withhold their contempt for this crudely materialistic argument. We do not wish to say that bodily activity is more important than spiritual, nor do we wish to present physical pleasure as our sole object in life. On the contrary, we want to say that often our bodies, as an instrument that serves spiritual activity, are often spoiled by various weaknesses and ailments

and are unable to fulfil their functions. We protest against
the fact that often we only pay lip service to spiritual improvement, but in practice we do not try to subjugate the body to the
spirit; abandoning ourselves to sensuousness, we derange our
bodies and do not allow our spiritual faculties to manifest themselves properly; for the deranged organs of the body become unfit to serve lofty spiritual activity. This is proved by constant
experience, it is proved by our inner consciousness, by our faith;
and it is confirmed by the results of modern research in natural
history. It is this necessity—of training the body to serve as an
instrument for proper spiritual activity—it is this truth, which has
even become threadbare from frequent repetition, the truth that
mens sana, a sound mind, must be *in corpore sano*, in a sound
body, that we intend to prove by pointing to the indisputable facts
of natural history. And it is in this sense that all our observations
on the inseverable connection between spiritual and bodily
activity must be understood.

But let us return to the objection mentioned above. In addition to its one-sided and narrow conception of health, it is fallacious also because it compares objects under not altogether equal
conditions. Difference of race and difference in occupation exercise
considerable influence on a man's potential degree of development
in all respects. If we could take health in the abstract, there would
be no need for us to refer to human beings, we could quote the
example of animals. Where will you find a stronger and healthier
organism than in the elephant, or lion, or even in the ox? It is
not for nothing that the saying goes: "He's as strong as an ox."
But the very structure of the organism of these animals differs
from ours and we shall therefore leave them alone. There are
worms which can be cut in halves and the two halves will crawl
in different directions as if nothing had happened; but we cannot
take these as examples. Nor can the Iroquois serve as an example
for European scholars. Moreover, it must be observed that sickness
did not, of course, facilitate the useful discoveries and researches
of these scholars. In the majority of cases sickness did not affect
the organs needed for their specialities (we may quote Beethoven
as an exception, but his hearing was not so badly affected at the
time he composed his finest works); in this case local afflictions
must be left out of account.[41] Byron, of course, was lame, but that

did not prevent him from being a great poet; similarly, weak sight was not a hindrance to many great scholars, philosophers, and so forth. But everybody will agree, of course, that external injury can least of all be called a sickness of the organism. On the other hand, everybody will agree that every morbid sensation in the body will, for a moment at least, disturb our spiritual activity, and that, consequently, if great scholars were absolutely sound in health they would do even more than they do when they suffer from various ailments.

It is said that the contrary is the case, that sometimes bodily sickness stimulates greater spiritual activity. Many examples are quoted. Several poets are mentioned who became conscious of their talents and revealed it to the world after they had become blind. Here, of course, Homer and Milton are brought up, and Pushkin's lines to the blind Russian poet are quoted:

> Bard, when the mundane world
> Vanished before thee in gloom
> Thy genius awakened in a flash,[42] etc.

Reference is also made to Ignatius Loyola who, when he was sick, heard the call to form his order; to Mohammed, who heard the call of Allah during fits of epilepsy; to the ascetics whose visions occurred as a result of the torments to which they subjected the flesh, etc. Thousands of examples could be quoted on this subject; and cases in which the antagonism between the spiritual and physical nature of man is revealed are also numerous. But in all this perplexity reigns. At first the crude materialists were to blame for this, but later, the dreamy idealists, in refuting the former, committed the same error. We intend to dwell on this in greater detail because we think that an explanation of precisely this point is most essential to convince one of the importance of a healthy organism not only for the bodily, but also for the spiritual activities of man.

We shall begin by saying that it is quite natural and inevitable that a man should note the antagonism between objects as soon as his consciousness is awakened. As long as we fail to note the difference between objects we exist unconsciously. The first act of consciousness is that we distinguish ourselves from the other objects in the world. This very distinction that we draw contains

a contrast, and the more we recognize our own independent existence the stronger this contrast becomes. Regarding himself as
something separate from everything else, man must necessarily
arrive at the conclusion that he has a right to live and act by
himself, to live a separate and independent life. Actually, however,
he constantly meets with insurmountable obstacles in the pursuit
of his own strivings, and realizing his impotence, but not yet
clearly realizing his connection with the universal laws of nature,
he places himself in opposition to the latter. It seems to him that
there are certain forces in nature hostile to man and constantly
fighting him. Gradually, this gives rise to the conception of dark
forces which are constantly doing man harm. And yet, once man
has already distinguished himself from nature, he cannot help
observing also her beneficial forces and thus, simultaneously
with the conception of dark forces, there arises the conception
of light and benign forces which protect man. This marks the
beginning of that dualism which we find at the basis of all natural religions; Vishnu and Siva, Ormuzd and Ariman, Belbog
and Chernobog (White God and Black God), etc., etc., are the
personification of man's original conceptions of the forces of
nature. Later on in man's development, as he acquired more experience, the general idea split up into numerous separate ideas,
which were applied to every single phenomenon. Thus arose the
conception of the conflict between light and darkness, warmth and
cold, sea and land [the earth and the pagan heaven] etc. Finally,
man turned from the external world to himself, and gradually
became conscious of a conflict between certain antagonistic impulses within his own nature. Unable as yet to grasp the idea of
universal unity and harmony, he also assumed the existence within
himself, as well as in nature, of different, mutually hostile principles. In his search for their origin, still almost completely under the influence of the impressions of the external world, he did
not hesitate to ascribe their origin to the hostile forces that he
had already noted in nature. Discovering within himself certain
vague strivings, a certain discontent with the external, he naturally concluded that within him there exists a special being,
superior to that which revealed itself in his external activities.
Hence the conclusion that there are two hostile beings in man
—one springing from the element of good, the inner and higher

element, and the other created by the evil, the external, coarse
and dark force. Thus arose that gloomy conception of the body
as the prison of the soul which existed among the peoples before
they adopted Christianity. Under Christianity the ancient dualism
gradually began to disappear and, to some extent, to lose its
potency in the public mind. But the Schoolmen of the Middle
Ages were reluctant to abandon the old concepts, and so they
clutched at dualism as an inexhaustible source of dialectical controversy. 'Indeed—what would there be to argue about if everything were so simple, natural and harmonious? Far better that
there should be two principles, two forces, two opposite propositions, with which, armed cap-a-pie with sophistries, one could
enter the arena of idle dialectics. It was these Schoolmen who
retarded the progress of general common sense, which, of course,
should have understood long ago, that the final object of knowledge is not struggle but conciliation, not antagonism but unity.
The Schoolmen of the Middle Ages tried to separate the soul
from the body and, looking upon it as a being that was totally
alien to the body, they began to speculate on the question as to
how the soul combined with the body. In ancient times Aristotle
also pondered over this question, but he, of course, could be
pardoned for this. He imagined that the body was crude matter
and that the soul was also matter, but of a very fine texture, and,
consequently, the question he raised might be to some extent
understood in the chemical sense. This explains the origin of
his excellent theory—*influxus physicus*, with which he explained
the connection between the soul and the body. The Schoolmen
of the Middle Ages could not subscribe to Aristotle's assumption
concerning the material nature of the soul. They were all Christians; most of them belonged to the clergy, and all believed in
the spirituality and immortality of the soul, and yet they discussed a question which could have arisen only on the basis of
Aristotle's assumption. How did the soul combine with the body?
—they asked. What place does it occupy in the body? By what
means is pain inflicted on the body conveyed to the soul? Through
what channels are thoughts and the desires of the will conveyed to the body?... In asking these questions the Schoolmen
failed to understand that in regarding the soul as an ideal being,
mechanically introduced into the body, they were themselves

dropping into the crudest materialism. If the soul occupies a definite place in the body, then, of course, it is material; if it combines with the body through certain external connections, we arrive at the same inevitable conclusion. To this error was added another, also pagan, that the body was under the influence of an evil force, through which all impurities enter the soul. On the basis of this contention the ascetics of the Middle Ages even excelled the Indians in the cruel and bloody torments they inflicted upon themselves in their religious frenzy. The degree of madness reached by them in the endeavour to subdue the flesh is known. And we also know how many witches and how many unfortunate people who were said to be "possessed" were burned to death at that time owing to the conviction that the devil had entered their bodies. . . .

In our days the successes achieved by the natural sciences, which have already rid us of many prejudices, enabled us to form a sounder and simpler idea of the relation between man's spiritual and corporal activities. Anthropology has clearly proved to us, first of all, that all our efforts to picture to ourselves an abstract spirit bereft of all material qualities, or positively to determine its nature, have always been, and always will be, absolutely fruitless. Science has also explained that all man's activities can be noted only to the extent that they are revealed in corporal, external manifestations and, consequently, that we can judge of the activities of the soul only by their manifestations in the body. At the same time we have learned that the simple substances that enter into the composition of our bodies have no separate existence of their own; consequently, the vitality we reveal depends not on this or that substance, but on a certain combination of all of them. With this precise knowledge it was now impossible to adhere to crude, blind materialism, which regarded the soul as a minute piece of the finest, ethereal matter; it now became impossible to raise questions concerning the organic life of man in the way they were raised by the ancient pagan philosophers and by the Schoolmen of the Middle Ages. A broader and clearer view was needed, it was necessary to bring about unity in what hitherto had been deliberately separated; it became necessary to generalize what had hitherto been pictured 'as separate [disconnected] parts. This elevation of apparent contradictions to natural unity is the great service rendered by modern science. Modern science alone refuted the scholastic dualist conception of man and began to study him as a complete, undivided whole, corporal and spiritual, without attempting to separate the two. It discerned in the soul the force which permeates and inspires the whole of man's body. Guided by this conception, science today no longer regards corporal activities separately from spiritual and *vice versa*. On the contrary, in all, even the most minute, corporal phenomena science discerns the action of the same force, which unconsciously takes part in the formation of blood, the assimilation of food, etc., and reaches the heights of consciousness in the functions of the nervous system, and mainly of the brain. Distinguished for its simplicity and for the truthful explanation it gives of the facts of life, in harmony with the highest Christian conception of man's personality as an independent individual, the view of true science is superior in still another respect. It establishes beyond doubt the truth that the soul unites with the body not by means of external connections, that it has not been accidentally introduced into the body and does not occupy a certain corner in it, but necessarily, firmly and inseparably merges with it, completely permeates it; that without it, without this inspiring force, it is impossible to conceive of the living human organism [and *vice versa*].

Once one understands this view, it is not difficult to understand in what sense sound health may be accepted as the supreme object of a man's development. If all spiritual activity inevitably manifests itself in external symbols, and if the organs of our body necessarily serve as the instruments of its manifestations, it is clear that the proper manifestation of spiritual activity needs properly developed and healthy organs. Much as he would like to heed good advice and see good examples, a blind and deaf man can no more fulfil his wish than a legless man can walk, a dumb man speak, and so forth. Similarly, if our nerves are deranged we cannot be calm and patient; if our brain is affected we cannot reason well, and so forth. In all these cases we are unhealthy, although we do not feel any acute physical pain. Nor can we call an organism a healthy one in which one side is developed too much at the expense of the other. Thus, an organism in which the development of the cerebral functions absorbs everything else

develops abnormally, morbidly. Also abnormal is the development of the organism in which the development of the nervous
system, and of the brain in particular, is restricted and stunted
by intense muscular activity. In this respect, therefore, pale,
emaciated, overeducated children, as well as savages who possess
enormous physical strength but are coarse and uneducated, are
both one-sidedly developed, and this one-sidedness may be called
the organism's lack of complete sound health. This, of course,
does not in the least prevent the proper functioning of those
organs which are properly developed, although it prevents the
development of complete harmony in the organism. That is why
we always see so much feverishness and convulsiveness in the
activities of enthusiasts whose feelings and imaginations predominate over their reason. That is why the intelligence of people who
spend all their lives in physical labour is so limited and dull;
animal health is not enough for man; he needs human health,
health in which the development of the body will not hinder
but facilitate the development of the soul. When that is not the
case we get one-sided, unhealthy development, in the course of
which—quite naturally—the morbid state of some organs stimulates others to intensified activity. Strictly speaking, every ailment may be defined as a disturbance of the proper relation
between the parts that make up our organism. Consequently, the
fact, for example, that the imagination is heightened when the
body is exhausted by disease does not contradict but rather confirms the general harmony of the organism. It has long been
noted that nature tries to compensate man for defects in some
organs by greater perfection in others. Thus, the blind are gifted
with good hearing and touch, the deaf frequently enjoy very
good sight, and so forth. The same thing must occur in the activities performed through the medium of the brain. The less
other activities are developed, the more the brain activities will
be developed. Thus, loss of sight necessarily compels the blind
man to drop certain public occupations and, in addition, deprives
him of the opportunity of obtaining new impressions through his
eyes. It is quite natural that, finding himself in such a state, a
blind man will turn to his subjective world and begin to analyze
the impressions he had received in the past. Similarly, a Loyola
might mentally draw up the grandest of plans in spite of his

physical weakness during convalescence. This is very natural: it
is well known that the enfeeblement of the body as a consequence
of prolonged starvation ends in delirium, and, in general, delirium
most often appears in sicknesses which exhaust the organism.
In such phenomena we should discern harmony rather than antagonism.

By treating man as a single whole, as an indivisible being,
as a true individual, we eliminate the innumerable contradictions
that the Schoolmen found between corporal and spiritual activity.
It goes without saying that if a man were dissected we would find
a host of irreconcilable contradictions, as we would find in everything else under such circumstances. What would happen if, for
example, we set out to find what part of a violin contains the
sounds that it emits—the strings, the bridge, the slits, or the deck.
What amusing arguments the attempt to settle this question, which
by its very nature cannot be settled, would lead to! Something
of the same kind happened to the Schoolmen who tried to contrast the body to the spirit. How can the soul rejoice when the
body feels pain?—they asked. How can the soul fail to note an
object when the eyes are looking at it? How can the soul feel
cold when the hand touches a warm object directly after a hot
one? etc. The contradictions were endless, and from them the
Schoolmen—without any grounds, incidentally—drew a rather
curious conclusion, viz., that the soul in man was quite separate
from the body; one functioned in accordance with its own laws
and the other in accordance with its own, quite different laws.
Absurd as this conclusion was, it was accepted on faith for a
long time until the results achieved by the natural sciences
helped to determine more precisely the organic nature of man.
Now nobody has any doubts that all efforts to draw a line of demarcation between the spiritual and corporal functions of man
are useless, and human knowledge can never achieve this. We
cannot learn of the existence of internal activity without material
manifestation, and the material manifestation takes place in the
body. Is it possible to separate an object from its characteristics?
And what remains of an object if we destroy our conception of
all its properties and characteristics? We get an absolutely simple
and logical explanation of the apparent antagonism within human nature when we treat man simply as a united, indivisible

organism. Then, the fact, for example, that we sometimes look and do not see is very simply explained. Vision is not merely the reflection of the visible object in our eyes; the main thing here is that the visual nerve should be irritated and convey the impression of the object to the brain. The seat of vision, as of all our senses, is in the brain; if, for example, the eye nerve is severed, objects will be reflected in the eye as before, but we shall not see them. Hence, there is nothing strange in the fact that when our mind is occupied with important thoughts, *i.e.*, when intense activity is going on in the brain, the feeble irritation of the visual nerve, sensitive enough in other cases, now becomes inadequate and fails to make the brain conscious of it. But as soon as the irritation of the nerve becomes too strong our attention is at once diverted from the subject of our thoughts and turns to the object which caused the irritation. In the same natural way physiology explains all the contradictions invented by the Schoolmen who, unbeknown to themselves, dropped into extremely crude materialism.

After these preliminary explanations we believe the reader is no longer left in perplexity as to what we mean by the healthy development of ·the organism, and why we attach so much importance to it. Generally speaking, it has become the custom in our days to echo the high-flown utterances of the poets, to complain about the materialism and the practical trend of the age. But we think that physicians and physiologists have far more grounds for complaining about the one-sided and short-sighted idealism of our times. Indeed, look at the contempt with which we regard physical labour, and what little attention we devote to the exercise of physical strength. True, we love beauty, litheness and grace, but here too our contempt for the simple and healthy development of the organism often finds expression. Often we like to see the dreamy, transcendental expression in faces, and the pallor that is "the sign of melancholy"; in bodily structure we like the waist that can be embraced with one arm, and as for small hands and feet, that goes without saying. There is nothing positively bad in all this, it cannot be asserted that a large foot is nicer than a small one, but still, our preference, which is based not on the conception of the symmetrical development of all organs of the human body but on some unaccountable caprice, is proof of a one-sided, false idealism. Muscular, strongly developed arms and legs awaken in us thoughts of physical labour which, as is well known, develop these members, and this is what we do not like. On the other hand, small, dainty hands show that the lady or gentleman who possesses them is not engaged in coarse toil, but in some gentler activity. And this is exactly what we want.... We are constantly betraying a distorted idealism. For example, we are very stern in our strictures of the conduct of other people and are very much inclined to demand that everybody should be the incarnation of virtue. Only very rarely do we pay any attention to a man's conditions, to the circumstances of his life, to various mitigating circumstances [but very often we say with amazing heroism: "He told a lie, that's enough, I think he is a dishonest man."] Well, is this not an idealistic line of thought?... What about our pleasures? We organize charity balls, charity lotteries, noble theatrical performances, also for charitable objects: can one fail to discern in this lofty strivings alien to material calculation? We admire all the arts and say that the strains of Verdi's operas, and Kalam's landscapes attune us to something lofty, pure and ideal. As a matter of fact all this, perhaps, merely conceals the pleasant satisfaction felt by the organs of hearing and vision and, perhaps, even a desire to drive off ennui; but we do not confess this, and so our striving after some ideal finds expression. We are ashamed to see things as they really are; we always try to beautify, ennoble them, and often take up a burden too heavy for us to carry. Who of us has not sometimes tried to give a shade of heroism, magnanimity or subtle wit to our simplest action, sometimes performed quite casually. Who has not adorned in the rosy colours of idealism the ordinary and very intelligible desire for a woman? And finally, how many educated people—we have our readers in mind—have spoken confidently and sometimes even with rapture about Homer and Shakespeare, perhaps about Beethoven, and Raphael and his Madonna, and yet, in their heart of hearts, have not understood what they were talking about? No, say what you like, the desire to play the idealist is very strong in us. The physicians and naturalists have "good reason" for their reproaches.

But in no sphere is this false and sterile idealism so clearly expressed and does so much harm as in the sphere of education. In what circles do we see any concern for adjusting education to the individual organism of a child? In what circles is education by demonstration commenced with children at an early age? Who seeks for his children a healthy development of their organism instead of the inculcation of all sorts of abstractions, often of a freakish kind? In the old days people loved to fatten their children; today they starve them so that they shall not become fat and stupid. In the old days education was not commenced until the child had reached the age of fifteen, as much as to say: let the children romp a little longer, school will not run away. Today, however, children are not allowed to romp, they are compelled to sit still and learn their lessons. There was a time when children were sent to bed early so as not to weary themselves; and they slept nearly twelve hours a day. Today, however, children are compelled to pore over their lessons until their heavy heads sink on their desks. Even a two-year-old boy has the prospect of going to school dinned into his head, and at five, and sometimes even earlier, attempts are made to knock into his head lofty ideas about his mission in life—to be an architect, an engineer, a general, a lawyer, and so forth. Perhaps this conceals within itself the crudest form of materialism, but its results are by no means beneficial for the child's physical health and development. Today it is by no means rare to find a mother who with pride and secret self-satisfaction relates how her son did not sleep at night, lost his appetite, and became as thin and dry as a matchstick during the period of his examinations. Needless to say, to take pride in one's children's diligence and love of knowledge is extremely praiseworthy—but we are sorry for the children.

One cannot fail to note a pseudo-idealistic trend combined with neglect of the organic development of children in their subsequent education. For example, parents would like their son to become a famous general. They, of course, realize that this object cannot be attained if their child should die, and so they try to guard him from death, that is to say, they do not permit him to romp and play, safeguard him against colds and draughts, muffle him up, keep him on a medical diet, and so forth. The child is, of course, feeble and sick, but he is safeguarded against accidental illnesses, although not always. The time to go to school arrives, and at once tales of heroic deeds and great historical examples are dinned into the child's head. Weakness and cowardice are shameful, he is told; he must always be brave and cool. Such were Leonidas of Sparta, Alexander of Macedon, Julius Caesar, and so forth. Look at the hardships Suvorov went through; look what dangers Napoleon faced; this is what Mucius Scaevola, Horatius Cocles, etc., etc. performed. The praiseworthy qualities and feats of these gentlemen and the eloquent admonitions of the parents create a strong impression on the child. He is ready to go to war and perform miracles of valour right now. But *right now*, unfortunately, he cannot even go into the garden because it rained yesterday and the ground is still damp. The boy would also be delighted to emulate Mucius Scaevola, but he is checked by the recollection of the hubbub that was raised all over the house a day or two before when the future hero had dropped some hot wax on his finger when sealing a letter. He himself roared so loudly that he was heard all down the street, his mother swooned, a doctor was hastily sent for, his finger was bandaged and the hero was kept in bed for two days. And so the boy realizes that it is rather difficult to become a Mucius Scaevola, and all the lofty admonitions to which he is treated are almost wasted, since they are intended to affect *only* the spirit, while utterly neglecting the body.

And this is what we do in everything that concerns the development of children. The children whose mission it is to study in general, to become *educated*, are the ones who suffer particularly from this. First of all they are compelled to pore over books and learn from them what they should really learn from actual experience. Thus, a boy who lives in St. Petersburg receives information about many things that surround him only when he begins to learn various subjects. From geography he learns that St. Petersburg is situated on the Neva, which flows into the Gulf of Finland, forming several islands in the process; from history he learns about the St. Petersburg Side, Peter the Great's cottage, and so forth; from natural history he learns of the existence of granite, etc. But think how long it takes before he comes to all these subjects if he follows our textbooks. It is not surprising that we hear anecdotes like the one we heard recently, which we will relate here for the sake of curiosity. A very *educated* boy was taken to high school. He passed the examination for the second form and went to live with his uncle. Next day, when his parents had gone, he complained at dinner that he could not eat anything because the uncle's Triphon was bad [Triphon ought to be flogged, he said.] There was nobody named Triphon in the uncle's house and so nobody could understand what the boy was complaining about, nor could he explain. All he did was to repeat his abuse of and complaints about Triphon. And so the problem remained unsolved. But the same thing was repeated the following day, and then only was it learned that the cook at the boy's parents' country house was named Triphon, and this *educated* boy, who had been prepared for the second form at high school, had never asked himself what Triphon meant, and did not know the meaning of the word cook!

All this clearly shows how little the necessity of connecting organic functions with the action of the internal spiritual faculties is understood among us. We din into children's heads an enormous amount of abstract concepts of different kinds that are totally alien to the children [God knows by whom and how invented, and often totally unnecessary], and yet we will not take the trouble properly and rationally to train those organs which are necessary to ensure that mental and spiritual activity properly proceeds. In our unpractical—and perhaps all too practical—dreams we forget that the human organism has appropriate physical conditions for every kind of spiritual action, that it is impossible to speak without a tongue, hear without ears, or feel and think without a brain. The latter is forgotten most often and, consequently, no care at all is taken among us properly to develop the activity of the brain during the child's education. And yet, this is the most important obstacle to the achievement of successful results in our education, which is undoubtedly extremely wise and moral, but one-sided as regards methods. The following is what Dr. Bock, a scholar very well known in Germany, has to say about this:

"Weak mental faculties and diseases of the brain," he says, "may be due not only to natural deficiencies, but also to insufficient nutrition of the brain and excessive mental strain. The latter, with its deplorable consequences, is particularly fatal to children whose brains are too soft and insufficiently developed to perform hard work. And yet, how often they are tortured with abstractions which are totally unintelligible to them at their age and their power of perception, how often feeble, anaemic children are expected to achieve success in their studies equal with healthy children! Add to this irrational rest and food unsuitable to the child's age, and you will understand that nothing can be more harmful than this kind of mental drilling!"

We find the same opinion expressed by Schnell, the author of the other book, the title of which is given at the beginning of this essay. He gives vent to the following tirade on this subject:

"Knowledge is acquired far more easily by natural than by artificial means, *i.e.*, the reading of books. Books burden the spirit with alien material and, therefore, often bring no benefit and upset the health of the spirit. Sicknesses of the brain that we meet with among children of an early age are rather often due not so much to premature education as to bad, unnatural methods of education; they are due to the fact that education is not commenced by practical demonstration, as it should be, but by stuffing the child's head with forms, abstractions and ideas which subsequently begin to decay, so to speak, and infect the entire structure of the brain. In later years, too, the superficial assimilation of abstract forms may completely dull receptiveness to healthy, sensual impressions, *i.e.*, to nature and to life. We already know that the incomplete, or imperfect, reception of impressions by the organs of external senses give rise to fantasies, *i.e.*, subjective impressions, or delusions. Similarly, fantastic images created by the imagination and the mind are due to the imperfect assimilation by the spirit of abstract forms, or to inadequate, unclear and insipid spiritual sustenance. Under such circumstances, the mind pictures to itself not objects that really exist in the external world, not actual things, but its own (subjective) products of fantasy, delirium, which gradually completely overpowers the mental forces. If the number of insane and semi-insane people whose mental derangement manifests itself either in lack of restraint and unruliness, or in slavish, apathetic and unthinking obedience, is actually increasing day after day, as psychologists tell us, it is not a historically necessary phenomenon arising from the present order of things, but the result of a parasitic spiritual life."

One may disagree with the last remark in the above passage, because the defects in education are, of course, a historical phenomenon which springs from the present order of things. But the author's protest against the abstract education that predominates in our times is fully justified. All the requirements and methods of modern education reveal utter contempt for the organic life of man as a man and not as a calculating machine, a machine for performing feats of valour, constructive work, heroism, honesty, universal learning, and so forth. By stuffing the heads of children with all sorts of abstractions we, of course, stimulate their brains to activity, but to one-sided and morbid activity, because we persist in ignoring the connection between the functioning of the brain and the condition of the entire organism. This unfavourably affects the mental and spiritual activities of man. Physiology has lately proved by a continuous series of researches and discoveries the undoubted connection that exists between man's spiritual life and the structure and development of his brain, and it is a great pity that to this day our educated public shows so little interest in the results obtained with the aid of the natural sciences. Having this in mind, we take the liberty of presenting here several commonly known facts related to our subject.

Moleschott, one of the most celebrated naturalists of modern times, was driven to the conclusion by his researches that thinking influences the material composition of the brain and, *vice versa,* the composition of the brain influences thinking. This conclusion is elaborated in one of his works in some detail, which we think it superfluous to quote here. We shall only remind the reader of the proposition, long known in comparative anatomy, that in the uninterrupted gradation of animals, commencing with the lowest organisms and ending with man, the size of the brain is in direct proportion to the mental faculties. The lowest animals have no real brain but only nerve nets, which represent rudiments of the brain. The smallest brains are found among amphibians and fish, the largest among dogs, elephants and apes, *i.e.,* among the animals who are distinguished for their intelligence. Man has a larger brain than all the other animals. The size of the brain considered here is, of course, relative, relative to the size of the body (those parts of the brain which form the central organs of locomotion and perception are not taken into account here). The mental faculties also stand in the same relation to the composition and the structure of the brain. Thus, the researches of Bibra have shown that the development of the thinking faculties of animals is determined by the amount of fat and phosphorous in the brain. The more fat and phosphorous the brain contains, the more perfect are those faculties. According to the

researches of another naturalist, intelligence and ease in thinking are in direct proportion to the weight of the brain. Cushke's
observations have shown that the higher an animal stands in the
scale of mental development the more winding and deeper are
the convolutions of the surface of the brain, and the more they
lack visible regularity and symmetry. All this applies perfectly
to man. His brain fat contains a larger quantity of phosphorous
than that of all other animals; his brain is heavier, and the convolutions are deeper and more peculiar. Differences in all these
respects are observed not only as between humans and the lower
animals, but also between humans of different tribes, of different
modes of life, of different ages and of different sexes. The amount
of fat in the brains of newborn children is relatively smaller than
in the brains of adults; in general, the infant brain is thinner,
softer, and contains more white matter than grey matter, which
increases only later with the development of the mental faculties.
Vogt asserts that the development of a child's mental faculties
proceeds strictly parallel with the development of the cerebral
hemispheres. In general, brain matter continues to develop and
grow in man up to the age of forty or fifty; in old age, however,
it begins to grow smaller, it shrinks, becomes viscous and more
watery. Accordingly, in old age we observe failing memory, loss
of quick and firm comprehension, etc.

The same relation is observed in the weight of the brain. The
weight of the ordinary human brain ranges from 3 to 3½
pounds.* Numerous observations have shown that a woman's
brain generally weighs from 1/4 to 1/6 of a pound less than the
brain of a man. This is in complete conformity with their mental
development: it is well known that (probably as a result of the
conditions of our civilization) women's reasoning faculties are
less developed than those of men. This difference exists also in
the weight of the brains of people of varying abilities. Thus, Cuvier's brain weighed over 4 pounds, and the brains of several
imbeciles weighed by Tiedeman weighed only from 1 to 2 pounds.

We do not think it necessary to deal with the differences between the skulls of Negroes and of other lower races of man and
the skulls of people among civilized nations. Who is not aware

---

* *I. e.*, Russian pounds: 1 pound—14.5 ounces.—*Tr.*

of the strange development of the upper part of the skull among these races, so much so, in fact, that among some of them, the New Hollanders for example, have no upper part of the brain at all? And who, at the same time, is not aware that as regards development of the mental faculties, these tribes are at an imcomparably lower level than the people of the Caucasian race?

We shall also point to remarkable facts which prove the inseverable connection that exists between the brain and the mind, and the spiritual life of men in general. A man's occupation influences the condition of his brain. Mental activity increases its volume and strengthens it in the same way as gymnastics strengthen our muscles. The observation of certain naturalists have shown that the brains of scientists, thinkers, etc., are firmer, contain more grey matter, and have more convolutions. In general, the front part of the skull of people belonging to the educated class is more developed than among the common people. Every mental derangement affects the condition of the brain. The evidence of medical men who have studied the corpses of the insane shows that injury to the brain is inevitably found in every case of mental derangement. Moreover, many undoubted cases have been met with of loss of memory accompanying local injuries to the brain, and what is particularly remarkable, often there was no complete loss of memory, but only loss of memory of certain objects. Some, for example, forgot events in certain years of their lives, others forgot one of the languages they had known very well before, others again ceased to recognize their friends, etc. Each of the above cases was due to local injury to the brain.

In general, the connection between spiritual activity and the functioning of the brain is recognized beyond a doubt in the works of all the best and most conscientious naturalists. Valentine says that if we slice the brain of any one of the mammals, the manifestations of its internal activity diminish in proportion to the diminution in the size of the brain; and when the so-called brain cavities are reached, the animal becomes dead to all sensibility. This proposition becomes absolutely obvious from the experiments of Flourens, who cut horizontal slices from the top of the brain of certain animals which can bear injury to the brain. He made such experiments on chickens, and by gradually slicing off the brain he brought them to a state in which they ceased to display all signs of higher vital activity. They even lost the ability of locomotion and all perceptiveness to external impressions. But life in them did not cease; it was sustained by artificial feeding, and the chickens vegetated like this for several months, and even gained in weight.

In face of all these facts, one cannot help admitting the importance of the proper development of the brain to ensure proper spiritual activity. And as man excels the lower animals most in that he possesses a more perfectly constructed brain, this organ of spiritual activity must be of exceptional importance for him. In this connection we may repeat the words of Dr. Bock:

"[Only] the higher and more perfect development of the brain distinguishes man from the lower animals; defects in the brain, imperfect development, or morbid changes in it, more or less weaken the mind, weaken the spiritual faculties, the ability to feel and the ability to move at will. The most important defects in the brain sometimes place men much below the animals. Consequently, a man's soul is conditioned primarily by a healthy brain."

But in order that the brain may be healthy and develop properly certain special conditions are needed. Not a single part of the human organism exists independently, without connection with the other parts; but no part of our body is so closely connected with its other parts as is the brain. Without going into details, it is sufficient to say that in it are concentrated the nerves of locomotion and sensation. The close connection that exists between the action of the brain and the general condition of the body will therefore be understood. Obviously, every change in the organism must also affect the brain, if not the thinking then the sensitive part. Physiological research has not yet fully explained the microscopic structure of the particles and the chemical composition of the brain; it is therefore impossible as yet to say what material changes in the organism are due to this or that aspect of the brain's activity. Nevertheless, it has now been reliably ascertained that in addition to protecting the brain from injury, two main conditions are essential for its development: *wholesome nutrition and proper exercise*. Nutrition for the brain is produced in the blood. Consequently, its proper nutrition requires proper blood formation, blood circulation and blood purification in the body. Examples of how deterioration of the blood harmfully affects the functioning of the brain are not rare. Such cases occur during overflow of the bile, delirium, rabies, etc. In addition to nutrition, the development of the brain needs exercise in the shape of the absorption of external impressions.

"A healthy brain," says Dr. Bock, "must develop its mental faculties gradually with the aid of the five senses and external impressions. The whole process of education is based on this. A man who was completely removed from the society of men immediately after birth will not have even a trace of human reason; surrounded, under the same circumstances, exclusively by animals, he will inevitably acquire all their habits, in so far, of course, as his human organism permits this."

The study of the history of the spiritual development of man undoubtedly confirms Bock's opinion, for it shows that the fewer external impressions a man obtains, the narrower is the circle of his conceptions and, consequently, the more restricted is his power of judgment. Many oppose this thesis on the grounds that man is born with conceptions and judgment, for if he were not he would be no different from the animals, whose outward senses are as perfect and, in some cases, even more perfect than man's. Furthermore, they say, if all conceptions were acquired from the outside world, children brought up under the same influences should be equally intelligent. This argument is utterly groundless; it disregards the fact that outward impressions are felt not by the sense organs, but by the brain. The brain of man differs from the brain of animals, and there is even some difference in the brains of different men. That certain specific features in body structure, temperament and disposition are inherited by children from their parents is a fact which, though not yet explained by natural science, is nevertheless fully proved. Hence, the same impressions often affect different people in different ways. For the purpose of comparison we can recall the remarkable fact presented by medicine. Medicine that is administered to the sick does not affect all the organs of the body in the same way, it mainly affects the particular organs for which it is intended; but the process by which the organism absorbs the medicine is the same in all cases; it enters the blood and with it spreads over the whole body. In its circulation, however, as the result of the operation of sometimes known and sometimes unknown chemical laws, it is attracted to one or another part of the body. Thus, it may be assumed that when the brain functions, certain impressions affect it more strongly than others, and the impressions which, so to speak, pass unobserved through the sense organs of one man may have a powerful effect upon another.

That a man does not develop conceptions within himself but obtains them from the outside world is proved beyond doubt by numerous studies that have been made of people who live under exceptional conditions. For example, those who are born blind have no conception of light or colour; those who are born deaf can have no conception of music. People born in forests, in the society of animals, and having had no association with human beings, are distinguished for their wildness and undeveloped conceptions. Sometimes this lack of development reaches the stage of almost complete absence of all signs of intellect, as was the case, for example, with the celebrated Kaspar Hauser, that "unsuccessful attempt at rational existence" as a German writer expressed it.

The same is confirmed by observations over children living even under normal conditions. In the first period of its life the infant displays no conscious activity. In the opinion of physiologists, it does not even feel pain or hunger; it takes its mother's breast, but it does so quite unconsciously, mechanically, simply as a consequence of a certain physiological process in its nerves. It cries and wriggles because its sensory nerves, on being irritated, pass the irritation on to the nerves of locomotion. Examples of such involuntary movement are not infrequently observed in corpses and in bodies in the vegetable kingdom. As regards consciousness, a newborn infant does not and cannot possess one.

"External impressions," says Bock, "produce no sensations or pain in an infant because its organ of sensation and consciousness, *i.e.*, its brain, is not yet able to function. An infant cries quite unconsciously because its irritated sensory nerves affect the nerves of the vocal organs. Consciousness and sensation appear later, only with the development of the brain."

How conscious life gradually develops in man is described in rather great detail in Dr. Bock's book. We think it will not be superfluous to present here his main ideas.

In Dr. Bock's opinion consciousness appears in the child rather early.

"Unfortunately," he says, "most parents think that reason, *i.e.*, the ability of the brain to feel, think and desire, appears not in infancy but much later and, therefore, it never occurs to them that a child at the breast already needs a proper education."

The education that Dr. Bock proposes, however, is not the abstract education that so much fuss is made about in our midst, but dietetic education. At first, the senses of the newborn infant are extremely dull, so that it cannot distinguish even its mother's milk from the bitterest substances, and only the fact that it becomes accustomed to sweet things gradually teaches it to distinguish between sweet and bitter. In the same gradual way, as a consequence of it becoming accustomed to impressions of a certain kind, it develops all its other senses. Consequently, at this stage it is easy to imbue the infant with many habits and requirements that may later become deep-rooted. The first sense that the infant develops is the sense of touch of its lips, with which it seeks for its mother's breast; later, sight, hearing, etc., develop. During the first months of life the infant's eyes are totally inactive; that is why its gaze is quite senseless and indefinite. In the fifth or sixth week the infant already begins to look at surrounding objects and, as a consequence, the first sensory impressions, that is to say, mental pictures, are made on the brain and gradually become more and more distinct. Gradually they become so distinct that the infant can conceive of them even when the objects themselves are not before its eyes. This marks the beginning of the functioning of the faculty of imagination. Hearing develops parallel with sight, and both organs help each other in their development, so that impressions created on the hearing, for example, induce the child to open its eyes and look in the direction from which the sound came. In the third month of its life the infant already manifests a desire to take hold of visible objects, but a complete absence is observed of any conception of distance and size, as well as of ability to exercise the muscles. The child reaches out for an object but usually *misses* it, and if the object is put into its hand, it is unable to hold it. But gradually the sense of touch develops in the infant. At three months the infant already begins to babble or "*gurgle*," as it is called. If the infant often hears the same word combined with the presence of any particular object, the two concepts—the name of the object and the

object itself—are combined in its mind, so that when it hears the
object named, it can picture its shape and understand what is
meant. Only the connection between objects and the order in which
actions are performed still remain strange to the infant; coherent
speech is altogether unintelligible to it. At the same time (*i. e.*, in
the fifth or sixth month) the infant begins to distinguish between
gentle and angry speech. Two months later it acquires a vague
understanding of the order in which certain things are done, and
why they are done. Having reached this stage of mental development, the child already attempts to talk, but this ability is acquired sooner or later, according to the degree in which its organs of locomotion are developed. The will develops last of all,
only in the second year, when the child is able to walk without
assistance, and when it already has a sufficient stock of impressions to enable it to form its own judgment and draw its own
conclusions. All this shows how important are the first impressions that are made on the child's brain for moulding its character
and future conduct. It has been observed that children whose
mothers or wet nurses chatted merrily and played with them in the
first months of their lives, later developed kind and cheerful dis-
positions. Many children who had long been kept in leading
strings and had not been allowed to walk without assistance grow
up to be irresolute in character and always lack confidence in
their own strength. Children who, in the first year of their lives,
were accustomed only to pleasant sensations and were relieved of
everything unpleasant the moment they cried, subsequently found
it very difficult to bear anything displeasing and lost their temper
at the slightest mishap. Most of the children who are *taught* to
speak, that is to say, have words repeated to them without showing
them the objects referred to, subsequently reveal extreme superficiality.

External impressions are still more important for children
entering their third or fourth year. Up to that time, in Bock's
opinion, reward and punishment, even corporal punishment, may
still be inflicted, not as a rational pedagogical measure, however,
but only out of consideration for the fact that the child's organs
of rational activity are not yet developed and animal spontaneity
still predominates. Thus, a lazy horse will steadily cover the entire journey if a loaded hay cart is proceeding in front of it;

thus, a horseman will put spurs to his horse to make it run faster. It is precisely in this sense that reward and punishment may be resorted to in the early, almost unconscious, life of the child. Beginning with the fourth year, however, they become superfluous and must be replaced by persuasion. In Dr. Bock's opinion, "the expectation of the usual reward for good conduct may imbue the child with the elements of covetousness, venality and egoism." Punishment, of course, frightens children and, according to Bock, "fear is the beginning of cowardice, hypocrisy and baseness." Beginning with the fifth, and particularly with the sixth year, the child must be taught to reason and to understand everything it does. Hence, a child should never be forced to do anything that is beyond its understanding, and of the reasonableness of which it cannot convince itself with the aid of the small stock of knowledge it has obtained from its observations of the outside world. The child's external senses must be exercised as much and as correctly as possible in order to enlarge the stock of impressions in its brain. If that is done, intelligent views, and judgment, of the various relations between objects, will inevitably arise in its mind of their own accord. Stuffing the child's head with various conceptions beyond its understanding, however, will only make it impossible for the child to analyze its sensations, subordinate them to its will or free itself from them.

"Many teachers," says Dr. Bock, "think, of course, that such an education cultivates noble and lofty sentiments in children, but in this they are mistaken. The result is entirely different, that is to say, it cultivates not men and women with noble sentiments, but sentimental dreamers who are totally unfit for practical life, and useless to themselves and others."

The few data we have quoted can, we think, give us some idea of the connection that exists between the functions of the nerves and brain and the mental activities of man. Incontrovertible facts clearly show that for correct thinking and expression of thoughts we must have a healthy and properly developed brain. Consequently, if we want the *mental* side of our beings to develop, we must not ignore the physical development of the brain.

But the question may arise in the mind of the reader: "What must be done for *moral* development, upon which the brain must exercise not direct but indirect influence?" On this point we have already quoted in passing several observations made by Dr. Bock, but here we can add a few more reflections. They are very simple and, therefore, will not be lengthy.

If we accept the ancient (and still generally accepted) division of man's spiritual faculties, we must consider not only the mind, but also the emotions and will. The emotions are usually attributed to the heart and are completely divorced from the brain. It cannot be said that this opinion is well grounded. Properly speaking, the heart is not in the least responsible for our emotions and passions. All that we have been accustomed to ascribe to the heart is engendered in the brain. But there are special *heart nerves* which run from the brain to the heart and are connected with all the other nerves of the body; hence, every irritation, however slight, and no matter where it may occur, or why, is immediately communicated by the brain, or spinal chord, to the heart nerves and causes the heart to beat faster. As it is easier for us to note the beating of the heart than the activity of the brain nerves, we ascribe all emotions to the heart. But the fact that the primary cause of all emotion is the brain can easily be proved by the following: emotion arises in us as a result of impressions produced upon us by objects in the outside world. But we can become conscious of these impressions only when they affect the brain. Otherwise, we would look at things and not see them; a severed nerve could be irritated by every possible means, but we would feel no pain, because the nerve is disconnected from the brain. Hence, it is obvious that, before it is reflected in the heart, every emotion must appear in the brain as a thought, as the consciousness of an impression, and then affect the organism and manifest itself in the beating of the heart. Consequently, emotion must be influenced by means of thought. Some feelings are more developed in us than others, some people feel one way, some another —all this is true. But the cause of this difference does not lie in the development of the heart, of that hollow muscle which pumps up the blood. The cause lies mostly in the difference in the original impressions obtained by our brain. If, for example, a man has been accustomed from early childhood constantly to hear melodious sounds, naturally, his musical sense will be developed; if a man was not accustomed since childhood to experience unpleasant sensations, then, of course, the slightest unpleasantness will upset his temper; if successful efforts were made to retard the free activity of a child's mind, the child will inevitably develop a feeling of repugnance for mental activity, etc. In general, it must be said, that our bad feelings are invariably the consequence of an incomplete, incorrect, or utterly distorted perception of impressions by the brain. Just as we fail to hear a moderate but fairly audible sound after hearing a loud sound, or see nothing when suddenly passing from a brightly lit to a dimly but sufficiently lit place, so we sometimes receive wrong impressions and, consequently, feelings, with regard to objects directly affecting our spiritual activity. A man who has been accustomed to hear constant praise is displeased, and even angry, when he is praised less than usual; he who is accustomed to a life of idleness and has experienced few strong impressions is frightened at the prospect of having to make the slightest effort and imagines that he is incapable of performing it; a man who has been accustomed from childhood to witness sordid and ugly scenes, finds pleasure in the company of a vulgar circle if it is just slightly more decent than the company he was used to. Thus, all our good and bad feelings and passions are entirely dependent upon the degree of development, and on the health or ill-health of the brain. The development of sympathetic feelings simultaneously with education, and predominance of egoistic feelings when education is lacking, are phenomena known to all.

On the basis of these data we may positively say that the efforts of many teachers to *influence the heart* of a child without imbuing it with sound conceptions are absolutely wasted. The result of such "influencing the heart" is usually, a man habitually amiable, but totally lacking firm and potent convictions. It can be emphatically asserted that only that kindness and nobility of feelings are absolutely reliable, and may be truly useful, which are based on firm convictions, on well developed thinking faculties. Without this, the morality of a *kindhearted* man, and particularly his usefulness to others, cannot be guaranteed. Let us remember that "an obliging bear is more dangerous than an enemy."

In the process of education, therefore, feeling develops of its own accord if mental perceptions are correct, consistent and clear. We often see how pleased children are when some new object, or some new idea, becomes clear to them. They seem to be

7*

bathed in light, their eyes shine, their faces beam, they begin to chatter in their ebullience, express opinions, devise plans, etc. This shows that they have grasped the idea with sufficient full-ness and clarity to rouse an inner feeling in them—and happy is the teacher who is often able to rouse his pupils to such a state. In this connection Mr. Schnell quite rightly observes:

"During lessons there is no need to deliver fervid speeches, to declaim, etc., to cause ideas to affect also the feelings of the pupil. All true teach-ing in itself supplies rich material for feeling, for knowledge enlightens not only the mind but also the heart, it animates and rejoices it. Knowl-edge and joy are closely akin."

As regards will, it more than feeling depends upon the im-pressions created upon our brain by the outside world. Every-body in our days understands that there is no such thing as abso-lute free will for man, that he, like all phenomena of nature, is dependent upon her eternal laws. Except for Mr. Bervi, the author of "A Physiologico-Psychological View," nobody today can say that man exists outside of the conditions of space and time, and can change the universal laws of nature at will. Everybody under-stands that man cannot do everything he pleases; consequently, his freedom is relative, restricted freedom. Moreover, the briefest reflection will convince anyone that there can be no absolutely free actions, actions dependent upon nothing but our will. In our decisions we are constantly guided by certain feelings or consider-ations. To assume the opposite, means assuming the possibility of action without cause.

Strictly speaking, it is impossible to assume the existence of will as a faculty separate from, innate and independent of other faculties. All its actions are determined, and are even inevitably produced, by that stock of knowledge which we have accumulated in our brain, and by the degree to which our nerves can be irri-tated. The instrument for the fulfilment of our wishes are the nerves of locomotion which run from the brain to all the muscles. Consequently, the degree to which the muscles are developed also determines our activity. The nerves of the muscles must also be connected with the brain, otherwise they will not obey us, and we shall not be able to move.

That desire appears first in the brain is proved by the fact that desire is always centred upon some object, or some goal. This shows that desire must have an object which must first create an impression on our brain, for it is impossible to desire anything of which we have no conception. Furthermore, the object must produce a pleasant impression, *i.e.*, one that will soothe and not irritate our natures: like everything else in the world, man strives only for what conforms to his nature in some respect or other, and turns away from what is repugnant to it. Thus, so-called freedom of choice really means the possibility, which exists in our minds, of comparing several objects and determining which of them is the best. Here it is very appropriate to recall the well-known aphorism that "every criminal is primarily a poor calculator." Indeed, most crimes and immoral acts are committed as a result of ignorance, of a lack of sound conceptions of things, inability to understand the existing state of affairs and the consequences of the given act. Only a few immoral acts are committed as the result of firm but false conviction. This enables us to distinguish frivolous conduct from grave error. Some immoral people justify themselves on the ground that their line of reasoning is correct and act accordingly. But the number of such people is not very large. Most people commit offences of various kinds because they have no definite conception of anything in particular and just waver between good and evil. When a man is in a good mood it seems to him that a certain act would be immoral. When that mood passes, the same act may appear to him to be moral. A man may feel he would like to take a glass of something for the sake of his stomach, but he knows perfectly well that he must not drink much. When in company, however, he will not refuse another glass, and another, and here his conceptions turn right the other way. As long as a man has money and is not in need he will think it dishonest to accept gratuities; but the same man may even solicit gratuities if hard pressed by want. In this way all bribetakers, frauds and blackmailers gradually acquire the habit and achieve a certain amount of skill in this art. Sometimes practice engenders theoretical convictions which harmonize with that practice. Most often, however, moral convictions remain in the head as abstractions, while practice proceeds on its own way. All this is because the conception of morality is not worked out in the minds of many people independently, but enters their minds in passing, from what they hear from others at a time when they are not yet capable of understanding such things. The conception of morality held by many people can be compared to our conception of the evil, for example, of smoking tobacco, drinking tea or coffee, etc. We have all heard something about these evils, but we have heard so much about other things too. It is rather difficult to acquire a clear and correct judgment about the harmfulness of tobacco and tea, and in what cases they are harmful, and we therefore content ourselves with rumours, and even these we often forget. One cannot recall the exhortations of medical men every time one smokes a cigarette or drinks a cup of tea; and besides, these admonitions may be wrong. Similarly, many people forget about morality in their everyday conduct. In general, caprice, which so many confuse with true freedom, means the very opposite, means slavish subordination to the first impression one receives. That is why children whose every caprice is indulged in, no matter how absurd, grow up to be as little free morally as the children in whom every manifestation of will, that is to say, every attempt to discuss things independently, had been suppressed at the very beginning of their lives.

Mr. Schnell quite rightly says concerning this:

"Mainly, we must safeguard ourselves and others from caprice. Whoever blindly obeys a passing mood, whoever is guided in his conduct only by caprice and fails to subordinate his will to the higher power of reason and justice, will be either weak and spineless, or a tyrant and oppressor of himself and others. This happens even with children.... Cruel men, the tormentors of mankind, have all been educated in this way. They are the most unhappy and most dangerous of men. They are not to be trusted, even though they themselves preach fraternity and lawful civil liberty; for caprice, which serves as the lever of all their actions, is also the source of injustice, cruelty and villainy."

The influence which organic development undoubtedly exercises on the mental and spiritual activities of man has long been the object of study by naturalists. The way this influence is exercised, and its very nature, is explained more and more clearly every day by the latest physiological researches. Basing ourselves on these researches, we may now boldly assert that the natural, correct and healthy development of all the forces of the organism means much more for mental activity than all sorts of artificial admonitions. The healthy state and normal development of the brain, however, affects our feelings and desires far more strongly and more often than all the moralizing platitudes and fervid exhortations that we have learned by heart, in most cases without any useful result.

In pointing, in this essay, to some of the results of physiological research, we have not gone into any detail to explain the structure of the organism in general, the composition and structure of our brain, the nervous system, etc. We refrained from introducing these details into our essay because they would have made it far too long and would not in any case have given the reader who is unfamiliar with anatomy and physiology a perfectly clear conception of the structure of our organism. Such a conception can be obtained only from books that deal specially with this subject. In fact, we wrote this essay only for people who are totally unfamiliar with physiology; those who have studied this subject to any extent will probably not find a single new fact or idea in it. . . . But even those who are unfamiliar with the present state of physiology may find this essay unsatisfactory precisely because of the absence of details. Stern critics will observe that, consequently, our entire essay is useless, and was written in vain! Anticipating such a conclusion, we hasten to say that we do not attach any special significance to our observations. Our only object has been to rouse in readers to whom the natural sciences are utterly strange, at least some interest in them, and at the same time to draw the attention of the public to two books which may very well serve as an introduction to physiology and to the process of human development. The readers may find all the details concerning anatomy and physiology that are lacking in this essay in Dr. Bock's *A Book on the Healthy and Sick Man*, which is written in an exceedingly simple and popular style. The application of the principles of physiology to education may be found in Schnell's book, in which many useful and correct ideas are expounded, although sometimes the author is carried away by dreams which, strictly speaking, are totally unnecessary for the proper organic development of man.

THE FIRST YEARS OF THE REIGN OF PETER THE GREAT

THE HISTORY OF THE REIGN OF PETER THE GREAT, BY N. USTRYALOV

St. Petersburg, 1858. In three volumes[43]

> "Peter acted entirely in the national spirit, bringing his country nearer to Europe and eradicating the transient Asiatic features which the Tatars had introduced."
>
> *(Otechestvenniye Zapiski, 1841. Critica.)*

THIRD AND LAST ESSAY

THE EVENTS that stirred Russia during Peter's childhood and early youth steeled his character and helped him to free himself of many of the prejudices of ancient Rūs. But these events were not enough to develop in Peter's mind a definite idea of the reforms of which Russia was then in need. Hence, his early activities do not reveal the steady pursuit of a preconceived and carefully elaborated plan. The young sovereign, and all those immediately around him, revealed a striving for something *different*, for something *new*, dissatisfaction with the existing order, a thirst for activity. It is evident, however, that nobody, not even Peter himself, had yet conceived of a definite ideal towards which to strive. Even the ultimate aim of the reforms—to give wider scope for the development of the people's natural forces, both material and spiritual—even this aim had not yet been clearly conceived by anyone in the period of Peter's reforms. Many details of the facts that we find in Mr. Ustryalov's *History of Peter the Great* clearly indicate this, and the evidence of the facts is fairly easily explained and confirmed by certain reflections. We shall first expound these reflections and then deal with the facts.

When studying the history of great men we usually yield to a slight illusion which obscures the clarity of our view. We are scarcely ever able clearly to distinguish the different periods in the life of a historical personage and picture him to ourselves in the full brilliance of his extraordinary qualities and deeds, the image of him as he went down into history. And often we include in his merits and demerits not only his actions, but also the consequences of these actions over which he may have had no control. A great military commander launches into war, calculating only the barest and surest chances; but during the war certain favourable circumstances arise which he did not anticipate, but of which he skilfully takes advantage. We readily believe that this military commander foresaw these circumstances, took them into account in drawing up his plans, and conducted his operations accordingly—and as a consequence, the greatness of this commander is exceedingly magnified in our eyes. A skilful ruler, prompted by the most natural sentiments, strove to enlarge the scope of his power and to reduce the power of his rivals; but we perceive in this the profound and clearly conceived idea of centralizing the state, and we extol the extraordinary farsightedness and wisdom of this ruler. Another ruler enacted a law which a hundred or two hundred years later exercised enormous influence upon the condition of the entire state; but we credit this subsequent influence to the genius of the ruler who, we assume, clearly foresaw all the consequences that would ensue from his law in the future, etc. In all such cases we confuse the results with the deed, and we ascribe the logical conclusion that we draw from the facts to the facts themselves. In the old days, men who were great in the sphere of poetry were judged in the same way. For example: after all the works of a poet had been analyzed and their main trend had been determined, it was said that the poet had set himself such and such themes and had developed them throughout the course of his life. Today this habit has been discarded in aesthetical analyses, for critics have convinced themselves that there can be no deliberate premeditation in a man's character or in his whole life. The works of a poet, or of an artist, reflect the impressions of his life, and their character is determined by the facts which constituted his existence. He does not act according to a definite plan drawn up for him in his childhood for the rest of his life, but follows the actual course of events, and reflects the demerits and merits, the sorrows and joys of the society and the times in which he lives. This is the view now held regarding men who are great in the sphere of poetry. Unfortunately, this view is rarely applied to great men in history, although it is even more applicable here than in aesthetics. To this day, after studying all the activities of a historical personage with all its innumerable consequences, we at once, by force of habit, conceive the idea that all the consequences that we have deduced had been truly and positively calculated by that personage beforehand. After that we begin to eulogize him without measure if we think that these consequences are good, or ruthlessly to condemn him if, for some reason, we dislike them. And yet both are groundless, or at all events exaggerated. The future is never as clear to us as the past; and the past, in its turn, never has the same power over us as the present. Hence, every contemporary statesman understands the relation between his actions and the facts of the past upon which they are based far more clearly than he understands their relation to remote consequences in the future. But the past does not serve him as a guide to the necessary historical continuity in which causes engendered in the distant past are linked up with effects that will appear in the distant future. This continuity is studied only in history, when both causes and effects have already culminated in a certain cycle of phenomena. For the contemporary statesman, however, the past serves as a stimulus only in so far as it still exists in the present, hindering or facilitating it. A certain measure, system, or state of affairs in general, is not changed when a genius realizes that it may lead to evil consequences several hundred years later because it had led to such consequences several centuries earlier. No, it is changed when it is no longer in harmony with the existing conditions, when its unfavourable influence is not only foreseen by a few but has become palpable to the majority. It is precisely in times like these that energetic men come forward, who at once take the lead of a movement and give it definite shape and unity. They alone are visible to us in the historical narrative, and to the inattentive they seem to be the sole and original cause of the events in which they are participants. But a closer examination always reveals that the course of history is quite independent of the will of individuals, that its course is determined by the character of the events and not by programs drawn up by this or that historical personage. On the contrary, the activities of all historical personages develop only under the influence of circumstances which preceded and accompanied their appearance in the historical arena. Hence, to ascribe to the outstanding leaders in history a clear conception of the remote consequences of their actions, or to ascribe their least significant and particular actions to one guiding idea of which they had been the representatives throughout their lives, means placing the individual will higher than the inevitable connection between and continuity of historical phenomena. More than that, it means standing in childish awe before great men and entirely forgetting that, after all, they are human, and, consequently, are subject to the same limitations of strength and knowledge that all humans are subjected to. We forget this when we ascribe to a man a clear conception and thorough knowledge of things about which he could have only vaguely surmised. Transcendental inspiration, sudden intuition, prophecy and clairvoyancy belong, as we know, to the realm of the conjurer's art. Indeed, however wise a man may be, even if he is a genius, he can draw up his plans only on the basis of the data that he has at hand. Hence, all great plans, lofty ideals and complicated designs are usually confined to the achievement of an *immediate* aim. Only when that aim has been achieved is the idea further developed, are plans enlarged, and the previous aim, in its turn, becomes the basis, the point of departure, for new aims, etc. But the farther the aim projects itself into the future, the more it is obliged to rest on events which have not yet occurred but are only contemplated, the more it departs from the world of reality and enters the sphere of fantasy. Every historical leader fully appreciates this and, naturally, he tries to avoid building these castles in the air. That is why we think that the boundless, world-embracing ideas that are ascribed to every act, even the simplest, performed by a great man put him in a queer, unnatural light. It, if you like to put it that way, raises him on a pinnacle that is inaccessible to ordinary mortals, and causes him to shine with a miraculous, supernatural brilliance. But this very thing robs him of his simple, human greatness, and converts him into something legendary, which the human mind cannot grasp. This is how fantastic tales about the doughty deeds which various heroes are alleged to have performed, and which elevate them

above ordinary humans, obliterate the truly human side of their
valour. In past history exaggerations of this kind were woven
into legends; in the present world of reality they lead to chicanery and trickery. These tricks baffle ignoramuses, but they
cannot deceive the educated. Great as the skill of a physician
may be, if he attempted on medical grounds to forecast how
long the children you hope to have will live, you, of course,
would not believe him.... Nor would you believe a gardener,
who, after having planted a tree, claimed that he knew how
many leaves that tree will bear in the following year. Similarly,
nobody believes a historical personage who urges them to adopt
a certain decision for the sake of the beneficial results that will
ensue from it centuries later. A man can induce his fellow men
to do anything only when he, as it were, is the incarnation of
the general idea, the personification of the requirements that
have already been created by preceding events. As is well known,
such requirements never extend very far into the future, and often
they are limited to the present day. Such, more or less, must be
the historical leader who acts as the representative of the general
movement. More remote requirements, which the masses do not
yet feel, may be understood and discussed by theoreticians and
philosophers, who, as a rule, stand outside the movement of the
present day; but such men do not, as a rule, appear in history
as the great promoters of the events of their times. They are
appreciated later, when their ideas are confirmed by facts and
become the ideas of the day, *i.e.*, conform to the mentality of the
majority. The practical leaders whom history extols usually
achieve success because they march firmly and undeviatingly to the
immediate goal, which is visible to all, leaving the *ultimate* goal
to the further course of events.

We deemed it necessary to give expression to these reflections
in order to obviate the perplexity which many reveal on finding
in Mr. Ustryalov's book clear evidence of the fact that, in launching upon his work of reform, Peter was far from being imbued with ideas of reform of a definite and far-reaching nature.
Up to now Peter has been usually depicted for us in the rhetorical terms borrowed from the eulogy of him composed by
Lomonosov. Peter has been presented to us in the supernatural,
impossible greatness of a semi-god and not as a great man; and

we have been accustomed to associate lofty ideas, world-embracing aims with the simplest and most casual of his actions. It
seemed to us that Peter contemplated reforming Russia when
he was still in his cradle; that he began to play at soldiers with
the view to forming a victorious regular army in Russia; that
when he ordered his little boat to be repaired he was already
inspired by the idea of building a navy, and that he struck up
a friendship with Lefort and visited Nemetskaya Sloboda* because he planned to "push Russia into the system of European
states" already in his earliest years. More than that, up to now
we have been trying to attach a special, a sort of mystical significance to every action that Peter performed, thus taking it
literally [and ridiculously] that Peter devoted *all his life* to the
welfare of his subjects. He drove about in a gig accompanied
only by his orderly: from this we at once draw the conclusion
that he did this in order to warn his people against living in
luxury. He worked with an axe: and we say that he was prompted to do so by his desire to set his subjects an example of industry. He forged a strip of iron: and it seems to us that the
sole reason for his doing so was that he wanted to encourage the
development of home industry.... It is all very well to invent
this now, and it is all partly true as regards its consequences:
Peter's simple way of life did indeed strike a blow at the luxury
in which the boyars lived, his example did indeed influence those
around him; but it would be exceedingly strange to assume that
one fine day Peter thought to himself: "I'll try and forge a strip
of steel; perhaps industry will develop in my realm as a result
of it." To think up fables of this kind may be becoming for those
who are incapable of more serious exercises. As far as Peter is
concerned, there is no need to regard every action he performed
as the fruit of a given theorem. We have already observed in the
preceding essay that Peter's nature was active rather than con-
templative. His actions directly expressed his vivacious, ardent
nature and not the fulfilment of a state program. If he was unable
to restrain himself even in foreign affairs and, flying in the face
of all the rules of etiquette, he hastened to visit an ambassador

---

* Literally—German village. The foreign quarter in the suburbs of
Moscow.—*Tr.*

he had been long expecting before the latter had called on him, how much more must his ardour and impatience have expressed themselves in minor and less important affairs? Nothing is easier for a biographer than to allow himself to be carried away by the ardent nature of an extraordinary man and to ascribe to the inspiration of lofty thoughts, profound considerations, etc., what was simply an expression of that ardent nature. There is nothing reprehensible in this, but still, it is wrong, and in our view it may prevent the formation of a correct opinion about a historical personage. We have already seen above how Mr. Ustryalov allowed himself to be affected in this way when he said that at the sight of a little boat the idea of reforming Russia flashed through Peter's mind like lightning. We have seen another example of this where Mr. Ustryalov tells us that brilliant plans of his future activities had already shaped themselves in Peter's mind in every detail even before he had reached the age of seventeen, and before he had struck up a friendship with Lefort. In our preceding essay we had occasion to say that such assumptions have no historical grounds. Now, further on in this essay, we shall see that Peter did not suddenly set to work on the reforms even after he became acquainted with Lefort, or even after Sophia was deposed, but that he worked them out in his mind gradually, step by step, to the degree that he acquired fresh knowledge and his own outlook expanded. Mr. Ustryalov himself presents us with the facts which prove this.

The first and the most undoubted fact that everybody emphasizes in the history of Peter's reign is his attachment to things foreign, his desire to draw Russia close to Europe. When did this fondness for foreigners develop, and to what extent did it possess his soul at the beginning of his reign? Since childhood, historians have asserted hitherto, assuming that Peter struck up his friendship with Lefort when he was still a child. Now Mr. Ustryalov has refuted the opinion that Peter, in his childhood, developed under the influence of Lefort. Consequently, the time when Peter began to think deeply of bringing Russia closer to Europe must be put at a somewhat later period. Incidentally, Mr. Ustryalov himself speaks very indefinitely about this and, if anything, gives one the impression that he too discerns already in Peter's childhood evidence of the brilliant design of which

Peter's whole life was an expression. We are forced to this conclusion by the following observations we have come across in
Mr. Ustryalov's book:

"Suddenly, as if out of the impenetrable darkness, Peter appeared
before the eyes of an astonished posterity betraying undoubted symptoms
of possessing some great although not yet altogether clear idea.... As
soon as the brilliant light of history was turned on Peter's majestic coun-
tenance [by this figure of speech Mr. Ustryalov means: from the moment the first information about Peter's life became available] we could
not fail to observe the profound idea that was already embedded in the
soul of the great Tsar, and to which he remained faithful to the end of
his days." ·

This outburst of eloquence does Mr. Ustryalov honour, but,
unfortunately, we were unable fully to grasp what "great idea"
the eloquent historian is referring to here. If he means the general idea of reforming the state, he is obviously allowing himself
to be carried away by his own eloquence and is forgetting the
facts. If he means the partial expression of the general idea of
reform, *i.e.*, his rapprochement with foreigners in order to learn
from them, then, even in that case, as we shall see later, facts
will have to be sacrificed to eloquence. If, lastly, by the great
idea to which Peter remained faithful to the end of his days the
eloquent historian means Peter's passion for things naval and
military, which developed in him before any other, it must be
said that even this passion did not prompt in the mind of the
youthful Peter those great designs which can really be described
as a profound idea. We shall see that the idea of building a
regular army and a fleet arose in Peter's mind later on. Here
are the facts, which we find in Mr. Ustryalov's book. We shall
start with Peter's attitude towards foreigners in the first period
of his reign.

The astrolabe which Prince Dolgoruky brought to Russia
Peter showed to Hulst, Hulst recommended Timmerman to him,
Timmerman found Carsten Brandt; Brandt introduced Kort to
the Tsar. In the Troitsky Monastery Peter met Lefort and Patrick Gordon. Through Gordon he learned of Megden and Vinius;
through Vinius he heard of Krevst, etc. Soon Peter is surrounded
by foreigners and thus the apparent grounds are created for the
view that Peter had from the very beginning of his reign dreamed
of Russia adopting European habits and customs. But is that the

case? Study closely the state of affairs. Immediately after Sophia
was deposed, Peter dismissed the dignitaries who had occupied the most important posts in the state during Sophia's
reign. Whom does he appoint in their place? The Naryshkins,
Lopukhins, Streshnevs, Romodanovskys, Golitsyns, Dolgorukys
and so forth, *i.e.*, the Tsar's relations, tutors, friends, all Russian
boyars of high birth. Not a single foreigner occupied an important post; they all remained with their regiments, as had been
the custom since the days of yore. More than that, Peter
showed very little sympathy for the foreigners when the opposition party launched a campaign against them in the beginning
of his reign. In the first days of his reign the heretic Kuhlmann was burnt at the stake in Moscow. This was followed
up by an ukase prohibiting the entry into Russia of a single
foreigner without the Tsar's permission. Early in 1689 Sophia had
issued a special manifesto inviting to Russia the French Protes-
tant émigrés whom Louis XIV had banished, but at the end of
that very same year Peter issued an ukase imposing restrictions
upon the entry of all foreigners into the country. All the frontier voyevodas were ordered closely to interrogate foreigners who
desired to enter as to the country they came from, their rank,
to whom they were going, and for what purpose, what acquaintances they had in Moscow, as to whether they had been in
Russia before, and whether they had credentials and travelling
permits from their respective governments. After this information was obtained a full report was to be sent to Moscow and
the voyevodas were to wait for the Tsar's ukase. They were not
to permit anybody to enter Russia without the Tsar's ukase. The
question arises: could such an ukase have been issued if Peter
had already made up his mind what role foreigners were to play
under his reign? It may be said that in this matter Peter yielded
to the demands of the opposition party; but the last thing Peter
can be accused of is being too compliant and yielding. His strong
personality was moulded at a very early age, and his firm determination, which recognized no obstacles, revealed itself in his
youth as strongly as it did in his maturer years. No, since he
consented to issue an ukase restricting the entry of foreigners
into Russia, it definitely shows that he had not yet at that time
determined his attitude towards foreigners. Peter was fond of

Lefort, Timmerman, Brandt and the others, he was fond of those foreigners whose acquaintance he made in the Nemetskaya Sloboda; but he did not at that time think of generalizing this sentiment, of extending it to all foreigners in general. He cherished Brandt as a yacht builder, Lefort served him as an example of a merry conversationalist and excellent *raconteur*, but not as a representative of European standards. In loving and- respecting his foreign friends Peter loved and respected them as *individuals*, without caring very much what standards they represented. This is evident from the fact that Peter connived at an attempt to restrict the religious freedom of the inhabitants of Nemetskaya Sloboda; it is also evident from the peculiar way in which he made amends to Gordon for a public insult which the latter had suffered. Here is what Mr. Ustryalov relates about this incident.

"Gordon, who had been invited to the festive board (February 28, 1690), on the celebration of the birth of the Tsarevich Alexei Petrovich, was obliged to leave the palace on the insistence of the Primate (Patriarch Joachim), who emphatically declared that the presence of foreigners was unseemly on such an occasion—an incident which must undoubtedly have caused Peter deep chagrin. Next day the Tsar consoled the offended general with a magnificent feast and friendly conversation in one of the suburban palaces. . . ."

Is it not clear that in this incident Peter's interest was as yet limited to Gordon's personality? He had yet taken no definite stand on the point as to whether it was seemly or unseemly for foreigners to be present at royal, solemn banquets; he yielded to the voice that demanded that the foreigner should leave the palace, and only on the following day, out of friendship for the foreigner, did he make amends for the affront the latter had suffered.

It might be assumed that Peter's compliance was due solely to his respect for the Patriarch Joachim, but at all events he must have disliked having to yield, and must, of course, have tried to take advantage of every opportunity to avoid having to do so. Nevertheless, we see that on the death of Joachim (in March 1690), although Peter wished to appoint in his place Markell, a kindly pastor, and one who was indulgent towards those of other faiths, he did not strongly insist on his choice. In conformity with the wishes of the Tsarina Natalya Kirillovna, Adrian was appointed Patriarch, "the only counsellor and intimate friend of the late Patriarch," as Mr. Ustryalov puts it, the man who penned the epistle fiercely denouncing the shaving of beards that we mentioned in our first essay.

In general, in the first period, Peter's fondness for foreigners seems to have been limited to the small circle of persons around him, and it was not prompted by any far-reaching considerations. It assumed a somewhat more general significance after Peter went to Archangel (as late as 1693) and inspected the Dutch and Hamburg ships there. It assumed real political significance only after the first Azov campaign, when Peter, taught by the experience of failure, began impatiently to invite to Russia foreign engineers, artillery experts, shipbuilders, ships' captains and so forth. This began in 1696, and in the same year young Russians were sent abroad, and the Tsar's own journey abroad was decided upon. Now, indeed, we see evidence of a real, considered conviction that we must learn from Europe, that we must borrow for Russia the useful knowledge and arts of the foreigners. But it is evident that neither Lefort's stories, nor a sudden mysterious flash of insight which some historians wish to ascribe to him, was sufficient to make Peter consciously and definitely aware of this intention. The matter is explained quite simply: the experience of several years had proved to Peter the inadequacy of the resources then available in Russia; the foreigners who were intimate with him showed him where larger resources could be obtained. He, on his part, proved to possess sufficient strength of character to be able to devote his subsequent activities to the zealous quest and acquisition of those resources, and to the elimination of what proved worthless when those resources became available. Peter did what nobody before him had dared to do, although, of course, the necessity of much that he introduced had been understood before him.

That Peter had no definite views in the early period of his reign concerning his future course of action is proved by his inaction during the first five years of his rule before the Azov campaigns. We know that Peter detested procrastination in all things; as soon as he had set himself a certain object he marched towards it with rapid and undeviating strides. No extraneous occupations or diversions, no external obstacles could divert him from his purpose, once he had set his mind on it. Hence, Peter's inaction previous to the Azov campaigns can be explained only by the absence of a clearly conceived idea, the absence of a definite goal. As the historian clearly and definitely testifies, "the first five years of Peter's reign were spent in military exercises, manoeuvres on land and water, firework displays and merry feasts. During that time *not a single* law of note was promulgated, *not a single* important decree was issued concerning *any branch* of public affairs." In support of this statement Mr. Ustryalov quotes from the complete code of laws the most important legislative acts and governmental decrees that were issued during the five years 1690-1694, and even among these *most important* acts we find several that are simply reaffirmations of ones previously promulgated. As for the degree of their importance, this may be judged from the fact that among them we find orders such as the following: one announcing a holiday in government offices from December 24 to January 8; an order to brand criminals with the letter V in case of a second conviction and banishment; an order prohibiting hackney coachmen from standing with their coaches in the Kremlin, etc.

True, Peter did not remain idle during this period. On the contrary, he himself, in more than one of his letters, mentions with pleasure the fact that he was working tirelessly. As early as 1689 he wrote to his mother from Pereyaslavl: "Your son, Petrushka, *engrossed in labour*, your blessing I pray." In 1695 he wrote to Romodanovsky from his camp near Azov: "We hope with your numerous and ardent prayers, with your orders and with *our labours and blood* to achieve this object." In the same year he wrote to Vinius from his camp near Azov: "We are toiling unceasingly under the yoke of Mars." In one letter to Romodanovsky he stated that he had not written for a long time because he had been "engaged in unceasing labour." In 1696 Peter wrote to Streshnev from Voronezh: "And we, in conformity with God's command to our forefather Adam, are earning bread by the sweat of our brow." At that time Peter was already engaged in building his fleet and, evidently, already attached an importance to his undertaking far greater than that of mere amusement. This was also understood by his entourage. In reply to Peter's letter, in which he had referred to our forefather Adam, Streshnev wrote:

8*

"Your Majesty writes that in conformity with God's command to
our forefather Adam you are earning bread by the sweat of your brow:
we know quite well that you are never idle, that you are always indus-
trious, *not for your own benefit, but for the benefit of orthodox Christians.*"

But we repeat—the idea that Peter was working for the public welfare took definite shape in the minds of his supporters, as
well as in his own mind, only in the period of the Azov campaign. Even the flattery of courtiers, which could not but exist
even during Peter's reign, became bolder and more florid only
at that time. After the capture of Azov, Romodanovsky wrote to
Peter in the following style:

"I know that you, My Lord, work harder than many others, and
do that which is desirable for us; and in all that you do I deem you to
be equal to many: to Peter in your faith in God, to Solomon in wisdom, to Samson in strength, and to David in glory, and what is most
important, while other men seek for better paths by much learning and
prolonged search, you, My Lord, achieve it with small effort, which,
however, is complete and thorough."

Even the courtiers of that time dared not speak to Peter in
this strain before the Azov campaign. Evidently, they too realized
that the time had not yet come to attach political importance
to Peter's occupations.... All the more strange would it be therefore if a later historian discerned in them profound ideas and intentions for the benefit of the state. One could argue in this way
only as long as the facts were kept concealed and were not
sufficiently explained; but now, the material brought to light
by Mr. Ustryalov proves beyond doubt that Peter's labours during the first years of his reign were mainly mechanical and
performed for his own amusement; they served him as a special
kind of diversion, as favourite exercises, and nothing more, or,
to express it in his own words, he *gratified his own desires.* Moreover, these labours frequently alternated with various amusements and holidays with his friends. We get an idea of the character of these amusements from the following description presented by Mr. Ustryalov.

"There were days when Peter abandoned all his occupations and with
his companions in his labours gave himself up to noisy revelry. He usually
invited his company to the house of Lefort, for whom he subsequently built
a magnificent palace on the River Yauza, sometimes to Lev Kirillovich
Naryshkin's house in Fili, to Prince Boris Alexeyevich Golitsyn's, to Peter

Vassilyevich Sheremetev's, or to General Gordon's, and made merry until long after midnight, with music and dancing and not infrequently with salvoes fired from cannon mounted around the house where the Tsar and his company were feasting.

"These feasts were always presided over by the Duma Secretary Nikita Moiseyevich Zotov, the Tsar's former tutor, who was nicknamed 'Prince-Pope, Patriarch of Pressburg, Yauza and of the whole of Kokui.' He strictly saw to it that the cups were drained to the bottom and by his own example encouraged the company to fight Ivashka Khmelnitsky,* the invisible, but crafty and dangerous foe who displayed his power by making some of the guests fall asleep on the spot and compelling them to spend the night in the host's house, by reducing others to such a state that they could reach their homes only with great difficulty, and by laying Gordon, for example, so low that he could scarcely come to three days after the feast.

"The only one to remain sound and unharmed was the Tsar, who on the next day already could be found at his, work with the rising of the sun. He was the leading spirit at the feasts, he invented all the practical jokes for the amusement of the company, was unassuming and friendly in his behaviour towards everybody and was not angry when contradicted; but he disliked both persistent contradiction and persistent flattery; he particularly disliked hearing ignorance praised, or science, art or his friends condemned, and often one vexatious or inappropriate word drove him into such a passion that even the wildest revelry was interrupted and the company sat silent and trembling. In such cases only Lefort was able to pacify the irate Tsar. A few minutes later his gloomy brow cleared, the storm subsided and the flowing bowl was attacked again amidst the thunder of cannon which shook the feasting chamber.

"Particularly merry was the feasting at Yuletide and Shrovetide. At Yuletide, accompanied by all his friends, called carol singers, numbering eighty and more, he visited boyars, generals and rich merchants and sang carols in praise of Christ, accepted presents and made merry for several days on end. At Shrovetide he invariably gave brilliant firework displays, which he himself arranged, making with his own hands in his workshop rockets, stars, wheels, crackers and fire pictures."

Mr. Ustryalov only vaguely indicates how often these feasts, banquets and other amusements of Peter's occurred. *There were days,* he says, and by this expression he seems to hint that such days did not occur often; but Mr. Ustryalov's subsequent narration clearly shows that the entire five years of 1690-1694 were almost a continuous series of military and naval exercises, usually accompanied by official entertainments. Peter ascended the throne in October 1689. According to Gordon, in January and

---

* *I. e.,* John Barleycorn.—*Tr.*

February 1690, he was already letting off fireworks. In the spring
the military exercises and manoeuvres began, during which, incidentally, Peter was scorched by the explosion of a grenade. In
the summer he lay sick; in the autumn he resumed the manoeuvres,
and in the winter he was again making fireworks for Christmas
and Shrovetide. The spring and summer of 1691 were devoted to
manoeuvres and to preparations for a sham fight, which was
fought in October and was wound up with a merry feast. In the
autumn and winter Peter travelled to and fro between Moscow
and Pereyaslavl-Zalessky, where he was having new ships built.
In the spring of 1692 he began to launch these ships, and not
satisfied with having only his favourite company at this ceremony, he summoned the Tsarinas—his mother and his wife—to
Pereyaslavl. They arrived from Moscow in August, and on August
14 a ceremonial banquet was given on the flagship. A week later
the launching of the ship was celebrated, and here endless feasting commenced. The Tsarina, Natalya Kirillovna, celebrated her
saint's day here and did not leave for Moscow until the beginning of September—not quite in good health, however. Peter
remained in Pereyaslavl a little longer and then returned to
Moscow, where he fell sick with dysentery "due to overwork and
probably excessive feasting," as the historian observes. His illness lasted until Christmas and caused grave anxiety. It was
then that some of Peter's favourites provided themselves with
horses to be able to flee from Moscow at the very first news of
Peter's death.

"But Providence saved Peter for Russia," continues his historian. "Just
before Christmas he began to recover, and at the end of January, although
not fully recovered, he rode through the town in the capacity of best man,
inviting guests to the wedding of a German goldsmith, presided at the
wedding feast, and unceasingly pressed drinks on the guests, although
he drank little himself."

At Shrovetide Peter, as usual, arranged a fireworks display
with fireworks of his own manufacture, and wound up with "a
sumptuous supper which lasted until three o'clock next morning."
Peter spent the spring of 1693 in building ships and in July he
went to Archangel. Here he lived until the middle of September,
waiting for the arrival of foreign ships, sailing in the White Sea,
and making the acquaintance of the foreigners who were living

in Archangel. Mr. Ustryalov says that while in Archangel Peter "readily accepted the invitations of foreign merchants and ships' captains to dinner and supper, and that he found great pleasure in their company, chatting with them over cups of foreign wine and questioning them about life in their respective countries." He also visited Afanasi, the Archbishop of Archangel, with whom as the "Dvina Records" tell us he discussed, among other things, "the navigation of seas and rivers by ships and other vessels, and revealed considerable knowledge." In October 1693, Peter returned to Moscow and engaged in preparations for another naval expedition to the White Sea, which was to take place the following spring.

"Meanwhile, he spent his evenings with his company in noisy revels, often far beyond midnight (Gordon: November 5, 1693, amused ourselves at Lefort's until six in the morning), feasted at weddings in the Nemetskaya Sloboda with officers, merchants and craftsmen of various callings."

In January 1694 Peter's mother died. Her death greatly affected Peter and his grief was as impulsive as were all his sentiments and strivings. "For three days he was plunged in grief and wept bitterly; on the fourth day he was already calmer and spent the evening with company at the house of his friend Lefort; next day—ditto, and then he set to work." In the spring he decided to go to Archangel again and wrote a letter to Apraksin informing him of his intention and requesting him, among other things, "not to forget the beer." He left for Archangel in April, "after a farewell dinner given by Lefort, at which they feasted *from midday to midnight.*" In June he left Archangel to visit the holy relics of the saints in the Solovetsky Monastery, but on the way he nearly perished in a gale. His return from this perilous journey was celebrated in Archangel with merry feasts which lasted several days.

"First the captain of an English ship invited Peter and his whole company to dinner, and according to Gordon, he spared neither wine nor gunpowder. Two days later Peter attended a birthday party at the house of Tikhon Nikitich Streshnev; from there he went on to the yacht *St. Peter*, which had been commissioned for Rear Admiral Gordon that very day, and made merry at his housewarming, spending the evening and the whole night until two o'clock in the morning at the Admiral's; next day he attended a big feast given by the voyevoda F. M. Apraksin."

Soon after this Peter celebrated his saint's day (June 29); the dinner table was laid in the Tsar's chambers and Peter spent the evening with the English captain John Grames, who entertained his guests most excellently. Several days later the launching of another ship was celebrated; here Vice-Admiral Buturlin treated everybody to a merry and lengthy feast. Ten days later the arrival of a Dutch frigate was celebrated. "The celebrations defied description; the entire *company* gathered on the ship and made merry there for a long time." When the feasting was at its height, adds Mr. Ustryalov, Peter decided to share his joy with his absent comrades and briefly informed them of the arrival of the frigate in a letter. "I shall write at greater length with the next post," wrote Peter at the conclusion of this letter. "Today we are making merry and it is inconvenient to write at length, and moreover it is impossible, for on such occasion honour is always done to Bacchus, who with his leaves covers the eyes of those who want to write at length." On his return from Archangel, Peter again *amused himself* in Moscow with the Kozhukhov manoeuvres, which, as was the custom, were wound up with a big feast. This was in October 1694. Soon after the Azov campaign was planned and Peter's amusements gave way to real, serious labours and military exercises.

We have taken these brief excerpts from several chapters of Volume II of Ustryalov's book in order to show how the young Tsar spent his time during those five years in which the historian notes a complete absence of state activity on his part. Having read these excerpts the reader will find it easier to understand the following observations made by Mr. Ustryalov concerning Peter's inaction at that time.

"Evidently," he writes, "the Tsar, still unskilled in the art of administering the state, and *devoted exclusively to his cherished ideas*, left affairs to run their usual course in the government offices and scarcely found time for lengthy conferences with his boyars; not infrequently he heard his ministers' reports and made his decisions in the cannon foundry."

We shall note that here Peter's *cherished ideas* mean, not, of course, ideas of reforming the state, but his passion for military and particularly naval affairs. Indeed, at that time Peter's passion for the sea was already developed to a high degree. For the sake of it he forgot everything, and he devoted himself to it with that enthusiasm and ardour which in general distinguished his impulsive nature. He constantly travelled to Pereyaslavl, and even in Moscow he worked on ships. For the launching of a ship he summoned his mother and his wife from Moscow; to see ships he went to Archangel, and once there, nothing could tempt him away from the place. His mother sent him letter after letter begging him to return soon, but in vain. "I beg of you, my light," she wrote, "heed the prayers of the one who bore you, come back to us as soon as you can, my joy, come without delay...." "Be gracious to me, my light, come back to us, my little father, without delay. Yea, yea, my light, great is my grief that I do not see you, my light, my joy." Peter did not heed the prayers of his sorrowful mother, for he was determined to wait for the arrival of the ships, and so he sent her soothing letters like the following: "I ask but one favour of you: why do you grieve for me? You were pleased to write that you have placed me in the care of the Mother of God; since I have such a shepherd, why do you grieve?" At that time Peter was equally indifferent to other matters outside the sphere of naval and military affairs. Thus, in 1694, while in Archangel, he received news from Vinius to the effect that there had been many fires in Moscow during his absence. Peter commenced the letter he wrote in reply to this with news about the new ship that had been launched "amidst the fumes of Mars' incense, and amidst the same incense, due honour was paid also to Bacchus." "How insolent is your Vulcan!" he continues. "He is not satisfied with being on land, but dares to show himself here in Neptune's realm, where he set on fire nearly all the ships lying in Konchukorie laden with merchandise for the fair, but thanks to our labours was greatly curbed." The jocular tone in which this letter was written shows that, immensely pleased with the launching of the new ship, Peter did not in the least take to heart the news about the fires in Moscow. He seemed to mention them only for the purpose of giving point to the mythological names with which his letter is punctuated.

But this is not all. Indulging in his passion for ships, Peter was even ready to sacrifice important political interests for it.... Thus, in the beginning of 1692, he, with his sixteen pupils, went to Pereyaslavl to lay the keel of a ship and refused to return to

Moscow even for the official reception of the Persian ambassa-dor. His ministers, Lev Kirillovich Naryshkin and Prince Boris Alexeyevich Golitsyn, were obliged to travel to Pereyaslavl and convince Peter of the necessity of according the ambassador the customary audience in order to avoid a quarrel with the Shah. Peter went to Moscow, but hurried back to his ships two days after he received the ambassador.

It is not surprising, therefore, that the historian notes the same inaction in foreign affairs as he notes in domestic affairs. Peter paid not the slightest heed to the constant danger which the Crimean Tatars constituted for Russia.

"Notwithstanding the urgent demands of the Polish King, which were backed by the requests of the Austrian Emperor," says Mr. Ustryalov, "Peter studiously refrained from taking resolute measures against the Crimean Tatars, in spite of the fact that, embittered by the campaigns of Prince Golitsyn, they gave us no respite, neither winter nor summer; he contented himself only with the protection of our southern frontiers, entrusting their defence to the Belgorod army under the command of boyar Boris Petrovich Sheremetev."

Nor is this all. Peter was almost ready to agree to the terms of the Bakhchisarai Treaty; it was only the demand for the pay-ment of an annual tribute to the Khan that restrained him. And yet how angry he was with Golitsyn for the failure of the Cri-mean campaigns....

Mr. Ustryalov believes that "Peter's irresolution in this case was due mainly to his intention first of all to learn the art of war in all its forms, in order to enter into combat with the enemy on sea and land with greater chances of success." But one can scarcely accept this explanation in full. There can be no doubt that, like every man of common sense, Peter was aware that troops were needed to wage war. One would have to be ex-tremely stupid to believe that an army is a mere toy to be used for brilliant parades and which war can only spoil. Peter did not think that way, of course. Nevertheless, we think there are no historical grounds for asserting that he *deliberately* ignored foreign affairs of state because he intended first of all to build a powerful army with which to fight the enemy. More than that, by desiring, as it were, to cover up Peter's temporary inactivity with such an excuse, we would be rendering a bad service to the

cause we are defending. Subsequent events proved that during
the period from 1690-1695 very little, almost nothing, was
done to form an army, or even to develop a navy in Russia. If
Peter was concerned about this, and concerned to such an extent
as to ignore the most important diplomatic relations for the
sake of it, would he have tolerated so many flaws and defects
as were revealed during the Azov campaign, the first serious
campaign that Peter undertook? We see how well Peter was able,
subsequently, to go into all matters, to take care of everything,
to foresee everything and to make timely arrangements for those
undertakings on which he had already decided. We see nothing
like this before the Azov campaigns. Obviously, before that time,
Peter's military exercises and amusements on sea and land were
still only an outlet for his *personal* passion, which so far was
not associated with any definite design. Nowhere does Peter
himself even as much as hint that in exercising himself in shipbuilding, the manufacture of fireworks and the organization of
sham fights he had any political objects in view.

"For several years *I gratified my desires* on Lake Pereyaslavl," he
wrote in his preface to the *Naval Regulations*, "but later that seemed to
me to be inadequate; then I went to Lake Kubenskoye, but the lake being
shallow, I did not like it. Then I began to beg of my mother to allow me
to go to sea. At first she refused, but later, *seeing how great was my
desire and exceeding eagerness*, she reluctantly gave permission."

After that, having seen the Dutch and English ships, Peter,
as he himself put it, bent all his thoughts to the building of the
fleet, and *"when, to avenge the insults of the Tatars, the siege
of Azov was undertaken, and when later the latter was happily
captured*, I, in conformity with my unalterable desire, did not
think long and soon set to work." Clearly, the idea of a navy
first flashed through Peter's mind only when he saw the foreign
ships in the White Sea, *i.e.*, in September 1693. This idea took
definite shape after the Azov campaign. Up to that time it had
been merely *a passion* for the sea, having nothing particular in
view except that of obtaining wider scope for himself.

The same must be said about the art of war on land. Peter
himself clearly testified in a letter he wrote to Apraksin before
the Azov campaign that for him the manoeuvres had been merely
a game.

"Although at that time, in the autumn," he wrote, "we exercised for five weeks near Kozhukhov in the game of Mars, *I had nothing in mind except play*; but this playing was the precursor of real action."

There can be no more direct and emphatic refutation of all the outcry raised by rash panegyrists about the grand designs and plans which Peter is alleged to have associated with his games. *"I had nothing in mind except play,"* he says to them plainly and sternly, fully conscious that his deeds need no flattering ornamentation with the figments of idle imaginations. When he was *playing* he was not ashamed to admit it: the time for serious business would come. When it did come the games proved of benefit to him in a way he himself had not suspected before.

But apart from Peter's own confession, we have factual evidence concerning the state of military affairs in Russia towards the end of the first five years of Peter's reign. This evidence is provided by the first Azov campaign. This campaign was undertaken without long deliberation. The conference at which it was discussed took place in the cannon foundry. Before the campaign started Peter expressed his views about it in a letter to Apraksin in the following terms: "We amused ourselves at Kozhukhov and now we are going to play at Azov." Peter took with him an army of 31.000 men consisting of new regiments and of Moscow Streltzi,* and against the Crimea, at his command, "there rose a vast mass of fighting men, mostly horsemen mustered in the ancient Moscow fashion, to the number of 120,000 men." Gordon with the Streltzi were sent to Azov ahead of the rest by the land route. It was calculated that he would arrive within three weeks, but the roads were so bad that the march lasted two months. It was found necessary, for example, to build a bridge across the Severny Donetz to enable the troops to cross; the bridge was built very slowly "owing to the indolence, disobedience and inefficiency of the Streltzi," as Gordon reported. Peter himself went by water, accompanied by Lefort and Golovin. From Moscow they proceeded on ships down the rivers Moskva and Oka. The voyage was not a happy one. The weather was stormy and the ships proved to be unfit, and so also were the pilots. Several times they struck sandbanks, and many ships

---

* Musketeers.—*Tr.*

were damaged so severely that they could barely reach Nizhni Novgorod. The progress of the fleet was so disorderly that, as Peter himself stated, some of the ships lagged three days behind the rest. and even then *barely managed to reach their destination.* All this was due to the carelessness of the foolish pilots, "and such were most of them in the caravan," adds Peter. The rest of the campaign proved to be no better. From Tsaritsyn the troops marched through the steppe, encountering extraordinary difficulties. The already exhausted soldiers were obliged for three days and nights to haul guns, ammunition and other heavy equipment because only five hundred cavalry horses were available and there were no artillery or pack horses. On top of all this a shortage of provisions was revealed in Panshino (a Cossack encampment) "due to the negligence of the Moscow contractors, who had failed to take measures for the timely delivery of supplies; of salt there was not even a pound."

After numerous adventures they managed to reach Azov. Here, as Peter expressed it, "hopes were reposed on the prayers of the holy apostles as upon a rock." But the very deployment of the troops revealed how unfit they still were. Gordon's division had scarcely occupied the height which had been assigned to it when the Turks opened fire and hurled themselves upon our cavalry, who were at once put to flight, but infantry came to their assistance. The historian adds: "the officers, and even colonels, were so terrified by the flying cannon balls that they begged their general to permit them to fortify themselves in trenches." Gordon had great difficulty in restraining his men from ignominious flight. In such a situation he waited for the arrival of Lefort and Golovin for three days. What had detained them? The fact that they lacked carts and waggons. To enable them to start out carts had to be sent them from Gordon's camp and this, in face of the numerous enemy cavalry, was a rather difficult operation.

Peter and Gordon were tireless; the Cossacks distinguished themselves by their bravery and greatly facilitated the siege operations by capturing two Turkish watchtowers, three versts above Azov, on both sides of the River Don. But this did not improve the fitness of the main body of troops. On the day after the watchtowers were captured the Turks terrified the Russians by attacking them when they were *resting after dinner*—"a custom which they never neglected either at home or in camp," as the historian observes. Referring to this Gordon wrote: "The Musketeers and foot soldiers, frightened by the attack, scattered over the field in panic such as I have never seen before." The consequence of this fear was that the Turks captured our redoubt, although it was subsequently recaptured by newly arrived regiments. Gordon proposed numerous measures for improving the chances of success of the siege, but his advice was not heeded and everybody behaved as if it were all a joke. Gordon was actually left without reinforcements, so that one day a part of his division was saved only by the sudden retreat of the Turks, who had been deceived by some ruse or other. "This sudden retreat," observes Gordon, "saved us from a grave disaster: our unit on the other side had no defences except *chevaux-de-frise*." Our generals were obviously bored and were afraid to fight. At the end of July they even sent a letter to the Pasha "in an endeavour to persuade him to surrender the city by the offer of *advantageous terms*." What those terms were is unknown.... The Pasha rejected the offer.

Bored by the siege, and losing hope of persuading the Pasha to surrender by the offer of *advantageous terms*, they began to talk about launching an assault. Gordon argued at great length in an effort to prove that an assault was premature; but again he was not heeded: Peter himself resolved to launch an assault. A call was made for volunteers; privates were promised a reward of ten rubles for every gun captured, and officers were promised special rewards. Two thousand five hundred Cossacks volunteered, but *not a single volunteer* came forward from the Musketeers or the foot regiments. To reinforce the volunteers fifteen hundred men were detailed from each division. Among the volunteers there were few officers, and even these were either too cocksure owing to inexperience, or extremely despondent. The assault was launched without scaling ladders or fascines. During the assault a column of Musketeers, which had been sent to support the attackers, was posted in the orchards and there calmly watched the efforts of their comrades. As a result, the assault failed, of course. Four Russian regiments lost fifteen hundred men, whereas the Turks lost only about two hundred....

After the unsuccessful assault siege operations were resumed, but were conducted in an extremely inefficient manner. Lefort, in particular, did nothing owing to his own carelessness and the lack of skill of his engineers. He made no effort whatever to establish lines of communication with Gordon's camp for mutual 'defence. The mine galleries which he began to dig were discovered by the enemy and wrecked. Gordon also damaged his own galleries by exploding an enemy countermine. In Golovin's division a young engineer (Adam Weide, we think it was) announced that he had driven a gallery right under a bastion and urged that it should be sprung. The council of war decided: to spring the mine and, as soon as the fortress wall collapsed, to occupy the breach with the troops posted nearest to the position. The mine was sprung. "Logs, planks and stones flew into the air and came down with all their weight upon our own trenches, in which thirty men were killed, including two colonels and one lieutenant colonel, and about a hundred men were injured. The fortress wall, however, remained undamaged."

As a last resort they wanted to try another assault, and to make success more certain it was decided to launch the assault immediately after mines, which were to be placed against the fortress, right in the centre, were sprung. It was resolved to launch the assault simultaneously on all sides, from the land as well as from the Don. Gordon argued that it was useless attempting to launch an attack from the river and advanced extremely weighty arguments in proof of his case, but in vain; he was not heeded, and the only answer he heard to his objections was the expression of nebulous hopes. A strange blunder was committed in deploying the troops for the attack. The Cossacks, who had proved their courage on so many occasions, were left to guard the camp against a possible attack by Tatars from the steppe; the foot soldiers and Musketeers were assigned for the assault, but, of course, they displayed no more courage now than they had done before. The second assault ended in the way that might have been expected. The mines damaged a part of the bastion, but inflicted probably more damage upon the Russians. "As in the former case, the stones that flew into the air rained down upon our approaches and crushed Colonel Ban, several officers and many lower ranks, and as many as a hundred men were injured." Again the assault was launched without scaling

ladders; the entire operation was conducted listlessly and with
no co-ordination. Lefort's unit, whose function it was to divert
the enemy's forces by attacking with his main forces the fortifications adjacent to the place to be attacked, moved up for this
purpose, but on discovering that there was no breach here, and
that even the ditch had not been filled in, he deemed it more
expedient to join Gordon's Musketeers who were passing through
the breach in the wall. The rest of the troops confined themselves to feint attacks and waited until the others had cleared the
way for them into the town. Noticing this, the Turks concentrated
all their forces at the breach, drove the Russian troops from the
rampart, and then hurled four hundred fierce Janissaries against
them. On catching sight of the Janissaries the Musketeers at
once turned tail and fled without waiting to be attacked, and
halted at the outer rampart, from which they were soon dislodged
and thrown into the ditch. Gordon sounded the retreat. . . . The
second and third assaults were equally unsuccessful. The soldiers advanced reluctantly and were unable to stand up against
the enemy. After sustaining heavy losses, all hope of capturing Azov this time had finally to be abandoned. On the day after
the second assault it was decided to raise the siege. This time our
trophies consisted of a single Turkish flag and one piece of iron
cannon.

The retreat was accompanied by worse hardships and difficulties than were encountered on the march to Azov. In the steppe
the retreating forces were constantly harassed by Tatar horsemen, and Gordon, whose force acted as the rear guard could scarcely maintain even the semblance of order among his troops. One
regiment, under the command of Swert, dropped behind. The
Tatars attacked it, broke it up completely and captured the colonel himself, as well as several regimental colours. This threw
the whole rear guard into utter confusion; only the Butyrsky
Regiment maintained order. The enemy ceased his pursuit on
reaching Cherkassk, but here frost and blizzards set in. The troops
marched through the deserted and barren steppe; men and
horses perished from hunger and cold. A month after the army
had passed, Pleyer, a courier from the Austrian Emperor, travelled in its tracks, and he reported that he could not look without a shudder upon the innumerable corpses which lay scat-

.tered along the route for a stretch of eight hundred versts, being devoured by wolves. ... Two months later, already at the end of November, the regiments entered Moscow, incidentally, in triumph. To symbolize victory, of course, "a Turk was led past the Tsar's councillors with his arms tied behind his back; to his wrists were attached heavy chains held by two men." By this [miserable] semblance of triumph Peter paid his last tribute to his former amusements, but he could not rest content with *such* a triumph.

The repeated failure at Azov taught Peter a great deal and compelled him to look at many things with entirely different eyes. He could not fail to realize the inadequacy and frivolity of that to which he had devoted himself with so much passion in the past. The Azov campaign too was partly the fruit of a passion, an attempt at playing at war against a real enemy; but this attempt was costly, and it proved a failure. It failed because no thought had been given before the war to the things that were necessary for success. Not a thought had been given to means of communication, provisions, artillery and engineering equipment, or to procuring capable officers; to rousing the fighting spirit of the troops, or to the proper organization of the regiments. From the first step to the last, extreme disorganization, disorder, weakness and blunders due to ignorance were revealed in everything. Peter could not help seeing that changes, swift and decisive, were needed before anything could be done for Russia. He could not help realizing now that success or failure in war did not depend upon skilful manoeuvres alone, that something else was needed. This thought must have pursued him at every step during his unsuccessful attempts to capture Azov, and it must have been strengthened by the news he received from the Belgorod army. He was informed that "it was impossible to do any trade at Kazikerman because the troops were not paid, the money had all gone, and there was also a shortage of arms." He was further informed that Sheremetev had complained about a shortage of "breaching guns," *i.e.*, siege artillery, and that orders had been given to send him such guns from Kiev, but, he wrote "there is no time to take them, it is too late." All such information clearly indicated to Peter that it was necessary to set up a properly organized military administration and to devote more attention

to the sinews of war than to bravery on the battlefield. He realized this, and from that moment a change was observed in his
activities. It cannot be said that at that time Peter already devoted his attention to all branches of state administration, that
he was fully and clearly conscious of all that had to be done
for the prosperity and glory of Russia, but at all events, as regards
military affairs, his views became clearer and broader after the
first Azov campaign. And here we see what a difference there
was between Peter's activities when they were directed towards
the achievement of some definite object, as was the case now,
and his activities when they were prompted merely by his personal pleasure, without any further object, as was the case with
his military and naval amusements before the Azov campaign.
In those games he merely studied the technique of the simplest
and most insignificant operations, and by means of physical labour,
interspersed with feasting and merrymaking, he seemed to be trying
to quench that inordinate thirst for activity which tormented him
owing to his failure to find a worthy object with which to satisfy
it. He failed to make the preparations needed for a successful
war precisely because he did not know what would come of this
game, and did not even think about it. If he had really refused
to enter into decisive negotiations with the Turks, and with the
Poles, only because he wanted first to prepare for war, he,
undoubtedly, would have prepared for that war during the five
years from 1690 to 1694. We see, however, that no such preparations were made, and that more was done during the six months
between the first Azov campaign and the second than had been
done during those five years. Thus, here too it becomes clear
how much Peter was dragged along by the force of events, how
he was gradually made wiser by the facts which occurred before
his eyes, and how his strivings revealed themselves and grew in
proportion as the facts of life indicated to him the new requirements of the state which had to be satisfied. His determination
to satisfy these requirements at all costs is his greatest merit.
But it must not be thought that Peter embraced all branches of
state activity in one brilliant flash of genius, and that he drew
up a complete plan of reform immediately after the Azov campaign. Not by any means. We see that, leaving numerous extremely important state problems and urgent requirements of Rus-

sia aside for the time being, Peter, on this occasion, turned his
attention only to what was most immediately and directly connected with the preceding events, and what was most in harmony
with his own personal inclinations. First of all he devoted attention to what could help to improve the army and to build up
our naval strength. The policy of basing the whole strength of
the state on the army was characteristic of that time, when the
higher conceptions of the welfare and greatness of nations had
not yet been worked out. It is not in the least surprising, therefore, that Peter too devoted his first care to the army and neglected the other interests of the country for the time being. Still
more comprehensible is his concern for the navy, for we know
that his passion for the sea was one of his strongest and most constant passions. He expressed his general ideas about the armed
forces very clearly somewhat later, in his ukase of 1702 inviting
foreigners to Russia. In that ukase Peter said that it had always
been his striving "to promote the people's welfare and, for that
reason, had introduced various changes and innovations." After
enumerating several of the new institutions and measures, the
ukase continues as follows:

"But fearing that the measures we have taken have not yet achieved
the perfection that we desire and that, consequently, our subjects cannot
yet enjoy the fruits of our labours in undisturbed peace, we have been
contemplating other methods, etc. For the fulfilment of these beneficial
intentions we have *endeavoured most of all* to improve as much as possible
our military establishments, *the bulwark and protection of our state*, so
that our army shall consist of men *familiar with the art of war and able
to maintain good order and discipline....*"

Such were Peter's plans and views even as late as 1702. He
regarded the army as the bulwark of the state and therefore concerned himself with it *most of all*; and of the army he demanded
nothing except knowledge of the art of war, good order and discipline. He regarded the formation of an army with the qualities
described as the *best* means of protecting the state and of promoting its welfare. This idea lived in Peter's mind to the end of his
days, but in the course of time it ceased to dominate all his
thoughts. Side by side with it there gradually matured the idea
that the other branches of state administration were also important. He never ceased to care for the army and the navy, but in

the subsequent period he also devoted much attention to the development of home industry, to financial affairs, to the improvement of the civil institutions—he established schools, planned the establishment of an Academy of Sciences, founded the Synod, and so forth. But for the time being, amazed at the imperfections of the armed forces, he was almost exclusively engaged with military affairs and, in particular, with the building of a navy.

On his way back from the first Azov campaign, while still in the steppe, near the banks of the Aidar, Peter sent a despatch to the Austrian Emperor informing him that he had taken up arms against the foes of Christianity, but had failed to capture the latter's principal fortress owing to a shortage of arms, ammunition and, above all, of skilled engineers. He therefore requested the Emperor to send several of his skilled engineers and sappers to Russia. Later on he wrote in the same strain to the Elector of Brandenburg. To the King of Poland he sent a demand that, in conformity with the treaty of alliance, he should undertake simultaneous and resolute operations against the enemy. This already showed that Peter now intended to go to Azov not to *play*, but for serious business. And indeed, he arrived in Moscow from Azov on November 22, 1695; on the 27th he issued orders for the mustering of another force for service at Azov, and on the 30th he wrote to Apraksin, the voyevoda of the Dvina Province, immediately to send all the shipwrights in Archangel to Voronezh.

"*Having failed to capture Azov,*" he wrote, "the council of generals has advised me on my return to build galleys for the next war; hence, I deem it expedient that you should send all your shipwrights here, for they will remain idle with you this winter, but here they can do much that is useful for the war; food and pay will be adequate, and when navigation opens (in Archangel) they will be sent back without delay; all this you may promise them; and provide them with vehicles and stocks of food for the journey."

Particularly noteworthy in this letter is Peter's serious and thoughtful concern to make the journey from Archangel to Voronezh profitable and comfortable for those he was summoning.

The actual recruitment of the army proceeded differently from the way it had done before. On December 13 the town criers in Moscow called for volunteers for the service from among men of all walks of life. "No few volunteers were found," writes the historian, "especially in the households of the gentry, which were filled with hundreds of idle and starving menials. Serfs flocked to Preobrazhenskoye and enlisted, some in the foot regiments and some in the Musketeers. Their wives and children were taken from their masters and quartered in Preobrazhenskoye." Moreover, Peter called upon the Hetman of Little Russia* to send him troops, and he also called for troops from the Belgorod army. Over all these troops a single commander-in-chief was appointed. This was not done during the first campaign, with the result that the operations of the various units were badly co-ordinated. In December, after issuing orders to have materials for building the ships stocked in Voronezh, Peter set to work to form a *naval regiment*, which consisted of four thousand men, partly new recruits and partly men transferred from the Semyonovsky and Preobrazhensky regiments. From March onwards he devoted himself almost exclusively to the building of ships.

Mr. Ustryalov informs us that, the statements the latest historians notwithstanding, even at that time Peter "did not yet think of building frigates and ships of the line. His ambitions were confined to a rowing flotilla of galleasses, galleys and fireships." Hence, here too Peter pursued only an *immediate* object: to build a flotilla with which to cut off Azov from the sea. The definite idea of a navy as "the cornerstone of Russia's might and the best means with which to open Russia's road to Europe" arose later. Peter's flotilla now consisted of thirty warships which had been built under his supervision and with his active participation during the course of March 1696. In the middle of April the troops arrived in Voronezh from Moscow, and a month later Peter was already at Azov. Here, at the very first step, Peter observed that the Turks were timid on the sea and were looking upon his galleys with some trepidation. It is not surprising that, as Mr. Ustryalov assumes, this convinced Peter of the advantage and necessity of building a fleet that could ride the waves not only of the Azov, but also of the Black Sea. We see that subsequently, during the negotiations with the Turks, Peter pressed very hard for the right of Russian ships to have free navigation of the Black Sea.

---

*The Ukraine.—*Tr.*

This time things went ever so much better at Azov, although until the arrival of the Austrian engineers we were able only to damage the buildings in the town with artillery, but could do nothing against the fortifications. Things did not always go altogether well in the actual fighting, as was the case, for example, on June 24, when the Russians, after repelling the Tatars, rushed in pursuit of them, as Peter himself described it, "in our great-grandfathers' way, without lining up in defensive military order," and, as a consequence, sustained heavy losses. Still, things were now far different from what they had been during the first siege. We could not, however, master the art of conducting siege operations, notwithstanding the presence of the Brandenburgers, who proved to be artillerymen and were skilled only in hurling bombs. Not knowing what to do, the commanders asked the foot soldiers and Musketeers to say what they thought would be the best way to capture Azov, and the latter advised that a high embankment be built up against the enemy's rampart, that the ditch be filled and the Turks dislodged from the fortress wall.

"Strange as this proposal was, reminiscent of the siege of Kherson by Grand Prince Vladimir in the 10th century," observes Mr. Ustryalov, "nevertheless, the Tsar's council accepted its idea and Gordon even clutched at it with great eagerness. . . . They set to work to build the embankment, and fifteen thousand men worked on it at night for over two weeks. . . . It goes without saying that this work entailed considerable losses for us, while the benefit derived from it was as yet small. At last, on July 11, the Austrian engineers arrived. They were amazed at the immense scale on which the work was being conducted, but were not very optimistic about its results. They relied more on sapping operations and the work of the batteries. They advised how mine galleries should be dug and how the batteries should be posted, and soon the well-aimed shots wrecked the palisades which Gordon had vainly tried to destroy. On the night of July 12, Russian foot soldiers were already able to occupy the corner bastion which the Turks had abandoned. A week later the Turks were no longer able to stand up against our cannonade and offered to surrender. The capitulation was decided on next day. The Turkish troops were allowed to leave with their arms. Peter occupied Azov, drew up plans for new fortifications for it, and then went off to look for a place on the Azov coast that would be convenient for a harbour for the future Russian navy. He found this place near Taganrog. Soon the troops returned home, and two months later, on September 30, marched into Moscow in solemn triumph. A month later (in the beginning of November) Peter decided to form *companies* to build ships which were to be completed by April 1698.

In the same month 'Peter sent numerous noblemen to Holland and other countries to study naval architecture and navigation.'"

In the beginning of the following month a Grand Embassy was sent to Europe, and Peter himself went with it, accompanied by volunteers who were to learn the art of navigation. This is how Peter acted when inspired by a definite and clearly conceived idea. Nothing could stop him, nothing could divert him from his plans. He disliked long reflection or procrastination, he disliked weighing difficulties and obstacles; once he had decided on a thing he pushed forward to the end in spite of everything. . . . "No sooner said than done," this proverb may be said to apply to all Peter's undertakings.

It is this firm and undeviating pursuit of his objects that most clearly reveals Peter's greatness. The ideas of reform arose in his mind gradually, one after another, of their own accord, precisely because he steadily and resolutely strove to carry out every undertaking he planned. He was determined to overcome, to remove or destroy, everything that might hinder him in his path, and he made use of everything that could help him to carry out his ideas. Thus, reforms and innovations were inevitable owing to the very nature of Peter's activities. He conceived of them even when he had no far-reaching designs in mind. It would be useless to seek for great and far-sighted political designs in his travels abroad. The object of these travels was nothing more nor less than the study of shipbuilding. Concerning them Mr. Ustryalov says the following:

"It was not the irresistible passion for things foreign fanned by Lefort, or the merry life he led in Nemetskaya Sloboda, as some authors say, not the far-reaching and long planned intention, also inspired by the same favourite 'to leave the kingdom in order to learn to be a better king' and to refashion Russia on the lines of European states, as other historians write, but his own conviction, the fruit of the brilliant idea that the navy must be the cornerstone of Russia's political might—this is what drew Peter to foreign lands in order, with the comrades who shared his labours, with the flower of the Russian nobility, to learn the extremely complex and extremely difficult arts of shipbuilding and navigation with which even the foreigners who came to Russia were scarcely familiar, for they possessed only their practical skill and were ignorant of the theoretical principles of these arts. Of course, the knowledge-loving Tsar did not think of confining his all-embracing curiosity to this: nothing useful, nothing that could be adopted for the Russian people could escape his eagle eye; but the thorough and profound study of shipbuilding and navigation in all their forms, from the adroit skill of the carpenter to the geometrical precision of the ship-wright, from the resourcefulness of the pilot to the admiral's ability to command—this was the true object of Peter's travels."

In this case too, Mr. Ustryalov's characteristic eloquence somewhat obscures the plain substance of the matter; but it is not difficult to get down to this substance with the aid of the facts and a few comments provided by Mr. Ustryalov himself. From these facts one thing is obvious: that common opinion notwithstanding, as our historian himself observes in another place, the only thing Peter sought abroad was the means of introducing and establishing the arts of shipbuilding and navigation in Russia, *probably not thinking* at that time of refashioning his entire state on the lines of the Western states. Basing ourselves on what Peter himself wrote in his preface to the Naval Regulations, we may even bluntly say that "he *did not think at all* about this." Here are his words, not written in his own hand, but corrected and supplemented in his own hand.

"In order that it (*i.e.*, shipbuilding) may be forever established in Russia, he decided to introduce this art among his people, and for this purpose sent many noblemen to Holland and other countries to study naval architecture and navigation. And what is most astonishing—*as if ashamed of lagging behind his subjects in this art, he himself undertook a journey to Holland,* and in Amsterdam, at the East Indian dockyard, gave himself up, together with other volunteers, to the study of naval architecture, perfected himself in it in a short space of time, thoroughly learned what a good shipwright should know, and by his own labour and skill built a new ship and launched it."

This is how Peter himself explained his journey abroad. It seems as though he was ashamed that his subjects were learning something that he did not know, and so he too went abroad to learn it. This reveals a lofty striving, not a political but a purely personal striving, prompted not by mature and deliberate designs and plans, but by his impetuous, impatient nature. He simply "had not the patience to ponder long over things" and wait until the men he had sent abroad came back with the new knowledge and organized the work of shipbuilding. Prompted by his love of the sea, devoted to the one thought that prevented him from dealing calmly with other questions he, without long reflection, decided to *give himself up to the task* to which all his thoughts were devoted. Everything else was relegated far into the background. That is why we believe that not only was Peter not yet thinking of refashioning the state on the lines of the European states, but that even the idea of the "cornerstone of the political might of Russia" was not, at all events, the main reason that prompted him to go abroad. The most far-reaching, and the latest of Peter's ideas at that time did not, we believe, go further than the possibility of successfully fighting the Turks. At all events, we are driven to this conclusion by a letter he wrote to the Patriarch from Amsterdam, in which he said:

"We in the Netherlands, in the city of Amsterdam, by the grace of God and your prayers, are alive and in good health, and following the commands of God to our forefather Adam, we are working; and we are doing so not from want, but in order successfully to learn the ways of the sea, so that, on completely mastering the art, we may, on our return, vanquish the foes of the name of Jesus Christ, and, by His grace, be the liberators of the Christians there. And for this I shall not cease to wish as long as I have breath in my body."

The idea of war against the Turks is expressed more than once in other letters that Peter wrote, as well as in the negotiations which the Grand Embassy conducted at different courts. But this idea had long been inspiring our policy, and did not represent any extraordinary great design. As regards the hopes and plans Peter based on a successful war against the Turks, this he nowhere expressed, and history can tell us absolutely nothing about it. It is no difficult matter for a historian to discern great and brilliant plans *after the event*, but these plans must have a positive factual basis, and this is lacking in the present case. True, we have the testimony of Shafirov of 1716, in his "Reflections on the Causes of the Swedish War," regarding the general object of Peter's journey abroad, but this testimony too must be regarded as belated. Shafirov says that Peter

"was prompted by his acute and naturally enlightened mind, and for his fondness for things new, to see with his own eyes the European civilized states, which neither he nor his ancestors had seen because it had not been the custom to do so in the past; his object was, after learning from personal observation, to build up his far-flung state on the lines of these states in political, military and other respects, and also, by setting a personal example, to stimulate his subjects to travel to foreign countries and learn their good customs and the languages necessary for this."

Commenting on this broad explanation Mr. Ustryalov rightly observes that it was easy for Shafirov to write like this eighteen years after Peter's journey, when many useful changes had already been introduced; and our historian expresses the following fully justified conviction.

"The idea of transforming the state arose in Peter's mind when he was already abroad, but *it remained for a long time vague and indefinite, and the changes in the state were introduced gradually, throughout the whole period of Peter's reign, in conformity with the lessons taught by experience.*"

If the historian traces this gradualness in the rest of his work more consistently than he has done in the volumes published so far, the next volumes of the history of Peter's reign will be extremely interesting. . . .

The fact that in going abroad Peter simply satisfied his own personal inclination and that he was not prompted by any lofty considerations of state is clearly evident from the entire history of his activities abroad, and particularly in Holland. We shall not, to prove this assertion, quote the whole of Mr. Ustryalov's comprehensive story; we shall merely point to certain particulars. Before the departure of the *Grand Embassy* Peter drew up a memorandum consisting of twelve points, indicating what the ambassadors should concern themselves with mainly while abroad. Mr. Ustryalov reproduced the authentic memorandum, and we find that it refers to nothing more than the enlistment of skilled naval officers, boatswains, sailors, shipwrights of every grade, and the purchase of guns and various supplies for the navy. To show in what detail Peter wrote concerning these matters, we shall quote the following items enumerated in the last two points.

"Purchase cloth for flags, pennants and vanes, white, blue and red, 1,000 or 900 arshins, of each colour the same quantity, and if the price is not high purchase more. Whalebone for vanes 15, cork for stopping the muzzle of guns 100 pounds, and if it is cheap 200 or 300 pounds; paint— yellow, and other colours, enough for 15 frigates, saws for long sawing 100, and for cross sawing 30, as per samples."

These detailed instructions clearly show what all Peter's thoughts were directed upon at that time, especially if we bear in mind that the ambassadors did not receive such detailed instructions on any other matters although, in all probability, they

needed them more on these matters. The reasons which prompted
this journey are brought out even more clearly by the life Peter
led while abroad and the letters he wrote there. Of the eighteen
months that Peter stayed abroad, nine were spent on work at the
shipyards in Holland and in England, five in travelling from
place to place, and four on visits to various towns, particularly
Vienna, Königsberg and Pillau, in connection with Turkish and
Polish affairs. It is obvious, therefore, that the main item in all
these travels was work in the shipyards, all the rest seems to have
been done in passing, by the way. Peter was so absorbed in this
work that frequently he could not find time to answer the letters
and dispatches he received from his boyars. Hard physical labour
required either long periods of rest or good refreshment. Sometimes Peter allowed himself a holiday and, staying away from
work, he made excursions by water into the surrounding countryside; but more often he resorted to refreshment and caroused
with his companions. In October 1697 he wrote to Vinius, urging
the latter not to be alarmed by the long absence of letters, "because this is due sometimes to lack of time, sometimes to my
absence, and sometimes Khmelnitsky* is to blame." What did
Peter learn in the Amsterdam shipyards, what was his chief
occupation there? He performed all the duties of a carpenter,
smoothing logs, planing planks, putting up rigging and doing
everything the shipwright under whom he was working ordered
him to do. Peter worked in Holland for about six months and
learned everything that "a good carpenter should know," as he
himself expressed it. At the end of that period he asked the ship-
wright to teach him "ship proportions," i.e., the art of designing
ships, but it turned out that "in Holland there was no theory of
this craft fully based on geometrical principles, they have only
a few general principles, all the rest being taken from long
practice." Naturally Peter was extremely displeased on discovering
this state of affairs, which came as a complete surprise to him,
"and he was extremely disgusted at having taken this long journey
without having achieved the desired object." Several days later
Peter learned that the real art of shipbuilding could be studied
in England, and soon after he set out for that country. Here he

---

* See footnote on p. 155.—Tr.

studied the English system of shipbuilding for over two months. Subsequently he said that "he would have remained nothing more than a carpenter (as Perry says—a bungler) had he not learned from the English." Peter was so displeased with the Dutch shipwrights that in December 1697, even before his arrival in London, he sent an order to Moscow to have all the Dutch shipwrights working in Russia placed under the supervision and guidance of Danish and Venetian craftsmen. To this the court official Protasyev sent the following reply, which fairly clearly expresses his naive astonishment on the receipt of Peter's unexpected order:

"Recently I laid the keel of a government ship of the old Dutch dimensions, *but cn hearing today that the Dutch are so stupid* that they know nothing about dimensions, I ordered them to leave the ship until the arrival of the craftsmen Your Majesty is sending."

Thus, even if we only assume that in working in Holland Peter was inspired with the idea of learning the art of shipbuilding with the object of building a powerful navy in Russia, we must regard the time he spent in the Amsterdam shipyards as almost wasted. Peter himself clearly stated that it had not been worth while going to Holland for that purpose, that the Dutch were poor shipbuilders, that they could not be entrusted with the task of supervising such work, let alone serve as teachers or set examples in the art of shipbuilding. Consequently, during his six months' stay in Holland Peter learned only the art of the ship's carpenter. Pondering over this, the question must arise in everybody's mind: was it necessary for Peter himself to learn to perfection the art of smoothing logs, carving blocks for pulleys, laying planks, etc., in order to build a navy in Russia? If it was not necessary, was it in keeping with Peter's character to spend so much time on unnecessary trifles when he was already being irresistibly drawn on by far-reaching and definitely conceived plans? We think it was not. Peter did not, for example, before the second Azov campaign, study all the subtleties of the arts of engineering and artillery, he did not devote whole years to the study of metallurgy when he turned his attention to this industry, he did not himself make soldiers' coats and hats when he established a regular army with new uniforms. But the art of smoothing logs is, of course, no more important for the building of a navy than the ability to make soldiers' greatcoats is for the establishment of a regular army with new uniforms. Consequently, we would be ascribing to Peter excessive concern for detail if we assumed that he could devote himself for so long, and with such close attention, to such trifling matters if he had higher interests in view. We might assume that Peter remained in Holland only because of his mistaken opinion about the skill of the Dutch, but he could not have remained in error for so long had he sought in Holland what his historians say he sought. He, undoubtedly, would have demanded from the Dutch shipwrights the knowledge which must have constituted the main object of his quest after he had been there a week and would have found that the Dutch did not possess this knowledge. But we see that he worked as a carpenter for over four months, evidently not even thinking of asking his teachers about the main principles of shipbuilding. This was so strange for Peter, so much out of harmony with his ardent and impatient character, with his eager curiosity, so contrary to his habit of marching straight towards his goal with rapid strides and ignoring extraneous circumstances, that his stay in Holland can be explained only by the fact that he had as yet no definite ideas and aims about building a navy. In this case Peter was simply carried away by his passion for the work of a ship's carpenter, a passion which at that time mastered him more strongly than all remote considerations. The strength of this passion is proved among other things by the eagerness with which he worked. While at an official banquet he learned that the East-India Company had decided to lay the keel of a new frigate for his exercises. No sooner did he hear this than he wanted to start work at once, and it was with difficulty that he was persuaded to wait until the end of the feast and the fireworks display that had been arranged in his honour. But scarcely were the last fires extinguished when Peter set out for Saardam, where he had left his tools. He was warned of the danger of sailing at night, but in vain; he would not hear of anything, and set out at eleven o'clock at night. At one o'clock next morning he was in Saardam. He packed his tools and returned to Amsterdam early in the morning and started work. So strong and irresistible was his passion for shipbuilding!... And this passion, proved beyond doubt by facts, does not in the least detract from the greatness of Peter's deeds, even if we regard it as the cause that prompted some of them which hitherto have been regarded as the fruit of certain considerations of state. We repeat that it is not so much what a historical personage planned as what he accomplished that is important for history. Augustus patronized poetry because he himself wrote tragedies; but his age was the Golden Age of Roman literature. Richelieu always dreamed of literary fame, surrounded himself with a crowd of flatterers and, even with certain views of his own literary career, founded the French Academy; but the period of Richelieu's administration was the period of France's glory, and the French Academy has remained as one of the finest monuments of his administration. Frederick William built an army because of his passion for parades and giant soldiers; but the army he built enabled his son to lay the foundation of Prussia's greatness. And in general, if we admit that all great men in history had their own particular passions, if we appreciate Augustus' fondness for poetry. Frederick's passion for playing on the flute. and Napoleon's fondness of chess, then why not admit Peter's passion for the art of the turner and the carpenter, especially of the ship's carpenter, which partly satisfied his passion for the sea? There would seem to be nothing strange or unnatural in this; but this alone can fully explain Peter's six months' stay in Holland.

The same absence of extraordinary considerations is revealed in Peter's living incognito, which former historians also represented as some inexplicable mystery. Mr. Ustryalov explains this very simply by the fact that Peter wanted to avoid the ceremonies and court etiquette,. which always wearied him. Nevertheless, he did not by any means wish to forego the advantages which his high position gave him during his travels. At all events, this was clearly revealed after the unpleasantness he experienced in Riga. At first Peter really intended to travel strictly incognito, and in order not to be recognized in Europe he even had recourse to a measure which was permissible only under the then prevailing conceptions of the rights of private persons: he ordered that all letters sent abroad from Moscow through the ordinary post be opened, and that all those which contained even one word about the Tsar's journey be detained! On the other hand, however, the Russian court demanded from the King of Sweden an explanation as to why Dalberg had not accorded due honours to the Moscow

Tsar who was a member of the Grand Embassy. Dalberg, who, it seems, naively took the Tsar's incognito literally, answered, with good grounds from his point of view, as follows: "We pretended that we were not aware of the Tsar's presence because we were afraid to incur his displeasure; in the suite nobody dared speak of him on pain of death." Objecting to this Mr. Ustryalov observed:

"A lame excuse! Strict incognito did not prevent the Duke of Courland, the Elector of Brandenburg, his spouse the Electress of Hanover, the High States of the Netherlands, the King of England, the Austrian Emperor and the Empress herself from according Peter the courtesy due to his position and to his personal qualities."

True, Dalberg was naive, but scarcely less naive were those historians who accepted Peter's incognito too strictly, *à la lettre*. Incidentally, it is interesting to note how Peter's incognito was revealed in Saardam. All the circumstances here show that Peter even did not wish to remain unknown, he only wanted everybody to pretend that they did not know him. One day, after his arrival in Saardam, he bought some plums, put them in his hat and ate them as he walked down the road. On one of the dykes a crowd of boys surrounded him and Peter felt a desire to tease them. He gave plums to some of them but not to others and, according to an eyewitness, he was amused to see the joy of the first and the disappointment of the latter. The boys who got no plums began to throw mud and even stones at Peter. Peter took refuge from them in an inn and angrily summoned the burgomaster. That same day a public warning was issued to the effect that nobody, on pain of severe punishment, was to insult distinguished foreigners who desired to remain unknown. And that same day also a guard was placed on the bridge that led to the house where the Tsar was living, because he had complained about the crowds which gathered to stare at him. Several days later a crowd surrounded him on the shore. This angered Peter and he severely slapped the face of a Dutchman who was standing closer to him than the others and staring at him. . . . All this, of course, had very little resemblance to incognito; if anything, it actually revealed to the Dutch people who it was that had appeared among them.

Speaking generally, it is quite wrong to regard Peter's simple way of living and absence of ceremony as something deliberate and calculated. We saw in the preceding essay that the ground for this simplicity was laid by Peter's upbringing, which from his earliest years removed him from court etiquette and developed in him a natural vivacity and impulsiveness. To the Russians of that time, of course, it seemed extraordinary and strange that their monarch should appear among them like an ordinary mortal, not surrounded with the Asiatic splendour with which his predecessors had always appeared. And not only the Russians; this was also unusual for the peoples of Europe of that time. They had all been accustomed to picture the Tsar of the Muscovites as some unapproachable, mysterious personage, inaccessible to his subjects; and suddenly, to their amazement, they saw the Tsar of the Muscovites behaving with a simplicity that none of *their* European kings ever descended to. And this amazement gave rise to widespread speculation and attempts to ascribe Peter's simplicity to various, more or less great and brilliant, impulses. Some said that he wanted thereby to crush the arrogance of the boyars and to strike a final blow at the rules of precedence. Others said that he wanted in this way to learn all the needs of his kingdom. Others again even said that it was due to the profound humility of the Tsar, who placed himself on the level of the lowest of his subjects and wished to excel them only in his industry and merits. The strangest of these assumptions, and the one which most contradicted the facts of history, was the last, which transformed Peter from the Tsar of Moscow into some sort of idealistic philosopher. It is certainly a noble idea humbly to recognize the worthlessness of all privileges acquired by birth and accident, to understand that every man, whoever he may be, is exalted only by his industry and personal merits, to understand this in theory and always to apply this conviction in practice. But however beautiful such a conviction may be, it can be revealed in the actions of some homeless Diogenes in his unceremonious behaviour towards an Alexander rather than in the life of the autocratic ruler of a large state. Peter was never such a profound theoretician as to seek for principles on which to base his actions in abstract ideas about the rules of humanity and the dignity of the human being. And even if he had worked out for himself that idealistic humility that is ascribed to him, he would, undoubtedly, have revealed sufficient strength of mind to remain loyal to that conviction to the end and to apply it to the extreme, even though that would have entailed renunciation of his power and might. But the whole point is that neither in this case nor in many others were Peter's actions dictated by abstract principles; they flowed directly from his lively nature. It was simply that the stiff forms of Asiatic splendour which had reigned at the court of his predecessors were irksome to him; he felt it embarrassing to submit to this burdensome etiquette, and he simply refused to submit to it. To him it was just as simple, natural and unimportant as his hitherto unusual familiarity with foreigners, his fondness for firing cannon, his excursions on the water, which started his passion for the sea. He took it all as a matter of course. It was the direct consequence of his upbringing and development and was not due to any striving to carry out certain remote and grand designs, or to philosophical convictions concerning certain abstract principles. Peter's whole life shows that he never thought of devoting himself to purely theoretical contemplation, and never sacrificed to it a single moment of useful practical activity, not a single strong impulse of his passionate nature. He never suppressed these impulses, but demanded full scope for them, despite all the simplicity and indulgence he displayed towards those around him. He cast aside the ancient obsolescent forms in which the supreme authority had been clothed before him, but the substance remained unchanged. Clothed in a sailor's jacket and wielding an axe he ruled his kingdom with a hand as hard and as powerful as that of his predecessors who were arrayed in purple and sat on a golden throne with a sceptre in their hand. Woe to the audacious fellow who amidst the jollities of a feast dared to forget himself in Peter's presence: in a flash there would arise before him not the boon companion, but the formidable monarch who had power of life and death over him. Peter allowed his friends many liberties, but all the more dangerous was it to exceed the bounds of what he would permit. In a moment of anger he would stick at nothing, and so terrible was the fear he inspired at such moments that, according to Mr. Ustryalov's evidence that we quoted above "even the wildest revelry was interrupted and the company sat silent and trembling." Peter revealed the same impatience and impetuousness during his travels. Even the fact that he travelled incognito scarcely restrained him in this respect, as is evident, for example, from the case of the boys in Saardam, and of the Dutchman whose face he slapped.

Thus, all Peter's activities that we have traced so far in Mr. Ustryalov's story show that his was a strong and extraordinary nature, but, contrary to current opinion, his far-reaching political designs and plans of reform did not arise in his mind early in his career. And even when they did arise these plans were not as universal and boundless as certain historians have described them. Not all branches of the administration were affected at once; not all the reforms were at once conceived in a harmonious system, with a definite schedule indicating what was to be done first and what was to follow. We say again that such schedules would be convenient for a thinker who was drawing up some plan, but it is rare for a real practical statesman to be guided by them. All the more difficult, therefore, was it for Peter to draw up such systems, for by his very nature he was not disposed towards long reflection; and besides, he found himself in a situation where preconceived programs could only have hindered him.

Incidentally, the mere comparison of the state of affairs in Russia at that time with what Peter was able to see abroad could have served him as a sufficiently clear indication as to the goal to which his activities must henceforth be directed. The strictly theoretical problem was extremely simple in this case. That much had to be altered and much newly introduced was understood in Russia before Peter's time, and anybody familiar with European conditions could have told Peter what the principal needs of his kingdom were that called for immediate satisfaction. Particularly profound thinking was not needed here; what was needed was uncommon determination, inflexible will in the struggle against obstacles, and the undeviating pursuit of a goal to the very end that a genius displays. It was these qualities that Peter's predecessors lacked, although they appreciated the necessity of a great deal of what Peter subsequently performed. Already in the reign of Mikhail Fyodorovich our government realized that Russians must learn the art of war from foreigners and therefore invited foreign officers to Russia; it was during his reign that artillery and men capable of handling it were brought from abroad. Alexei Mikhailovich felt that a navy was needed, and he even had a ship built with the aid of foreign shipwrights. Trade with foreigners had been conducted for a long time, and Fletcher already wrote in his time that "the Russian tsars see in this trade a means of filling their treasury." Many in our country thought about foreign trade, and precisely overseas trade, as is evidenced, for example, by a preface written to a textbook on arithmetic which Karamzin believes was published in 1635. In this preface the various benefits to be derived from arithmetic are enumerated to encourage the study of it. It says *inter alia:*

"With the aid of this art merchants *carry on trade in foreign countries* and acquire a knowledge of all merchandise and commerce, of all systems of weights and measures, of geometry, become versed in navigation, and are well able to count."

Even the Turks understood that for a navy and for trade we needed the sea, and this explains their firm and unyielding insistence during their negotiations with us upon their exclusive rights to navigation in the Black Sea. The need for spreading education, and precisely of the European type, among the people was felt in this country from the time of Ivan Grozny, who sent Russians abroad to study, and particularly from the time of Boris Godunov, who sent a whole expedition of young men abroad to study, who contemplated founding a university, and for this purpose invited foreign scholars to Russia. We do not see these plans continued in the subsequent reigns, but the idea that we must learn from the foreigners dwelt in the public mind nevertheless. Koshikhin says with indignation that "the Russian boyars are afraid to send their children to foreign countries to study." Even in matters of less importance for the state, in matters of a more private nature, Peter had predecessors who, timidly, half-heartedly and slowly, began what he completed quickly and resolutely. For example, we know that the confinement of women to their chambers became less strict already in the reign of Alexei Mikhailovich. Soon after Sophia loudly proclaimed the rights of women. Similarly, the wearing of foreign clothing was already permitted by Fyodor, who himself wore *Polish* clothing. The introduction of various public amusements borrowed from foreigners already began in the reign of Alexei Mikhailovich. The point was, however, to complete, or at all events to continue quickly and resolutely, what had been begun. But none possessed

10*

the energy to do so except Peter. At the first failure Peter's predecessors lost heart and dared not continue their efforts; some, daunted by the difficulties, did not even dare commence. Thus, Alexei Mikhailovich abandoned the idea of building a navy when the first ship he built was burnt by Stepan Razin. Similarly, Godunov abandoned the idea of establishing a university with foreign tutors only because, as Karamzin tells us, "the clergy made representations to him to the effect that Russia enjoyed the blessings of peace owing to the unity of her laws and language, and that diversity of language may lead to diversity in thought, which would be dangerous to the Church." He also stopped sending young men abroad because the results of sending out the first party were not happy. Peter was not of that type; nothing could divert him from any purpose he had once decided on. His strong will was able to surmount all obstacles. It is this strength of character that most of all constituted his greatness; and it was such a character that Russia needed at that time.

Peter's father, Alexei Mikhailovich, was distinguished for his kindness and concern for the welfare of his subjects. But he lacked the energy that was needed to rid himself completely of the influence of the evil persons who surrounded him and who transformed his good intentions into evil. His successor, Fyodor, was an ailing man of weak character, totally unable to wage a persistent struggle against the old order of which he too disapproved. As a consequence, there was no unity and firmness in his administration. The government itself realized that things were going badly and it could not vigorously defend the existing order against the grumbling and discontent that was rising everywhere. Nevertheless, it dared not launch a determined struggle against the old order and its supporters; it merely confined itself to a few measures against abuses that were already too glaring to be ignored. But this was not enough, because these abuses were rooted in the very nature of the situation at the time, in the absence of freedom for the development of the forces of the people, in the ignorance and corruption of the men who were entrusted with the power of government, of administering justice and meting out punishment, in the general lack of education in every respect. This situation could not be changed merely by ukases prohibiting on pain of severe punishment extortion, wrang-

ling over precedence, or the unauthorized devastation of the country in time of war. A bolder and more determined blow had
to be struck at these evils by means of more general and deep-
going measures; but it was precisely for this that all of Peter's predecessors lacked strength. Of course, having the welfare of their
people at heart, they constantly revealed the most beneficial and
noble strivings, but these strivings, which testified to the goodness
of their hearts, were rarely carried out in the way they desired.
They themselves were unable personally to supervise the fulfilment of their intentions because, in conformity with the custom
prevailing in Rūs before Peter's time, they stood inaccessibly
remote from the people, while the men who surrounded them
exercised their power and influence for their own selfish ends.
These men greatly misrepresented the situation to kindhearted
Alexei and succeeded in persuading him to drop many of his
excellent intentions designed to benefit the people. This pernicious influence of the higher boyars was so glaring that it could
not be concealed even from the people. During the rebellion of
Stepan Razin a rumour was abroad to the effect that the Tsarevitch
Alexei had fled to the Don, carrying a message from the Tsar
to the Don Cossacks requesting them to help him to rid himself
of the crafty boyars. This rumour drew many to the side of the
rebel leader. This shows that the people felt the yoke of boyar
influence. The good Tsar alone, concerned for the welfare of the
subjects, had no suspicion that his favourites were the most
dangerous opponents of his beneficial designs. As a consequence,
things went from bad to worse. Sullen discontent began to find
outlet in open rebellion, and internal disorder increased year
after year. Fyodor's brief reign could do nothing to improve
matters, and when Peter took over the reins of government the
conditions in Russia were as follows.

Abroad Russia was humiliated: she had suffered numerous
setbacks in dealings with the Poles, she paid heraj—*remembrances*
in our language—to the Crimean Khan, she had lost territory
in the Gulf of Finland and had allowed a half of Little Russia,
which had voluntarily submitted to her, to slip out of her hands.
The Crimean campaign conducted by Prince Golitsyn, which had
been extolled by Sophia, brought still further disgrace upon
Russian arms and made us a laughingstock of the Poles, Turks

and Germans. If we analyze the causes of this we shall find, of course, that it was all due to internal disorder. The art of war was at the lowest level. Foreigners were invited to Russia to drill the Russian troops in the foreign manner, but this was done in a haphazard and negligent way. It often turned out that the foreigners were either totally ignorant themselves or were unwilling to do anything, and were found to be *"absent"* even during campaigns. Not being inspired by any strong sentiments and having no clear conception even of their duties, the troops entirely lost the martial spirit. This was proved during Golitsyn's Crimean campaign, and even later, during the Azov campaigns, which Peter himself led. Ignorance of engineering and gunnery was so complete that even Timmerman, who exploded mines in such a way that they injured our own troops, was regarded as an expert. There was no fleet either for war or commerce; there were even no decent ships or pilots to navigate rivers. Foreign trade was entirely in the hands of foreigners and the Russian merchants only suffered loss from their monopoly. The state revenues were small; as a consequence of the numerous shortcomings and disorder prevailing in the reign of Alexei Mikhailovich and of Sophia, arrears accumulated everywhere; rights of ownership became confused and a subject of controversy. The ukases of 1683 ordering the compilation of new registers of serfs to replace those that had been destroyed in the Chancellery for Serf Affairs during the May rebellion,[45] the return to their owners of serfs they had released under duress during that rebellion, the search for fugitive serfs, the resumption of the registration of the population, etc., all these ukases seem to have been of little use. The disorders continued, everything was in a state of confusion, the treasury was exhausted. As the historian observes, even at the time when Peter went abroad "our finances were in such a low state that they scarcely sufficed to meet the most urgent requirements." The entire administration was distinguished for its ignorance and corruption. Far from doing something to pacify the people, it seemed to go out of its way to irritate them. We know what happened during the reign of Alexei Mikhailovich as a result of the tyranny and extortion of the officials who enjoyed the protection of Morozov and Miloslavsky; and we also know the consequences of the issue of copper coinage and the selfish

manipulations of the rich boyars in connection with it. In the
preceding essay we saw how the injustices and acts of violence
committed by the commanders of the Musketeers prepared the
ground for the first Musketeers' mutiny. Equally remarkable was
the zeal of the boyars in antagonizing the Dissenters, which subsequently brought forth such bitter fruit. We have not dealt
with this subject in our essays because we have been trying to
trace only those events which occurred during the period of Peter's
adolescence, and which had marked influence upon his development. In a general survey of the state of Russia at that time,
however, attention must be paid to the position of the Dissenters,
for it throws a glaring light on the degree of education and
humanity that prevailed in the administration in that period.
We shall refrain from expressing our own opinion on this subject but take the liberty of quoting just one page from Volume
I of Mr. Ustryalov's *History of Peter's Reign.*

"The measures the Tsarevna took to eradicate the principal evil, the
schism, only helped to aggravate it. After the rebellion of Nikita Pustosvyat[46]
the following order was issued: to search for the Dissenters all over the
country and, depending upon the degree of their guilt, to hand some over
to the Ecclesiastical Court and others to the Civil Court on the charge of
committing crimes against the state. About two years later decrees were
issued containing instructions as to how these were to be dealt with: those
who persisted in their error were to be subjected to cruel torture to compel
them to say who their teachers were, and if they refused to renounce their
schismatic doctrines they were to be burnt to death in log cabins and their
ashes blown to the winds; those who rebaptized infants or adults on the
ground that their first baptism was invalid, were also to be burnt in log
cabins; those who gave refuge to Dissenters, or being aware of their where-
abouts had not reported them, were to be punished with the knout and
banishment. Thus, persecution was instituted all over the country: it
brought forth bitter fruit: the fanatics became more fanatical than ever;
large crowds of armed people attacked the monasteries and kept the
Tsar's troops at bay for whole months, and at last, driven to desperation,
they perished in the flames of the churches that they themselves had set
on fire. . . . Those events make sad reading, and the legislators of that time
seem to be all the more guilty for the reason that while they ruthlessly
persecuted unfortunate errors of thought and conscience, they themselves
paid tribute to absurd prejudices: the chief of them, Prince Golitsyn, the
Tsarevna's first guide and counsellor, believed in magic and witchcraft. . . ."

Together with ignorance and cruelty, embezzlement of state
funds and bribery were rampant everywhere, and this, as Koshi-

khin expressed it, reduced all faith and invocations to nought. In
the army administration the officials kept back the pay of subordinates and forced them to serve their private needs: they compelled them to acquire at their own expense equipment that should
have been supplied by the government, etc. In the civil courts
everything could be obtained by bribery and it was difficult to
find an honest man. Protasyev, for example, whom Peter had
appointed chief supervisor of the construction of the fleet, was
found to be taking bribes on a vast scale. It was notorious that
Emelyan Ukraintsev, the best diplomat and ambassador in the
first period of Peter's reign, also took bribes. Evidence of extortion, practised even by men in Peter's immediate entourage,
appeared even later and always drove the Tsar into a frightful
rage. But the disease was so widespread that even Peter could
not eradicate it. It manifested itself not only in internal affairs,
but also in relations with foreign states. Bribery served as a
substitute for military prowess and diplomatic skill. We shall
remind the reader that at Azov the Russians tried to induce
the Pasha to surrender the town by offering *advantageous terms;*
the same device was resorted to on the Pruth very much later.
Nefimonov, the Russian minister in Poland, who was there in
1696, at the time the king was chosen, advised, in a despatch
to Peter that, following the example of the Austrian Emperor, he
should send to Poland "a plenipotentiary ambassador with a
fairly large sum of money for presents. The Poles, however,"
he added, "love Moscow sables more than money." The whole
of life in Rūs at that time consisted more in satisfying the crude,
animal needs of man than in satisfying his higher interests. The
lower classes of the people lived in poverty, the result of which
was drunkenness and robbery. The upper classes were steeped
in rude arrogance and wallowed in luxury, consisting in idleness,
eating and drinking and in wild carousing, which often reached
such a degree that they indulged in open robbery. Zhelyabuzhski's
memoirs provide no few cases of princes and boyars being caught
in the act of robbery. What the intellectual level of the upper
classes was like we saw in a preceding essay. What their domestic life was like can be seen from Koshikhin's work. An interesting feature is the list which Mr. Ustryalov gives in his book of

the items of food allowed Tsarevna Sophia when she was *incarcerated* in the Novodevichy Monastery.

"To her and her few servants were issued *daily*: one vedro* of excise mead and one of March beer, two vedros of small beer (and at Christmastide and on Easter Sunday a vedro of brown vodka and five quarts of aniseed vodka), four steam boiled sterlet, six soup sterlet, two pikes, one bream, three roaches, thirty perch and carp, two portions of white fish, two portions of caviar, two portions of herrings, four plates of salted sterlet, a portion of beluga and a commensurate amount of bread: white, green, Krasnoselsky, buns, scones, rolls, pastry, pies, loaves, nut oil and spices, and also for one year: half a pood** of Canary sugar, a pood of medium sugar, four pounds of candy, white and red, four pounds of hard bake candy, three pounds of confectionery, etc."

Why the Tsarevna should have been supplied with this enormous quantity of food, and particularly of beer, can be explained only by the habits of life of those times. On the other hand, the Moscow boyars were famous for their hospitality, and they were inordinately proud of their wealth and breeding, although the most thoroughbred of them, according to Koshikhin, often "sat in the Tsar's council stroking their beards and saying nothing, for the Tsar appointed many of the boyars not for their wisdom, but for their birth, and many of them were illiterate and unlearned."

It was these *unlearned* men that Peter had to bring face to face with Europe, for whom, already at that time, much that the Russian courtiers had never conceived of was common and natural. On becoming acquainted with foreigners, and learning from them, Peter strode far ahead of his boyars, who were steeped in selfishness, arrogance and ancient custom. People abroad looked upon Russia as upon a great *potentiality*, although they realized that for the time being she could not compare with Europe. Peter too soon realized this, and it became his task to bring the potentiality nearer to reality. From the outside this seemed an extremely easy task. This, for example, is the tone in which the Polish ambassador Karlowicz spoke to Peter in 1699, in urging him to make war on Sweden.

"It is for His Royal Majesty to determine," he wrote in the memorandum he submitted to Peter, "whether he shall gain boundless profit,

---

* Vedro—2.70 gallons.—*Tr.*
** Pood—36.11 lbs.—*Tr.*

achieve world fame, open flourishing trade with Holland, England, Spain, Portugal and with all the northern, western and southern countries of Europe, and what is most important, and what no sovereign has achieved so far, open through Russia a trade route between the East and the West with exclusive rights to all the profits. By this means His Royal Majesty will enter into close communication with the foremost monarchs in Christendom, gain importance and weight in the general affairs of Europe, build up a formidable navy, and raising Russia to the position of the third naval power, compel the French King to abandon his dreams of a French monarchy, thus gaining world-wide fame sooner than by subjugating the Turks and the Tatars. If, on the opening of a war for the Spanish Succession, or for any other cause, he sends to the assistance of England and Holland ten to twenty thousand troops with a considerable fleet, the allies will regard His Royal Majesty with exceptional respect; and meanwhile, the Muscovites will learn the art of war at other people's expense and then, no longer needing foreign officers, will wage war against the Turks and the Tatars with the greatest success. The other advantages will be best of all weighed by His Royal Majesty's lofty mind."

During Peter's time ideas of this kind may have sounded new to the Russian courtiers, but in Europe this view of Russia had been current for a long time, except, of course, for the few high sounding hyperboles which Karlowicz permitted himself in pursuit of his object. During his travels in Europe Peter could not fail to see the importance that was attached in Europe to the kingdom of Russia because of its geographical situation and its vast homogeneous population. Peter's predecessors too had been aware of this, as is evident from certain diplomatic documents; but the rulers of Russia before Peter lacked the determination to take due advantage of their position. They seemed to be confessing to themselves all the time that while they had the strength, they lacked the will. Peter, however, having from his earliest years seen disorder reigning in his kingdom, was more conscious than his predecessors that his strength was not as great as it seemed; but he possessed the will and the determination to use at least the strength he had. And he used it in spite of all the obstacles ignorance and indolence placed in his way. Not relying on the effectiveness of exhortations, and carried away by his ardour and impatience, he often resorted to violence. He himself started everything, supervised everything and pushed everything forward, because he was too impatient to wait until his assistants got going in their "Moscow forthwith" manner. Often he had no one

at all to help him, and at times the men he most relied upon
only spoiled the job they were given to do. Peter did not lose
heart, but he vented his wrath upon those who failed to execute
his orders properly. Here, in passing, we may mention an incident to illustrate the kind of men Peter had at his command
to carry out his intentions, and to show how far our political
sagacity at that time lagged behind European diplomacy, an
example of which we saw in Karlowicz's memorandum. This incident occurred during the second Azov campaign, that is to say,
only three years before Karlowicz came as an ambassador to
Moscow. In this campaign, as is well known, Peter waited a long
time for the arrival of the Austrian engineers, who were several
months late. Asked why they came late, the engineers answered
that nobody in Vienna expected that the Russian troops would
start out so early, and that Kuzma Nefimonov, the Russian ambassador at the court of Vienna, had not told them anything,
and knew nothing himself, about the progress of military operations. It transpired that Ukraintsev, who was then in charge
of the Department for Foreign Affairs, had not informed Nefimonov about the movements of the army for fear that *he would
divulge such information* if he received it. . . . Peter was extremely annoyed by this strange argument and forthwith wrote the
following original letter to Vinius, Ukraintsev's brother-in-law:

"I am extremely displeased by the fact that your brother-in-law is
keeping Kuzma (Nefimonov) in ignorance about our war. Is it not a disgrace? Whenever he is asked about anything he has to confess he does
not know. . . . And yet he was sent on such an important mission (to conclude a treaty of alliance). In his letters to Nikita Moiseyevich about
Polish affairs, which are not so important, he tells him what to do, but
about the Austrians, upon whom the hopes of the entire alliance rest,
he forgot. He writes as follows: 'I don't tell him anything about the
army so that he, Kuzma, should not blab.' What a fine argument! Is he
in his senses? He is entrusted with state affairs, but he is not told what
everybody else knows! Tell him (Ukraintsev) that what he fails to write
on paper I will write on his back."

Such were the best representatives of ancient Rūs, whose
mission it was to carry out Peter's plans before the eyes of Europe, which at that time, owing to the political situation, was
watching Russia more closely than at any other time. How puny
the ideas of the farsighted and cautious Chief of our Department

for Foreign Affairs looks in comparison with, say, the bold and
far-reaching plans of Patkul, part of which were formulated in
Karlowicz's memorandum! ... What could Peter do with men of
that type except what he threatened to do at the end of the letter
quoted above? No kindness of heart, no good intentions, no theoretical perspicuity could have helped him if he had not possessed
that powerful character, which often expressed itself unevenly,
impulsively and stormily, but which always pushed things forward with bold and determined strokes. This character, which
was moulded in the stormy period of the early part of his life,
Peter revealed quite early; everybody soon became convinced
that once he got going Peter would not do things by halves; and
he soon became the representative and promoter of those new
ideas which had long been maturing among the people and could
not find satisfaction. All those who were discontented with the
old order turned their gaze hopefully upon Peter and gladly
followed him, for they saw that on his banner was inscribed that
same hatred of the deep-seated evil, that same struggle against
the obsolete past and that same love for the light of education
which the people themselves vaguely felt. On the other hand,
notwithstanding their crudeness and ignorance, the representatives
of the old order also guessed that Peter would not treat them
any too kindly, and realizing that by his very nature he would
stand no nonsense, they lay low. And so, Peter appears in our
history as the personification of the people's needs and aspirations, as the man who concentrated within himself the desires
and forces that were diffused among the masses. This is the
secret of the success that always accompanied his undertakings,
notwithstanding all the obstacles that were raised in his path
by the ignorance and selfishness of the ancient party—and this
too is the answer to the riddle as to why at that time Peter devoted little attention to what were the most important conditions
for promoting the happiness of the people: the spread of education among all classes of the people, and the creation of conditions for the free and unfettered development of all the productive forces of the country. Clearly, even if he had wished
to devote himself to these matters Peter could not have concentrated upon them: the people's past had not yet sufficiently prepared the conditions that would have enabled the desire for real

and serious education and for the improvement of economic conditions to manifest itself strongly and effectively among the
masses. It was still necessary, first of all, to open the eyes of the
masses, to take a look at others, to realize that education and
properly defined social relations, different from ours, did exist
in the world, and then to set to work to assimilate these as far
as ability and strength would allow. This explains why all Peter's
activities were directed to the task of bringing Russia nearer to
Europe. Probably Peter did a great deal towards this without
having this object in view; but this result came of its own accord,
from the natural order of things. Peter was a strong driving
force: nevertheless, he did not determine the direction of the
movement... that was determined by the course of history, as it
has been always and everywhere.

But Peter's greatness as a powerful driving force of events
in the given direction is truly amazing. He became the head of
the movement on the very first day of his reign and he swept all
obstacles from his path. Naturally, his sister's ministers and
favourites were not to his liking, and so he dismissed them all
in one day and put his own friends and supporters in their place.
But most of these new dignitaries also followed the old customs,
they too were imbued with the old boyar arrogance, were involved
in quarrels over precedence, were fond of Asiatic ceremonies
and were steeped in crude prejudices. Even after Peter's reforms,
not long before the Peace of Nystadt, some of them still sighed
for the good old days of Muscovy. In many things they could
not understand Peter, who had already learned from Timmerman and Brandt, and there were many things on which they
could give him no advice. Bored by their inertness and extreme
narrow-mindedness, Peter made friends with the countrymen of
Timmerman and Brandt, and soon Lefort and Gordon became
his best friends, and the company at Nemetskaya Sloboda his
favourite company. The narratives of the foreigners and his study
of military and naval affairs, revealed a new world to Peter, and
he examined this new world for five years, as if testing his
strength, forgetting everything to the exclusion of his favourite occupations, which for the time being were only his private occupations. But later he decided to subject these occupations to a
serious test, not as amusements, but in real affairs, and so he

set out for Azov. This undertaking had as yet almost no state
significance, but it awakened Peter's genius for affairs of state.
He realized that his ships were bad, his troops were bad and the
laws that were passed were bad; he also realized that his foreign
friends were extremely bad too. This, one would think, would
have marked the triumph of the opposition party: its reproaches
and sinister forecasts would seem to have been justified. Some
told the Tsar that God was punishing him for his fondness for
heretics, others assured him that the *old ways* were really better
than following the cunning devices of foreigners, and others
again argued that all the foreigners were scoundrels and traitors,
and therefore, all should be put to death, or banished. For all
this there was glaring proof and evidence: the ships which the
foreigners had built were unseaworthy, the troops which they
had trained were unable to stand up against the enemy, the
mines they laid blew up to our own injury, and lastly, there
had actually been traitors among the foreigners, who deserted
us for the Turks. Clearly, all the evil came from the foreigners;
at all events, no good came from them.... But Peter refused
to listen to all this; he argued differently: the whole trouble was
that there were too few foreigners, and these few were inefficient; more foreigners, and more efficient ones, were needed. And
so he sent messages to different countries requesting that skilled
men be sent to him.... And to these men he entrusted his engineering operations, he placed his artillery in their charge, and
he commissioned them to build a fleet. The need for a fleet had
also been indicated by the Azov campaign, and Peter, already
devoted to his passion for navigation, set to work to build a fleet
with the greatest ardour. But to build a fleet money was needed
and his treasury was depleted; since a fleet was to be built it
had better be a good one, but who could tell what the foreign
shipwrights would be like? For a fleet we must have a sea, but
we had no sea. What was to be done? Anybody else would have
stopped to ponder, anybody else would have abandoned these
ideas in face of the insurmountable obstacles. But Peter was
never daunted by great obstacles; to such trifles he refused to
pay any attention. The treasury is depleted? But what are *companies* for? In November 1696 Peter ordered all owners of estates and patrimonies to build ships—church owners one for every

eight thousand serf households, and secular owners one for every ten thousand serf households—the ships to be ready by April 1698; and all people engaged in commerce were together to build twelve bombarding ships by the same date. And so the problem was solved. Those who refused to obey this order, or those who defaulted, were to be deprived of their villages, of their lives and of their households. And all the ships were ready within sixteen months.... Even more were ready than were at first required. A year later Peter found that there would not be enough ships if only one ship was built by each company, and so he issued an ukase to the effect that every two companies should build an extra ship. And they were built.... Since the skill of the foreign shipwrights was doubtful, Peter sent messages to all countries requesting that the *best and most skilled* craftsmen be sent him; and to be able to judge the quality of their work he sent Russians abroad to learn the arts of shipbuilding and navigation, and he himself followed them abroad for the same purpose. Since there was no sea, Peter sent Ukraintsev to Constantinople to secure right of navigation in the Black Sea. When that failed, we turned in the other direction—to the Baltic.

Peter behaved in exactly the same way in choosing his collaborators. The venerable greybeards he had chosen before were found to be lacking in energy, and they sympathized little with Peter. So Peter looked round for other people among all classes of society, and in the embassy that went abroad with him we already find the names of Peter Shafirov and Alexander Menshikov. Some may say: "So Peter had men with him who were capable of rendering him effective and intelligent assistance." Yes, but when do such men not appear? Let us recall the just observations of Karamzin:

"Military leaders, ministers and legislators are not born in any particular reign, they are chosen. To be able to choose one must have discernment, and only great men can discern men—and Peter's servants helped him amazingly on the battlefield, in the Senate, and in the Cabinet."

To this we will add that sometimes it is not so much the choice of men as putting them in the required places that is difficult, and in this respect Peter probably encountered more difficulties than anybody else in his position. To put the men he

chose in the positions they merited he was obliged to break down
a thousand obstacles. First of all, these were men of low degree,
of unknown birth, hence, their elevation offended the aristocratic
pride of the boyars, and their quarrels over precedence could
easily affect their relations in government service. Moreover, all
these were young men. By elevating them and entrusting them
with important affairs Peter flew in the face of ancient custom,
by which age was regarded as a sufficient guarantee of a man's
wisdom and knowledge while youth was condemned to serve as the
errand boys of the ancients. To this we must add that the new
men whom Peter chose were heart and soul in favour of the
innovations against the old order; and this inevitably still further roused the hostility of the highborn boyar grandees who
looked down with contempt upon everything that was not coloured
with the hoary tints of ancient birth and rank. How much more
was their ire roused when foreigners appeared among those whom
the Tsar had chosen! Here superstition and patriotism came to their
aid; here they expected to see the people on their side. But
Peter was not daunted by their impotent ire and boldly proceeded
along the path he had chosen, "paying no attention," as Mr. Ustryalov says, "to the marked vexation of the boyars who were esteemed
for their grey hairs and devotion, to the stern admonitions of the
universally revered Patriarch, to the superstitious horror of the people, and paying no heed to the tender reproaches of his mother or the
upbraidings of his wife, whom he still loved." And it was not only
their words and grumbling that Peter ignored; he was not even
daunted by discontent when it assumed the form of armed rebellion.
Two weeks before Peter's departure on his journey the plot hatched
by Sokovnin and Tsikler was discovered. Peter had them and their
principal accomplices executed over the coffin of Ivan Mikhailovich
Miloslavsky, which was disinterred; on the Red Square he had
erected a pillar of brick with iron spikes on which the heads of the
executed men were stuck; around the pillar their bodies were laid,
and so they remained for several months. The relatives of the executed men were flung into jail in remote towns. All this, notwithstanding, two weeks later he started out on his journey abroad.
During his absence another rebellion broke out, provoked rather
by the unwise, or perhaps, even really tyrannical conduct of officials than by any definite designs to preserve the old order. In March

1698 a hundred and seventy-five Musketeers who had deserted their regiments on the Lithuanian frontier arrived in Moscow and complained that they were being starved and oppressed. The boyars ordered them to return to their regiments before April 3, but on that day four hundred men appeared before the boyars demanding various exemptions and privileges and refused to return to their regiments. They were driven out of the city by force. On learning of this Peter censured Romodanovsky for "not having investigated this matter." Indeed, the Musketeer deserters who were permitted to go back, or rather, were *sent back*, to their regiments, incited the rest, and in June a real mutiny broke out, the Musketeers marched on Moscow. They did not manage to do any harm for they were soon subdued: one hundred and thirty were hanged, one hundred and forty were flogged and banished, and two thousand were sent to prison in various towns. But Peter was not content with this. He wanted to eradicate completely everything that might still offer dangerous opposition to his strivings. He recalled the horrors of the early years of his life, he recalled that the Musketeers had been the supporters and the tools of his sister, and he decided immediately on his return home from abroad to root out this evil which gave him no rest. In this case he regarded the Musketeers as the representatives of the opposition party and the accomplices of those whom he regarded as his evil-wishers, beginning with his sister and his wife, and he therefore decided to use the Musketeers as an example of how frightfully and cruelly he could punish his opponents. "I will interrogate them more sternly than you have done," he said to Gordon. And indeed, in September and October 1698, there took place that ruthless investigation, the details of which, as communicated by Mr. Ustryalov, must rouse horror in readers of our times. Every day thousands of Musketeers and men whom they had denounced were tortured in several dungeons for hours at a stretch to compel them to state the causes and objects of the mutiny. At first all of them displayed amazing heroism and refused to speak even during confrontations, even on the *rack*, on the *wheel*, under every kind of torture, even *by fire*. Many died under torture without saying anything, except that they had marched on Moscow because they had been starved and oppressed by the officers, and also because they had heard rumours to the effect that the Tsar had died abroad. But Peter could not be put off so easily. He had the tortures continued, he stuck at nothing, he even summoned his sisters for interrogation, and he himself drew up the points on which the interrogation was to proceed, namely: was it not Sophia who called the Musketeers to Moscow? Did she send a letter? Did they want to put her on the throne? When the question was put in this blunt way there were fewer disavowals; many confessed, but vaguely and indefinitely, as if they themselves did not fully understand what they were confessing. At last one of them related the whole story of the receipt of a letter from Sophia (which, however, was not confirmed by the subsequent investigations), and after that the whole investigation was concentrated upon this circumstance. At last, a considerable number of the Musketeers confessed to having political designs and to having been incited by Sophia.* Then the executions commenced. According to certain sources, as many as four thousand men were executed. According to Mr. Ustryalov "the Red Square was carpeted with beheaded bodies; the walls of Byely and Zemlyanoi towns were strung with hanging bodies." Shortly afterwards, one thousand and sixty eight corpses were carted out of Moscow and laid along different roads. In addition, enormous numbers of men were banished. Not content with this, and wishing to exterminate the rebels, Peter decided, to use his own expression, to *cashier* the entire Musketeer force. In 1699 the Musketeers were reduced to the status of civilians (possadskiye); they were prohibited from entering military service, and those who enlisted without stating that they had previously served in the Musketeers, were to be banished.

---

* Not wishing to deal with this subject at too great length we shall not go into the details of the investigation. But it would be very interesting to make it the subject of a legal investigation with the object of deciding whether the historian should attach more credence to the earlier disavowals of the Musketeers, or to the testimony that was wrung out of them by cruel torture. On the one hand, if the disavowals and silence of the Musketeers was deliberate and not due to the fact that they really knew nothing, and, therefore, could not say anything, then their heroism exceeds that of Mucius Scaevola and Regulus. On the other hand, it is well known that confession under torture cannot be regarded as being very reliable. An examination of the whole investigation, the records of which have been preserved, would probably render possible a calmer and more dispassionate conclusion at the present time than was possible at that time.—*N. D.*

This is how Peter acted against those who dared to oppose his undertakings, or reveal sympathy for his opponents. But action of this kind could not, of course, have been successful had not Peter, in all his activities, represented that nascent movement which had already defeated the old and obsolete past. Let us recall the fatal embitterment that was caused by, and the deplorable consequences that usually ensued from, the much milder severity of his predecessors. But in giving rein to his indomitable and implacable will, Peter was conscious of his strength. This explains why he boldly and bluntly proclaimed his demands and as plainly and threateningly announced in advance the punishment to which recalcitrants were liable. He already had wider and more definite plans in view on his return home from abroad than he had had before his departure, and, consequently, he began to act with greater determination; for by that time he already had formed in his mind certain ideas concerning certain subjects which had been suggested to him by what he had seen abroad. Thus, immediately on his return he, together with that skilled and experienced mariner Kreyss, found that the ships which had been built by the companies were unsatisfactory. On some the armaments and rigging had to be improved, on others the hulls themselves needed alteration, others again had to be completely remodelled because they were too unsteady, while others were totally unseaworthy. Orders were immediately issued to the *companies* which had built the ships to make the necessary alterations under the supervision of English craftsmen. A fleet was now *imperatively* necessary for Peter because our diplomacy had proved to be exceedingly inefficient in the negotiations at the Austrian court, and the Russians were faced with a war with the Turks with whom all our allies had made a separate peace, leaving us to face them alone. Peter was not afraid of the prospect of war, he even welcomed it, and no doubt he would have not been so compliant to the Turks had not Patkul's designs against Sweden called forth the Northern War which diverted Peter's attention to the north.

While engaged in the task of building the fleet, no longer as a carpenter but as an admiral and director, Peter now began to devote more attention to other departments of the state administration. Thus, on the suggestion of Kurbatov, who had borrowed

11*

his ideas from abroad, *stamp duties* were introduced as a means of increasing state revenues and at the same time of reducing false denunciations. With the same end of increasing revenues in view, the entire system of collecting taxes, customs and excise duties, was reformed in 1699. A special *Bailiff's Chamber* was set up to supervise the collection of taxes, and the rates of taxation were doubled. Notwithstanding the increase in taxation, the reform was welcomed by everybody, because, as Peter himself stated in his ukase (of January 30, 1699), up till now the trading class had been "the helpless victim of arrogant lawlessness and shameless extortion, so that as a result of official red tape, voyevoda impositions and bribery, trading people had been reduced to utter ruin, many enterprises had to be closed, they had no means of paying taxes, and the state exchequer suffered no little loss as a result of arrears in taxes and the dropping off of trade license fees." And Mr. Ustryalov adds in commenting on this ukase: "The example of Holland had proved to the Tsar that the prosperity of the trading class served as one of the main sources of the wealth of the state and that trade could flourish only if it developed freely and independently without the interference of outside authorities, which is burdensome at all times and was particularly so under the conditions then prevailing in Russia." It is very probable that the example of Holland was one of the things that prompted Peter to set up the Bailiff's Chamber, although it cannot be said that he at that time fully realized what effect the intervention of outside authorities had upon the prosperity of industry and, consequently, upon the welfare of the state everywhere, and particularly here in Russia. At all events, Peter had not yet turned his attention to the reform of these *authorities*.

The influence of Peter's journey abroad was manifested first of all in his desire to change certain social relationships. He had seen that the mode of life in other countries differed from that in Russia, and, of course, he was pleased by the simplicity and absence of ceremony in the relations between men and women in the West, by the happy family circle, and by the public amusements in which women always participated. He wanted to introduce the same thing in Russia, and in order to make Russians resemble Europeans in externals as well, he first of all devoted

himself to the task of changing their appearance. This seemed
to him a trifling task after all the things he had done, and in
which he had proved his strength. He even started this as a mere
jest in the belief that the people who had willingly sacrificed
their means for building a fleet, who had seen the superiority of
the foreigners in various sciences and arts, who by the Tsar's
command had abandoned their pompous and frigid pride, who
had travelled abroad, or had heard the detailed narratives of
eyewitnesses about foreign lands—that these people would not
put up a fight for their long gowns and beards. But it turned
out that the resistance in this case was more stubborn than in
others. The obsolete past, losing its privileges, wanted at least
to preserve its outward symbols and therefore fought harder for
the symbols than for the actual substance. On hearing that the
boyar Golovin had appeared at the court of Vienna with a shaven
chin Caesar Romodanovsky exclaimed: "I refuse to believe that
Golovin was as mad as that." The Patriarch wrote that "those
who have shaven their beards shall not be given Christian burial
nor be mentioned in the church's prayers." More than that,
according to our historian, "the stupid priests fanned the superstitious horror of the mob by secret admonitions and even
dared in their parishes audaciously to denounce the Tsar. Thus,
in the town of Romanov, the priest Vikula, in making the rounds
of the houses with the sacred icon in the Troitskaya Sloboda
during Holy Week, came to the house of the soldier Kokorev,
but would not allow him to kiss the Holy Cross, calling him an
adversary and an infidel because his chin was shaven. When
Kokorev pleaded in justification: 'Nowadays in Moscow the boyars and princes shave by command of the Tsar,' Vikula roundly
denounced even the Tsar." In general, no previous demand that
Peter had made had aroused so much grumbling and open discontent as the command to shave off beards. But Peter had already decided that beards must come off, and nothing on earth
could make him alter his decision. He did not want Russians to
appear repulsive to foreigners, and as the historian tells us, "the
more stubbornly the Russians clung to their beards the more
hateful these beards became to Peter as the symbol of ossified
prejudice, as a sign of haughty ignorance, as a permanent obstacle to friendly relations with the foreigners and to the borrow-

ing of all that which was useful from them." As was his custom, Peter put his order about the shaving of beards into execution forthwith. His first attempt to do so was rather comical—which is proof that at first Peter had thought that this was an easy matter. On the day after he returned to Moscow from abroad the most celebrated boyars came to his palace to welcome him. Peter received them very kindly, kissed and embraced them, chatted with them and suddenly, to their indescribable amazement, he clutched each one by the beard and cut it off. The first to be subjected to this humiliating operation were those high dignitaries *Caesar* Romodanovsky and *Generalissimo* Shein. Then came the turn of the others, except Streshnev and Cherkassky, whom the Tsar spared. Five days later a similar scene was enacted at a feast in Shein's mansion; here the Tsar's jester acted as the barber. Three days later, at a feast given by Lefort, the boyars appeared already without beards. "The ebullient Tsar," Mr. Ustryalov tells us, "did not wish to see bearded men around him either in the palace, in the army or in the shipyards. The boyars, courtiers, soldiers and shipwrights were obliged to yield to the indomitable will of the Tsar." Soon a tax on beards was introduced and was extended to the common urban people, and even to peasants. In spite of the expectations and wishes of the supporters of the old order, even this passed off quietly; there were no rebellions anywhere. The people were loth to abandon an ancient custom, but their regret could not have been profound because this custom did not express any reasonable or vital necessity.

The same thing happened with the ancient Russian costume, against which Peter launched a campaign at the same time. In this respect too the Tsar was influenced by his journey abroad; it roused in him a definite dislike for the Russian costume which, as Mr. Ustryalov observes, "he had had no great liking for before, primarily because the long gowns, capes and cloaks with sleeves two yards long hindered him in climbing ships' masts, in wielding the axe, in marching with the soldiers, in short, was totally out of harmony with his lively, impetuous and tireless activities." But what prompted him most in this respect was this desire of his to bring the Russians closer to the foreigners. Peter was convinced that the ancient costume would be a hindrance to this object, and so he decided to deal with the gowns and cloaks as he had dealt with the beards.

"At first, at merry feasts he cut off the long sleeves of the courtiers and refused to have around him long gowns any more than beards. Soon after he had foreign uniforms made for the newly established regular army, and then he issued strict orders to the effect that all boyars, courtiers, servicemen, clerks, and traders should wear Hungarian and German clothing before Epiphany, and at all events not later than Shrovetide in the year 1700. The same applied to boyars' ladies who came to visit the Court from the provinces. Soon this order was extended to the womenfolk of merchants, Musketeers, soldiers, priests and deacons."

At the same time Peter reformed our coinage, which was an extremely inconvenient one. The idea of doing so had also occurred to him while abroad, particularly in London, where he had made repeated visits to the Mint. Before Peter's time our coinage was extremely ugly and of irregular shape, so that it was very easy to clip and counterfeit, and this explains why coiners flourished in ancient Rūs, notwithstanding the stern laws that were passed against them. Peter combated this evil by different means: he introduced coins of a better mintage and as a result counterfeiting declined. Another evil was that the only coins current at that time were silver kopeks. On the one hand, owing to the complete absence of gold and silver coins of larger denominations the government encountered no few difficulties in its financial transactions, particularly abroad. On the other hand, the poor class of the people suffered from a shortage of small money. Peter decided to introduce copper coins; kopeks, *dengas* and *polushkas*, in spite of the fact that an attempt to do the same in the reign of Alexei Mikhailovich had extremely deplorable consequences. Later, he began to coin *chervontsys*,* silver half rubles, quarters, and finally rubles. All these coins at once went into circulation at a rate fixed by the government.

Peter did not act with the same swiftness and determination in two other important branches of state administration, *viz.*, in issuing a code of laws and taking measures for the education of the people. That Peter had these matters in mind is evident from the fact that in February 1700 he ordered the setting up in Moscow of a commission to draw up a new code, and that in a

---

* Gold ten-ruble pieces.—*Tr.*

conversation with Adrian he expressed his intention of reforming the Slavonic-Greek-Latin Academy into something in the nature of a university. But evidently Peter did not devote himself very closely to these questions, for he soon turned his thoughts away from the commission and the academy towards his favourite occupations. In the course of fourteen years the commission succeeded in examining only the first three chapters of the code, and the idea of establishing schools and an academy found application only in the establishment of a School of Navigation. Soon the Tsar's attention was for a long time deflected from internal affairs by the war against Charles, but of course Peter's lack of attention to the Laws' Commission and to the establishment of schools cannot be ascribed to this accidental circumstance. We have seen what his character was like, the vigour with which he carried out the most difficult undertakings. Even at that time he could have issued the necessary orders, or have undertaken himself, to invite teachers from abroad, as he had done in the case of shipwrights; he could have had schools, high schools and universities built in the same way as he had a fleet built, and he could have established museums and libraries as he had established a regular army.... But there is a limit to human might. Peter could have set in motion those forces of his people which were ready to move, but he could not call forth before their time those forces which were still too feeble to be set in motion. As a man whose will expressed the requirements and aspirations of the people, Peter possessed that instinctive *tact* which distinguishes historical leaders of his type from the uninvited fanatics, who often take the figments of their distorted imaginations for the true requirements of their age and people, and who undertake fruitless tasks that are beyond their strength. Peter was aware that he possessed strength enough to accomplish a great deal, but he was also aware of the limits of his strength. He came to a harvest that had been prepared for ages, and he realized that he could reap this crop which his predecessors had left untouched. But at the same time he was aware that, after all, the *producing* force here was this soil on which he was about to reap. He was able more or less quickly and successfully to reap and gather all that had grown on it, but he could not at his own will compel the grain to grow. It was first necessary to sow, and he sowed all he could. But what could he, at that time, sow in the field of civil law and public education in Russia? The sowing was of necessity meagre, and this explains why Peter displayed so little energy in his undertakings in this field. The people were, as yet, little prepared for this, and Peter was the representative of his people. Could he have become deeply imbued with something which had not yet become a profound and imperative requirement in the mind of the people themselves?

The war against Sweden deflected Peter's thoughts from legislation and education and indicated to him a field that was closer to his constant occupation and strivings. We shall endeavour to trace the manifestations of his thoughts and character during this war when the continuation of Mr. Ustryalov's work, which we are eagerly looking forward to, appears.

The third volume of Mr. Ustryalov's *History of Peter's Reign* ends with the rupture with Sweden, and with this we shall conclude our comments, the object of which was to acquaint our readers with the nature of the facts collected in Mr. Ustryalov's book. Avoiding general deductions and a detailed discussion of Peter's importance in our history, we tried only to group the facts bearing on the same subject that are dispersed in chronological order throughout Mr. Ustryalov's book. This chronological order is a specific feature of Mr. Ustryalov's book that will strike the eye of every reader of the *History of Peter's Reign*. It could have been one of its greatest merits had it been carried through consistently, *i.e.*, had the author refrained entirely from all argument and expression of opinion and confined himself entirely to relating the facts. But in his book Mr. Ustryalov sometimes reveals an inclination to express a certain view. We often come across rhetorical and sonorous phrases which ornament the plain truth of events. There is even evidence in some places of a *selection* of the facts, so that sometimes his narrative does not at all create the impression that is produced by the document appended at the end of the book, and to which the historian himself refers. Hence, being artificial and inconsistent in its application, this chronological method detracts from rather than adds to the merit of Mr. Ustryalov's book. We think it would have been better had the historian taken the trouble to group the facts contained in the history of Peter's reign and illuminate them with a general idea, not ascribed to or forced upon them from outside, but one strictly and logically deduced from these facts. Then the general impression would have been livelier and fuller, the facts would not have been lost for the reader because of their scattered and seemingly casual nature. Mr. Ustryalov could have thrown a true and brilliant light on all the events that occurred during Peter's reign. Having at his command a vast mass of material which had been available to no one before him, he found himself in a more favourable position than anybody else even in the working up of these materials and therefore could have told us more than anybody else could do. Unfortunately, he did not make the fullest use of the advantages of his position, but confined himself to the labour, after the manner of Karamzin, of collecting materials, arranging them in a connected and harmonious way, and relating them in an eloquent style. Lending his work mainly a biographical character, he paid no attention to the general problems of the history of the country and Peter's times, and thus, depriving himself of the weapon of higher historical criticism, he was unable to abandon the rut followed by previous panegyrists, whom he himself censures in the introduction to his *History of Peter's Reign*.

All these are defects which cannot be described as insignificant; but it must be observed that *such* defects may be found only in a serious and fundamental work such as Mr. Ustryalov's work really is. We ask why Mr. Ustryalov has not done more, precisely because we see how much he has done. The very importance of his book determines the amount and magnitude of the requirements that we expect him to fulfil. If his work were less remarkable, if it were mediocre, nobody would have thought of reproaching him for the absence of what one so naturally seeks and often does not find in Mr. Ustryalov's work. At all events, as a collection of valuable materials unknown to the public hitherto, as the fruit of many years of conscientious labour, as a harmonious and living picture of the events of Peter's reign, Mr. Ustryalov's book will long remain one of the finest adornments to our historical literature. We say once again, in conclusion, that for the history of Peter's reign, Mr. Ustryalov's book will have the importance of Karamzin's history. Its importance will not fade even when the time comes for a pragmatic history

of modern Russia under Peter's reign. The future historian, even
if he does not utilize Mr. Ustryalov's ideas and views, will at
all events find in his book much valuable material and numerous authentic documents. The appendices, almost as large as the
text of the history, lend and always will lend it important and
permanent significance. Many of them really throw a new light
on events, others enable one to form definite and firm opinions
concerning matters which formerly had been judged only on the
basis of assumptions. All this lends Mr. Ustryalov's book extreme
importance, and we hope that our readers will not be vexed with
us for having for so long engaged their attention with a review
of this remarkable work which the Russian public had been expecting so long.

THE WORKS OF V. BELINSKY[47]

OUR LITERARY world could have received no gladder news than that which has only just reached us from Moscow. At last the works of Belinsky are being published! The first volume is already printed and has been received in St. Petersburg; the next, it is said, are to follow soon. At last! At last! ...

Whatever happens to Russian literature, no matter how luxuriantly it may blossom forth, Belinsky will always be its pride, its glory, its adornment. To this day his influence is felt in everything beautiful and noble that appears in our country; to this day every one of our foremost literary men admits that for a considerable part of his development he is indebted, directly or indirectly, to Belinsky.... [It is scarcely possible to find in literary circles of all shades five or six sordid and vulgar individuals who would dare to utter Belinsky's name without respect.] In all parts of Russia there are people who are filled with enthusiasm for this genius, and, of course, these are the finest people in Russia! ...

For them, undoubtedly, no news that we receive can be so glorious as the news that the works of Belinsky are being published. We have been waiting for them for a long time and at last our expectations are to be gratified! How many pure and happy moments his essays will recall to our minds—the moments when we were full of youthful, selfless impulses, when Belinsky's vigorous words opened for us an entirely new world of knowledge, reflection and activity! Reading him we forgot the pettiness and vulgarity of everything around us, we dreamed of different people, of different activities, sincerely hoped one day to meet such people and rapturously promised to devote ourselves to such activities.... [Life deceived us as it deceived him, but to this day we cherish the memory of those days of holy rapture, of that inspired thrill, of those pure and unselfish passions and dreams which, perhaps, are never destined to come true, but with which to this day we find it difficult and painful to part....]

Russia still knows little of Belinsky. He rarely signed his essays with his own name, and now that his works are being published it transpires that even literary men cannot point with certainty to all the essays he wrote. Many readers learned his name more from articles written about him after his death. But now that his works have been collected and are being published, it will be possible for all readers to become more closely acquainted with this man, with his views and aspirations, with the influence he exercised on our entire literature during the past twenty-five years. And on acquainting themselves with him the readers will be convinced that much of what they admired in others belongs to him, came from him; many of the truths upon which our opinions now rest were asserted by him in a fierce struggle against the ignorance, falsehood and malice of his opponents and amidst the somnolent apathy of an indifferent public.... Yes, Belinsky is the incarnation of our highest ideals; and Belinsky is the incarnation of the history of our social development [he too is a severe, bitter, indelible reproach to our society].

Sovremennik passed into the hands of the present editors[48] with the assistance of Belinsky, and he never left *Sovremennik* until the day of his death. *Sovremennik* was the first to speak of Belinsky after a long silence[49] [due to the situation then prevailing in literature]. The ideas of that brilliant critic, and his very name, have always been sacred to us, and we deem ourselves fortunate when we can speak of him. Therefore, in hastening to inform our readers of the joy we feel over the publication of his works, we do not renounce the right to speak about him in greater detail in connection with this publication, although much has already been said about Belinsky in the essays "The Gogol Period in Literature" published in *Sovremennik* in 1856.

The first volume of the works of Belinsky now published contains the critical and bibliographical essays he published in *Molva* and *Teleskop* in 1834 and 1835. The edition, which belongs to Messrs. Soldatenkov and Shchepkin, is extremely neat and the price is low. A volume of 530 pages in the usual Shchepkin format costs only one ruble, and this will be the price of all the subsequent volumes. There can be no doubt that the entire edition will be sold out quickly even if it is printed in twenty thousand copies!

WHAT IS OBLOMOVSHCHINA?

OBLOMOV, A NOVEL BY I. A. GONCHAROV

Otechestvenniye Zapiski, Nos. I-IV, 1859[50]

> Where is the one who in the native lan-
> guage of the Russian soul could pronounce
> for us the mighty word "forward"? Century
> after century passes, and a half a million stay-
> at-homes, lubbers and blockheads are immersed
> in deep slumber, but rarely is a man born in
> Rûs who is able to pronounce this mighty
> word. . . .
>
> *Gogol*

OUR PUBLIC waited for Mr. Goncharov's novel for ten years.
Long before it appeared in the press it was spoken of as a work
that was something out of the ordinary.[51] People began to read it
with the widest expectations. And yet, the first part of the novel,
which was written as far back as 1849[52] and is remote from
the current interests of the present day, seemed dull to many. At
that time *A Nest of the Gentry* appeared, and everybody was
charmed by its author's poetical and highly attractive talent. Many
dismissed *Oblomov* from their minds, many were even wearied
by the exceedingly subtle and profound psychological analysis
that runs through the whole of Mr. Goncharov's novel. Those
people who are fond of superficial and entertaining action found
the first part of the novel tiring because, right to the very end,
its hero continues to recline on the couch, on which they found
him at the opening of the first chapter. Those readers who favour
the accusatory trend were dissatisfied because our official public
life was not touched upon at all in the novel. In short—the first
part of the novel created an unfavourable impression upon many
readers.

There seemed to be many indications that the entire novel
would be a failure, at all events among our public, which is accustomed to regard all poetical literature as a source of entertainment, and to judge works of art by first impressions. This

time, however, artistic truth soon prevailed. The subsequent parts of the novel obliterated the first unfavourable impression among those who had received such impressions, and Goncharov's talent, thanks to its irresistible influence, vanquished even those who were least sympathetic towards him. The secret of this success, it seems to us, lies as much in the power of the author's artistic talent as in the exceedingly rich content of the novel.

It may seem strange that we discern an exceptionally rich content in a novel which, by the very character of its hero, contains hardly any action. But we hope to make our idea clear in the course of this essay, the main object of which is to formulate certain observations and deductions which, in our opinion, the content of Goncharov's novel necessarily calls for.

Undoubtedly, *Oblomov* will evoke considerable criticism. Some of it will probably be of the proofreader type, which will discover some flaws in the language and style; some of it will be pathetic and contain numerous exclamations about the charm of the scenes and characters, and some of it will be of the apothecary-aesthetic type, which will carefully scrutinize the novel to see whether all the dramatis personae have been prescribed the precise and proper doses of such and such qualities, and whether these personages always take these doses in strict conformity with the prescription. We do not feel the least desire to enter into such subtleties, nor, in all probability, will the reader grieve very much if we refrain from racking our brains over the problem as to whether such and such a sentence harmonizes with the character of the hero and his position, or whether several words should have been transposed, etc. Therefore, we do not think it will be in the least reprehensible if we engage in more general reflections concerning the content and significance of Goncharov's novel, although, of course, the *true critics* will reproach us again for having written an essay not on Oblomov, but only *in connection with* Oblomov.

We think that in the case of Goncharov more than of any other author, it is the critic's duty to formulate the general deductions he draws from the author's work. There are authors who undertake this task themselves and explain to their readers the purpose and significance of their works. Others do not express their intentions positively, but relate their story in such a way

that it turns out to be a clear and correct embodiment of their
ideas. The aim of every page of the works of such authors is to
make the reader understand, and one would have to be very dull
indeed not to understand.... But the fruit of such reading is
more or less complete (according to the degree of talent displayed
by the author) *agreement with the idea* that underlies the given
work. All the rest evaporates two hours after the book is read.
With Goncharov it is entirely different. He gives you no deductions, and evidently does not set out to do so. The life that he
depicts serves him not as a subject for abstract philosophy, but as
a direct object in itself. He is not concerned about the reader,
or about the deduction that you draw from his novel: that is your
business. If you are mistaken—blame your own shortsightedness
but not the author. He presents you with a living image and guarantees only that it resembles reality; the task of defining the
merit of the objects depicted is yours: it is a matter of complete
indifference to him. He does not display the ardour that lends
the utmost strength and charm to other talents. Turgenev, for
example, talks to us about his heroes as if they were people close
to his heart; he extracts their ardent sentiments from their
breasts, he watches over them with tender sympathy and painful
anxiety, shares the joys and sorrows of the characters he has
created, and is himself carried away by the poetical environment
in which he is always so fond of placing them.... His enthusiasm is contagious: he irresistibly captures the sympathies of
his readers, rivets their thoughts and sympathies to the narrative
from the very first page and compels them to feel, to live through
themselves, the scenes in which his characters appear before
them. Much time may pass and the reader may forget the plot
of the story, lose the connection between the details of the various
incidents, forget the characteristics of individual personages and
situations, and even forget everything that he has read, but he
will always retain and cherish the lively and gratifying impression he obtained from reading this story. There is nothing like
this about Goncharov. His talent does not yield to impressions.
He does not burst into lyrical song on seeing a rose and on hearing a nightingale; these things will strike him, he will halt, look
and listen for a long time and become immersed in reflection....
What processes go on in his soul at such times we can never learn

exactly.... But he begins to sketch something.... You look coldly upon the as yet indistinct outlines.... Gradually they become
clearer, clearer and more beautiful ... and suddenly, as if
by a miracle, a rose and a nightingale emerge from those lines
in all their beauty and charm. You not only see them; you can
also smell the fragrance of the rose and hear the song of the
nightingale.... Now sing lyrical songs if the rose and the nightingale inspire you to do so; the artist has drawn them and
stands aside, satisfied with his work; he will add nothing to it....
"It is no use adding anything," he thinks to himself. "If the
image tells your heart nothing, what can words tell you?..."

This ability to convey the complete image of an object, to
finish it like a piece of sculpture, represents the strongest side
of Goncharov's talent. And this is what particularly distinguishes
him among contemporary Russian writers. It serves as an easy
clue to all the other features of his talent. He possesses the amazing ability at any given moment to halt a fleeting phenomenon
of life in all its fulness and freshness and hold it in front of
him until the artist has taken complete possession of it. We are
all struck by a bright ray of life, but it instantly vanishes almost before it affects our minds. That ray is followed by others
from other objects, and these also vanish as swiftly, leaving hardly any trace. And so, the whole of life passes, gliding over the
surface of our minds. But not so with the artist; he is able to
discern something in every object that is near and dear to his
heart; he is able to halt the instant something particularly strikes
him. The sphere accessible to the artist may be wide or
narrow, his impressions may be livelier or more profound, his
expression of them may be more passionate or more calm, according to the nature of his poetic talent and the degree to which
it is developed. Often the poet's sympathies are drawn towards
one particular quality of objects and he tries to find and bring
out this particular quality, he makes it his main task to express
it in the fullest and most vivid manner possible, and on this
he mainly exercises his artistic powers. So artists appear who
merge the inner world of their souls with the world of external
phenomena, and who see all life and nature through the prism
of the moods that dominate themselves. Thus, some subordinate
everything to the sense of plastic beauty, others depict mainly

tender and attractive features, others again, in every image, in every description, reflect humane and social strivings, etc. But Goncharov displays none of these leanings to any marked degree. His is a different quality: a serene and all-embracing poetical world outlook. He does not devote himself to one thing to the exclusion of all others; or rather, he devotes himself to all things equally. He is not impressed by one aspect of an object, by one phase in an event; he turns an object round and examines all its sides, he waits until all the phases in an event have occurred, and then proceeds to work them up artistically. The consequence of this is, of course, that the artist's attitude towards the objects he depicts is calmer and more dispassionate, his outline of even trifling details is more distinct, and he devotes an equal amount of attention to all the particulars of his narrative.

That is why some think that Goncharov's novel is too long drawn out. Perhaps it is too long drawn out. In the first part Oblomov lies on the couch; in the second part he goes to visit the Ilyinskys and falls in love with Olga, and she falls in love with him; in the third part she realizes that she had been mistaken in Oblomov and they part; in the fourth part she marries Oblomov's friend Stolz, and Oblomov marries the landlady of the house in which he rents his lodgings. And that is all. No external events, no obstacles (except perhaps the raising of the bridge across the Neva which put a stop to the meetings between Olga and Oblomov), no extraneous circumstances intrude into the novel. Oblomov's indolence and apathy are the sole springs of action throughout his whole story. How could this be stretched into four parts? Had another author taken up this subject he would have treated it differently: he would have written about fifty easy and amusing pages, would have invented a lovely comedy, would have ridiculed his indolent hero, would have admired Olga and Stolz, and there the matter would have ended. The story would not have been the least bit dull, although it would not have been of any particular artistic significance. Goncharov set to work in a different way, however. He did not lose sight of a phenomenon that had once caught his eye without tracing its progress to the end, without discovering its causes, and without discerning the connection between it and all other surrounding phenomena. His aim was to elevate to a type an image that has accidentally flashed past him; to give it generic and permanent significance. Consequently, for him, there was nothing empty or insignificant in anything that concerned Oblomov. He lovingly devoted himself to everything and drew everything distinctly and in detail. Not only the rooms in which Oblomov lived, but also the house in which he only dreamed of living; not only the dressing gown he wore, but the grey frock coat and bristling side whiskers of his valet Zakhar; not only the way Oblomov writes a letter but also the quality of the paper and ink of the letter the village elder wrote to him—all is brought in and depicted with the fullest distinctness and relief. The author cannot even pass by Baron von Langwagen, who plays no role whatever in the novel; he writes an entire page of extreme beauty about the baron, and would have written two and even four had he not exhausted his subject in one. This, perhaps, slows down the action, wearies the unsympathetic reader, who demands that he be irresistibly carried away by thrills. Nevertheless, this is a precious quality in Goncharov's talent which helps him to achieve truly artistic delineation. When you begin to read him you find that many of the things he writes are seemingly not justified by strict necessity, they seem to be out of harmony with the eternal requirements of art. But you soon begin to accustom yourself to the world he depicts and in spite of yourself you admit that everything he describes is legitimate and natural; you put yourself in the place of the dramatis personae and begin to feel that they could not act otherwise in the places and circumstances they found themselves and, in fact, should not have done so. The tiny details which the author constantly introduces, and which he draws with such loving care and extraordinary skill, at last begin to exercise a certain charm. You transport yourself entirely to the world into which the author carries you, and you find in it something that is dear to you; not only the external form, but the innermost soul of every person and of every object reveals itself to you. And having read the whole novel you feel that your thoughts have been enriched by something new, that new images, new types have been deeply engraved upon your heart. They haunt you for a long time, you feel you want to ponder over them, you want to ascertain [their] significance and their relation towards your own life, your own character and inclinations. What has become of your listlessness and weariness? Vigorous thoughts and fresh sentiments awaken in you. You are ready to read many of the pages again, to ponder over them and to argue about them. This, at any rate, is how Oblomov affected us. We read *Oblomov's Dream* and several scenes over and over again; we read the whole novel almost right through twice, and on the second occasion we liked it almost better than on the first. Such is the charm of these details which the author introduces into the action and which, in the opinion of some, *drag out* the novel.

Thus, Goncharov stands before us primarily as an artist who is capable of bringing out the fulness of the phenomena of life. To depict them is his calling, his delight; his objective art is not thwarted by theoretical prejudices or preconceived ideas, it does not yield to any one set of sympathies to the exclusion of others. It is serene, sober and dispassionate. Is this the highest ideal of artistic endeavour, or is it, perhaps, a defect which reveals the artist's dulled perception? It would be difficult to give a categorical answer to this question; at all events, it would be unfair to do so without reservations and explanations. Many dislike the poet's calm attitude towards reality and are ready forthwith to censure sharply the unsympathetic nature of such a talent. We realize that such censure is logical and, perhaps, we ourselves are conscious of a wish that the author would tickle our senses more, would thrill us more. But we are also conscious of the fact that this wish is of a somewhat Oblomov nature and that it springs from the inclination always to have a guide—even in matters of feeling. It is unfair to ascribe to the author a dull perception only because impressions do not send him into lyrical raptures but remain silently hidden in the depths of his soul. On the contrary, the more swiftly and impetuously impressions are expressed, the more often they prove to be superficial and fleeting. We see numerous examples of this at every step in people who are endowed with an inexhaustible stock of verbal and mimical fervour. If a man is able to nurse, to nurture the image of an object in his soul and then present it fully and vividly, it shows that his keen perception is combined with profound feeling. He does not express himself prematurely, but nothing in the world is lost to him. For him all that which lives and moves around him, all that which enriches nature and human society

By some miraculous means
Lives in the depths of his soul.[33]

He reflects every phenomenon of life like a magic mirror; at any given moment, and in obedience to his will, they halt, become motionless, and assume rigid, immobile shapes. It seems as though he can halt life itself, rivet forever and present to us its most elusive moment, so that we may gaze at it constantly for our instruction or enjoyment.

This power, developed to its highest perfection, is, of course, worth all that we call the attractiveness, charm, freshness or vigour of a talent. But this power also varies in degree and, moreover, it can be directed towards objects of different kinds, which is also very important. Here we disagree with the advocates of so-called *art for art's sake*, who believe that the excellent delineation of a tree leaf is as important, say, as the excellent delineation of a human character. Subjectively, this may be right: two artists may possess talent as such to an equal degree and only their spheres of activity may be different. But we shall never agree that a poet who wastes his talent on exemplary descriptions of leaf buds and brooks can be as important as an artist who is able with equal talent to reproduce, say, the phenomena of public life. We think that for literary criticism, for literature, and for society itself, the question of what the talent of an artist is spent on, of how it is expressed, is far more important than that of the degree and quality of the talent he possesses in himself, in the abstract, in potentiality.

How was Goncharov's talent expressed, what was it spent on? This question can be answered by an analysis of the content of his novel.

Apparently, Goncharov did not choose a wide field for his delineations. The story of how good-natured and indolent Oblomov lies and sleeps, and of how neither friendship nor love can awaken and make him get up, is, after all, not such an important one. But it reflects Russian life; in it there appears before us the living contemporary Russian type presented with relentless severity and truth; it reflects the new word of our social development, pronounced clearly and firmly without despair and

without puerile hopes, but in full consciousness of the truth. This
word is—*Oblomovshchina*; it is the key to the riddle of many of
the phenomena of Russian life, and it lends Goncharov's novel
far greater social significance than all our exposure novels possess. In the Oblomov type and, in all this Oblomovshchina, we
see something more than a successful production by the hand of a
strong talent; we see a product of Russian life, a sign of the times.

Oblomov is not altogether a new personage in our literature,
but never has he been presented to us so simply and naturally as
he is in Goncharov's novel. Not to go too far back into the past,
we shall say that we find the generic features of the Oblomov
type already in Onegin; and then we find them repeated several
times in the best of our literary productions. The point is that
this is our native, national type, which not one of our serious
artists could brush aside. But in the course of time, as social
consciousness developed, this type changed its shape, established
a different relationship with life and acquired a new significance.
To note these new phases of its existence, to determine the substance of its new significance, has always been an enormous
task, and the talent who succeeded in doing it always did a great
deal for the advancement of our literature. This is what Goncharov has done with his *Oblomov*. We shall examine the main features of the Oblomov type, and then we shall try to draw a slight
parallel between it and several types of the same kind which
have appeared in our literature at different times.

What are the main features of the Oblomov character? Utter
inertness resulting from apathy towards everything that goes on
in the world. The cause of this apathy lies partly in Oblomov's
external position and partly in the manner of his mental and
moral development. The external position is that he is a gentleman: "he has a Zakhar, and another three hundred Zakhars," as
the author puts it. Ilya Ilyich (Oblomov) explains the advantages of his position to Zakhar in the following way:

"Do I fuss and worry? Do I work? Don't I have enough to eat? Do
I look thin and haggard? Am I in want of anything? Have I not people
to fetch and carry for me, to do the things I want done? Thank God,
I have never in my life had to draw a pair of stockings on. Do you think
I would go to any trouble? Why should I?... But I need not tell you
all this. Haven't you served me since childhood? You know all about
it. You have seen how tenderly I was brought up. You know that I have

never suffered cold or hunger, that I have never known want, that I don't have to earn my bread and, in general, have never done any work."

Oblomov is speaking the absolute truth. The entire history of his upbringing confirms what he says. He became accustomed to lolling about at a very early age because he had people to fetch and carry for him, to do things for him. Under these circumstances he lived the idle life of a sybarite even when he did not want to. And tell me, pray, what can you expect of a man who grew up under the following circumstances:

"Zakhar—as his (Oblomov's) nurse did in the old days—draws on his stockings and puts on his shoes while Ilyusha, already a boy of fourteen, does nothing but lie on his back and put up one foot and then the other; and if it seems to him that Zakhar has done something not in the right way, he kicks him in the nose. If disgruntled Zakhar takes it into his head to complain, he gets his ears boxed by the adults. After that Zakhar combs Ilya Ilyich's hair, helps him on with his coat, carefully putting his arms into the sleeves so as not to incommode him too much, and reminds him that he must do so and so and so and so: on waking up in the morning—to wash himself, etc.

"If Ilya Ilyich wants anything he has only to make a sign—and at once three or four servants rush to carry out his wishes; if he drops anything, if he reaches for something he needs and cannot get at it, if something has to be brought in, or it is necessary to run on some errand—he sometimes, like the active boy he is, is just eager to run and do it himself, but suddenly his mother and his father and his three aunts shout in a quintet:

"—'Where are you going? What for? What are Vaska and Vanka and Zakharka here for? Hey! Vaska, Vanka, Zakharka! What are you all dawdling there for? I'll let you have it!...'

"And so Ilya Ilyich is simply not allowed to do anything for himself. Later on he found that this was much more convenient and he learned to shout himself. 'Hey, Vaska, Vanka, bring me this, bring me that! I don't want this, I want that! Go and bring it!'

"Sometimes he got tired of the tender solicitude of his parents. If he ran down the stairs, or across the courtyard, a half a score of voices would shout after him desperately: 'Ah, ah! Hold him! Stop him! He will fall and hurt himself! Stop, stop!...' If he took it into his head to go out into the hall in the winter, or open the casement window, he would again hear cries of: 'Oh, where are you going? How dare you? Don't run, don't walk, don't open the window; you'll hurt yourself. You'll catch cold....' And Ilyusha would sadly stay at home, tended like an exotic flower in a hothouse, and like the latter under glass he grew slowly and listlessly. His strength, which vainly tried to find an outlet, turned inwards, wilted and faded."

Such an upbringing is by no means exceptional or strange in the educated section of our society. Not everywhere, of course, do Zakharkas help little gentlemen to put on their stockings, etc. But it must not be forgotten that Zakharka is thus exempted from these duties by special indulgence, or because of higher pedagogical considerations, and that this is quite out of harmony with the general course of domestic life. Perhaps the little gentleman dresses himself, but he knows that for him it is a pleasant exercise, a whim, that he is by no means obliged to dress himself. In fact there is no need for him to do anything. Why should he trouble? Has he not people to fetch things for him and do everything he needs?... That is why he will never tire himself with work, whatever people may tell him about work being a necessity and a sacred duty: from his earliest years he sees that all the domestic work in his home is performed by flunkeys and housemaids, and all that Papa and Mama do is give orders and scold the servants if they don't carry out the orders properly. And so, the first conception forms in his mind—that it is more honourable to sit with folded arms than to fuss around with work. ... And all his subsequent development proceeds in the same direction.

The effect this position of the child has upon his entire moral and intellectual development will be understood. Its internal strength necessarily "wilts and fades." Even if the child tests that strength sometimes, it is only in whims and arrogant demands that others should obey his orders. It is well known that the satisfaction of whims develops spinelessness and that arrogance is incompatible with the ability really to maintain one's dignity. Becoming accustomed to make unreasonable demands, the boy soon loses the power to keep his wishes within the bounds of the possible and practical, loses all ability to make means conform with aims and is therefore baffled by the first obstacle that calls for the exercise of his own efforts for its removal. When he grows up he becomes an Oblomov, possessing the latter's apathy and spinelessness to a greater or lesser degree, under a more or less skilful disguise, but always with the same invariable quality—a repugnance for serious and independent activity.

An important factor here is the mental development of the Oblomovs, which, of course, is also moulded by their external position. From their earliest years they see life turned inside

out, as it were, and until the end of their days they are unable
to understand what their relation to the world and to people
should reasonably be. Later on much is explained to them and
they begin to understand something; but the views that were
inculcated in them in their childhood remain somewhere in a
corner and constantly peep out from there, hindering all new
conceptions and preventing them from sinking deep into their
hearts.... As a result, chaos reigns in their heads: sometimes a
man makes up his mind to do something, but he does not know
how to begin, where to turn.... This is not surprising: a normal man always wants to do only what he can do; that is why
he immediately does all that he wants to do.... But Oblomov...
is not accustomed to do anything; consequently, he cannot really
determine what he can do and what he cannot do—and consequently, he cannot seriously, *actively*, want anything.... His
wishes always assume the form: "how good it would be if this
were done," but how this can be done he does not know. That
is why he is so fond of dreaming and dreads the moment when
his dreams may come in contact with reality. When they do, he
tries to shift the burden of doing things to another's shoulders;
if there are no other shoulders, why then, *perhaps* it will get
done *somehow*....

All these features are splendidly noted and concentrated with
extraordinary strength and truth in the person of Ilya Ilyich
Oblomov. It must not be imagined that Ilya Ilyich belongs to
some special breed of which inertness is an essential and fundamental feature. It would be wrong to think that nature has
deprived him of the ability to move of his own volition. This
is not the case at all. Nature has endowed him with the same gifts
as she has endowed all men. As a child he wanted to run about
and play snowballs with other children, to get one thing or another himself, to run down into the gully, to reach the near-by
birchwood by crossing the canal, climbing over fences and jumping across ditches. When everybody in the Oblomov house was
taking his or her customary afternoon nap he would get up to
stretch his legs: he "ran to the gallery (where nobody was permitted to go because it threatened to collapse any moment), ran
round the creaking floor, climbed up to the dovecote, wandered
down to the end of the garden and listened to a beetle droning

and followed its flight with his eyes until it was far away."
Sometimes he "got into the canal, grubbed about, found some
roots, peeled off the bark and ate them with the utmost relish,
preferring them to the apples and jam that Mama used to give
him." All this might have served as the elements of a gentle
and quiet character, but not of a senselessly indolent one. Besides, gentleness which grows into timidity and the habit of
offering your back for others to climb on is by no means a natural characteristic of a man, but purely an acquired one, just
like insolence and arrogance; and the distance between these
two characteristics is not so great as is usually believed. Nobody
is so able to hold his nose in the air as a flunkey is; nobody
treats his subordinates so rudely as one who is obsequious towards his own superiors. With all his gentleness, Ilya Ilyich
does not hesitate to kick Zakhar in the face when the latter is
putting on his shoes; and if he does not do the same to others
later on in life, it is only because he anticipates opposition which
he would have to overcome. Willy-nilly he confines his activities to his three hundred Zakhars. If he had a hundred, a thousand times more Zakhars, he would meet with no opposition,
and he would boldly kick in the face everybody who had any
dealings with him. Conduct of this kind would not be evidence
of a brutal nature; Oblomov himself, and all those around him,
would regard it as very natural and necessary.... It would not
occur to any of them that it is possible and necessary to behave
differently. But unfortunately, or fortunately, Ilya Ilyich was
born a small country squire with an estate that provided him
with an income that did not exceed ten thousand rubles in as-
signats; consequently, he could mould the destiny of the world
only in his dreams. But in his dreams he was fond of giving
himself up to bellicose and heroic ambitions.

"Sometimes he liked to picture himself an invincible general, compared with whom not only Napoleon but even Yeruslan Lazarevich was a
nonentity; he would picture a war and its cause: for example, Africans
would come pouring into Europe, or he would organize new crusades and
would fight, decide the fate of nations, sack towns, show mercy, execute,
perform acts of kindness and generosity."

Sometimes he would picture himself as a great thinker or
artist who is followed by admiring crowds.... Clearly, Oblomov

is not a dull, apathetic type, destitute of ambition and feeling; he too seeks something in life, thinks about something. But the disgusting habit of getting his wishes satisfied not by his own efforts but by the efforts of others developed in him an apathetic inertness and plunged him into the wretched state of moral slavery. This slavery is so closely interwoven with Oblomov's aristocratic habits that they mutually permeate and determine each other, so that it becomes totally impossible to draw any line of demarcation between them. This moral slavery of Oblomov's is, perhaps, the most interesting side of his personality, and of his whole life.... But how could a man enjoying the independent position of Ilya Ilyich sink into slavery? If anybody can enjoy freedom, surely he can! He is not in the civil service, he does not go into society, and he has an assured income.... He himself boasts that he does not have to bow and scrape and humiliate himself, that he is not like "others" who work tirelessly, fuss and run about, and if they do not work they do not eat.... He inspires the good widow Pshenitsyna with reverent love for himself precisely because he is a *gentleman*, because he shines and glitters, because he walks and talks so freely and independently, because "he is not constantly copying papers, does not tremble with fear that he might be late at the office, because he does not look at everybody as if asking to be saddled and ridden on, but looks at everybody and everything boldly and freely, as if demanding obedience." And yet, the whole life of this gentleman is wrecked because he always remains the slave of another's will and never rises to the level of displaying the least bit of independence. He is the slave of every woman, of every newcomer; the slave of every rascal who wishes to get him under his thumb. He is the slave of his serf Zakhar, and it is hard to say which of them submits more to the power of the other. At all events, if Zakhar does not wish to do a thing Ilya Ilyich cannot make him do it; and if Zakhar wants to do anything he will do it, even if his master is opposed to it—and his master submits.... This is quite natural: Zakhar, after all, can at least do something; Oblomov cannot do anything at all. It is needless to speak of Tarantyev and Ivan Matveyich, who do everything they like with Oblomov in spite of the fact that they are far inferior to him both in intellectual development and in moral qualities.... Why is this? Again the answer is, because Oblomov, being a gentleman, does not wish to work, nor could he even if he wanted to; and he cannot understand his own relation to everything around him. He is not averse to activity as long as it is in the form of a vision and is far removed from reality: thus, he draws up a plan for the improvement of his estate and zealously applies himself to this task—only "details, estimates and figures" frighten him, and he constantly brushes them aside, for how can he bother with them!... He is a gentleman, as he himself explains to Ivan Matveyich:

"Who am I? What am I? you will ask.... Go and ask Zakhar, he will tell you. 'A gentleman' he will say! Yes, I am a gentleman, and I can't do anything! You do it, if you know how, and help if you can, and for your trouble take what you like—that's what knowledge is for!"

Do you think that in this way he is only shirking work, trying to cover up his own indolence with the plea of ignorance? No, he really does not know how to do anything and cannot do anything; he is really unable to undertake any useful task. As regards his estate (for the reorganization of which he had already drawn up a plan), he confesses his ignorance to Ivan Matveyich in the following way:

"I don't know what barshchina* is. I know nothing about husbandry. I don't know the difference between a poor muzhik and a rich one. I don't know what a quarter of rye, or oats is, what its price is, in which months different crops are sown and reaped, or how and when they are sold. I don't know whether I am poor or rich, whether I will have enough to eat next year, or whether I shall be a beggar—I don't know anything!... Therefore, speak and advise me as if I were a child...."

In other words: be my master, do what you like with my property and leave me what share of it you think best.... And that is what happened: Ivan Matveyich nearly grabbed Oblomov's entire estate, but unfortunately Stolz prevented him.

But Oblomov was not only ignorant of agricultural matters, he not only failed to understand the state of his own affairs: that would have been only half the trouble!... The main trouble was that he could see no meaning in life in general. In the Oblomov world nobody asked himself: why life, what is life, what is its

---

* Corvée, or labour rent, paid by the serf in work performed on the squire's demesne.

meaning and purpose? The Oblomovs had a very simple conception of life.

"They conceived it as an ideal of repose and inaction, disturbed at
times by various unpleasant accidents such as: sickness, losses, quarrels
and, incidentally, work. They tolerated work as a punishment imposed
on our ancestors, but they could not love it, and they always shirked it
whenever possible, deeming this permissible and right."

This is exactly how Ilya Ilyich looked upon life. The ideal
happiness that he described to Stolz consisted in nothing more
than a life of plenty, with conservatories, hothouses, picnics in
the woods with a samovar, etc.—a dressing gown, sound sleep
by way of a rest in between—idyllic walks with a meek but
plump wife, gazing at the peasants at work. Oblomov's mind
was so moulded from childhood that he was able, even in the
most abstract arguments, in the most utopian theories, to halt
in the present and never leave this *status quo* in spite of all arguments. In depicting his conception of ideal bliss Ilya Ilyich
never thought of asking himself what its inherent meaning was,
he never thought of asserting its lawfulness or truth, he never asked
himself where these conservatories and hothouses were to come
from, who was to maintain them, and on what grounds he was
to enjoy them. ... Failing to put such questions to himself, failing to clear up his own relation to the world and to society,
Oblomov, of course, could not grasp the meaning of his own
life and, therefore, found everything he had to do irksome and
tedious. When he was in the civil service he could not for the
life of him understand why all those documents were being
written; and failing to understand, he could think of nothing
better than to resign and do no more writing. He went to school,
but he could not understand the purpose of this instruction:
and failing to understand, he piled his books up in a corner and
indifferently watched the dust accumulating on them. He went
into society, but he could not understand why people visited
each other; and failing to understand, he gave up all his acquaintances and lolled on his couch for days on end. He tried to
become intimate with women, but he began to ask himself what
could be expected of them, what one should expect of them; and
after pondering over the matter, and failing to find an answer,
he began to avoid women. ... Everything bored and wearied

him, and he lolled on his couch filled with utter contempt for the "human ant heap," where people worried and fussed, God knows what about. . . .

Having reached this point in explaining Oblomov's character we deem it appropriate to turn to the literary parallel we drew above. The foregoing reflections have brought us to the conclusion that Oblomov is not a being whom nature has completely deprived of the ability to move by his own volition. His indolence and apathy are the result of upbringing and environment. The main thing here is not Oblomov, but Oblomovshchina. Perhaps Oblomov would even have started work had he found an occupation to his liking; but for that he would have had to develop under somewhat different conditions. In his present position he cannot find an occupation to his liking because he sees no meaning in life in general and cannot rationally define his own relations to others. This is where he provides us with the occasion for comparing him with previous types, which the best of our writers have depicted. It was observed long ago that all the heroes in the finest Russian stories and novels suffer from their failure to see any purpose in life and their inability to find a decent occupation for themselves. As a consequence, they find all occupations tedious and repugnant, and in this they reveal an astonishing resemblance to Oblomov. Indeed, open, for example, *Onegin, A Hero of Our Times, Who is to Blame?, Rudin, Unwanted,* or *Hamlet from Shchigry County*[54]—in everyone of these you will find features almost identical with Oblomov's.

Onegin, like Oblomov, gives up society because he was

> Weary of inconstancy
> And of friends and friendship too.

And so he took to writing:

> Abandoning wild gaiety
> Onegin stayed at home,
> He picked his pen up with a yawn
> And wished to write, but diligence
> To him was loathsome; nothing
> From his pen would come.

Rudin too launched out in this field and was fond of reading to the chosen "the first pages of the essays and works he intended to write." Tentetnikov[55] also spent many years writing "a colossal work that was to deal with the whole of Russia from all points of view," but in this case too, "this undertaking was confined mainly to thinking: his pen was bitten to shreds, drawings appeared on the paper, and then everything was thrust aside." Ilya Ilyich was not behind his brothers in this respect; he too wrote and translated—he even translated Say. "Where is your work, your translations?" Stolz asked him later. "I don't know, Zakhar put them away somewhere. They are lying in the corner I suppose," Oblomov answers. It appears, therefore, that Ilya Ilyich may have done even more than the others who had set down to their tasks as determinedly as he had.... Nearly all the brothers in the Oblomov family set to work in this field in spite of the difference in their respective positions and mental development. Pechorin alone looked down superciliously upon "the storymongers and writers of bourgeois dramas"; but even he wrote his memoirs. As for Beltov, he must certainly have written something; besides, he was an artist, he visited the Hermitage and sat behind an easel planning to paint a large picture depicting the meeting between Biren who was returning from Siberia and Münnich who was going to Siberia.... What came of this the reader knows.... The same Oblomovshchina reigned in the whole family....

As regards "borrowing wisdom," *i.e.*, reading, Oblomov also differs little from his brothers. Ilya Ilyich has also read something, and has not read it in the way his late father used to read: "I haven't read a book for a long time," he would say, "let's have a look at one." And he would pick up the first book that came to his hand.... No, the ideas of modern education have affected even Oblomov: he reads intelligently, and chooses what to read.

"If he hears about some remarkable work he feels an urge to become acquainted with it; he looks for it, asks for it, and if it is brought to him soon he will begin to read it, and an idea begins to form in his mind about the subject; one more step, and the idea would be complete, but before you can look round he is already lying on the couch, gazing apathetically at the ceiling, while the book is lying next to him not read to the end, and not understood.... He had cooled towards it quicker than the desire to read it had seized him: he never took up an abandoned book again."

Is it not the same with the others? Onegin thought of appropriating other people's ideas and began by

> Lining his shelf with a detachment of books,

and settling down to read. But nothing came of it. He soon got
tired of reading and

> His books, like his women, he deserted
> And across the shelf with its dusty crew
> He a black crape curtain drew.

Tentetnikov read books in the same way (because he was accustomed to having them always at hand); he read mostly while
having his dinner "with the soup, with the sauce, with the roast,
and even with the pie...." Rudin also confessed to Lezhnev that
he had bought some books on agriculture, but had not read even
one to the end; he became a teacher, but found that he knew too
few facts, and concerning some monument of the 16th century
he was proved wrong by a teacher of mathematics. He, like Oblomov, could grasp easily only general ideas; as for "details,
estimates and figures," he always brushed them aside.

"But this is not yet life, it is only the preparatory school
for life," mused Andrei Ivanovich Tentetnikov as he, together
with Oblomov and the whole of that company, plodded through
a host of useless subjects, unable to apply even an iota of them
to actual life. "Real life is in the service." And so, all our heroes, except Onegin and Pechorin, go into the service; and for
all of them this service is a useless and senseless burden, and all
end up by resigning, early and with dignity. Beltov was fourteen
years and six months short of qualifying for a clasp because,
after working with intense zeal for a time, he soon cooled towards office work and became irritable and careless.... Tentetnikov had some high words with his chief, and, moreover, he
wanted to be useful to the state by personally taking over the
management of his estate. Rudin quarrelled with the head master
of the high school at which he served as a teacher. Oblomov
disliked the fact that all the members of the staff spoke to the
chief "not in their natural but in some other kind of voices,
squeaky and disgusting." He rebelled at the idea of having
to explain to his chief in this voice why "he had sent a
certain document to Archangel instead of Astrakhan" and so

he resigned.... Everywhere we see the same Oblomovshchina....

The Oblomovs resemble each other very closely in domestic life too:

> Sound sleep, a stroll, an entertaining book,
> A forest glade and a babbling brook,
> A dark-eyed beauty,
> Young and fresh to kiss sometimes,
> The bridle of a restive steed,
> Dinner to suit his fastidious needs,
> A bottle of light wine,
> Solitude, tranquility,
> Holy is the life Onegin leads....

Word for word, except for the steed, this is the kind of life that Ilya Ilyich regards as the ideal of domestic bliss. Oblomov does not even forget the kissing of a dark-eyed beauty.

"One of the peasant women," muses Ilya Ilyich, "with a tanned neck, her sleeves rolled up above her elbows, her sly eyes shyly drooping, just a little, only for appearance sake, resisting the squire's embraces, but actually enjoying them ... but ... so that the wife doesn't see, God forbid!" (Oblomov imagines that he is already married)....

And if Ilya Ilyich had not been too lazy to leave St. Petersburg for his country seat he would undoubtedly have tried to achieve his cherished idyll. In general, the Oblomovs dream of an idyllic, idle bliss which will cost them no effort: "Take delight in me, but expect nothing more," they seem to say. Pechorin is active enough, heaven knows, but even he believes that real bliss lies in calm and sweet repose. In one passage of his memoirs he compares himself to a starving man who "falling asleep from exhaustion, dreams of sumptuous food and sparkling wine; he consumes the airy gifts of his imagination with the utmost relish and feels refreshed ... but no sooner does he awake than his dream vanishes, and he feels twice as hungry and as desperate as before...." In another passage Pechorin asks himself: "Why did I not take the path that destiny had opened for me and where quiet joys and spiritual calm awaited me?" He himself believes that it was because "his soul had accustomed itself to storms and craved for seething activity...." But he is always displeased with the struggle he is waging, and he himself is constantly saying that he indulges in all this disgusting debauchery only because he cannot find anything better to do.... And

since he cannot find anything to do and, as a consequence, does
nothing and is pleased with nothing, it shows that he is disposed
more to idleness than to activity.... It is the same old Oblomovshchina....

The attitude of all the Oblomovs' towards other people, and
towards women in particular, also has certain common features.
They hold all people in contempt because of the petty labours
they engage in, because of their narrow concepts and shortsighted
strivings. "They are all common labourers," is the supercilious
comment even of Beltov, the most humane of them. Rudin naively
imagines that he is a misunderstood genius. Pechorin, of course,
tramples everybody under foot. Even Onegin has two lines written
about him. which read:

> He who has lived and thought grows scornful
> And must at heart all men despise.

Even Tentetnikov, meek though he is, felt on entering his office for the first time "as if, for some misdemeanor, he had been
degraded from the upper class to the lower," and on arriving in
the country he soon tried, like Onegin and Oblomov, to get un-
acquainted with all the neighbours who had hurried to make his
acquaintance. And our Ilya Ilyich yields to no one in his contempt
for people: this is so easy that it requires no effort whatever. In
front of Zakhar he smugly compares himself with "others"; in
conversation with his friends he expresses naive surprise that
people should worry so much, compel themselves to go to work,
to write, to read newspapers, to go into society, and so forth. In
conversation with Stolz he expresses his sense of superiority over
other people in the most categorical terms.

"They say that life is to be found in society. A nice life, to be sure!
What can you find in it? Anything that can interest the mind and the
heart? Where is the hub around which all this turns? There's no hub.
There's nothing profound that can touch you to the quick. They are all
lifeless, dormant people are these men of the world and of society. Worse
than I am!..."

And Ilya Ilyich proceeds eloquently to dilate on this subject
in a way that would be worthy of Rudin himself.

In their attitude towards women all the Oblomovs behave in
an equally disgraceful manner. They are totally incapable of
loving and they have no more idea about what to seek in love

than they have about what to seek in life in general. They are not averse to philandering with a woman as long as she seems to them to be a doll moved by springs; nor are they averse to enslaving a woman's heart... why not? This pleases their gentlemanly natures exceedingly! But no sooner does the affair become in any way serious, no sooner do the gentlemen begin to suspect that they are dealing not with a doll, but with a woman who may demand that they should respect her rights, than they turn tail and fly for their lives. The cowardice of all these gentlemen is amazing! Onegin, who was able "early in his life to disturb the hearts of hardened coquettes," who sought women "without ardour and deserted them without regret," showed the white feather in front of Tatyana, showed it twice—once when he took a lesson from her, and again when he gave her a lesson. After all, he liked her the moment he set eyes on her, and had she loved him less deeply he would not have permitted himself to adopt that tone of stern mentor towards her. But he saw that he was playing with fire and began to talk about his spent life, his bad character, about her falling in love with somebody else in future, and so forth. Subsequently, he himself explains his conduct by the fact that "noticing the spark of tenderness in Tatyana, he did not wish to believe her," and that

> His bleak and barren freedom
> He did not wish to lose.

With what beautiful phrases he covered up his own cowardice!

As we know, Beltov too dared not go to the end with Krutsiferskaya and fled from her, although for quite different reasons if we are to believe what he says. Rudin entirely lost his head when Natalya tried to get something definite out of him. He dared not do any more than advise her to "be resigned." Next day, he wittily explained to her in a letter that he "had not been in the habit" of dealing with women like her. Such also was Pechorin, an expert in matters of the feminine heart, who confessed that he loved nothing in the world but women, and that for them he was prepared to sacrifice everything in the world. He too confesses firstly, that he "cannot love women who have character: what business have they to have character?" And secondly, that he can never marry.

13*

"However passionately I might love a woman," he says, "if she makes me only feel that I must marry her—goodbye to love. My heart turns to stone and nothing warms it again. I am ready to make every sacrifice except that; I am ready to stake my life. even my honour twenty times, but I will never sell my liberty. Why do I cherish it so much? What do I want it for? What am I preparing myself for? What do I expect from the future? Absolutely nothing. It is a sort of innate fear, an inexplicable presentiment," and so forth.

Actually, it is nothing more than Oblomovshchina.

Do you think that Ilya Ilyich has not in him a Pechorin and Rudin, not to speak of an Onegin element? Indeed he has, and how much of it! For example, he, like Pechorin, is determined to *possess* a woman, to compel her to make all sorts of sacrifices to prove her love. At first, you see, he had no hope that Olga would agree to marry him and proposed to her very timidly. She answered something to the effect that he should have proposed long ago. This embarrassed him, it was not enough that Olga had accepted him, and so—what do you think?... He began to question her to find out whether she loved him enough to become his mistress! And he was vexed when she said that she would never agree to anything like that; but her explanation and the passionate scene that followed calmed him.... In the end his cowardice so overcame him that he was even afraid to see Olga; he pleaded indisposition, that the bridge was raised and he could not cross the river, he gave Olga to understand that she might compromise him, and so forth. Why? Because she wanted him to decide, to act, and this was not his habit. Marriage itself did not frighten him as much as it frightened Pechorin and Rudin; his habits were more patriarchal. But Olga wanted him to settle the affairs of his estate before they were married; that would have meant *sacrifice*. He would not make that sacrifice, of course, and proved himself a true Oblomov. He on his part, however, was extremely exacting. He played Olga a trick that one might have expected from Pechorin. He took it into his head that he was not very prepossessing in appearance and, in general, not attractive enough to make Olga love him very strongly. And so he began to suffer, he could not sleep at night, and finally. mustering all his energy, he wrote Olga a long letter in the Rudin style, in which he repeated the old and threadbare story which Onegin had told Tatyana, which Rudin had told Natalya, and which even

Pechorin had told Princess Mary, namely, "I am not made in such a way that you could be happy with me. In time you will love another, more worthy than I."

> Again and again will maiden fair
> Change her dreams and fancies....
> You'll love again—but do take care,
> Learn to keep yourself in hand;
> Not everyone, like I, will understand....
> And innocence may lead you to despair.

All the Oblomovs like to humiliate themselves, but they do so in order to have the satisfaction of being contradicted, of hearing praise from those to whom they are speaking deprecatingly about themselves. They delight in this self-abasement; all are like Rudin, concerning whom Pigassov says: "He begins to revile himself and grovel in the mud, and you feel sure that he will never look people in the face again. But nothing of the kind! He soon becomes so merry that you think he has been swilling vodka!" In the same way Onegin too, after reviling himself in Tatyana's presence, begins to parade his generosity. And Oblomov behaves in the same way when, after writing Olga a lampoon about himself, he felt "not so depressed, almost happy...." And he concludes his letter with a sermon, similar to that with which Onegin concluded his speech: "Let your relations with me," he wrote, "serve you as a guide in your future normal love," and so forth. Ilya Ilyich did not, of course, continue his self-humiliation before Olga to the end: he rushed to see what impression his letter made upon her, he saw her weeping, he was satisfied and—could not refrain from presenting himself before her at this crucial moment. But she proved to him what vulgar and miserable egoism he displayed in that letter, which he had written "out of concern for her happiness." Here his courage oozed out completely, as indeed it does with all the Oblomovs when they meet a woman who is superior to them in character and intelligence.

"But, profound people will protest and say, in spite of the selection of apparently similar facts, that there is no sense in the parallels you have drawn. In defining character, it is not so much outward manifestations that are important as the motives which prompt a man to do this or the other. As regards motive, how is it possible not to see the vast differ-

ence between Oblomov's conduct and that of Pechorin, Rudin and the
others?... Oblomov does everything by inertia, because he is too lazy
to move, and too lazy to resist when he is pushed; his whole object is not
to move a finger unnecessarily. The others, however, are prompted by a
thirst for activity, they undertake everything with the greatest zeal, they
are always

> Prompted by a restless spirit,
> A yearning for a change of scene,[56]

and suffer from other ailments that are symptoms of a strong character.
If they do nothing that is truly useful it is because they cannot find activities commensurate with their strength. They, as Pechorin puts it, are
like genii chained to the clerk's desk and doomed to copy documents.
They tower above the realities of life and, therefore, have a right to hold
life and men in contempt. Their whole life is a negation, a reaction against
the present order of things; Oblomov's life, however, consists in passive
submission to existing influences, a conservative repugnance to all change,
an utter lack of internal reaction due to his nature. Can these men be
compared? What! Put Rudin on the same plane as Oblomov!... Denounce
Pechorin for being as much a nonentity as Ilya Ilyich!... This is evidence
of complete lack of understanding; it is absurd—it is a crime!..."

Good God! We have indeed forgotten that one must keep a
sharp lookout when dealing with profound people; they are sure
to draw conclusions that you did not even dream of. If you intend
to bathe in the river and a profound person standing on the bank
with his hands tied boasts that he is a splendid swimmer and
promises to go to your rescue if you should drown, don't dare
say: "But my dear friend, your hands are tied! Had you not better first get somebody to untie your hands?" Don't dare to say
that because the profound person will at once flare up and say:
"Ah! You say that I can't swim! You are praising the one who
tied my hands! You don't sympathize with people who rescue
the drowning!..." And so on and so forth.... Profound people
can be very eloquent and profuse in drawing the most unexpected
conclusions.... And so it is in this case: they will at once jump
to the conclusion that we wanted to place Oblomov on a higher
plane than Pechorin and Rudin, that we wanted to justify his
indolence, that we are unable to see the inherent fundamental
difference between him and the preceding heroes, etc. We
hasten to explain ourselves to the profound people.

In all that we have said we had Oblomovshchina in mind
rather than the personality of Oblomov and the other heroes.

As regards personalities, we could not fail to see difference in temperament of, say, Pechorin and Oblomov, Pechorin and Onegin, or Rudin and Beltov.... Who will deny that there is a difference in personality among men (although, perhaps, not nearly as great and as important as is usually supposed). The point, however, is that weighing heavily upon all these persons is the same Oblomovshchina, which imposes upon them the indelible impress of indolence, idleness and utter uselessness. It is highly probable that under other conditions of life, in a different society, Onegin would have been a really good fellow, Pechorin and Rudin would have performed doughty deeds, and Beltov would have proved to be a man of excellent qualities. But under other conditions of development Oblomov and Tentetnikov too, perhaps, would not have been such drones, and would have found some useful occupation.... But the point is that at the present time they all have one common feature—a barren striving for activity, the consciousness that they could do a great deal but will do nothing.... In this respect, they resemble each other to an astonishing degree.

"I look back upon the whole of my past life and involuntarily ask myself: What have I lived for? Why was I born?... There must have been some reason, I must have had some lofty mission, because in my soul I feel that I possess boundless strength. But I failed to realize what this mission was, I allowed myself to be tempted by hollow and ungratifying passions; I emerged from the crucible hard and cold like iron, but I had forever lost the ardour of noble striving—life's finest flower."

That was Pechorin.... And here is how Rudin reasons about himself.

"Yes, nature was bounteous with her gifts to me; but I shall die without having done anything worthy of my powers, without leaving any beneficial trace. All my wealth will be wasted: I shall not see the fruit of the seeds I have sown."

Ilya Ilyich is not behind the rest. He too "painfully felt that some good, bright element was buried within him as in a grave, perhaps dead now, or lying idle like gold in the depths of the mountains, and that it was high time that this gold served as coin. But this treasure lies buried deep down under a heavy weight of rubbish and refuse. It was as if somebody had stolen the treasure which the world and life had bestowed upon him and had buried it in his own soul."

Do you see—a *treasure* was buried in his soul, but he was never able to reveal it to the world. His brothers, younger than he, "are roaming over the world

> Seeking great deeds to perform,
> Since the heritage of their wealthy sires
> Had freed them from life's petty cares. . . ."[57]

Oblomov too, when he was young, dreamed of "serving while his strength lasted, because Russia needs hands and heads to develop her inexhaustible resources. . . ." And even now, "he is responsive to universal human suffering and is capable of enjoying the pleasures of lofty thoughts"; and although he does not roam the world in quest of great deeds to perform, he nevertheless dreams of activity of world-wide importance, looks down with contempt upon the common labourer and ardently exclaims:

> No, I shall not waste my soul
> In the ant heap labours of men. . . .

He is no more idle than all the other Oblomov brothers, he is only more candid than they—he makes no attempt to cover up his idleness even with talk about society, and strolling along Nevsky Prospect.

But what causes the difference in the impression produced upon us by Oblomov and the heroes we referred to above? The heroes seem to us in their different ways to be strong natures crushed by an unfavourable environment, whereas Oblomov is a drone, who will do nothing even under the most favourable circumstances. But in the first place, Oblomov's temperament is extremely phlegmatic and naturally, therefore, he makes feebler attempts to carry out his plans and to resist his hostile environment than the more vigorous Onegin or jaundiced Pechorin. Actually, however, they are all equally unable to resist the forces of their hostile environment, all equally sink to the level of nonentities when real and serious activity confronts them. In what way did Oblomov's environment open up for him a favourable field for activity? He had an estate which he could have put in order; he had a friend who urged him to take up practical activity; there was a woman who was superior to him in vigour and clarity of views, and who loved him tenderly. . . . But tell me, which of the Oblomovs was destitute of all this, and what did they do with it

all? Both Onegin and Tentetnikov pottered about on their estates; and about Tentetnikov, the muzhiks even said at first: "Sharp-
eyed, isn't he!" But soon those same muzhiks tumbled to the fact
that their squire, although keen at first, understood nothing, and
would do nothing practical.... But what about friendship?
What do they all do with their friends? Onegin killed Lensky;
Pechorin is always quarrelling with Werner; Rudin succeeded
in repelling Lezhnev and failed to take advantage of Pokorsky's
friendship.... And did not each of them meet many Pokorskys
in the course of his life? What did they do? Did they combine for
some common cause, did they form a close alliance to defend
themselves against their hostile environment? Nothing of the
kind.... Everything was swept to the winds; it all ended in the
same old Oblomovshchina.... It is needless to speak of love.
Everyone of the Oblomovs met a woman superior to himself (because Krutsiferskaya is superior to Beltov, and even Princess
Mary is, after all, superior to Pechorin), and everyone of them
ignominiously fled from her love, or did his best to make her
dismiss him.... How can this be explained if not by the pressure
that despicable Oblomovshchina exercised upon them?

In addition to difference in temperament, there is also a
great difference in age between Oblomov and the other heroes.
We are not speaking of age in years: in that respect they are
almost equal, Rudin was even two or three years older than Oblomov. We have in mind the age in which they appeared. Oblomov appeared at a later period and, therefore, to the younger
generation, our contemporaries, he must look much older than
the previous Oblomovs at his age.... When he was still at the
university, at the age of seventeen or eighteen, he was already
conscious of the same strivings, became imbued with the same
ideas that inspired Rudin at the age of thirty-five. After that
only two roads lay open before him: either activity, real activity—not with the tongue, but with the head and heart and
hands together, or simply lying down with folded arms. His
apathetic nature brought him to the latter: this is bad, but at all
events there is no falsehood and pretense here. If he, like his
brothers, had begun to talk loudly about what he only dares
dream of now, he would have felt day after day the same annoyance that he felt on receiving the letter from the village elder,

and on receiving notice to quit from his landlord. In the old days phrasemongers who talked loudly about the necessity of this or that, about lofty ambitions, etc., were listened to with awe. Then, perhaps, Oblomov too would not have been averse to talking. . . . But nowadays all phrasemongers and schemers are confronted with the demand: "Why not try your hand at it yourself?" This the Oblomovs cannot stand. . . .

Indeed, how one feels the breath of the new life when, after reading *Oblomov*, one ponders over the circumstances that called this type into being in literature. It cannot be ascribed solely to the talent of the author and to the breadth of his views. We find talent and views of the broadest and most humane kind among the authors who portrayed the earlier types that we referred to above. But the point is that thirty years have passed since Onegin, the first of them, appeared. That which existed in embryo at that time, what was expressed only in vague hints and whispers, has now assumed firm and definite shape, it is being expressed openly and loudly. Phrases no longer count; society itself feels the need of real deeds. Beltov and Rudin, who were imbued with strivings that were truly lofty and noble, not only did not feel the urge to enter into mortal combat with the environment that was crushing them, they could not even conceive of such a combat as an early possibility. They entered a dense and unexplored forest, trod dangerous bogs, saw various snakes and reptiles creeping at their feet, and they climbed trees—partly to see if there was a road near by, and partly to rest and to escape for a while the danger of being sucked into the bog or of being stung. The people who followed them waited to hear what they would say and looked up to them with awe as pioneers. But these pioneers saw nothing from the heights to which they had climbed: the forest was too vast and dense. Meanwhile, in climbing the trees they scratched their faces and hurt their feet and hands. . . . They are in pain, they are weary, they must rest by making themselves as comfortable as possible among the branches. True, they do nothing for the common weal, they have seen nothing, and have said nothing; those standing below must hew and clear a road for themselves through the forest without their aid. But who would dare to cast stones at those unfortunate ones to make them drop from the height on which they have ensconced themselves with such difficulty, having the common weal in mind? They meet with sympathy, they are not even called upon to help to clear the forest; theirs was a different mission and they have performed it. If nothing has come of it, it is not their fault. In the past, every author could regard his Oblomov as a hero from this point of view, and he was right. To this we must add that the hope of finding a way out of the forest to the road was long cherished by the whole crowd of wayfarers, and that belief in the farsightedness of the pioneers who had climbed up the tree also lasted for quite a long time. But little by little the situation cleared and took a different turn: the pioneers have got accustomed to the tree and like it; they argue very eloquently about different ways and means of getting out of the bog and the forest; they have even found some kind of fruit on the tree and are enjoying it, throwing the rind to the ground below; they invite a few chosen ones from the crowd to join them, and these climb the tree and remain there, not to look out for the road, but only to gobble the fruit. These are the Oblomovs in the proper sense of the term.... And the poor wayfarers standing below sink into the bog, they are stung by snakes and frightened by reptiles, swinging branches slash their faces.... At last the crowd decides to set to work and calls those who had climbed the tree later to come down again, but the Oblomovs make no reply and go on gorging themselves with fruit. The crowd then appeals to the former pioneers to come down and assist in the common effort, but the pioneers merely repeat the old argument that it is necessary to find the road, that clearing a road through the forest would be useless toil. The poor wayfarers then see their mistake and say with a gesture of disgust: "Ekh! You are all Oblomovs!" After that they set to work in real earnest: they fell trees, use the logs to build a bridge across the bog, clear a track, kill the snakes and reptiles that creep on to it, and give no further thought to those wiseacres and strong characters, the Pechorins and Rudins, upon whom they had formerly reposed their hopes, and whom they had so much admired. At first the Oblomovs calmly look on at the general activity, but later, as is their habit, they become alarmed and begin to shout.... "Oh! Oh! Don't do that! Stop!" they howl when they see the people setting to work to cut down the tree on which they are ensconced. "Don't you

realize that we may be killed and that with us will perish those
beautiful ideas, those lofty sentiments, those humane strivings,
that eloquence, that fervour, that love for all that is beautiful
and noble that have always inspired us? Stop! Stop! What are
you doing?...." But the wayfarers have heard these beautiful
phrases a thousand times, and they go on with their work without
paying the slightest attention to them. The Oblomovs still have
a means of saving themselves and their reputations, namely, to
climb down the tree and join the others in their work; but, as
they are in the habit of doing, they lose heads and are at a loss
what to do.... "What's this, all of a sudden?" they keep asking
themselves in their despair, and go on hurling their impotent
curses at the stupid mob which had lost all respect for them.

But the crowd is right! Once it has realized that it is necessary to set to work in real earnest, it makes no difference to
it whether a Pechorin or an Oblomov stands before it. Again, we
do not say that under the given circumstances Pechorin would act
exactly in the same way as Oblomov; by virtue of the same circumstances he may have developed in another direction. But the
types which great talent has created are long lived; even today
there are people who seem to be copies of Onegin, Pechorin,
Rudin and the others, and not in the way in which they might
have developed under other circumstances, but exactly in the way
they were depicted by Pushkin, Lermontov and Turgenev. It is
only in the public mind that they become more and more transformed into an Oblomov. It cannot be said that this transformation has already taken place. No, even today thousands of
people spend their time talking, and thousands of others are willing to take this talk for deeds. But the fact that this transformation has begun is proved by the Oblomov type which Goncharov
has created. His appearance would have been impossible had society, at least some section of it, realized what nonentities all
those quasi-talented natures are, which it had formerly admired.
In the past they decked themselves in cloaks and wigs of different fashions and were attractive because of their diverse talents;
but today Oblomov appears before us in his true colours, taciturn,
reclining on a soft couch instead of standing on a beautiful pedestal, wearing a wide dressing gown instead of an austere cloak.
The questions: *What is he doing? What is the meaning and pur-*

pose of his life? have been put plainly and bluntly without being obscured by any secondary questions. This is because the time for social activity has arrived, or will arrive without fail. . . . And that is why we said in the beginning of this essay that we regard Goncharov's novel as a *sign of the times.*

Indeed, look at the change that has taken place in public opinion concerning the educated and smooth-tongued drones who were formerly regarded as genuine leaders of society.

Before us stands a young man, very handsome, adroit and educated. He moves in high society and is successful there; he goes to theatres, balls and masquerades; he dresses and dines magnificently; he reads books and writes well. . . . His heart is stirred only by the daily events in high society; but he also has ideas about higher problems. He is fond of talking about passions,

> About age-old prejudices
> And the fatal secrets of the grave. . . .[58]

He has some rules of honour: he can

> A lighter quit rent substitute
> For the ancient yoke of barshchina,[59]

sometimes he can refrain from taking advantage of an unsophisticated young woman whom he does not love, and he does not overrate his successes in society. He stands sufficiently high above the society in which he moves to be conscious of its vapidity; he can even abandon this society and retire to his seat in the country, but he finds it dull there too, and does not know what to turn his hand to. . . . Out of idleness he quarrels with his friend and thoughtlessly kills him in a duel. . . . Several years later he returns to society and falls in love with the woman whose love he had formerly spurned because it would have meant surrendering his freedom to roam about the world. . . . In this man you recognize Onegin. But look more closely . . . it is Oblomov.

Before us stands another man with a more ardent soul, with wider ambitions. This one seems to have been endowed by nature with all that which were matters of concern for Onegin. He does not have to worry about his toilet and his clothes, he is a society man without that. He does not have to grope for words or sparkle with tinsel wit, his tongue is naturally as sharp as a razor.

He really despises men, for he is aware of their weaknesses. He can really capture the heart of a woman, not for a fleeting moment, but for long, perhaps forever. He can sweep away or crush every obstacle that rises in his path. In only one matter is he unfortunate: he does not know which path to take. His heart is empty and cold to everything. He has tried everything; he was sated with all the pleasures that money could buy when still a youth. He is weary of the love of society beauties because it has brought no solace to his heart. Learning has also wearied him because he has seen that it brings neither fame nor happiness; ignorance is bliss, and fame is a matter of luck. The dangers of the battlefield too soon bored him because he saw no sense in them, and quickly became accustomed to them. And lastly, he even grows tired of the pure and simplehearted love of an untamed girl of whom he is really fond because even in her he finds no satisfaction for his impulses. But what are these impulses? Whither do they lead? Why does he not yield to them with every fibre of his being? Because he himself does not understand them and does not take the trouble to think about what he should do with his spiritual strength. And so he spends his life jeering at fools, disturbing the hearts of unsophisticated young ladies, interfering in the love affairs of other people, picking quarrels, displaying valour over trifles and fighting duels over nothing at all.... You remember that this is the story of Pechorin, that he himself has explained his own character to Maxim Maximich to some extent, almost in the same words.... Please look closer: here too you will see Oblomov....

But here is another man who is more conscious of the path he is treading. He not only knows that he is endowed with great strength, he knows also that he has a great goal before him.... It seems that he even suspects what kind of goal it is and where it is situated. He is honourable, honest (although he often fails to pay his debts), ardently discusses not trifling matters, but lofty subjects, and asserts that he is ready to sacrifice himself for the good of mankind. In his mind all problems have been solved, and everything is linked up in a living harmonious chain. He enraptures unsophisticated youths with his overpowering eloquence, and hearing him speak they too feel that they are destined to perform something great.... But how does he spend his life?

In beginning everything and finishing nothing, attending to everything at once, passionately devoting himself to everything, but unable to devote himself to anything.... He falls in love with a girl who at last tells him that she is willing to give herself to him although her mother has forbidden her to do so—and he answers: "Good God! Your Mama disapproves! What an unexpected blow! God, how soon!... There is nothing to be done, we must be resigned...." And this is an exact picture of his whole life.... You have already guessed that this is Rudin.... No, even he is now Oblomov. If you examine this character closely and bring it face to face with the requirements of present-day life you will be convinced that this is so.

The feature common to all these men is that nothing in life is a vital necessity for them, a shrine in their hearts, a religion, so organically merged with their whole being that to deprive them of it would mean depriving them of their lives. Everything about them is superficial, nothing is rooted in their natures. They, perhaps, do something when external necessity compels them to, for Oblomov goes visiting the places that Stolz drags him to, he buys music and books for Olga and reads what she compels him to read; but their hearts do not lie in the things they do merely by force of circumstances. If each of them were offered gratis all the external advantages that they obtain by their work they would gladly give up working. By virtue of Oblomovshchina, an Oblomov government official would not go to his office every day if he could receive his salary and regular promotion without having to do so. A soldier would vow not to touch a gun if he were offered the same terms and, in addition, were allowed to keep his splendid uniform, which can be useful on certain occasions. The professor would stop delivering lectures, the student would give up his studies, the author would give up writing, the actor would never appear on the stage again and the artist would break his chisel and palette, to put it in high-flown style, if he found a way of obtaining gratis all that he now obtains by working. They only talk about lofty strivings, consciousness of moral duty and common interests; when put to the test, it all turns out to be words, mere words. Their most sincere and heartfelt striving is the striving for repose, for the dressing gown, and their very activities are nothing more than an *honourable dressing gown* (to use an expression that is not our own) with which they cover up their vapidity and apathy. Even the best educated people, people with lively natures and warm hearts, are prone in their practical lives to depart from their ideas and plans, very quickly resign themselves to the realities of life, which, however, they never cease to revile as vulgar and disgusting. This shows that all the things they talk and dream about are really alien to them, superficial; in the depth of their hearts they cherish only one dream, one ideal—undisturbed repose, quietism, Oblomovshchina. Many even reach such a stage that they cannot conceive of man working willingly, with enthusiasm. Read the argument in *Ekonomicheski Ukazatel* to the effect that everybody would die of starvation resulting from idleness if by the equal distribution of wealth people were robbed of the incentive to accumulate capital. . . .

No, all these Oblomovs have never converted into flesh and blood the principles with which they were imbued; they have never carried them to their logical conclusion, have never reached the border line where words are transformed into deeds, where principle merges with the inherent requirements of the soul, disappears in it and becomes the sole spring to a man's conduct. That is why these people are always telling lies, that is why they are so bankrupt when it comes to definite action. That is why abstract views are more precious to them than living facts, why general principles are more important to them than the simple truths of life. They read useful books in order to keep themselves informed about what people are writing; they write inspiring articles in order to admire the logical construction of their own arguments; they make bold speeches in order to hear their own sonorous phrases and to win the approbation of their auditors. As regards the next step, the object of all this reading, writing and talking—they don't want to know anything about it, or do not trouble much about it. They are constantly saying to us: this is what we know, this is what we think—as for the rest, let others worry, it is no business of ours. . . . As long as there was no work to be done they could still fool the public with this sort of thing, they could still strut about and boast: after all we are worrying, walking, talking, and so forth. This is what the success achieved in society by men like Rudin was based on. More than that: they could indulge in debauchery, philandering, punning and theatricals, and to argue that they were reduced to this because there was no field for wide activities. At that time Pechorin and even Onegin must have appeared to be men endowed with boundless spiritual strength. But now all these heroes have been pushed into the background, they have lost their former significance, they have ceased to mislead us with their enigmatic natures and the mysterious disharmony between them and society, between the greatness of their strength and the insignificance of their deeds. . . .

> Now the riddle has been answered,
> A word for it has now been found.[60]

That word is—*Oblomovshchina*.

Now, when I hear a country squire talking about the rights of man and urging the necessity of developing personality, I know from the first words he utters that he is an Oblomov.

When I hear a government official complaining that the system of administration is too complicated and cumbersome, I know that he is an Oblomov.

When I hear an army officer complaining that parades are exhausting, and boldly arguing that marching at a *slow pace* is useless, etc., I have not the slightest doubt that he is an Oblomov.

When, in the magazines, I read liberal denunciations of abuses and expressions of joy over the fact that at last something has been done that we have been waiting and hoping for for so long, I think to myself that all this has been written from Oblomovka.

When I am in the company of educated people who ardently sympathize with the needs of mankind and who for many years have been relating with undiminished heat the same (and sometimes new) anecdotes about bribery, acts of tyranny and lawlessness of every kind, I, in spite of myself, feel that I have been transported to old Oblomovka. . . .

Stop the loud declamations of these people and say to them: "You say this is bad and that is bad, but what is to be done?" They do not know. . . . Propose some simple remedy to them and they will say: "What's this, all of a sudden?" They will say this without fail, because the Oblomovs cannot answer differently. . . .

Continue the conversation with them and ask: what do you intend
to do? They will give you the answer that Rudin gave Natalya:

"What is to be done? Resign ourselves to our fate, of course. What
else can be done? I know only too well how bitter, hard and unbearable
this is, but judge for yourself. . . ." and so forth.

You will get nothing more out of them because all of them
bear the brand of Oblomovshchina.

Who, then, will in the end, shift them from the spot to which
they are rooted by the mighty word "forward!" which Gogol
dreamed of, and for which Rūs has been longing and waiting
for so long? So far we find no answer to this question either
in society or in literature. Goncharov, who understood and was
able to reveal our Oblomovshchina to us, could not, however,
avoid paying tribute to the common error which is prevalent in
our society to this day: he set out to bury Oblomovshchina and
deliver a panegyric over its grave. "Farewell old Oblomovka,
you have outlived your time," he says through the mouth of Stolz,
but what he says is not true. All Russia which has read, or will
read, *Oblomov* will disagree with him. No, Oblomovka is our
own motherland, her owners are our teachers, her three hundred
Zakhars are always at our service. There is a large portion of
Oblomov within every one of us, and it is too early to write our
obituary. We and Ilya Ilyich have not deserved the description
contained in the following lines:

"He possessed what is more precious than intelligence: an honest
and loyal heart! This is natural gold; he has carried it untarnished through
life. Jostled on every side, he fell, cooled, at last fell asleep, worn out,
disillusioned, having lost the strength to live, but not his honesty and
loyalty. His heart has never uttered a single false note, no mud has stuck
to him. No bedecked lie will ever flatter him, and nothing can divert him
to a false path; let an ocean of baseness and evil surge around him; let
the whole world poison itself with venom and turn upside down—Oblomov
will never bow down to the idol of falsehood, his soul will ever remain
pure, bright and honest. . . . His is a soul that is crystal clear; there are
few men like him; he is a pearl among the mob! You could not bribe
his heart with anything, you can rely on him always and everywhere."

We shall not dilate on this passage, but every reader will
observe that it contains a great untruth. Indeed, there is one good
feature about Oblomov, namely, he has never tried to fool any-

body; but that is part and parcel of his indolent nature. But pray, in what *can he be relied on*? Only, perhaps, when nothing need be done; here he will certainly distinguish himself. But if nothing need be done we can do without him. He would not bow down to the idol of evil! But why not? Because he was too lazy to get up from his couch. And if he were dragged from his couch and forced to his knees in front of that idol he would not have the strength to get up. He cannot be bribed with anything. But what is there to bribe him for? To make him move? Well, that is a really difficult task. Mud would never stick to him! Yes, as long as he lies alone on his couch everything goes well; but as soon as Tarantyev, Zaterty and Ivan Matveyich arrive—brr! What awful and disgusting things begin to take place around Oblomov. They eat him out of house and home, they drink up his wine, they drive him to drink, they induce him to sign a false promissory note (from which Stolz, somewhat unceremoniously, in the Russian manner, releases him without trial or investigation), they ruin him and say his peasants are the cause of it, they extort enormous sums of money from him for nothing at all. He suffers all this in silence and, for that reason, of course, never utters a false note.

No, the living must not be flattered like that, and we are still alive, we are still Oblomovs. Oblomovshchina never abandoned us; it is still with us *at the present time, when*, and so forth. Which of our authors, journalists, men of education and public leaders, which of them will not agree that Goncharov must have had him in mind when he wrote the following lines about Ilya Ilyich:

"He knew the delights of lofty thoughts; his heart was responsive to universal human suffering. Sometimes, deep down in his heart, he wept bitterly over the misfortunes that mankind endured, he experienced unknowable and nameless suffering and grief, and he was conscious of a striving towards something in the remote distance, probably towards that world to which Stolz sometimes drew him. Sweet tears roll down his cheeks. Sometimes he is filled with contempt for human vices, for falsehood, for slander, for the evil that has spread over the world, and he burns with a desire to draw mankind's attention to its sores—and suddenly ideas flare up in his mind, heave and toss in his head like the waves of the sea and then grow into an intention and set his blood on fire—his muscles twitch, his sinews become tense, the intention is transformed into a striving: moved by moral force, he quickly assumes two or three postures in one minute

14*

and with flashing eyes he half rises in his bed, extends an arm and looks around like one inspired. . . . Behold the striving is materializing, it is about to become a deed. . . . And then, good Lord! What miracles, what beneficial consequences could be expected from this sublime effort! But the dawn appears, it passes away, evening sets in, and with it Oblomov's wearied strength turns to repose: the storm and excitement in his heart die down, his mind becomes more sober, his blood flows less rapidly through his veins. Silently and pensively Oblomov turns over on his back, gazes mournfully at the sky through the window and bids a sad farewell to the sun which is setting in splendour behind somebody's four-storey house. How many times has he said farewell to the setting sun in this way?"

Will you not agree, educated and noble-minded reader, that the above lines truly depict your own well-intentioned strivings and your useful activity? The only difference that one may find here is the stage you will reach in your development. Ilya Ilyich reached the stage of half rising in his bed, extending an arm and looking around. Others do not get so far; they only reach the stage when ideas toss about in their head like the waves of the sea (they constitute the majority); others reach the stage when their ideas grow into intentions but do not reach the degree of strivings (there are fewer of these); others again reach the striving stage (but these are extremely few). . . .

And so, following the trend of our times, when the whole of our literature, as Mr. Benedictov expresses it, is a

. . . torment to our flesh,
Chains of poetry and prose,[61]

we humbly confess that much as Mr. Goncharov's praise of Oblomov may flatter our vanity, we cannot regard it as being justified. Oblomov irritates the fresh, young and active man less than Pechorin and Rudin do, but he is a disgusting nonentity, nevertheless.

Paying tribute to his times, Mr. Goncharov provided an antidote to Oblomov in the shape of Stolz; but as regards that individual, we must repeat the opinion that we have always expressed, namely, that literature must not run too far ahead of life. Stolzes, men of an integral and active character, every one of whose ideas becomes a striving and is transformed into deeds the moment it arises, do not yet exist in our society (we have in mind the educated section of society, which is capable of lofty strivings;

among the masses, where ideas and strivings are confined to a few and very practical objects, we constantly come across such people). The author himself admits this when he says about our society:

"There! Eyes have opened after slumber, brisk, wide footsteps, animated voices are heard.... How many Stolzes with Russian names must appear!"

Many must appear, there can be no doubt about that; but for the time being there is no soil for them. And that is why all we can gather from Goncharov's novel is that Stolz is a man of action, always busy with something, running about, acquiring things, saying that to live means to work, and so forth. But what he does and how he manages to do something worth-while where others can do nothing, remains a mystery to us. He settled the affairs of the Oblomov estate for Ilya Ilyich in a trice—but how? That we do not know. He got rid of Ilya Ilyich's false promissory note in a trice—but how? That we know. He went to see the chief of Ivan Matveyich, to whom Oblomov had given the promissory note, had a friendly talk with him, and after this Ivan Matveyich was called to the chief's office, and not only was he ordered to return the note, but was also asked to resign. It served him right, of course: but judging by this case, Stolz had not yet reached the stage of the ideal Russian public leader. Nor could he have done so; it is too early. For the time being, even if you are as wise as Solomon, all you can do in the way of public activity is, perhaps, to be a *philanthropic tavern licensee* like Murazov, who performs good deeds with his fortune of ten million, or a generous landlord like Konstanzhoglo[62]—but further than that you cannot go.... And we cannot understand how in his activities Stolz could rid himself of all the strivings and requirements that overcame even Oblomov, how he could be satisfied with his position, rest content with his solitary, individual, exclusive happiness.... It must not be forgotten that under his feet there was a bog, that the old Oblomovka was near by, that he would have had to clear the forest to reach the highroad and thus escape from Oblomovshchina. Whether Stolz did anything in this direction, what he did, and how he did it—we do not know. But until we know we cannot be satisfied with his personality.... All we can say is that he is not the man who "will be able to pronounce in a language intelligible to the Russian soul that mighty word: 'forward!' "

Perhaps Olga Ilyinskaya is more capable of doing this than Stolz, for she stands nearer to our new life. We have said nothing about the women that Goncharov created, nothing about Olga, or about Agafya Matveyevna Pshenitsyna (or even about Anissya or Akulina, women also with peculiar characters), because we realized that we were totally unable to say anything coherently about them. To attempt to analyze the feminine types created by Goncharov would be to lay claim to expert knowledge of the feminine heart. Lacking this quality, we can only admire Goncharov's women. The ladies say that Goncharov's psychological analysis is amazing for its truth and subtlety, and in this matter the ladies must be believed.... We would not dare to add anything to their comment because we are afraid of setting foot in a land that is completely strange to us. But we take the liberty, in concluding this essay, to say a few words about Olga, and about her attitude towards Oblomovshchina.

In intellectual development, Olga is the highest ideal that a Russian artist can find in our present Russian life. That is why the extraordinary clarity and simplicity of her logic and the amazing harmony of heart and mind astonish us so much that we are ready to doubt even her imaginary existence and say: "There are no such young women." But following her through the whole novel we find that she is always true to herself and to her development, that she is not merely the creation of the author, but a living person, only one that we have not yet met. She more than Stolz gives us a glimpse of the new Russian life; from her we may expect to hear the word that will consume Oblomovshchina with fire and reduce it to ashes.... She begins by falling in love with Oblomov, by believing in him and in the possibility of his moral transformation.... She toils long and stubbornly, with loving devotion and tender solicitude, in an effort to fan the spark of life in this man and to stimulate him to activity. She refuses to believe that he is so incapable of doing good; cherishing her hopes in him, her future creation, she does everything for him. She even ignores conventional propriety, goes to see him alone without telling anybody, and, unlike him, is not afraid of losing her reputation. But with astonishing tact she at once discerns every false streak in his character, and she explains to him why it is false and not true in an extremely simple way. He, for example, writes her the letter we referred to above and later assures her that he had written it solely out of concern for her, completely forgetting himself, sacrificing himself, and so forth.

"No," she answers, "that is not true. If you had thought only of my happiness and had believed that for it it was necessary that we should part, you would simply have gone away without sending me any letters."

He says that he fears that she will be unhappy when she learns that she had been mistaken in him, ceases to love him, and loves another. In answer to this she asks him:

"Where do you see my unhappiness? I love you now and I feel good; later I will love another, hence, I will feel good with him. You need not worry about me."

This simplicity and clarity of thought are elements of the new life, not the one under the conditions of which present-day society grew up. . . . And then—how obedient Olga's will is to her heart! She continues her relations with Oblomov and persists in her love for him, in spite of unpleasantness, jeers, etc., from outside, until she is convinced of his utter worthlessness. Then she bluntly tells him that she had been mistaken in him and cannot combine her fate with his. She continues to praise and pet him while she rejects him, and even later, but by her action she annihilates him as no other Oblomov was ever annihilated by a woman. Tatyana says to Onegin at the end of the romance:

> I love you (why conceal it?),
> But to another my troth is plighted,
> To him forever I'll be true.

And so, only formal moral duty saves her from this empty-headed fop; if she were free she would have flung her arms around his neck. Natalya leaves Rudin only because he himself was obdurate from the very outset, and on seeing him off she realizes that he does not love her and she grieves sorely over this. There is no need to speak of Pechorin, who managed only to earn the *hatred* of Princess Mary. No, Olga did not behave to Oblomov in that way. She said to him simply and gently:

"I learned only recently that I loved in you what I wanted you to have, what Stolz pointed out to me, and what he and I conjured up. I loved the future Oblomov! You are unassuming and honest, Ilya; you are tender ... like a dove; you hide your head under your wing—and you want nothing more; you want to coo in the loft all your life. ... But I am not like that: that is not enough for me; I want something more, but what—I don't know!"

And so she leaves Oblomov and strives towards her *something*, although she does not quite know what it is. At last she finds it in Stolz, she joins him and is happy; but even here she does not halt, does not come to a dead stop. Certain vague problems and doubts disturb her, there are things she is trying to fathom. The author did not fully reveal her emotions to us and we may err in our assumptions concerning their nature. But it seems to us that her heart and mind were disturbed by the spirit of the new life, to which she was immeasurably nearer than Stolz. We think so because we find several hints of this in the following dialogue:

"—'What shall I do? Yield and pine?' she asked.

"—'No,' he answered. 'Arm yourself with firmness and serenity. We two are not Titans,' he continued, embracing her. 'We shall not follow the Manfreds and Fausts and challenge disturbing problems to mortal combat, nor shall we accept their challenge. We shall bow our heads and wait humbly until the hard times pass, and life, happiness, will smile again. ...'

"—'But suppose they never leave us: suppose grief disturbs us more and more?' she asked.

"—'Well, we'll accept it as a new element of life. ... But no, that cannot be, it cannot happen to us! It is not your grief alone, it is the common ailment of mankind. You have suffered only one drop. ... All this is frightful when a man loses his grip on life, when he has no support. But in our case. ...'"

He did not specify the *our case*, but it is evident that it is *he* who does not wish to "challenge disturbing problems to mortal combat," that it is *he* who wants to "humbly bow his head. ..." She is ready for this fight, she longs for it and is always afraid that her tranquil happiness with Stolz may grow into something that resembles the Oblomov apathy. Clearly, she does not wish to bow her head and wait humbly until the hard times pass, in the hope that life will smile again later. She left Oblomov when she ceased to believe in him; she will leave Stolz if she ceases to believe in him. And this will happen if she continues to be tormented by problems and doubts, and if he continues to advise her to accept them as a new element of life and bow her head. She is thoroughly familiar with Oblomovshchina, she will be able to discern it in all its different shapes, and under all masks, and will always be able to find strength enough to pronounce ruthless judgment on it. . . .

REALM OF DARKNESS

THE WORKS OF A. OSTROVSKY.
Two volumes, St. Petersburg 1859.[63]

I

> What sort of a trend is this? Before you
> can look round they have a story out. If
> only there were some sense in it. . . . Still,
> there has been a lot of noise, so there must
> have been some reason for it.
>
> *Gogol*

No MODERN Russian writer has met with such a strange fate
in his literary career as Ostrovsky. His first work (*A Picture
of Domestic Bliss*) passed entirely unnoticed; the magazines did
not say a single word either of praise or blame of the author.
Three years later Ostrovsky's second work appeared: *Our Own
Folks—We'll Settle It Among Ourselves*; everybody greeted the
author as an entirely new man in literature and immediately
recognized him as a writer of extraordinary talent, as the best
representative of the dramatic art in Russian literature since Gogol.[64] But owing to one of those accidents which are strange to
the ordinary reader but a cause of extreme annoyance to an
author, and which occur so often in our poor literature, Ostrovsky's play was not produced in a single theatre and did not even
get detailed and serious consideration in any journal. *Our Own
Folks* was first published in *Moskvityanin* and later it was published in book form, but the literary critics totally ignored it.
And so, this comedy vanished for a time, as if it had been thrown
into the sea. A year later Ostrovsky wrote another comedy: *The
Poor Bride*. The critics spoke respectfully of the author, repeatedly mentioned the fact that he had written *Our Own Folks*,
and even observed that they were paying him this attention more
for his first comedy than for his second, which they all regarded as being inferior to the first. Later every new work of Ostrovsky's that appeared caused some stir in the journalistic world,
and soon two literary parties, one radically opposed to the other,

were formed in connection with them. One party consisted of
the young editorial board of *Moskvityanin*, which proclaimed
that "with his four plays Ostrovsky has created a people's theatre in Russia," that he is a

> Poet, herald of new truth,
> Of a new world the creator,
> A new word has he brought us,
> Though serving ancient truth,

and that this ancient truth depicted by Ostrovsky is

> Simpler, but more precious,
> More beneficial for the heart

than the truth contained in Shakespeare's plays.[65]

The above lines were published in *Moskvityanin* (No. 4, 1854)
with reference to the play *Poverty Is No Crime*, and with particular reference to one of the personages in that play, Lyubim
Tortsov. Many at the time laughed at the eccentricity of these
lines, but this was not an expression of poet's licence; it was
a fairly correct expression of the critical opinion of the party
which went into raptures over every line Ostrovsky wrote. Unfortunately, this opinion was always expressed with such an
amazing arrogance, vagueness and ambiguity that the opposite
party found it impossible even to enter into serious controversy over
it. Those who eulogized Ostrovsky claimed that he had introduced
a *new word*; but when asked: "What is this new word?" they
refrained from answering for a long time. When they did answer
eventually, they said that the *new word* was nothing more nor
less than—what do you think?—*nationality*! But this "nationality"
was dragged on to the stage with reference to Lyubim Tortsov
and woven around him so clumsily that the critics who were unfavourable towards Ostrovsky immediately pounced upon this,
and poking their tongues out at the clumsy eulogists they taunted
them, saying: "So your *new word* applies to Tortsov, to Lyubim
Tortsov, to that drunkard Tortsov! So the drunkard Tortsov is
your ideal!" etc. It goes without saying that it is not quite the
proper thing to poke the tongue out in a serious discussion of
the works of Ostrovsky, but it must be confessed that scarcely
anybody could keep a straight face on reading lines like the
following about Lyubim Tortsov;

The lively images of a poet
The comedian in flesh and blood has clothed....
That is why a single current
For the first time runs through all.
That is why the theatre rings from roof to floor
With one loud cry of
Heartfelt joy.
Lyubim Tortsov stands there, alive,
Proud, with head erect,
Clothed in a dilapidated cloak,
With beard dishevelled,
Unhappy, drunk, emaciated,
But with a Russian heart so pure.
Is it comedy that weeps before us,
Or tragedy chuckling with him?—
We cannot tell, nor do we care!
Hasten to the theatre! crowds are pushing through the doors,
Life is flowing in full flood:
Russian songs resound quite freely,
A man there weeps and laughs at once,
All the world's there, full of joy and life.
And we, plain and humble children of the age,
No longer fear but rejoice at man's destiny:
A warm glow fills the heart, we breathe freely,
Lyubim Tortsov to us points out the road! (Where to?)
Great-Russian life is feasting on the stage,
Celebrating the beginning of the triumph
Of our great Russian tongue
In stirring refrain and *playful* song.
The Great-Russian mind, the Great-Russian view,
Like Mother Volga wide and *free.*
Glowing, free, a joy to us, who would eschew!
A life of morbid deception....

These lines were followed by a denunciation of Rachel and of
those who admired her and thereby revealed the *spirit of blind
and slavish imitation.* She may be talented, she may be a genius, exclaimed the author of the above lines, "but her art does
not *suit our street!*" We are not like others. he said, we need
truth. And he took the occasion to revile Europe and America
and to praise Rūs in the following poetical strain:

Let falsity be dear to aged Europe
Or to *toothlessly youthful* America,
Ailing like an aged dog....
Our *Rūs is strong!* Much ardour and strength has she;
Rūs loves truth, and upon her

The Lord bestowed
The gift of understanding truth.
She alone today a refuge gives
To all that which ennobles man! ...

Needless to say, outbursts of this kind, associating Tortsov with what ennobles man, could not lead to a sound and dispassionate discussion of the subject. They only gave the critics of the opposite trend good reason for expressing noble indignation and for exclaiming in their turn about Lyubim Tortsov:

"And this is what some people call a *new word*; this is presented as the finest flower of our literary productions of the past few years! What has Russian literature done to deserve *this ignorant abuse*? It is true that it has not yet uttered such a *word*, that it has never dreamed of such a hero, but this is because it is still imbued with the old literary traditions which do not permit such a corruption of taste. *Lyubim Tortsov could appear on the stage in all his hideousness* only at a time when those traditions were passing into the realm of oblivion.... What is surprising and incomprehensible is that the figure of a drunken Tortsov could become an ideal, that people should want to take pride in it as if it were the purest expression of nationality in poetry, that Tortsov should serve as a criterion of success in literature, and that we are all called upon to love him on the pretext that he is 'one of our own,' that he lives 'in our street'! *Does this not reveal a corrupted taste and utter forgetfulness of all pure literary traditions? After all, there is such a thing as shame, there is such a thing as literary decency,* which remains even after the finest traditions have sunk into oblivion. *Why should we disgrace ourselves* by calling Tortsov 'one of our own' and extolling him as our poetic ideal?" (*Otechestvenniye Zapiski,* No. VI, 1854.)

We have quoted this passage from *Otechestvenniye Zapiski* because it shows how much harm the polemics between his detractors and his admirers have always done to Ostrovsky.* *Otechestvenniye Zapiski* was always an enemy camp for Ostrovsky, and its attacks were mainly directed against the critics who extolled his works. The author himself has always stood aloof until quite recently, until *Otechestvenniye Zapiski* announced that he, and also Mr. Grigorovich[66] and Madame Eugenie Tour,[67] *had already*

---

* Incidentally, our readers may with great benefit to themselves pass over the whole story about the critics' opinion of Ostrovsky and commence reading our essay from the second half. We are confronting Ostrovsky's critics with each other mostly in order that they may admire each other.

ended their poetical careers. (See *Otechestvenniye Zapiski*, No. VI, 1859.) And yet it was Ostrovsky who had to bear the brunt of the charge of admiring Lyubim Tortsov, of being hostile to European education, of admiring the good old days before Peter the Great, etc. Upon his talent fell the shadow of some sort of Old Believer-ism, almost of obscurantism. His defenders, however, kept on talking about a *new word*, without, however, pronouncing that word, and proclaimed that Ostrovsky was the foremost modern Russian writer because he had a *special world outlook*. . . . Their explanation of this special world outlook was extremely muddled, however. Most often they made shift with phrases like the following:

"Ostrovsky alone in the present literary epoch *has his own firm, new, and at the same time ideal world outlook with a specific shade* (!) resulting from the conditions of the epoch as well as, perhaps, from the nature of the poet himself. *Without the slightest hesitation* we call this shade a fundamentally Russian world outlook, sound and serene, humorous without being morbid, straightforward without running to extremes, and, lastly, ideal, in the true sense of idealism, without false grandiloquence or equally false sentimentality" (*Moskvityanin*, No. 1, 1853).

"Thus he wrote—darkly and listlessly"[68]—without explaining in the least the specific features of Ostrovsky's talent or his importance in modern literature. Two years later the same critic started out to write a series of articles on "Ostrovsky's Comedies and their Importance in Literature and on the Stage" (*Moskvityanin*, No. 3, 1855), but he wrote only the first article and even that was more a display of pretentious claims and bold assertions than of real knowledge. Quite unceremoniously he expressed the opinion that present-day critics *were simply not big enough* to deal with Ostrovsky's talent, and that this explains why they found themselves in such an awkward predicament. He even claimed that *Our Own Folks* was not reviewed only because it already contained the *new word* which the critics could see, but *could not get their teeth into*. . . . One would have thought that the author of this article would definitely know the reason for the critics' silence about *Our Own Folks* without going into abstract speculations! Then, after expounding his views on Ostrovsky, the critic goes on to explain what, in his opinion, the *originality of the talent* that he discerned in Ostrovsky consisted in—and this is his definition. "It expressed itself—1) *in the new way of life* which the author describes and which nobody had dealt with before him, *if we leave out of account several essays by Veltman*[69] *and Lugansky*[70] (fine predecessors of Ostrovsky forsooth!!); 2) in the author's *new attitude* towards the life and the personages he depicts; 3) in his *new manner* of depicting life; 4) *in the novelty of his language—its colourfulness* (!), *specificalness* (?)." And that is all. The critic does not explain these propositions. Later on in the article he hurls a few more contemptuous remarks at the critics; he says that *"this life* (which Ostrovsky depicts) *tastes bad to them, so does his language, and his types—tastes bad to them because of their own condition"*—and then, without explaining or proving anything, the critic calmly goes on to discuss the Annals, *Domostroi* and Pososhkov[71] in order to present "a review of the attitude of our literature towards nationality." And with this the critic who took up the cudgels on Ostrovsky's behalf against the opposite party ends. Soon after sympathetic praise of Ostrovsky reached the limit where it took the shape of a weighty cobblestone thrown at one's head by an obliging friend: the first volume of *Russkaya Beseda* contained an article by Mr. Terti Philippov[72] on the comedy *You Can't Live As You Like*. Sometime ago the *Sovremennik* exposed the scandalously savage nature of this article, the author of which advocated that a wife should readily submit to being beaten by her drunken husband, and praised Ostrovsky for, as the author alleged, sharing this opinion and for expressing it so vividly.... Among the public this article roused universal indignation. In all probability Ostrovsky (who on this occasion again suffered as a consequence of the attentions of his unrecognized critics) was himself displeased with this article; at all events, since then he has given no grounds for having such things thrown at him again.

Thus, the enthusiastic admirers of Ostrovsky have not done much to explain his significance and specific features of his talent to the public; they have only prevented many from taking a plain straight look at him. Incidentally, enthusiastic admirers are rarely of real use in explaining the real significance of a writer to the public; in this respect, the detractors are far more reliable: in looking for defects (even where none exist) they,

after all, present their own demands and enable one to judge
to what extent the writer has or has not satisfied them. As regards Ostrovsky, however, his detractors have proved to be no
better than his admirers. If we were to sum up all the reproaches that have been hurled at Ostrovsky from all sides for ten
whole years, and which are being hurled at him today, we would
positively have to abandon all hope of understanding what his
critics wanted of him and what they thought of him. Each one
put forward his own demands, and in doing so he reviled others
who put forward opposite demands; and each invariably used the
merits of one of Ostrovsky's works as a stick with which to beat
another of his works. Some rebuked Ostrovsky for having deviat-
ed from his original trend and, instead of giving a vivid picture
of the vulgar life of the merchant class, he began to idealize it.
Others, on the contrary, praised him for this idealization, but
made the reservation that they regarded *Our Own Folks* as being
not sufficiently thought out, one-sided, and even false.* When
the subsequent works of Ostrovsky appeared, complaints about
the author's alleged sentimental embellishment of the banal and
colourless reality from which he had taken the subjects for his
comedies were accompanied, on the one hand, by praise for this
very embellishment** and on the other hand, by criticism to the
effect that he depicted this sordid life with daguerreotype faithfulness.*** This contradiction in the fundamental views on Os-

---

* Thus, in reviewing *Poverty Is No Crime*, one critic rebuked Ostrovsky for having been in his first work, "a pure satirist: while depicting
evil he showed nothing that counteracted it." *Moskvityanin*, No. 5, 1854.
A critic in *Russkaya Beseda* expressed himself in still sharper language.—*N. D.*

** One critic expressed his preference for the comedy *Poverty Is No
Crime* over that of *Our Own Folks* because in *Poverty Is No Crime*
"Ostrovsky is no longer merely a satirist—side by side with the evils of
a false civilization he sees in this same environment a complacent and
simple life strongly bound with our native traditions and customs; and in
the clash between these two hostile principles all his sympathies are
naturally with the latter" (*Moskvityanin*, No. 5, 1854). A critic in
Russkaya Beseda also expresses approval of Ostrovsky for having after
Our Own Folks changed his *unfavourable* attitude towards life for a
sympathetic attitude, and instead of the gloomy scenes we saw in *Our
Own Folks* other scenes appear, the creation of which was inspired by
different, brighter impressions of life.

*** Thus, a writer in *Otechestvenniye Zapiski*, in reviewing the same
comedy *Poverty Is No Crime*, rebukes Ostrovsky not only for having

trovsky's literary activity would have been sufficient in itself to mislead simplehearted people who might have taken it into their heads to trust the critics in their judgment of Ostrovsky. But the contradiction was not confined to this; it also extended to the numerous particular comments on the various merits and demerits of Ostrovsky's comedies. The diversity of his talent and the wide range of problems dealt with in his works constantly provided pretexts for the most contradicting reproaches. Thus, as regards his *A Lucrative Post*, for example, he was criticized for not making the bribetakers he described *sufficiently loath-some*,* and as regards his *The Ward*, he was criticized for making the personages depicted in that book *too loathsome*.** In the case of *The Poor Bride, Don't Get into Another's Sleigh, Poverty Is No Crime* and *You Can't Live As You Like*, Ostrovsky was obliged to listen to criticism from all sides to the effect that he had sacrificed the dramatic finish of these plays to his fundamental purpose,*** and in connection with the same works the

___

"depicted the most sordid sides of reality *in their genuine colours*, but also for elevating them to ideals." Evidently, the critic was displeased with the fact that the sordid sides of reality were depicted at all. Complaints on this score were always heard to the accompaniment of complaints on the score of idealization, and more recently these have even been expressed in the following form: "Under Mr. Ostrovsky's pen, comedy has lost its artistic significance and has become merely a copy of real life" (*Atenei*, No. 8, 1859).

* "These persons who are brought on to the stage should rouse in the reader, or spectator, a feeling of repugnance, but in themselves they excite only compassion. Bribery, that social sore, is not brought out in very vivid and disgusting colours in their conduct.... The author should have shown how bribetakers and embezzlers of state funds are tormenting, disgracing and ruining our long-suffering and beloved mother Russia everywhere, at home and abroad" (*Atenei*, No. 10, 1858).

** "All the persons in *The Ward*, except Nadya, are not persons at all, but abstract and condensed doses of various kinds of human slime, which have a most depressing and unpleasant effect upon the reader's mind" ("Spring," an article by Mr. Akhsharumov).[73] In reviewing *You Can't Live As You Like*, he expressed the following opinion about *Our Own Folks*: "*Our Own Folks* is, of course, a work which bears the impress of unusual talent, but it is conceived under the powerful influence of a negative view of Russian life, partly softened by artistic execution, and in this respect it must, regrettable though this is, be attributed to the consequences of the *natural trend*" (*Russkaya Beseda*, No. 1, 1856).—*N. D.*

*** "Carried away by the nobility and novelty of *his tasks*, the author did not allow them to mature sufficiently in his heart, did not allow them to ripen to the proper stage of fulness and clarity.... Had Ostrovsky squeezed author heard advice to the effect that he should not content himself with slavishly copying nature, but strive to *widen his mental horizon*.* Not only that, he was even criticized for devoting himself exclusively to the true portrayal of reality (*i.e.,* execution) without troubling about the *idea* that runs through his works. In other words, he was criticized for the absence, or insignificance, of the *purposes* which other critics regarded as being too broad, as far exceeding the means for achieving them.**

In short, it is difficult to conceive of any middle stand that one can take in order to, at least to some extent, harmonize the demands that have been presented to Ostrovsky for ten years by different (and sometimes by the very same) critics. On the one hand he was criticized for painting Russian life in too gloomy colours, and on the other for embellishing it, piling on the powder and rouge. On the one hand he was criticized for

---

his play into a smaller frame, had he moderated somewhat his extremely *noble and broad tasks*, had he not thrown in all at once everything that he had pondered over and felt in relation to the chosen dramatic situation, the play would have been more harmonious and complete, although it may have lost a little of its dynamic force" (*Moskvityanin*, No. 1, 1853, review of *The Poor Bride*).

"By choosing the dramatic form for achieving *his purpose*, the author undertook the obligation to meet all the requirements of this form, *i.e.,* first of all, to give the reader, or spectator, the impression of a dramatic collision and action, and thereby impress upon his mind the main idea that runs through the comedy.

"*In this respect we cannot be quite satisfied with Mr. Ostrovsky's new play,*" and so forth (*Moskvityanin*, No. 5, 1854, review of *Poverty Is No Crime*).

"In the works of Mr. Ostrovsky the *purposes* are not only correct but full of profound meaning, and are always sound in moral respects... and we cannot help regretting that this particular work *You Can't Live As You Like*, so beautifully conceived and so beautifully arranged from the dramatic aspect, is weaker in its execution than all the other works written by Mr. Ostrovsky up to now" (*Russkaya Beseda*, No. 1, 1856).

* We find slavish imitation not only in the language of the new comedy, but in almost its entire content, in the conception of the whole, as well as in its details. In vain will you seek in it even one ideal feature: you will not find it either in the personages or in the action.... We would like the author first of all to emerge from that close circle in which he has confined his activities up to now and widen his mental horizon to some extent" (*Otechestvenniye Zapiski*, No. 6, 1854).

** This found exceptionally vivid expression in an insolent article recently published in *Atenei*. The concluding words of the critic were as follows: Mr. Ostrovsky's works, while picturing real life, are in themselves

being too didactical, and on the other for the absence of any
moral principles in his productions.... On the one hand he
was criticized for too slavishly copying reality, and on the other
for misrepresenting it. On the one hand he was criticized for
displaying too much concern for outward finish, and on the
other for being careless about this finish. On the one hand he
was criticized because the action in his plays is too slow, and
on the other because the changes are too fast and because the
preceding actions do not prepare the reader for these changes.
On the one hand his characters are too ordinary, and on the
other they are too excep.ional.... And often all this was said
about the same productions by critics who evidently must have
agreed on fundamental views. If the public were obliged to
judge Ostrovsky only on the basis of what the critics have been
writing about him for ten years, it would have been totally at
a loss to know what, finally, it should think about this author.
At one moment, according to these critics, he is a flag-wagging
patriot, an obscurantist; at another moment he is the direct successor to Gogol in his best period. At one moment he is a Slavophil, at another a Westerner; at one moment he is the creator
of the people's theatre, at another a shopkeeper Kotsebu, at

---

lifeless; they contain *neither ideas*, nor action, nor truly poetic characters.... In fairness to the author it must be said that in his plays (the comedies depicting the life of the merchant class) he presents us with a
fairly true picture of merchant and middle-class life—but that is all. One
of his plays stands out from the rest, namely, *The Poor Bride*, but then
it is the worst one of the lot. As regards *wealth of ideas* and diversity
of characters, we can say nothing consoling. It is sufficient to learn that
one play served as the pretext, so to speak, for another by way of a
contrast. Thus, the comedy *Our Own Folks—We'll Settle It Among Ourselves* has a counterpart in the shape of the drama *You Can't Live As
You Like*, which also might have been called *Our Own Folks—We'll Settle
It Among Ourselves*. *The Poor Bride* served as the pretext for writing the
comedy *Don't Get Into Another's Sleigh*, or *The Rich Bride*; very close
to them is the comedy *Poverty Is No Crime*, which could quite justly be
called *The Poor Bridegroom. From this it is evident how well Mr. Ostrovsky's imagination is supplied with a stock of ideas, and of images
with which to express them.*[7]

We shall remind the reader that for a long time those who eulogized
Ostrovsky expressed amazement precisely at the inexhaustible richness of
his imagination in creating numerous new types and dramatic situations;
from this it will be clear how ineffective the favourable criticism has been
in explaining this author's significance.

15*

another an author with a new and original world outlook, at another a man who fails to understand the reality which he copies. Far from giving a complete characterization of Ostrovsky, nobody, so far, has even indicated the features that constitute the main idea of his productions.

What is the cause of this strange circumstance? "There must have been some reason!" Perhaps Ostrovsky has, indeed, changed his direction so often that his character has been unable to take definite shape to this day? Or perhaps, on the contrary, he, from the very beginning, as the critics in *Moskvityanin* assert, reached a height which is beyond the understanding of contemporary critics? In our opinion, it is neither the one nor the other. The reason for the confusion of opinion about Ostrovsky that prevails up to now is that a determined effort has been made to present him as the representative of a certain set of convictions, and he has been either punished for disloyalty to these convictions or praised for remaining faithful to them. All the critics have admitted that Ostrovsky possesses remarkable talent and, as a consequence, all the critics wanted to see in him a champion and vehicle of the convictions which they themselves held. People with a touch of the Slavophil about them were extremely pleased with the excellent way in which he depicted Russian life, and to spite the corrupting West, they unceremoniously proclaimed Ostrovsky an admirer of the "*good old days*" *of Russia.* As a man who really knows and loves the Russian people Ostrovsky has, indeed, given the Slavophils considerable ground for regarding him as "one of their own," and they took immoderate advantage of this. This, in turn, gave the opposite party good ground for regarding him as an enemy of European education and as a writer who belonged to the retrogressive trend. Actually, however, Ostrovsky has never been either one or the other, at all events, in his writings. Perhaps he has been influenced by the study circle to recognize certain abstract theories; but this influence could not destroy his true sense of the realities of life, could not entirely close for him the road to which his talent pointed. That is why Ostrovsky's productions have constantly slipped away from the two totally different yardsticks with which attempts were made to measure them from two opposite ends. The Slavophils soon discerned in Ostrovsky features which did not in the least serve the purpose of preaching humility, patience, devotion to the customs of our ancestors and hatred for the West; and so they deemed it necessary to rebuke him either for failing to express his views fully, or for yielding to the *negative* view. The most absurd of the critics in the Slavophil party has very categorically stated that everything would have been all right with Ostrovsky were it not for the fact that "sometimes he lacks determination and boldness in executing his plan: he seems to be hindered by the false shame and the timid habits which he has imbibed from the *natural trend*. This explains why he, not infrequently, starts on something *lofty* and *broad*, but is frightened away from his plan by the vision of the *natural* yardstick that rises before his eyes. He ought to give free reign to his happy fancy but he, as it were, is frightened by the height to which he must climb, and the image comes out unfinished" (*Russkaya Beseda*). On the other hand, people who went into raptures over *Our Own Folks* soon observed that in comparing the ancient principles of Russian life with the new elements of Europeanism discerned in the life of the merchant class, Ostrovsky always inclines towards the former. This displeased them, and the most absurd of the critics in the so-called *Western* party also expressed his opinion in the following very categorical terms:

"The didactic trend which determines the character of these productions prevents us from conceding that they reveal true poetic talent. This trend is based on those principles which our Slavophils call national. It is to them that Mr. Ostrovsky, in his comedies and drama, has subordinated the thoughts, the sentiments and the free will of man" (*Atenei, 1859*).

These two opposite statements may provide us with the key to the problem as to why the critics have been unable up till now to regard Ostrovsky simply and straightforwardly as a writer who depicts the life of a certain section of Russian society, but always regard him as a preacher of a morality that conforms with the conceptions of this or that party. The critics should have abandoned this ready-made yardstick and have taken up Ostrovsky's productions simply in order to study them with the determination to take from them what the author himself gave. But had they done that, they would have had to abandon their

desire to enlist him in their own ranks, they would have had
to push their prejudices against the opposite party into the
background, they would have had to ignore the smug and rather
insolent sallies of the opposite side... but this would have
been extremely difficult for either party. And so Ostrovsky, falling a victim to the polemics between them, struck several wrong
chords to please both sides, and thereby confused them all the
more.

Happily, the public paid little attention to the squabbles
among the critics and read Ostrovsky's comedies, went to the
theatre to see those that were permitted to be staged, read the
plays again, and thus became fairly well acquainted with the
productions of their favourite comedy writer. Thanks to this,
the task of the critic is much easier now. There is no need to
review each play separately, to relate its contents, to trace the
development of the action scene by scene, to pick up little flaws
by the way, to praise apt expressions, and so forth. Readers are
already well aware of all this: all know the contents of the
plays, the minor defects have been discussed over and over again,
the public long ago picked up the apt expressions which have
now gone into our common speech as popular sayings. Nor is
it necessary, or convenient (unless one has the courage that was
displayed by the *Atenei's* critic, Mr. N. P. Nekrasov of Moscow)
to ascribe to the author one's own line of thought: it is now
obvious to every reader that Ostrovsky is not an obscurantist,
not an advocate of flogging as the basis of family morality, not
a champion of the disgusting morality which preaches infinite
patience and renunciation of the rights of one's own individuality—nor is he a blind and embittered lampooner who tries
at all costs to expose to our shame the *dirty stains* of Russian
life. Of course, each one is free to do as he pleases; but recently
a critic has tried to prove that the main idea that runs through
the comedy *Don't Get Into Another's Sleigh* is that it is immoral
for a merchant's daughter to marry a nobleman, that it is much
more respectable for her to marry her equal in obedience to her
parents' commands. The same critic decided (very energetically) that in the drama *You Can't Live As You Like*, Ostrovsky
preaches that "complete resignation to the will of one's seniors,
blind faith in the justice of ancient laws, and complete renun-

ciation of human liberty, of all claim to the right to express one's human feelings, are all superior to the thoughts, feelings and the free will of man. The same critic very wittily observed that "in the scenes of *A Holiday Dream Before Dinner*, superstitious belief in dreams is ridiculed...."* But now two volumes of the works of Ostrovsky are in the hands of readers—who will believe such a critic?

Thus, assuming that our readers are familiar with the contents and the development of Ostrovsky's plays, we shall merely try to recall the features that are common to all his productions, or to most of them, to reduce these features to a common denominator, and use this as the criterion with which to determine the significance of this writer's literary activities. By doing so we shall be merely giving a general outline of what the majority of our readers have known for a long time, but which many of them, perhaps, have not properly brought together in a harmonious whole. We deem it necessary, however, to warn the reader that we do not ascribe any program to the author, we do not draw up for him any preliminary rules to guide him in planning and executing his works. In our opinion, such a method of criticism is extremely offensive to an author whose talent is universally recognized and who has already won the love of the public and a certain share of significance in literature. Criticism which consists in showing what a writer *should* have done, and to what extent he has done what he *should* have done, is still useful at times in relation to an author who is just beginning, who is showing some promise, but is proceeding along an absolutely false path and, therefore, needs guidance and advice. But, in general, such criticism is unpleasant, because it places the critic in a position of a pedantic schoolteacher setting out to examine a schoolboy. One cannot permit oneself to indulge in such pedantic criticism of an author like Ostrovsky. Every reader would be quite justified in saying to us: "Why are you worrying yourself to death over what should have been in one place and what is lacking in another? We refuse to recognize your right to lecture Ostrovsky; we are not in the least interested in your opinion as to how he should have written his play. We read

---

* You will find all this in *Atenei*.

Ostrovsky and we love him; what we want the critics to do is
to explain to us what it is that so often unaccountably thrills
us, to explain our own impressions to us and put them in some
order. If, after this explanation, our impressions prove to be
erroneous and their results harmful, or if it turns out that we are
ascribing to the author something that should not be ascribed
to him, then let the critics set to work to rectify our errors; but,
we insist, they must be rectified on the basis of what the author
himself presents to us." We think that such a demand would
be quite just, and we therefore consider it best to apply to Ostrovsky's productions *realistic* criticism, which consists in reviewing what his productions present us with. Here we shall not
enquire why Ostrovsky does not depict his characters as Shakespeare depicted his, why he does not develop his comical scenes
as Gogol did his,* etc. All demands of this kind are, in our
opinion, as superfluous, futile and groundless as, for example,
the demand that Ostrovsky should be a comedian of passions,
and that he should give us types like Molière's Tartuffe and
Harpagon, or that he should follow the example of Aristophanes
and give his comedies a political significance. We do not deny,
of course, that it would be better if Ostrovsky combined within
himself the merits of Aristophanes, Molière and Shakespeare;
but we know that he does not, we know that this is impossible,
and still we recognize Ostrovsky as a remarkable figure in our
literature and are of the opinion that he, just as he is, is not at
all bad and deserves our attention and study. . . .

Similarly, the realistic method of criticism does not permit
the practice of ascribing to an author other people's ideas. Before
its judgment stand persons whom the author has created and the
actions he ascribes to them. The realistic critic must say what
impression these persons make upon him, and he can indict the
author, only if this impression is incomplete, vague and ambig-
uous. He will never permit himself to draw a deduction like
the following: this person is devoted to ancient prejudices, but
the author has depicted him as benevolent and by no means
stupid, consequently, the author intended to present ancient prejudices in a good light. No, the first thing a realistic critic takes

---

* Clever critics have actually hurled such reproaches at Ostrovsky. . . .

cognizance of is the fact that the author depicts a benevolent and by no means stupid person who is imbued with ancient prejudices. Then the critic goes on to investigate whether such a type of person is possible, and whether it exists; on finding that it is true to reality the critic will proceed to express his own views as to the causes which engendered such a type, etc. If the author of the work under review has given these causes, the critic uses them and is grateful to the author; if he has not, he does not point a dagger at his throat and demand how he dared depict such a person without explaining the causes of his existence? The realistic critic treats the work of an artist in the same way as he treats the phenomena of real life; he studies them in the endeavour to define their norm, to collect their essential, characteristic features, but he does not ask fussily why oats are not rye and coal not diamonds.... True, there may have been scientists who engaged in experiments to prove that oats became transformed into rye; there have also been critics who tried to prove that if Ostrovsky had altered such and such a scene in such and such a way he would have been a Gogol, and if he had depicted such and such a person in such and such a way he would have been a Shakespeare.... We believe, however, that such scientists and critics did not do much to promote science and art. Far more useful were those who brought to the knowledge of the public a few hitherto concealed or not quite clear facts of life, or of the world of art, which is the portrayal of life. If nothing of this nature has been done in relation to Ostrovsky up to now, we can only regret this strange circumstance and endeavour to fill the gap as far as our strength and ability will allow.

But to finish with the former critics of Ostrovsky, we shall now gather together those observations upon which they were nearly all agreed, and which may deserve attention.

First, everybody agrees that Ostrovsky possesses the gift of observation and the ability to paint a true picture of the habits of life of those classes from whose ranks he took the subjects of his productions.

Second, everybody has noted (although not everybody has done justice to) the aptness and truthfulness of the language of the people in Ostrovsky's comedies.

Third, all the critics agree that practically all the characters in Ostrovsky's plays are quite ordinary people, that they are in no way distinguished and do not rise above the banal surroundings in which they find themselves. Many censure the author for this on the grounds that such people must necessarily be colourless. Others, however, have rightly found very striking typical features in these ordinary persons.

Fourth, all are agreed that most of Ostrovsky's comedies "lack (as one of his enthusiastic admirers puts it) economy in the plan and structure of the play," and that, as a consequence (in the words of another of his admirers), "the dramatic action in his plays does not develop consistently and continuously; the plot of the play does not merge organically with its idea and seems to be somewhat extraneous."

Fifth, none of the critics likes the rather abrupt, *casual* climaxes in Ostrovsky's comedies. As one critic put it, at the end of the play "it seems as though a gale sweeps through the room and turns the heads of all the characters in it."

This, we think, is all that the critics have agreed upon up to now in their criticism of Ostrovsky.... We could have devoted the whole of our essay to the amplification of these unanimously accepted propositions and perhaps, by doing so, we would have chosen for ourselves a gratifying task. Our readers would have found it somewhat tedious, of course, but we would have got off very easily; we would have earned the sympathy of the aesthetic critics and even—who knows?—might have earned for ourselves the reputation of a keen judge of artistic beauty and of artistic flaws. Unfortunately, we do not feel that it is our mission to *cultivate the aesthetic tastes of the public*, and therefore, we ourselves would have found it a tedious task to act the schoolteacher and to talk at great length, and very profoundly, about the most subtle shades of art. We shall leave this to Messrs. Almazov,[75] Akhsharumov and their ilk and confine ourselves here to the task of summing up the results we have obtained from a study of Ostrovsky's works from the standpoint of the reality he depicts. But before doing that we want to make a few observations concerning the relation between an author's artistic talent and his abstract ideas.

Diverse as the works of a talented artist may be, one can always note something common to them all which characterizes each of them and distinguishes them from the works of other writers. In the technical language of art it is customary to call this the artist's *world outlook*. Vain would be our attempts to reduce this world outlook to definite logical schemes, to express it in abstract formulae. As a rule these abstractions do not exist in the artist's own mind; not infrequently he even expresses in abstract discussions ideas that are the very opposite of what he expresses in his artistic activity—ideas which he accepts on faith, or which he acquires by means of false, hastily constructed and superficial syllogisms. His actual world outlook, the one that provides the clue to his talent, must be sought in the living images that he creates. It is here that we find the material difference between the talent of the artist and that of the thinker. In substance, thinking power and creative ability are both characteristic of and equally necessary for the philosopher and the poet. The greatness of a philosophical mind and the greatness of poetic genius equally consist in the ability at a glance to grasp the essential features of an object, distinguish them from the casual ones and organize them properly in one's mind, to master them in such a way as to be able freely to call them forth for every possible combination. But the difference between the thinker and the artist is that the latter's power of perception is much more vivid and powerful than that of the former. Each fashions his world outlook on the basis of the facts that succeeded in reaching his mind. But a man with keener powers of perception, an "artistic nature," is powerfully affected by the very first fact of a certain kind that presents itself in surrounding reality. He has not yet worked out any theory that would enable him to explain this fact, but he realizes that there is something here that merits special attention, and he examines this fact with keen interest, he assimilates it, nurtures it in his soul, at first as a single image, and then he adds other kindred facts and images to it, and finally creates a type which expresses the essential features of all the particular phenomena of this kind which he has observed before. The thinker, on the other hand, is not affected so quickly and so powerfully. The first fact of a new kind does not produce a vivid impression upon him; in most cases he scarcely notices this fact and passes it by as if it were a strange accident, without even taking the trouble to assimilate it. (We are not, of course, discussing personal relationships: a philosopher may fall in love, lose his temper and grieve at the first appearance of a *fact* as quickly as the poet.) Only later, when numerous kindred facts accumulate in his mind, does a man with a low power of perception pay attention to them at last. But here the numerous particular images which he had previously collected and which imperceptibly rest in his mind enable him at once to mould them into a general conception and thus immediately to transfer the new fact from the realm of living reality into the sphere of abstraction. And here a proper place is found for the new idea among a number of other ideas; its significance is explained, deductions are drawn from it, etc. In the process the thinker—or to put it more simply, the man who reasons—utilizes both the real facts and the images which have been reproduced from life by the art of the artist. Sometimes these very images even help the man who reasons to form correct ideas about some of the phenomena of real life. Thus, the *importance of artistic activity among other manifestations of social life* becomes absolutely clear: by concentrating the facts of real life, by focussing them, as it were, the images created by the artist greatly facilitate the formulation of correct ideas about things and the dissemination of these ideas among men.

Hence it is clear that the principal merit of the author-artist lies in the *truth* of the images he creates; if they were not true, false conclusions would be drawn from them and false ideas would result. But what is the *truth* of artistic images? Strictly speaking, writers never invent *absolute falsehood*: even with respect to the most absurd novels and melodramas it cannot be said that the *passions* and banalities that are depicted in them are absolutely false, *i.e.*, impossible even as monstrous accidents. But the *falsehood* of novels and melodramas of this kind lies precisely in that they make the accidental and false features of real life, which do not constitute its substance, its characteristic features. They are false also because, if we formulated theoretical ideas on their basis, we would arrive at absolutely false ideas. For example: there are authors who devote their talent to describing voluptuous scenes and dissolute adventures; they depict volup-

tuousness in such a way as to make it appear that it alone constitutes true human happiness. It goes without saying that such
a deduction would be absurd, although, of course, there are people
who, due to the degree of their development, are incapable of
conceiving of any other kind of happiness.... There have been
other writers, still more absurd, who have extolled the virtues of
the warlike feudal barons who shed rivers of blood, burned down
cities and plundered their vassals. There was no downright
falsehood in the descriptions of the facts that were performed by
these robbers, but they were presented in such a light, and were
so highly praised, that it is clearly evident that the soul of the
author who extolled them lacked the sense of human truth. Thus,
all one-sidedness and exclusiveness prevents the artist from fully
conforming to truth. Consequently, the artist must either keep
his simple, childishly direct outlook on the whole world intact, or
(since this is absolutely impossible in life) must save himself
from one-sidedness by broadening his outlook as much as possible, by assimilating those general ideas that have been worked
out by the men who reason. In this way the link between science
and art may find expression. The free transformation of the loft-
iest speculations into living images and, at the same time, full
understanding of the higher, general meaning of every, even the
most particular and accidental, fact of life, is the ideal which
represents the complete merging of science and poetry which
nobody so far has achieved. But the artist who is guided by correct principles in his general ideas has this advantage over the
undeveloped, or falsely developed, writer, that he can freely
yield to the suggestions of his artistic nature. His direct feelings
will always truly guide him to his object; but when his general
ideas are false, a conflict will inevitably arise within him, doubts
and irresolution will beset him, and although his works may not
be utterly false as a result of this, they will nevertheless turn
out to be weak, colourless and inharmonious. On the other hand,
when the artist's general ideas are correct and fully harmonize
with his nature, this harmony and unity are reflected in his works.
Reality is then reflected in his works more brightly and vividly,
it can more easily lead the man who reasons to draw correct deductions and, consequently, they will be of more importance in
life.

If we apply all the foregoing to the works of Ostrovsky, and
if we recall what we said above about his critics, we shall have
to admit that his literary activity has not been altogether free
from that vacillation which takes place owing to the lack of harmony between the artist's inner feelings and the abstract ideas he
has acquired from outside. It is this vacillation that explains
why the critics could draw totally opposite conclusions concerning the meaning of the facts that are presented in Ostrovsky's comedies. The accusation that he is preaching renunciation of free will,
idiotic humility, resignation, etc., must, of course, be ascribed
mostly to the dull-wittedness of the critics, but it shows also that
the author himself has not sufficiently safeguarded himself against
such an accusation. And indeed, in the comedies *Don't Get Into
Another's Sleigh, Poverty Is No Crime* and *You Can't Live As You
Like,* the undeniably seamy sides of our old-fashioned way of life
are presented in the course of the action in such casual circumstances
as to make one think that they were not at all bad. The fact that
these casual circumstances serve as the basis of the above plays
shows that the author must have attached more importance to
them than they really deserved, and this wrong view affected
the completeness and vividness of the works themselves. But even
here the author did not lose his artistic feeling, and for that reason, the particular situations and the individual characters that
he depicts are always distinguished for their unadulterated truth.
Only on very rare occasions has obsession with an idea led Ostrovsky to overdraw certain of his characters or dramatic situations,
as he did, for example, in that scene in *Don't Get Into Another's
Sleigh* where Borodkin offers to marry the dishonoured daughter
of Rusakov. Throughout the play Borodkin appears as a good
and noble man of the old-fashioned type, but this last act of his
is entirely out of keeping with the mentality of people of which
he is a representative. The author, however, wanted to ascribe
to this person all sorts of good qualities, and among these he
included one from which the real Borodkins would in all probability shrink with horror. But there are extremely few overdrawn
scenes of this kind in Ostrovsky's plays; the artist's sense of truth
constantly saves him. Far more often he seems to have sacrificed
his idea precisely because he wanted to remain true to reality.
Those who persisted in regarding Ostrovsky as a supporter of

their party often complained that he failed to bring out strikingly, enough the idea which they wish to see in his works. For example: wishing to see in *Poverty Is No Crime* the apotheosis of humility and obedience to seniors, some critics complained that the climax of the play does not follow logically from the moral virtues of the humble Mitya; but the author realized the practical absurdity and artistic falsehood of such a climax and therefore introduced the casual intervention of Lyubim Tortsov. Similarly, in the case of Pyotr Ilyich in *You Can't Live As You Like*, the critics complained that the author had not given that person that expansiveness and generosity which, they claim, is characteristic of the Russian, particularly when he is on the spree. But the author's artistic intuition told him that his Pyotr, who regained consciousness at the sound of the church bells, represents not the expansive devil-may-care Russian nature, but rather, the low tavern-frequenter. Rather amusing criticism was also heard with reference to *A Lucrative Post*. Some critics asked why Ostrovsky had brought out a disreputable gentleman like Zhadov as the representative of honest striving; they were even angry because Ostrovsky's bribetakers are so banal and naive, and they expressed the opinion that "it would have been far better to have brought to public trial those who *deliberately and adroitly* create, develop and foster bribery and obsequiousness, and *vigorously* oppose, in every way they can, the infusion of fresh elements into the state and social organism." And the exacting critic added: "We would have been the keenest and most ardent spectators of that now turbulent, now skilfully sustained conflict of the two parties" (*Atenei*, No. 10, 1858). This wish, although just in the abstract, nevertheless showed that the critic totally failed to understand the realm of darkness which Ostrovsky depicts, and which itself forestalls all perplexity as to why such and such persons are banal, why such and such situations are casual, and why such and such conflicts are weak. We have no wish to thrust our opinions upon anyone, but it seems to us that Ostrovsky would have transgressed against the truth had he ascribed to Russian life phenomena totally alien to it, had he taken it into his head to present our bribetakers as a properly organized and conscious party. Where will we find such parties in our country? Where have you found the traces of deliberate and premeditated

action? You may be quite sure that if Ostrovsky had invented
such persons and such actions, his play as a whole would have
remained lifeless and false, no matter how dramatically the plot
may have begun, and no matter how vividly all the characters
may have been brought out. Even as it is there is already a false
note in that comedy in the person of Zhadov, but in this case
too, the author realized this before all the critics did. In the
middle of the play he begins to remove his hero from the pedestal
on which he had placed him in the first scenes, and in the last
act he shows that he is totally unfit for the struggle which he
wanted to undertake. Far from blaming Ostrovsky for this, we
regard it as evidence of the greatness of his talent. He undoubtedly felt the beautiful things that Zhadov talked about, but at the
same time he also felt that to compel Zhadov *to do* all these beautiful things would have meant presenting a distorted picture of
actual Russian reality. Here the requirements of artistic truth
saved Ostrovsky from being carried away by external tendencies
and helped him to keep away from the road which Messrs. Sollogub and Lvov[76] have taken. The example of these mediocre phrase-
mongers shows that it is not at all difficult to make a mechanical doll and call it an *honest government official;* but it is difficult
to breathe the breath of life into it and compel it to speak and
act in a human way. Ostrovsky too tried to depict the honest government official and was not always successful in overcoming
this difficulty; nevertheless, in his comedy, human nature reveals
itself more than once through Zhadov's high-sounding phrases.
It is this ability to discern nature, to delve deep down into a
man's soul, to grasp his feelings quite apart from depicting his
external, official relations, that we regard as one of the chief and
best characteristics of Ostrovsky's talent. That is why we are
always ready to absolve him from the charge that in depicting
character he deserted some fundamental motive which the profound critics imagined they had found in it.

Similarly, we absolve Ostrovsky from the charge that the
climaxes in his comedies are casual and apparently unreasonable.
How can you have reason when it does not exist in the life that
the author depicts? There can be no doubt that Ostrovsky could
have presented more weighty reasons than the sound of church
bells to persuade a man to give up drink; but what could he do

when Pyotr Ilyich is a man who is impervious to reason? You cannot put your own head on another man's shoulders; you cannot alter popular superstition. To ascribe to it a meaning it does not possess means distorting it and misrepresenting the very life in which it manifests itself. The same applies to other cases: to create unyielding dramatic characters who steadily and firmly pursue a particular goal, to invent a strictly co-ordinated and subtle plot would mean ascribing to Russian life something that it does not contain. Speaking conscientiously, none of us has ever met sinister intriguers, systematic rogues and conscious Jesuits. If a man among us does act basely, he does so mostly because of weakness of character; if anybody does engage in fraudulent speculation, it is mostly because the people around him are very stupid and credulous; if anybody does oppress others, it is mostly because it costs no effort—everybody is so yielding and submissive. Our intriguers, diplomats and rogues always remind me of a chess player who said to me: "It's all nonsense when they say that it is possible to think out your game in advance: players boast that they do, but it is not true. Actually, it is impossible to see more than three moves ahead." And this player has beaten many an opponent. This shows that the others were unable to see even three moves ahead, and merely sat and stared at what was under their noses. This is what our entire Russian life is like: whoever can see three steps ahead is regarded as a sage, and he can fool and enmesh thousands of people; and yet they want an artist to depict Tartuffes, Richards and Shylocks in Russian skins. In our opinion such a demand is totally inapplicable in our case, and it smacks very much of scholasticism. According to the demands of scholasticism there must be nothing casual about a work of art: everything in it must be strictly co-ordinated, everything must develop consistently from one given point of departure with logical necessity and *also naturalness*! But suppose *naturalness* precludes *logical consistency*? In the opinion of the Schoolmen it is wrong to choose subjects in which casualness cannot be adapted to the requirements of logical necessity. In our opinion, however, every subject, no matter how casual it may be, is fit for an artistic production, and in dealing with such subjects one must for the sake of naturalness sacrifice even abstract logic, fully confident that life, like nature, has its own logic, and that this logic may turn out to be far better than the one we often impose upon it. . . . Incidentally, this problem of the theory of art is still very new, and we have no wish to present our opinion as an indefeasible rule. We are merely taking this opportunity to express it in connection with the productions of Ostrovsky, who everywhere tries to remain true to the facts of life and even displays a certain amount of contempt for logical consistency, and whose comedies are nevertheless entertaining and possess an inner meaning.

Having uttered these passing remarks, we must make the following reservation before dealing with the main subject of this essay. In recognizing faithfulness to life as the chief merit of an artistic production, we thereby point to the criterion by which we gauge the *merit* and importance of every phenomenon in literature. The degree to which an author's eye penetrates the very substance of phenomena, and the extent to which he embraces the different sides of life in his work, determines the degree of his talent. Without this, all our talk will be useless. For example: Mr. Fet possesses talent and Mr. Tyutchev possesses talent; how can we determine their relative importance? Obviously, only by examining the range each one has reached. When we do that we shall find that the talent of one is capable of manifesting itself to the full only in catching fleeting impressions from serene nature; whereas the other, in addition to this, is capable of expressing ardent passion, grim energy and profound thought, stimulated not only by elemental phenomena, but also by moral problems and the interests of social life. Properly speaking, all this should serve as the criterion of the talents of both poets. Readers would then be able without the aid of aesthetical (usually very nebulous) arguments to understand what place this or that poet occupies in literature. This is what we propose to do with the works of Ostrovsky. The whole of the foregoing exposition has brought us to the admission that faithfulness to reality, living truth, is always observed in Ostrovsky's works and stands in the foreground, overshadowing all sorts of tasks and hidden motives. But this is not all; even Mr. Fet very faithfully expresses indefinite impressions of nature, but this certainly does not mean that his poems occupy an important place in Russian literature. Hence, to say something definite about Ostrovsky's talent one must not confine oneself to the general conclusion that he faithfully depicts reality; it is also necessary to show how wide is his sphere of observation, how important are the aspects of the facts that interest him, and how deeply he penetrates them. To do this it is necessary to subject the contents of his productions to a realistic examination.

The general considerations which should guide us in such an examination are the following:

Ostrovsky is able to peer into the depths of a man's soul, he is able to distinguish his *nature* from the deformities and excrescences introduced from outside; hence, outside pressure, the weight of the whole environment that presses down upon a man is felt in his works far more than in many stories, the contents of which are absolutely outrageous, but the external, official side of which completely obscures the internal, human side.

Ostrovsky's comedies do not show the higher classes of our society; they are confined to the middle classes and therefore cannot provide the clue to many of the ugly scenes that are depicted in them. Nevertheless, they easily suggest numerous analogous thoughts concerning the life with which they do not directly deal. This is due to the fact that the types in Ostrovsky's comedies often possess not only merchant or government official features, but also the common national features of the people.

Public activity is scarcely dealt with in Ostrovsky's comedies, and this is undoubtedly due to the fact that our civic life, while abounding in formalities of every kind, provides scarcely any examples of real activity in which the *human being* can freely and broadly express himself. On the other hand, Ostrovsky's comedies bring out with extreme fulness and relief two kinds of relationships to which a man in this country can still devote his soul, namely, *family* relationships and *property* relationships. It is not surprising, therefore, that the subjects and the very titles of Ostrovsky's plays deal with the family, bridegrooms, brides, riches and poverty.

All the dramatic collisions and catastrophes in Ostrovsky's plays take place as a result of the conflict of two parties, namely, *the old and the young, the rich and the poor, the arrogant and the timid.* Clearly, by the very nature of the case, the climax of such conflicts must be fairly abrupt and smack of casualness.

16*

With these preliminary remarks we shall now enter into the world that is opened for us by Ostrovsky's works and examine the people who inhabit this *realm of darkness*. You will soon see that it is not for nothing that we call this realm *dark*.

II

> Where there is more strictness there
> is more sin. You must judge humanely.
>
> *Ostrovsky*

Before us are the sad submissive faces of our younger brothers whom fate has doomed to an existence of dependence and suffering. Sensitive Mitya, kindhearted Andrei Bruskov, the poor bride Maria Andreyevna, dishonoured Avdotya Maximovna and unhappy Dasha and Nadya, stand before us meek and despondent, silently resigned to their fate.... This is a world of suppressed, softly sighing grief, a world of dull, aching pain, a world in which reigns the silence of the prison or the grave, disturbed at rare intervals only by a muffled, impotent complaint, which subsides almost the moment it is uttered. Here there is neither light, nor warmth, nor space; this dark and close prison reeks of dampness and decay. Not a sound penetrates it from the free world outside. not a ray of light pierces the gloom. At rare intervals only a spark flashes from that sacred fire that burns in every heart until it is quenched by the influx of the mud of daily life. This fire barely smoulders in the stench and dampness of this prison; but sometimes it flares up for an instant and sheds the light of truth and kindness upon the dismal figures of the captives languishing in this prison. Thanks to these momentary flashes we see that it is our brothers who are suffering here, that these seemingly inhuman, dumb, filthy beings have certain human features—and our hearts shrink with pain and horror. These unhappy prisoners are silent; they sit in a state of lethargic stupor, and do not even rattle their chains; they have almost lost the power to realize their tragic situation; nevertheless, they feel the weight of the burden that lies upon them, they have not lost the power to feel their pain. If they bear it silently and motionlessly, it is because every cry, every sigh they utter in this stinking pool catches in their throats and causes excruciating pain to shoot through their chests; every movement of their fettered bodies threatens to increase the burden and the torment of their situation. And nowhere can they look for joy, nowhere can they seek relief: over them rages the irresponsible and senseless *tyranny* represented by various types of Tortsovs (Bolshovs), Bruskovs, Ulanbekovs and the like, who recognize no reasonable rights or demands. Only their savage and revolting shouts disturb this gloomy silence and cause a frightful stir in this melancholy graveyard of human thought and freedom.

But all these miserable creatures are not corpses, they were not born nor are they living in dark graves. In their early, carefree childhood, long ago, the free light of day shone in their eyes, if only for a brief period. They recall this golden age even in their fetid prison and in their bitter bondage to tyranny. The savage and unbridled shouts of some tyrant, the broad sweep of his angry gestures, remind them of the wide spaces of a life of freedom, the proud impulses of a free mind and ardent heart—impulses which have been deadened in these unhappy martyrs, but which have not been crushed entirely. And so a black residue of discontent, impotent rage, dull fury begins to disturb the depths of this gloomy pool; it wants to rise, and ruffling the murky surface it makes it still uglier and more horrible. There is no space or freedom here for living thought, for an inspiring word, for a noble deed; the heavy seal of the tyrant's veto has been placed upon audible, overt and wide activity. But as long as a man is alive it is impossible to crush his desire to live, *i.e.*, to express himself in some way in external activity. The more this striving is suppressed the more distorted is the form in which it expresses itself; but it *cannot cease* to manifest itself as long as the man retains some power to think. So powerful is tyranny in this dark realm of the Tortsovs, Bruskovs and Ulanbekovs, however, that many of the people actually become stupefied; they lose the power to think, they lose the will and even the power to feel—all that constitutes intellectual life—and they vegetate in imbecile impotence, merely performing the functions of animal life. But there are also tenacious natures: these collect the venom of their discontent deep down in their hearts in order to release it when opportunity offers; but meanwhile they silently

creep and crawl like snakes and crouch like toads. ... They are
dumb, silent, inconspicuous; they know that every rapid and
sweeping movement will cause excruciating pain to shoot through
their fettered bodies; they realize that even if they could tear
their chains off they could not escape from their prison and would
only lacerate their limbs to no purpose. And so they work stealthily and silently, twisting, turning, squeezing, resorting to every
possible manoeuvre in the endeavour imperceptibly to free a
hand in order later to file through their chains. ... And so, a
stealthy, sporadic movement commences, with furtive glances over
the shoulder to see whether they are being observed; they resort
to deception and knavery, to pretence and malice fiercely directed
against everybody around them, each caring only for himself,
striving only to achieve relief for himself. Here there are no plans
conceived in anger, no deliberate determination to conduct a
methodical underground struggle, there is even no sign of any
exceptional cunning, there is only an unconscious manifestation
of the instinct of self-preservation stimulated by external circumstances, by no means deliberate, and not properly co-ordinated with anything. Just as tears involuntarily and unconsciously
appear in our eyes from smoke, emotion or horse-radish, just as
our eyes involuntarily screw up when they suddenly encounter a
powerful light, just as our bodies involuntarily shrink from cold,
so these people involuntarily and unconsciously turn to this
stealthy, hypocritical and crudely selfish activity, owing to the
impossibility of engaging in activity that is open, honest and
altruistic. ... We cannot blame these people, although it would
be as well to be on our guard against them: they know not what
they do. In constant fear of being bullied and punished, brought
up like slaves in constant fear of being left without a crust of
bread, living like slaves, they exert all their strength to acquire
one of the principal virtues of the slave—shameless cunning. Why
should they feel ashamed? What truth, which rights should they
respect? Tyranny reigns over them, crushes and kills them senselessly, shamelessly, and without respect for any of their rights.
People brought up under such a rule cannot develop a sense of
moral duty or of the true principles of honesty and justice. That
is why the most outrageous fraud appears to them to be a praiseworthy deed, the most despicable cheating is merely a clever

trick. They can cheat you, rob you, even murder you, and all
the time remain sincerely affable and polite to you, preserving
an imperturbable cordiality, and numerous truly virtuous qualities. There is neither malice nor perfidity in their natures; but
they must rise to the surface somehow, extricate themselves from
this decaying quagmire into which powerful tyrants have plunged
them. They know that it is possible to get out into the fresh
air which these tyrants breathe so freely by means of deception
and money; and so they resort to cunning, flattery and deceit,
in a small way at first and later in a big way, but always stealthily, and in fits and starts, in order to pocket other people's
property. What matters it to them that it is other people's property? Have they themselves not been robbed of all they possessed, of *their will* and of *their reason*? Why, then, should they
stop to ponder over what is honest and what is dishonest? Why
should they not want to cheat others for their own personal
profit?

Thus, in the realm of darkness that Ostrovsky depicts, external submission and dull, concentrated grief that reaches the
stage of downright imbecility and the most deplorable obliteration
of personality are interwoven with slavish cunning, with the most
despicable deception and the most shameless perfidy. Here nobody
can trust another: at any moment you may expect your friend to
boast about how skilfully he has cheated or robbed you; a partner in a profitable speculation may quite easily get hold of all the
money and documents and get his partner locked up in the debtors' prison; a father-in-law will cheat his son-in-law out of his
dowry; a bridegroom will cheat the matchmaker; the bride will
deceive her father and mother, a wife will deceive her husband.
Nothing is sacred, nothing is pure, there is no justice in this dark
world: the savage, unreasonable and unjust tyranny that reigns
over them has driven all sense of honesty and justice from their
minds.... These cannot exist where tyrants have shattered and
have arrogantly trampled upon human dignity, the freedom of
the individual, faith in love and happiness and the sacredness
of honest toil.

And yet right near by, only on the other side of the wall,
there is another life, bright, clean and enlightened.... Both sides
in the realm of darkness are aware of the superiority of this life,

and they are frightened by it at one moment and attracted by it another. But the principles of this life, its inherent strength, are totally unintelligible to the wretched creatures who have grown unaccustomed to all reasonableness and truth in their daily relationships. Only the most crude and superficially striking manifestations of this enlightened life are intelligible to them. Only these manifestations do they attack when they take it into their heads to *dislike* education, and only *these do they copy* when they are fired with the passion to live *like the gentry.* The old tyrant will shave off his beard and get drunk on champagne instead of vodka; his daughter will sing *passionate* love songs and flirt with army officers; his son will carouse with ballet dancers and buy them costly clothes and shawls. This is all their code of education amounts to.... On the other hand, even those who are afraid of the new world, when they meet the foolish Vikhorev or Balzaminov, are glad to accept him as a representative of the educated section of society and use him as the butt for their raillery against the new fashions.... And so, through the whole life of the *tyrants* and through the entire life of suffering of the *oppressed* runs this struggle against the tide of the free new life which, of course, will one day flow over the age-old accumulations of mud and convert the marsh into a bright and magnificent river, but which today as yet only stirs up this mud, becomes itself submerged in it, and with it decays and stinks.... At present, the new principles of life are only disturbing the minds of all the inhabitants of the realm of darkness like a distant vision, or a nightmare. Even for those who dare to *copy the new fashions* this life is hard to bear, as every nightmare is hard to bear even if you see the most tempting things in it. And exactly like after a nightmare, even those who would seem to have freed themselves from the tyrant's yoke and have managed to recover their feelings and consciousness—even those cannot feel quite at home in their new situation and, failing to understand either true education or their own mission in life, they are unable to retain their rights, dare not set to work, and sink once again into the old resignation to their fate, or else plunge into shady transactions with falsehood and tyranny.

Such is the general impression that is created by Ostrovsky's comedies as we understand them. To bring out some of the feat-

ures of this faint sketch in somewhat greater relief we shall
remind the reader of several particulars which will serve to confirm and explain what we have said. In this essay we shall confine ourselves to depicting the moral corruption, the shamelessly
unnatural human relationships that we find in Ostrovsky's
comedies, and which are the direct consequences of the tyranny
that crushes everything.

We open the first page of *The Works of Ostrovsky*. We are
in the house of the merchant Puzatov, in a room furnished without taste, with portraits on the walls, birds of paradise, multi-
coloured drapery and bottles of liqueur. Maria Antipovna,
Puzatov's sister, a girl of nineteen, is sitting at her embroidery
and singing "Black Colour, Dismal Colour." Then she soliloquizes:

"There, the summer is passing, it is already September, and you are
sitting within these four walls like a nun in a convent. And you mustn't
even go near the window. What is there interesting in that?"

The girl's life is certainly far from interesting: the house
is ruled by that tyrant and swindler Puzatov, Maria Antipovna's
brother, and when he is not at home his mother, a shrewish old
woman, pious, good-natured, and ready to sell a man for a kopek,
keeps an eye on her daughter and on her son's young wife. With
these people the young women find no joy, no repose and no
freedom; they must die of ennui and vexation with the constant
grumbling of the old woman and the caprices of the master of
the house. Involuntarily they begin to seek clandestine amusements and, of course, they find them. This is what Maria Antipovna says immediately after she utters the above complaint about
her fate:

"Very well, don't let us out. Lock us in! Tyrannize over us! But
sister and I will ask permission to go to the convent for vespers. We'll
dress up and go to the park, or to Sokolniki. *You've got to be cunning
with these people.* . . ."

Here you have the first example of that involuntary and unnecessary cunning. What does it matter to us how this line of
argument arose in Maria Antipovna's mind, what particular circumstances caused her to develop an inclination for cunning?
We know the *general* cause of this mood; it is very clearly in-

dicated to us by Ostrovsky himself. And we see that far from
being an exception, Maria Antipovna is a most ordinary and
perhaps universal phenomenon in this respect. We need no other
explanation of her early misconduct. But Ostrovsky takes us into
the very heart of this family, he compels us to be present during
the most intimate scenes, and we not only understand but painfully feel with our hearts that here there can be no relationships
except those based on deception and cunning on the one side, and
savage and shameless despotism on the other. The scenes between
Maria Antipovna and Matrena Savishna, Puzatov's wife, and
between the two and the cook, reveal all the disgusting dissoluteness
upon which the whole of that house rests. Matrena Savishna tells
Maria that she must not encourage officers to ride past her window
because it will give her a bad reputation, which she will never be
able to get rid of. Meanwhile, however, the two have already sent
the cook to some young men who had invited them to Ostankino
and had asked them to bring a bottle of Madeira with them. All
this, of course, is done stealthily, and with fear and trembling, because although Puzatov is not at home, his mother spies upon
them and hinders all their movements. As soon as Maria sees
Darya the cook through the window as she is returning from her
errand she exclaims in a frightened voice: "Oh, sister! I hope Mama does not catch her!" Mama does indeed catch Darya, but
Darya is smart too and finds a plausible excuse: "I went to get
some milk," she says. "I ran down to the shop." This time they
manage to deceive their wardress. But during the conversation
between the young women and the cook a slight noise is heard
behind the scenes. The cook listens intently and then exclaims:
"Good Lord, the master's come!..." And indeed, Puzatov's voice is
heard calling in the hall: "Wife! Hey, wife! Matrena Savishna!..."
The wife goes to the door and enquires: "What's happened?" The
husband answers: "Good afternoon! And you thought God knows
what has happened? ..." This outburst already gives you an idea
of the conjugal relations between Antip Antipich and Matrena Savishna. Clearly, he regards his wife as a rubber doll with which
children amuse themselves: they stretch its legs and flatten or
stretch its head to see what it will *look like*. It has never occurred
to Puzatov that his wife has any human rights, and he has never
thought it necessary to respect her personality. His relations with her

are limited to his carnal appetites and to the exercise of his tyranny over her. He says that his wife, "when she dresses up, is better looking than any lady—more buxom, 'pon my word! The others are all such scraggy things, nothing worth looking at for our sort, if you'll excuse me for saying so. But look at her, isn't she grand?... What I mean is—her figure... and all the rest...." And as regards his duties to his wife, to obtain her love he confines himself to the same thing. This is what he says: "The idea that she should ever want to give up a handsome man like me for somebody else!..." Why does he think himself handsome? Here are his own words: "It's different with a good merchant, filled out and rosy-cheeked like me. There's somebody to love, not like those weedy fops...." But perhaps in this he is right: it is not for nothing that the magazines publish cartoons of beautiful camelias in dress coats, gentlemen who live on other people's wives!... And if Matrena Savishna, unbeknown to her husband, visits young men in Ostankino, it of course only shows partly that her development has taken a somewhat wrong direction, and partly that she suffers too much from her husband's tyranny. And this tyranny finds expression in the following way, for example. While waiting for his tea, Antip Antipich runs his eye round the room and at last, finding nothing better to do, plays the following trick:

Antip Antipich (*sternly*): Wife! Come here!

Matrena Savishna: What next?

Antip Antipich: Come here, I tell you! (*banging his fist on the table*).

Matrena Savishna: Have you gone mad, or what?

Antip Antipich: What shall I do with you? (*rapping the table with his knuckles*).

Matrena Savishna: Whatever is the matter with you? (*timidly*) Antip Antipich....

Antip Antipich: Aha! That scared you, didn't it? (*laughs*). It's all right, Matrena Savishna. I was only joking (*sighs*). What about the tea, is it ready?

You see, *joking in this way* only because he was bored! He found it tedious waiting for his tea.... One can understand what kind of feelings even the most unexacting wife can have towards a husband like that.

But Antip Antipich is progressive and humane compared

with his mother. He considers it proper to beat his wife only when he is drunk, and even then he doesn't quite approve of it. In giving his sister's hand to Shiryalov he asks him: "You're quiet when you're drunk, aren't you? You don't fight, do you?" But his mother, Stepanida Trofimovna, does not even recognize this limit. She scolds her son for not keeping a tighter hand on his wife. "My late husband," she says, "much as he loved and petted me, always kept a whip on a nail in the bedroom in case it was needed." Her son has no whip, and she regards this as a sign of moral degradation.... But even without a whip his wife deems it necessary to play the hypocrite before her husband: she kisses him with feigned tenderness, nestles up to him, begs permission of him and her mother-in-law to go to vespers, although she herself reveals some symptoms of the tyrant and says that "the man is not born yet that could shut me up." Deception and pretence reign supreme in that house, and they are presented to us as a special kind of religion, which we could call the *religion of hypocrisy*.

Leaving his wife in peace for a while, Puzatov turns his attention to his sister and tries to find a fiancé for her. Here too he makes various modest remarks about her figure, which causes the no less modest girl to hasten from the room. Then follows an intimate consultation concerning her fate between mother and son. The mother proposes Shiryalov as a suitable fiancé, and in support of her proposal she says: "He may be old and a widower, but look at the money he's got, Antipushka, so much that he doesn't know what to do with it. And besides, he's so respectable and God-fearing, an exemplary merchant and highly respected." To this the son answers laconically: "But *too much of a rascal*, Mother." One would think that Puzatov respects honesty and dislikes knavery, but nothing of the kind. He has his own conception of ethics which permits of rascality, but only within certain limits, although he cannot say definitely what those limits are.... It just seems to him that such and such a man *is not yet too much of a rascal*, and that such and such a man *is already too much of a rascal*. And where there is too much rascality his conscience begins to trouble him, although even this does not make very much difference. The following is the way mother and son formulate their own moral

concepts. In answer to the son's remark about Shiryalov's rascality Stepanida Trofimovna says:

"But my dear, why do you say he is a rascal? *He goes to church
every holiday, and even gets there before everybody else. He keeps the
fasts; during Lent he does not even take sugar with his tea—only honey,
or raisins. Not like you, my dear.... Suppose he does cheat now and
again, what of it? He's not the first and he won't be the last: he's a
businessman, and that, Antipushka, is what keeps business running.
It's not for nothing that they say: 'If you don't cheat, you can't sell.'"*
    A n t i p   A n t i p i c h: You're right! *Why not cheat a friend when
the opportunity occurs?* There's nothing wrong in that. But *my dear,
sometimes your conscience pricks you (scratches his head).* It's the
truth I'm telling you. *And sometimes you think of the hour of death.
(Silence.)* I can do a man down no worse than he when the chance occurs. *But then, I will tell him afterwards:* look, I says, so and so, I did
you out of a bit. Why last year, for example, in settling accounts with
Sava Savich I did him out of five hundred rubles and afterwards I said
to him: look here, Sava Savich, I says, you missed a half a thousand,
but it's too late now, brother, I says, *you ought to keep your wits about
you. He was angry for a bit, but we were soon friends again. After all,
it's not so important.*

You see, therefore, that Puzatov does not regard his frauds
as a vice, he does not even regard them as cheating, but simply
as an artful trick that one can even boast about. And those whom
he cheats are of the same opinion: Sava Savich was angry because he allowed himself to be done in, but later, when his offended pride was soothed, he became friends with Antip Antipich
again. Here cheating is normal and necessary, like killing in
war. Life is so arranged in this realm of darkness that constant
enmity reigns among its inhabitants. Here everybody is at war
with everybody else: a wife with her husband for his tyranny,
the husband with his wife for her disobedience or failure to
please him; parents with their children because the children want
to think for themselves, and the children with their parents because they are not allowed to think for themselves; masters with
their employees, superiors with their subordinates war against
each other because the former want to suppress everything with
their tyranny and the latter cannot find scope for their legitimate
strivings; business people fight to prevent others from robbing
them of the profits of their enterprise, which is always based on
the exploitation of others; idlers fight to prevent from slipping out

of their power the people by whose labours they live, strut about
and grow rich. And all these people combine their forces to
fight the honest people, the people who may open the eyes of
the oppressed toilers and teach them to raise their voices and
demand their rights. As a consequence of this, the realm is in a
constant state of siege, everybody strives only to save himself
from danger and to lull the vigilance of the enemy. On all faces
are written fear and distrust; the process of human thinking
deviates from its natural course and the place of sound conceptions is taken by special conventional considerations which are
distinguished for their brutality and utter contradiction to
human nature. It is common knowledge that the logic of war
differs fundamentally from the logic of common sense. Military
cunning is praised as proof of intelligence directed towards the
extermination of one's neighbours; killing is extolled as the highest valour man can display; successful plunder—the capture
of a camp, of a baggage train, etc.—exalts a man in the eyes
of his rivals. And yet, the laws of all countries provide for
penalties for fraud, robbery and murder. More than that, the
laws of all countries recognize mitigating circumstances, and
sometimes murder itself is excused if the reasons that motivated
it were too irresistible. But what mitigating circumstances can be
pleaded when, for example, Hungarians or Slavs go to war
against Italians in order that Austria may continue to oppress the
latter. What frightful punishment should be meted out to every
Hungarian and Slav, officer or private, for every shot he fires
at French and Sardinian soldiers! But such is the power of the
universal blindness that inevitably affects men in certain situations that murder and plunder during war, far from being punished, is extolled and rewarded. It is in this state of insane
blindness that all the inhabitants of the realm of darkness who
face us in Ostrovsky's comedies find themselves. They are constantly at war with their entire environment. Therefore, do not
demand and do not expect from them the rational thinking that
you would expect from men in a calm and peaceful state. Puzatov formulates the following military syllogism: if I don't
smash you, you will smash me, so it is better that I should
smash you. What can you say in answer to this syllogism? Does
it not arise automatically in the mind of every man who finds

himself in the embarrassing position of having to choose between victory and defeat? It is not surprising, therefore, that in relating how he had underpaid a German shopkeeper who had presented him with a bill, Puzatov should argue in the following way: "What, give him the whole lot? Why should I? No, honesty comes later. *They charge any price they like, and fools believe them. And I'll do it again next time if he does not ask me for a promissory note.*" You see, therefore, that this is just an ordinary game: whoever plays more skilfully wins.

But Puzatov dislikes cheating for cheating's sake, unnecessary cheating, cheating without hope of gain; incidentally, he dislikes it also because this sort of cheating reveals not a serious mind engaged with important interests, but sheer frivolity. As for Shiryalov, whose rascality exceeds all bounds, he disapproves of him mainly because he does not distinguish between war and peace, because he would shoot during an armistice, and would even fire on his own side. "He's like a Jew," says Puzatov, "he would cheat his own father. Yes he would. He just waits for the chance to cheat someone. And yet, he pretends he's a saint." But in this case Puzatov's disapproval must not be taken seriously: just as he is reviling Shiryalov, this very same merchant comes to pay him a visit. Antip Antipich not only receives his guest very politely, not only listens attentively to his stories about the carousals indulged in by his son, Senka, which compel the old man himself to marry, and about the rascally tricks that he, Shiryalov himself plays, but in the end offers the rascal his sister's hand and settles the matter on the spot, without Maria Antipovna's knowledge and consent. What were his motives in doing this? We find the answer to this in the few words that Antip· Antipich utters when Shiryalov leaves. "What a rascal he is," Puzatov says to himself with a wink. "He's a sly beast! What a Lazarus he pretended to be! Makes out that Senka is to blame!... But what's the use of pretending— it's merely an old man's caprice.... Well, it suits us all right! We shall only be too pleased! *The only point is, Paramon Ferapontich, who is going to be cheated over the dowry? That's a dark business. Mother and I are no fools either....*" And so the matter turns out to be very simple: an opportunity presents itself to get his sister off his hands on very *favourable* terms; why not take advantage of it? It will be a good thing for the sister too. After all, she will be settled!...

Such are the people, such are the human relationships that are presented to us in *A Family Picture*, Ostrovsky's first play. In it we find the elements of much that is more fully and vividly brought out in his later comedies. At all events, it is evident that already at that time the author was amazed at the harsh and unfriendly relationships that exist among most people in our society, even among those who are most closely related to each other. Here too is partly indicated the cause of this harshness and enmity: the senseless tyranny of some and the timid evasiveness and inactivity of others. Here too we get an extremely vivid and distinct presentation of the consequences of this unnatural state of things—widespread cheating and fraud, both in domestic and public affairs.

In *Our Own Folks* we already see the religion of hypocrisy and rascality, the same senseless tyranny of some and the same deceptive submissiveness and slavish cunning of others, only with wider ramifications. Here we get several degrees of oppression, we see indications of a certain system in the distribution of tyranny, we get an outline of its history. The chief tyrant, the despot who rules with an iron hand all those who are closely related to him and puts *no restraint* upon himself is Samson Silich Bolshov. What fear he inspires in the whole house! Agrafena Kondratyevna, his wife, threatens her grown-up daughter that she will "complain to Father," and the daughter answers: "That's what God made you for, to complain; you yourself don't amount to very much to me." And when the threat is repeated she retorts still more sharply: "That's all you can say, to Father, to Father! You are very cocky when he's here, but try and be cocky when he's away!" It is evident that both for his wife and his daughter Samson Silich is something in the nature of a bogey, and although each tries to frighten the other with this bogey they together constitute a tacit, covert and spontaneous opposition to him. Being extremely dull-witted, Agrafena Kondratyevna cannot herself define her own feelings, and she expresses the suffering she undergoes only with groans and sighs. But Lipochka, the daughter, says quite unceremoniously: "Mama changes her mind seven times a week; and Papa, when he's not

drunk, doesn't say a word, but when he's drunk he'll knock you
about if you get in his way.... How can an educated young
lady stand it all!" The domestic servants are all imbued with
the same gloomy and timid feeling: the houseboy Tishka complains of the thumps he gets from his master; Fominishna, the
cook, holds the following conversation with Ustinya Naumovna,
the matchmaker who is trying to find a husband for Lipochka,
Bolshov's daugher:

Ustinya Naumovna: Sit down, Fominishna—your feet are old,
they must ache.

Fominishna: Oh, Mother mine! I've no time. We're in awful
trouble: the master hasn't come home from town yet, and we're in a terrible fright, he may come home drunk. And good Lord, what a terror
he is! It's awful to think that such wicked men are born!

Ustinya Naumovna: Everybody knows that it's as hard to get
on with a rich man as it is with the devil.

Fominishna: Oh, the trouble we've had with him. One night
last week, for example, he came home drunk and started a row. It was
something awful! Smashed up the crockery.... "You such and such,"
he yelled, calling us awful names, "I'll kill you all!"

And indeed Samson Silich drives the fear of God, so to
speak, into all his domestics. When he arrives everybody peers
anxiously into his face trying to guess what mood he is in. Here
is a little scene which shows the dread he spreads throughout
the house. Fominishna rushes into the room and shouts:

Fominishna: Samson Silich has come, and he's drunk!
Tishka: Heavens, now we're in for it!
Fominishna: Run for Lazar, Tishka, quick, be a good boy!
Agrafena Kondratyevna (*appearing on the stairs*): Look,
Fominishna my dear, where's he going?
Fominishna: Heavens! It looks as if he is coming in here! I'll
lock the door, by God I will, let him go upstairs. You sit here, my dear.

It turns out, however, that Samson Silich is not drunk;
Fominishna only thought he was. But the noteworthy thing is
how this despotism that reigns over everybody confuses all concepts, erases all distinctions: the mother, the daughter, the cook,
the mistress of the house, the houseboy and the master's head
shop assistant—all, in a moment of distress, merge into one, in
the oppressed party, concerned only with protecting itself. Fominishna, who at other times beats and bullies Tishka, begs of
him to run quickly, and calls him a good boy; Agrafena Kond-

ratyevna turns pitifully to the cook and asks her: "Look, Fominishna my dear..." and Fominishna looks at her sympathetically and prepares to protect her by locking the door.... Only Lazar Podkhalyuzin, the head shop assistant, who is bound to his employer by some dark tacit alliance, and who is himself preparing to become a little despot, stands somewhat aloof from this fear which everybody feels when entering Bolshov's house. In Podkhalyuzin we see another tyrant of a lower order, so far held in check by severe oppression, but already beginning to raise his head.... In a conversation with Podkhalyuzin the matchmaker says: "You know what a devil that Samson Silich is. Why, before you know it he'd crush your bonnet." But Podkhalyuzin answers confidently, as if conscious of his power: "No, he won't crush anything." When Tishka threatens to complain to his master about him because he had beaten him, he retorts still more emphatically: "You'll tell the master! What do I care for the master! If it comes to that I'll..." but he does not finish the sentence. Evidently he has not forgotten what a devil Samson Silich is. Incidentally, even Podkhalyuzin behaved in this cocksure manner only when all the arrangements which Bolshov had made to declare himself a bankrupt were already in his hands. He felt that he was in the position of a man who had pushed his prison warder into the cell from which he has himself just managed to escape. But the prison warder still possesses the key of the prison gates: Podkhalyuzin has still to gain possession of them and that is why, feeling that he is no longer a prisoner, but aware that he is not yet entirely free, he continuously swings backwards and forwards from smug elation to anxiety and combines insolence with obsequiousness. He has already gained possession of Bolshov's house and shops; he still has to obtain all the old man's possessions and also to marry his daughter, who suits him very much, and he bases his hopes of success precisely on Bolshov's willfulness. He does not make long explorations or hatch particularly malicious plans, he merely induces the matchmaker to persuade Lipochka's present fiancé, a gentleman, to give up the match while he himself gets into Bolshov's good graces by his obsequious tone and expressions of sympathy for him. His train of thought is very simple.

"Knowing Samson Silich's character," he soliloquizes, "knowing what he is, this may very easily happen. He's that kind of man that once something gets into his head you'll never knock it out again. Just like what it was three years ago, when he wanted to shave his beard off: how Agrafena Kondratyevna begged of him with tears in her eyes to let it alone, but he said: 'No! I'll let it grow again afterwards, but I'm going to have my own way now!' and he went and shaved it off. So it will be in this case: whether I please him, or he takes it into his head himself—we'll go to the altar tomorrow, and nobody will dare say a word."

Clearly, the entire plan is extremely simple: all the time he's playing on Bolshov's despotic nature. Nor can there be any exceptional cunning in this; laws are not passed for fools, still less for self-willed tyrants, and consequently, it is *hard to get on with them* as Ustinya Naumovna expresses it. Podkhalyuzin is aware that he is taking a chance. "Whether I please him *or he takes it into his head himself*," he says—both contingencies are equally probable and equally improbable. As regards *pleasing*, one does not have to be very cunning for that: lie to him about your obedience, gratitude, your happiness to serve such a man and your own insignificance compared with him—nothing more is needed to win the favour of a stupid and despotic old man. Of all the different kinds of everyday diplomacy this is the lowest, it is no more than calculating only the next move in a game of chess. Bolshov falls to this artless trick because his self-willed habits have long ago deprived him of all intelligence, they have deprived him of the ability to look at things plainly and soberly. He regards himself as the supreme law and the focus of all that comes within the scope of his activities. Within his own family circle he expresses this with cynical bluntness. Concerning his daughter he says: "She's mine, I can do as I like with her." That is why compelling her to marry Lazar Podkhalyuzin against her will seems to him to be no more than an amusing experiment. "Go in," he says to Lazar, "*we'll play a joke on them*." The joke is that he suddenly announces to his wife and daughter that Lazar is Lipochka's fiancé. They all lose their heads: the mother, the matchmaker, Fominishna and the girl herself, who, however, being *educated*, found the strength to express her determined opposition and to shout: "I won't! I won't! I'll never marry a disgusting fellow like that!" It goes without saying that nothing could come of

17*

this opposition: Samson Silich is not the kind of man who can
be turned from his purpose, and, in addition, Podkhalyuzin
eggs him on by saying craftily: "It looks as though it won't be
as you wish, Dad." These words are enough to make Bolshov
forcibly join the hands of the betrothed and to answer in the
following manner: "Why won't it if I wish it? *What am I a
father for if not to command?* Have I fed her all this time for
nothing?" As you see, Bolshov recognizes only one paternal
duty: to command his children. True, he fed his daughter, but
that was out of charity, and for this the daughter must show
her gratitude by completely renouncing her own will. He is the
same in all his dealings. He, himself, for example, becomes
aware that Podkhalyuzin is a rascal, but that doesn't concern
him because Podkhalyuzin is his head shop assistant and works
for his profit. Without the slightest hesitation he reproaches him
for being ungrateful and points to facts like the following:
"Remember, Lazar, how many times I have caught you doing
dishonest things. But I did not dismiss you, I did not disgrace
you all over the town, did I? I made you my head shop assistant, I gave you my whole fortune, why, I gave you my daughter with my own hands." And all this in the hope that Lazar
would continue to defraud and make money out of everybody,
except, of course, Bolshov himself. It is the same with Rispolozhensky, a court clerk, a drunkard who dabbled in shady affairs, sometimes on behalf of Bolshov. Samson Silich taunts him
with having been expelled from the court and very sternly observes that he ought to have been exiled to Kamchatka. When
Rispolozhensky asks him: "Why to Kamchatka?" Bolshov answers sharply: "Why? For your rascality! You don't think you
ought to be rewarded for it, do you?" But this stern view of the
activities of a government official who had been dismissed from
service did not prevent Samson Silich from soliciting his services in the matter of the fraudulent bankruptcy that he was
planning. It seems as though Bolshov exempts himself from
the operation of those moral rules which he considers obligatory
for others. This strange phenomenon (which, however, is met
with so often in our society) is due to Bolshov's ignorance of
the true principles of the social contract, that he does not recognize collective responsibility for a man's rights and duties to-

wards other men and, like Puzatov, he looks upon society as an enemy camp. "All I am concerned about is to arrange my own affairs in the best possible way. As for who causes others to suffer, or who makes profit, that's no business of mine. If anybody suffers, it's his own fault. It shows that he doesn't keep his wits about him." This sums up Bolshov's entire line of reasoning, and it was this that prompted him to declare himself a bankrupt. Critics have complained that Ostrovsky did not, in his comedy, fully and clearly explain the specific influences which prompted Bolshov to proclaim himself a bankrupt, that he did not show the successive stages by which he arrived at this decision, and how this harmonized with the general features of his character. "Fraudulent bankruptcy," said the critics, "is a far worse crime than simple cheating, theft or murder. It combines all these three types of crime, but it is worse than all of them because it is committed deliberately, after long preparation, and calls for crafty patience and the most insolent presence of mind. Only a man with false *convictions*, or one subject to exceptionally unfavourable moral influences, would venture to commit a crime like that. Ostrovsky not only fails to show us anything of this, but he even presents Bolshov's bankruptcy simply as a whim, simply that he *did not wish* to pay." All these arguments, while being quite true theoretically, are totally inapplicable to Russian life. The whole point is that our life does not facilitate the cultivation of any convictions; and if anybody does acquire convictions it does not permit him to apply them. Only one conviction flourishes in our society, namely, the conviction that one need not have (or at all events, need not display) moral convictions. This conviction Samson Silich possesses, although he is not fully conscious of it; and it is a consequence of this conviction that he favours Lazar, has dealings with Rispolozhensky, and resolves to proclaim himself a bankrupt. In general, it must be said that only this conviction enables people to retain some spark of life in our "realm of darkness": with its aid careers are made, profitable matches are arranged, fortunes are made and universal respect is acquired. If this, the sole *conviction*, were not developed in the "realm of darkness," everything would come to a standstill, everything would fall asleep, would stop dead. True, in this realm there are also people with *firm* moral principles, with *honest* and *sacred* convictions; but, unfortunately, all these people are of the Oblomov type. They even acquire these very convictions not in the course of practical activity, not in the struggle against everyday injustice, but by reading good books, in ardent conversations with friends, while making fervent vows to women, and while dreaming noble dreams on their couches. It so happened that these people were not drawn into practical activity in their youth, and so they had plenty of leisure in which to ponder over their relation to the world and over the moral principles of their conduct! Standing aloof from practical activities, their reflections led them to beautiful ideas; but they remained unfit for practical affairs and proved to be utter nonentities when they came in contact with some of the things, and some of the people, from the "realm of darkness." At first people were somewhat frightened of them when they appeared with Onegin's eyeglass, in Pechorin's austere cloak, and with Rudin's fervent speeches; but afterwards they realized that these were all Oblomovs and that while they may be dangerous to certain young ladies, they were not in the least dangerous to practical men. And so these men of honest strivings and independent convictions (which, incidentally, they often failed to act up to because they were so unpractical) remained outside of life. And if it cannot be said that they remained as pure as doves in their collisions with the birds of prey around them, it can be affirmed, at all events, that they proved to be as impotent as doves. As regards those inhabitants of the "realm of darkness" who possessed the strength and the habit to engage in practical affairs, they, from the very outset, took a path which could not possibly lead them to pure moral convictions. The active man never found here a field for peaceful, free and useful activities; before he knew where he was he found that, in some way or another, he had wandered into the enemy camp, and that in order to save himself he must deceive his enemies in some way, he must at least pretend that he was a voluntary deserter. Then he began to resort to cunning in order to escape the vigilance of his enemies and to save himself from them. If he was successful he devised unfriendly actions against them, partly in revenge and partly to safeguard himself against fresh dangers. How, under these circumstances, could he develop

a correct conception of the relations between men? How could
he cultivate respect for human dignity? Here everybody is made
to pay for the injustice perpetrated by another, everybody is
doing me mischief for something for which I am not in the
least to blame, and I am obliged to fight to keep everybody at
bay even when I have no wish to fight anybody. Willy-nilly a
man ceases to discriminate and begins to fight everybody who
comes in his way, even though he is aware that, strictly speaking,
there is no need to fight anybody. Involuntarily the comparison
between life in the "realm of darkness" and fierce war rises up
in one's mind again. In war it is not wrong for a soldier to kill
an enemy soldier who has not fired a single shot into our camp:
the bullet happens to hit him, and that is all there is to it. The
conscience of the soldier who killed does not prick him. Similarly, it is not wrong for the merchant to cheat an absolutely
honest man who has never done anybody the slightest harm. It
is enough that he was buying goods; commerce is like war: if
you don't cheat you can't sell!... Apply this to the landowner
and to the government official in the "realm of darkness," apply
it to whomever you will, it will be the same thing: all are in a
state of war, and nobody's conscience will prick him for cheating and appropriating other people's property precisely because
nobody has any moral convictions, and all live as circumstances
dictate.

Thus we find a profoundly true, characteristically Russian
feature in the fact that in his fraudulent bankruptcy Bolshov is
not prompted by any particular *convictions*, and he is not conscious of any *deep inner struggle* except the fear that criminal
proceedings may be taken against him.... In the abstract all
crimes seem to us to be horrible and extraordinary; but in particular cases they are most often committed very lightly and are
prompted by extremely simple causes. A man is convicted by a
criminal court on the charge of robbery and murder; you would
think that he is a monster. But you look closer and you find
that he is not a monster at all, but a very ordinary man, even
kindhearted. He does not in the least believe that there is anything praiseworthy in robbery and murder; and the crime he committed was not preceded by a severe and prolonged struggle
with himself; he committed it casually, scarcely conscious of

what he was doing. Speak with people who have seen many
criminals; they will tell you that this is very often the case.
Why is this? Because crime is not a product of human nature,
but of a man's abnormal relation to society. And the more pronounced this abnormality is the more often are crimes committed even by respectable characters, and the less deliberate and
methodical, the more casual, almost unconscious, are these
crimes. In the "realm of darkness" that we are discussing, the abnormality of social relationships reaches the utmost limit, and
it is quite understandable therefore that its inhabitants should
lose all conception of morality. They understand only the external, juridical aspect of crime, an aspect which they justly hold
in contempt if they can evade it in one way or another. Of the
internal aspect, of the consequences a crime may have for other
people and for society as a whole, they do not think at all. In
planning his fraudulent bankruptcy Bolshov does not think of
the harm this may do to his creditors, of the likelihood of a number of men being reduced to beggary. This does not enter his
head even when he is already in the debtors' prison. He says that
he is afraid to look at the icon of the Iberian Mother when he
passes the Iberian Gates; he complains that the street urchins
jeer and point the finger of scorn at him; he is afraid of being
exiled to Siberia—but about the people he has ruined, not a word.
Is it surprising, therefore, that he decides so lightly to commit
a crime, the abominable nature of which he even fails to understand? All he sees is that "*other people do the same.*" And for
him this is not merely a phrase in justification of himself, not
merely an example, as one of Ostrovsky's stern critics asserted.
No, it is the clue to Bolshov's entire morality. He sees that others
declare fraudulent bankruptcies, embezzle his money, and then
build themselves mansions with ornamental turrets and purchase
spanking equipages; and so he at once applies the common
rule: "Cheat or be cheated." It is no use arguing that Bolshov's
own creditors had not declared fraudulent bankruptcies and
had done him no harm; it does not matter who suffers as long
as he profits. Here it is like in a battle, it is no use attempting
to discriminate between individuals. Now, if nobody cheated, *i.e.,*
if there were no war, Samson Silich would live peacefully and
honestly and would not cheat anybody. But how is he to behave

when everybody around him is cheating? Who will benefit by
his honesty? If he does not cheat, others will, what difference
does it make? The following is a dialogue between Bolshov and
Podkhalyuzin on this subject:

Bolshov: You'd do me a favour, Lazar, if, in your spare time, you
would draw up my balance sheet for me, if you made up the accounts of
the retail trade with the gentry, and whatever else there is there. We
trade and we trade, brother, but we don't seem to get a kopek out of it.
Perhaps the salesmen are stealing the stuff and taking it home, or giving
it to their relatives, or to their mistresses. They ought to be pulled up.
What's the use of trading if there is no profit in it? Perhaps they don't
know the business? It's high time they did though.

Podkhalyuzin: How can that be, Samson Silich? How can
they not know the business? Am I not always in town myself and explaining things to them?

Bolshov: Yes, but what do you explain to them?

Podkhalyuzin: Well, of course, I try to see that everything is
in order, just as it should be. I says to them, I says: now, boys, keep your
eyes open. When an opportunity occurs, don't miss it. If a customer turns
up who's not so bright, or if a young lady takes a fancy to some particular
colour and pattern, stick another ruble or two on the yard.

Bolshov: *You know, brother, how the Germans fleece our gentry
when they go to their shops. We, of course, are not Germans, we are Orthodox Christians, but we also like to eat pie.* Isn't that so?

Podkhalyuzin: Of course it is. And I also says to them, I says,
you must also measure more naturally: pull and stretch the stuff a bit,
but God forbid, don't tear it; we don't have to wear the stuff, I says.
And if their wits have gone wool gathering, who's to blame? I says. You
can just miss a yard.

Bolshov: *What does it matter? The tailors steal the stuff, anyway!*
Ekh, Lazar! Profits are low nowadays! Not like what they were in the
old days.

The point is clear: Samson Silich's morality is based on the
rule: better that I should steal than that others should steal.
Perhaps this rule is not of dramatic interest—that may be as the
critics please; but it is applied on an extremely wide scale in
many spheres of our life. In conformity with this rule one takes
a bribe for doing an injustice and salves his conscience with the
plea: if I don't take it another will. Another clings to his ma-
norial rights and argues: if my steward does not oppress the
peasants the local sheriff will. Still another will cringe before
his superior and argue to himself: if I don't behave in this way

he'll find somebody else and I'll only lose my job. In short, you will find people behaving according to this rule whichever way you turn. One extends hospitality to scoundrels, another cheats a rich simpleton, a third acts as an informer and a fourth seduces a young woman—and all justify themselves with the same virtuous plea: *"If I don't do it another will."* It would seem to be clear that this plea is not urged here merely by way of example. . . . It is nothing more nor less than the expression of the crudest and most repulsive egoism, and of the complete absence of any higher moral principles.

It is in response to the promptings of this egoism that Bolshov plans a fraudulent bankruptcy. In this case even his egoism can be excused: not only has he seen others grow rich by going bankrupt, but he himself has suffered loss owing to the bankruptcy of some of his debtors. He talks bitterly about this to Podkhalyuzin:

"You've got to understand what business is, Lazar! Do you think money is lying around just waiting to be picked up? When it comes to paying they tell you to go and whistle for your money. Take a promissory note, they say; but what can you take from them when they haven't got anything? I've got a hundred thousand rubles' worth of notes like these, all dishonoured, and they keep mounting up every year. I'll sell you the whole lot for fifty kopeks silver if you like! You couldn't find those debtors even if you searched for them with bloodhounds: some are dead and some have run away, but there's nobody to put in the ditch.* Even if you put them in the ditch, Lazar, no good comes of it. Some of them settle down in it so snugly that you can't even smoke them out. I'm all right here, they say, you clear out!"

Buttressing himself with arguments of this kind Bolshov thinks he has a perfect right to play a little joke on his creditors. At first he is only overcome by a vague desire to avoid paying his debts in one way or another—at one time they amounted to quite a lot. He racks his brains in an effort to find out "how to set the wheels going," but neither he nor his adviser Rispolozhensky can think of anything. When he consulted Rispolozhensky, the latter answered: "It depends on circumstances." But suddenly the idea occurs to them to compel the creditors to compound the debts at the rate of twenty-five kopeks in the

---

* The debtors' prison—*Tr.*

ruble, to offer a little more to those who protest, and in the last resort to pay the full amount. Bolshov says:

"That's right, it won't do any harm to bargain with them: if they won't take twenty-five they'll take fifty, if they won't take fifty they'll take seventy with both hands. Even that will leave us a profit. You can say what you like, but I have a daughter waiting to get married—ready to sign the marriage contract and get out of the house, so to speak. And it's high time I retired: I'd lie around and rest and send all business to the devil."

As you see, Bolshov's decision is prompted by good motives and reveals no sign of a vicious nature; he wants to squeeze as much as he can out of his creditors because he has a daughter who is waiting to get married and he himself wants to retire. . . . What is there particularly revolting about that? Why should Bolshov feel any qualms of conscience? He regards his new plan as one of those pieces of deception of which he has seen so many in the course of his life, and which to him are all part of the day's work. Only one thing disturbed him a little, namely, that he might not carry off the deal successfully. He is a little bit afraid, and therefore wants to strike a bargain with his creditors by offering them twenty-five kopeks in the ruble. But Podkhalyuzin says to him: "In my opinion, Samson Silich, rather than pay twenty-five kopeks it would be better to pay nothing at all." To this Bolshov readily agrees. "I think you are right," he says. "Courage *won't astonish anybody*; the best thing is to bring the deal off quietly. *Then let the Lord judge after the Second Advent.* But it's going to cause a lot of trouble." But not a word, not a hint about the immorality of the plot against his creditors. He only recalls the "judgment of the Lord," but even that is only by the way, for form's sake: the "Second Advent" is of no more significance here than that which Bolshov attaches to "the mercy of God" in his well-known statement: "Bonaparte may be all right, but we place our trust mostly in the mercy of God, *but that is not the point now*." Precisely—that is not the point now: Bolshov is not concerned about the judgment after the Second Advent (who knows when that will be?), but about the trouble ahead in connection with the deal he has on hand. The trouble which he anticipates disturbs him very much: by his very nature he shrinks from trouble. He does not mind cheating somebody at one stroke, even if he does it in the most shameless manner; but he is unable to think, to scheme, to prepare for a fraudulent deal a long time ahead, *to set the wheels going,* to display chronic shamelessness—not because he is, in general, incapable of displaying shamelessness and craftiness, he has more than enough of the one and the other—but simply because he is unable to think about anything seriously. He himself admits this, and in a moment of vexation he even says to Rispolozhensky: "That's the whole trouble, brother. We merchants are such fools, we don't understand anything, and this just suits leeches like you." We may even say that all Bolshov's willfulness springs from the fact that he is unaccustomed to independent and conscious activity, for which, however, his undoubted natural intelligence inclines him. We cannot see from the comedy how Bolshov grew and was brought up, what influenced him in his youth; but it is clear to us that he was brought up under influences that did not favour healthy, independent development. His actions constantly reveal the absence of *a mind of his own;* it is evident that he is not accustomed rationally to rouse himself to activity and to give an account to himself of his actions. His present situation, however, and his whole nature, which oppression has not completely broken and which has preserved the spirit of contradiction, calls for independent action, and this finds expression in stubbornness and willfulness. It is well known that stubbornness is a sign of weak character; similarly, tyranny is sure proof of inner impotence and of a slavish mind. The tyrant is always trying to *prove* that nobody is his master and that he can do exactly as he pleases. A really independent man of strong spirit never wants to prove this: he brings the strength of his character into play only where it is needed; he does not waste it in experiments on absurd undertakings. Bolshov delights in asserting that he can do as he pleases and that nobody is his master; but this only shows that he himself is not quite sure of this. ... It is evident that his personality which, perhaps, is not weak by nature, had been severely oppressed at one time and he has therefore lost a large part of his natural spiritual strength. That is why, on becoming his own master, he was unable to put restraint upon himself. He seems to be a terrible tyrant, but that is only because he meets with no opposition from any side; he could not withstand opposition. ... Ostrovsky brings

this feature out very clearly in another of his comedies and so
we shall return to it again later on. But it is also to be observed
in Bolshov who, even when deciding to take such a step as declar-
ing a fraudulent bankruptcy, not only tries to avoid all the trouble
this step involves, but simply does not know what he is doing;
he surrenders his gains and even his will in this deal and leaves
everything to fate.... Podkhalyuzin and Rispolozhensky, working hand in glove, arrange things so that instead of coming to
an arrangement with his creditors Bolshov decides to declare himself a bankrupt. For the sake of appearances, however, Podkhalyuzin tries to dissuade him from this step. What does Bolshov
say in reply? Flaring up he says: "What, pay money! Where
d'you get that idea from? *I'd rather burn everything than pay*
them a kopek. Take the goods away! Sell all the bills! *Let any-*
body who wants to grab the stuff! I won't pay a kopek!" Podkhalyuzin says regretfully that "ours was a splendid business,
but now everything will go to rack and ruin." But Bolshov shouts:
"What's that got to do with you? It wasn't your business....
You do your best—I'll not forget you." What made him flare
up like that? One would think it was the outburst of a strong
nature, that his is an indomitable will.... But in the first place,
what rouses in him such determination that acts to his own disadvantage; and why does his will express itself only in bawling
at Podkhalyuzin and not in active participation in the arrangement of this deal? Secondly, Bolshov himself soon surrenders
his will. When Podkhalyuzin explains to him that "there may
be trouble," that he may be deprived of his estate, and that legal
proceedings may be taken against him, Bolshov answers: "There's
nothing to be done about it, brother. Evidently it is God's will.
You can't go against that." To this Podkhalyuzin replies: "You
are right, Samson Silich." But actually it is not "right," it is
very absurd. Bolshov not only wants to shirk all moral responsibility, he even tries not to think about what he is undertaking.
The decision he took became deeply embedded in his mind, but
somehow it failed to link up with anything in his thoughts and
ideas and it remains alien and dead to him. He even tries to make
out that it was not his decision but "such is the will of God. You
can't go against that." This feature is very common in our society,
and Ostrovsky brings it out with great subtlety and truth. It

alone tells us a great deal and depicts Bolshov's character better than it could have been depicted in a number of lengthy monologues. This beclouded reasoning and abhorrence of thinking, this weakness of will when any risky step has to be taken—all of which gives rise to that stupid and desperate fatalism and willfulness which is even an obstacle to personal gain—stand out in strong relief in Bolshov's character and very easily explain why he transferred his estate to Podkhalyuzin, his head shop assistant and son-in-law—an act which some critics were prone to regard as an inexplicable burst of generosity and an imitation of King Lear. Indeed, there is a superficial resemblance between Bolshov's action and that of Lear, but this is only to the degree that a comedy may resemble a tragedy. Lear also seems to us to be a victim of unnatural development; his action—which is prompted by the proud consciousness that he is great *in himself* and not because of the power he wields—is also a punishment for his arrogant despotism. But if we take it into our heads to compare Lear with Bolshov we shall find that one of them is from head to foot an English king, while the other is a Russian merchant; in one everything is grand and luxurious, in the other everything is feeble and petty, all calculated in small change. Lear is indeed a strong character, and the universal obsequiousness that is displayed towards him merely gives his character a one-sided development, makes it capable not of great deeds of love for the common weal, but solely of satisfying his own personal whims. This is quite intelligible in a man who is accustomed to regard himself as the fount of all joy and sorrow, the beginning and the end of all life in his kingdom. Owing to his superficially wide field of action and the ease with which all his wishes are executed, his spiritual strength finds no expression. But now his self-admiration exceeds all the bounds of common sense; he ascribes all the luxury and respect he enjoyed as king to his own personality and he decides to renounce his power, convinced that his people will continue to stand in fear and trembling before him even when he was no longer their king. This insane conviction induces him to transfer his kingdom to his daughters and, as a consequence, he passes from his barbarously senseless position to that of an ordinary mortal to experience all the suffering that accompanies human existence. It is here, in the struggle that follows, that the best sides of his character are revealed; here we see that he is capable of generosity, tenderness, sympathy for the unhappy, and of the most humane justice. The strength of his character is revealed not only in the imprecations he hurls at his daughters, but also in his realization of the wrong he had done Cordelia, in the regret he expresses for his former arrogance, and in the repentance he feels for having thought so little about the unfortunate poor and for having loved true honesty so little. It is this that makes Lear so profoundly significant. On looking at him we at first feel hatred for this wanton tyrant, but as we watch the drama unfold we become more and more reconciled to him as a man, and we end with being filled with indignation and burning anger *not against him,* but *for his sake* and for the sake of the whole world; we feel anger against the savage inhuman conditions which can make even men like Lear such wanton tyrants. We do not know what impression *King Lear* makes upon others; at all events, this is the impression it always makes upon us.

One critic asserted that Ostrovsky also wanted to raise his Bolshov to a similar height of tragedy and for this purpose took Samson Silich out of the debtors' prison in the fourth act and made him beg his daughter and son-in-law to pay his creditors twenty-five kopeks in the ruble for him. This argument reveals a complete failure to understand not only Shakespeare and Ostrovsky, but the moral aspect of dramatic situations in general. In our opinion, Bolshov is not in the least raised in the eyes of the reader, and does not in the least lose his comical character in the last act. There is a tragic element in the last scenes, but it is a purely superficial element, as it is in the case, for example, of the appearance of the gendarme in the *Inspector General....* But do we find here that inner tragedy that can compel one to sympathize with Bolshov and reconcile one with his personality? Where are the traces of that inner struggle that would clean and brighten Bolshov's slime-covered tyrannical nature? There are no such traces, and the comedy was not written with the object of indicating them; we regard the last act merely as the final brilliant stroke which put the finishing touches to Bolshov's character— the natural development of which was checked by the crushing hostile environment, and which remained impotent and insignificant under circumstances favourable for wide and independent activities as well as in the distress which again oppressed it. In our opinion Bolshov does not cease to be comical even in the last act: not a single ray of light penetrates his dark soul after the change in his fortune which he had brought upon himself. He does not in the least realize how basely he has acted, he is not tortured by internal shame; he is tortured only by superficial shame: his creditors drag him to court, street urchins point the finger of scorn at him.

"To think of me being in the ditch!" he says. "Think of me being led through the streets under escort! Why, they know me in this town for forty years, for forty years everybody bowed low to me, and now the street urchins point the finger of scorn at me!"

This is what is uppermost in his mind, and next to it comes the thought of the Shrine of the Iberian Mother, but even that is only a fleeting thought: it is soon driven out by the fear that he might land in Siberia. These are his words:

"And we shall have to pass the Shrine: how will I be able to look at the Holy Mother? You know, Lazar: Judas also sold Christ for money as we sell our consciences for money.... *And how was he punished for it?... My crime, they'll say, was premeditated, with malice aforethought.... They'll send me to Siberia. Good Lord! If you won't give me the money for my sake give it to me for Christ's sake (weeps)."*

What a pity it is that *Our Own Folks* is not produced on the stage! A skilful actor could bring out with striking power the comical nature of this self-willed man who lumps together the Iberian Mother, Judas, banishment to Siberia and appeals for the sake of Christ.... The comical nature of this tirade is enhanced by the preceding and subsequent dialogues in which Podkha-lyuzin, with amiable nonchalance refuses to pay more than ten kopeks in the ruble for Bolshov, and Bolshov now rebukes him for his ingratitude, now threatens to have him sent to Siberia, reminding him that they will both end up in the same way, now asks him and his daughter whether they have a spark of Christianity in them, now curses himself for having made a fool of himself and quotes the proverb: "The servant punishes herself if she does not reap well," and, at last, turning to his daughter he says to her in a mocking tone:

"Well, now you will be rich. You will live like a lady. You will go to parties and balls—and please the devil! But don't forget, Olympiada Samsonovna, that there are cells with iron bars where unfortunate prisoners sit.... Don't forget us unfortunate prisoners."

In our opinion, this scene very closely resembles the scene in the *Inspector General* where the City Governor rails at the merchants for having forgotten how he had helped them in their fraudulent deals. The only difference is that in Ostrovsky's play the comical features are somewhat more subtle and, moreover, it must be admitted that the inherent comicalness of Bolshov's personality is obscured somewhat in the last act by the unfortunate situation in which he finds himself, as a consequence of which the penetrating critics ascribe to Ostrovsky ideas and aims which in all probability he had never even dreamed of. A critic's moral conceptions must indeed be fine if he believes that the author depicted Bolshov in the last act in the way he did in order to win the spectators' *sympathy* for him.... In our opinion, Bolshov looks more banal and insignificant at the end of the play than throughout the whole of the preceding action. We see that even misfortune and imprisonment have done nothing to bring him to his senses, that they have not awakened human sentiments in him; and we rightly conclude that evidently they have expired within him and will sleep the sleep of the dead forever. Even now he says that the creditors should be given twenty-five kopeks in the ruble—it is a lot, but what can one do when they will not take less.

"They'll keep me in the ditch for about eighteen months, march me through the streets under escort every week and, for all you know, transfer me to a regular prison, and then I'll be glad to pay fifty kopeks."

Does not this reveal the comical impotence of this character, which dares not take a bold step and is unable to stand a prolonged struggle? Does it not reveal the moral insignificance of this man who throughout the whole play never once betrays a sense of right and duty? More than that: in his coarse heart even the sentiments of the father and husband are deadened; we see this in the first acts of the play, and we see it in the last. His wife's grief does not touch him in the least, and the outrageous rudeness of his daughter does not offend his feelings as a father. Olympiada Samsonovna says to him: "I lived with you for twenty

years, Dad, and never saw the light of day. Do you expect me
to give you back your money and walk about in cotton frocks
again?" Bolshov can think of nothing better to say in answer to
this than to cast in the teeth of his daughter and son-in-law the
involuntary gift he made them when he transferred his estate
to them: "I am not asking you for charity, I am asking for what
is my own," he says. Is not this relation between father and
daughter comical? And the moral which Bolshov draws for himself from the whole business is the highest pinnacle he could rise
to in his moral development: "Don't chase after more, be content with what you have! If you chase after more, you will lose
what you already have!" What a degree of moral virtue these
words indicate! A man who has suffered as a result of his own
fraudulent bankruptcy can find no other moral lesson in these
circumstances than that contained in the maxim: "Don't chase
after more for you may lose what you have!" And a moment later he adds to it his regret that he had failed to bring
off his deal and quotes the proverb: "The servant punishes herself
if she does not reap well." How strongly this expresses the absolute thoughtlessness and moral degradation of this character,
which, judging by the fear he drove into the hearts of everybody
around him, may have seemed a strong one in the beginning of
the play!... And yet, critics were found who decided that the
last act of *Our Own Folks* ought to rouse the spectators' sympathy for Bolshov!*

---

* We shall take the liberty of quoting another passage from the
curious article by Mr. N. P. Nekrasov of Moscow which was published in
the *last* issue of *Atenei*, and which partly explains why this learned journal was so short-lived. "The question arises, why should Bolshov appear
on the stage again after he has been imprisoned for fraud? Did the author wish to rouse sympathy for him by showing how really humiliating it
is for a merchant to be in the ditch? But everybody has a perfect right
to ask: *why does Bolshov deserve sympathy?* What is the purpose of the
whole of the *tearful* fourth scene in the last act? Probably to say to the
esteemed public: 'You see how unwise it is for a merchant to cheat; in
the end he only cheats himself.' What a beautiful idea, what a lofty moral
principle!..."

Obviously, the critic is not much superior to Samson Silich in the
understanding of moral principles and consequently took Bolshov's words
that we quoted above: "Don't chase after more, you may lose what you
have," as the main idea of the play. Confusing thus Bolshov's ideas with
the ideas of the author of the play, the critic begins to admonish Os-

But what lesson does this personage in the comedy teach us? Can his significance be limited to the moral: "See what bad men there are in the world?" No. That would be too little for the principal character in a serious comedy, too little for the talent of an author of Ostrovsky's calibre. The moral significance of the impression one obtains from a careful examination of Bolshov's character is far more profound. We have already had occasion to observe that one of the distinguishing features of Ostrovsky's talent is his ability to delve deep down into a man's soul and note not only his line of thought and conduct, but also the very process of his thinking, the very birth of his desires. This same ability is revealed in the delineation of Bolshov's character; the author's psychological observations resulted in an extremely humane view of what apparently were the most sordid sides of life, and in a profound respect for the moral dignity of human nature, a respect which he communicates to his readers. In Bolshov, that *fraudulent* bankrupt, we see nothing vicious or monstrous, nothing that would justify our regarding him as a monster. The author takes us away from the official, legal point of view and shows us the substance of the act that is committed, causes the dishonest scheme to take shape and grow before our eyes. And what do we see in the unfolding of this scheme, which is so horrifying from the legal point of view? Not a shadow of diabolical malice, not a sign of Jesuitical cunning! Everything is so simple,

---

trovsky in the following way: "Does the author realize how dangerous it is to subordinate art to reality? Is he aware how degraded the moral aspect of his play is? Can a truly artistic production be based on the maxim: 'Don't cheat so that ye shall not be cheated,' or 'Don't dig a pit for others, you might fall into it yourself,' or to keep nearer to our comedy: 'Don't cheat because cheating does not always pay.' How is the moral dignity of man redeemed here? Does it at least ridicule cheating as the base side of human nature? No.... The comedy does not tell us how cheating (no matter what shape it may assume) is abhorrent to man's moral nature, it merely tells us that, notwithstanding the defects in our laws governing debts, merchants are sometimes caught in the traps they lay for others and for this are put into prison and then banished to Siberia. Yes, it cannot be denied that such things happen. But why repeat them on the stage?..." And immediately after this naive question the critic triumphantly exclaims: "This is how Mr. Ostrovsky adjusted the action he chose to the idea of his play!..."

Now that *Atenei* has ceased publication we think that Mr. "N. P. Nekrasov of Moscow" might successfully write for Mr. Balashevich's *Oryel*.[77]—N. D.

good-natured and absurd: Samson Silich is not a child begotten of hell, but simply a crude animal, all the sympathetic sides of whose nature were stifled in his youth, and who developed no moral concepts. His character lacks what is called individual initiative, or free self-prompting to activity; he just browses through life without calculating or speculating much. He becomes a tyrant because he meets not with firm opposition, but with constant submission from those around him; he cheats and oppresses others because he feels only that it is pleasant to *himself*, but is incapable of feeling how hard it is for *them;* he dares to declare himself bankrupt because he has no conception whatever of the social significance of such an act. To him even the law is not the representative of supreme truth, but only an external obstacle, a boulder which should be removed from the road. His conscience lies not in his inner voice, but in the jeers of passers-by, in his glance at the Iberian Mother, in his fear of banishment to Siberia. In short, you clearly see that Bolshov's criminal, outrageous conduct is due precisely to the fact that the human is not developed in him. He is abhorrent to us precisely because he is almost completely destitute of human elements, and at the same time he is vulgar and comical because even the rudiments of humanity that were in his nature were warped. But the very fact that he is abhorrent and vulgar owing to his undeveloped character points to the necessity of proper and free development and rehabilitates for us the dignity of human nature, convinces us that baseness and crime are not inherent in human nature and cannot be the result of natural development.

The achievement of this result is greatly facilitated by the entire development of the action of the play and by all the persons grouped around Bolshov. There are no particularly intricate machinations in any part of the play, no artificial development of the action to please scholastic theories to the detriment of the real simplicity and lifelikeness of the characters. All the personages act conscientiously according to their lights, and not one of them sinks to the tone of the hero in melodrama. Here a shameful goal is not achieved by means of the highest mental abilities and most noble of spiritual forces in their highest development; on the contrary, the entire play clearly shows that it is the lack of this development that leads people to such abominations. All the personages are obviously inbued with one human striving, namely, to free themselves from the tyrant's yoke under which all grew up and lived. On the surface, Bolshov freed himself from this yoke, but the traces of his upbringing which restrict his thoughts and will remain with him all his life and convert him into a wanton despot. And so contagious is the absurd way of life in the "realm of darkness" that every individual, however oppressed he may be, tries to oppress others the moment he has freed himself ever so little from another's yoke. These savage relationships are very skilfully traced throughout the whole of Ostrovsky's comedy; that is why we say that in it we see a whole hierarchy of tyrants. Indeed, Bolshov holds unchallenged sway over all of them; Podkhalyuzin is afraid of his employer, but he already bullies Fominishna and thumps Tishka; Agrafena Kondratyevna, a simplehearted and rather stupid woman, fears her husband like the very devil, but she too deals rather vigorously with Tishka and also bullies her daughter, and if she had the power she would certainly keep a tight hand over her. Look how she lets herself go in the second scene of the first act. "Do you think I have no power to command you!" she shouts at her daughter. "Tell me, you hussy, why is there such an envious look in your eyes? Do you want to be smarter than your mother? Goodness gracious, what next? If you're not careful I'll send you to the kitchen to wash, the dishes! I'll sew a sack cloth sarafan and make you wear it. Yes I will, and in a trice too!"

Lipochka makes a stinging retort, but Agrafena Kondratyevna says: "Yield to your mother! If you say another word I'll sew your tongue to your heel!" But Lipochka finds spiritual strength in the consciousness that she is *educated*, and she therefore pays little heed to her mother; in her quarrels with her she is always the victor: she taunts her with being ill-bred; she bursts into tears and her mother becomes alarmed and begins to pacify her offended daughter. Lipochka clearly betrays a disposition towards the crudest and most outrageous despotism. She says to her mother: "I can see that I am more educated than others. What should I do, encourage your foolishness? Certainly not!" And when she becomes engaged to Podkhalyuzin she says to him: "The old folk have had their good time, *it's our turn now....*" Tishka is the only one who so far reveals no striving to dominate; on the contrary, he is the butt of all the tyrannical inclinations of the whole house. "In our house," he complains, "if it's not one then it's the other, if it's not the master then it's the mistress who thumps me. And then there's that shop assistant Lazar, and Fominishna, and ... every swab that comes along orders me about." The consequence of this ordering about and the constant thumpings are already to be seen in Tishka: he has already learned to cheat and steal. And when he has stolen enough money he, too, of course, will begin to tyrannize as wantonly and as cruelly as he was tyrannized. Ostrovsky very skilfully forecasts his career in the few words that Tishka utters in the scene where he finds himself alone and counts the money.

"Fifty kopeks silver—Lazar gave me that (for bringing him some vodka on the quiet); ten kopeks Agrafena Kondratyevna gave me when I fell from the belfry the other day; a quarter that I won playing heads and tails, and a ruble the master left on the counter the day before yesterday...."

Such are Tishka's sources of gain: running for vodka, falling from the belfry, gambling and stealing. What moral sense can he develop when leading a life like this? How can he sympathize with the sufferings of others if he is consoled with ten kopek pieces when he falls from the belfry? Obviously, in time he will grow up to be a Podkhalyuzin.... The very soil of this "realm of darkness" is such that no other produce will grow on it!

But what is Podkhalyuzin himself? He is a shrewd, deliberate rascal with developed ideas! Does he contradict the general impression the comedy creates which forces us to admit that all the crimes that are committed in that milieu are due to a beclouded understanding and the under-development of the human side of people's characters? Not in the least. Podkhalyuzin definitely convinces us that this impression is correct. We see that he is still tolerable precisely to the degree that he has been touched by the breath of humane ideas. He does not recklessly plunge into rascality, he carefully plans his undertakings. We see that a feeling of revulsion rises in him against cheating in its naked form; he tries to cover up his rascality by means of

various sophistries and looks for some moral justification for
it in order to preserve some semblance of legal honesty in the
very act of cheating. Some things he never stops to think about,
as for example, giving the customers at the shop short measure and cheating them in other ways—there he acts quite coolly, without any qualms of conscience. But when an extraordinary occasion arose, an opportunity to make a big haul out
of his master's estate, he begins to reflect and tries to justify
himself.

"You must have a conscience, they say," he argues with himself. "Yes,
of course *you must have a conscience, but what is a conscience?* Everybody has a conscience when dealing with an honest man; *but when a man
cheats others, how can you have a conscience towards him?* Samson Silich
is one of the richest merchants in town, and now he has started all this
business, just as a pastime, as you might say. But I am a poor man! If
I try to make a little extra out of this business there can be nothing
sinful about it *because he himself is dishonest, he goes against the law.*
Why should I pity him? Since the opportunity has come, why should I
miss it? *He follows his line, I shall follow mine.* I would do much more
to him, but there's no opportunity for that!"

You see, therefore, that Podkhalyuzin is not a monster either;
he too has a conscience, but he has his own view about what a
conscience is. He, like all the rest, is misled by the state of war
that reigns throughout the "realm of darkness"; he regards his
fraud not as a fraud, but as a shrewd deal, perfectly fair in
itself, although unlawful from the legal point of view. He dislikes downright dishonesty: he promised the matchmaker two thousand rubles and gives her only a hundred, but that was on the
grounds that she did not deserve any more. He pays Rispolozhensky in dribs and drabs, and only after he has paid him several
hundred rubles does he refuse to pay any more on the grounds
that he "ought to know when to stop." He does not object to
paying Bolshov's creditors, but he thinks that twenty-five kopeks
in the ruble is too much. In this case he even has an ostensible
justification for his conduct: he remembers what Bolshov himself
told him and quotes his words against him. In betrothing his
daughter to Podkhalyuzin, Samson Silich conducts the following
dialogue with his future son-in-law:

B o l s h o v: It's my money, I earned it myself ... I can give it to
whomever I like.... But what is there to talk about? Don't look a gift

horse in the mouth! Take everything, only feed me and the old lady, and pay the creditors at ten in the ruble.

Podkhalyuzin: It's not worth talking about, Dad. Don't I understand? We're our own folks—we can settle it among ourselves.

Bolshov: Take everything I tell you, and that's all there is to it! Nobody can tell me what to do! Only pay the creditors. Will you pay?

Podkhalyuzin: Why, of course, Dad, the very first thing.

Bolshov: Only take care—don't pay them too much. *You may be fool enough to give them everything.*

Podkhalyuzin: Don't worry, Dad, we'll settle it It's our own folks we're dealing with, isn't it?

Bolshov: That's right. *But don't give them more than ten in the ruble. It's quite enough for them.*

Podkhalyuzin understood this argument perfectly well and politely reminds Bolshov of it when the latter comes to him from the debtors' prison. He thinks that the creditors' claim for twenty-five kopeks in the ruble is unfair; he thinks that they have "become too perky; if they're not careful they'll get only eight in the ruble, spread over five years!" Taken up with this idea he treats his father-in-law hospitably, joins him in reviling the creditors and expressing the hope that they could "get rid of them somehow," because "God is merciful"; but he refuses to pay what the creditors demand because they are "demanding an impossible price." From his own point of view he is not acting either dishonestly or cruelly, he is merely sensible and firm. He even displays a considerable degree of generosity in agreeing to pay on Bolshov's behalf fifteen kopeks in the ruble instead of ten, and even decides to go to the creditors himself to persuade them to accept the offer. Obviously, he is not altogether destitute of compassion and of some glimmerings of conscience, but he wants to make as much as possible out of the deal and hopes to conclude it with the utmost gain for himself. It is here that the petty cheat, the direct product of the despotic yoke which he has borne since childhood, is most strikingly revealed in Podkhalyuzin. He lacks the determination of the downright scoundrel to refuse to pay anything and leave Bolshov's business entirely to its fate in order to undertake new ventures, with new worries and risks; he lacks also the shrewd calculation which distinguishes rascals who operate on a large scale and which induces them to accept even the minimum gain out of every speculation in order to get it off their hands. A shrewd swindler, operating on a large scale, and deciding to embark upon a transaction like fraudulent bankruptcy, would not miss an opportunity to settle the deal by a payment of twenty-five kopeks in the ruble; he would finish the affair at once with this profitable deal and be satisfied. And why shouldn't he be satisfied after obtaining gratis three-fourths of another's property? Everybody would be satisfied with such a result except our Russian home-grown swindler. A real swindler, one who had made swindling his profession, does not haggle over and try to make a fortune out of every fraudulent deal, he does not try to make another kopek out of an affair from which he has already gained rubles; he knows that another deal lies in the offing after this one, and after that a third, and so forth, and that is why he hastens to finish with one deal in order, having made as much out of it as he could, to take up the next. But our petty cheat, who was born and brought up under the senseless yoke of tyranny, behaves quite differently. He lacks the expansiveness that everybody, for some reason, admires so much in the Russian; on the other hand he betrays a great deal of fatuous miserliness. Some people may discern the expansiveness of the Russian character in Podkhalyuzin's conduct too: "You see the kind of man he is," they may say. "Once he decides to take another man's property he is determined to take as much as possible, not three-fourths, but nine-tenths...." But actually, it is precisely here that Podkhalyuzin betrays a lack of enterprise and self-confidence. He looks upon his swindle as a windfall which, perhaps, may never come to him again. That is why he is reluctant to part with his affair and waits to see whether it is possible to squeeze a little more out of it: he did not take risks for nothing! He is so unaccustomed to take risks and they worry him so much that he is afraid even to think of undertaking another of the same kind.... All he is concerned about is getting well settled down, after which he will go in for petty cheating, as he promises to do in his concluding address to the audience in the first edition of the comedy: "And we'll open a little shop! I'll be glad of your custom. You can send a little child, you may be sure we'll not cheat him even out of a kopek."[78] This means that he will be satisfied with the practice that he had formerly *explained* to Bolshov's assistants.... Unless, of course, another *opportunity occurs* where something will lie around unguarded; then he will grab as much as he can.

Thus, even Podkhalyuzin is not a monster, is not the quintessence of abomination. He is most disgusting in the scene where, with tears in his eyes, he assures Bolshov of his devotion, and so forth. But here he is trying to ingratiate himself with Samson Silich not so much out of greed as to wheedle a promise out of him to give him the hand of his daughter whom, it must be observed, Podkhalyuzin loves dearly and sincerely.... He clearly proves this by the way he treats her in the fourth act, that is to say, when she is already his wife.... Is it only craftiness of this kind that we excuse in the most moral of heroes of the most romantic novels when resorted to for the sake of love?

There is no need to dilate on the fact that Lipochka does not spoil the general impression of the play, in spite of her moral depravity. Some people are of the opinion that the way she treats her mother and the scene with her father in the last act overstep the bounds of the comical and are extremely disgusting. We totally disagree with this because we cannot regard the relationships in a family like that of Bolshov's as sacred. Lipochka too bears the impress of the despotism that reigns in the house: it is only this despotism that creates these hard and heartless natures, this cold and repelling attitude towards one's own kith and kin; only such a despotism can explain the complete absence of the concept of morality that we observe in Lipochka. But, with the exception of what has remained in her as a result of the despotism that has oppressed her, she is no worse than the majority of our young ladies not only among the merchant class, but also among the aristocracy. Are there many of them who do not devote their whole lives to mere externals, who do not find solace for their grief in fine dresses, do not seek oblivion in dancing and do not dream of dashing officers? If I have had occasion to converse with three educated young ladies in my life you may be sure that from two of them I certainly heard a repetition of Lipochka's well-known monologue:

"It's altogether different when you are with an officer! They're charming, they're a dream! And their moustaches, their epaulettes, their uniforms! They even have spurs with bells on them!... How can you compare a military man with a civilian? You can see at once that a military man is smart, lithe and everything. But a civilian! He looks as if he has no life in him...."

How can one blame young ladies who deliver monologues of this kind for anything? Is it not clear that everything Lipochka does, she does because of her total lack of moral and mental development and not because of malice or natural brutality? What is there in the personality of this unfortunate girl that should rouse our ire?

What, in general, should rouse our ire in *Our Own Folks*? Not the people, and not their particular actions, but the deplorable senselessness that weighs down upon all their lives. As we have seen, the people are presented to us in the comedy in their human and not in the legal aspect, and for this reason the impression which even their crimes produce upon us is softened. Officially we see here a fraudulent bankrupt, a still more fraudulent shop assistant who robs his employer, and a malicious daughter who coldheartedly sends her father to prison—and we brand all these persons as scoundrels and monsters. But the author of the comedy leads us into the domestic life of these people and reveals their souls to us, conveys to us their logic, their views of things, and in spite of ourselves we become convinced that they are neither villains nor monsters, but all very ordinary people, like all other people, and that the crimes which astonish us are not due to their exceptional characters which are naturally inclined to villainy, but merely to the inevitable result of the environment in which the people we accuse were born and now live. This conviction awakens in us respect for human nature and for human personality in general, laughter and scorn for the warped characters who act in the comedy and who, from the official aspect, rouse our horror and disgust, and lastly, profound, relentless hatred of those influences which retard and distort so much the normal development of personality. This brings us straight to the question: what are those influences, and how do they operate? The comedy tells us clearly that all the pernicious influences are, in this case, the savage, lawless tyranny of some over others. The way these influences operate is very clearly demonstrated in the comedy. We have seen that Bolshov is by no means a strong character, that he is incapable of waging a

prolonged struggle and, in general, dislikes exertion of any kind;
we have also seen that Podkhalyuzin is a shrewd fellow, not in
the least devoted to his employer; we have seen that none of
the people in the family are kindly disposed towards Samson
Silich except, perhaps, his wife, who is a stupid old woman and
an utter nonentity. What, then, prevents them from forming an
open opposition to Bolshov's tyranny? Is it the fact that they
are materially dependent upon him; that their welfare is bound
up with his? But if that is the case, why does not Podkhalyuzin,
who is working in his employer's interests, dissuade him from
taking the dangerous step which he is planning because of his
ignorance, "just like that, as a pastime?" Is it because Podkhalyuzin, of course, hopes to make something for himself out of
this deal? Yes—but it is precisely here that the absurd relationships that are depicted in *Our Own Folks* reveal themselves in
all their horrid nakedness. You see, it is not a matter of the
personality of the tyrant who oppresses his family and all those
around him. In himself he is impotent and a nonentity; he can
be cheated, pushed out of the way, and even thrown into the
debtors' prison.... The matter is that tyranny does not disappear with his removal. Its action is contagious; its germs infect
even the victims of this tyranny. Lawless, it saps confidence in
law; black and false at its very root, it extinguishes every ray
of truth; senseless and capricious, it kills all common sense and
all capacity for rational and useful activity; rude and oppressive, it destroys all love and trust; it even destroys trust in oneself and weens one from honest and overt activity. It is this that
makes it dangerous to society! It would not be difficult to destroy
the tyrant if honest people energetically set out to do so; but the
trouble is that, under the influence of tyranny, even the most
honest people become petty and wear themselves out in slavish
inactivity, and the work of society is performed only by people,
the human side of whose characters is least developed. These
people's conceptions are utterly corrupted by the influence of
tyranny and, as a consequence, their activities are also petty,
private and crudely egoistic. Their aim is not to destroy the tyranny from which they suffer so much, but to overthrow the
tyrant somehow and step into his shoes. And so Bolshov lands in
the debtors' prison and his place is taken by Podkhalyuzin,

who prospers by working to the same rules that Bolshov adhered to.*

Such are the general conclusions that we draw from the comedy *Our Own Folks—We'll Settle It Among Ourselves.* We have dealt with this comedy at such exceptionally great length for many reasons. Firstly, nothing serious had been said about it up to now; secondly, the brief comments that were made about it in passing always revealed a rather strange conception of the meaning of the play; thirdly, the comedy in itself is not one of the most striking and consistent of Ostrovsky's works; fourthly, not having been produced on the stage, it is less known to the public than his other plays.... Furthermore, it called for a more detailed examination also because it depicts the mobile, roguish characters which have developed under the yoke of tyranny. Such are all the personages in this play, except Agrafena Kondratyevna. They willingly submitted to tyranny, their minds became warped, they themselves became accomplices in the abominable deeds that were engendered by the despotic yoke. To analyze this moral corruption is a much more complex and difficult task than to point to the mere collapse of a man's inner strength under the weight of external oppression. And it is precisely characters of the latter category, crushed, deadened, robbed of all energy and mobility, that we mostly meet with in Os-

---

* Incidentally, in the new edition of Ostrovsky's plays, even Podkhalyuzin does not prosper. At the end of the play he is taken away by a policeman and he is faced with the prospect of being sent to Siberia. We think that this addendum is totally superfluous. The author was, of course, prompted to make it not by his convictions, but by his desire to please certain exceedingly strict Puritans who demanded that vice should be punished without fail. But we have seen that what matters here is not persons, and not the external fact, but life itself, the very ties that hold this life together. Furthermore, we know that even if Podkhalyuzin can be punished, it can only be for his error in not having made a clean job of his fraudulent deal. Besides, he still has one recourse open to him: when the policeman comes he offers him a drink and starts a conversation in the hope of coming to some arrangement with him. But the policeman is not to be tempted and he takes Podkhalyuzin away. We know, however, that Podkhalyuzin's fate does not depend upon the policeman, and that not everybody in the realm of darkness is so incorruptible as this extraordinary police officer.... In fact, bearing in mind the relationships that exist in the society in which Podkhalyuzin operates, we are almost certain when the curtain drops that he will find an easy means of wriggling out of the situation and of justifying himself.—*N.D.*

trovsky's subsequent comedies, to which we must now turn. In reviewing the later comedies we shall try to trace the deadening influence of tyranny more briefly and devote our attention mainly to one aspect of it, namely, the slavish position of our women in the family. Then, in connection with the same question of tyranny, and even in direct dependence upon it, we shall investigate the significance of those forms of education which disturb the inhabitants of our "realm of darkness" so much; and lastly, we shall examine the means which many of the heroes in this realm employ to consolidate their material well-being. But the examination of all these questions, and the demonstration of their direct connection with tyranny—as it is revealed in Ostrovsky's comedies—must serve as the subject of another essay.

And now, in concluding our review of *Our Own Folks*, we can only ask our readers: will they deny that Ostrovsky's images, which we have analyzed in such detail, are true to life and presented with artistic skill? And if these personages, and the life they lead, are true to life, do not our readers think that the aspects of Russian life which Ostrovsky depicts for us are worthy of the artist's attention? Will they venture to assert that the reality that he depicts is only of minor and petty significance and can produce no important results for a person who thinks?... The answers to these questions may show whether we have achieved our object in analyzing the facts presented to us in Ostrovsky's comedies.... As far as we are concerned, we have no desire to thrust any opinion upon anyone, we even refrain from expressing either admiration or censure of Ostrovsky's works. We only study the phenomena he depicts and explain what significance they have for us. Our readers will decide for themselves, in conformity with their own observations of life and with their own conceptions of law, morality and the requirements of human nature, whether our judgment is correct, and also what significance lies in the vital facts we have taken from Ostrovsky's comedies.

III

All is drear and desolate around. . . .
Of leaf not a rustle, of brook not a sound.
In vain to the prophet for some shade doth he pray,
There is nothing around but scorching sand.
A tufted kite o'er the deserted land
Plucks and tears at its unfortunate prey.

Lermontov

In reviewing Ostrovsky's comedy *Our Own Folks—We'll Settle It Among Ourselves,* we drew the readers' attention to certain features of Russian life, mainly the life of the merchant class, which are reflected in that comedy. We expressed the opinion that the basis of Ostrovsky's humour lies in depicting the senseless influence that *tyranny*, in the broad sense of the term, exercises upon domestic and social life. The behaviour of Samson Silich Bolshov towards all those around him shows us that this tyranny is in itself impotent and senile, that it possesses no moral strength; but its influence is frightful because, being in itself senseless and unjust, it distorts the common sense and conception of justice of all those who come in contact with it. That comedy shows us also that the influence of tyrannical relationships fosters roguery and chicanery, crushes all the humane strivings of even good characters, and develops a narrow, exceptionally selfish and hostile attitude toward one's neighbours. One must have the mind of a genius, the pure heart of an infant and a will of titanic power to dare to enter into a real and effective struggle against this environment, the absurdity of which only helps to develop egoistic sentiments and perfidious strivings in every live and active character.

But even all the virtues we have enumerated are not enough to enable one to emerge from such a struggle unvanquished: in addition, one must have absolutely sound health, an iron constitution and—what is the main thing—an absolutely sound financial position. And yet, owing to the way things are arranged in the "realm of darkness," all its evils, all its falsehood, bring suffering and privation precisely to those who are weak, exhausted, and whose lives are insecure; for the rich and powerful, however, this same falsehood serves to sweeten life. How would it profit them to expose this falsehood, to combat these evils? Can the merchant

Bolshov, for example, be expected to urge his head shop assistant
Podkhalyuzin to ruin him by acting honestly and dissuading his
customers from buying his shoddy goods and by refraining from
overcharging them? It is far more likely, of course, that the head
shop assistant would act in this way of his own accord if he
became conscientious. But he is bound to his employer; he is
well fed and well clothed thanks to his employer's charity, and
he can "get on in the world" if his employer takes a liking to
him. If the employer does not take a liking to him, however,
what is a shop assistant with an unpractical conscience? A mere
nonentity!... And so Podkhalyuzin begins to weigh up the
chances of his position. He is not a genius, not a hero and not
a Titan; he is a very ordinary mortal. And he cannot be expected
to enter a practical protest against his environment, against cen-
tury-old customs, against ideas which had been dinned into his
head as sacred when he was still a small boy and had no ideas
about anything.... Clearly, he must submit to the morality that
reigns in his environment, to proceed along the path which has
been trodden by others.... He cannot be expected to try a new and
unexplored road when he already has a trodden path before him.

On the other hand, being a live and active character, Podkhalyuzin too sets himself certain vital questions and tasks. These
tasks are usually very petty and the questions are not profound,
for his horizon is very limited. He sees before him his tyrannical
employer who does no work, drinks and eats and indulges in his
pleasure, is never bullied by anyone but is constantly bullying
everybody else, and he believes that this repulsive person has
achieved the ideal of happiness, the highest pinnacle that men
can reach. Of what goes on outside the narrow circle of the everyday life that he constantly observes round him he has only a vague
idea and, indeed, he cares little about it, being of the opinion that
this is something entirely different and does not concern men of
his standing.... And having decided that, having drawn for himself such a borderline which he must not overstep, Podkhalyuzin
very naturally tries to adjust himself to the circle in which he
must act, and so he wriggles and crawls. This does not cost him
much effort; he has been accustomed to do this since childhood.
When you get a yardstick across your back, or get your head
punched, you will wriggle and crawl whether you like it or

not. ... After suffering every kind of torment and coming to
believe at last that this is in the regular order of things, he suppresses his own live strivings in the hope that one day his turn
will come. Meanwhile, his moral development takes its course, a
logically inevitable course under these circumstances. Finding that
his personal strivings meet with hostility on every hand, he gradually becomes convinced that his personality, as well as that of
everybody else, must indeed be in conflict with its environment,
and therefore, the more he takes from others the more he will
satisfy himself. This is the starting point for the development of
that constant state of siege in which every inhabitant of the "realm
of darkness" who enters into practical activity with the object
of achieving something inevitably finds himself.... The higher
rules of morality, which are equally binding on all, exist for him
only in the shape of a few excellent maxims and commandments
which are never applied in real life; the sympathetic side of his
character remains undeveloped; the conceptions of social solidarity and the equilibrium between rights and duties which science
has worked out is alien to him. His very ideals (for Podkhalyuzin
has ideals, just as the City Governor in the *Inspector General* has)
are crude, dull, ugly and inhuman. The City Governor dreams
of the time when he will be a General and compel City Gover-
nors to wait for him for five hours. Similarly, Podkhalyuzin
thinks to himself: "Dad has had his fling—it's time he stopped.
It's our turn now." If only the opportunity occurred to achieve
his ideal! He would soon make others be afraid, cringe, lie and
suffer as he was afraid, cringed, lied and suffered until he had
secured for himself the right to tyrannize....

It is painful to trace a career like that; it is painful to see
human nature warped like that. Nothing would seem to be worse
than that savage and unnatural development that characters
like Podkhalyuzin's undergo as a consequence of the tyranny
that oppresses them. But in Ostrovsky's subsequent comedies
we see a new side of this same influence, a side that is scarcely
less gloomy and ugly than the one we pointed to in our previous
essay.

This new side presents itself to us in oppressed and downtrodden characters. We see such characters more or less clearly defined
in nearly all of Ostrovsky's comedies. Even Agrafena Kondratyevna

in *Our Own Folks* belongs to this category, but here she does not play a prominent role. More vivid are the characters in the subsequent comedies, of Mitya in *Poverty Is No Crime*, of Bruskov's children in *Shouldering Another's Troubles*, and of the young women in nearly all of Ostrovsky's comedies. Avdotya Maximovna, Lyubov Tortsova, Dasha and Nadya are all innocent and downtrodden victims of tyranny and this flattening out, *obliteration* of their human personality that is effected by life has a no less depressing effect upon our hearts than the warped human natures of rogues like Podkhalyuzin. In the play he appears in we see some sparks of life, some sparks of independence, momentary flashes of hope. Here, however, there is unperturbed silence, impenetrable gloom; we see before us lifeless beauty in a desert land, and the pervading silence of the grave is disturbed only by the movements of a kite plucking and tearing its prey in the sky.... It gives you an eerie feeling as if you were in a graveyard, or in the house of a Dissenter merchant on the eve of an important holiday!

To reveal the manifestations of the downtrodden and submissive character in various situations and circumstances we shall now review those of Ostrovsky's comedies which depict the life of the merchant class that followed *Our Own Folks*, beginning with *Don't Get Into Another's Sleigh*.

In mentioning this play, however, we deem it necessary to remind the reader of what we said in the first essay concerning the significance of artistic activity in general. *Don't Get Into Another's Sleigh* evoked the most diverse opinions concerning Ostrovsky's *convictions*. Some extolled him for having assimilated the splendid views of the Slavophils concerning the charms of Russian life in the good old days; others expressed indignation at the fact that, as they claimed, Ostrovsky came out as an opponent of modern education. All these arguments may have grieved Ostrovsky mainly for the reason that in concentrating their attention on his views, the critics entirely forgot about his talent, and about the persons and situations he presented. In relation to Ostrovsky, this was sheer discourtesy. We admit that one cannot review the works of Count Sollogub without asking what he *intended to convey* in his *The Government Official*, for *The Government Official* is nothing more nor less than a fashionable, legal, not

even idea, but simply phrase, presented as a drama without the
slightest sign of talent. It would be permissible to treat in this
way the poems of Mr. Rosenheim, for example: there is no poetry
in a single one of his verses, consequently, the only criterion we
can apply to his poems is the relative importance of the ideas they
are supposed to express. Thus, without entering into a discussion
of his artistic merits, we may, for example, praise Mr. Rosenheim[79]
for the fact that *The Thunderstorm,* which he recently published in *Russkoye Slovo,* is written on a subject that is free from
the vulgarity of his elegies on government officials and tavern
licensees. Here we may quite calmly concentrate our attention solely on the views which the author wished to express in the play.
Ostrovsky's comedies, however, call for a different type of criticism, because, they all possess artistic merit, no matter what theories the author holds. We have already observed that the artist,
in his works, accepts, develops and expresses general ideas in a
way that is entirely different from that of ordinary theoreticians.
The artist is not concerned with abstract ideas and general principles, he is concerned with living images in which ideas manifest
themselves. In these images the poet may, imperceptibly even to
himself, grasp and express their inherent meaning long before
his mind can define it. Sometimes the artist may even fail to grasp
the meaning of what he himself is depicting. It is precisely the
function of critics to explain the hidden meaning of the images
the artist creates, but in analyzing the images which the poet presents they have no authority whatever to probe into his theoretical views. In the first part of *Dead Souls* there are passages
which, in spirit, closely resemble the *Correspondence,*[80] but this
does not deprive *Dead Souls* of its general meaning, which so
strongly contradicts Gogol's theoretical views. And Belinsky, in
his criticism, did not concern himself with Gogol's theories as
long as he dealt with him simply as an artist; he attacked Gogol
only when he proclaimed himself a preacher of morals and came
before the public not with a vivid story, but with a book of admon-
itory advice. . . .

We shall not compare Ostrovsky's importance with that of
Gogol in the history of our development; we shall observe, how-
ever, that no matter what theories influenced their composition,
Ostrovsky's comedies always contain profoundly true and vivid

19*

features which prove that the sense of truth never abandons the artist and never permits him to distort reality to suit a theory. That being the case, the fundamental features of the artist's world outlook could never be entirely destroyed by errors of judgment. He may have taken for his images facts of life which did not express a certain idea in the best possible way, he may have given them an arbitrary connection, he may have interpreted them not quite correctly, but if his artistic intuition has not betrayed him, if truth has been preserved in his productions, it is the critic's duty to utilize it in order to explain reality and also to characterize the author's talent, but not to rebuke him for ideas which, perhaps, he had not yet entertained. The critic must say: "Here are persons and scenes depicted by the author, this is the subject of the play, this, in my opinion, is the meaning of the facts of life the artist describes, and this is the degree of their importance in social life." Such a judgment will automatically show whether the author's own views concerning the images he has created are correct. If, for example, he has tried to raise one of the personages to the level of a universal type and the critic proves that the importance of this character is extremely limited and small, it will follow clearly that the author has spoilt his production by his false views concerning the hero. If he makes several facts dependent upon each other and the critic proves that these facts are never dependent upon each other in this way, but are dependent upon entirely different causes, it will again be self-evident that the author has failed to understand the proper connection between the phenomena he depicts. But here too the critic must be extremely cautious in drawing his conclusions. If, for example, the author rewards the villain at the end of the play, or if he depicts a stupid man as a noble one, it by no means implies that he wants to justify scoundrels, or regards all noble men as fools. All that the critic should be concerned with in this case is whether the man whom the author has depicted as a noble fool is really such in conformity with the critic's conception of wisdom and nobility; and secondly, whether the importance the author attaches to such persons is really the importance they possess in real life.

Such, in our opinion, should be the attitude of the realistic critic towards artistic productions; such, in particular, should be his attitude towards the author in reviewing his literary activities as a whole. In discussing an individual production a critic may unduly concentrate on particulars and blame the author for that which he had failed to bring out clearly enough. In a general characterization, however, particulars may be left aside, and the author's general world outlook and the way it found expression in his works as a whole should be put in the forefront. The way this is expressed is indicated by the subjects and phenomena which attracted his attention and sympathy and served as the material for his images.

Having given this explanation, we can now say that we are not in the least inclined to regard *Don't Get Into Another's Sleigh* as an apology for ancient patriarchal life or an attempt to prove the superiority of Russian lack of education over European education. We could even find something that is the very opposite of this in the comedy, but we have no wish to do this either; we shall merely point to the fact which serves as the basis of the play. We have already seen that the keynote of Ostrovsky's plays is the unnatural social relationships which arise from the tyranny of some and the oppression suffered by others. . . . The artist's sentiments, outraged by this order of things, attack it in its most diverse manifestations and pillory it before the very society in which this order of things exists. The following is one of these forms.

There lives in Russia a tyrannical merchant who is kindhearted, honest and even clever in a way—but he is a tyrant. He has a daughter who has no rights whatever as far as he is concerned, as is the case with every daughter of every tyrant. As her rights as an independent person are not recognized, she is deprived of everything which can protect personality in social life: she is uneducated, she has no voice even in domestic affairs, she is unaccustomed to see people with her own eyes, she has no conception of the right of free choice even in matters of the heart. Although an adult, she still behaves like a minor. like an unreasonable child. Her very love for her father, paralyzed by fear, is incomplete, unintelligent, and lacking in candour, so that, unbeknown to her father, she imbibes the ideas of her aunt, an elderly spinster who had been a milliner's apprentice on Kuznetsky Most,* and repeating her aunt's words she assures herself that she is in love with a

---

* A fashionable shopping centre in Moscow.—*Tr.*

young scamp, a retired Hussar officer who has recently arrived in town. The Hussar asks for the daughter's hand, the father refuses, the Hussar elopes with the girl, and the girl, while eloping with him, protests all the time that she is doing wrong and that she ought to return to her father. At the very first post station, however, the Hussar officer learns that the father will not give his absconded daughter a kopek, and of course, he at once deserts the poor girl. She returns home, the father scolds her severely and wants to lock her up in the house, so that she may not go out into the world again and make a laughingstock of him; but a young merchant, who had been in love with her for a long time, and whom she had loved before meeting Vikhorev, agrees to marry her, and all ends well.

Such is the gist of the plot in *Don't Get Into Another's Sleigh*. What is its meaning? Does it give the slightest ground for dilating on the subject of the advantages of the old way of life, and for the charge that the play expresses Slavophil tendencies? We think not. Its meaning is that tyranny, no matter how moderately it may be expressed, even if it develops into a mild tutelage, still leads at least to the loss of personality by the people who are subjected to its influence; and loss of personality is diametrically opposed to all free and rational activity. Consequently, a man who loses his personality under the influence of the tyranny that oppresses him may unwillingly, unconsciously, commit any conceivable crime and perish simply because of his foolishness and lack of independence.

This meaning of the facts we have related, a meaning which strikes the eye before anything else, does not stand out vividly enough in the comedy because in the forefront stands the contrast between clever and staid Rusakov and kind and honest Borodkin on the one hand, and that featherbrained nonentity Vikhorev. The critics pounced upon this contrast and in their reviews made assumptions that the author, perhaps, had never dreamed of. He was accused almost of obscurantism, and even to this day some critics have not forgiven him for the fact that though uneducated, Rusakov is a kind and honest man for all that.* Indeed, allowing

---

* Since we wrote our first essay, in which we spoke about Ostrovsky's critics, two more articles about him have appeared in the magazines. One

himself to be carried away by his indignation with the superficial
education of gentlemen like Vikhorev who lead simple Russian
people astray, Ostrovsky did not bring out with sufficient power
and clarity *the reasons* why Russians are infatuated with such
gentlemen. But it cannot be said that the author completely forgot
these reasons; the plain and natural meaning of the facts did not
escape him, and we find features of those relationships, which we
designate by the general term tyranny, scattered throughout the
comedy *Don't Get Into Another's Sleigh.* If these features were
more vivid, the comedy would have been more integral and definite; but even in its present shape it cannot be said to contradict
the main features of the author's world outlook. He turned a ray
of external light upon the dark lives of the Rusakovs and
smoothed and straightened out some of their coarser features; but
if we look closely we shall find that even in this smooth shape
the substance remains the same. We shall endeavour to point out
some of the features of Rusakov's relations with his daughter and
those around him; we will see that the basis of the whole story is
the very same tyranny which serves as the basis of all domestic
and social relationships in this "realm of darkness."

Maxim Fedotich Rusakov—this finest representative of all the
charms of the old way of life, a very intelligent old man, *the
Russian soul*, which the critics of the Slavophil and Koshikhin
persuasion used to bring up in order to shame our post-Peter epoch
and all our modern education—this Rusakov, in our opinion, is
a living protest against this dark, senseless and basically immoral
existence. In Bolshov we saw a wretched character who had been
the victim of the influence of this existence; Rusakov seems to
show us what effect this influence has even upon honest and mild
characters. . . . And indeed, a natural kindness and even delicacy
breaks through Rusakov's coarseness. He treats everybody kindly
and talks tenderly to his wife and daughter; when Dunya swoons
on learning that he has definitely rejected Vikhorev (incidentally,
we think this scene is overdrawn), he is frightened and forthwith
agrees to alter his decision for her sake. More than that, his head

---

is of a dithyrambic character, but the other repeats all the absurdities
that were ascribed to Ostrovsky in the past and ends by advising him to
"think, think and think." Both articles, however, are destitute of all significance.—*N. D.*

is well screwed on his shoulders and common sense cannot be
knocked out of it. He does not say bluntly: "It must be so
because I wish it," but tries to give reasons for his decisions. But
this is all that he has been able to preserve of the good qualities
of his character; beyond that he is a tyrant. It is evident that
owing to the natural mildness of his character Rusakov meekly
submitted to the existing order of things and recognized its lawfulness from the very outset; hence, there was no need to teach
him this with kicks and cuffs. This explains why even in old age
he does not display that hostility and severity that we observe in
the other tyrants whom Ostrovsky depicts, and this also explains
why he even reasons with his subordinates and juniors when he
talks to them. But life in the "realm of darkness" in which he
grew up contributed nothing in the way of reason to his education; there is no reason in that life, and so Rusakov sank into
the same state of unreason, into the same gloom, in which all his
fellows who are less endowed by nature are groping.

It is interesting to note the level of morality to which he
succeeded in raising himself. Submission, patience, respect for
experience and tradition, keep to your own circle—such are his
maxims. He worked them out in a crudely empirical way by
comparing facts, but he deduced no ideas from them, because his
mind is fettered by the most stubborn and fatalistic conception of
destiny which rules human affairs. He appears on the stage with
the trite sentence on his lips: "You must go to the old folks for
advice—an old man will never give you bad advice." And in
answer to Borodkin's request for his daughter's hand he says:
"I must think about this very carefully because I shall have to
answer to God for my daughter." On these grounds he settles the
fate of his daughter in the following way: "Can a girl be trusted
to know whom she likes or dislikes? No, that's wrong. The man
must please *me*. I shall not give her to the man she loves, but to
the man *I* love. Yes, I'll give her to the man I love." This smacks
very strongly of tyranny, but in Rusakov it is softened by the
following argument: "How can a girl be trusted? What has she
seen? Whom does she know?" This argument is a fair one in
relation to Rusakov's daughter, but it never enters the head either
of Rusakov or of any of his fellows to ask: "Why has she seen
nothing, and why does she know nobody? What need was there

to keep her in such blissful ignorance that anybody who comes
along can deceive her? ...." If they were to put these questions to
themselves their answer would show once again that the root of
the evil is nothing more nor less than their own tyranny. Rusakov
is quite satisfied with his position and has no wish to climb into
the circle of the gentry, and he regards education as the exclusive
privilege of the gentry. Consequently, he keeps his daughter in
such a position that she remains, as he himself expresses it, a
ninny. In answer to Vikhorev's request for his daughter's hand, he
says: "Look for an educated young lady for yourself and leave
our ninnies to us, we shall find young men for them of a cheaper
kind." There is a touch of irony in these words, but Rusakov
continues in a graver tone, but in the same strain: "What sort of
lady can she be? Judge for yourself, young man. She has been
living within these four walls all her life and has never seen
the world.... There's nothing you can love her for. She's
a simple girl, uneducated, and no match for you at all. You
have relatives and friends, they will all laugh at her as a ninny.
And you yourself will find that she is more bitter to you than
wormwood.... D'you think I'd put my daughter into such
slavery?"

The saddest thing about this argument is that it is absolutely
true. Indeed, it would not be a very happy life that would await
Avdotya Maximovna if she married a *gentleman* even if he were
not a scapegrace like Vikhorev. She has indeed been brought up
in such a way that she is scarcely human. What is the highest
praise her own father can express about her? That "all you can
see in her eyes is love and meekness. *She will love any husband.
We must find her one who will love her.*" This means goodness
that is indifferent and submissive, the kind of goodness that is
developed in soft characters under the yoke of domestic despotism,
and the kind that pleases tyrants most. For people who are accustomed to base their activities upon common sense and adjust
them to the requirements of justice and the common welfare, such
goodness is abhorrent, or at all events pitiful. It is easy to understand that if a person agrees with everybody, it shows that he has
no convictions of his own; if he loves everybody and is everybody's friend, it shows that he is indifferent to everybody; if a
young woman would love any husband, it clearly shows that her

heart is not even a piece of flesh, but merely a soft piece of dough into which you can stick anything. . . .

For a man who is not infected with the virus of tyranny, the charm of love lies in that the will of another being merges harmoniously with his own without the slightest coercion. The charm of love is often so incomplete and inadequate precisely because love is won by a sort of blackmail, deception, because it is purchased with money, or, in general, acquired by external and extraneous means. Love can be truly sincere only when there is internal harmony between the lovers, and when that exists, it serves as the basis and the pledge of that social well-being that the future development of mankind holds out for us, by the establishment of fraternity and equal rights among men. But tyranny cannot allow even the sentiment of love to remain free from its yoke; it senses some sort of danger for itself in its free and natural development, and therefore tries to kill first of all that which is the basis of love—personality. For this purpose the tyrants invent their own morality, their own rules of life, according to which, the more personality is obliterated, indistinguishable and unnoticeable, the nearer it approaches the ideal of human perfection. "He has such a splendid character that he will suffer uncomplainingly any insult, he will love the most unworthy of men"—such is the highest praise the tyrant can conceive of. In our opinion, however, such a person is trash, a jellyfish, a mere rag; he may be a good *man* only in the flunkey sense of the term. He is not fit to be anything else, and one may expect as much mischievous as honest conduct from him—it will all depend upon the hands he falls into. Being a tyrant, Rusakov refuses to admit all this and persists in his argument: "All evil in the world is due to lack of restraint. We, in our time, feared and respected our elders—that was much better . . . they don't thrash young people nowadays, more's the pity. There's nothing like leather." No matter what he may talk about—respect for elders stands in the forefront. He is angry even with Vikhorev mostly because the latter "doesn't know how to speak to his elders." And in spite of his mildness, when his daughter dares to attempt to reason with him, he bawls: "How dare you talk to me like that?" And then he says to her sternly: "This is my last word, Avdotya. Either you marry Borodkin, or I disown you!" And to make his command effective he reinforces it with the following rebuke: "I brought you up. I guarded you like the apple of my eye.... Sin entered my soul, I was proud of you.... God has punished me for my sin." Speaking impartially, this mode of address cannot be described as humane; but in our "realm of darkness" even this is fairly mild, and Rusakov may be justly described as one of the better type of tyrant.

But look at the nature that Avdotya Maximovna cultivated under the influence of this meek tyrant! It is difficult to picture to oneself a more pitiful girl. Actually, she is comical rather than pitiful, just as Sophia Pavlovna, with her love for Molchalin, or Sophia Sergeyevna (in Mr. Potekhin's[81] *The Latest Oracle*) with her tender passion for Zilberbach were comical. But one must not laugh at Avdotya Maximovna; her environment is too gloomy. When we wander alone at midnight through a dark churchyard among the tombs and a figure suddenly springs up from behind one of the tombstones and makes a funny face at us it frightens us: funny as that face may be, it is hard to force a laugh at that moment. So it is with the comical in our "realm of darkness." In itself it is simply amusing; but when one sees the tyrants and the victims they have crushed in the darkness, all desire to laugh passes away.... Throughout the play Avdotya Maximovna is in a state of extreme agitation; it may be absurd and foolish agitation, nevertheless, it rouses in us not a desire to laugh, but a feeling of compassion. After all, the poor girl is not to blame if she has been deprived of moral backbone and has been brought up in such a way as to need leading strings all her life. She is good at heart, she is of a confiding nature, as are all the unhappy and oppressed who have not yet become hardened; a yearning for love has been roused in her, but it lacks scope, reasonable support and a worthy object. She has not developed a real conception of what is good and what is evil, she has not cultivated a respect for the promptings of her own heart; on the other hand she has developed the conception of moral duty only to the degree that enables her to recognize it as an external, coercive force. And it is in this state that the poor girl rushes from place to place, not knowing where to lay her head. She loves her father, but at the same time fears him and does not even altogether trust him. She likes Borodkin, but she is told that he is an uneducated fellow and so she is at a loss, she does not know what to think, and at last conceives a

dislike for him. Then Vikhorev comes along, who possesses nothing but insolence and a doll's face. She is enchanted by him. But
here too she torments herself in vain; not for a moment is she on
firm ground, but seems to be drowning, rising to the surface for
an instant only to sink again ... and you wait on tenterhooks
expecting her to go down for good. ... The moment she appears on
the scene at the end of the first act Vikhorev informs her that her
father had betrothed her to Borodkin, but she answers naively:
"Don't worry. I shall not marry Borodkin." "But what if your
father orders you to?" Vikhorev asks her. "No," she says, "he
cannot force me to marry him." "But suppose he does force you,
what then?" "Then," she answers idiotically, "I really don't know
what I shall do. ... It's a real misfortune!" Vikhorev, who is
absolutely unscrupulous, proposes that she should elope with him.
She is horror-stricken and exclaims: "Oh, no, no! How dare you
suggest such a thing? Not for all the treasures in the world!" Why
is she so horror-stricken? Simply because, you see, "My father
will curse me! How will I be able to live after that?" Consequently, in her simplicity, she suggests that Vikhorev should go and
speak to her father. Vikhorev thinks it is of no use, and she tries
to encourage him with the following argument: "What shall I do?
This must be my unhappy fate. ... Aunty consulted the cards
yesterday and they showed something bad. Oh, how I cried!"
Vikhorev threatens to go to the Caucasus and seek death, but she
pleads with him: "No, don't go! What terrible things you say!"
In short, the girl is beset by fear on all sides: the threat of her
father's curse, the evil forecast of the cards, and the prospect that
the Circassians may kill her darling Vikhorev. If only the poor
girl had something within her to counteract all these horrors! She
is simplehearted and believes everything: her father's curse, the
cards and Vikhorev—that he will go and face death; and she
equally fears them all. ... She tells the truth about herself in the
beginning of the second act: "I walk about like a shadow. I can't
hear my own footsteps ... my heart tells me that nothing good
will come of all this. Alas, I know it only too well. Oh, the tears
I shall yet shed!" Is it surprising that she should shed tears in
such circumstances? ...

To crown it all it appears that she is, after all, in love with
Borodkin; she used to meet him and could not tear herself away

from him, waited for him at the wicket gate, sat with him through
the long autumn evenings, and she is even sorry for him now, but
she cannot drive away the thought of Vikhorev's extraordinary
beauty. Incidentally, she is very displeased with herself and says:
"I wish I had never set eyes on him." But what tortures her most
is the thought of going to her father and asking for his consent to
her marriage to Vikhorev. She prepares for this with exceptional
solemnity, compels Vikhorev to take an oath that he really loves
her, and then tells him that in proof of her love for him she dares
to go to her father herself to ask for his consent to their marriage.
"If you only knew what it is costing me," she adds, and the next
scene fully explains and justifies her fear, which is possible and
explicable only under the relationships upon which the whole of
the domestic life of the Rusakovs is based. One would think that
there was nothing more natural and easy than for a daughter to
express her wish to her father who loved her tenderly. But Avdotya
Maximovna, while reiterating that her father loves her, is aware
of the scene that may follow such a confession to her father, and
her kind, downtrodden nature trembles and suffers in anticipation
of it. Indeed, "How dare you?" "I brought you up and tended
you!" "You're a ninny!" "You have not my blessing!" and similar
raillery came pouring down on the poor girl's head like hail, so
much so that even her weak and submissive soul is suddenly
roused to offer a mild protest, which finds expression in an involuntary, unconscious change in her feelings: her father's command to marry Borodkin rouses in her a revulsion of feeling towards the latter. "I was sorry for Vanya up till now, but now I
hate him. . . . I hate him!" But this is the utmost limit the girl's
reaction can reach; beyond that she cannot go in her resistance to
another's will and—she swoons. Then follows the sentimental
scene in which Rusakov's heart softens and he agrees to give his
daughter to Vikhorev—provided, however, the latter takes her
without a dowry. Overjoyed, Avdotya Maximovna hurries to the
church to meet Vikhorev and to tell him the joyful news, and
Vikhorev takes her away. . . . The subsequent action indicates that
Vikhorev kidnapped Avdotya Maximovna, and this circumstance
appears to be extremely important for old Rusakov; but it is
not so important for us, because we see in the comedy the scene
between the kidnapped girl and Vikhorev at the inn. From this

scene we may confidently conclude that even if Vikhorev did force
Avdotya into the carriage, he did so only to save time, for she
would not have been able to resist him had he stopped to persuade
her to go with him. At the inn she pleads with him: "Victor
Arkadich, darling, I am ready to go through fire and water with
you, only let me go back to Papa.... What's going to happen to
him?" and so forth. But her pleading is overpowered by Vikhorev's will. He begins to persuade and caress her a little, and she
at once exclaims: "My darling! My life, my joy! I'll go anywhere
with you! *I'm not afraid of anybody now, and I'm not sorry for
anybody.* I'd fly away with you right now!" After that she remembers her father again, and again, of course, to no purpose. It had
been a frightful effort for her to decide to go away with Vikhorev,
but once having fallen into his hands she is afraid to leave him.
Not once did she display a strong determination that would testify
to the independence of her character; she has never dared to go
beyond meek complaints, humble supplication. When Vikhorev
spurns her on learning that she is not getting a dowry she shows
some signs of resentment and says: "You will never know what
happiness is for insulting a poor girl like me, Victor Arkadich!"
But she is immediately frightened by her own words and she
adopts a humble tone, in which one would like to discern a note of
irony, however out of place it may have been in Avdotya Maximovna's situation. Kindness of heart combined with utter inability
to express anger against evil and dull submission to her fate are
expressed in the words of the unhappy girl:

"God will punish you for me; I wish you no harm. Find a rich wife
for yourself, but one who will love you as I love you; live happily with
her, and I, a simple girl, will go on living somehow, spending my life
within four walls, cursing my fate."

And this humanely-pathetic tirade is addressed to Vikhorev!
And Vikhorev thinks to himself: "Why not have a bit of fun when
fun costs so little." And on top of all this, at the end of the play
Rusakov, overjoyed that his daughter has learned her lesson and
is more strongly than ever imbued with the principle of obedience
to elders, pays the debt Vikhorev owes at the inn at which he
stayed. Here too, as you see, the law of the tyrant prevails: If I
wish to I can punish; if I wish to I can pardon.... I obey no one
—not even the rules of justice.

Such, then, is the position and development of the two principal characters in the comedy *Don't Get Into Another's Sleigh.*
Do you like it? Would you like to be in Avdotya Maximovna's
shoes? Or perhaps you would like to play the part of Rusakov
and reduce one of your dear ones to the position in which we
find Avdotya Maximovna? If you would, then, of course, you must
admire the patriarchal ways, the purity and happiness of the life
that Ostrovsky depicts in this comedy. If you would not, then this
play must appear to you to be a strong protest against tyranny
even in the phase in which it can still deceive many people by
some of the features of goodness and reason which it possesses.

"But," we may be told, "the misfortune which befell the Rusakov family is no more than an extraordinary episode in that
family's life. Until Vikhorev's arrival peace and quiet reigned in
the family. The cause of all the trouble were the new ideas which
Arina Fedotovna, Rusakov's sister, had brought from Kuznetsky
Most. Rusakov himself says to her: 'It's your doing, aren't you
pleased? I brought her up in fear and in virtue, and she was as
pure as a dove. You came with your poisonous ideas. You did
nothing all day long but talk nonsense ... all your talk was just
silly. You ought not to have been allowed into a decent family—you
are poison and temptation!' And indeed throughout the play, you
see very clearly and consistently how this poison gradually permeates the girl's soul and disturbs the serenity of her tranquil life.
At the end of the play we see how the vital force of simple patriarchal relationships regains the upper hand over the cancer of
present-day semi-education, brings the prodigal daughter back
to her father's house and triumphs in the person of Borodkin. by
restoring the girl's natural rights among all her kinsfolk. Evidently, this is the meaning the author himself wanted to put into
the play, and the impression it makes upon everybody is not that
of a protest against the old way of life but reconciliation with it."

In answer to this we must say that we do not know what precisely the author had in mind when he planned this play; but in the
play itself we see features which cannot be regarded as praise of
the old way of life. If these features are not so vivid as to strike
the eye of everybody, if the play creates a double impression, it
only proves (as we have already observed in the first essay) that
the author's general theoretical convictions at the time he wrote

the play were not in complete harmony with what his artistic nature had imbibed from the impressions of real life. If, however, we look upon the author not as a theoretician but as a reproducer of the phenomena of real life, we shall not attach exceptional importance to the theories he holds. The main thing is that he should be conscientious and not distort facts to suit his views. If he is conscientious the true meaning of the facts will reveal itself in his productions spontaneously, although, of course, not as vividly as when artistic effort is assisted by the power of an abstract idea.... As regards Ostrovsky, even his opponents say that he always paints a true picture of real life; hence, we may leave aside as minor and personal the question as to what the author's intentions were when he wrote the play. Let us suppose that he had no particular intentions, that he was merely struck by an episode of the kind that often occurs in the "realm of darkness" and made it his business to describe it; he simply recorded this episode and left it to the critics and the public to judge its meaning. The critics decided that the meaning of the play is—that it exposes the harm of semi-education and praises the fundamental principles of the Russian way of life. In our opinion this is partly wrong and partly inadequate. The real meaning of the play is as follows.

Rusakov is the finest representative of the old way of social life, the tyrannical way of life. By nature he is kind and honest, his thoughts and deeds are bent towards good, and this explains why we do not see in his family the horrors of oppression that we see in the families of other tyrants whom Ostrovsky himself has depicted. But this is a purely accidental, exceptional phenomenon; actually, the principles upon which the life of the Rusakovs is based provide no guarantee of well-being. On the contrary, by destroying the rights of personality, and by placing fear and submission at the foundation of education and morality, those principles can only breed tyranny, oppression and deception. Rusakov is a casual exception, and for that reason the first insignificant incident destroys all the good his family enjoys as a result of his personal virtues. He believes that all the evil is due to the insinuations of Arina Fedotovna, but he is simply shifting the blame from the guilty to the innocent. Here we have the same syllogism that we heard only very recently from the opponents of literacy. "The literate peasants are rogues and schemers, they cheat the illiterate; hence, peasants should not be taught to read and write." Formulated correctly this syllogism will read as follows: "Illiterate peasants are cheated by the literate; hence, all peasants should be given the opportunity to learn to read and write so as to be able to guard themselves against deception." It is the same in this case: Arina Fedotovna tempted and deceived Rusakov's daughter. What follows from this? That the girl should have been given the means with which to guard herself against temptation. She should have been given the opportunity to discover life for herself, she should have been brought among people, and she should have been trained to think and act independently. A girl who was educated and accustomed to society would not have yielded to vulgar Arina Fedotovna, and would not have succumbed to the wiles of the featherbrained Vikhorev. But to have given her a real, human education would have meant recognizing her right of personality, would have meant renouncing the rights of the tyrant and running in the face of all the traditions upon which life in the "realm of darkness" is based. This Rusakov would not and could not do. [He is kind and clever enough not to go to extremes, not to abuse the tyrant's power to the extent that his fellow tyrants do, but he lacks the strength of mind and character to renounce the main principles of his way of life.] He stops at a given point and he discusses fairly correctly everything that emerges from it: he quite rightly observes that it is easy to deceive his daughter, and that the kind of talk that Arina Fedotovna indulges in may be harmful for her; that an uneducated merchant's daughter would not be happy if she married a gentleman, and so forth; but all his arguments reveal that unreasonable, dull conservatism which constitutes one of the distinguishing features of the obstinate tyrant. He has accepted the existing order of things and will not even admit that this state of things can or should be changed. He realizes that his daughter is uneducated and for that reason is unfit to be a lady, but he expresses not the slightest regret that he had not educated her. According to his lights that is how it should be: a merchant's daughter must remain a merchant's daughter; as for being a lady, one must be born for that. He also realizes that his daughter is unable to judge people and is therefore enchanted by that featherbrained ne'er-do-well Vikhorev; but this does not suggest to him that he should have taught her, at least to some extent, to form her own judgment about things. On the contrary, he is convinced that it is a good thing that she can fall in love with anybody who comes along. The right to choose people according to one's own taste, the right to love some and not love others, can belong, in all its scope, only to him. Rusakov, all the rest must adorn themselves with meekness and submission—such are the rules of tyranny. [Kind and clever though he is, Rusakov, as a tyrant, cannot tolerate any material changes in his relationships with those around him, he cannot even conceive of the necessity of such a change. All the evil in the family is due to the fact that, being afraid to allow his daughter freedom of opinion and the right to act independently, Rusakov restricts her thoughts and feelings and keeps her in the state of a perpetual infant, almost that of an imbecile. He realizes that evil exists and wishes that it did not exist, but in order to remove it he must first of all abandon his tyranny, he must part with his conception of his rights over the mind and will of his daughter; but this is beyond his strength, he cannot even conceive of it.... And so he throws the blame on others: at one moment Arina Fedotovna is to blame for having brought her poison into the house, at another it is simply due to the devil's mischief. "The enemy of the human race," he says, "tempts us with all sorts of temptations...." But he refuses to understand the very simplest truth, namely, that if you want a man to fight his enemies successfully you must not subdue his inner strength, you must not tie him hand and foot.]

And for this tyranny of her father's the girl must sacrifice all that might have provided her with a bright, truly happy and meaningful future. Notwithstanding his love for his daughter, Rusakov's general outlook on life could not but affect his daughter's development. He succeeded in safeguarding her from everything that enables a person to safeguard himself and. as a consequence, he failed to safeguard her. One would think that he could not have done better: the girl was brought up "in fear and in virtue," as Rusakov puts it, she read no bad books, she hardly saw anybody, she left the house only to go to church, rebellious thoughts about disobedience to elders and the rights of one's heart could not have penetrated her mind from anywhere, and

she was as remote from claiming personal independence as from
the idea of—going into military service.... What could have been
better? Had she lived calmly and serenely according to the plan
Rusakov had drawn up for her once and for all, nothing, it would
seem, could have corrupted this absolutely meek creature, this
submissive dove, and diverted her from the true path. But precarious, fleeting and insignificant is everything that has no foundation and support within a man, in his mind and conscious determination. Only those family and social relationships can be
strong which flow from inner conviction and are justified by the
voluntary and rational agreement of all those who participate in
them. Tyranny, even in the person of its best representative such
as Rusakov is, refuses to recognize this—and therefore suffers
cruel defeat at the very first casual episode, at the very first miserable little intrigue, even at some simple frolic bereft of any
definite meaning. What could be more insignificant and senseless
than Arina Fedotovna's arguments? Who could have appeared
more vulgar and absurd than Vikhorev in the eyes of Avdotya
Maximovna? Nevertheless, these two vulgar people disturb the
harmony of the Rusakovs' domestic life, compel the father to
curse his daughter and the daughter to leave her father, and then
place the unhappy girl in a position which, in Rusakov's opinion,
involves not only grief and shame for the girl herself for the rest
of her life, but general disgrace for the whole family. And in
this tyrant's way of life, with its patriarchal customs, there is not
even power of reconciliation in this case, because not only is formal virginity violated here, but the very principle of obedience.....
To restore the rights of the innocent but dishonoured girl the
generous behaviour of Borodkin is required, behaviour that is
quite exceptional and incompatible with the morals of this milieu,
in which ignorance and tyranny create both the extraordinary
thoughtlessness with which Avdotya Maximovna behaves and the
impossibility of reconciliation.

Thus, we may repeat our conclusion: Ostrovsky's comedy
Don't Get Into Another's Sleigh shows us—irrespective of whether
the author intended it or not, or even in spite of him—that as long
as tyrannical conditions exist at the very foundations of social
life, the kindest and most noble personalities will never be able
to do anything; and the well-being of the family and even of

20*

society as a whole will remain precarious and in no way safeguarded against the most insignificant fortuities. Our analysis of
Rusakov's character and relationships has demonstrated this truth
in application to a case where a decent character figures as a tyrant and is befogged by its own rights. In Ostrovsky's other comedies we find even stronger evidence of this same truth applied
to the other half of the "realm of darkness," the dependent and
oppressed half.

[The lines we put at the head of this essay may to some extent apply to Rusakov too: he too has good intentions, he too
wishes to do good to others, but "in vain for some shade doth he
pray," and shrivels in the scorching rays of tyranny. But those
lines apply still more to those unfortunates, who, being endowed
with splendid hearts and the purest of strivings, writhe under the
yoke of tyranny, which kills all thought and feeling in them. It
is with them in mind that we remembered the lines

> In vain to the prophet for some shade doth he pray,
> There is nothing around but scorching sand,
> A tufted kite o'er the deserted land
> Plucks and tears at its unfortunate prey.][82]

IV

> It all comes mostly from lack of restraint,
> and perhaps also from stupidity.
>
> *Ostrovsky*

In the hard lot of Rusakov's daughter we see much that is
unreasonable; but here our impression is softened by the fact that,
after all, tyranny does not oppress her so crudely. Far more absurd and cruel, we think, is the fate of the oppressed people who
are depicted in the comedy *Poverty Is No Crime*.

Poverty Is No Crime very clearly reveals to us how an honest
but weak character is stifled and killed by the burden of senseless tyranny. Gordei Karpich Tortsov—Lyubov Gordeyevna's father, Lyubim Tortsov's brother and Mitya's master—is a tyrant
in the full sense of the term. He is overbearing, proud, and as his
wife, Palageya Yegorovna, says of him, he has no sense. The
whole house trembles before him. He became particularly terrible

after he struck up a friendship with Afrikan Savich Korshunov and began to "adopt the new fashion." It is on this friendship and Gordei Karpich's passion for the new fashion that the plot of this comedy is based. Our readers will, of course, remember that Tortsov wants to give his daughter in marriage to Afrikan Savich, although the daughter loves the shop assistant Mitya and is loved by him. . . . On these grounds the critics assumed that Ostrovsky wrote *Poverty Is No Crime* with the object of showing how harmful are the consequences for a merchant's family when it departs from the old customs and is carried away by a new fashion. . . . For this some critics immoderately praised Ostrovsky, while others ruthlessly reviled him. We shall not stop to argue with either of these groups of critics nor analyze the correctness or fallacy of their assumptions. We shall even grant that Ostrovsky really had the intention that is ascribed to him; this point interests us little at present. What interests us far more is that Gordei Tortsov presents us with a new shade, a new species of tyranny; here we see how the tyrant accepts education, that is to say, those casual and insignificant forms of education which alone can reach his understanding. This is what we shall discuss now.

Tyranny and education are in themselves opposites and, therefore, a collision between them must obviously end in the subordination of one to the other: either the tyrant imbibes the principles of education, and in that case he ceases to be a tyrant, or he converts education into a servant of his whims, and of course, remains the ignoramus that he was before. It is the latter that happens to Gordei Karpich, as it happens to nearly all tyrants. He has no idea that the first step towards education is the subordination of his willfulness to the demands of reason and respect for the same demands in others. On the contrary, he thinks that all education, all logic, exists solely for the purpose of implicitly serving his whims. This explains why he understands only the crudely material, purely external aspect of education.

"What," he asks, "do these ignoramuses drink? Cordials, cherry brandy and stuff like that. They don't know that champagne is the stuff to drink!" "What ignorance they show at the table: the dishes are served by the houseboy or the kitchen maid!" "All I can see in this town," he says, "is ignorance and lack of education. That's why I want to move to Moscow. I shall *follow all the fashions* there."

Believing that following the fashion is the sum and substance of education, he keeps on bothering his wife to make her, in her old age, wear a bonnet instead of a kerchief, to arrange fashionable evening parties with music, and to abandon all her old habits. But he sees no need whatever to change his attitude towards his domestics, to allow common sense at least some part in his domestic life. Gordei Karpich becomes more exacting, but he allows no more scope for activity to those around him than he did before. His wife complains that "it is impossible to talk to him with his overbearing character," especially after he *took over* this education. "Before, he had some sense," says Palageya Yegorovna about him, "but now everything seems to have turned topsy-turvy in his head. . . ." His wife has no right even to talk to him about the fate of their daughter: "He looks at me like a wild beast and doesn't say a word, as if I wasn't her mother. . . . Yes, it's true . . . I daren't say a word to him. All I can do is talk to some stranger about my grief, have a good cry and relieve my heart, and that's all. . . ." Gordei Karpich's attitude towards all his other domestics is also coarse and tyrannical to the highest degree. All he demands from his daughter is that she should not dare to disobey him. When she asks him not to make her marry Korshunov, he answers: "You ninny, you don't understand what happiness awaits you. . . . For one thing, you will live in society and not in this backyard. *And for the other—you must do as I tell you.*" To this the daughter answers: "I don't dare disobey you." Gordei Karpich unceremoniously bullies his shop assistant Mitya and for no reason whatever. On learning that Mitya sends money to his mother, Tortsov says to him: "You'd do better if you spent it on yourself. God knows, your mother doesn't need much, she's not used to luxury. She probably cleaned out the pigsty herself. . . ." Gordei Karpich thinks it is a great crime for the shop assistant to send his mother money and not have a new suit made for himself! . . . But he does not think of raising the zealous assistant's salary! Even humble Mitya complains about this: "The pay Gordei Karpich gives me is small, but I get plenty of insults and abuse. And he's always taunting me with my poverty, as if I were to blame. . . . But he doesn't raise my pay." In general, Gordei Karpich is constantly displaying rudeness and lack of restraint, and to a very strong degree. Bursting into the room where his shop assistants

are having a singsong he bawls at them: "What's this singing?
Yelling like a lot of boors!..." and pours out a stream of abuse.
In the second act, where Palageya Yegorovna has arranged a social evening to which she has invited some mummers, Arina dashes
into the room and exclaims: "The master's come!" and everybody
present gets up in a fright. Gordei Karpich comes in and greets
his wife and the guests in the following way: "What's this rabble
doing here? Clear out! Wife! Receive a guest!..." The guest
is Afrikan Savich, who somewhat restrains Gordei Karpich's
ire.... Clearly, Gordei Karpich has not even acquired that superficial education that is expressed in manners and politeness. He
may put on a new suit of clothes, buy new *furnisher*, and develop
a passion for *chempain*, but he refuses in any way to change his
personality, his character, even his manner of treating people and
[in all his habits] he remains true to his tyrannical nature.
[We see in him a rather curious example of the way education
affects every tyrant. It would seem that the man had taken a good
road, that he had realized the defects of his former mode of life,
had grown indignant with ignorance and had realized the superiority of education in general.... A consoling fact! Granted
that he still realizes all this vaguely, faintly and not very definitely, but after all he has made a start, the former stagnation
has been disturbed, his activities have taken a new direction....
Perhaps, he will proceed farther along this road, his temper will
become milder and his whole life will assume a new character....
But no, don't expect this....] In any other person education awakens sympathetic strivings, softens character, develops respect for
the principles of justice, etc.; but in a tyrant, education itself,
logic, virtue, assume peculiar savage and ugly features. Starting
out from the assumption that his tyranny must be law for everybody and everything, the tyrant is glad to enjoy what education
has produced for man's comfort, he is glad to demand from
others that his will shall be obeyed better, in conformity with the
successes of the various sciences, the introduction of new inventions, etc. But there he stops. Don't expect him to impose any
restriction upon himself in view of his appreciation of the new
demands of education, don't even think that he could cultivate
serious respect for the laws of reason and the deductions of science;
all this is incompatible with a tyrant's nature. No, he will always

look down with contempt upon thinkers and scientists, as upon
common labourers, whose duty it is to provide the materials for
the convenience of his tyranny, [in the new successes of education he will always seek pretexts for claiming new rights for
himself] but he will never recognize the duties that these same
successes of education impose upon him. He cannot behave otherwise without ceasing to be a tyrant, for the first demand of education is precisely that he should abandon his tyranny; and for
Gordei Karpich Tortsov to abandon his tyranny would mean becoming an utter nonentity. And so, he amuses himself at the expense of those around him: he taunts them with their ignorance
and persecutes them every time they display any knowledge or
common sense. He learns that educated girls talk well, and so he
rebukes his daughter for not being able to talk; but when she
begins to talk he bawls at her: "Shut up, you ninny!" He saw that
educated shop assistants dress well, and so he is angry with Mitya
because the latter wears shabby clothes, but he continues to pay
him a mere pittance. . . . And so he is in everything in his life—
and it is the revelation of this attitude of the tyrant towards education that principally makes the personality of Gordei Karpich
interesting for us. We totally fail to understand how certain critics could arrive at the conclusion that in this person, and in the
comedy *Poverty Is No Crime* in general, Ostrovsky wanted to show
the harmful effect new conceptions have upon the old Russian
way of life. . . . From the whole comedy it is clear that Gordei
Karpich did not become so coarse, frightful and absurd only after
he had been to Moscow and had adopted the new fashion. Actually, he had been the same tyrant before; now, however, he was
merely making several new demands. . . .

It is under the influence of such a man, and of relationships
such as these, that meek characters like Lyubov Gordeyevna and
Mitya develop, demonstrating what degree obliteration of personality can reach, and how oppression makes even the most sympathetic and self-sacrificing characters totally incapable of independent activity. Mitya is capable of self-sacrifice: he himself suffers
want in order that he may help his mother; he bears all Gordei
Karpich's insults and does not want to leave him because he loves
his daughter; braving his employer's anger he gives Lyubim Tortsov shelter in his room and even gives him money to buy a drink

to get over the effects of a drinking bout. In short, Mitya is so
self-sacrificing that one would think that no sacrifice and no
danger would be too much for him. . . . No less kindhearted is
Lyubov Gordeyevna. Her love for Mitya cannot be expressed in
words, it seems as though she would gladly give her life for him. . . .
If these people were normal, if they possessed free will and at least
a little energy, nothing could separate them, or at all events they
would not separate without a severe and terrific struggle. But see
how the whole story of the Tortsov family unfolds. At the very
moment when Mitya proposes to Lyubov Gordeyevna and they
are preparing to go and ask for her father's blessing, Lyubov
says to Mitya: "But suppose Papa will not agree to our marriage,
what then?" Mitya answers: "What's the use of meeting trouble
halfway? We are in God's hands. I don't know what you think,
but life will not be worth living without you." Lyubochka can
find nothing to say in answer to this. How vividly the impotence
and the oppression from which these young people suffer are depicted here! They are afraid even to think of taking some independent step, and they try to drive out of their minds even the
very thought of the obstacles that confront them. She says in horror: "Suppose Papa will not agree?" And he answers: "We are
in God's hands! . . ." Clearly, they are incapable of carrying out
their intentions if they meet with the slightest obstacle. And indeed, that very same evening Gordei Karpich comes home with
Korshunov, orders his daughter to caress and kiss Korshunov, and
tells her that he is to be her husband. Palageya Yegorovna is
horror-stricken and in response to some unconscious impulse she
clutches her daughter by the hand and shouts: "She's my daughter, I shan't give her up! Don't torment a mother's heart, Gordei
Karpich! Stop it, father! . . . You have worn out my soul." But
Gordei Karpich bawls threateningly: "Wife! You know me! What
I say I do!" and the wife falls silent. Now the daughter raises
opposition. She begins by falling at her father's feet and saying:
"Papa! I dare not disobey you. . . . Papa, don't make me unhappy
for the rest of my life! Think it over, Papa! I'll do anything you
want, but don't make me, against my will, marry a man I do not
love." The opposition ceases with the humble statement after the
father's stern refusal: "I submit to your will, father." With that
she bows and goes to her mother, while Korshunov tells the ser-

vant girls to sing a wedding song.... The struggle turns out to
be not very stubborn or prolonged, but even this demonstration
of her own desires speaks a great deal for Lyubov Gordeyevna.
Only extreme grief, only severe spiritual pain could have induced
her to open her mouth to pronounce words that ran counter to
her parent's will. But here too, think of the words she utters!
"Think it over!" "Don't make me unhappy!" What a wretched
position to be in! To be unable even to think of the possibility
of doing something independently, to repose all one's hopes in
the decision of another, in another's charity, at a time when dire
misfortune threatens one! ... How warped human nature must
become in this horrible family, where even the instinct of self-
preservation assumes such a slavish form! ...

The third act opens with a feast to celebrate the engagement
between Lyubov Gordeyevna and Afrikan Savich. Gordei Karpich
has had his way. Arina, the old serving-woman, reviles the future
husband and bewails the fate of the young girl. Palageya Yegorovna mournfully complains that her daughter is going to her
doom. Mitya comes to say goodbye; he has decided to go to his
mother to get over his misfortune. Palageya Yegorovna's tears and
complaints, however, anger him, and he taunts her with her cowardice and impotence. "It's no use complaining," he says, "you
are giving her away yourself. Rather than shed tears, you'd do
better not to give her away. Why are you ruining the girl? Why
are you putting her into slavery? Isn't it a sin?" and so forth.
The only answer Palageya Yegorovna can make is: "I know all
that, but I have no say in the matter. You ought not to blame
me, but pity me, Mitya." Mitya's heart is softened by these words
and he proceeds to tell her how much he loves Lyubov, and Palageya exclaims: "Oh, you poor boy! I can see how much you are
suffering! ..." She sympathizes with his grief in a way one
sympathizes with a person whose misfortune is beyond repair—
as if she had heard that Mitya had had his arms cut off, or that
his mother had died.... Suddenly Lyubov Gordeyevna comes in
and Mitya's heart is so touched that he tells Palageya Yegorovna
to wrap her daughter up as warmly as possible against the night
as he intends to take her to his mother and marry her. This is a
very bold decision, but it is not a serious and thought-out plan,
and it is doomed to perish as soon as it is born. Mitya himself

characterizes this impulse in the following words: "Ekh, make room for my soul—it wants to go on the spree! If I have to answer for it, at least I'll know that I've had a bit of fun." And so this is nothing but an outburst of wild desperation, of which even the most timid people are capable for an instant. But Mitya has not the strength to persist in his demand, and meeting with the refusal of both the mother and the daughter he very soon abandons his intention with the remark: "Well, evidently it was not fated to be so." As for Lyubov Gordeyevna, she is so crushed that she cannot even think of the possibility of agreeing to Mitya's proposal. . . . This is not surprising: she stands very much closer to Gordei Karpich and has felt the influence of his tyranny much more than Mitya. That is why she uncomplainingly puts up with every torment rather than disobey her father. "No, Mitya, it cannot be," she says. "Don't torment yourself in vain; don't break my heart. . . . It pains me enough as it is. . . . Go, and God be with you." And Mitya goes away, knowing that "by marrying Korshunov, Lyubov Gordeyevna is going to certain doom." Lyubov too knows that, and so does her mother—but all sadly and dully submit to their fate. . . . To such a degree has tyranny warped their human natures, crushed every independent feeling, deprived them of all ability to stand up for their sacred rights, their right to the inviolability of their feelings, independently to respond to the promptings of their hearts, to enjoy mutual love! . . .

If it were an irresistible power, a character of a higher order that dominated over these unhappy people! But this is not the case! . . . Gordei Karpich is not only extremely narrow-minded, he is also craven and fainthearted. This is also an inalienable and inevitable attribute of the tyrant. The tyrant raves, storms and yells as long as he meets with no opposition, or as long as opposition is timid and irresolute. . . . But he has no prop to support him in a long and serious struggle. He demands and commands, but he does not really understand either the real significance of his commands, or on what they are based. . . . Moreover, he is always beset by a vague, indefinite doubt about his rights; he has a vague feeling that many of his claims cannot be sustained by any right, or by any general law. . . . Fearing that others may become aware of this, he resorts to the customary weapon—intimidation. How this weapon serves to conceal every kind of paltriness, falsehood and sordidness, in short, weakness of every kind, is well known. A teacher who is rather ignorant himself tries to be very stern with his pupils to discourage them from asking him questions. An incompetent or dishonest chief of a department puts on an air of importance in order to discourage his subordinates from judging him too freely. A gentleman who possesses no real dignity tries to win the respect of his valet by sternness and rudeness.... Thanks to the general apathy and complacency that prevail among people, this behaviour nearly always successfully achieves its object. Sometimes somebody is prompted by a desire to ask his chief, or his teacher, why and wherefore?— but he sees that the one or the other is totally inaccessible, and so, waving his hand in disgust, he says: "Oh, to the devil with him! He'll only insult me for nothing at all!" As a consequence, and because people reason in this way the arrogant, stupid and dishonest tyrant continues undisturbed to enjoy all the advantages of his insolence and all the marks of ostensible respect from those around him. Universal compliance raises the pride of the tyrant and even lends him real strength. It compensates him for his lack of a sense of his inner dignity. Thus, for example, the gentleman who carts refuse out of the city could, in spite of the utter worthlessness of this refuse, demand an immense sum of money for it if he saw that people, because of some inexplicable illusion, attached some particular value to it.... But it is only an illusion of this kind that sustains the importance of the tyrant. As soon as he encounters strong and determined opposition his strength fails him, he begins to be afraid and loses his head. At first he will still show courage and obstinacy, but this is due entirely to habit. Accustomed to meet with dumb obedience, he at first refuses to believe that anybody could seriously oppose his will. Consequently, regarding every voice that expresses even a hint of a desire to limit his power as being due to a misunderstanding, he gives vent to his rage and tries to intimidate his victims even more than before, and in this way, in the majority of cases, he succeeds in subduing or crushing all discontent. But as soon as he sees that he is really not feared, that the opponent really intends to enter into determined combat with him, that the issue is "rather perish than yield," he immediately retreats, becomes milder, shuts up and transfers his rage to other objects, or to other people who are to blame only for the fact that they are weaker.... Everybody who has gone to school, who has been in government service, has carried out private commissions and, in general, has had dealings with men, has probably, more than once in the course of his life, come across tyrants of this kind and can confirm the practical justice of our remarks. Beware of contradicting an angry or incompetent superior *in passing*; you will be overwhelmed with a flood of extremely offensive abuse and threats. More than that, later on you will be pursued by your superior's unfavourable opinion about you: you are a liberal, you are disrespectful to your superiors, your head is stuffed with all sorts of fantastic ideas, he will say about you.... But if you want to serve and do business honestly, don't be afraid to enter into a serious and determined conflict with tyrants. In ninety-nine cases out of a hundred you will gain the upper hand. Only make up your mind beforehand not to stop halfway, make up your mind to carry on the fight to the end, even if it involves real danger for you, such as losing your place, or losing certain privileges. Your very first attempt to express your own opinion will be met by the tyrant raising his voice, but you continue in spite of that. Your opinion will be met either with abuse or with censure, more or less discourteous, according to the importance and the habits of the person you are addressing. But do not let this daunt you; raise your voice to the same pitch that the tyrant raises his, speak as forcibly as he does, assume an increasingly resolute tone in proportion as his ire rises. If the conversation ends that first day, resume it the next, and the day after that, and don't go over the old ground again, but continue from where you left off the day before. If you do that you may be sure that you will win the day. The tyrant will hate you, but he will fear you more. He will be glad to get rid of you and ruin you, but knowing that you will give him a lot of trouble, he will himself try to avoid fresh conflicts with you, and, in fact, will become extremely compliant. In the first place he lacks the inner strength to wage an open struggle on equal terms; and in the second place, he is, in general, unaccustomed to persistent and persevering effort. And to fight a man who boldly and persistently challenges you calls for no little effort....

And so, as a tyrant, Gordei Karpich is extremely fainthearted and lacks stamina. As substitutes for all the qualities of the really strong character he possesses unbridled tyranny and dull-witted stubbornness. This explains and justifies the apparent suddenness of the climax which Ostrovsky gave the comedy *Poverty Is No Crime*. When this comedy appeared all the critics attacked the author for having given the play an arbitrary denouement. The sudden change in Gordei Karpich, his quarrel with Afrikan Savich, and the attention he pays to Lyubim Tortsov's demands seemed unnatural to them all. Furthermore, they claimed that the author had endowed Tortsov with generosity and had artificially ennobled his character. We think there is no need now to go to the trouble of proving that Ostrovsky had no such intention; the character of his literary activities has taken definite shape and in one of his subsequent works he himself pronounced the word which in our opinion can best serve to indicate the trend of his satire. To ridicule tyranny in all its forms, to pursue it to its last refuge, even where it assumes the mask of nobility and generosity—this, we are convinced, is the real goal to which Ostrovsky's talent is constantly directed, quite independently of the views and theoretical convictions he may temporarily hold. In three of his comedies the tyrants he depicts are prompted by generous impulses, and in every case they are silly, superfluous or offensive. In *Don't Get Into Another's Sleigh*, Rusakov's heart softens towards his daughter, he magnanimously changes his mind and consents to his daughter marrying Vikhorev. Why should he do this? He is apparently convinced that this marriage will be fatal for his daughter. He had proved this only a few moments earlier with fairly sound arguments; only a few moments before he had displayed firmness and had threatened to withhold his blessing if he were disobeyed. All of a sudden he generously yields! What is this due to? Partly to kindness of heart and paternal love, but mostly to the absence of firm foundations for the decision he had previously made. A man who knows what he is doing and has his heart in what he is doing will not abandon his purpose in response to a momentary whim. This same Rusakov would refuse to shave off his beard or put on a dress suit, in spite of all the pain this refusal would cause his daughter. But as regards his daughter's fate, his convictions are not even as strong and as definite as they are as regards wearing a beard and a dress suit. That is why he can change his mind so easily in a matter that concerns his daughter, although in the eyes of some critics this is a piece of touching generosity, like his payment of Vikhorev's debts!

Tortsov's generosity is also distinguished for its irrationalness. He is immensely fond of his future son-in-law, Afrikan Savich. "Can you understand me now?" he asks him, and it seems as though he wants nothing more than that his son-in-law should understand him. To please him he seals his friendship with him, he sacrifices his daughter, spurns her prayers and her mother's tears and apparently humbles himself and allows his future son-in-law to treat him somewhat patronizingly. But Lyubim Tortsov gets nasty with the future son-in-law; the latter takes offence at this and rather rudely makes Tortsov feel it by concluding his speech to him with the words: "No, now *you* come begging to me to take your daughter." Gordei Karpich flies into a rage on hearing these words and bursts out with the question: "What! I go begging to you?" And Korshunov adds fuel to the fire by saying: "You will. I know you. You are dying to arrange a wedding for your daughter that will rouse the envy of the whole town. You'd put a noose around your neck to be able to do that, but nobody wants to take her.... That's your trouble." With these words Korshunov upsets his own apple cart; he employs the very method that tyranny cannot possibly stand, and which, in its turn, is nothing but the absurd product of tyranny. One tyrant says to another: "You wouldn't dare do a thing like that," and the other answers: "Yes, I would." Here the dispute is over the question: which of the two is the most stubborn? And if one of the disputants is trying to get something out of the other, the victor, of course, will be the one who is called upon to give. This will not cost the victor much effort; all he has to do is to stand pat and refuse to give. It is the same in this case. On hearing Korshunov say: "You won't dare," Gordei Karpich says:

"After hearing words like that from you I don't want to have anything more to do with you! I have never bowed down to anybody in all my life. If it comes to that I'll give her to anybody *I please*. With the dowry I shall give her any man will take her.... There! I'll give her to Mitka!"

And in his rage he repeats over and over again: "Yes, I'll give her to Mitka! To spite him I'll give her to Dimitry!..." Korshunov goes off in a huff and the domestics are all astonished, for so accustomed are they to Gordei Karpich's unreasonableness that they think he really intends to do what he says. Mitya, with the naiveté of a downtrodden youth who is very credulous and scarcely understands the true meaning of what is going on around him, even addresses himself to Tortsov in the following terms:

"Why to spite him, Gordei Karpich? Things like this are not done for spite I don't want anything done for me out of spite, I'd rather be in torment all my life. If you are that way inclined give us your blessing in the proper way, with a father's love."

But these naive words only rouse Tortsov to angry expostulation, of course, for he has no intention whatever of giving his daughter to Mitya.

"What! What!" he shouts. "You are glad to jump at the opportunity, are you? *How dare you even dream of such a thing?* Do you think you are her equal? Remember *whom you are talking to!*"

Mitya goes down on his knees before him, but this humiliation fails to disarm Gordei Karpich, he goes on raving. The supplications of his wife and daughter are also unavailing. But here Lyubim Tortsov, the reprobate who has already given Gordei Karpich so much trouble and whom he cannot handle at all, comes to their aid. He talks to him in the same tone that Korshunov had talked to him: "Go down on your knees and thank me for having shamed you," and Palageya Yegorovna adds: "You're right, Lyubimushka, we ought to go down on our knees and thank you...." One might have expected Gordei Karpich to get stubborn again to spite his domestics, and to think of something else also *out of spite*, but he only enquires in perplexity: "What am I, a monster or what, in my family?" From this you gather that generosity is beginning to gain the upper hand, now that he has gained his point in driving Korshunov out of the house and his vanity has been appeased for the time being. Moreover, he is already worn out by the strain he has put himself to and is unable to muster fresh strength for another struggle. And here the meek supplications of his wife are reinforced by the arguments and persistent requests of his brother Lyubim, who talks to him boldly and resolutely, holding nothing back, and reinforcing his requests with proofs taken from his own experience. Gordei Karpich's mind seems to become beclouded; he looks around as if trying to grasp what is going on around him and wondering what to do, as if seeking within himself for support in this struggle, but he can find nothing except his own tyrannical will. And it is this that finds expression in his last retort: "I don't care what you say, I don't want to listen to you." But Lyubim does not attach any particular importance to this retort and keeps on persisting. Gordei Karpich is utterly confused and exhausted, everything around him gets mixed up in his head, he cannot collect his thoughts which never hang very closely together, but which have now scattered in all directions.... At this critical moment he becomes maudlin, he bursts into tears, and thanking his brother Lyubim for his admonition, he gives his blessing to the future happiness of his children.... Taking advantage of his present frame of mind his nephew Guslin, whom he had forbidden to marry, asks for permission to do so and receives it. Gordei Karpich says: "Now, all of you, ask for whatever you want. I am a different man now!..."

What amazing generosity! Just think of it! You get the impression that an Oriental potentate is standing before you saying: "Everything is in my power!... At a mere sign from me your head will fly from your shoulders. At a mere word from me magnificent palaces will spring up out of the ground for you. Ask for whatever you desire. I can take half the world and give it to whomever I please...." The difference is only one of dimensions, the substance is the same as that contained in the words of Tortsov. Put him on the throne of some Caliphate and he will behave there in the same way as he behaves in his family. He will tyrannize, will spurn all human rights and recognize no law except his own will, and now and again will astonish everybody by his generosity, which will also be based on the same idea, namely: "Look! You have no rights whatever. Everything is entirely in my power. I can punish and I can pardon!..." Happy are we, readers, that we are living at the present time when such outbursts of generosity are impossible! ... They can be taken advantage of at certain moments in the way Mitya and Lyubov Gordeyevna took advantage of Karpich's outburst. They gained their point, although, of course, Gordei Karpich will not remain generous for

long, he will repent later on and blame them for his decision....
Such gains are unreliable. When you plan your future life you do
not, of course, base your plan on the possibility of winning a
fortune in a lottery. Similarly, it would be unwise in rational and
conscious life to count on winning the generosity of the tyrant.
It will be much better if there is none of that sweeping generosity
of the grand gentleman which old flunkeys, whose servility reached
the point of idiocy, went into raptures over. Let that which is mine
by right be sacred and inviolable, let me have the opportunity of
exercising my mind and will freely and rationally, always and not
only when I receive the gracious permission of some Gordei Karpich
Tortsov....

But in none of these comedies is the impotence and inherent
triviality of tyranny brought out with such astonishing force as in
Shouldering Another's Troubles. Here you have everything—rudeness, lack of honesty, cowardice and outburst of generosity and
it is all accompanied by such dull stupidity, that even those who
are most favourably disposed towards Slavophilism could not approve of Tit Titich Bruskov and merely observed that, after all,
he has a kind heart.... Agrafena Platonovna, the landlady of the
house in which the schoolteacher Ivanov and his daughter live,
speaks of Bruskov as of "a savage man, domineering, hardhearted,
to put it in a nutshell—a tyrant." Ivanov asks what she means by
tyrant, and she answers:

"A man who won't listen to anyone. You can hit him over the
head with a cudgel, but he won't budge. He'll stamp his foot and shout:
'Do you know who I am?' and everybody in the house must fall down
at his feet and lie there, otherwise it'll go hard with them...."

Continuing to describe him she says: "As for roguery, he's
certainly a shrewd old fellow; but rogue as he is, he's ignorant.
He's a terror only at home. Outside of his house you can do
anything you like with him, because he's a perfect fool, and can't
say boo to a goose." And indeed, as the play unfolds you find
that what Agrafena Platonovna says is right. She herself gets out
of him, as easily as anything when he comes to the Ivanovs' apart-
ment, a thousand rubles in return for a signed statement by his son
Andrei Titich promising to marry Ivanov's daughter. This statement is worthless, Ivanov and his daughter know nothing about
it and make no claims on it; the whole thing was arranged by the

landlady who wanted to be their benefactress. . . . But Bruskov is
so ignorant, so steeped in the customs of the "realm of darkness,"
that he does not seem to mind a bit. In the first place, he always
expects to be cheated, because he himself is always ready to cheat
others. That is why, glancing at the paper which Agrafena Platonovna shows him, he says quite calmly: "It's downright robbery.
You're a nice one!" and begins to haggle, not in the least put out
by the deal, but only expressing surprise at the trick that had been
played on his son. In the second place, he is terribly afraid of
going to court, because, although he relies on his purse, he is not
sure whether the case will go for or against him—all he knows is
that if he loses he will also have to pay a lot of money. And so,
when Agrafena Platonovna says: "It will have to take its legal
course now," he scratches his head and says: "Legal course?
No, better let's settle it between ourselves." And it is, indeed, much
easier for him to do that, because he is quite accustomed to deals
of this kind. On returning home from the Ivanovs he discusses this
point with his wife in the following way:

T i t   T i t i c h: Nastasya! Would anybody dare offend me?
N a s t a s y a   P a n k r a t y e v n a: Nobody would dare offend you,
Kit Kitich. You are the one to offend people.
T i t   T i t i c h: I can do people wrong, and I can forgive them, or
compensate them. I have paid out lots of money in that way in my time.
N a s t a s y a   P a n k r a t y e v n a: Lots of money, Kit Kitich, lots.
T i t   T i t i c h: Shut up!

Bruskov's lack of a clear conception of moral principles is
revealed in the way he permits himself to treat Agrafena Platonovna and the Ivanovs after he paid the money and gained possession of his son's written promise of marriage. Agrafena Platonovna tries to get him out of the house, but he sits down and becomes abusive, advancing the following argument: "No, wait. *At
least let me have a good swear for my money.*" But that is only to
relieve his feelings; he does not mean to be offensive when he
swears, and besides he himself has not been touched on the raw.
When Ivanov arrives and, knowing nothing of what had gone before, looks inquiringly at Bruskov, the latter addresses him in the
following terms: "What are you looking at me like that for?
There's nothing written on my face, brother. You could take money
from me all right. *The least you can do is to give me a little treat*

for my money." Ivanov asks him to go, and he becomes abusive
again. Ivanov orders him to go, and he retorts: "What are you
shouting for? *I don't mean any harm, I am only joking.*" Ivanov
insists that he should go, but Bruskov goes up to him, slaps him on
the back and says: "Come home with me. *We'll have a drink and
be friends. Why should we quarrel?*" Ivanov is beside himself with
rage now, and Bruskov looks at him dourly and observes: "My!
Isn't he riled?" and he leaves the house swearing again.... When
he arrives home he orders Zakhar Zakharich, a court clerk and a
confirmed drunkard, to draw up a petition "that will get three men
sent to Siberia." "I want it," he says, "and I don't care how much
it costs me." But here Ivanov arrives on the scene. In the meantime
he has learned about the whole business and brings back the money
that Agrafena Platonovna took and asks for the son's written promise. Bruskov at once jumps to the conclusion that Ivanov wants
the paper back in order to squeeze more money out of him, but
the old schoolteacher touches his heart and he turns to the clerk
and asks: "Shall I return it to him, Zakharich? Shall I?" "No,
no, no!" answers Zakhar Zakharich, but Bruskov suddenly makes
up his mind and says: "But I say give it back! ... You shut up!
Don't dare say anything! ..." He returns the paper and Ivanov at
once tears it up. Several moments later Bruskov arrives at the conclusion that "money and all that—is dirt" and therefore his son
may marry Ivanov's daughter even if she is poor.... "My word
is law," he says, and he sends his son to the schoolteacher to ask
for his daughter's hand. "But he won't agree, Dad, I'm sure he
won't!" the son answers. "I order you to go, do you hear?" Tit
Titich retorts. "How dare he refuse when I wish it? ... Don't dare
talk to me in that fashion," he adds. "If he refuses, don't let me
set eyes on you again! ..."

The remarkable thing about all this is that the whole story is
so absurd.... Looking at it soberly we must admit that everybody
in the story wants the impossible, or rather, they do not know what
they want. Without consulting the Ivanovs, Agrafena Platonovna
induces Andrei Bruskov to make the written promise of marriage
and extorts money from his father. Tit Titich wants to get the
Ivanovs exiled to Siberia on the basis of this document, which, in
his own interests, he ought to destroy. Ivanov strongly insists not
merely that the document should be destroyed, but that it should be

returned to him, although he does not need it in the least, and
thereby rouses Bruskov's just suspicions.... All this is utterly
senseless and absurd, as is Bruskov and the entire life he leads.
But the absurdest thing of all is the part played by Andrei Titich,
Bruskov's son, the cause of all the trouble, who, as he himself
expresses it, is "wandering around as if dazed," and complaining
that their home is "quite different from decent people's" and that
he had been "brought up to be a monster and not a human being."
Indeed, it is funny to see what they are doing with him. The lad
is well over twenty, nature has not deprived him of intelligence,
he knows the business of his father's factory better than anybody,
he knows what is wanted a long way ahead and, moreover, he
has a bent for learning and is fond of art—"has a passion for
the violin"—in short he is a grown-up lad, kindhearted and intelligent, grownup enough to want to get married and yet ... he
has to "hide from father." No sooner does he hear the dread announcement: "The master's come!" than he shouts: "Mum! Mum!
Hide me from Dad!" and runs to his mother's bedroom to hide.
What is the reason for this? The reason is that his father has
decided to force him to marry against his will ... and so he wants
to save himself by running away, you see! A splendid means he
chose to do so, indeed! And the only reason why his father wants
to force him to marry against his will is that he wants to do so....
Incidentally, the mother suggests another reason: the young woman
he has found for his son is very rich "and we," according to
Nastasya Pankratyevna, "want a bride with a lot of money *because—we ourselves are* rich!" This is incontestable logic! ... And
Andrei Titich can advance no strong argument against it. His
father has already reduced him to such a state that he regards
himself as "good for nothing." The treatment he receives at his
father's hands must indeed be nice if we are to judge by what he
tells Lizaveta Ivanovna, Ivanov's daughter. "My wings have been
clipped, or rather cut off," he says. He must marry not the girl
of his choice, but the one his father chooses for him.

"And if I say, 'Dad, I don't like the girl,' he says, 'I'll send you to
the army,' and I've got to shut up." "And not only in this matter," he
adds. "He won't let me have my way in other matters either. When I
was younger I wanted to study, but he wouldn't let me!"

Lizaveta Ivanovna advises him to choose an opportune moment to have a heart-to-heart talk with his father, to tell him that he has ability, that he wants to study and so forth. To this Andrei replies:

"He'll give me such a heart-to-heart talk that I won't know where to hide. Do you think he doesn't know that it is better to be educated than ignorant? But he wants to have it all his own way.... It's mere caprice on his part, mere envy that he is uneducated and thinks I want to be more educated than he."

Now is it possible to talk reasonably with people like that? The father knows that it is better to be educated than ignorant, the son knows that the father knows this, the son wants to acquire education, but the father forbids him, and he dare not disobey! ... The father admits that he is uneducated, he realizes that this is bad, but he is afraid that his son may avoid this evil! ... The son knows that his father forbids him to study only because of his own ignorance, but he deems it his duty to submit to this ignorance! ... Who can disentangle the idiotic confusion which the tyrant has introduced into his family relationships? Who will dare to cast a ray of light into the outrageous gloom of this inexplicable logic of the "realm of darkness"? One would think that Andrei Titich is as insane as his brother Kapitosha, who is another interesting product of the domestic discipline that prevails in the Bruskov house. ... But everybody around him says that Andrei Titich is intelligent; he himself reasons intelligently about his brother. "He [his father] won't let me go to the theatre because, he says, we already have one in the family who is mad on the theatre. But he is not mad from going to the theatre; he's mad *because they beat him too much when he was little....*" Andrei has not been brought to such a state, but for all that he gives the impression of being not quite right in the head. If only he would resign himself to his condition, as hundreds and thousands of others do! But no, he refuses to do that, and this drives his father and mother to despair. The mother grieves over him even more than she does over her other son, the imbecile. Kupidosha's condition seems to disturb her little, it seems quite natural and understandable to her, she even finds amusement in it. What grieves her more is that he smokes very strong tobacco.

"Our Kupidoshka is quite mad on the theatre," she explains to her guest Nenila Sidorovna. "And he smokes such strong tobacco that it's simply impossible to breathe. Nobody ought to smoke such tobacco indoors, not under any circumstances! It's enough to make anybody sick.... So he spends his time mostly in the kitchen. *Sometimes it is so dull that I call him and he begins to rant like an actor, and so he amuses me a little.* He sings bass in the choir, and his voice is so loud that it sounds like gunfire."

Thus, the son's imbecility even provides some pleasant moments for the mother! ... But Andrei's intelligence causes her very grave misgivings.

"He is getting quite out of hand," she says. "He's always complaining about this, that and the other. 'I want to study,' he says.... But what does he want a lot of learning for? *He's saucy enough as it is, and if he gets any education it'll be impossible to talk to him. He'll lose all respect for his mother. It's enough to drive anybody out of the house....*"

Thus, part of Bruskov's tyrannical habits pass to his wife, although only in words, and Andrei, in spite of all his love of learning and all his natural gifts, must grow up an ignoramus in order to retain respect for his father and mother. They, poor things, realize that an intelligent and educated man cannot respect them! ...

But if Andrei Titich is really an intelligent young man, why does he not dare to satisfy his passion for learning and even in this case dare to be a little disobedient? After all, there have been cases in Russia of lads with a passion for learning who have thrown up everything and have gone to study, not caring a straw for the opinion of their parents, or about how they were going to obtain their livelihood.... Yes, but those lads must in some way have shielded themselves from the deadening influence of tyranny, they were not cowed in their childhood and, as a consequence, they were able to develop a certain amount of determination to enter into the battle of life, to develop some strength of will. Nothing of this kind can be expected of Andrei and Kapitosha Bruskov. These unfortunate lads were beaten in childhood, and are constantly being bullied and often made a laughing stock of even now, when they are grownup. How could bright and independent intelligence and strong determination develop in them? Andrei Titich, perhaps, possesses only enough determination to storm and rage later on like his father, to bully others in revenge for having been bullied by others.... And so, this

outrageous hierarchy passes from generation to generation, and
he who rises to the top tramples upon and crushes those who
remain down below. What else can he do? This dense crowd of
indolents who pushed his worship to the top is his only prop in
life; willy-nilly he is obliged to crush them with his own weight
more or less, otherwise he will fall at the feet of others again
and, who knows, may be trampled upon. . . . And who wants to be
trampled upon?

But here a question of an entirely different kind may arise,
namely: why do these indolents so persistently support above
themselves a man who has done them nothing but harm? Why
does Mitya humble himself so before Tortsov? Why does Andrei
torment himself so without daring to utter a word of protest to
Tit Titich? And so forth. Why does the whole of society tolerate
in its midst so many tyrants who are preventing the development
of all order and truth? The society which is brought up under
the influence of the Tortsovs and Bruskovs has no determination
to fight. But one cannot help admitting that if the tyrant by himself is inherently infirm, which is the case, as we have seen above,
his importance can be sustained only by the support of others.
Hence, no exceptional heroism is required here; let society with-
draw this support from him, let the crowd which presses closely
together in order to support a Tortsov or a Bruskov spread out
a bit, and he will fall, and really be trampled upon if he persists
in his claim to tyranny. . . . Why, then, has society tolerated for
so many scores and hundreds of years this impotent, decayed and
decrepit phenomenon, which the best and truly educated section
of society has long regarded as obsolete? There are two important reasons for this which are clearly brought out in Ostrovsky's
comedy, and to which we now intend to draw our readers' attention.

V

> With patience bear your burden
> And beg without complaint.
>
> *Lomonosov*[83]

The first reason which restrains people from opposing tyranny is, strangely enough, *respect for the law*, and the second is the
need for material security. At a first glance the two reasons we

have put forward must, of course, seem absurd. The very opposite would appear to be the case: the absence of respect for the
law and disregard for material well-being would seem to explain
people's indifference to all the claims of the tyrant. Those who
reason on the basis of abstract principles could now advance the
following argument: "Tyranny recognizes no law except its own
arbitrary rule. The consequence of this is that all who are subjected to its influence gradually lose respect for the law, no longer
regard the actions of the tyrant as wrong and outrageous and,
therefore, suffer them with a fair amount of indifference. Moreover,
in the distribution of wealth of every kind, the tyrants, according
to their custom, always cheat them, take the lion's share for themselves and leave them scarcely anything. Since they tolerate this,
it shows that they have already lost an interest in their own welfare, that they have grown accustomed to having nothing and
care little about extricating themselves from this situation....
In view of the indifference all these Mityas and Andreis display
towards their material interests, it is not surprising that the tyrants
bully them when prompted by the whims of their 'rotten imagination,' as Gordei Karpich expresses it."

Notwithstanding its apparent soundness, this argument is extremely shallow. How is it possible to assume that people can
lose all interest in themselves, in their own welfare? And why?
Because it entered somebody's head to rob me of my wealth! ...
No, this might be said only if all those who were oppressed by
the tyrant were extremely pleased with their position. But we
see that Mitya, Andrei, Kapitosha, Avdotya Maximovna and Lyubov
Gordeyevna are all very discontented with their lot. Consequently,
it is not their indifference that keeps them in their present condition, but something more profound.... This something is respect for the law. If it were not for that respect, that is to say, if
the oppressed side really became convinced that there was no
order and no law, and that law and order were unnecessary, it
would behave quite differently. The orders of the tyrant would
be obeyed only as long as it was to the advantage of the obedient
to do so, and as soon as Tortsov encroached upon the well-being
of Mitya and the other assistants, they would, without thinking
twice, "overthrow" him.... They outnumber and are stronger
than Gordei Karpich.... But they quietly submit to him pre-

cisely because he is the master and must be respected. The fact that
he cheats and insults them they regard as the lawful attribute of
his position. . . . It was not in irony, but, on the contrary, in a
marked tone of awe that Nastasya Pankratyevna says to her husband: "Nobody would dare offend you, Kit Kitich. You are the one
to offend people. . . ."

This turn of affairs is very strange, but such is logic in the
"realm of darkness." In this case, however, it is precisely the
blindness of these people that explains the situation. What is respect for law in the general sense, in our meaning of the term?
It is not something fixed and formed, it is not an absolute principle of morality clothed in a certain form fixed for all time. Its
origin is very simple. On entering society I acquire the right to
a certain share of certain benefits which are available to all its
members. For this I pledge myself to pay by striving to increase
the total sum of benefits available in that society. This pledge
follows logically from the general conception of justice which
is inherent in human nature. But in order more successfully to
achieve the common goal, i.e., to increase the sum of general benefits, people adopt a certain line of conduct and guarantee it by
certain provisions which prohibit anybody from arbitrarily hindering the common effort. On entering into society I must accept
these provisions and promise not to violate them. Consequently,
I enter into something in the nature of a contract with society,
not an expressed or formulated contract, but a tacit one. Hence,
if I violate the laws of society and at the same time enjoy their
benefits I violate part of the stipulations of the contract, the stipulations that are irksome for me, and I become a liar and a
cheat. By the rule of just retribution, society may deprive me of
the right to participate in the benefits of the other stipulations,
which I regard as advantageous and compel me to pay for what
I have enjoyed without any right to do so. I myself feel that such
a decision would be just and that my conduct was unjust—now
this is exactly what is meant by my respect for the law. But I do
not feel that I have transgressed against respect for law if I renounce the stipulations (which, it must be observed, by their very
nature cannot be laid down for any given term in this case), if
I voluntarily renounce their benefits and, therefore, renounce their
obligations. For example, if I join the army I might rise to be

a general, but being a private I would be obliged, in conformity
with the rules of military discipline, to salute every officer. But
if I do not join the army, or if I resign from it, I thereby renounce the military uniform and the hope of rising to be a general, and, on the other hand, regard myself as free from the
obligations to raise my hand to the peak of my cap on meeting
every officer. But take the peasants in remote villages—they bow
low to everybody they meet wearing foreign clothes. They may do
this voluntarily, or it may be an expression of their particular
conception of respect for law! ... We do not recognize this sort
of respect; we feel that we are right when, if we are not in government service, we do not go to the office every day, and when,
receiving no pay, we make no deductions for the benefit of dis-
abled soldiers, etc. Similarly, we would feel that we were right if,
for example, we arrived in a Mohammedan country and, while
submitting to its laws, did not embrace the Islamic faith. We would
say: "The laws of the country protect us from those forms of
violence and injustice which are regarded as illegal here and may
injure our well-being, therefore we recognize them in practice.
But we do not feel obliged to go to a Mosque because we feel no
desire to pray to the Prophet, we feel no need for the truth and
consolation of the Koran, and do not believe in Mohammed's
paradise with all its houris. Consequently, we shall not enjoy the
benefits of Islam, nor do we wish to do so." We would be acting
correctly in this case in conformity with respect for law in the
true sense of the term.

Thus, laws are of conventional validity in relation to ourselves.
But this is not all: they are in themselves neither eternal nor
absolute. In accepting them as conditions which have evolved from
the experience of the past we do not by any means pledge ourselves to regard them as perfect and to reject all other conditions.
On the contrary, by its very nature, my contract with society includes the obligation to try to find the best possible laws. From
the point of view of the general, natural rights of man, every
member of society must constantly strive to secure the improvement of the existing laws and the abolition of those which have
become harmful or superfluous. All that is needed is that the
changes in the laws for the common good shall be subject to
common judgment and receive common consent. If, however, that

common consent is not obtained, the individual has the right to argue and prove the correctness of his own proposals, and lastly, to refrain from participating in all matters concerning which he regards the existing rules as fallacious.... Thus, the very respect for law eliminates stagnation and immobility in social organization; it gives scope and work for the mind and will; this very respect for law often calls for the violation of the formal status.

This is how respect for law is understood and explained by enlightened people, by people who, like ourselves, participate in the benefits of civilization. But it is not so understood by those ignorant people whom Ostrovsky depicts for us. In his "realm of darkness" the situation is entirely different. It is ruled by certain forms, fixed and defined for all time. Here learning is confined to a very close circle, there is scarcely any work to do for the mind; everything proceeds mechanically, in a definite order fixed for all time. Hence, it is quite logical that here children never grow up, but remain children until they mechanically move into the places of their fathers. It is also logical that those who serve as the intervening links between the tyrant and the oppressed have no definite personality of their own, but acquire their character from the position in which each finds himself: one day he cringes before his superiors and another day he, in his turn, looks down with contempt upon his inferiors. They are just like mechanical dolls: if you turn them one way they bow, if you turn them the other way they stand up straight and throw their heads back.... Nastasya Pankratyevna seems to wilt in the presence of her husband, she dare not breathe, nevertheless she bawls at her son: "How dare you?" and "Who are you talking to?" We see the same thing with Agrafena Kondratyevna in *Our Own Folks*. The same thing is repeated in another class with Yusov in *A Lucrative Post*. And all this is due to their lack of inner independence, to their downtrodden natures. From his earliest years a man had it dinned into his head that he in himself is nothing, that he is only an instrument of another's will and, consequently, he must not reason but only obey, obey and submit. The only object upon which he can still direct his mind is gaining the ability to adjust himself to circumstances. Whoever is able to do that is saved, he will rise to the top.... Those who are unable to do so are doomed—they will be crushed....

As a consequence of this mental ossification the active side of respect for law completely vanishes in the "realm of darkness" and only the passive side remains. Some Tishka has learned by rote that he must obey his elders and he remains only with this in his mind, and will remain so for the rest of his life.... It is a postulate of pedagogics that for children who are not yet capable of grasping abstract ideas the teacher is the personification of the moral law and, therefore, the child must trust the teacher. But it is the duty of the teacher, the rules of pedagogics go on to say, to make himself superfluous for the child as soon as possible by teaching it to understand the moral law in its true essence independently of the teacher's authority. All the inhabitants of the "realm of darkness" fear this latter rule like fire and murder, and all try to act in the very opposite spirit. "Listen to the old man, the old man will never give you bad advice," says even the best of them, Rusakov, and he too refuses to recognize the rights of education which teaches a man to distinguish between good and evil without the advice of others. And that is why respect for law finds expression only in obedience and patience; all the rest remains quite beyond the reach of the inhabitants of the "realm of darkness" until he himself becomes a tyrant. Tishka sweeps the floor in Bolshov's house, runs to bring Podkhalyuzin vodka and steals rubles from his master—and all this is quite lawful in his opinion.... It is the elders who send him for vodka and elders must be obeyed; this is irrefutable logic. He is not told to steal, but that does not matter—stealing is also sanctioned by the elders: how many times have the shop assistants boasted in his presence about some adroit trick they have carried off, how many times have they told him to say nothing to their employer about their shady tricks, how many times has the master himself explained to the assistants how to cheat customers! ... All this has left its impression upon this quick-witted boy—and hence all the abominations which calmly exist within him side by side with profound respect for the law.... And this is the means with which he is fighting his way out of his state of insignificance; and he is beginning himself to tyrannize with an absolutely clear conscience, for he regards tyranny as being just as legitimate as his former humiliation.

Of course, not everybody rises to the top. In fact, only very few succeed in doing so. For that one must have a fairly strong character and the ability to turn it inside out in the most unnatural way. One must suppress all one's sympathetic sentiments, dull one's mind and, in addition, bind one's arms and legs for several years and at the same time be able to sacrifice one's own pride and personal profit when necessary, make a clean job of every deal and play adroit tricks. ... Not many can do that. ... True, there are any number who try to do this, but not all have the stamina of, for example, Pavel Ivanovich Chichikov—and without stamina you can gain nothing here. ... That is why most of the people who fall under the influence of the tyrant prefer simply to suffer in the dull hope that somehow things may change. ... They lack the inner strength that could rouse them to oppose evil, nor can they possess it, for they have never had the opportunity really to learn what was evil and what was good. ... That is why they have no sense of justice and no conception of higher moral virtue; they only possess a respect for law in the accepted and narrow sense of the term. For them behaviour and the phenomena of life are divided not into good and evil, but only into the permitted and not permitted. What is permitted, what is sealed by a positive law, or simply by a command. is good to them. When there are no positive commands about certain things, they find themselves in a quandary. That is why they are always so timid and slow whenever any new question or phenomena calling for a change in the existing system arises. ... Here painful misgivings overcome these poor oppressed beings who, under the influence of tyranny, have lost all ability to think. On learning that a rule which they have followed has been abolished or has become extinct, they are completely at a loss to know where to turn or what to do—and they are overjoyed to meet the first newcomer who offers to lead them. It goes without saying that this first newcomer is, in the majority of cases, a rogue and a tyrant, and the bigger the rogue the denser is the crowd of "simpletons" who wish to be guided by another's mind and live under another's will, even if that of a tyrant. ...

The thoughts we have just expressed are not the fruit of any ready-made theory, they are simply the deductions that logically follow from the phenomena of the Russian way of life as depicted in Ostrovsky's comedies. There can be no doubt that the artist

had no intention of bringing out the ideas that we are now de-
ducing from his comedies; but they follow from his plays automatically and are expressed with amazing truth. The personages
in his comedies always remain true to the position in which they
have been placed by tyrannical rule. They do not utter a single
word that would raise them above the level of that way of life,
they always retain the main features of their type as moulded by
life itself. Even the best of the characters in Ostrovsky's comedies lack that boldness of virtue which we could demand of them
under other circumstances, but which they cannot possibly possess
under the yoke of tyranny. Only as feeble embryo do we see in
them the beginnings of a higher moral development; but these
beginnings are so faint that they cannot serve as the stimulus
and justification of practical activity. That is why all the moral
grounds of action of the honest people in Ostrovsky's comedies
are superficial and extremely restricted; that is why they all re-
volve around obedience to another's will, without the inner conviction that what they are doing is right. Thus, Avdotya Maximovna, in refusing to elope with Vikhorev advances only the one
argument that her father will curse her; and when she does run
away with him she grieves only over the fact that "my father
will disown me, and the whole town will point the finger of scorn
at me." In the case of Lyubov Gordeyevna, this superficial submission to duty uninspired by inner conviction is expressed even
more strongly. This, for example, is what she says to Mitya in
justification of her decision to marry Korshunov:

"I must not disobey my father. My father wishes me to marry. I must
obey him. *Such is the lot of us girls. It must be so, for that has been the
custom for ages.* I don't want to oppose my father's wishes *and have people
talking about me and pointing at me as a bad example.* Although it breaks
my heart to do so, at all events, I know *I shall live according to the law*
and nobody will be able to laugh at me."

There is not the shadow of a hint in these words about the
moral significance of her behaviour, but there is the word
"law".... But the nature of this law, and how common sense
applies it to the present case, this girl cannot discuss: her upbringing under the yoke of tyranny has made her totally incapable
of discussing such things.
    Obedience is elevated to the plane of the supreme, absolute

law by the tyrant himself, and even more persistently than by the
oppressed side. . . . This is quite logical: in the first place the
tyrant also almost entirely lacks true moral concepts and, consequently, he cannot properly distinguish between good and evil,
and, consequently, must be guided by his own caprices. In the
second place, the absolute obedience of others is very much to
his advantage, because, having achieved that, he can do exactly
as he pleases. But here too, of course, the logic of the tyrant
differs very much from general human logic. According to general
logic, if a man does establish any particular rules and demands,
even arbitrary ones, he should respect them himself in the given
cases and circumstances equally with everybody else. But the tyrant does not reason in this way. He thinks he has a right to
violate whenever he pleases even those rules which he himself
recognizes, and in conformity with which he judges others. And
so dark is the mind in the "realm of darkness" that not only the
tyrant, but all those who are wronged and oppressed by him,
regard this state of affairs as being quite natural. This curious
aspect of the organization of the "realm of darkness" is best expressed in the comedy *You Can't Live As You Like*. From the
literary point of view, this play is regarded as inferior to the
others; it is said that its conception is weak, that some of the
situations are artificial, and so forth. We shall refrain from dealing with it at great length here not because it does not merit
lengthy treatment, but, firstly, because our essay is already too long,
and secondly, the play itself is a very simple one—as regards both
the plot and the characters—so that there is no need to say much
about it, particularly after what has already been said above. The
gist of the play is as follows: Pyotr Ilyich is a drunkard, he tyrannizes over his wife, deserts her and takes a mistress. When the
wife hears about this she decides to leave her husband and go back
to her parents, but a common court of good old folks pronounces
her to be the guilty one. . . . On the way home she meets her father
and mother at an inn. She tells them about her grief and adds
that she has left her husband in order to go to live with them
because all her patience has given out. The father is amazed on
hearing of such libertarianism. "What do you mean, with us?
Why with us?" he exclaims. "No! Come, I'll take you back to
your husband." Dasha says: "No, father, I shall not go back to

him," and the father, believing that his daughter has taken leave
of her senses, admonishes her in the following way:

"Try and understand, you ninny, try and understand! How can I
take you home? Why, he's your husband! ... (*Gets up from the bench*).
Come, what's the use of talking nonsense, what can't be!... How can
you run away from your husband, you ninny? D'you think I am not
sorry for you? Well, let's all weep together over your grief—this is all
we can do to help you! What can I do? I can weep with you, but that's
all. Why, I am your father, my child, my darling child! (*Weeps and
kisses her*.) Try to understand, my darling daughter: those whom God
hath joined let no man tear asunder. Our fathers lived this way and
never complained or grumbled. Are we wiser than they? Come, let's go
back to your husband."

These inhuman words were prompted simply by the old man's
total inability to understand how it is possible for a wife to leave
her husband! He cannot possibly conceive of such a thing. To
him the idea is so absurd that he does not even know how to
argue against it. It would be the same with us if, for example,
we were told that man ought to walk on his hands and take his
food with his feet! What argument would we advance against
that? ... All the old man can do is go on repeating: "How can
that be? ... Try and understand what this means.... How can
you leave your husband? What do you mean? ..."

One would think that the same argument would apply to the
husband too, but no, he is above the law! ... He is his wife's
master. and he tyrannizes over her as much as he pleases even
when he is guilty before her and knows it. He learns that his
wife has heard about his "beauty," the "beauty" hears that he is
married, and refuses to have anything more to do with him. What
does he do? Is he ashamed to present himself to his wife? Is he
repentant? Nothing of the kind! When he gets home he even vents
his spite on his wife for having been dismissed by his "beauty"....
One would have thought that this would have outraged the feelings
of the poor wife's parents: in front of them he, who is entirely
to blame, raves and storms and, beside himself with rage, he even
threatens to cut his wife's throat and rushes out into the street
with a knife.... Dasha says to her father: "You can see for yourself what a sweet life I lead with him." But the father advises
her to "bear it, wait!" "What shall I wait for, what can I expect
from him when even his own father has disowned him?" answers

Dasha, shielding herself under the cloak of authority. "Never mind, bear it," the father reiterates, and then tries to present her misfortune as just retribution for her own disobedience, for having married without her parents' consent. This is what he says:

Agafon: This is too bad, this is too bad! Oh, oh, oh! It's too bad! But are you in the right? Didn't you run away and leave your old parents? Tell me, didn't you? Ought you have done a thing like that? Does the law allow you to do things like that? The devil tempted you! You are inhuman. So now bear, bear it! Take this punishment meekly and gratefully!... What are you thinking of doing, eh? What are you thinking of doing? Run away! Is that the proper thing to do? Where have you seen husband and wife living separately? Well, suppose you leave him, run away from him and he becomes desperate—who will be to blame then? Who? Suppose he falls sick—who will nurse him? Why that's your first duty. And when his last hour comes and he wants to bid you farewell and you in your pride have left him....

Dasha (*throwing herself on his neck*): Father!

Agafon: So think it over, daughter dear, think it over well.... (*Weeping*.) We are so foolish! Oh, how foolish we are! And proud!

Note how kind and sensitive this old man is, and also how hardhearted, only because he has no conception of the moral value of personality and is accustomed to subordinate everything only to the external laws established by tyrants. It is not because he is hardhearted, or angry, but simply because he is naive that he rebukes his daughter for the past at a time when her heart is breaking. And what arguments he advances! He does not say your husband will suffer, fall sick, and so forth. Won't you be sorry for him? or something else in the same strain prompted by the heart. No, he advances quite other grounds: "Who will *be to blame?*" And "This is *your first duty*...." And on the grounds of this purely superficial morality he urges his daughter to "bear it, bear it, everything will turn out well."

And indeed a fatuous fortuity occurs to justify the old man's words in exactly the same way as in the case of the merchant's wife who "went and died after her silly old dog had been howling for three nights running. What further proof would you have?"

Mad with drink, Pyotr Ilyich rushes to the Moscow River with a knife in his hand, seeing nothing and understanding nothing. Suddenly he hears the sound of church bells calling worshippers to morning prayers. Mechanically he raises his hand to cross himself, sees the knife and suddenly realizes that he is standing

on the brink of a hole in the ice.... Fear overtakes him, his
intoxication is dispelled in an instant, he remembers the admonitions of his father and goes back home full of repentance. After
hearing his tale Dasha's father says to her in a tone at once smug
and tender: "I told you so, little daughter, didn't I! ..." And
that is the end.

When one ponders over this story it seems to acquire a frightfully fantastic significance. Some critics asserted that this scene
indicates how beneficial for the people is the sound of church
bells, and how in most desperate moments a man is saved by the
pious habits that were inculcated in him in his childhood. It is
needless to say how strange this interpretation is. No, we see something entirely different in this drama relative to the general idea
that runs through all Ostrovsky's productions. Repentant Pyotr
Ilyich reveals to us the joyless and hopeless position into which
he himself and all those connected with him have been plunged
by the tyrannical way of life. Pyotr Ilyich's father admonishes
him, his aunt pleads with him, his wife, whom his behaviour is
killing, supplicates him, his friend reasons with him, the girl for
whose sake he deserts his wife rejects him—but all this has no
effect upon him. He is totally unconscious of the living principles
of morality, his heart is absolutely coarse and dull. Even his love
is savage and outrageous! He falls in love with Dasha and takes
her away from her father, but several months later he is already
tyrannizing over her and regards her unassuming and self-sacrificing love as the bane of his existence. He is madly in love with
Grusha; but what does he do when she jeers at him and orders
him to leave her? He goes to Yeromka, who has an acquaintance
who tells fortunes, and asks him whether he can "put a charm
over the girl to make her love me; *so that I should be able to
lord it over her as much as I please and not have her lording
it over me.*" This is what he is striving for, such is the nature of
his love: to be able to lord it as much as he pleases over the
woman he loves! ... It is terrible to think that all the inhabitants
of the "realm of darkness," as far as we know them from Ostrovsky's plays, have such tyrannical inclinations, if they are not
themselves downtrodden to the point of completely losing their
own personalities.... What can bring these wretched people to
their senses, what can rescue from them those unfortunates who

22*

are compelled to suffer from them? Nothing, positively nothing
in the way of ordinary means. Their concepts and characters cannot be changed in any natural way. Something extraordinary,
something extreme, violent, even if absolutely absurd, is needed
to sober them. It so happened that Pyotr Ilyich reached the brink
of the hole in the ice on the Moscow River just when the church
bells were calling worshippers to morning prayers, and this
brought him to his senses. But suppose this had not happened? ...
He would have continued his miserable existence with his wife
for many years more, as many in the "realm of darkness" continue it. And even now what guarantee is there that his repentance is lasting? Is there anything in his character that shows
promise of moral reformation? It goes without saying, of course,
that a drunkard must sleep off the effects of his drinking bout,
that a man who drinks until he reaches a state of delirium tremens
should give up drinking for a time, should take a rest and recu-
perate his strength. But is it for long? Do not forget that Pyotr
Ilyich's repentance was prompted by the phantoms and monsters
which he saw in his delirium. ... He may assert, and all his neighbours may believe him, that a water sprite or some other sprite,
led him on; but we know positively that all this is the figment
of a perverted imagination, of an overheated brain. What guarantee of future moral reformation can there be here? While he still
feels exhausted after the recent drinking bout, and while the horror of that event is still vivid in his mind, he will keep a guard
on himself. ... But later on he will return to his old ways, and
knowing that consciousness of the necessity of leading an honest
and useful life is totally undeveloped in him, we can be certain
that this is what he will do. ... And the poor woman, his wife,
will have to bear her bitter lot as before, unless another miracle
happens. And the old folks, her father and mother, will continue
to grieve for her and urge her to bear it! ... Life is now easier
for them, for they have already become completely depersonalized,
they are thoroughly imbued with the doctrine that you must

> With patience bear your burden
> And beg without complaint.

But will the unhappy woman whose young nature still retains
some remnants of life, and who still, at times, protests, even if

feebly, against the dark force which unjustly and senselessly
oppresses her, be able to bear it?...

Certainly not. She will inevitably fall, fall not in the sense
of the term which in the vulgar language of our artificial morality is applied to the full enjoyment of love, but in the real sense
of the term, in the sense of losing her moral purity and strength.
A man may fall in this way equally with a woman; but for a
loving woman's nature there is a road to this fall which may
tempt her at any moment, and only one step along this road may
make her a criminal in the eyes of society and seal her doom.
This road is intercourse with a man. A man too may seek in
intimate intercourse with a woman a refuge from the gloom and
the abominations which surround him in his practical life. Here
he finds repose and peace; here he seeks oblivion. But for a man
such relations are not fatal; everybody regards them as innocent
diversions, they leave no stain upon a man's character as far as
society is concerned. He can break off these relations at any moment, return to his business relationships and enter into his customary environment without in the least having lost his moral
prestige. But it is different in the case of a woman. Having once
taken a false step she, by virtue of the prevailing morality, loses
all possibility of peacefully returning to the former road. She is
humiliated, degraded, cast out; all doors are closed to her, at all
events until she arrogantly hurls in the face of society her shame
ornamented with the gold of some tyrant. Then, perhaps, people
will bow and cringe to her. But even in that case her nature must
undergo profound moral corruption. Thus, whichever road a girl
takes, she meets with difficulties and dangers; and every road she
takes must lead to the loss of her moral dignity. If she has not
yet become utterly coarse and vulgar she will be weighed down
by want and universal contempt, and she will be defenceless
against every man she meets, so that involuntarily and imperceptibly, she must accustom herself to deception, to idleness and to
living on other people.... Later, if she is lucky, when she has
grown accustomed to her situation, calmly sells her emotions and
enjoys luxurious idleness, open admiration, envy and the baseness of those around her will completely drive every kind sentiment out of her heart and plunge her into the very depths of depravity.... If she is not lucky, then ... well, moral people do

not even talk about such women, at least not when they are sober. . . .

But even such women were once pure and moral beings, worthy of the respect of the primmest Puritan champion of formal virtue. How did their fall come about? What caused them to step on to the wrong road? What decided their "first step"? One may speculate about this a great deal, but we do not wish to speculate; we ask these questions only because we find plain answers to them in Ostrovsky's comedies. Absence of active moral development, lack of inner support, and the yoke of tyranny outside of them— these are the causes which in the "realm of darkness" lead to immorality among women, as well as immorality among men. We have already seen how the absence of moral independence and dislike for everything that is called forth by tyranny find expression in vivacious and physically passionate characters. Puzatov's wife and sister have no other interest in life but that of deceiving him and surreptitiously carousing with young men after asking for and receiving permission to go to church. Lipochka Bolshova has a craze for army officers, is afraid of her father, does not care a brass tack about her mother, later marries Podkhalyuzin and coolly allows her father to be taken to the debtors' prison so as to avoid paying his creditors twenty-five kopeks in the ruble out of his own estate. . . . We have also seen how sweet and tender women fall and are crushed under the tyrant's yoke. Avdotya Maximovna, who remains a child even in her maturity, unable to understand either herself, her own position, or the people surrounding her, yields to the insinuations of Arina Fedotovna and is charmed by Vikhorev. . . . Lyubov Gordeyevna, who does not even dare to confess to her father that she loves Mitya, is ready to marry Korshunov, for whom she only feels fear and disgust. No less immoral is the position of Dasha, who is obliged to give her husband vodka, and when he is drunk he beats her. . . . But these are all facts of the past; we see before us already stifled personalities and we can only picture to ourselves the agony through which these young souls must have passed before they sank to this condition. But there is one play of Ostrovsky's in which we hear the whispering of a pure heart at the very moment when it is only just feeling the approach of an impure thought, a play which explains to us the whole process of the spiritual struggle that preceded the unwise passion of the girl who is crushed by the power of tyranny.... Our readers, of course, remember this play, for it appeared this year and attracted universal attention. We have already discussed this play in *Sovremennik* and therefore we shall say here only that which can directly help to explain our idea. Nadya, Ulanbekova's foster daughter, a kindhearted and intelligent girl, is imbued with very modest and very honest strivings. She dreams of domestic bliss with a man she loves, tries to "ennoble" herself so that no man may be ashamed to marry her, dreams of the good order she will keep in the house of the man she marries, tries to behave modestly, keeps away from that young gentleman, Ulanbekova's son, and even expresses astonishment at the pertness with which the young ladies of Moscow talk about their beaux and about the Guardsmen. "But how do they know all this?" she asks herself in amazement.... In short, this is a girl who under other circumstances would come up to the ideal of very many people. She wants with all her heart to be a good wife and a good housekeeper, and considering her character she could be one. Give her a little education and she will be a good mother and bring up her children well. But she lives in the house of Ulanbekova, of that outrageous tyrant in feminine attire, and everything must be lost for poor Nadya. The personality of Ulanbekova presents a striking example of tyranny transferred from the merchant's house to a different sphere. Here it is stronger, its influence is wider and, therefore, still more revolting. The merchant confines his tyranny to his domestics and to the people closely around him; he cannot act the tyrant in public, because as we have seen, being a tyrant, he is craven and fainthearted in the presence of every independent person. Heaven knows that Tit Titich Bruskov is tyrant enough, but even he does not dare to take too many liberties with Ivanov, and when he gets home he confesses that "they got the better of me only because I was in their house; had they come here, I'd have put them in their place." Pyotr Ilyich, with his ungovernable temper, after being dismissed by his "beauty," also lets himself go only when he returns home. "They laughed at me and drove me out! ... But here I am at home. I'll smash everything to smithereens!" he shouts in a frenzy. Thus, many of the merchant tyrants are "angry, but not strong," and society cannot suffer much from them. But the generic features of tyranny remain the same in all spheres, and the wider the sphere the more frightful and harmful it is. Ulanbekova's sphere of action is fairly extensive. In the first place she has numerous domestics—foster daughters, dependents, housekeepers, housemaids and flunkeys.... Then she has her serfs. Moreover, she is an important person in the county and exercises considerable influence. She decides other people's marriages, finds jobs for her dependents and saves them from legal prosecution.... As for the quality of her influence, that may be judged by certain of its features. She asks the Chief Constable to find her godson Negligentov a situation as head clerk, but the Chief Constable says that there are no vacancies. Ulanbekova takes offence at this and says to him: "Evidently you don't understand who is making the request." The Chief Constable is obliged to promise to find a vacancy. In this connection Vassilisa Peregrinovna, one of Ulanbekova's dependents, argues as follows:

"I simply can't imagine how he dared to oppose your wish. Now I can see how uneducated he is! Even suppose Negligentov doesn't deserve to have anybody bother about him, considering the way he lives, but for your sake the Chief Constable ought to do everything in the world for him, no matter what a rascal he is.... He's your godson and, of course, he ought not to listen to any talk.... Everybody knows, my benefactress, that you can pull a man out of the mire if you want to, but if you don't want to, he will die in obscurity even if he is as wise as Solomon. And he would only have himself to blame, because he would not do you a service...."

The utter cynicism of this tyrant's morality and logic is brought out here in strong relief. Here the personality of the tyrant is the moral hub of the entire world; from it everything goes out, and to it everything must return. There are no rights except the personality of the tyrant, no moral rules except that of serving his will.... Thus, the question of law is here presented with shameless bluntness: the law is nothing but the will of the tyrant; all must obey him, but nothing must restrict his actions.... What kind of life can people lead under such a morality? ...

This is the kind of life they lead. Ulanbekova keeps her foster daughters under strict lock and key. If one of them dare open her mouth she says to her:

"I hate to hear people arguing with me, I simply hate it, and that is all there is to it! I cannot permit anyone to argue with me. I have been accustomed from my earliest years to have every word of mine obeyed, and it's high time you knew that! It is very strange to me, my dear, that you should dare argue with me. I can see that I have spoilt you and you are becoming impudent...."

On the other hand, according to old Potapich, she dresses her foster daughters well and does not compel them to do any work. "I want everybody to envy them," she says. When they grow up she will choose husbands for them. Potapich tells Leonid, Ulanbekova's son, about this in the following way:

"She'll say: 'I have found a young man for you and the wedding will be on such and such a day,' she'll say; and that's final, of course, not one of them will dare say a word! Whomever she orders them to marry they'll have to marry, because, Sir, I see it this way: who would care to tolerate disobedience from anybody he has brought up? But sometimes it happens, Sir, that *the young man doesn't like the young lady and the young lady doesn't like the young man, and then doesn't she get angry!* ... *She fair loses her temper....* She wanted to marry off one of her foster daughters to a shopkeeper in town, but he, being unpolished, took it into his head to object. I don't like the girl, he said, and I don't want to get married. So she went to complain to the Chief Constable and to the priest, and they made the fool change his mind."

In Potapich's view, this means that the mistress "extends her solicitude to all." What prompts this solicitude? Ulanbekova herself tries to answer this question in the *sermon* which she reads with great emotion, with tears in her eyes, as Potapich tells us, to her foster daughters when she marries them off.

"You have been living with me in wealth and luxury and did not have to do anything," she says. "Now you are marrying a poor man, and so, live the rest of your life in poverty; work and do your duty. Forget how you lived with me, because I did not do this for your sake, I did it only for my own amusement. You must never think of living such a life again, but always remember how lowly you are and what station in life you came from...."

Do not think that this is said with malice or sarcasm. Not at all! It springs from Ulanbekova's fulness of heart and sincere conviction. She too has no particular bent for evil; the whole trouble is that, confined within the circle of her ideas, she can recognize nothing but herself. Everything seems to her to have been created to serve her, in the same way as the corn in the field exists not for itself, but to serve the needs of man.... What can you do with concepts like these?... That she is really inclined to do good is proved by the way she protects the husbands of her former dependents. Potapich says that in those cases where her dependents were married to court clerks the husbands are doing well.

"Because if they want to dismiss him from his job, or they have dismissed him, he at once complains to our lady, and *she stands up for him and even worries the Provincial Governor about him.* After that the court clerk can go on the booze and do anything he likes and not be afraid of anybody. . . ."

Of course you will say that this too is wrong, but still it is evident that Ulanbekova is not a tormentor, not a wicked woman, but a sympathetic, benevolent and charitable woman.

It was due to her benevolence (and for no other reason) that she took it into her head to marry Nadya to the drunkard Negligentov. She puts it very simply to Vassilisa Peregrinovna:

"You say that he is leading a bad life. All the more reason to hurry up with the wedding. Nadya is a girl with good principles and she will restrain him. If he doesn't marry soon his bachelor life will lead him to a bad end."

Nadya is present during this conversation and hears what Ulanbekova says, but she dare not utter a word of protest. . . . At last, she supplicates and weeps, but she is rebuked for this. Ulanbekova says to her:

"Your tears mean absolutely nothing to me. Once I have decided to do a thing I will have my own way and will not listen to anybody in the world!. . . And know for the future that your obstinacy will lead to nothing, you will only make me angry."

All this is said politely and gravely, but, of course, this does not make it easier for Nadya. In this case tyranny hides its fists and whip, but it is no better for this, perhaps even worse. In one of Ostrovsky's plays we see exactly the same scene in a merchant's family. There it is much coarser, nevertheless it is not so revolting. The following is a scene in *Incompatibility of Temperament,* where Karpich informs his daughter about the forthcoming wedding of his niece and he discusses this subject with his wife Ulita Nikitishna. For the sake of comparison we shall quote this scene in full; it is a very short one.

Karp Karpich: There! We shall have a wedding, too, soon. Matrena was found in the garden with the shop assistant, so I want to marry them (*Matrena covers her face with her sleeve*); I'll give him a thousand rubles and pay for the wedding.

U lit a N i k i t i s h n a: All you want is a drinking party, and that's why you are arranging this wedding.

Karp Karpich: Well, what else?

U lit a N i k i t i s h n a: Nothing else.

Karp K a r p i c h (*sternly*): No, no, you speak up!

U lit a N i k i t i s h n a: I've nothing more to say, honest!

Karp Karpich (*more sternly*): No, you speak up, I'll hear what you have to say.

U lit a N i k i t i s h n a: What's the use of talking? You won't listen anyhow.

Karp Karpich: What is there to listen to? Nothing you can say is worth listening to. Ekh, Ulita Nikitishna! (*Wagging his forefinger at her threateningly*): I told you to keep quiet! I want the girl to feel, but you come along with your talk.... (*Matrena covers her eyes with her other sleeve*). This is the third niece I am marrying off in this way. I am a benefactor to all our relations. There's another little one. I'll take her in Matrena's place and put her on her own feet too.

In this scene we have abuse, threats and violence, in short tyranny in full swing ... but it has not developed here to the same stage of virtuosity as in the case of Ulanbekova. Here Matrena marries the shop assistant with whom she was discovered in the garden—the case is clear and simple. Probably Karp Karpich married off his other nieces in the same way. If he could have thought of some other way of marrying them to somebody they did not want, or to those who did not want them, perhaps the idea would have pleased him very much ... but he is not yet subtle enough for inventions of that sort. Ulanbekova, however, can enjoy this luxury. Moreover, Karp Karpich's manners are different; he is more rude to his wife than Ulanbekova is to her dependents, he does not allow her to speak, and perhaps he even beats her sometimes; but at all events his wife can make some remarks, whereas Nadya remains absolutely dumb in Ulanbekova's presence. You see what little joy there is under the civilized form of tyranny!

It is this blow, delivered with such a cool and staid mien, that rouses in Nadya that bitter desperate feeling that compels a person to rush headlong wherever it may be—into the water, or into the arms of the first newcomer! In Ostrovsky's play this feeling is brought out with amazing power and vividness; such profoundly true pictures are rarely to be found in our literature.

We have already reproduced this scene in *Sovremennik*, but we cannot refrain from reminding our readers of several of its passages.

"I don't understand myself what has suddenly happened to me," says Nadya. "As soon as the mistress told me today that I must not dare object, but marry the one she tells me to, I felt my heart would break. I thought to myself: Good Lord, what is my life worth! (*Weeps.*) What's the good of my living honestly, of my taking care to avoid an evil word, or even an evil glance?... I became angry even with myself. I thought to myself: Why should I take care of myself? I won't, I won't!... But my heart nearly stopped beating—I felt that if she said another word I'd die on the spot."

This confession clearly shows into what a hopeless position tyranny places all those who have the misfortune to come under its influence. Nadya has not been trained to keep control over herself and to remain true to her conceptions by virtue of her inner conviction of their truth and power; her modesty and honesty have a direct object, namely, to ·preserve herself for marriage. . . . But her natural feelings are suddenly outraged by the command to marry a drunken and filthy scoundrel. . . . All her maidenly dreams are shattered, her hard lot rises before her in all its pitiless coarseness. She had dreamed of being with her betrothed, of sitting with him like a princess, of every day being a holiday, of how she would live after her wedding as if in paradise. proud of her new life . . . but now different thoughts run through her mind; she is crushed by tyranny and sees no prospect before her other than this same tyranny.

"To think," she says, "of this disgusting fellow tormenting me, lording it over me, exercising his power over me! It would be a living death! I'd get old without having lived. . . . Honest, it would be better to go with the young gentleman. . . ."

And, indeed, in her "desperation," as she expresses it, she finds that she likes Leonid, who has been courting her for a long time. . . . Formerly she avoided him, but now she goes out into the garden to him at night and rushes into his arms. He takes her on a boat to a lonely island. Vassilisa Peregrinovna spies on them and reports them to Ulanbekova. Ulanbekova flies into a towering rage and immediately sends a message to Negligentov (whom she had ordered out of the house because he had arrived drunk, and thereby had shown disrespect to her) saying that the wedding between him and Nadya must take place at the earliest date....

Here Leonid comes on the scene with his regrets.... But he has already breathed the air of tyranny and cannot do anything practical. This play, *The Foster Daughters*, shows, in passing, but with astonishing truth, how the plague of tyranny that pervades the entire atmosphere of the "realm of darkness" imperceptibly, but inevitably, infects even the freshest of natures. Leonid is a lad of eighteen, by no means malicious, and not at all stupid: his character is not yet fully moulded. But see what his manners are already, how he is already spoiled to the roots, how everything around him is facilitating his further corruption, how everything is operating to convert him into a disgusting tyrant. What are his conversations with Potapich alone worth! He observes to Potapich as his eyes wander over the estate: "All this will be mine!" And Potapich answers: "Yes, Sir, all, and all of us will be yours.... We will have to serve you, just as we served the late master, because you are of the same blood.... That's quite natural...." When Leonid tells Potapich that he does not intend to go into the service because "they'll make me do a lot of writing"... Potapich expresses approval of this too. "You are right, Sir," he says, "why should you work? That wouldn't do! You'll be found a place worthy of a gentleman, an easy one. The clerks will do all the work and all you'll have to do is to give them orders. And, of course, promotion will come in the regular way...." Then Leonid complains that the young women avoid him, and Potapich tells him that this is because his Mama wants to preserve him, and the young women too. Then he adds:

"Why, of course, Sir, your Mama must be strict, because she is a lady. But why should you bother your head about her? You should behave as all young gentlemen do. You should not miss any opportunity. Why should you lag behind the others? That would be a disgrace."

Leonid: What you say is right, but I don't know how to talk to girls.

Potapich: But why do you have to talk to them a lot? What sciences can you discuss with them? Do they understand anything? It's the usual thing—you are a gentleman, and that's all there is to it....

Leonid quickly imbibes these concepts. In the scene with Nadya in the garden he turns out to be a spoiled and empty-headed boy, nothing more; but in the last scene, when he hears about his mother's rage and about the fate that threatens Nadya, he is simply repulsive.... He fusses around, asks in what way he can help, apparently pities Nadya, but actually he no longer cares a brass tack for her.... There was one thing he could do to help the girl in her misfortune. Ulanbekova was angry mainly because her favourite footman, nineteen-year-old Grishka, had been out of the house all night. When he arrived in the morning he went to sleep in the hayloft, not in the least disturbed by his mistress' ire. It was necessary to tell him to go and apologize to Ulanbekova. This would have pleased the lady and would have put her in a frame of mind to listen to intercession on Nadya's behalf. Vassilisa Peregrinovna caustically suggests to Leonid that he should go and urge Grishka to go to Ulanbekova, but after a moment's reflection the boy answers: "No, that would be doing him too much honour...." And after deciding Nadya's fate by this answer he again begins to ask "What can be done?" and presses his sympathies upon Nadya.... At last Nadya loses all patience and says to him: "Why should you worry about a trivial thing like this? You are going to St. Petersburg soon; have a good time there. As for me, what business is it of yours?" Leonid is offended by this and asks Nadya: "Why do you talk to me like that?" "Because you are still a mere boy," answers Nadya, and she concludes with the words: "It would be better if you went away! As for me, if my patience gives out, why the pond is not far off! ..." Leonid, somewhat embarrassed, but inwardly pleased that he can get out of the mess, says: "You are right. It'll be better if I go and visit our neighbours for a week ..." and he leaves Nadya, who only the day before had thrown herself into his arms on the impulse of the same feeling which is now making her want to throw herself into the pond....

And so, this is why people fall, this is the cause of the moral corruption that so thoroughly permeates the whole of the tyrants' "realm of darkness"!

"As long as I thought I was a human being like all human beings, my thoughts were different," says Nadya. "But as soon as they began to treat me as if I were a doll, and I saw that I had no freedom and no protection, I fell into despair.... What became of fear and shame?... If I live only for a day, that day will be mine, I thought to myself, and I don't care a scrap what happens after that...."

And with these thoughts in her mind the girl rushes to her doom, and actually enjoys life only for a matter of an hour or so.... Even that is taken away from her, for the recollections of the previous day's scene of love are already marred, poisoned by Leonid's present behaviour. *"To whom* did I surrender myself, *on whom* did I waste my pure virginal caresses?" the unhappy girl must now ask herself, and the shame of her bitter error will pursue her longer and more persistently than her grief over her lost virginity. Strictly speaking, the immorality of her behaviour lies only in that she, on the impulse of the moment, disposed of herself foolishly.... But what else could she do?... It was not only respect for law that restrained her from open rebellion against her "benefactress," but simply impotence, the impossibility of her rebelling. Where was she to go, where and how could she seek protection and above all, how was she to live?... She had but one other alternative to what she did, and that was to drown herself in the pond.... But there's no great pleasure in that either!...

Here there is revealed to us the other reason we mentioned as to why tyranny, which is weak in itself and has been inwardly decayed for a long time now, can still hold on so tenaciously. Respect for law, which has become purely passive and petrified, has been transformed into stupid reverence for another's will, could not have been so meekly and submissively retained by the oppressed people in face of all the absurdities and abominations of tyranny were it not supported by something more virile and substantial. Indeed, it is being constantly supported by the fact that people are prompted by the inevitable urge and need to ensure their material existence. It is this need, combined with the stupid and irrational respect for law, that to a very large degree enables tyranny to flourish. If the respect for law entertained by the inhabitants of the "realm of darkness" were not so petrified and passive, their urge to improve their material existence would, of course, have led to different results. Mitya would not tearfully complain about his master behind his back and remain dumb in his presence because he regards his will as law; he would deem it quite legitimate to demand an increase of pay from him. Podkhalyuzin himself would not cheat his customers and give them short measure in obedience to his master's will as the supreme law

and stealthily pocket a few kopeks; he would simply demand a
share in Bolshov's profits, because actually he manages all his
affairs. In that case, of course, there would have been no need
for Bolshov to declare himself a bankrupt; in fact, he would have
found that tyranny did not pay. On the other hand, if men did
not have to strive after material wealth, Andrei Titich would, of
course, not have trembled so before his father, Nadya need not
have lived in Ulanbekova's house, and even Tishka would have
had no respect for Podkhalyuzin. . . . But at present the situation
is as follows: every man is in need of material wealth, but all
the material wealth has been seized by the tyrants, so that the
weak and oppressed side, being under the influence of the tyrant,
is dependent on the tyrannical charity of a Tortsov or an Ulanbekova. They could be called upon to disgorge what they possess
without any right, but respect for law prohibits the violation of
the respect due to them. . . . What follows from this? What follows is clear, one would think: it is necessary to "beg without
complaint" that the tyrant should live and let live. . . . But in
order that this plea may be successful, it is necessary to win the
tyrants' good graces, and to win their good graces you must agree
with them in all things, submit to them, and "with patience bear
your burden" if necessary. . . . And of burdens it is necessary to
bear quite enough, judging by the "stern character" of a Gordei
Karpich or a Madame Ulanbekova, and also by their impenetrable
stupidity. . . . And for all this you must prepare yourself, train
yourself, that is to say, *remould* your own character, *knock the
nonsense, i.e.*, your own convictions, out of your head, you must
resign yourself, *i.e.*, abandon all thoughts about your own rights
and human dignity. The tyrants themselves effectively perform all
these operations upon all the people who are born within the
sphere of their influence. That is why they always have at hand so
many submissive Mityas and Andreis, obsequious Potapiches, and
so forth. If anybody, even after being tamed by the tyrant, still
retains some sense of personal independence, and if his mind
still retains some ability to form its own judgment, then that personality and that mind has a trodden path before it. As we have
seen, by its very nature, tyranny is stupid and ignorant and, consequently, nothing is easier than to cheat any tyrant. A man who
has preserved some remnants of a mind of his own will unfailingly

take this path against the tyrants in the "realm of darkness" as soon as he launches upon any practical activity. Hence the saying: "A clever man cannot help being a rogue."

Thus, the tyrants have two categories of pupils and clients under them—live and lifeless. The lifeless are downtrodden and inert, and lie motionless without making any independent effort: if they are dragged from one place to another well and good, if not, they lie and rot.... The live ones, on the contrary, try to push as near and as conveniently as they can to the tyrant, and if they are successful, they try to trip him up in order to. get on his back and play the tyrant themselves. And the new tyrant is worse, more dangerous and more long-lived than the old one, because he is more cunning than the old one, and has been taught by his bitter experience. And so it all goes on: one tyrant succeeds another, in a different form, more civilized, as Ulanbekova is more civilized than Bruskov, for example, but in substance making the same demands and possessing the same character. The live characters on the oppressed side plunge into roguery in order to make their own positions secure, while the lifeless ones try by means of their inertness and submissiveness to win the good graces of the tyrant in order to obtain a drop of the life-giving water (which, incidentally, he gives them very rarely, so as to prevent them from becoming too much alive).

From these brief and simple remarks it is not difficult to understand why the brunt of the burden of tyrannical relationships in this "realm of darkness" is borne mostly by women. In our preceding essay we promised to deal with the slavish position which women occupy in the Russian family as depicted in Ostrovsky's comedies. We think we have dealt with this sufficiently in the present essay. It only remains for us to say a few words about the causes of this, and to point to another comedy, concerning which we have not said a word up to now, namely, *The Poor Bride*.

Our society is arranged in such a way that nearly everywhere women occupy the position that parasites occupied in ancient society: she always lives on another. This in itself explains the offensive opinion about women that is formed in society.... True, the "masters of the house" in this "realm of darkness," men like Bruskov, Bolshov, and others, also live on others, but

these have an unwritten but universally recognized *right* to be
parasites. Moreover, they even justify themselves on the grounds
of political economy: they own capital (how obtained is nobody's business!) and they have a right to the interest on this capital.... If the profits of their trade are somewhat excessive they
are not to blame, it is due to the absence of severe competition.
Lastly, we must take into consideration the fact that by general
consent, and by his own conviction, the tyrant is the beginning,
the centre and the head of everything that goes on around him;
hence, although he himself may do nothing, the activities of others
belong to him. It is he who grants the right to and provides the
means for activity; without him the other people are nothing, as
Yusov says in *A Lucrative Post.* "If they pay attention to you,
you are a man; but if they don't pay any attention to you—what
are you?" Hence, it is useless talking about the idleness of the
tyrants. We must discuss the other half of the "realm of darkness," the half that we have called the oppressed. Here all work,
more or less. This work is not free, not independent of course:
the workers are dependent in everything upon the whims of the
tyrant, and are often compelled to do not what they ought to do
or what they want to do.... Let us remember how eager Andrei
Bruskov is to go and study, how Mitya yearns to "educate himself," and how their desires are thwarted. Hence, their activities
are also greatly restricted precisely because their position is insecure, because they are materially dependent upon the whims of
a tyrant.... But at all events they still have some hope that the
tyrant will not suddenly take it into his head to disown them and
drive them out of his house; after all, they are doing something
and are useful to the tyrant. Let us suppose that Tortsov cared
nothing for his shop assistants as Vishnevsky, in *A Lucrative Post,*
cares nothing for his subordinates and can dismiss them any day.
But somebody would have to be put in their place; consequently,
in general, Tortsov needs men and, therefore, if only because of
his conservatism, will not idly dismiss men who far from opposing him do everything to please him. Moreover, however second-
rate and dependent the occupations of men may be, they nevertheless call for a certain degree of development and consequently,
even in the opinion of men of the Bruskov type a boy must from
his earliest years acquire far more knowledge than a girl. Andrei

Bruskov, for example, is the chief man in his father's factory, consequently, he had to learn at least something, even if he did not receive a systematic education. But concerning the daughters, the mother of this same Andrei very naively observes: "What's daughters! *Daughters can be locked up and there's less trouble with them. We don't have to educate them or anything.*" All that daughters need, in her opinion, is a guard to keep them away from young men until they are married; after they are married their husbands will guard their wives from strangers. ... We have seen in all Ostrovsky's comedies that we have reviewed so far that the inhabitants of this "realm of darkness" express the most utter disdain for women, and this disdain is all the more hopeless for the reason that it is quite good-natured. It is not even accompanied by that ire a certain gentleman, for example, betrayed in criticizing a merchant who dared to write about the peasant problem. Supercilious as this ire may have been, it nevertheless betrayed a certain apprehensive attention, a vague realization that the opposing side possesses a certain amount of strength; here the tone of disdain was artificial. There is nothing artificial in the tone of the relationships between husband and wife and between father and daughter in the "realm of darkness" of Ostrovsky's comedies. These gentlemen do not get angry about the claims of womanhood, they do not seriously protest against it; they even allow their wives to argue with them. ... It is simply that they cannot find room in their heads for the idea that a woman is also human, their equal, and endowed with rights. Why, the women themselves do not think so! "What's a woman! A hen is not a bird and a woman is not human" they repeat with Nichkina in *A Holiday Dream.* She does nothing, acquires nothing, plays no role in society, and occupies no place in public affairs. Whatever she may be she is by virtue of being her father's daughter, or her husband's wife. ... And she uncomplainingly submits to this because she thinks it should be so, because it has been so for ages and, consequently, such is her lot. ... The feeble attempts she makes to express her importance are confined only to talk similar to that in the following dialogue between Ulita Nikitishna and Karp Karpich in *Incompatibility of Temperament.* We quote this dialogue because, in addition to confirming the correctness of our views, we think it is an example of the skill with which

23*

Ostrovsky is able to convey the most elusive features of banality
and stupidity that pervades the whole of the "realm of darkness,"
and which, together with tyranny, constitute the main basis of its
way of life.

Ulita Nikitishna (*brewing the tea*): Nowadays *moir antique*
is all the fashion.

Karp Karpich: What's this *moir antique?*

Ulita Nikitishna: It's a kind of dress cloth.

Karp Karpich: What do I care.

Ulita Nikitishna: Oh, I just happened to mention it.... But
if Serafimochka were to get married, I would certainly have a dress made
of it.... All the ladies are wearing it.

Karp Karpich: Why, are you a lady?

Ulita Nikitishna: Certainly, I am a lady!

Karp Karpich: Would you believe it? I can't bear that word
when you call yourself a lady!

Ulita Nikitishna: Why, what's the matter with that word—
lady? What is there ... (*searching for a word*) shameful about it?

Karp Karpich: I don't like it, that's all!

Ulita Nikitishna: But is Serafimochka a lady?

Karp Karpich: Of course, she's a lady. She's educated, and her
husband was a gentleman. But what about you? You were simply a woman all the time, but now your husband's rich you call yourself a lady.
You be a lady in your own right.

Ulita Nikitishna: But after all ... what do you mean?

Karp Karpich: I told you to shut up, didn't I! (*Silence.*)

Ulita Nikitishna: When did that battle take place?

Karp Karpich: What battle?

Ulita Nikitishna: Well, that one, not long ago. Don't you
remember?

Karp Karpich: Well, what about it?

Ulita Nikitishna: Weren't a lot of men of common rank promoted to officers?

Karp Karpich: But they were not women, were they? Everybody is rewarded according to his merits.

Ulita Nikitishna: But that town woman who comes here says
that when her nephew graduates from the university she will be a lady.

Karp Karpich: Don't believe what she says.

Ulita Nikitishna: And they say that in some countries there
are women's regiments.

Karp Karpich (*laughs*): Guards! (*Silence.*)

Ulita Nikitishna: They say it's a sin to drink tea.

Karp Karpich: How can that be?

Ulita Nikitishna: Because it comes from a heathen country.

Karp Karpich: But lots of things come from heathen countries.

Ulita Nikitishna: Well, here's an example: bread comes from a Christian land, and we eat it at the proper time. But when do we drink tea? Respectable people go to morning prayers, but we stay at home and drink tea. We should be at evening prayers now, but here we are drinking tea. That's why it's a sin.

Karp Karpich: Drink it at the proper time then.

Ulita Nikitishna: Still....

Karp Karpich: Still... you shut up. You've got no brains, but you love to talk. Shut up, I tell you! (*Silence.*)

Ulita Nikitishna: How happy Serafimochka is! When she married a gentleman she became a lady, and now that she is a widow she's still a lady. If she marries a prince now, I suppose she'll be a princess.

Karp Karpich: Only because of her husband though.

Ulita Nikitishna: And if Serafimochka marries a prince, do you mean to tell me I won't be anything? After all, I'm her mother.

Karp Karpich: One only gets mixed up talking to you. I have some business to think over, but you come along with your silly talk. A whole lifetime is not enough to hear all the silly stuff you women have to say. When I say: shut up!—it cuts the matter shorter.

After this conversation Karp Karpich observes to himself: "If you didn't drive fear into women, you'd never be able to manage them...." They do everything to tempt a man, he says, and "an inexperienced young man may be captivated by their charms, but to a man who has reached understanding, and a more solid age, feminine charms mean nothing, he even finds them disgusting...." This is how everybody in the "realm of darkness" looks upon women, and even then they think they are being gracious to them.... It is evident that survivals of Oriental views still have a tight hold here. Women are not openly sold in the market place as they used to be in the Orient, but it cannot be said that they are not sold at all; and the mode of selling them is still rather cynical and shameless, as can be seen from the few examples of marriage brokers that are depicted in some of Ostrovsky's comedies. We shall not stop to deal with these personages because we have already abused our readers' patience far too much, but we cannot refrain from mentioning the matchmaking scene in *The Poor Bride*. This comedy as a whole is distinguished for its simplicity and plainness, and for the absence of all sharp features, such as, for example, the widow Kukushkina's discourses in *A Lucrative Post*. Nevertheless, the betrothal of the girl, the mother's concern about getting her married, and the talk about likely husbands—can all strike horror in a man who pon-

ders over the comedy.... Anna Petrovna, Maria Andreyevna's
mother, is a weak, ailing and forgetful woman, as she describes
herself. Every step she takes clearly shows that she was brought
up and has lived the greater part of her life under tyranny, which
has robbed her of all capacity and taste for independent activity.
She cannot think, she does not know to whom to turn, or what
to do; she fusses and rushes about all to no purpose, and is constantly lamenting the fact that her daughter has been unable to
find a husband for so long. Conscious of her own utter insignificance, she keeps on repeating:

"How we can get on in the house without a man I really can't
understand.... What do we know, being here alone?... The other day,
for instance, the constable brought a paper. Who knows what it is about?
That's how unfortunate we women are! I run around like a fool all day
long.... All the morning I have been trying to count up my money, but
I can't make head or tail of it.... How we can get on without a man
I really do not know. It's worse than misfortune."

As you see, she is such a nonentity that in all probability
she would not dare say a word to her husband, or to anybody
stronger-minded than herself. But the atmosphere of tyranny has
infected her too, and ignorant and witless though she is she decides the fate of her daughter, bullies her, scolds her, reminds her
that it is her duty to obey her mother, and shows no sign of understanding of what human feelings and a living personality are.
All these are direct and manifest symptoms of a tyrannical upbringing, which proves only how easily it affects even the most
incapable. It is evident, therefore, that tyranny knows neither sex,
age nor station in life. Women, who, in general, are downtrodden and despised in the "realm of darkness" can also act the
tyrant. And how! We have the example of Ulanbekova.... Young
boys and old men, merchants, government officials and squires,
everybody you will, begin to tyrannize at the first opportunity....
Take a man who is despised by all, who has been beaten and insulted a thousand times, who trembles before everybody and seems
to be so meek and humble that he would not even cause a ripple
in a pond!... And yet, if only one son is born to him, or if a
dependent, a servant or a subordinate falls into his hands, he
immediately begins to tyrannize over him, while continuing to
tremble before every passer-by who fails to bow to him.... That

is the way things are in the "realm of darkness," such are the
rules of its hierarchy; here even the personal character of a man
is of little importance.... "Almost everything is due to lack of
restraint or to stupidity," as Borodkin puts it.

In our first essay on the "realm of darkness" we tried to show
that the worst of crimes are committed in this realm, and the most
inhuman relationships are established between people, not out of
malice or spite, but simply because of the stupidity and ossification of the extremely narrow and vague ideas of its inhabitants.
Reminding our readers of this, we shall here merely observe that
Anna Petrovna is a very striking example of this *immorality due
to stupidity*. Her treatment of her daughter is profoundly immoral: she is constantly badgering Masha and reduces her to a frightful state of nervous irritation, to hysterics, with her ceaseless
complaints and taunts:

"I brought you up, I reared you, and this is how you reward me!...
You are sticking to your caprice and won't find a husband, and your mother must grieve in her old age.... Why, we have nothing! What shall I
do in my old age, find a place as a cook? You only want to go gallivant-
ing, but you've forgotten your mother, you don't want to do anything for
her.... Well, perhaps some good people will turn up who will take care
of an old woman!"

Maria Andreyevna hears such reproaches every day and every
hour. What kind of a mother can it be who has such a mercenary
regard for her daughter? Does she not clearly reveal traces of a
tyrannical disposition which has only lightly affected her, which
is not in the least inherent in her nature, but which nevertheless
has made her intolerable to all those around her? Such a personality and such conduct ought to rouse repugnance in our
hearts.... But Anna Petrovna disarms us by her extraordinary
good nature and stupidity. She is not positively immoral, she
merely lacks morality; her organism is destitute of all humane
principles. To get her daughter married is her monomania. What
can you do about it? The fact that she insists on Masha marrying
Benevolensky is due to two causes: firstly, that Benevolensky un-
dertakes to plead for them in the Senate; and secondly, that she
cannot conceive that it is not a matter of indifference to her
daughter as to whom she marries. When Masha tells her that she
dislikes Benevolensky, she simply cannot understand how that

can be and at first brushes the objection aside with the remark that Masha's head is stuffed with all sorts of nonsense and that she will change her mind twenty times yet. And later, when Masha repeats her objection, she says that it is only her daughter's "caprice," that she is doing it "only to spite her mother." It must be observed, however, that she herself does not know or approve of Benevolensky in the least. In the final scene, when all is over, she suddenly thinks of asking Masha: "Do you like him? I must confess we rushed this matter a little. Who can tell what he's like? You can't peep into his heart." What can you do with such simplicity? You can't even get angry with it. . . . You can only look on and wonder, and gaze more sadly at the environment in which characters like these arise and vegetate.

It is in such an environment that Maria Andreyevna, a simple and undeveloped girl, but one possessing a delicate and noble character, lives in torment. Her torment is due mainly to the fact that her mother is eager to get her off her hands, and not satisfied with the services of marriage brokers, she herself hunts around for a husband for her. The delicacy with which all this is done is evident, for example, from the letter which Anna Petrovna receives from her friend, good old Dobrotvorsky.

"As for the point you asked me about," he writes, "I visited the office you mentioned: there are no bachelor officials there suitable for Maria Andreyevna; there is one, but I doubt whether you will like him, because he is very tall, very much above the average, and pock-marked. But from inquiries I made about him of the secretary and of his fellow officials, I gather that he is a man of good morals, does not drink, and as far as I can understand would make a very desirable match. Would you like me to look in other offices? If so, I will do so with the greatest pleasure."

And Anna Petrovna compels Masha to read this letter! Naturally, the poor girl is offended, but the mother cannot possibly understand what there is to be offended at!

But why does the unfortunate girl tolerate all these insults? What keeps her in this bog? Clearly, the fact that she is a *poor bride*, she has nowhere to turn, and can do nothing except wait for or seek a profitable match. Marriage is her occupation, her work, her career, her mission in life. In the same way as a day labourer must look for work, an official for a post, and a beggar

for alms, so must this girl look for a husband.... Present-day
liberals laugh at this, but it would be interesting to know what
a girl who does not get married is to do in our society? If we
ponder over the matter we will find that Anna Petrovna is quite
right when she asks:

"What is an unmarried woman?" and answers: "Nothing!... Of what
importance is she? It's bad enough to be a widow, but to be a spinster
is altogether too bad! A woman must live with a husband, keep house,
bring up children; but what will you do if you remain an old maid?
Knit stockings?..."

These words are stupidly true, and they provide a fairly emphatic answer to the question: why do women in our society occupy such a slavish position in the family, and why does tyranny
oppress them with exceptional force?

A woman may acquire a certain degree of independence if
she has money. Ostrovsky depicted this aspect of a woman's life
in his play *Incompatibility of Temperament*. Elegant Paul is extremely attentive and submissive to his wife because he hopes to
wheedle money out of her. But in women's hands even money
seems not to have the same importance as in men's hands. The
image of some tyrant's wealth very soon merges in our minds
with the image of his personality, and this is probably because,
after all, he himself disposes of his money and puts it in circulation. Consequently, in entering into relations with a rich man,
everybody tries to get the largest possible *share* of his profits;
but in entering into relations with a woman who has money, they
directly work to *gain possession of all her fortune*. The personality of the woman is of no importance whatever. This is perfectly
well understood by Serafima Karpovna who strictly follows the
admonitions of her father. On getting married she promises in
advance not to give her husband any money. "What will I be without any capital? I'll be nothing," she says, and to this her father
answers with a significant "of course!"... She keeps her word
after she is married. When her husband asks her for money she
leaves him, goes to her father and sends her husband a letter in
which, among other things, she expounds the following philosophy:

"What will I be when I have no money? I will be nothing! If I have
no money and I fall in love with somebody that somebody won't love me.

But if I have money and I fall in love with somebody that somebody will love me, and we shall be happy...."

After all, Serafima Karpovna is right!...

But it is very rare for a woman to gain possession of money. It may happen in the case of a woman who marries a rich man and soon becomes a widow. How else can a woman gain possession of money? And what can she do with money even if she does gain possession of it? Squander it in fashionable shops or else distribute it among monasteries, according to her age and inclinations. More than that she cannot do. It is far better to utilize this money for some practical purpose.... Even the law allows a woman only one-fourteenth part of an inheritance; and apart from the law she is not even entitled to that.... In any case, a woman does not hold her money long.... Unless, perhaps, she buys herself a good husband.... But even that scarcely ever happens. Rich brides are always courted by Vikhorevs, Baranchevskys, Balzaminovs and Prezhnevs.... All these gentlemen belong to the type which Neuyedenov in *A Holiday Dream* describes as follows:

"One will go into the service, to any job he can find, serve for a little while, nose around a bit and then find that the job is too hard for him, that he hasn't enough brains for it, that he hadn't studied hard enough, can't add two and two, that his laziness was born before him and yet he wants to live like a gentleman. So he promenades the streets and goes to fêtes in the hope of finding a fool with money...."

Indeed, all these gentlemen are handsome and so silly that it gives one nausea to think of them. The majority of them have served, or wish to serve, in the army, have a vent for tyranny, and are extremely pleased when they are regarded as educated men. But their ignorance is in every respect equal to that of the actual tyrant, and it is only thanks to the tyrannical system which prohibits the lower classes, and women in particular, from receiving an education that saves them from looking ridiculous in this milieu. In reviewing *Don't Get Into Another's Sleigh* we dealt fully enough with the reason why Avdotya Maximovna allowed herself to be enchanted by Vikhorev. Here we shall merely point to a similar relationship between Maria Andreyevna and Merich in *The Poor Bride*. We have already said that we would not examine the particular artistic merits of the scenes and personages in Ostrovsky's comedies and, therefore, we shall not enter into a detailed examination of Merich's character; but we cannot help observing that we are amazed at the skill with which Ostrovsky succeeded in depicting this decent, not evil, not disgusting, but from head to foot banal person. He is not copied from a type of which we have several examples in the best of our literary productions; he is not Onegin, not Pechorin, not even Grushnitsky, he is not the *unwanted man* in general. All these, after all, have something within them which they imagine is their own possession. The only trouble with them is that they are shallow characters and lack serious development, so that nothing can deeply penetrate their minds, and there is nothing to which they can devote themselves heart and soul. But Merich even lacks shallow convictions; all truth, all serious sentiments and strivings seem to bounce off him; he gives the impression not only of never having lived a conscious life, but even of having not the faintest idea what a conscious life is.... Infinite banality, unornamented and unvarnished, banality in its natural form, is expressed in every word, in every gesture of his. ... And this person becomes the object of the love of an intelligent and sensitive girl! ... Such is the inevitable consequence of the tyrannical system of education, which deems it its duty to bind and constrict a young character as much as possible, and to keep it in impenetrable darkness for as long as possible....

Maria Andrevevna is poor, and Merich, of course, does not marry her; he too is one of those who need rich brides. But cases occur in the "realm of darkness" when unwise poor men marry poor girls.... Then hell is let loose! ... Ostrovsky depicts this hell very well in *A Lucrative Post*. Our readers, of course, remember the story of young Zhadov, the nephew of an important personage, who displeases his uncle with his liberalism and loses his favour, later marries good-looking and kind, but poor and foolish Pauline, and after suffering want and his wife's reproaches for some time goes to his uncle again and begs him to find a lucrative post for him. The best feature of this comedy, in our opinion, is the way it depicts family relationships and shows how these relationships influence public activity. Interesting also is the inner, spiritual side of the lives of those people whom we officially despise and brand as pettifoggers and bribetakers. Here, one of the main features of Ostrovsky's talent is brought out in full strength, namely, his ability to peer into the soul of man and depict his human side regardless of his official position. We dealt with this at great length when we discussed *Our Own Folks* and, therefore, we shall here touch only upon some of the features that are specifically characteristic of government officials. The complacency and the exceptional brand of scrupulousness of bribetakers are depicted by a few fleeting strokes in *The Poor Bride* in the person of genial Dobrotvorsky; but in *A Lucrative Post* these features are brought out more vividly in the persons of Yusov and Byelogubov. These persons suggest to us the idea that all their lawless actions are merely the consequence of the false position they occupy in society, and of the false conceptions they have acquired as a result of the false position they occupy. And the false position they occupy is, in its turn, the result of the one general cause of all the abominations prevalent in the "realm of darkness," namely, tyranny. It is even more disgusting and revolting among government officials than among the merchants, because in the former it is always the public interest that is affected, and tyranny is hidden under the cloak of right and law. Moreover, here we already see innumerable shades and degrees, and the higher it goes the more this tyranny becomes inwardly arrogant and more ruinous for the public good, but it is more handsome and dignified in form. When Yusov was a boy the minor officials treated him as if he were a pup; Yusov is not so rude to Byelogubov: Vishnevsky talks with Yusov in such a dignified tone that far from shocking us it fills us with awe. But all the trouble in Vishnevsky's department is due to the fact that he himself is infected with the germs of tyranny and all the others follow his example. None of them recognizes any law, honesty not one of them can understand, intelligence they define in no other way than the ability to get rich, and the highest virtue in their eyes is submission to the will of superiors. Simplehearted Yusov confesses that he does not behave proudly towards anybody, only he dislikes the superciliousness of the educated people of the present day. "With them," he says, "I am strict and exacting. I make it a rule to keep a tight hand on them for the benefit of the service, because they do a lot of harm." It is not surprising that he should hold such views, for he himself "was an errand boy for a couple of years, ran all sorts of errands: for vodka, for pies, for kvass for somebody to get over a headache in the morning after the night before—and I sat not on a stool but on a stack of papers near the window, and wrote with ink not from an inkwell but from an old pomade jar. And yet I got on in the world." And now he confesses that "all this is not due to ourselves, it comes from above! ..." He oppresses educated people not out of malice, or out of roguery, but because he is really convinced that they do harm to the service.... The same conviction is held by Byelogubov who says: "What's the use of learning when a man knows no fear, when he doesn't tremble before his superiors?" They cannot think otherwise, because everything around them confirms their opinion at every step. Even those *educated people* who challenge their opinion often prove by their conduct how wrong they are in their behaviour! This was the case with Zhadov. At first Byelogubov seems to shrink before Zhadov and admits that he feels some power in his intellectual superiority. He has a vague feeling that it is not always pleasant to humble oneself and cringe, to depend on another's whims and to renounce one's own will. Seeing that Zhadov is much freer and more independent in his behaviour, Byelogubov almost envies him. When his fiancée asks him why he is putting off their wedding, although Zhadov is not putting off his, he answers:

"His is an entirely different case. He has a rich uncle, and he himself is educated, he can get a place anywhere. He can even go as a school-teacher—he can always earn his bread But what can I do? Until I am promoted to chief clerk, I can do nothing...."

But on receiving this place, while Zhadov has lost his, Byelogubov begins to feel a smug pity for Zhadov, which he expresses to him when he meets him in the tavern. What, then, did Zhadov get out of his *studying without fear?* Only that he tormented himself, tormented his wife for a whole year and at last went to his uncle to beg for Byelogubov's place.... And his uncle gives him a good dressing down.... "There you are, look at the hero!" he says. "A young man who has been shouting at all the cross-roads about bribetakers and talking about a new generation comes to us to beg for a lucrative post where he can take bribes! ... A fine new generation, indeed!"

In general, Vishnevsky, having firmly taken his stand on the *status quo*, very logically shatters all Zhadov's noble phrases and proves to him as definitely as twice two are four that it is impossible to support oneself and one's family honestly under the present system. Honest methods of acquisition yield too little, and even these are withheld from those who refuse to please and want to contradict. This is not an unfortunate accident but stern necessity, which follows logically and inevitably from the tyrannical system that prevails in the "realm of darkness." "He may be as wise as Solomon, but if you dislike him, he will remain insignificant, and he will only have himself to blame for not being able to win your favour." This is the entire law and the entire philosophy of the "realm of darkness"! It is not at all surprising, therefore, that on hearing that legal proceedings are to be taken against the entire staff of Vishnevsky's department, Yusov expresses his sincere conviction that "this is a punishment for our sins, *punishment for our pride*...." Vishnevsky gives a similar, but somewhat more rational explanation. "My rapid advancement and noticeable enrichment armed powerful people against me," he says.... Agreeing to this explanation, both administrators feel no qualms of conscience concerning the legality of their actions.... And why should they feel any qualms of conscience when their actions, like all their concepts and strivings, harmonize so well with the general course of affairs and arrangements in the "realm of darkness"?...

"But surely there must be some way out of this gloom.... Ostrovsky, who has so truthfully and fully depicted the 'realm of darkness' to us, who has shown us all the diversity of features of its inhabitants, has enabled us to peep into their souls and catch glimpses of certain human features, should also have indicated to us the possibility of leaving this slough of despond and of coming out into the free light of day.... As it is, it is simply horrible to remain faced with a dilemma that cannot be solved: either to die of starvation, jump into the water, or go mad, or else kill all thoughts and will in ourselves, cast aside all moral dignity and become the slavish instrument of another's will, a bribetaker and a scoundrel, in order to be able to live an untroubled life.... If this is all that this splendid author's artistic activity indicates to us, it is very sad! ..."

Sad, but true. But what is to be done about it? We have to admit that we have not found a way out of the "realm of darkness" in Ostrovsky's productions. Shall we blame the artist for this? Would it not be better to look around and present our demands to life itself, which is dragging on so listlessly and monotonously around us? ... True, we find it hard to breathe under the deadly pressure of the tyranny which rages in different shapes from the first to the last pages of Ostrovsky's works; but on finishing our reading and laying the book down, and on leaving the theatre after seeing one of Ostrovsky's plays, do we not see in real life around us innumerable Bruskovs, Tortsovs, Ulanbekovas and Vishnevskys, and do we not feel their deadly breath?... Let us then thank the artist for having given us the opportunity at least to see this realm of darkness in the light of his vivid pictures. That is already a great deal.... The way out of it must be found in life itself; literature only reproduces life, it never portrays that which does not exist in reality....

Incidentally, attempts are made in real life to escape from the darkness; one must not ignore these attempts in Ostrovsky's comedies. The only trouble is that these attempts are horrible and, moreover, they remain mere attempts. We find no personages in Ostrovsky's plays who are entirely free from the mud of everyday life. Mykin in *A Lucrative Post* may be free from it because he takes no part in the public service in any way, but "does a little teaching." But we learn so little about him from his conversation with Zhadov that we cannot give any guarantees for him. There is also a girl in *The Poor Bride* who is so attractive and highly moral that one feels like running after her and never parting from her once we have caught up with her. But this girl is already stained with the mud of other's vices. This is Dunya, with whom Benevolensky had lived for five years before he married, and who has now come to stand among the crowd unnoticed amidst the fuss and bustle of the wedding to take a look at the bride of her recent lover. She meets Benevolensky in an anteroom, something in the nature of a pantry; with her is her friend Pasha, whom she has only just told in a few words how Benevolensky used to storm and rave at her when he was drunk.... Benevolensky catches sight of her, is embarrassed and asks her to behave decently. She answers: "Do you want me to start a row? I will in a minute!" "You

fool, you ninny, what do you mean?" Benevolensky exclaims in a
fright, but she reassures him at once by promising never to come
again. He tries to get her out of the house, and the following scene
ensues, which reveals to us the girl's feelings, which are amazingly
pure and noble:

B e n e v o l e n s k y: What business have you here, Dunya? Take
a look at the bride and go away.

D u n y a: I have seen her already. She's a lovely girl, Pasha, I must
say she's lovely!... (*To Benevolensky*): But will you be able to live
with such a wife? Take care you don't ruin her life. That would be a sin.
Settle down and live decently. You mustn't treat her as you treated me:
live with me all those years and suddenly disappear (*wipes the tears from
her eyes*).

P a s h a: And you said you were not sorry....

D u n y a: But I loved him once, didn't I?... We had to part some
time, we couldn't live together all our lives. *It's a good thing he's marrying; perhaps he'll live decently now.* But still, just think of it, Pasha, we
lived together five years.... After all, it's a pity.... I wasn't very happy
with him, that's true.... I was all tears most of the time.... More shame
than anything. And so, my youth has passed away and I've no happy
remembrances of it.

P a s h a: What can you do about it, Dunya?...

D u n y a: Oh, but there were times when I was so happy when he
came!... *Take care now, live decently!*

B e n e v o l e n s k y: Why, yes, of course!

D u n y a: You'd better! *This time it's for life, not like what it was
with me....* Well, goodbye! Don't think bad of me. I'm afraid you've
nothing good to remember me by. What a fool I am, breaking into
tears like this! Let's forget it, Pasha! Let's put our sorrow on the
shelf!

B e n e v o l e n s k y: Goodbye, Dunya!

D u n y a: Adieux, monsieur! Come on, Pasha (*exeunt*).

Greater purity of moral sentiment we do not see in any other
personage in Ostrovsky's comedies. This is no longer the dispassionate kindness that distinguishes Bruskov's daughter, not the
sheeplike meekness that we see in Lyubov Gordeyevna, nor the
unsophisticated conceptions by which Nadya is guided.... Here,
the power of conscious determination can be discerned in every
word; not the entire soul of this girl has been crushed or killed,
on the contrary, it is exalted, illuminated by the consciousness of
the good that she does by renouncing her claim to Benevolensky.
Indeed, it would have been quite easy for her to give vent to her

feelings and cause a scandal at the wedding, but she did not want
to do that. She frankly pays tribute to the bride's beauty, and her
heart begins to fill with pleasure at the happiness her former lover
has achieved. Overflowing with good will, she is glad that he is
marrying, because it holds out the promise of his moral reformation.... And then there is that kindly, pure solicitude for the
other girl, her rival.... And lastly what a gracious charm of
character is expressed in that "put our sorrow on the shelf," and
in those affected parting words in which, however, we cannot fail to
discern the grief and bitterness of her still loving heart.... Yes,
this girl has preserved the purity of her heart and all the nobility
that a human being can achieve. But what is she in our society?
Is she not despised and rejected by it? And is it not to this re-
jection, to this separation from the gloom of tyranny which pervades our social environment that we must attribute the nobility and clarity of her heart that radiates so gratifyingly before us?...

There is another personage in Ostrovsky's comedies who is
distinguished for his moral strength. This is Lyubim Tortsov. He
is a filthy drunkard and a boor; life has broken him, and he has
allowed himself to sink very low. But this very life which deprived
him of ready means of existence, degraded him and reduced him
to want, did one good thing for him in that it broke in him the
element of tyranny. He is Gordei Karpich's brother, and as he
himself relates, was even a worse tyrant than he when he was
young. But when he was obliged to play the clown in the cold
street in order to turn a penny, to beg for alms, and to live on
the charity of his brother, human feelings, the consciousness of
truth, love for the poor, and even respect for work awoke in him.
In begging his brother to allow his daughter to marry Mitya he adds:

"He will provide me with a corner to live in; I have had more than
enough of cold and hunger, I can't stand it any more. My youth is gone.
It is hard for me to play the clown in the cold street for a crust of
bread. I must try to *live honestly* at least in my old age. Up to now I have
cheated people; begged for alms and spent what I got on drink. *I will
get some work, and I will have my own bowl of soup....*"

These aspirations and confessions show that want did actually
bring about a change in Lyubim Tortsov's character and compel

24—1241

him to be as ashamed of his former tyrannical habits as of his recent dissoluteness.

The example of Tortsov partly indicates to us a way out of the realm of darkness. If the other brother, Gordei Karpich, were taught a similar lesson by having to beg for a crust of bread for the sake of Christ, he too would probably feel a desire "to have some work" in order to live honestly. . . . But it goes without saying that it cannot enter the head of any of those around Gordei Karpich to subject him to such a trial, and consequently, the power of tyranny will continue to keep in darkness all who are in his power!

But what about the light of education? Will it not dispel this gloom at last? Beyond the slightest doubt! . . . But remember what we said about the way the tyrant imbibes education. . . . Remember also the effect of education upon V.khorev, Balzaminov, Prezhnev, Lipochka, Kapochka, Ustenka and Arina Fedotovna. . . . Look around you—what scenes, what conversations astonish you! In one place Rispolozhensky tells the story about a country where lived a venerable old man with twelve daughters, all quite young, and how he went to the crossroads to beg for charity from generous passers-by: in another place a decked-out bear dances with a goat in a drawing room; in another Yeromka performs magic and the ringing of church bells serves to bring about moral rectification; and in still another place we hear people say that it is a sin to drink tea, and so on and so forth. . . . And the talk we hear! Nastasya Pankratyevna says that a lot of learning is harmful, and Nenila Sidorovna catches this up and says: "Oh yes, about learning: our neighbour sent her son to school and he poked his eyes out." Or else Nenila Sidorovna says: "Young man, listen to your elders, you don't know how cunning people are"; and Nastasya Pankratyevna confirms this. "Yes, yes," she says, "somebody stole our coachman's coat—before you could wink. . . ." Or take this, for example:

Nichkina: Yes, and tell me this: they say that King Pharaoh with his troops comes out of the sea every night.
Balzaminov: That is quite probable.
Nichkina: But where is that sea?
Balzaminov: Not far from Palestine, I suppose.
Nichkina: Is Palestine a big country?

Balzaminov: Yes, very.

Nichkina: Is it far from Tsargrad?

Balzaminov: No, not very.

Nichkina: About sixty versts, I suppose. They say it's sixty versts from all such places.... But Kiev is farther.

And recall the conversation between Karp Karpich and Ulita Nikitishna about ladies! ... And the conversation between the coachmen about the Austrians! Or even the conversation between Vikhorev and Baranchevsky about industry and political economy; the conversation between Prezhnev and his mother on how to behave in company, or between Nedopekin and Lisavsky (in *A Young Man's Morning*) about beauty and education, or between Kapochka and Ustenka about politeness in company (in *A Holiday Dream*). That's education for you! It has produced enough gentlemen like Nedopekin and Vikhorev, and young ladies like Lipochka and Kapochka. But the tyrant will never permit it to do any more!... As it is they say that educated people must be kept under a tight hand for the benefit of the service!... And what sort of educated people do they see? Who has frightened them? Zhadov! But Zhadov himself confesses that he has no will, that he lacks energy....

The tyrants must indeed be weak if they are afraid of Zhadov! ... That is a good omen! ...

And at this good omen we shall stop at last. We do not wish to draw any general conclusions regarding Ostrovsky's talent. Our object was to show *what* his artistic feeling grasps in Russian life, and *how* it grasps it, *how* he conveys what he perceives and feels, and what importance we should, in our conceptions, attach to the phenomena he depicts in his productions. In Ostrovsky's plays we have found a complete picture of Russian life with Podkhalyuzin's frock coat, Vikhorev's gloves, Nadya's handkerchief wet with tears, Zhadov's walking stick and Tortsov's tyrannically ugly cap.... We have left much unsaid, of some things we have spoken at very great length; but let the readers who have had the patience to read this essay to the end forgive us. [Both the one and the other was due mostly to the mode of expression—partly metaphorical—to which we were obliged to adhere. In discussing Ostrovsky's personages we, of course, wished to point to their significance in real life, but after all, we were obliged to deal mainly with the

24*

products of the author's imagination and not directly with the phenomena of real life. This explains why the general meaning of the idea that was revealed called for lengthy discussion and repetition of the same thing in different ways—in order to be understood and at the same time keep to the figurative form which we were obliged to adopt for our essay by virtue of the nature of the subject. . . . Some things, however, could not be satisfactorily conveyed in this figurative form, and we therefore thought it best not to deal with them at all.] Incidentally, many of the deductions and conclusions which we have left unexpressed here should suggest themselves to the reader whose patience and attention have held out to the end of the essay.

CHENSKY'S COURTSHIP OR
MATERIALISM AND IDEALISM

St. Petersburg 1859

THE INEVITABILITY OF IDEALISM
IN MATERIALISM BY Y. SAVICH

Atenei, No. 7, 1859[84]

CHENSKY'S COURTSHIP cannot be explained without reference to
the essay by Mr. Savich, and Mr. Savich's essay cannot be
properly appraised without referring to *Chensky's Courtship*. That
is why we have decided to combine these two works. although one
is a Moscow product and the other, judging by its appearance
comes from St. Petersburg. Incidentally, the idealists say that we
"must not judge by appearances," and one cannot but agree with
this side of their doctrine. It is quite possible that *Chensky's
Courtship* belongs to Moscow, as does Mr. Savich's essay, and
Atenei itself. But it is also quite possible that Moscow, in spite of
its reputation for hospitality, is a terrible idealist. After all, it is
well known that

> It is pleasant to a sumptuous feast
> To add profound conversation.

Can there be a better subject for conversation than idealism
and materialism when the entire honourable company has fed well
and is in a good humour? ... Idealism and materialism! Oh, how
much material for pleasant conversation this excellent subject provides!... Firstly, a man can retire into the realm of pure thought
where nothing impure, nothing real, disturbs him.... Nothing,
because *materialism* itself is not *realism* at all; no, it is nothing
more than a pleasant abstraction, something like a pretty model
of a locomotive, on which one cannot ride, of course, but, which,
on the other hand, requires no water, fuel, nor workers.... Secondly, idealism and materialism make a pleasant subject for con-

versation because it enables one to exercise one's wits and dialectical powers in demonstrating the antagonism between these two
principles. Thirdly, it is a good subject for conversation because
the controversy, while not reaching the point of irritation over
vitally important matters, can however, slightly tickle the self-
esteem of the opponents, and thereby pleasantly sustain the conversation. In short, as Balzaminov in Ostrovsky's play says—"it is the
most pleasant subject for conversation in company." The only subject that can be more *"fascinating"* than this is, perhaps, the question which Ustenka raises in the same play: *"What is harder to
bear—to wait for something and never receive it, or to have something and lose it?"*[85]

But why do people pompously and profoundly write about
idealism and materialism? Why don't they confine themselves to
this *fascinating* subject in drawing-room discussions and leave
literature alone? If they don't, we may again be faced with the
danger of being inundated with essays such as: "The Inevitability
of Classicism in Romanticism," "The Love of a Mysterious Stranger for a Beauty Who Conceals Her Name—or Nominalism and
Realism," "A Comparative Analysis of the Importance of *These*
and *Those* for Society," etc. Has not this subject been discussed
enough? Is all this not yet absurd enough for our literature at the
present time, when the dawn of the future... and so forth?...We
thought that we had finished with dualism long ago; we were
hoping that the indivisible human being could now be torn apart
only in Mr. Kikodze's book on psychology.... We thought that it
was beneath the dignity of an educated man, nowadays, seriously
to concern himself with the antagonisms between the two opposite
principles in the world and in man. Since the now commonly
known truth became widespread, namely, that force is an inevitable
quality of matter, and that matter exists for our minds only to
the extent that some kind of force is revealed in it—since that time,
we have been of the opinion that all these Ormuzds and Arimans
were totally superfluous.... But no! Mr. Y. Savich tries to prove
the contrary to us. He imagines that materialism is widespread
among us—not the materialism that recognizes force as the indis-
pensible quality of matter, but a materialism which denies all
force. Consequently, he vigorously takes up the cudgels on behalf
of idealism against materialism. Why? We can explain this only

by assuming that Mr. Savich and the author of *Chensky's Court-ship* (if both productions are not from the pen of the same au-thor. . . .) have failed to develop their ideas verbally in profound conversation and want to make up for this in literature. The lack of direct acquaintance with their assumed opponents is noticea-ble even in the methods both authors employ, as well as in their views on the substance of their subject. Their main thesis is: "Every fool is a materialist; *ergo,* materialists are fools." And then follows a very ingenious development of this syllogism. But perhaps you will not believe that a scientific essay published in a scientific magazine can be based on such a syllogism? You even suspect that this syllogism is not presented quite in the way we present it even in the comedy *Chensky's Courtship.* We under-take to prove that what we say is true. We shall start with *The Courtship.*

The sum and substance of the comedy is that Chensky, a re-tired cavalry captain, has relations with Princess Lapina, a very wealthy lady of advanced age. He succeeds in making a fortune out of her and, in addition, obtains from her on a promissory note a loan of several million rubles which he invests in commerce. One day, while out for a ride with the elderly lady, he contrives things so that she falls out of the carriage and, as the result of this, she soon dies, leaving a will in favour of her niece Onina. But Chen-sky manages to get hold of all her papers, conceals the will and his own promissory note, and draws up another will, in which all the property is left to him. And there the matter would seem to end. But Chensky is a materialist, and therefore, he must be a fool. Consequently, he is quite at a loss what to do with the elderly lady's will and his own promissory note, now that he has gained possession of them. At last, being a materialist, *i.e.,* a fool, he thinks of the following device to extricate himself from his predicament: he decides to marry the old princess' niece—the daughter of an indigent professor. Then, he argues to himself, everything will be covered up, and the law will be restored by means of joint possession; the promissory note for three million rubles will go with the poor girl's dowry. What a materialistic (meaning foolish) calculation, is it not?

And so Chensky presents himself to the Onins. Here he meets with idealism. The girl's father, the retired professor Onin, dilating at length on antagonistic principles of some kind or other, says:

"Everything depends upon principles: they are the basis of our actions. A man who obeys the spiritual principle is noble in his actions and is capable of the greatest self-sacrifice: he seems to be unconscious of our perishable body. A sensuous man is inclined towards coarse pleasures, he is selfish and capable of the meanest actions. All the evil in us springs from a lack of living feeling, of living faith. Among the coarse masses of the people, unconscious formalism is a common occurrence: among them man has not yet developed, among them the animal still reigns, among them simple human feeling must assume a material form to become intelligible; but if this same form passes into a higher strata of society only as a form, if conscious feeling fails to gain the upper hand there, or. . . ."

But what are we doing? We began by quoting the words of Onin in *Chensky's Courtship* and ended with a quotation from Mr. Savich's essay. . . . But there is really no difference, so let it remain as it is. . . . Perhaps our readers will see for themselves where Onin ends and Mr. Y. Savich begins??

And so Onin is an idealist. He has a sister living with him, a learned lady who is a student of Ancient Egypt. Onin's daughter is also an idealist. Clearly, they cannot take a liking to Chensky. What makes things worse is that Liza Onina already has a fiancé, Molvin, who is also a rabid idealist. This Molvin says:

"We know that the qualities of matter are not employed just anyhow, that they are inevitably directed towards a previously designed object, which is determined by the *idea of organization*. I may be told that this idea springs from the qualities of matter itself, even if it is an organic cell, which, if placed under certain conditions, can develop at the expense of its environment *in one particular way and in no other*. I can accept this too. But while it can develop only *in one particular way and in no other, the idea* which underlies the formation of these conditions has already determined the image of the future individual with all the minutest details of its subsequent structure. Consequently, this individual is the direct product of the idea, which is realized in him, assuming the form of matter, *subordinating matter to itself*, converting it into its tool." (*Atenei*, p. 283.)

But what's this? We have again quoted a passage from Mr. Savich's essay instead of *Chensky's Courtship*. . . . How can one help doing that, however, when the two are so much alike? . . . Molvin says the same thing, only more tersely, and even more intelligently. Here is what he says:

"The basis of everything is the idea. It is necessarily engendered in our souls; we introduce it into nature; it guides our reasoning, and with its aid we correct everything."

Hence, the only difference between Molvin and Mr. Y. Savich is that Molvin regards the idea as something produced by man, and which he introduces into nature, whereas, according to Mr. Savich, the idea is some sort of special animal, which exists separately, independently, of man's consciousness and subordinates matter to it. Which of these two idealists is the more sensible one is not a difficult question to answer. But we shall continue our story about Chensky's courtship.

Chensky presents himself to the Onins and begins by paying Liza compliments like the following:

C h e n s k y: You are in the bloom of youth. Your cheeks are like two buns.

O n i n a: What a comparison!

C h e n s k y (*laughing*): I wanted to say, like two well-browned cutlets.

Chensky has to talk like that because he has a materialist (*i.e.*, foolish) conception of things. But the author compels him to say things which are so materialistic (*i.e.*, foolish) as to make one suspect that the author himself is infected with materialism (as he himself understands it). At his very first meeting with Onina, Chensky tells her that he very much likes her "half-bared shoulder," and makes an attempt to touch it. Then he expresses his admiration for her figure: "So slim and yet so plump!" and in doing so drops to his knees. In this posture he is discovered by Molvin, and he at once offers the latter fifty thousand rubles as an inducement to cede his fiancée to him. Naturally, Molvin rejects this offer, and then Chensky begins to work upon Liza's father. It must be said that the poor professor had once borrowed from his relative, Princess Lapina, thirty thousand rubles for the education of his daughter. Why did he need such an enormous sum of money? And how could he have borrowed such a sum considering his own meagre resources? There can be only one answer to this question: Onin is an idealist. It is common knowledge that idealists are incapable of spending money wisely. It is not surprising, therefore, that Onin spent the thirty thousand rubles on his daughter's education without even having her taught that it was indiscreet, while alone with Chensky, at their first meeting, to play the harp and sing to him the following song:

> Abandon all labour, abandon all care,
> *Lay your head on your darling's white breast,*
> *Her passions overpowering give her no rest,*
> And love shines warm from her eyes.
> And when her harp she takes up to play
> *By ardent desires she is carried away,*
> And a dream is woven in the strains she brings
> Out of the golden strings.

Here, of course, in addition to bad verse, we also have ideal-ism; but it is evident that Liza Onina has her own conception of what idealism is....

Taking advantage of the fact that Onin was in debt to the Princess, Chensky, as her heir, demands immediate payment, threatening to put Onin into prison if this was not forthcoming. Here Onin's idealism reveals itself to the full. He begins by mor-alizing in the following strain: debts must certainly be paid; *"failure to pay debts is a peculiar form of theft."* But when Chensky forthwith demands payment, Onin answers with emotion: "Permit me to tell you that if the Princess were alive, she would have cancelled this debt. She often hinted at this in her letters to me." Now is not this idealism admirable? Having no means, he bor-rows thirty thousand rubles from a rich relative in the hope that she would cancel the debt! This is a pinnacle of idealism which, besides Onin, only Mr. Y. Savich could reach in *Atenei.* Mr. Sa-vich, on his part, is also of the opinion that there is a limit beyond which neither cool calculation nor intelligence, but only some sort of formless and limitless feeling is needed. This is what he says:

"Where human intellect ends feeling begins as the continuation of intellect, as a persistent, *but vain* (alas) striving towards the figurative (in Koshansky's textbook on rhetoric?)[86] expression of some idea, which, by its nature, is *incompatible with anything that presupposes limitation* and, therefore, passes into something that is formless and limitless. (Is this clear? The payment of a debt presupposes the limitation of the idea of borrowing; hence, as Onin feels, payment is incompatible with bor-rowing!) It does not seek facts, it does not demand theories; it carries within itself truth, faith (that the debt will be cancelled) and love, and believes and loves without denial, without explanations." (Indeed, Onin believed that the debt would be cancelled solely on the basis of the hints contained in the Princess' letters.)

These are the lofty sentiments (which for some unknown rea-son Mr. Savich calls *"religious"*) that guide Onin. But Chensky, being a materialist, agrees to cancel the debt only on the condition that Onin consents to give him his daughter in marriage. Onin tries to persuade his daughter to agree to the match, but in this he is unsuccessful. As a consequence, the professor is dragged to prison as a defaulting debtor. But here upon the scene comes Princess Lapina's maid, Darya Semyonovna Tumina, with whom Chensky, while living at the Princess' house, had had intercourse— *because it was cheap*, as he expressed it—and had seven children with her. On learning that Chensky was seeking the hand of Onin's daughter, this Tumina goes to the professor, denounces Chensky and depicts his materialism in the most awful colours. For example, she relates the following incident about him:

"We had a footman named Fyodor," she said, "he was very tall, and he rode out with the Princess and attended her when she went for a walk. Once, when Chensky was fasting and had already been to Confession, Fyodor did something that displeased him. What did Chensky do? He gave Fyodor a thrashing, and so he could not go to Holy Communion. This happened three times in three weeks, and Chensky had to fast for three weeks."

This awful example of *materialism* horrifies everybody. After that, to prevent the marriage between Chensky and the professor's daughter, and also to take revenge on Chensky, Tumina breaks open the latter's strongbox, removes the promissory note, the Princess' will and the will which Chensky himself had fabricated, and brings all this to Onin just at the moment when Liza, terrified by the fate that awaited her father, agrees to marry Chensky. Here, of course, are present Molvin, and also a police officer, who must now drag not Onin but Chensky to prison. But all those present, being true idealists, turn out to be so generous that they not only refrain from handing Chensky over to justice, but even allow him to retain possession of all the money he had gained by his commercial operations and confine themselves only to compelling him to marry Tumina. Thus, the idealists gain affluence and happiness, fully rewarded for their worship of an idea, and the materialist is the loser—which was the point to be proved. . . .

It is obvious, one would think: all that can be said to Chensky in conclusion is that he is a fool, and if the idealists in the *Courtship* also turn out to be rather foolish, all the worse for

Chensky. He must be even more foolish than they if he allowed them to get the better of him.

But probably, in spite of the foregoing passages we quoted from *Atenei*, you are still not fully convinced that Mr. Savich handled the materialists in exactly the same way as the author of *Chensky's Courtship* handled them. We assure you, however, that he did. You see, from the very outset he presented the problem in the following manner: if a philosophical system is to penetrate deeply into the public mind it must "by its nature, and in application, be *provable without proof, by the force of truth alone.*" Then he asks: "Where is there such a system?" It turns out that all systems are strong by proof; there are no unprovable systems. From this it is perfectly clear to Mr. Savich that "truth is not given to the sages," and that it is necessary to seek another, *general, universal* truth, which will be not only unprovable, but to which all probabilities advanced by shortsighted wisdom will be opposed. Then follows abuse of those who seek provable truth by means of experience and not by faith in a universal, unprovable truth:

"Our times," says Mr. Y. Savich bitterly, "have become exceptionally exigent and exacting; nowadays mere words are not believed, all speculation is abandoned in disgust (*quelle horreur!*) and only that which science or experience make provable and demonstrable is accepted (*horreur, horreur!*).... The young generation is proud of its new convictions; it claims to have taken them from science.... Among us science comes first, and we, without arguing much, watch it in silence and merely point to new sources of light for the benefit of those who wish to become enlightened quickly, in conformity with the prevailing fashion. Nowadays there is a fashion for everything; ready-made convictions are acquired more easily than ready-made clothing, and they please everybody all the more for the reason that they fit everybody. What are these convictions? The negation of everything that cannot be strictly proved by experience...."

After enumerating the horrors that arise from such confidence in experience Mr. Savich exclaims: "It is impossible to enumerate all the evils, and besides, what is the use? Every one of the new people feels that he lacks something, that he has lost something that is very precious to him! The young generation coldly looks ahead, coldly looks around; but do not believe this bold indifference, do not call it maturity," and so forth.... Mr. Savich then goes on to assert that the young generation merely pretends to believe in science and experience, but actually longs for "universal, unprovable truth."

But pray—what is science to trust her like this? Listen to Mr. Y. Savich. According to him, the ardent partisans of science, intoxicated by success, hasten to express their hopes on the most important questions concerning the world and man and, carried away more and more by their enthusiasm, pronounce with a comical air of importance an emphatic verdict—*such a crude, such an ugly, such an inhuman verdict!*... You will be surprised, reader, (observes Mr. Y. Savich *himself*). This stern judgment of *what is called the successes of science* (probably what is meant here are those very *modern ideas* against which Messrs. Barkov and Kulzhinsky, and their fraternity,[87] are arming themselves!) may sound strange to you. But keep calm! There is still plenty of junk, old and new, in its storehouse—and you need not take everything for gold. But what should be taken for gold and what for junk? How can we know which is which? Does not Mr. Savich reject and scorn all *proof and external symptoms*? ... Listen to this:

"Only that remains true treasure, the precious attainment of science, which emerges pure from the spiritual crucible, from our minds—the only possible test when dealing with subjects of supreme spiritual significance. But if concepts which contradict our consciousness, our reason, our feelings are offered you as truth, will you accept them solely because they are offered you in the name of science? You cannot if you are not frivolous and vain," and so forth.

Let us translate these idealistic phrases into common language. They will read as follows:

"You wish to study because you realize that you are not sufficiently educated. But do not think that science must broaden your views, group things that are familiar to you in a different way, present them to you in a new light, make accessible to your mind things of which formerly you have not been conscious, arouse in you new sympathies and new antipathies unknown to you before. No, not at all! You must take from science only that which will always harmonize with your *mind*, your *reason*, your *sentiments* at the stage at which they are at the time you begin to study science. Hence, if you are told that the earth revolves around the sun, that the sun is bigger than the earth, that certain stars which you see are even bigger than the sun, and so forth, 'will you believe

this simply because you are told all this in the name of science?
You cannot if you are not frivolous and vain.' Similarly, in the
world of moral principles—if you are at a stage of development
reached by Mr. Dimman in his *Science of Life*, or by Mr. Miller-
Krasovsky in his pedagogics[88]—you will perhaps remain at that
stage if you are not frivolous, and so forth. Let science talk to
you about various philanthropic ideas in education, let it present
to you a theory of new social relationships based upon honesty
and truth and not upon obsequiousness and self-effacement; you
must not accept such arguments because our minds are already
imbued with opposite principles, and if you betray those principles
you will prove that you are frivolous, or vain."

What a triumph for Mr. Dimman, for Colonel P. S. Lebedev,
for Mr. Barkov, and for all the possible Mitrofanushkas of our
times! Mr. Y. Savich in *Atenei* permits them to refrain from studying, not to believe in science, to scorn it if it dares to say anything
in opposition to their individual consciousness and feelings. If the
consciousness and feelings of the tavern licensee make him think
that the spread of sobriety is fatal for the state, if the consciousness and feelings of the American cotton planter command him
to regard the oppression of Negroes as sacred and inviolable, if the
bribetaker's consciousness and feelings conjure up criminal indict-
ments against those who denounce bribery, then those people are
right in rejecting all the logical convictions worked out by the
social sciences! According to Mr. Savich, these people should be
admired as men who are not frivolous, and not vain. But why talk
about these people? Mr. Savich's authority permits every ignoramus to neglect his studies and to hold science in contempt. What,
indeed, is the use of studying if I dare not, and must not, take from
science anything that is out of harmony with what I know and feel
now? What will I gain by it? Far better to rest content with
universal unprovable truth, which, to Mr. Savich's deep chagrin,
cannot be found in any philosophical system, and indulge in *self-
realization* "in which the supreme organic unity of the conscious
idea finds expression," as Mr. Savich puts it, none too clearly on
page 286.*

---

* Here is what he says, with all his italics. "The idea is the *direct*
product of all-embracing reason, *indivisible* in its substance but

In general, Mr. Y. Savich goes so far in his idealism that he completely loses sight of human needs and all the requirements of common sense. He frantically clings to his unprovable truth and, indeed, does not prove it in the least. On the other hand, he resorts very largely to rhetoric even where it is totally unnecessary. Indeed, was it not possible to explain the dignity of man in simpler and more restrained terms than those which Mr. Savich uses in the following lines? (*Atenei*, p. 284):

"There can be nothing more beautiful, nothing loftier and nobler than man! If you only study him more deeply you will agree with me; see how the bright ray of the divine substance has passed through matter in infinite myriads of forms of life, subordinating everything *absolutely and implicitly* to its indefeasible laws, and only in the person of man, illuminating its own self with its light, saw, recognized itself, *felt God**— became man. How much light *pours* from there. . . . This is the seat of the soul of man—the sacred cradle of virtue, justice, reason and love!. . . But, just God! How thy people have departed from thee, what bad use they are making of freedom and reason—thy finest gifts!. . . How many centuries have passed in vain, distinguishing themselves in no way, or else shamefully distinguished for man's self-forgetfulness, his failure to understand divine truths, and abuse of freedom and reason. . . . Yes, much evil cries for justice and, it would seem, the history of mankind alone is sufficient to give one the right to deny that man possesses a soul, divine reason. . . .—Man trampled himself in the mire, he himself turned away from his God and renounced himself; but for all that, truth shines in his soul and it cannot be covered up by any sophistry. But it is time to wake up! It is time we looked deeper into ourselves, it is time we ascertained for ourselves where this light comes to us from, and why, even with an accidentally caused flash of it, our hearts beat so *anxiously*, passions whisper so *timidly*, audacious thoughts are subdued, and a man feels *disconcerted*, *awkward*, as if he were *ashamed* of himself. . . . *Happy*** moments! Who

---

infinitely productive; consequently, the whole of nature, the whole of the visible world, is a living book in which supreme reason has recorded its divine truths. From this it follows that the study and the discovery of the laws of reason which are expressed in the whole of the empirical world constitutes the substance of science. The idea, personified by man, and *living within him*, constitutes the substance of his reason, as the conscious idea of divine reason, which, in man achieves its highest organic unity expressed by *self-realization*."

We leave it to the reader to decide what predominates in this excerpt —rhetoric or nebulous exposition. Incidentally, these two qualities are very closely related to each other!. . .—*N. D.*

* Author's italics.—*N.D.*

** Just think of what happiness consists in!. . . A man is happy precisely when he feels *ashamed*, *awkward*, *disconcerted* and *anxious*!. . . Oh,

is not acquainted with you? Who has not been aware of you at least once in his life?..."

In addition to eloquence, Mr. Savich is distinguished for the intricacy of his thinking, which in some places even threatens to pass into profundity. Listen, for example, to the way he explains the relation between reason and matter by means of arithmetical analogies.

"Subtract a fraction from a unit and the unit will become a fraction; subtract all the fractions and the unit will become a 0, where you will find neither end nor beginning. So it is here: *oneness* on the one side, *infinite generality on the other*, while the parts are intermediaries between the one and the other, between the general and the one. The reader may, perhaps, jokingly reproach me for having reduced the infinite generality of reason to a cipher; but if, joking aside, we examine the importance of the cipher, it will not be difficult to convince oneself that the cipher exists neither in the sense of a whole, nor in the sense of parts, *although its incomprehensible existence is no less real for all that*."

Well, would you not like to examine more closely this "incomprehensible real existence of a non-existent cipher"? What a splendid problem to work on after a sumptuous dinner to stimulate the digestion! What a triumph for the unprovable, universal truth, which Mr. Savich revealed in *Atenei*! ... It is not surprising that he exclaims in his essay: "Here is truth, here it is in all the grandeur of its beauty and might! And we have been groping like the blind," and so forth.... And then follow again the old assurances that all those who seek proof for truth are downright fools....

And yet, strangely enough among these fools, among these unfortunates who fail to understand universal truth, Mr. Savich found a theory, which he disliked only because it is too lofty and too idealistic! ... You will not believe it, of course, and therefore we shall once again quote Mr. Savich himself. He expounds the theory which, he says, the materialists (meaning fools) accept, and this is the way he compels them to express their convictions (p. 275):

"Among us now, as somebody expressed it recently, in the forefront stands man and his direct existence—good. *We have convinced ourselves*

Mr. Savich! It is not surprising that he, already in last year's *Atenei*, wrote about "the relation of ideal human bliss to ideal canine happiness"!—*N. D.*

(!) that nothing is absolute, that everything has only relative importance and value. To be honest, generous and just, all we need know is our kinship with mankind; for this we need neither your principles, nor a soul with some kind of innate conceptions of good and evil. All this is too abstract for us. Good and evil are relative concepts; not that which pleases me alone is good, but that which pleases you and everybody else; and when everybody feels well, believe me, we too will not feel bad. This, then, is absolute good, and in the same way you may even find absolute evil, which, evidently, has not occurred to our philosophers. Each for all and all for each—this is our principle, and it is leading us not to false happiness."

After expounding his opponents' thoughts, Mr. Savich presents his own refutation in the following form:

"A splendid rule, if it is indeed a rule and not simply a highfalutin phrase; but, unfortunately, it serves as a screen for such a vacuum, such a *tabula rasa*, that we make so bold as to expose it and to display the other side of this splendid mantle, in which our present age is draping itself. We have never had any doubts about the existence of a feeling which forgets itself for the sake of all, which prefers public welfare to private interest; *we have always believed in the beneficial nature of such a feeling, but we have known it only as an exception to the common rule, carefully noted among rare historical examples; nobody would ever dare base the solidarity of human relationships upon it; a different, a more reliable basis, must be sought for this.*"

The meaning of this answer seems to be clear. Put in other words it would read as follows: "You, Messrs, materialists, want to base common good on the foundation of mutual interests, on the natural inclination of men to participate in public affairs. In theory you are right, but your hopes are too idealistic. We idealists are of the opinion that such a merging of private with public interests is a brilliant exception, which is recorded in history as a rarity. Don't dare to assure us that it was your science, your theory that brought you to such results; this is impossible. . . . It is too good and too lofty. . . . How can your science achieve such heights? Here some other foundation is absolutely necessary. . . . We idealists could indeed draw such beneficial results, but we refrain from doing so because we believe them to be only exceptional, rare phenomena. That being the case, how dare you attempt to do anything of the kind?"

Thus, a change of roles takes place: the *materialists* are reproached for being too *idealistic*. What can the poor fellows

do who are first scolded and then exposed as being incapable
of achieving what they have already achieved. This is another
repetition of the old story about the teacher who scolded a pupil
for having solved an arithmetical problem too quickly. "How
could you solve it when I myself have not yet finished my calculations!" "I solved it by a different method." "What other methods
can you have, you are still a fool, a mere whippersnapper, you
don't know anything. I might think up some other method because
I am a teacher. . . . But yet you see I am working on the problem
by the old method. . . . What's the use of you trying other methods?" "Still I have solved the problem you set me, and have
solved it correctly." "Nonsense! It's not true. It only seems to be
so, because all the proof is adduced and the conclusion is correctly
drawn. . . . But actually, it is far beyond you. What is needed here
is universal truth, proof without proof, nonsense that is sense," and
so forth.

How should one argue with a mentor of this type? Would it
not be better to leave him in the blissful conviction that he alone
possesses the key to truth and that whoever disagrees with him is
an utter fool? And would it not be better for us to finish in the
same way with Mr. Savich—with Mr. Savich who is so eloquent
and consistent?

But in taking our leave of him, and of the author of the comedy *Chensky's Courtship* (if they are not the same person), we
take the opportunity to draw several general conclusions concerning idealists and materialists as depicted by the authors whose
works we have reviewed.

1) According to *Chensky's Courtship*, idealists like to live at
other people's expense by borrowing money and not returning it.

2) Materialists are very [religious and fast for three weeks
at a stretch, depriving themselves of Holy Communion] for being
hot-tempered.

3) Idealists like to believe in hints, especially when those hints
promise the cancellation of debts.

4) According to *Chensky's Courtship*, and also according to
Mr. Savich, materialist is the synonym for fool; materialists forge
wills and keep the forgeries with the genuine wills which have
not been drawn up in their favour; they also keep intact their own
promissory notes, which they have stolen from their creditors. . . .

5) According to Mr. Savich, "every individual of the idealist is the direct product of the idea which is realized in him, assuming the form of matter."

6) The materialists are no good mainly because they are too idealistic, and regard as a general ethical requirement what the idealists can only wonder at as a rare exception.

7) From all this it follows that idealism is inevitable in materialism, as Mr. Savich conceives it, and that these two principles are very tangled and mixed up—if not in the world, then at any rate in the minds of Mr. Savich and the author of *Chensky's Courtship* (if they are not the same person).

WHEN WILL THE DAY COME?

ON THE EVE, A NOVEL BY I. S. TURGENEV,
Russki Vestnik, No. 1-2, 1860.[89]

> [Schlage die Trommel und fürchte dich nicht.
>
> *Heine.*]

AESTHETICAL criticism has now become the hobby of sentimental young ladies. In conversation with them the devotees of pure art may hear many subtle and true observations, and then they can sit down and write a review in the following style. "Here is the content of Mr. Turgenev's new novel" (follows a summary of the story). "This faint sketch is enough to show how much life and poetry, of the freshest and most fragrant kind, is to be found in this novel. But only by reading the novel itself can one obtain a true idea of that feeling for the most subtle poetical shades of life, of that keen psychological analysis, of that profound understanding of the hidden streams and currents of public thought, and of that friendly and yet bold attitude towards reality which constitute the distinguishing features of Mr. Turgenev's talent. See, for example, how subtly he has noted these psychological features" (then comes a repetition of a part of the summary, followed by an excerpt from the novel); "read this wonderful scene which is depicted with such grace and charm" (excerpt); "recall this poetical living picture" (excerpt), "or this lofty and bold delineation" (excerpt). "Does not this penetrate to the depths of one's soul, compel the heart to beat faster, animate and ornament our lives, exalt before us human dignity and the great, eternal significance of the sacred ideas of truth, goodness and beauty! *Comme c'est joli, comme c'est delicieux!*"

We are unable to write pleasant and harmless reviews of this sort because we are little acquainted with sentimental young ladies. Openly confessing this, and disclaiming the role of "cultivator of the aesthetic tastes of the public," we have chosen for ourselves a different task, one more modest and more commensurate with our abilities. We simply wish to sum up the data that are scattered throughout the author's work, and which we accept as accomplished facts, as phenomena of life that confront us. This is not a complicated task, but it is one that must be undertaken because, what with the multiplicity of their occupations and the need for relaxation, people are rarely willing to go into all the details of a literary production, to analyze, verify and put in their proper places all the figures that combine to make this intricate report on one of the sides of our social life and then to ponder over the result, over what it promises, and what obligations it imposes upon us. But such verification and reflection will be very useful in the case of Mr. Turgenev's new novel.

We know that the devotees of pure aesthetics will at once accuse us of wanting to thrust our own views upon the author and to set tasks for his talent. We shall therefore make the following reservation, tedious though it may be to do so. No, we have no wish to thrust anything upon the author; we say at the very outset that we do not know what object the author had in view, or what views prompted him to write the story that constitutes the contents of the novel *On the Eve*. The important thing for us is not so much what the author *wanted* to say, as what he *said*, even unintentionally, simply in the process of truthfully reproducing the facts of life. We prize every talented production precisely because it enables us to study the facts of our own lives which, without these facts are so little exposed to the gaze of the ordinary observer. To this day there is no publicity in our lives except official publicity; everywhere we encounter not living but official persons, persons who are serving in one sphere or another; in government offices we meet clerks, at balls we meet dancers, in clubs—cardplayers, in theatres—hairdressers' clients, and so forth. Everybody hides his spiritual life as far away from the public gaze as possible; everybody looks at us as much as to say: "I have come here to dance, or to show my coiffure. That being the case, be satisfied with the fact that I am going about my business, and please don't take it into your head to question me about my feelings and my ideas." And indeed, nobody makes any attempt to make anybody confess, nobody is interested in anyone; everybody in society goes his own way, regretting that he must come together with oth-

ers on official occasions as, for example, a first night at the opera,
an official banquet, or at a meeting of some committee or other.
Under these circumstances, how is a man who does not devote
himself exclusively to the observation of social habits to study and
learn what life is? On top of all this there is the variety, even
opposites, in the different circles and classes of our society! Ideas
which have become banal and out of date in one circle are still
hotly debated in another; what some regard as inadequate and
weak, others regard as excessively sharp and bold, and so forth.
We have no other way of knowing what is defeated, what is victorious, or what is beginning to permeate and predominate in the
moral life of society than through literature, and mainly through
its artistic productions. The author-artist, although not troubling
to draw any general conclusions about the state of public thought
and morality, is always able to grasp their most essential features,
throw a vivid light upon them and place them before the eyes of
thinking people. That is why we think that as soon as it is recognized that an author-artist possesses talent, *i.e.*, the ability to feel
and depict the phenomena with lifelike truth, this very recognition
creates legitimate ground for taking his productions as a basis for
the discussion of the milieu, the epoch, which prompted the author
to write this or that production. And here the criterion of the
author's talent will be the breadth of his conception of life, the
degree to which the images he has created are permanent and
comprehensive.

We have deemed it necessary to say this in order to justify
our method, namely, to interpret the phenomena of life itself on
the basis of a literary production, without attributing to the author
any preconceived ideas or aims. The reader perceives that we regard as important precisely those productions in which life is expressed as it is and not according to a program previously drawn
up by the author. We did not discuss *A Thousand Souls*,[90] for
example, because, in our opinion, the whole social side of this
novel was forcibly adjusted to a preconceived idea. Hence, there is
nothing to discuss here except the degree of skill the author displayed in composing his work. It is impossible to rely on the truth
and living reality of the facts delineated by the author because his
inner attitude towards these facts is not simple and truthful. We
see an entirely different attitude of an author towards his subject

in Mr. Turgenev's new novel, as indeed we see in most of his novels. In *On the Eve* we see the inescapable influence of the natural course of social life and thought, to which the author's own thoughts and imagination were involuntarily adjusted.

In expressing the view that the main task of the literary critic is to explain the phenomena of reality which called a given artistic production into being, we must add that in the case of Mr. Turgenev's novels this task acquires a special meaning. Mr. Turgenev may be rightly described as the painter and bard of the morality and philosophy which have reigned among the educated section of our society during the past twenty years. He very soon divined the new requirements, the new ideas that were permeating the public mind, and in his works he, as a rule, devoted (as much as circumstances would permit) attention to the question that was about to come up next, and which was already beginning vaguely to stir society. We hope to trace the whole of Mr. Turgenev's literary activity on a future occasion, and so we shall not deal with it at length now; we shall only say that it is to this sensitiveness that the author displays towards the living strings of society, to this ability of his to respond forthwith to every noble thought and honest sentiment which is only just beginning to penetrate the minds of the best people, that we largely ascribe the success which Mr. Turgenev has always enjoyed among the Russian public. It goes without saying that his literary talent too has contributed a great deal to this success, but our readers know that Mr. Turgenev's talent is not of the Titanic kind, which by sheer poetic expression alone captivates you, thrills you and compels you to sympathize with a phenomenon, or an idea, with which you were not in the least inclined to sympathize. Not a turbulent and impulsive power but, on the contrary, gentleness and a kind of poetic moderation are the characteristic features of his talent. That is why we believe that he could not have roused the general sympathy of the public had he dealt with questions and requirements that were totally alien to his readers, or which had not yet arisen in society. Some readers would have noted the charm of the poetical descriptions in his novels, the subtlety and profundity with which he portrayed different individuals and situations; but there can be no doubt that this alone would not have been enough to make the author's success and fame permanent. Even the most attractive

and talented narrator must, if he fails to display this responsive attitude towards modern times, share the fate of Mr. Fet,[91]
whom people praised at one time, but of whose work only
about a half of his best poems are remembered by only about a
half a score of admirers. It is his responsive attitude towards
modern times that has saved Mr. Turgenev and has guaranteed
him permanent success among the reading public. A certain profound critic once rebuked Mr. Turgenev for having in his works
so strongly reflected "all the vacillations of public thought." We,
on the contrary, regard this as the most vital feature of Mr. Turgenev's talent; and we believe that it is this feature of his talent that
explains the sympathy, almost enthusiasm, with which all his
productions have been received up till now.

Thus, we may boldly assert that if Mr. Turgenev touches upon
any question in a story of his, if he has depicted any new aspect
of social relationships, it can be taken as a guarantee that this
question is rising, or soon will rise, in the mind of the educated
section of society; that this new aspect is beginning to make itself
felt and will soon stand out sharply and clearly before the eyes
of all. That is why, every time a story by Mr. Turgenev appears,
our curiosity is roused and we ask: what sides of life are depicted
in it, what questions does it touch upon?

This question arises now, and in relation to Mr. Turgenev's
new novel it is more interesting than ever. Up to now Mr. Turgenev's path, in conformity with the path of our society's development,
has proceeded in one, fairly clearly defined, direction. He started
out from the sphere of lofty ideas and theoretical strivings and
proceeded to introduce these ideas and strivings into coarse and
banal reality, which had digressed very much from them. The hero's
preparations for the struggle, his sufferings, his eagerness to see
the triumph of his principles, and his fall in face of the overwhelming power of human banality have usually been the centres of
interest in Mr. Turgenev's stories. It goes without saying that the
background of this struggle, that is to say, the ideas and strivings,
was different in each story, or was expressed more definitely and
sharply with the progress of time and change of circumstances.
Thus, the unwanted man's place was taken by Passinkov; Passinkov's place was taken by Rudin; Rudin's place was taken by
Lavretsky. Each of these persons was bolder and more perfect than

his predecessor, but the substance, the basis of their characters and their entire existence was the same. They introduced new ideas into a certain circle; they were educators and propagandists—even though it was for one woman's soul, but propagandists nevertheless. For this they were highly praised and, indeed, in their time they were evidently greatly needed; and their task was extremely difficult, honourable and beneficial. It is not surprising that they were so popular, that their spiritual sufferings roused so much sympathy and their fruitless efforts so much pity. It is not surprising that nobody at that time even thought of observing that these gentlemen were splendid, noble and intelligent, but, at bottom, idle people. Depicting them in various situations and conflicts, Mr. Turgenev himself usually treated them with moving sympathy; it was evident that his heart ached for their sufferings, and he always roused the same feeling among the bulk of his readers. When one motive for this struggle and suffering began to look inadequate, when one feature of nobility and exaltation of character began to show signs of banality, Mr. Turgenev was able to find other motives and other features, and thereby again strike at the heart of his readers, and again rouse admiration and sympathy for himself and for his heroes. The subject seemed to be inexhaustible.

Lately, however, demands entirely different from those which Rudin and all his fraternity roused have made themselves heard fairly distinctly in our society. A radical change has taken place in the conceptions of the majority of educated people in relation to these personages. It is now not a question of changing the particular motives, or the particular principles, underlying their strivings, but of the very substance of their activities. During the period in which all these enlightened champions of truth and virtue, these eloquent martyrs to exalted convictions, were parading before us, new people have grown up, for whom love of truth and honest strivings are no longer a novelty. The conceptions and strivings for which, in the past, the best people had to fight, to hesitate over and to suffer at a mature age, these new people imperceptibly and steadily imbibed in their childhood.*

---

* We have already been rebuked once for our partiality for the young generation and our attention has been drawn to the banalities and trivialities to which the majority of its representatives devote themselves. But we have never dreamed of defending all young people indiscriminately,

As a consequence, the very character of education in our present young society, has assumed a different hue. The conceptions and strivings which, in the past, were the hallmark of the progressive person, are now regarded as the primary and essential attributes of the most ordinary education. You will hear a high-school boy, a mediocre cadet, and sometimes even a seminary student a little above the average, expressing convictions which formerly Belinsky, for example, was obliged to defend in heated controversy. And the high-school boy, or cadet, expresses these convictions—which were formerly arrived at with such difficulty and struggle—quite calmly, without any particular ardour or smugness, as if any other convictions were impossible and even quite inconceivable.

Nobody among respectable people now expresses astonishment and admiration on meeting a man who belongs to the so-called progressive trend, nobody looks into his eyes with mute awe, nobody shakes hands with him mysteriously and gives him a whispered invitation to meet a close circle of the chosen in his home to discuss the point that injustice and slavery are fatal for the state. On the contrary, anybody who reveals a lack of sympathy for publicity, unselfishness, emancipation, and so forth, arouses instinctive astonishment and contempt. Today even those who dislike progressive ideas must pretend to like them in order to gain admission to decent society. Clearly, under such circumstances, the former sowers of the seeds of good, people of the *Rudin* type, lose a considerable part of their former credit. They are respected as old teachers, but rarely is anybody with an independent mind disposed to listen again to those lessons which were learned so eagerly in the past, in the period of childhood and initial development. Now something different is needed; it is necessary to go further.*

---

for this would not have been in conformity with our object. Banality and triviality is a characteristic of all ages and of all times. We did speak, and we speak now, of chosen people, the best people, not of the crowd; for Rudin, and all the men of his type, belong not to the crowd, but to the best people of our times. Incidentally, we shall not be wrong in saying that the level of education has, after all, risen lately, even among the bulk of society.—*N. D.*

* This view may seem to be contradicted by the extraordinary success which has been achieved by the publication of the works of some of our authors of the 'forties. A particularly striking example of this is Belinsky, whose works, in an edition of 12,000 copies, it is said, were quickly sold

"But," we may be told, "society has not yet reached the limit of its development; further mental and moral improvement is still possible. Consequently, society needs leaders, preachers of the truth and propagandists, in short, men of the Rudin type. Let us assume that everything of the past has been accepted and absorbed by the public mind, but that does not preclude the possibility that new Rudins, the preachers of new and higher trends, will appear, who will fight and suffer again, and again rouse sympathy for themselves in society. This subject is indeed inexhaustible and may constantly bring fresh laurels for a writer like Mr. Turgenev."

It would be a pity if observations such as these found confirmation at the present time. Happily, we think, they are refuted by the latest trend in our literature. Speaking abstractly, it cannot be denied that the view that ideas in society are in a constant process of movement and change and, consequently, that there is a constant need for preachers of these ideas, is quite correct; but we must also bear in mind that society does not live exclusively for the purpose of arguing and exchanging ideas. Ideas and their gradual development are of importance only because, engendered by already existing facts, they always precede changes in actual reality. A certain state of affairs creates a need in society; this need is recognized; following the general recognition of this need an actual change must take place in the direction of satisfying this generally recognized need. Thus, after a period of *recognition* of certain ideas and strivings a period must arise in society in which these ideas and strivings are *carried out*; reflection and talk must be followed by action. The question now arises: what has our society done during the past twenty to thirty years? So far, nothing. It studied, developed, listened to the Rudins, sympathized with them in their setbacks in the noble struggle for convictions, prepared for action, but did not do anything. . . . So much that is beautiful has accumulated in the minds and hearts of men; so much that

out. In our opinion, however, this very fact serves to confirm our view. Belinsky was a progressive among progressives; none of his contemporaries went further than he, and where 12,000 copies of the works of Belinsky can be sold out in several months the Rudins can find positively nothing to do. Belinsky's success proves not that his ideas are new for our society and call for much effort to disseminate, but that they are now precious and sacred for the majority, and that their advocacy now no longer calls for heroism or exceptional talent on the part of the new men.—*N.D.*

is absurd and dishonest has been discovered in the present order of society; the number of people who "regard themselves as standing above surrounding reality" is growing year after year, so that soon everybody, perhaps, will be standing above reality. . . . One would think that there were no grounds for wishing that we should continue forever to proceed along the painful road of discord, doubt and abstract grief and consolation. It would seem to be clear that now we need not people who will "raise us still higher above surrounding reality" but who will raise, or teach us how to raise, reality itself to the level of the rational demands that we have already recognized. In short, we need men of action and not of abstract, and always somewhat Epicurean, argument.

This was recognized, although vaguely, by many on the appearance of *A Nest of the Gentry*. On this occasion too Mr. Turgenev's talent, together with his true sense of reality, helped him to emerge from a difficult situation in triumph. He succeeded in depicting Lavretsky in such a way that it seemed out of place to treat him with irony, although he actually belongs to the type of idlers that we look upon with ridicule. The drama in his situation is no longer the struggle against his own impotence, but in his collision with concepts and customs, the fight against which is enough to daunt even a bold and energetic man. He is married, but has left his wife; he falls in love with a pure, angelic woman who has been imbued with concepts that make the loving of a married man a heinous crime. Nevertheless, she loves him, and his claims continuously and frightfully torture her heart and conscience. A situation like this cannot help giving rise to deep and bitter reflection, and we remember how painfully our hearts throbbed when Lavretsky, in bidding farewell to Lisa, said to her: "Oh, Lisa, Lisa! How happy we could have been!" And when she, already at heart a nun resigned to her fate, answers: "You can see for yourself that happiness depends not on us but on God." In reply to this he says: "Yes, because you . . ." but he does not finish what he wants to say. . . . We remember that readers and critics of *A Nest of the Gentry* admired many other things in that novel; but what interests us most in it is this tragic collision of Lavretsky, whose passivity, precisely in this case, we cannot but excuse. Here it seems as though Lavretsky, as if contradicting one of the generic features of his type, is scarcely even a propagandist. Beginning with his first meeting with Lisa, when she is going to morning prayers, he, throughout the story timidly yields to her unshakeable conviction and never dares to enter into a cool argument with her in order to shake those convictions. But this too, of course, is due to the fact that in such a case propaganda is the very thing which Lavretsky, and his entire fraternity, fears most. In spite of all this, it seems to us (at least it seemed to us when we were reading the novel), that the very situation in which Lavretsky finds himself, the very collision which Mr. Turgenev chose for this novel, and which is so familiar in Russian life, should [serve as powerful propaganda and] prompt in the mind of every reader a number of thoughts concerning the significance of an entire complex of concepts which govern our lives. From various published and spoken comments we now know that we have not been altogether right; Lavretsky's situation was either differently interpreted or quite misunderstood by many readers. That there is something genuinely and not artificially tragic about him was understood, however, and this, together with its artistic merits, gained for *A Nest of the Gentry* the unanimous admiration of the whole of the Russian reading public.

After *A Nest of the Gentry* there were grounds for apprehension concerning the fate of Mr. Turgenev's new work. The path of creating exalted characters who are compelled to resign themselves to the blows of fate has become very slippery. Amidst the admiration expressed for *A Nest of the Gentry* voices were heard expressing dissatisfaction with Lavretsky, from whom much more was expected. The author himself deemed it necessary to introduce Mikhalevich into his story in order to rebuke Lavretsky for his indolence. And Ilya Ilyich Oblomov, who appeared at the same time, definitely and bluntly explained to the entire Russian public that it is now far better for a man who lacks will and energy to refrain from making people laugh; that it is far better for him to remain lying on his couch than to make a lot of fuss and noise and bother, to argue and beat the wind for whole years and decades. The people who read *Oblomov* recognized his kinship with those interesting personages, the "unwanted men" and realized that these men were indeed already unwanted, that they were of no more use than good old Ilya Ilyich. "What will Mr. Turgenev create now?" we asked ourselves, and we sat down to read *On the Eve* with the utmost curiosity.

On this occasion too the author's feeling for the present did not fail him. Realizing that the former heroes had already done their work and could no longer win the sympathies of the best section of our society as they had done in the past, he decided to abandon them, and sensing in several fragmentary manifestations the spirit of the new demands of life, he stepped on to the road along which the progressive movement is proceeding at the present time. . . .

In Mr. Turgenev's new novel we meet with situations and types that differ from those we have been accustomed to find in his previous works. The social demand for action, for real action, incipient contempt for dead, abstract principles and passive virtue are expressed in the whole structure of the new novel. Everybody who reads this essay has undoubtedly read *On the Eve*, hence, instead of summarizing the story we shall only make a brief sketch of its principal characters.

The heroine of the story is a girl of a serious turn of mind, possessing an energetic will and a heart filled with humane strivings. Her development has been very peculiar owing to special domestic circumstances.

Her father and mother were very narrow-minded but not vicious; her mother was even favourably distinguished for her kindness and soft heart. From her childhood Helena was free from the yoke of that domestic despotism which crushes so many beautiful characters in the bud. She grew up alone, without friends, absolutely free; no formalism restricted her. Nikolai Artyomich Stakhov, her father, was a rather dull-witted person, but he regarded himself as a philosopher of the sceptical school and kept himself aloof from domestic life, at first only admiring his little Helena, who revealed unusual abilities at an early age. While she was little, Helena worshipped her father. But Stakhov's relations with his wife were not altogether satisfactory. He married Anna Vassilyevna for her dowry, he had no feeling towards her whatever. he treated her almost with contempt and left her for the society of Augustina Christianovna, who fooled and fleeced him. Anna Vassilyevna, a sick and sensitive woman, after the type of Maria Dmitriyevna in *A Nest of the Gentry*, meekly bore her lot but could not refrain

from complaining about it to everybody at home and, incidentally,
even to her daughter. Thus, Helena soon became her mother's
confidante, one to whom to pour out her woes, and involuntarily
she became the judge between her and her father. Owing to Helena's
impressionable nature this greatly influenced the development of
her inner strength. The less she could do practically in this matter
the more work she found for her mind and imagination. Compelled
from her earliest years to watch the relationships between those
she loved, participating with both heart and mind in the explanation
of these relationships and in passing judgment upon them, Helena
early trained herself to think independently and to form a conscious
opinion about everything around her. The domestic relationships
of the Stakhovs are very briefly sketched in Mr. Turgenev's novel,
but this sketch gives us profoundly true indications which explain
a great deal in the early development of Helena's character. She
was an impressionable and clever child; her position between
her mother and father early prompted her to serious reflection and
early raised her to an independent, authoritative role. She placed
herself on the level of her elders and put them before the bar of
her judgment. Her reflections were not cold, however; her whole
soul merged with them, because the matter affected people who
were extremely close and extremely dear to her, whose relationships
were bound up with her most sacred sentiments and her most vital
interests. That is why her reflections directly affected the disposition
of her heart. She ceased to worship her father and acquired a
passionate attachment to her mother, whom she regarded as an
oppressed and suffering being. Her love for her mother, however,
did not rouse the contrary feeling of hostility towards her father,
who was neither a villain, a positive fool nor a domestic tyrant.
He was just an ordinary mediocrity, and Helena cooled towards
him instinctively and later, perhaps, consciously decided that there
was nothing lovable about him. But soon she observed that her
mother too was a mediocrity, and passionate love and respect for
her gave way in her heart to a mere sense of pity and condescen-
sion. Mr. Turgenev very aptly describes her attitude towards her
mother when he says that she "treated her mother as if she were
an ailing grandmother." The mother admitted to herself that she
was beneath her daughter; the father, however, as soon as his
daughter began to surpass him in intellect, which was not a very

difficult matter, cooled towards her, decided that she was queer, and dropped her.

Meanwhile Helena's feelings of sympathy and humanity grew and expanded. Of course, the pain she felt at the sight of the suffering of others was originally caused in her childish heart by the downtrodden appearance of her mother long before she began to understand what the trouble was about. This pain was always with her, it accompanied her at every step she took in her development, it gave an exceptionally pensive bent to her thoughts, and it gradually called forth and defined in her active strivings, all of which she directed towards a passionate and irresistible yearning for the good and happiness of all. This yearning was still vague, her strength was still feeble when she found fresh sustenance for her reflections and dreams, a new object for her sympathy and love; we refer to her strange acquaintance with the beggar girl, Katya. She befriended this girl when she was over nine years of age, clandestinely met her in the park, brought her sweetmeats, gave her shawls and ten kopek pieces (Katya would not take toys), sat with her for hours eating the girl's stale bread with a sense of joyous humility; she listened to the stories the girl told, learned her favourite song and with concealed awe and fear heard her threaten to run away from her wicked aunt and go and live *in God's full freedom*; and she herself dreamed of putting a knapsack on her back and running away with Katya. Katya soon died, but Helena's acquaintance with her inevitably left deep traces upon her character. A new side was added to her pure, human, sympathetic disposition, a side which cultivated in her contempt for, or at all events stern indifference to, the superfluous luxuries of the life of the rich, a feeling which always penetrates the soul of a person, who is not entirely spoilt, at the sight of helpless poverty. Soon Helena's whole soul was thirsting with desire to do good, and at first this desire was satisfied with the customary acts of charity that were accessible to her. "The poor, the hungry and the sick beckoned to her, stirred and pained her; she saw them in her dreams, she questioned all her acquaintances about them." Even "all ill-treated animals, the emaciated backyard dogs, kittens condemned to death, young sparrows which had fallen from their nests, and even insects and reptiles found a protector in Helena; she herself fed them and never felt disgust for them." Her father called all this banal sentimentality, but Helena was not sentimental, for sentimentality is characterized precisely by an abundance of sentiment and words accompanied by a complete absence of effective love and sympathy. Helena always tried to express herself in action. She could not tolerate empty caresses and tenderness and, in general, attached no value to words that were unaccompanied by deeds, and respected only practical and useful activity. She was not even fond of poetry and had no judgment of art.

But the active strivings of the soul mature and grow strong only if there is scope and freedom for them. One must test one's strength several times, suffer reverses and collisions, learn to know what various efforts cost and how various obstacles have to be overcome in order to acquire the courage and determination which are necessary for an active struggle, in order to learn one's strength and be able to find commensurate work for it. Notwithstanding the freedom of her development, Helena could not find sufficient outlets for her strength and was unable to satisfy her strivings. Nobody prevented her from doing what she wanted to do, but there was nothing to do. She was not restricted by the pedantry of systematic education and was therefore able to educate herself without acquiring the multitude of prejudices that are inseparable from systems, courses, and routine education in general. She read a great deal and with interest, but reading alone could not satisfy her; the only effect it had upon her was that her power of reasoning developed more than her other powers, and her intellectual requirements even began to exceed the living strivings of her heart. Nor could the giving of alms, tending pups and kittens, and protecting flies from spiders satisfy her. When she grew older and wiser she could not fail to see how shallow this activity was, and moreover, these occupations called for very little effort and could not fill her life. She wanted something bigger, something higher, but what it was she did not know; even if she did know she could not set to work at it. This explains why she was always in such a state of agitation, why she was always expecting and looking for something, and that is why her very appearance became so peculiar.

"Her whole being, the expression on her face, her *attentive and somewhat timid, clear but unsteady gaze, her smile which seemed to be strained, and her low uneven voice* expressed something nervous, electrical, something *impulsive and hasty....*"

Clearly, she is still beset by vague doubts about herself, she has not yet determined her role. She has realized what she does not need and remains proud and independent amidst the habitual circumstances of her life; but she does not yet know what she needs, and above all she does not understand what she must do to achieve what she needs, and that is why her whole being is strained, uneven and impulsive. She is waiting, living on the eve of something. ... She is ready for vigorous, energetic activity, but she is unable to set to work by herself, alone.

This timidity, this virtual passivity of the heroine combined with her abundance of inner strength and her tormenting thirst for activity astonishes us and makes us think that there is something unfinished about Helena's personality. But this very unfinished state of Helena's personality, her lack of a practical role, reveals precisely the living connection between Mr. Turgenev's heroine and the whole of the educated section of our society. In the way Helena's character is conceived, at bottom, it is an exceptional one, and if she were indeed presented everywhere as expressing her views and strivings she would have been alien to Russian society and would not have had that intimate meaning for us that she has now. She would have been a fictitious character, a plant unskilfully transplanted to our soil from some foreign land. But Mr. Turgenev's true sense of reality did not permit him to make the practical activities of his heroine fully coincide with her theoretical concepts and the inner promptings of her soul. Our public life does not yet provide an author with the materials for this. At present we observe throughout our society only an awakening desire to get down to real work, a realization of the banality of the various beautiful toys, of the lofty phrases and inert forms with which we have amused and fooled ourselves for so long. But we have not yet emerged from the sphere in which we were able to sleep so peacefully, and we do not yet know very well where the exit is; if anybody does know, he is still afraid to open the door. This difficult and painful transitional state of society inevitably leaves its impress on works of art that are produced under these conditions. There may be individual strong characters in society, individuals may achieve a high level of moral development, and so such personalities appear in literary productions. But all this remains only in the portrayal of the characters of these persons, it is not carried over into life; the possibility of its existence is assumed, but it is not seen in real life. Olga, in *Oblomov*, appeared to us to be an ideal woman whose development had gone far beyond the rest of society; but where is her practical activity? She seems to be capable of creating a new life and yet she lives amidst the same banality in which all her women friends live because she cannot get away from this banality. She likes Stolz because he is an energetic and active character, and yet, notwithstanding all the skill displayed by the author of *Oblomov* in depicting character, he reveals to us only Stolz's abilities, but he gives us no opportunity to see how he applies them; he has no firm ground under his feet and floats before our eyes in a sort of mist. In Mr. Turgenev's Helena we now see another attempt to create an energetic and active character, and it cannot be said that the author's portrayal of this character is unsuccessful. If we have rarely met women like Helena, many of us, of course, have observed even in the most ordinary women the embryo of one or other of the essential features of Helena's character, the potential development of many of her strivings. As an ideal personage, constituted of the finest elements that are developing in our society, Helena is intelligible and close to us. Her strivings are defined for us very clearly; she seems to serve as an answer to the question and doubts of Olga, who, while living with Stolz, is yearning and longing for something which she herself cannot define. The portrait of Helena explains this longing, which inevitably overcomes every decent Russian, no matter how good his own circumstances may be. Helena is thirsting to perform good deeds, she is looking for the means to create happiness around herself, because she cannot conceive of herself enjoying peace of mind, let alone happiness, if she is surrounded by suffering, unhappiness, poverty and the humiliation of her dear ones.

But what activities commensurate with these inner demands could Mr. Turgenev provide for his heroine? It is difficult to answer this question even in the abstract, and it is probably still less possible for a Russian author of the present day to create such activities in his art. There is no scope for such activities, and the author is, willy-nilly, obliged to compel his heroine to display her lofty strivings in a shallow way, by giving alms and saving abandoned kittens. She is unable, and afraid, to undertake activities which call for great strain and struggle. All around her she sees one thing oppressing another, and precisely because of her humane and sympathetic disposition she tries to keep aloof from everything in order to avoid oppressing others herself. At home her influence is not felt at all; her father and mother are like strangers to her; they stand in awe of her authority, but she never offers them advice or instruction, or makes demands of them. She has a companion living in the house, a young, good-natured German girl named Zoya, but Helena keeps aloof from her, scarcely ever speaks to her, and their relations are very cold. There is also the young artist Shubin, about whom we shall speak in a moment; Helena annihilates him with her withering criticism, but she never dreams of exercising any influence over him, although this would have been extremely beneficial for him. There is not a single in- stance throughout the story where the yearning to do good induces Helena to intervene in the affairs of those around her and to exercise her influence in any way. We do not think that this is due to a casual oversight on the author's part. No, up to very recently we saw, not among women but among men, a special type who towered and shone above society and took pride in standing aloof from the surrounding milieu. "It is impossible to keep pure in this environment," they said, "and besides, this environment is so shallow and banal that it is far better to keep out of it." And they did indeed keep out of it; they did not make a single energetic attempt to improve this banal environment. Their self-exclusion from it was regarded as the only honest way out of their situation, and was glorified as an act of heroism. Naturally, having such examples and concepts before him, the author had no better means of depicting Helena's domestic life than by describing her as stand- ing entirely aloof from that life. As we have said, however, in the story Helena's impotence is attributed to a special cause, which springs from her feminine, humane sentiments: she dreads all col- lisions not because she lacks courage, but because she is afraid that she may offend or harm somebody. Having never experienced a full and active life, she still imagines that her ideals can be achieved [without a struggle], without causing anybody any harm. After one incident (when Insarov heroically threw a drunken German into a pond), she made the following entry in her diary:

"No, he will stand no nonsense, and he has the courage to take up the cudgels on another's behalf. But why that anger, those quivering lips and that venom in his eyes? But perhaps it cannot be otherwise? Perhaps a man, a fighter, cannot remain meek and mild?"

This simple idea had only just entered her mind, and then only in the form of a question which she is unable to answer.

In this state of indefiniteness, of inaction, in spite of a continuous yearning for something, Helena lives until she reaches the age of twenty. Sometimes she feels exceedingly depressed; she realizes that she is wasting her strength, that her life is empty. She says to herself: "If I got a place as a serving maid I would feel much better, I am sure." This feeling of depression is intensified by the fact that she meets with no sympathy from anybody, she can find no one to support her. Sometimes it seems to her that she wants something that nobody else wants, that nobody in all Russia is thinking about. . . . She becomes frightened and the need for sympathy grows stronger, and she longs intensely and agitatedly for another soul that would understand her, that would respond to her innermost sentiments, that would help her and teach her what to do. A desire arises within her to surrender herself to somebody, to merge her being with somebody, and the lone independence in which she stands among those immediately around her becomes repugnant to her.

"From the age of sixteen she lived her own life, but it was a lonely life. Her soul flared up and died down alone, she beat her wings against the bars like a bird in a cage; but there was no cage, nobody restricted her, nobody restrained her, nevertheless, she struggled and pined. Sometimes she did not understand herself; she even feared herself. Everything around her seemed to her to be either senseless or unintelligible. 'How is it possible to live without love? But there is no one to love,' she mused, and these thoughts, these sensations frightened her."

It is in this state of mind and heart that she comes upon the scene in the story, in the summer, at a country house in Kuntsevo. In a short space of time three men appear before her, one of whom attracts her whole soul. Incidentally, there is a fourth man, introduced casually, but not one of the unwanted type, whom we shall also count. Three of these gentlemen are Russians, the fourth is a Bulgarian, and him Helena regards as her ideal. Let us look at all these gentlemen.

One of these young men, who, in his own way, is passionately in love with Helena, is the artist Pavel Yakovlevich Shubin, a

handsome and graceful youth of about twenty-five, good-natured
and witty, merry and ardent, carefree and talented. He is a distant
relative of Anna Vassilyevna, Helena's mother, and therefore stands
very close to the young girl and hopes to win her affections. But
she always looks down superciliously upon him, regards him as a
clever but spoiled child who can never be taken seriously. Shubin,
however, says to his friend: "There was a time when she liked
me," and indeed there is much about him that is likeable. It is not
surprising that for a moment Helena attached more importance to
the good sides of his character than to the bad ones; but she soon
discerned the *artistic* side of this character, she realized that everything about him was ephemeral, that there was nothing constant
and reliable about him, that his entire make-up was a mass of
contradictions: indolence crushed his talent, and waste of time
later called forth fruitless contrition, caused spleen and roused
self-contempt. which, in its turn, served to console him for his
failures and fostered his pride and conceit. Helena realized all this
instinctively, without tormenting perplexity, and therefore, her
decision regarding Shubin was absolutely calm and dispassionate.
"You think that everything about me is pretence, you do not believe that I have repented, you do not believe that I can weep
sincerely!" said Shubin to her one day in an outburst of despair.
She does not answer: "I do not believe." She says simply: "But
I do believe you have repented, Pavel Yakovlevich, and I believe
your tears, but it seems to me that your repentance amuses you,
and so do your tears." Shubin shuddered as he heard this simple
verdict, which must indeed have stabbed deeply into his heart.
He had never imagined that his impulses, contradictions and
sufferings, his tossing from one side to another, could be interpreted and explained so simply and truthfully. After hearing
this explanation he even stopped making himself an "interesting
person." And indeed, as soon as Helena has formed an opinion
about him he ceases to interest her. It is a matter of indifference to her whether he is present or not, whether he remembers or has forgotten her, whether he loves or hates her. She
has nothing in common with him, although she is not averse to
praising him sincerely when he does something worthy of his
talents. . . .

Another begins to occupy her thoughts. He is of an entirely

different type. He is uncouth, old-fashioned, his face is ugly and even funny in a way, but it expresses a thoughtful and kindhearted character. Moreover, according to the author, "his entire uncouth figure bears the *impress of decency.*" This is Andrei Petrovich Bersenev, a close friend of Shubin. He is a philosopher, a scholar, reads the history of the Hohenstaufens and other German books, and he is modest and capable of self-sacrifice. In answer to Shubin's exclamation: "We want happiness, happiness! We shall win happiness for ourselves!" he says sceptically: "As if there is nothing higher than happiness!" and then comes the following dialogue between them:

"For example?" Shubin asked and halted.

"Well, take this, for example. We two, as you say, are young, we are good fellows. All right, let's admit that it is so. Both of us want happiness. But is the word 'happiness' the one that will unite us two, induce us to extend a hand to one another? Is it not a selfish word? What I want to say is: is it not a word that disunites us?"

"But do you know any words that unite?"

"Yes. Quite a number. And you know them, too."

"What words are these? Tell me."

"Well, take the word art, since you are an artist. Then there is country, science, freedom, justice."

"And love?" Shubin asked.

"And love is a uniting word, but not the love that you are now yearning for, not love that means pleasure, but love that means sacrifice." Shubin frowned.

"That's all right for the Germans. I want love for myself. I want to be number one."

"Number one," Bersenev echoes. "But I think that the entire mission of our lives is to make ourselves number two."

"If everybody behaves as you advise," said Shubin with a plaintive grimace, "nobody will eat pineapples, everybody will leave them all for others."

"That shows that pineapples are not essential. But don't be afraid, there will always be people who will even take bread out of another's mouth."

This conversation shows what noble principles Bersenev professes, and how his soul is capable of what is called self-sacrifice. It expresses sincere readiness to sacrifice his happiness for the sake of one of those words which he calls "uniting words." Consequently, it was inevitable that he should win the sympathy of a girl like Helena. But it at once becomes evident why be cannot capture her soul, fill her whole life. He is one of the heroes of passive virtue, a man capable of bearing a great deal, of sacrificing a great deal, of acting in a noble manner in general when opportunity occurs, but he will not be able and will not dare to undertake broad and bold activity, a free struggle, an independent role in any cause. He wants to be number two because he thinks that this is the mission of every living being; and indeed his role in the story to some extent reminds one of Bizmenkov in *The Unwanted Man*, and still more of Krupitsyn in *Two Friends*. Although in love with Helena, he becomes the mediator between her and Insarov, with whom she has fallen in love; he generously helps them, nurses Insarov when he is sick, renounces his own happiness for the sake of his friend, although not without some heartache, and even not without complaint. He has a kind and loving heart, but everything goes to show that he will always do good not so much because of the promptings of his heart, as because he thinks it his *duty* to do good. He holds that one must sacrifice one's happiness for the sake of one's country, of science, and so forth, and thereby condemns himself to remain an eternal slave and martyr to an idea. He draws a line between his happiness and his country, for example; he, poor fellow, cannot rise sufficiently to be able to understand that the good of his country is inseparably bound up with his own happiness, and to be unable to conceive of happiness for himself apart from the well-being of his country. On the contrary, he seems to be afraid that his personal happiness may hinder the well-being of his country, hinder the triumph of justice, the achievements of science, and so forth. That is why he is afraid to wish for happiness for himself, and owing to the nobility of his principles he decides to sacrifice his happiness for the sake of his ideas and, of course, thinks that this is an act of magnanimity on his part. Clearly, such a man is capable only of passive nobility. He cannot merge his soul with any great cause, he cannot forget the whole world for the sake of a favourite idea, that idea cannot inflame him and he cannot fight for it as if he were fighting for his own joy, his own life, his own happiness. ... He does what duty bids him, he strives for what he regards as just on principle; but his actions are listless, cold, and hesitant, because he is always doubting his strength. He finished his course at the university with distinction, he loves science, he is constantly studying and wishes to become a professor.

What could be simpler? But when Helena asks him about his professorship he deems it necessary to display praiseworthy modesty: "I, of course, know only too well how much I still lack to be worthy of such a lofty ... I want to say that I am too little prepared for it, but I hope to obtain permission to go abroad. ..." Exactly like the introduction to an academic speech: "I hope, ladies and gentlemen, that you will kindly excuse the dryness and colourlessness of my exposition," and so forth.

And yet the professorship about which Bersenev speaks in this way is the object of his cherished dreams! When Helena asks him whether he will be quite content with his position when he is appointed to a university chair he answers:

"Quite, Helena Nikolayevna, quite! What higher calling can there be? Think of it! To follow in the footsteps of Timofei Nikolayevich[92]. ... The very thought that I shall engage in such activities fills me with joy and embarrassment. ... Yes, embarrassment which ... which springs from the consciousness of my own weakness."

The same consciousness of his weakness first induces him stubbornly to refuse to believe that Helena has grown to love him, and then to grieve that she has grown indifferent towards him. This same consciousness can be discerned when, in recommending his friend Insarov, he, among his other merits, mentions the fact that he does not borrow money. The same consciousness can even be discerned in his reflections about nature. He says that nature awakens in him a sort of disquietude, anxiety and even melancholy, and he asks Shubin:

"What can this mean? Does the consciousness of our utter imperfection, of our lack of clarity grow stronger in her presence, before her face, or is that which she gives us inadequate for us, while the other ... what I mean to say is ... she lacks what we need?"

Most of Bersenev's reflections run in this air-beating romantic style. And yet, in one passage of this story we are told that he argued about Feuerbach. It would have been extremely interesting to hear what he had to say about Feuerbach! ...

And so, Bersenev is a very good Russian nobleman, trained in the principles of duty, who later plunges into scholarship and philosophy. He is far more practical and reliable than Shubin, and if he were led along some road he would go willingly and straight ahead. But he is incapable of leading not only others, but even himself: by his very nature he lacks initiative; he failed to acquire it during his upbringing and he failed to acquire it in later life. At first Helena feels an attraction for him because of his kindness and the serious subjects he discusses with her. She is even ashamed of her own ignorance, because he is always bringing her books that she cannot read. But she cannot become completely attached to him, she cannot surrender her soul, her fate, to him; she instinctively realizes even before she meets Insarov that Bersenev is not the man she needs. And indeed, we may confidently assert that Bersenev would have been scared had Helena thrown herself upon his neck, and he would certainly have fled on various extremely noble pretexts.

Incidentally, living in a wilderness, as it were, Helena was for a moment enchanted with Bersenev and already asked herself whether he was not the man for whom her soul had been yearning for so long, the man who was to relieve her of all her perplexities and point out to her the path of activity. But Bersenev himself introduces Insarov to her and the enchantment vanishes. . . .

Strictly speaking, there is nothing extraordinary about Insarov. Bersenev and Shubin, Helena, and even the author of the novel himself, describe him in negative terms. He never tells lies, he never breaks a promise, he does not borrow money, he is not fond of talking about his achievements, he never puts off the execution of a decision once adopted, his deeds never contradict his words, and so forth. In short, he has none of the features for which any man with claims to respectability should bitterly reproach himself. But in addition to this, he is a Bulgarian whose soul is filled with a passionate desire to liberate his country, and to this idea he devotes himself entirely, openly and confidently, it represents the ultimate goal of his life. He does not think that his personal happiness can come into collision with his life's object; such an idea, so natural for the Russian nobleman-scholar Bersenev, would never enter the head of this simple Bulgarian. On the contrary, he is striving for the liberation of his country because to him it means ensuring his own peace of mind, the happiness of his whole life; if he could have found satisfaction in anything else he would not have concerned himself about his enslaved country. But he cannot conceive of himself separately from his country.

"How can one be content and happy when one's countrymen are suffering?" he thinks. "How can a man remain calm while his country is enslaved and oppressed? What pleasure can he find in any occupation if that occupation does not lead to the alleviation of the lot of one's poor countrymen?"

Thus, he pursues his cherished cause quite naturally, without posing, without any fanfaronade, as naturally as eating and drinking. For the time being he can do little in the way of putting his idea into execution, but that cannot be helped. At present he has little to eat and sometimes even starves, but for all that the food, although scanty, is essential for his existence. So it is with the liberation of his country: he studies at the Moscow University in order to become thoroughly educated and to become intimate with the Russians, and throughout the story he is content for the time being with translating Bulgarian songs into Russian, compiling a textbook of Bulgarian grammar for Russians and a Russian grammar for Bulgarians, keeps up a correspondence with his fellow countrymen, and intends to return to his country in order to prepare for an insurrection on the very first outbreak of an Eastern war (the action of the story takes place in 1853). This, of course, is meagre sustenance for Insarov's active patriotism, but he does not regard his stay in Moscow as real life, and does not consider his feeble activities satisfactory even for his personal strivings. He too lives *on the eve* of the great day of liberation of his country, in which his being will be illumined by the consciousness of happiness, life will become full and already be real life. He looks forward to this as to a festival, and this explains why it never enters his head to entertain any doubts about himself, or coolly to calculate and weigh how much he will do, and to the level of which great man he will rise. It is a matter of total indifference to him whether he will be a Timofei Nikolayich or an Ivan Ivanich; whether he will be number one or number two does not worry him. He will do what his nature prompts him to do; if his nature is such that no better will be found, he will be number one, he will march at the head; if men stronger and bolder than he are found, he will follow them, and in both cases he will remain true to himself. Where he will stand and how far he will go will be determined by circumstances; but he wants to go, and he cannot help going not because he is afraid of failing to perform some

duty, but because he would die if he were unable to go. It is this
that constitutes the enormous difference between him and Bersenev.
Bersenev is also capable of making sacrifices and of performing
heroic deeds, but in this he resembles a generous girl who consents
to marry a man she hates in order to save her father. She looks
forward to the wedding with smothered pain and unwilling submission to her fate, and would be glad if something happened to prevent it. Insarov, however, looks forward to his feats of heroism,
to the day when he can engage in his self-sacrificing activities with
eagerness and impatience, like a young man in love looking forward to the day of his wedding with the girl he loves. Only one
anxiety disturbs him, and that is that something may happen to
put off the wished-for day. Insarov's love for the freedom of his
country lies not in his mind, not in his heart, nor in his imagination: it permeates his whole being, and whatever else penetrates
his being is transformed by the power of this feeling, submits to
it and merges with it. That is why, notwithstanding his quite ordinary abilities, notwithstanding the lack of brilliance in his nature,
he is immeasurably superior to, charms and influences Helena ever
so much more than brilliant Shubin and clever Bersenev, although
both are also noble and loving characters. Helena makes the following extremely apt observation concerning Bersenev in her diary
(on which the author did not spare his profundity and wit):

"Andrei Petrovich may be more learned than he (Insarov), he may
even be more intelligent, but I don't know why it is—*he looks so small in
his presence.*"

Is it necessary to relate the story of how Helena and Insarov
were drawn together, the story of their love? We think not. Our
readers probably remember this story well, and besides it cannot
really be told. We are afraid to touch this tender poetical creation
with our cold rough hands, we are even afraid to offend our readers' feelings, which, undoubtedly, have been stirred by the poetry
of Turgenev's narrative, with our dry and unfeeling account of it.
Mr. Turgenev, the bard of pure and ideal feminine love, peers so
deeply into the young virgin soul, understands it so fully and depicts its finest moments with such inspired emotion, with such an
ardour of love, that we actually feel in this story the quiver of
her maidenly breast, her tender sighs, her moist glance, every throb

of her agitated heart, so that our own hearts melt and stop beating from deep emotion, tears of happiness rise to our eyes more than once, and something bursts from our breasts as if we were sitting beside an old friend after a long parting, or had returned home to our native land after a sojourn in foreign parts. This feeling is both sad and joyful: it conjures up bright recollections of childhood, gone never to return, the proud and joyous hopes of youth, the ideal, harmonious dreams of a pure and mighty imagination as yet untamed or degraded by the trials of mundane experience. All this has passed never to return; but the man is not yet lost who can return to these bright dreams if only in recollection, to this pure and youthful intoxication with life, to these grand and ideal plans, and then shiver at the sight of the sordidness, banality and pettiness in which his present life is passing. And blessed is the one who can rouse such recollections in others, who can awaken such sentiments in another's soul.... Mr. Turgenev's talent has always been distinguished for this; his stories always create this pure impression of their general construction, and therein, of course, lies their essential importance for society. This importance is inherent in *On the Eve* because of its portrayal of Helena's love. We are certain that our readers will be able, without our aid, to appreciate the charm of those passions, those tender and languorous scenes, those subtle and profound psychological details with which the love of Helena and Insarov is depicted from beginning to end. Instead of relating the story we shall recall Helena's diary, her waiting for Insarov to come to say goodbye, the scene in the chapel, Helena's return home after that scene, her three visits to Insarov, especially the last,* then her parting from her mother and her country, her departure, and lastly, her last

---

* There are people whose imaginations are so sordid and corrupted that in this charming, pure and profoundly moral scene, so full of the passionate merging of two loving beings, they see only material for voluptuous scenes. Judging everybody by themselves, they even howl that this scene may have a bad influence upon morals because it rouses impure thoughts. But let them howl. After all, there are people who feel only sensuous excitement at the sight of a statue of Venus of Milo; and on seeing a picture of the Madonna they say with a lascivious smirk: "She's... [fit for] ...you know...." But art and poetry are not for such people, nor is true morality. Everything in their minds is transformed into something disgustingly impure. But give these scenes to an innocent, pure-hearted maiden to read; you may be sure that she will gain from this reading nothing but the brightest and most noble thoughts.—*N. D.*

stroll with Insarov along the Canal Grande, her visit to the opera
to hear *Il Traviata* and her return. This last episode strongly im-
presses us by its strict truthfulness, and by the infinite sadness of
its charm; we think it is the most touching, the most charming passage in the whole story.

We shall leave our readers to enjoy the recollection of the entire
development of the story while we return to Insarov's character, or
rather, to the relationship in which he stands to the Russian society
around him. We have already seen that here he does almost nothing
to achieve his principal aim; only once do we see him go off on a
journey of sixty versts to Troitsky Posad, to reconcile his com-
patriots who had quarrelled among themselves, and at the end of
his stay in Moscow it is mentioned that he travelled all over the
city clandestinely visiting various personages. But it goes without
saying that he has nothing to do while living in Moscow. To do
anything real he must go to Bulgaria. And he does go, but death
intercepts him on the road, and so we see no activity on his part
in the story. From this it is evident that the purpose of the story
is not to depict for us an example of civic, *i.e.*, public heroism,
as some critics try to assure us. Here there is no reproach aimed at
the Russian young generation, no indication as to what a civic hero
should be. Had this been the author's object he should have brought
his hero face to face with his cause—with parties, with the people,
with the alien government, with those who share his views, with
the enemy force.... But the author did not wish, and as far as
we are able to judge from his previous works, was unable to
write a heroic epic. His object was entirely different: from all
the Iliads and Odysseys he borrowed only the story of Ulysses' sojourn on the island of Calypsos and further than that he does not
go. After making us understand and feel what Insarov is, and in
what environment he finds himself, Mr. Turgenev devotes himself
entirely to describing how Insarov is loved, and what came of this
love. At the point where love must at last make way for real civic
activity he cuts the life of his hero short and ends his tale.

What then is the significance of the *Bulgarian's* appearance in
this story? Why a Bulgarian and not a Russian? Are there no
such characters among Russians, are Russians incapable of loving
passionately and persistently, incapable of recklessly marrying for
love? Or is this only a whim of the author's imagination, and it

is useless seeking any particular meaning in it? As much as to
say: "Well, he went and took a Bulgarian, and there's an end to it.
He might just as well have taken a Gypsy, or a Chinese,
perhaps. . . ."

The answers to these questions depend upon one's views concerning the entire meaning of the story. We think that the Bulgarian's place here could indeed have been taken by a man of some
other nationality, by a Serb, a Czech, an Italian or a Hungarian,
but not [by a Pole or] a Russian. [Not a Pole, because a Pole is
entirely out of the question. But why not a Russian? That is the
question at issue, and we shall try to answer it to the best of our
ability.]

The point is that the principal personage in *On the Eve* is
Helena, and it is in relation to her that we must examine the other
personages in the story. She expresses that vague longing for
something, that almost unconscious but irresistible desire for a new
way of life, for a new type of people, which the whole of Russian
society, and not only its so-called educated section, now feels.
Helena so vividly expresses the finest strivings of our present
society and she brings out the utter hollowness of the common
everyday life of this society in such prominent relief. that one
involuntarily feels like drawing a detailed parallel. [Here all
would be in their place: Stakhov, who is by no means malicious,
but is featherbrained and stupidly puts on airs: Anna Vassilyevna,
whom Shubin calls a hen; the German companion towards whom
Helena is so cold; dreamy but sometimes profound Uvar Ivanovich,
who is disturbed only by the news of the counter-bombardment;
and even the mean footman, who reports Helena to her father when
everything is all over].... But parallels of this kind, while undoubtedly revealing a playful imagination, become overstrained and
ludicrous when they go into great detail. We shall therefore refrain
from going into details and confine ourselves to a few observations
of a most general nature.

Helena's development is not based on deep learning, or on
wide experience of life; the finest, the ideal side of her character
blossomed, grew and matured at the sight of the meek sufferings
of the person who was dear to her, at the sight of the poor, the
sick and the oppressed, whom she found and saw everywhere,
even in her dreams. Is it not with impressions like these that all

the best characters in Russian society grew and were moulded?
Is it not in the character of every truly decent person [in this
country] to hate all violence, tyranny and oppression, and to wish
to help the weak and the oppressed? We do not say: "*activity*
in protecting the weak from the strong" because this is not the
case; we say *wish,* which is exactly the case with Helena. We too
are glad to perform a good deed when it concerns only the positive
side, *i.e.,* when it does not call for a struggle, when no outside
opposition is anticipated. We give alms, arrange theatrical performances for charitable purposes, and even sacrifice part of our
fortunes if need be; all on the condition, however, that the matter
ends here, that we will not have to encounter and combat all
sorts of unpleasantness for the sake of some poor or wronged
person. We have the "desire actively to do good," and we have
the strength to do it; but fear, lack of confidence in our strength
and, lastly, our ignorance of what is to be done, constantly check
us and, without knowing why, we suddenly find ourselves outside
of social life, cold and alien to its interests, exactly like Helena
and all those around her. And yet the *desire* still seethes in everybody's breast (we mean in the breasts of those who do not strive
artificially to suppress it) and we are all seeking, thirsting, waiting... [waiting for someone to tell us what is to be done]. It is
with the anguish of perplexity, almost of despair, that Helena
writes in her diary:

"Oh, if only somebody said to me: this is what you must do! Be good—
that is not enough. Do good ... yes, that is the main thing in life. *But how
is one to do good?*"

Who in our society, conscious of possessing a loving heart,
has not, in his torment, put this question to himself? [Who has
not confessed to himself that all the forms of activity in which his
desire to do good has manifested itself, as far as it was possible,
have been insignificant and pitiful? Who has not felt that there
is something different, something more lofty, that we could have
done, but did not do because we did not know how to proceed
about it?]... Who can solve our doubts? [We long for this solution, we seek it eagerly in the bright moments of our existence,
but we cannot find it anywhere. It seems to us that everybody
around us is either tormented by the same perplexity that torments
us, or has crushed his own feelings in his heart and confines him-

self to pursuing only his petty, selfish, animal interests. And so life passes, day after day, until it dies in a man's heart, and day after day a man waits and hopes that the next day will be better, that his doubts will be solved tomorrow, that somebody will tell us how to do good. , . .

Russian society has been longing and waiting like this for quite a long time; and how many times have we, like Helena, erred in thinking that the one we had been waiting for had arrived and then cooled off?] Helena became passionately attached to Anna Vassilyevna, but Anna Vassilyevna turned out to be a spineless nonentity. . . . At one time Helena felt well-disposed towards Shubin in the same way as our society at one time became enthusiastic about art, but it turned out that Shubin lacked real content, there were only sparkle and whims about him; and absorbed in her searching, Helena could not stop to admire trinkets. For a moment she was interested in serious learning, in the person of Bersenev, but serious learning turned out to be modest, beset by doubt, learning that was waiting for a number one to lead him. What Helena needed was a man without a number, a man who was not waiting for a lead, an independent man, who irresistibly strove towards his goal and carried others with him. At last such a man appeared in the person of Insarov [and in him Helena found her ideal, in him she found the man who could tell her how to do good.

But] Why could not Insarov have been a Russian? After all, he does nothing in the story, he only intends to do something; this much a Russian could have done. Insarov's character could have been encased in a Russian skin, particularly in the way it expresses itself in the story. In the story his character expresses itself in that he loves strongly and resolutely; but is it impossible for a Russian to love in this way?

[All this is true, nevertheless the sympathies of Helena, of the girl as we understand her, could not turn towards a Russian with the same justification and with the same naturalness as they turned towards this Bulgarian. All Insarov's charm lies in the grandeur and sacredness of the idea which permeates his whole being. Thirsting to do good, but not knowing how, Helena is instantly and profoundly captivated by the mere relation of his aims, even before she has seen him. "Liberate one's country," she says, "these are words that one even fears to utter—they are so grand!" And she feels that she has found the word her heart has been longing for, that she is satisfied, that no higher goal than this can be striven for, and that her whole life, her whole future will be filled with activities if only she follows this man. And so she tries to study him, she wants to peer into his soul, to share his dreams, to learn the details of his plans. He has only one idea: his country and its freedom, an idea which is constantly with him and has merged with his being; Helena is satisfied, she is pleased with the clarity and definiteness of his aim, the serenity and firmness of his heart, with the grandeur of the very idea, and soon she herself becomes the echo of this idea which inspires him.

"When he talks about his country," she writes in her diary, "he seems to grow and grow, his face becomes handsomer, his voice becomes like steel, and it seems as though there is not a man in the world before whom his eyes would droop. And he not only talks, he has done things, and will do things. I will ask him about it. . . ."

Several days later she writes again:

"But it is strange, though, that up till now, until I was twenty, I have never loved anybody! It seems to me that D (I will call him D, I like that name: Dmitri) has such a serene soul because he has devoted himself entirely to his cause, to his dream. Why should he worry? Whoever devotes himself to a cause entirely . . . entirely . . . entirely, knows little worry, he has nothing to answer for. It is not what *I want*, it is what *it* wants."

Realizing this she wants to merge herself with him in such a way that *not she* should want, but that *he*, and *that* which inspires him, should want. We can fully understand her position; and we are sure that the whole of Russian society, even if it is not yet carried away by the personality of Insarov as she is, will understand that Helena's feelings are real and natural.

We say that society will not be carried away, and we base this statement on the assumption that *this* man Insarov is, after all, an alien to us]. Mr. Turgenev himself, who has so thoroughly studied the finest part of our society, did not find it possible to make him *our man*. Not only did he bring him from Bulgaria, but he refrained from making his hero sufficiently endearing to us merely as a man. This, if you look at it even from the literary standpoint, is the main artistic defect in the novel. [We know one of the principal reasons for this, one over which the author had no control, and therefore we are not blaming Mr. Turgenev for this. Never-

theless], the pale sketch of Insarov affects the impression we obtain
from the story. The grandeur and beauty of Insarov's idea are not
brought out with full force [so that we are not imbued with it
sufficiently to compel us to exclaim with proud inspiration: we
shall follow you!] And yet this idea is so sacred, so exalted. ...
Far less humane, even utterly false ideas, vividly brought out in
artistic images, have exercised a feverish effect upon society; the
Charles Moores, the Werthers and the Pechorins had a crowd of
imitators. Insarov will have no such imitators. True, it was difficult
for him to express his ideas fully, living as he did in Moscow and
doing nothing; he could not indulge in rhetorical outpourings!
But from the story we learn little about him even as a man; his
inner world is inaccessible to us; what he does, what he thinks,
what he hopes for, what changes his relationships undergo, his views
on the course of events, on life that is sweeping past our eyes, are
concealed from us. Even his love for Helena is not fully revealed to
us. We know that he loves her passionately, but how he becomes
imbued with this passion, what it is about Helena that attracts him,
how deep this passion is, when he becomes aware of it and decides
to go away—all these inner details about Insarov's personality, and
many others which Mr. Turgenev is able to depict with such subtle
poetic skill, are kept from us. As a living image, as a real personality, Insarov is extremely remote from us, and this explains why
On the Eve produces upon the public such a faint and partly even
unfavourable impression compared with Mr. Turgenev's previous
stories, which portray characters whom the author had studied
down to the minutest detail, and for whom he had felt such a
lively sympathy. We realize that Insarov must be a good man and
that Helena must love him with all the ardour of her soul because
she sees him in real life and not in a story. But he is near and dear
to us only as a representative of an idea, which attracts us, as it
did Helena, like a flash of light and [lights up the gloom of our
existence. That is why we understand how natural are Helena's
feelings towards Insarov, that is why we ourselves, pleased with
his indomitable loyalty to an idea, fail to realize at first that he
is depicted for us only in pale and general outline.

And yet some want him to be a Russian! "No, he could not be
a Russian!" exclaims Helena herself in answer to a regret that
had arisen in her own heart that he was not a Russian. Indeed,

there are no such Russians, there should not and cannot be such, at all events at the present time. We do not know how the new generations are developing and will develop, but those that we see in action today have not by any means developed in such a way as to resemble Insarov. Every individual's development is influenced not only by his private relationships, but by the entire social atmosphere in which it is his lot to live. One social atmosphere will develop heroic trends, another will develop peaceful inclinations, a third irritates, a fourth soothes. Russian life is so well arranged that everything in it induces calm and peaceful slumber, and every sleepless person seems, and not without good reason, to be a troublesome character and absolutely unwanted by society]. Indeed, compare the conditions under which Insarov's life begins and passes with those met with in the life of every Russian.

Bulgaria is enslaved, she is groaning under the Turkish yoke. We, thank God, are not enslaved by anybody, we are free, we are a great people who more than once have decided with our arms the destinies of kingdoms and nations; we are the masters of others, but we have no masters....

In Bulgaria there are no social rights and guarantees, Insarov says to Helena: "If only you knew what a bounteous land my country is, and yet she is being torn and trampled upon. We have been robbed of everything: our church, our rights, our land; the vile Turks drive us like cattle, we are slaughtered...." Russia, on the contrary, is a well-ordered state, she has [wise] laws which protect the rights of citizens and define their duties; here justice reigns and beneficent publicity flourishes. Nobody is robbed of his church, and religion is not restricted [not in any way], on the contrary, the zeal of preachers [in admonishing the errant] is encouraged; far from anybody being robbed of rights and land, these are even granted to those who hitherto have not possessed them; [nobody is driven like cattle].

"In Bulgaria," says Insarov, "every peasant, every beggar, and I—we all want the same thing, we all have the same goal." [There is no such monotony]in Russian life [in which] every class, even every circle, lives its own separate life, has its own separate goal and strivings, has its own appointed place. With the [good] social order prevailing here each one need be concerned only with the pursuit of his own welfare, and for this purpose there is no need whatever to merge with the whole nation in one common idea, as they do in Bulgaria.

Insarov was still an infant when a Turkish Aga kidnapped his mother and afterwards murdered her, and then his father was shot because he wanted to avenge his mother by stabbing the Aga. Which Russian could ever gain such impressions in his life? Can anything like this be conceived of in Russia? Of course, criminals may be found anywhere, but if, in this country, an Aga kidnapped and afterwards killed another man's wife, the husband would not be allowed to avenge her, because we have laws, before which all are equal, and which punish crimes irrespective of persons.

In short, Insarov imbibed [hatred for enslavers and discontent with the present state of things with his mother's milk. There was no need for him to exert himself, to resort to a long series of syllogisms to be able to determine the direction of his activities. Since he is not lazy, and no coward, he knows what to do and how to behave. There is no need for him to take up many tasks at once. And besides] his task is so *easily understood*, as Shubin says: "All you have to do is to kick the Turks out—that's not much!" Moreover, Insarov knows that he is doing right not only in his own conscience, but also before the court of humanity: his idea will meet with the sympathy of every decent man. Try and picture something like this in Russian society. It is inconceivable. ... Translated into Russian, Insarov would turn out to be nothing more than a robber, a representative of the "anti-social element," with whom the Russian public are so familiar from the learned investigations of Mr. Solovyov,[93] which have been published in *Russki Vestnik*. Who, we ask, could love such a man? What well-bred and clever girl would not flee from him in horror?

Is it clear now why a Russian could not have taken the place of Insarov? Characters like his are, of course, [born in Russia in no small number, but they cannot develop as freely and express themselves as frankly as Insarov does. A contemporary Russian Insarov will always remain timid and dual-natured, he will lie low, express himself with various reservations and equivocations ... and it is this that reduces confidence in him. Sometimes he may even prevaricate and contradict himself, and it is well known that people usually prevaricate for their own gain, or out of cowardice.

What sympathy can one feel towards a covetous man and a coward, especially when one's soul longs for action and seeks for a great mind and a strong hand to lead it?

True, minor heroes appear among us who somewhat resemble Insarov in courage and in sympathy for the oppressed. But in our society they are ludicrous Don Quixotes]. The distinguishing feature of a Don Quixote is that he does not know what he is fighting for, or what will come of his efforts, and these minor heroes display this feature to a remarkable degree. [For example, they may suddenly take it into their heads that it is necessary to save the peasants from the tyranny of the squires and simply refuse to believe that there is no tyranny here at all, that the rights of the squires are strictly defined by the law, and must remain inviolable as long as these laws exist; that to rouse the peasants against this tyranny means not liberating them from the squires, but making them, in addition, liable to a penalty under the law. Or, for example, they may set themselves the task of protecting the innocent from miscarriages of justice, as if the judges in this country administer the law according to their own arbitrary will. Everybody knows that in this country everything is done according to the law, and that to interpret the law one way or another it is not heroism that is needed, but skill in legal quibbling. And so our Don Quixotes simply beat the air. . . . Or they may suddenly take it into their heads to eradicate bribery, and what a torment they will make of the lives of poor officials who take ten kopeks or so for some little service rendered! Our heroes who will set out to protect sufferers will make the lives of these poor officials unbearable. It is, of course, a noble and lofty task, but do these unwise people deserve our sympathy? We are not referring to those cold slaves to duty who act in this way simply in their official capacity; we have in mind Russians who really and sincerely sympathize with the oppressed, and are even ready to fight in their defence. But it is these who turn out to be useless and ludicrous, because they fail to understand the general character of the environment in which they are operating. How can they understand it when they themselves are in it, when their tops, so to speak, are pushing upwards, while their roots are, after all, embedded in this very soil? They want to alleviate their neighbours' sufferings, but these sufferings spring from the very milieu in which both the sufferers and the would-be

alleviators of suffering live. What can be done here? Turn this
whole milieu upside down? If so, they will have to turn themselves
upside down. Get into an empty packing case and turn it upside
down with yourself inside it! What efforts you will be compelled
to exert! If you stand outside of the packing case, however, you
can easily turn it over with just one push. Insarov's advantageous
position is that he is not inside the packing case; the oppressors of
his country are the Turks, with whom he has nothing in common.
All he has to do is go up and push them as hard as his strength
will allow. The Russian heroes, however, belonging, as a rule, to
the educated section of society, are themselves vitally connected
with what must be overthrown. They are in the position of what
a son of a Turkish Aga, for example, would be if he'took it into
his head to liberate Bulgaria from the Turks. It is difficult even to
conceive of such a situation; but even if it occurred, if this son of
an Aga wanted to avoid appearing like a stupid and ludicrous
fellow, he would have to renounce everything that connects him
with the Turks—his faith, his nationality, his relatives and friends,
and the material advantages of his social position. It must be
admitted that this is frightfully difficult, and determination of this
kind requires a somewhat different development from that which
the son of a Turkish Aga usually receives. It is not much easier
for a Russian to be a hero. This explains why sympathetic and energetic characters in this country content themselves with petty and
unnecessary bravado and fail to rise to real and serious heroism,
i.e., renouncing the entire complex of concepts and practical relationships which bind them to the social milieu. Their timidity in
face of the host of enemy forces is reflected even in their theoretical development; they are afraid, or are unable, to delve down
to the roots, and setting out, for example, to punish evil, they only
attack some minor manifestation of it and wear themselves out
frightfully before they have time even to look for the source of
this evil. They are reluctant to put the axe to the tree on which
they themselves grew, and so they try to assure themselves, and
others, that all the rot is only on the surface, that it is only necessary to scrub it off and all will be well]. Dismiss a few corrupt
officials from the service, appoint trustees over a few squires'
estates, and expose the tapster at one tavern who is selling diluted
vodka and justice will reign supreme, the peasants all over Russia

will live in bliss, and the tavern licensing system will become a splendid thing for the people. Many sincerely believe this and do indeed waste all their strength on efforts of this kind, and for this they quite seriously regard themselves as heroes.

We were told about a hero of this type who, it was said, was a man of extraordinary energy and talent. While still a student at the high school he started a row with one of the tutors because the latter was appropriating the paper intended for the use of the students. The affair took a bad turn; our hero managed to get into trouble also with the school inspector and the headmaster and was expelled. He began to prepare to enter the university and meanwhile gave private lessons. At the very first house at which he gave these lessons he saw the mother of his pupils slap the face of her housemaid. He flared up, raised a scandal in the house, called the police and formally charged the mistress with cruelly ill-treating her servant. A lengthy investigation ensued, but, of course, he could not prove anything and barely escaped severe punishment for laying false information and for slander. After that he could get no more private lessons. With great difficulty, thanks to somebody's special intercession, he obtained a situation in the government service. One day he was asked to copy a decision of an extremely absurd nature. Unable to restrain himself, he challenged this decision. He was told to hold his tongue, but he persisted in his protest. After that he was told to clear out. Having nothing to do, he accepted the invitation of an old school chum of his to stay in the country with him during the summer. When he arrived in the village and saw what went on there he began to tell his friend, his friend's father, and even the steward of the estate and the peasants that [it was illegal to compel the peasants to perform *barshchina* for more than three days, that it was outrageous to flog them without trial and sentence, that it was dishonourable to drag peasant women into the house at night, and so forth. The upshot was that the peasants who had agreed with what he had said were flogged, and] the old squire ordered the carriage to be brought round for him and asked him to leave and never show his face in those parts again if he wanted to keep a whole skin. Pulling through the summer somehow, our hero entered the university in the autumn, and he succeeded in doing so only because, at the examinations, he was given innocuous questions to answer which gave him no scope for argument. He

took up medicine and really studied hard; but during his practical
course, when a professor expounded the intricacies of the science
at the bedside of a patient, he could never restrain himself from
interrupting when the professor revealed the obsolescence of his
views, or quackery; as soon as the latter said anything of that
nature he at once butted in and tried to prove that he was talking
nonsense. As a result of all this, our hero was not allowed to
remain on as a post-graduate student, was not sent abroad for
further study, but was appointed to a hospital in some remote
district. No sooner did he arrive there than he exposed the superintendent and threatened to lodge a complaint against him. One day
he caught the superintendent red-handed and lodged a complaint,
but for this he received a reprimand from the head doctor. When
he received this reprimand he, of course, protested very loudly and
was soon dismissed from the hospital.... After that he received an
appointment to go with some expedition or other, and here he
took up the cudgels on behalf of the soldiers and quarrelled with
the chief of the expedition and with the official in charge of the
food supplies. As his protests were unavailing, he sent a report to
headquarters complaining that the men were being starved owing
to the malpractices of the officials and that the chief of the expedition was conniving at this. When the party reached its destination
an investigator arrived and interrogated the soldiers. The latter
stated that they had no complaints. Our hero became indignant,
was disrespectful to the General Staff doctor, and a month later
was reduced to the rank of assistant feldscher. He remained in this
post for two weeks, but unable to stand the deliberately brutal
treatment to which he was subjected, he shot himself.

An extraordinary case, a strong and impulsive character, is that
not so? And yet, look what he perished for. There was nothing in
his actions that would not represent the direct duty of any honest
man in his place; but he must possess considerable heroism to act
in this way, he must have self-sacrificing determination [to die
for the sake of doing good. The question arises: since he possessed
this determination, would it not have been better to have exercised
it for some bigger cause, so that something really useful might
have been achieved? The whole trouble is, however, that he did
not realize the necessity and the possibility of such a cause, and
he did not understand what was going on around him, he refused

to see the conspiracy that went on around him, he refused to see
what went on before his very eyes, and imagined that every manifestation of evil that he noticed was nothing more than an abuse,
which could only be a rare exception, of the system which in itself
was splendid. Holding views such as these, the Russian hero can,
of course, do nothing more than confine himself to petty details
without thinking of the general, whereas Insarov always subordinated the particular to the general, convinced that the particular
too, "will not get away." Thus, in answer to Helena's question as
to whether he avenged his father's murder, he said:

"I did not search for the murderer. I did not search for him, not
because I could not kill him—I would have done that with a clear conscience—but because there is no time for private vengeance when the
liberation of a nation is at stake. One would have hindered the other.
But the murderer will not get away. His time will come too."

It is this love for the general cause, this premonition which
gives him the strength coolly to bear private wrong, that makes
the Bulgarian Insarov far and away superior to all the Russian
heroes, who have no conception whatever of a general cause.

Incidentally, even of such heroes there are very few in this
country, and most of these do not hold out to the end. Far more
numerous among the educated section of our society is another
category of men—those who indulge in reflection. Among these
there are also many who, although able to reflect, understand nothing, but of these we shall not speak. We wish to point only
to those men who really have bright minds, men who after a long
period of doubt and searching, attained the integrity and clarity
of ideas which Insarov attained without exceptional effort. These
people know where the root of evil lies and they know what must
be done to put a stop to evil; they are deeply and sincerely
imbued with the idea they attained at last. But they no longer
possess the strength for practical activity; they have strained themselves to such an extent that their characters seem to have sagged
and become enfeebled. They welcome the approach of the new way
of life, but they cannot go out to meet it, and they cannot satisfy
the fresh sentiments of a man who is thirsting to do good and is
looking for a leader.

None of us finds ready-made the humane concepts for the sake
of which one must subsequently wage a life and death struggle.

That is why we all lack that clarity, that integrity of views and actions which are so natural in say, Insarov. In his case, the impressions of life which affect his heart and rouse his energy are constantly reinforced by the demands of his intellect, by the whole theoretical education which he has received. With us, it is entirely different]. An acquaintance of ours, a man of progressive opinions, and also burning with desire to do good, but one of the meekest and most innocuous men in the world, told us the following about his development to explain his present inactivity.

"As a boy," he said, "I was of a very kind and impressionable nature. I used to weep bitterly when I heard of some misfortune, I suffered at the sight of another's suffering. I remember that I could not sleep at night, I lost my appetite and could not do anything when anybody was sick at home. I remember that I used to be driven into a sort of frenzy at the sight of the tortures to which a relative of mine subjected his son, my chum. All that I saw and all that I heard developed in me a feeling of grave discontent. Very early in life, my soul became troubled with the question: "Why is everybody suffering like this? Is there no way of alleviating this suffering into which everybody seems to be plunged? I hungrily sought an answer to these questions. And soon I found an answer, a rational and systematic one. I went to school. The first maxim that I was given to copy was the following: 'True happiness lies in a clear conscience.' When I asked what conscience is, I was told that it punishes us for bad behaviour and rewards us for good behaviour. From that time onwards all my attention was concentrated on the task of learning what behaviour was good and what was bad. This was not a difficult matter. The code of morality already existed in the copybook maxims, in parental admonitions, and in a special textbook. 'Respect your elders,' 'Don't rely on your own strength, for you are nothing.' 'Be content with what you have, don't strive for more,' 'By patience and obedience will you win universal love,' and so forth—this is what I wrote in my copybook. I heard the same thing at home, and from all those around me. From various textbooks I learned that there can be no perfect happiness on earth. In so far as happiness is possible at all, it is achieved in well-ordered states, and my country is the most well-ordered state in the world. I learned that Russia is now not only great and bounteous, but also that the most perfect order reigns here, that it is only necessary to obey the laws and the behests of one's elders, and also to be moderate, and the greatest well-being awaits every man, no matter of what station and rank. I was overjoyed at all these discoveries and eagerly clutched at them as the best solution for my doubts. I took it into my head to verify them with my inexperienced mind, but much of this was beyond my powers. What I was able to verify in this way turned out to be correct. And so, trustfully and enthusiastically I devoted myself to this newly-discovered system, directed all my strivings towards it, and at the age of twelve I was already a little philosopher and a stern supporter of law. I reached the conviction that a man is himself to blame for all the misfortunes that beset him—either he was not cautious, nor careful enough, or was not content with little, or was not sufficiently imbued with respect for law and the will of his elders. I did not yet have a clear conception of what the law as such, was, but it was personified for me in every superior and every elder. This explains why, in that period of my life, I always supported my teachers, my superiors, and so forth, and was a favourite with my superiors and elders. One day my classmates nearly threw me out of the window. A teacher, addressing the whole class, said: 'You pigs!' There was a frightful uproar when the class was over, but I defended the teacher and argued that he had a perfect right to say what he did. On another occasion one of our classmates was expelled for being rude to a superior. Everybody was sorry for him because he was one of the best boys in the class. But I maintained that he had fully deserved his punishment and expressed astonishment at the fact that a clever boy like he could not understand that obedience to elders is our first duty and the first condition of happiness. And so, day after day, my conception of law became more firmly fixed, and I gradually grew accustomed to regarding most people only as instruments for the execution of orders from above. At the same time, I broke off living connection with the human soul, the sufferings of my fellow men ceased to trouble me, and I stopped seeking means for alleviating them. 'It's their own fault,' I said to myself, and I became conscious of a feeling akin to anger and contempt towards people who were unable calmly and contentedly to enjoy the benefits of our public order. Everything that was good in my nature was turned to a different purpose, the purpose of supporting the rights of our elders over us. I felt that in this lay self-sacrifice, the renunciation of one's independence; I was convinced that I was doing this for the public good, and I regarded myself almost as a hero. I know that many remain at this stage, but others change slightly and assure everybody that they have changed completely. Happily, I did indeed have to alter my course rather early. At the age of fourteen I was already an elder to some people—in the classroom and at home—and, of course, I was a very bad one. I could do everything that was demanded of me, but I did not know what I should demand, or how. On top of all this I was stern and aloof. Soon, however, I became ashamed of this and began to put my previous conceptions about elders to the test. The occasion for this was provided by an incident that re-awakened living sensations in my deadened soul. Being an elder brother, and clever, I used to give lessons to one of my sisters. I was given the right to punish her for laziness, disobedience, and so forth. One day her mind wandered for some reason and she would not understand what I was telling her. I ordered her to go down on her knees. She at once collected her thoughts and assuming an attentive air asked me to repeat what I had said. But I insisted that she should first carry out my order—go down on her knees. She was obstinate and refused. I then caught her by the arm, pulled her off her seat, and placing my elbows on her shoulders pressed down with all my might. The poor girl sank down on her knees and shrieked, for, as her knees bent, she sprained her ankle. I was frightened, but when my mother began to scold me for treating my sister in this way, I coolly argued that it was her own fault, that had she obeyed my order at once, nothing would have happened. In my heart of hearts, however, the incident pained me, the more so that I was very fond of my sister. It was then that the thought entered my mind that elders too may be wrong and do stupid things, and that it was necessary to respect the law as such and not as it is interpreted by various individuals. I then began to criticize the actions of people, and I jumped from conservative irresponsibility into the *opposition légale.* For a long time, however, I attributed all evil solely to particular abuses, and these I attacked not in the interests of the urgent requirements of society, not out of sympathy for the sufferings of my fellow human beings, but simply for the sake of the positive law. [At that time, of course, I would have argued very heatedly against cruelty to Negroes, but, like a certain Moscow publicist, I would have strongly condemned John Brown for wanting to liberate the Negroes contrary to the law]. I was very young then, however, [probably younger than that esteemed publicist] my thoughts roamed and wandered; I could not halt here, and after much reflection I at last realized that even laws may be imperfect, that they are of relative, transient and particular importance and should undergo change with the passage of time and upon the demands of circumstances. But again, what inspired me to reason in this way? The supreme, abstract law of justice, and not the promptings of the living feeling of love for my fellow men; not my consciousness of those direct and imperative needs to which the life that is passing before us is pointing. And what do you think? I took the final step: from the abstract law of justice I passed to the more real demand of the good of mankind; at last I reduced all my doubts and speculations to one formula: man and his happiness. But this formula had already been engraved in my soul during my childhood, before I began to study various sciences and to write copybook maxims. Needless to say, I understand it better now and can prove it more thoroughly; but at that time I felt it more, it was bound up with my whole being, and I think I was ready to do more for it then than I am now. Now I try not to do anything that contradicts the law that I now recognize, I try not to deprive people of happiness, but I confine myself to this passive role. If, however, my childish sentiments and dreams had developed unhindered and had grown strong, I might have been able to rush in search of happiness, to bring it nearer to people [to destroy everything that hindered it]; but those sentiments and dreams were being crushed and deadened for some fifteen years. I am returning to them only now, and I find them pale, thin and weak. I must revive them completely before I can put them into action; but who knows whether I shall succeed in reviving them!..."

We think that this narrative contains features that are by no means exceptional. On the contrary, they may serve as a general indication of the obstacles the Russian encounters in his path of independent development. Not all become attached to copybook maxims to an equal degree, but nobody escapes their influence, and they have a paralyzing effect upon all. To rid themselves of them a man must spend a great deal of his strength and lose a great deal of self-confidence in this constant struggle with this ugly confusion of doubts, contradictions, compromise, twists and turns, and so forth.

[Thus, whoever among us has retained strength for heroism need not be a hero; he sees no real goal before him, he does not know how to set about his task and, consequently, he can only play the Don Quixote. He who knows what to do and how to do it has put all that was in him into the effort of knowing, and therefore cannot take a practical step towards activity. Consequently, he refrains from all intervention, as Helena does in the domestic sphere. Even then Helena is bolder and freer than the others, because it was only the general atmosphere of Russian life that affected her; as we have said already, she escaped the impress of the routine of school education and discipline].

This is what explains the fact that the best of the people that we have seen in our present-day society so far are capable only of understanding the desire to do good that consumes Helena [and of sympathizing with her, but they are not capable of satisfying that desire]. And these are the progressives, these are the men we call "public figures"; the majority of intelligent and impressionable people, however, flee from civic glory and devote themselves to various muses. Take even Shubin and Bersenev in *On the Eve.* They are splendid characters [both can appreciate Insarov and even follow him with all their heart and soul; if only they had had a slightly different development and a different environment they too would not sleep]. But what can they do here [in this society? Re-shape it] after their own fashion? But they know of no fashion, and they have no strength. To patch up [something in it], cut off and cast aside little bits of the sordid side [of the social order]? But is it not a repulsive task to draw the teeth of the dead? And besides, what is the use? Only heroes of the type of those gentlemen the Panshins and Kurnatovskys are capable of doing that.

Incidentally, here we can say a few words about Kurnatovsky, who is also one of the finest representatives of the educated section of Russian society. He is a new species of Panshin, only without social and artistic talents, and more businesslike. He is very honest and even generous. In proof of his generosity Stakhov, who is thinking of him as a husband for Helena, mentions the fact that as soon as he was able to live comfortably on his salary he at once renounced in favour of his brothers the annuity which his father had granted him. In general, there is a great deal of good in him; even Helena admits this in describing him in a letter to Insarov. The following is her judgment, from which alone we can obtain some idea of Kurnatovsky; he takes no part in the action of the story. Helena's narrative is so complete and to the point, however, that we need nothing more and so, instead of paraphrasing her letter to Insarov, we shall quote it in full.

"Congratulate me, dear Dmitri, I have a fiancé. He dined with us yesterday. Papa made his acquaintance, at the English Club I think it was, and he invited him home. He did not come yesterday as my fiancé, of course, but dear kind Mama, to whom Papa had expressed his hopes, whispered into my ear what sort of guest he was. His name is Yegor Andreyevich Kurnatovsky. He is a senior secretary in the Senate. I'll first of all describe him. He is short, shorter than you are, and well built. He has regular features, close-cropped hair and long side whiskers. His eyes are small (like yours), brown and restless, his lips are broad and flat. There is always a smile in his eyes and on his lips, a sort of official smile, it looks as if it were on duty. He is modest in his demeanour, speaks distinctly, in fact everything about him is distinct. He walks, laughs and eats as if it were some formal business. 'How closely she has studied him!' you must think as you are reading this. Yes, I did study him in order to be able to describe him to you. And besides, why should not one study one's fiancé? There is something like iron about him . . . something dull and empty, and at the same time, honest. Indeed, they say he is very honest. You, too, are like iron, but not in the way he is. He sat next to me at table and Shubin sat opposite to us. At first they discussed certain commercial undertakings. They say that he is an expert in these matters and that he had nearly resigned the service in order to take over a large factory. What a chance he missed! Then Shubin began to talk about the theatre. Mr. Kurnatovsky stated, without false modesty, I must confess, that he understood nothing about art. This reminded me of you. . . . But I thought to myself: No, Dmitri and I don't understand art in a different way. It seemed as though Mr. Kurnatovsky wanted to say: 'I don't understand anything about art, nor is it necessary, but it is permitted in a well-ordered state.' Incidentally, he seems rather indifferent towards St. Petersburg and to *comme il faut*. Once he even called himself a proletarian. 'We are the common labourers,' he said. I thought to myself: If Dmitri had said that

I would not have liked it, but let him say it if he wants to! Let him brag! He was very polite to me, but all the time it seemed to me that a very very condescending high official was talking to me. When he wants to praise anybody he says about him that he *has rules*—this is his favourite expression. He must be self-confident, diligent, and capable of self-sacrifice (you see, I am unbiassed), *i.e.*, he is capable of sacrificing his own profit, but he is a great despot. Woe to the one who falls into his hands! At dinner the discussion turned to bribery....

"'I fully realize,' he said, 'that in many cases the people who take bribes are not to blame. They cannot do otherwise. But once they are caught they must be crushed.'

"I exclaimed:

"'What, crush an innocent person!'

"'Yes, for the sake of the principle.'

"'What principle?' inquired Shubin. Kurnatovsky looked confused, or surprised, I am not sure which, and said that that needed no explanation. Papa, who, it seems to me worships him, interjected and said that of course there was nothing to explain and, to my disappointment, the subject was then dropped.

"Bersenev came in the evening and I had an awful argument with him. I have never before seen our good Andrei Petrovich so excited. Mr. Kurnatovsky did not at all deny the benefits of learning, universities, and so forth ... but yet, I can understand Andrei Petrovich's indignation. The other one seems to look upon all this as some kind of gymnastics. When dinner was over Shubin came up to me and said: 'This man and somebody else' (he cannot utter your name) 'are both practical men, but look at the difference between them. The somebody else has a real, living ideal, created by life itself, but this one has not even a sense of duty: he is simply an honest official, and his practicalness has no content.' Shubin is a clever man and I took note of his wise words for your sake. But what can there be common between you two? You *believe*, but he does not, because one *cannot believe* only in oneself."

Helena grasped Kurnatovsky's character at once and commented on it quite favourably. But study this character closely and call to mind the business people of your acquaintances who are honestly striving for the common good. Probably many of them will be worse than Kurnatovsky; whether any will be found better than he it is hard to say. But why is this? Precisely because life, our environment, does not make us either clever, honest, or active. We must borrow wisdom, honesty and vigour for activity from foreign books [which, moreover, must be brought into harmony with the Code of Laws]. It is not surprising that this difficult task chills the heart, kills all the living spirit in a man and transforms him into an automaton which steadily and unfailingly performs what it is supposed to do. And yet, we repeat, these are the best. Beyond them commences a different stratum. On the one hand, we have the utterly somnolent Oblomovs who have entirely lost even the charm of eloquence with which they enchanted young ladies in the past; on the other, we have the active Chichikovs who are unslumbering and tireless in their heroic pursuit of their narrow and sordid interests. Still further in the distance loom the Bruskovs, Bolshovs, Kabanovs and Ulanbekovas, and all this evil tribe claims a right to the life and will of the Russian people.... [How can you expect heroism here? And if a hero is born, where is he to obtain the light and wisdom to enable him to expend his strength in the service of virtue and truth instead of wasting it? And even if he at last acquires this light and wisdom, how can he, weary and broken, display heroism? How can a toothless squirrel nibble its nuts? No, better not give way to temptation, better] choose some abstract speciality that is remote from life and bury yourself in it [and suppress that ignoble feeling of instinctive envy of people who are alive and know what they are living for].

This is exactly what Shubin and Bersenev do in *On the Eve*. Shubin flies into a rage when he hears of Helena's marriage to Insarov and begins to rave:

"Insarov.... Insarov.... What's the use of false humility? Suppose he is a fine fellow, suppose he does stand up for himself; but are we such downright rotters. Take me, am I a rotter? Did God leave me destitute of everything?" and so forth....

And then [poor fellow] in the next breath he turns to art: "Perhaps," he says, "I, in time, will become famous for my work...." And indeed, he begins to develop his talent and eventually becomes a splendid sculptor. And Bersenev, kind, self-sacrificing Bersenev, who so sincerely and gladly nursed Insarov when he was sick, who so generously served as the intermediary between him, his rival, and Helena—even Bersenev, that man with a heart of gold, as Insarov expressed it, cannot refrain from bitter reflections when he finally becomes convinced of the mutual love between Insarov and Helena.

"Let them!" he says. "It was not for nothing my father used to say to me: 'We two are not sybarites, not aristocrats, my boy. We have not been pampered by fate and by nature. We are not even martyrs. We are just toilers, toilers, toilers. And so put on your leather apron, toiler, and sit down at your bench in your gloomy workshop! And the sun, let it shine for others. We, too, in our lowly lives have our pride and our happiness!'"

What venomous envy and despair these unjust reproaches breathe—envy of whom and of what, no one can say!... Who is to blame for all that has happened? Is it not Bersenev himself? No, Russian life is to blame. "If we had sensible people among us," as Shubin said, "this girl would not have left us, this sensitive soul would not have slipped through our fingers like a fish into the water." But sensible and foolish people are made by life, by its general structure at a given time and in a given place. The structure of our life proved to be such that Bersenev could find only one [means of salvation]: "To drain his mind with fruitless learning." This is what he did and, according to the author, scholars highly praised his essays: "On Certain Specific Features of Ancient German Law in the Matter of Juridicial Punishment" and "On the Significance of the Urban Principle in Civilization." It is a good thing that he found salvation at least in this....

But Helena found no resource [in Russia] after she met Insarov [and conceived of a different life]. That is why she could neither remain in Russia nor return home after her husband's death. The author understood this perfectly well, and preferred to leave her fate unknown rather than bring her back to her father's house and compel her to live for the rest of her life in sad loneliness and idleness in her native Moscow. Her mother's appeal, which reached her almost at the moment she lost her husband, failed to soften her repugnance for this banal, colourless and inactive life. "Return to Russia? What for? What shall I do in Russia?" she wrote to her mother, and went off to Zara [to be swallowed up by the waves of insurrection].

What a good thing it was that she took this decision! Indeed, what awaited her in Russia? Could she have an object in life, or even life itself here? Return to the unfortunate cats and flies? Give to beggars money that she herself did not earn, but obtained God knows how? Rejoice at Shubin's successes in his art? Discuss Schelling with Bersenev, read *Moskovskiye Vedomosti* to her mother, and see *rules* parading in the public arena in the shape of various Kurnatovskys [and nowhere see real deeds performed, or even feel the breath of a new life....] And gradually, slowly and painfully wilt, wither and die?.... No, once [having tasted a different life], having breathed a different air, it was easier for her to rush into danger, however grave, than to condemn herself to this painful torture, to this slow execution.... And we are glad that she escaped from [our] life and did not confirm by her own example that hopelessly mournful and heart-rending prophecy of the poet which is so [invariably and ruthlessly] confirmed by the fate of the finest, the chosen characters in Russia:

> Remote from nature and the sun,
> Remote from light and art,
> Remote from life and love
> Your youth flashes by,
> Your living feelings die,
> Your dreams fade away.
> And your life will pass unseen
> In a deserted, nameless land,
> In an unchartered land—
> And vanish like a cloud of smoke
> In the dull and foggy sky
> In autumn's boundless gloom....[94]

It remains for us now to sum up the various features scattered through this essay (for the incompleteness and incoherence of which we ask our readers to excuse us) and draw a general conclusion.

Insarov, being consciously and completely engrossed by a great idea [of liberating his country and being ready to play an active part in this], could not develop and reveal his talents in present-day Russian society. Even Helena, who was able to love him so fully and merge herself completely with his ideas, could not remain in Russian society, even among her near and dear ones. And so, there is no room among us for great ideas and great sentiments?... [All heroic and active people must fly from us if they do not wish to die of idleness, or perish in vain? Is that not so?] Is this not the idea that runs through the novel that we have reviewed?

We think not. True, we lack an open field for wide activity; true, our life is spent in petty affairs, in scheming, intriguing, scandalmongering and meanness; true, our civic leaders are hard-

hearted and often thickheaded; our wiseacres will not do a thing
to achieve the triumph of their convictions, our liberals and reformers base their schemes on legal subtleties and not on the
groans and cries of their unhappy fellow men. All this is true,
and all this is seen to some extent in *On the Eve*, as well as in
dozens of other novels that have appeared recently. Nevertheless
we think [that *today* there is already room for great ideas and
sentiments in our society, and that the time is not far distant when
it will be possible to put these ideas into practice].

The point is that, bad as our present way of life is, the
appearance of types like Helena has proved to be possible. And
not only have such characters become possible in life, they have
already been grasped by the artists' mind, they have been introduced into literature, they have been elevated to a type. Helena
is an ideal personage, but her features are familiar to us, we
understand and sympathize with her. What does this show? It
shows that the basis of her character—love for the suffering and
the oppressed and a desire to do good [and weary search for the
one who could show how good can be done]—all this is at last
being felt in the best section of our society. And this feeling is
so strong and so near to realization that it is no longer, as before,
dazzled either by brilliant but sterile minds and talents, by conscientious but abstract learning, by official virtues, nor even by
kind, generous but passive hearts. To satisfy our feeling [our thirst,
something more is needed; we need a man like Insarov—but a
Russian Insarov.

What do we need him for? We ourselves said above that we
do not need hero liberators, that we were a nation of rulers, not
of slaves....

Yes, we are safeguarded against outside dangers; even if we
were obliged to wage an external struggle we can be calm about it.
We have always had sufficient heroes to perform deeds of valour
on the battlefield, and the raptures which even at the present day
our young ladies go into at the sight of an officer's uniform and
moustaches is irrefutable proof that our society knows how to
appreciate these heroes. But have we not many internal enemies?
Is it not necessary to wage a struggle against them? And is not
heroism needed for such a struggle? But where are the men among
us who are capable of action? Where are the men of integrity who

have been from childhood imbued with a single idea, who have merged themselves with that idea so thoroughly that they must either achieve this triumph or perish in the attempt? There are no such men among us, because up to now our social environment has been unfavourable for their development. It is from this environment, from its banality and pettiness, that we must be liberated by the new men whose appearance is so impatiently and eagerly awaited by all that is best, all that is fresh in our society.

It is as yet difficult for such a hero to appear; the conditions for his development, and particularly for the first manifestations of his activity, are extremely unfavourable, and his task is far more complicated and difficult than Insarov's. An external enemy, a privileged oppressor can be attacked and vanquished far more easily than an internal enemy, whose forces are spread everywhere in a thousand different shapes, elusive and invulnerable, harassing us on all sides, poisoning our lives, giving us no rest, and preventing us from surveying the battlefield. This internal enemy cannot be combated with ordinary weapons; we can liberate ourselves from him only by dispelling the raw, foggy atmosphere of our lives in which he was born, grew up and gained strength, and by surrounding ourselves with an atmosphere in which he will be unable to breathe.

Is this possible? When will it be possible? Of these two questions a categorical answer can be given only to the first. Yes, it is possible, and for the following reasons. We said above that our social environment suppresses the development of personalities like Insarov. But now we may add the following: this environment has now reached the stage when it itself can facilitate the appearance of such a man]. Eternal banality, pettiness and apathy cannot be the lawful lot of man, and the people who constitute our social environment and who are fettered by its conditions have long ago realized the harshness and absurdity of these conditions. [Some are dying of ennui, others are striving with all their might to go away, to escape from this oppression]. Various ways of escape have been invented, various means have been employed to infuse some animation into the deadliness and rottenness of our lives, but they have all proved to be feeble and ineffective. Now, at last, concepts and demands are appearing, such as those that we saw in the case of Helena; these demands meet with sympathy in society; nay, more, efforts are being made to put them into effect. This shows that the old social routine is passing away [a little more vacillation, a few more powerful words and favourable factors, and active men will appear!]

Above we hinted that in our society the determination and energy of a strong character are killed at their birth also by that idyllic admiration of everything in the world, by that proneness for indolent self-satisfaction and somnolent repose with which every one of us, when still a child, meets everything around us, and to inculcate us with which every effort is made by means of various counsels and admonitions. Lately, however, things have changed very much in this respect too. Everywhere, and in all things, we observe the growth of self-realization, everywhere the unsoundness of the old order of things is understood, everybody is waiting for [reform] and rectification, and nobody now lulls his children to sleep with songs about the inconceivable perfection of the present state of things in every corner of Russia. On the contrary, today everybody is waiting, everybody is hoping, and children are now growing up imbued with hopes and dreams of a brighter future, and are not forcibly tied to the corpse of the obsolete past. When their turn comes to set to work they will put into it the energy, consistency and harmony of heart and mind of which we could scarcely obtain even a theoretical conception.

[Then a full, sharp and vividly depicted image of a Russian Insarov will appear in literature. We shall not have to wait long for him; the feverishly painful impatience with which we are expecting his appearance in real life is the guarantee of this. We need him, without him our lives seem to be wasted, and every day means nothing in itself, but is only the eve of another day. That day will come at last! At all events, the eve is never far from the next day; only a matter of one night separates them.]

GOOD INTENTIONS AND ACTION

TALES AND SHORT STORIES
BY A. PLESHCHEYEV
Moscow 1860. Two volumes.[95]

AT ONE TIME Mr. Pleshcheyev's tales and short stories were published in all our best magazines. They were read and then forgotten. They never roused any discussion or controversy, either among the public or among literary critics: nobody praised them particularly, nor did anybody condemn them. In most cases, people read them and were pleased, and there the matter ended. . . .

The very authentic fact we have just mentioned does not, of course, testify to any exceptional originality, or vivid talent, on the part of the author; nor, evidently, does he himself lay claim to these qualities. Consequently, we too can save ourselves the task of indulging in extremely tedious aesthetical reflections on the merits and demerits of Mr. Pleshcheyev's literary talent. We have done this more than once in reviewing the literary activities of other writers, but the cudgels were taken up against us on their behalf by partisans of the "eternal" beauties of art who believe that the works of Mr. Turgenev, or of Mr. Maikov, for example, cannot be discussed without bringing in Shakespeare or Dante as criteria with which to gauge them. Nobody, we think, will take up the cudgels against us on behalf of Mr. Pleshcheyev: everybody understands that it would be ridiculous, in discussing ordinary magazine stories, to get up on stilts and, stumbling at every word, pompously preach to the author and to the reader the vague principles of home-grown aesthetics. We believe that this feeble method is out of place also in reviewing the novels of Madame Kokhanovskaya,[96] Turgenev's *First Love*, Mr. Pisemsky's *Thousand Souls*, etc. But there are gentlemen who are so submerged in patriotic aesthetics that they believe that great importance can be attached to the work of our best talents from the same point of view as that from which the works of Homer and Shakespeare are held up to the wonder of the ages. Much as we respect our first-class talents, we deem it inexpedient to appraise them from this point of view, and, therefore, in reviewing Russian novels, verses, etc., we have always tried to point not to their "eternal and absolute" artistic merits which time will never destroy, but to the direct significance they have for us, for our society, and for our times. To write a pamphlet proclaiming that Homer's epic has been resurrected in a more perfect form in *Dead Souls,* to proclaim Lermontov a Byron, to elevate Ostrovsky above Shakespeare—all this is not new in Russian literature. In fact, more than this has happened; probably nobody now remembers who it was in our country who wrote historical novels better than Walter Scott, who in our country was placed on a par with Goethe, whose Finnish girls were prettier than Byron's Greek maidens, who in Russia resurrected Corneuille's magnificent genius, who grew the tender roses of Theocritus in the snow, etc., etc. And yet, all this has been proclaimed in Russian literature, and even roused controversy and discussion. Today, people try to refrain, as far as possible, from playing this comical names game; but the substance of the present-day aesthetical arguments about the "eternal, human, world" merits of our writers constantly remind us of the naive exclamations that were uttered in the old days about Russian Homers and our native Byrons. . . .

Since nobody thinks of attaching great world importance to Mr. Pleshcheyev's talent, we can calmly refrain from expressing aesthetical judgment upon him and turn to the question which interests us ever so much more, namely, the nature of the content of his works. Mr. Pleshcheyev has written rather a great deal: before us lie two volumes containing eight stories; they do not contain *Cigarette* and *Friendly Advice,* which the author published in 1848 and in 1849, nor do they contain *Pashintsev (Russki Vestnik,* Nos. 21-23, 1859), nor *Two Careers (Sovremennik,* No. 12, 1859), nor *His Mission (Svetoch,* Nos. 1-2, 1860)—three long stories which the author published after these volumes appeared. These, too, could almost have made up two similar volumes. All were read without displeasure, and for some time engaged the attention of a certain section of the Russian public on a par with the works of other authors who had not aroused the suspicion of being geniuses. Well, did this mass of printed paper express any-

thing? Have these half a score of long and short stories any relation
to what is today engaging public attention in this country? Or are
these stories merely reading exercises, like the works of Messrs.
Kamensky, Voskresensky, Vonlyarlyarsky,[97] and some of the latest
names which may be not unknown to some of the readers of
Sovremennik? . . .

We are pleased to say, in answer to this question, that
Mr. Pleshcheyev's stories cannot by any means be placed in the latter category. They are throughout permeated with a social element,
and this distinguishes them from the innumerable colourless tales
of the 'thirties and 'fifties. The stories of those times, as is known,
were distinguished for the fact that in them man figured not as
a social but as an isolated being. To develop his plot the author
needed two, three or four persons—and these two, three or four
persons appeared in the story, without any relation to the rest of
the world, as if they were living on an uninhabited island, where
everything they needed appeared for them by the wave of a magic
wand. For the purpose of the climax there usually appeared, nobody knows where from, a mysterious *deux ex machina* in the
shape of a rich uncle, an irate superior, a fire, a flood, a philanthropic aristocrat, and so forth. Incidentally, this was more often
the case in the 'thirties; in the 'fifties the heroes who were stranded
on uninhabited islands usually became disillusioned and departed
from the island, leaving the heroines to weep and grieve, and there
the matter ended. . . . All these tricks affected Mr. Pleshcheyev little
because he commenced his literary activities in the 'forties—
when the Goremykas, Poor Folks and the Pinnacles and Nooks of
St. Petersburg were in fashion in literature—and he resumed them
only in recent years, when the trend that exposed our social evils
was in full bloom.[98] Throughout the [wretched] colourless 'fifties,
Mr. Pleshcheyev did not appear in the press,[99] thus escaping the
necessity of fleeing with his heroes to an uninhabited island; he
remained in the real world of petty government officials, school-
teachers, artists, small squires, young ladies and gentlemen of the
middle class, and so forth. Apparently, he is fairly well acquainted
with this little world, and he describes it with complete candour.
Following the career of every hero in Mr. Pleshcheyev's stories you
can see that he is connected with his environment, that this little

world weighs upon him with its demands and its relationships; in short—you see that the hero is a social and not an isolated being. The social element is present in every story. . . .

Such is the principal merit of Mr. Pleshcheyev's stories; but it must be admitted that he possesses this merit on a par with very many of our present-day writers of fiction. That man is entirely dependent upon the society in which he lives, and that his conduct is determined by the position in which he finds himself—this has now become the almost inevitable starting point for every narrator who possesses a grain of common sense. Further—that the arrangement of our social environment is not altogether satisfactory, and that our everyday relationships do not at all favour the normal development and free healthy activities of man—is also the subject of very many stories, written even by the most mediocre of writers. The disharmony between a man [who is the least bit decent,] and surrounding reality has become the common theme of present-day literature. All parties, all trends, all shades of literary opinion agree on this point. Whether you take *Russki Vestnik,* or *Biblioteka dlya Chteniya, Syn Otechestva* or *Moda,* in all of them you will find the same thing. Consequently, to depict the antagonism between honest strivings and the banality of one's environment is no longer, by itself, enough to win general sympathy; the picture must be vivid and strong, new situations must be dealt with, new aspects of the subject must be revealed—and only when it does that will the story enjoy permanent success and the author move into a prominent place in literature.

Mr. Pleshcheyev's stories do not rise above the level that has been established by the general run of productions of that school of writers which, perhaps, after its chief representative, may be called the Turgenev school. The theme that constantly runs through the works of all the members of this school is that *"environment ruins a man."* This is a good and very effective theme, but up till now our writers have not been able to make good use of it. Sometimes the man who is "ruined by his environment" is depicted in the stories of the Turgenev school fairly vividly, but the description of the "environment" itself, and of its relation to man, is pale and feeble. The Shchedrin school took up the task of depicting "environment"—but that school took up only the official aspect of the subject, and even then (and this is the main thing) its

extremely petty manifestations. This explains why all our stories—
accusatory or artistic, it makes no difference—always leave much
unsaid and—what is most important—always leave room for two
questions: on the one hand—what are they striving for, these
people who cannot harmonize with their environment? And on the
other hand—what causes the antagonism of this environment to
every honest striving, and upon what, in this matter, does its
strength rest?

However much we may dabble in abstractions to answer these
questions, they will not be cleared up until the facts of social life,
upon which the very substance of the matter depends, are digested
by the public mind. This digesting of facts is constantly going on
in life itself; but fiction too may be useful in [quickening and]
giving greater fulness to the conscious work of society. And the
more the images it depicts are presented with artistic fulness and
strength, the more useful will it be. Up to now the "ruinous environment" school has failed to give us truly artistic stories, precisely
because it never achieved complete harmony between the two
elements, the struggle between which makes up the content of the
story. You have seen the man who is ruined, but you have not been
given a full and vivid picture of the force that ruins him, why it
is ruining him [and why he allows himself to be ruined]: of [all]
this you have found in the stories only hints, but certainly not
full answers. Thus, the execution in these stories has always been
far below the idea which could have given them vitality; and this
explains why all the stories of this type have only temporary historical significance, which disappears forthwith, as soon as somewhat new combinations of everyday relationships and new demands
upon life arise in society.

For the time being, the stories we are discussing are being
read today, although not with the same interest as they were read
fifteen years ago. But even today questions arise which the heroes
in the stories of this kind are totally unable to answer. On reading Mr. Pleshcheyev's stories, for example, a fresh reader with
common sense will at once ask himself: what do these well-intentioned heroes want? What are they worrying so much over? To
find an answer to his questions the reader will examine the circumstances which are the cause of the misfortunes the noble heroes
suffer. But here we shall not find anything definite: everything is

so nebulous, fragmentary and shallow that it is impossible to discern any general idea, impossible to grasp the object in life these gentlemen pursue. They get very excited (like Kostin) over Frederika Bremer[100] and George Sand, and thereby earn the displeasure of the "environment"; they open the eyes (like Gorodkov) of the big chief to the misdeeds of their immediate superiors and, as a result, find themselves in disfavour; they declaim (again like Kostin) about the benefits of accusatory literature, and thereby antagonize people upon whom they are dependent.... All this shows that they have good aspirations, that they want people to live a better life on earth, and want everything that hinders the common good abolished. But have they a clear conception of what must be done to achieve what they desire? Do they realize what duties devolve upon themselves, once they are convinced that it is necessary to achieve the goal which seems to them sacred and lofty? No, they are always distinguished for a most infantile and most complete failure to understand where they are going, and how to get there. The only good thing about them is their wish that somebody should come along and pull them out of the bog into which they are sinking, fling them on his back and carry them to a clean and bright spot. They would not resist this form of transportation; on the contrary, they would be very pleased with it. But one must agree that they do not deserve any particular credit for it, and that if there are people who even lack a desire to leave the bog, this gives us no right to regard those who *wish* to leave it as heroes.

We may be told that Kostin, Gorodkov and the others are not presented to us as *heroes and ideals*, but that we are merely shown how life with its grindstones sometimes crushes and grinds good aspirations, the germs of goodness and honesty. But we are not imperatively demanding the *ideal*; all we want is that these people should be more *definite* and *conscious*. And we want this because we want to sympathize with the honest personages in these stories; but it is very difficult for us to sympathize with people who are insignificant, colourless, passive, people who are neither fish, flesh nor fowl.... Even from the artistic standpoint, a story should, in depicting a struggle, present antagonists whose strength is more or less equal. But instead of that we get a picture of a huge monster which is called "bad environment," or "banal reality," against

which are arraigned chubby little infants, naive, ignorant, incapable and credulous, and because of their inner impotence are really
entirely dependent upon their "environment." We shall be told
that there are no other people, that this is exactly what our environment makes of all the people who fall into it. Granted, but in
that case what should a writer do? He should include his heroes in
this "environment" and treat them with the same spirit of condemnation that he treats everything that surrounds them. If our environment is not only bad in itself but kills everything good that
falls into it, and if the evil in it is so potent that it has been impossible up to now to find a sufficiently strong and active character
to stand up against it and have his own way, if that is the case,
clearly, it is no use seeking anything in this environment except an
object for the most ruthless satire. Thus, the author's attitude
towards his noble youths will be entirely different; he will not
attempt to rouse his readers' sympathy for their dreamy and indefinite aspirations; rather will he strive to rouse their ridicule over
the fact that these youths concern themselves with nothing but their
abstract and practically useless fantasies. Mr. Pleshcheyev's heroes,
for example, usually go into the civil service; there they find themselves out of harmony with their colleagues, or else find their way
blocked at every turn, and finally they resign. After that they try
their hand at literary work, but for this they lack talent. Then,
only two means of obtaining a livelihood are left open to them:
to give lessons, or else work as copyists. This is all they can do,
this is all they are capable of. If they could at least handle a pair
of oars they could hire themselves as boatmen on the Neva or on
the Volga; or if they had a little gumption they could find jobs as
janitors; or they could go and lay cobblestones, or go about with
a barrel organ or a peep show, if they cannot stand their own environment any longer.... But they are incapable of doing anything, they cannot show their noses anywhere. And yet they rush
into battle, take up the cudgels for the happiness of mankind, want
to be public figures.... But, we ask, what can they do, these feeble
armchair philosophers? They are all dreamers, but not men of
action, not even schemers. Their dreams are very fine, noble and
bold; but anyone of us may say to them: "What do we care whether you have dreamed or not?" and end the conversation with
them there. Arguing psychologically, of course, one cannot help

respecting the fine spiritual qualities of a Kostin, or a Gorodkov, but we take the liberty of thinking that their contribution to the public cause will be no more valuable than that of the other youths whom Mr. Pleshcheyev tells us about in his other stories. Why, then, do they deserve our sympathy? Why write touching stories about their dreams and inner sufferings, which lead to nothing useful?

For writing these cruel lines we, of course, will be accused of being rude and hardhearted, of lacking sympathy for lofty strivings, and of fatalistically worshipping facts. We admit the justice of these and similar reproaches in advance, and placing ourselves in the hands of fate, we shall continue with our explanation.

It is true, we attach no practical importance to the beautiful strivings of the soul as long as they remain mere strivings. It is true, we attach value only to facts, and judge the merits of people only by their deeds. The reason why we judge in this way is very simple. We regard as beautiful strivings all the natural, unspoiled strivings of human nature; and we regard all beautiful strivings as a result of the natural, normal requirements of man. If a requirement is artificial, we consider it bad, pernicious, or ridiculous, no matter how beautiful and magnificent it may be. If it is true that Nero set fire to Rome in order to have living material for his description of the burning of Troy, then magnificent as such a spectacle may have been and aesthetical its object, we shall regard such a fantasy as disgusting, as something abhorrent to normal human nature. Equally disgusting are, for example, the self-mutilation indulged in by fakirs, the Brahmin's contempt for the pariah, club law, etc. All this is disgusting (and in some cases, also ridiculous) precisely because it constitutes a distortion of human nature. Briefly to define the substance of human nature proper is no easy matter, but at all events, there can be no doubt about one thing, namely, its capacity to develop. To be able to develop it must avoid all collisions and hindrances. And for this, evidently, it commands a man not to hinder other men, for by doing so he hinders himself, checks and restricts his own development. Thus, in recognizing that man has [only one] ability to develop and [only one] inclination for activity (of whatever kind) and rest, we, from this alone, can draw the direct deduction—on the one hand, a man's natural demand

that no one should restrict him, that he should be allowed
to enjoy his own inalienable resources and the free [unappropriat-
ed] gifts of nature; on the other hand—the equally natural realization that he too must not encroach upon the rights of others and
hinder other people's activities. This is the very simple law by
which a bird makes no attempt to build its nest in the place
where another bird is building one, by which a flock of sheep
peacefully shares the meadow in which it is grazing, etc. And it is
this law which is the core of all the strivings for independence
and strict justice, all human sentiments, all antipathy towards
violence and tyranny [despotism and slavery]. All these qualities
are by no means the supreme perfection worked out in the course
of thousands of years of civilization and achieved with great effort
in universities, academies and aesthetics. On the contrary, these
qualities [*should* be] possessed by every man, even at the lowest
stage of development. [Let us recall, say, Karamzin, our unforget-
table historiographer: according to him, even "savage peoples
love freedom and independence."] As regards human sentiments,
i.e., as regards not hindering others and not depriving others of
anything—we find this principle in operation even among wild
animals; wolves do not rush upon one another to seize their prey,
but prefer to obtain their own prey; jackals and hyenas live in
whole packs and sanguinary wars are extremely rare among them
[; in general—dog does not eat dog].

[But wolves steal sheep. Does that not show that the principle
of not restricting another's activities is undeveloped among
them?—] That is why we do not say that respect for what belongs
to others and for the feeling of humanity have been [(among
wolves and among men)] the result of certain lofty ideas. We
deduce them from the simple calculation of what pays best: "better
that I should go about my own business than hinder others; I will
gain more that way and life will be easier." It is on this ground
that a wolf does not fight another wolf, but steals a sheep which
nobody has yet stolen, and over which no bother will arise. It does
this from a natural impulse—hunger; in the same way a man plucks
a flower, catches fish, kills and roasts a duck or a partridge. Here
there can be no struggle with one's own kind, no hostile collisions
with those of one's own species—this is what we are talking about.
A man who has sat patiently a whole day angling for a tiny perch

will not poach fish in another man's preserves, for he knows that
this will lead to trouble. And, on the other hand, a man who owns
the preserves can look on calmly at other anglers fishing in the
free parts of the river, but will not remain unconcerned if anybody
were to poach in his preserves. Here the natural demand that he
should not be interfered with and that his rights should not be
encroached upon even prompts him to fight—and here too, the
same principle of what pays best applies: in order not to lose the
opportunity to act freely and unhindered I must prevent all interference; but if the interference is already occurring, then I must
at once eliminate it, otherwise all freedom of action is destroyed,
all possibility for natural development ceases.

We have made this digression in order to show how simple
and natural for man are the strivings and concepts which are
usually ascribed to the heroes in our stories as something exceptional, superior, raising them above the level of the crowd. If we
look at it simply and dispassionately, we shall find that the desire
to rid ourselves of restrictions and love for independent activity
are inalienable attributes of man, no less than the desire to drink,
eat and to love a woman. There was a time when it was possible
to amaze people with all sorts of tricks, and those who [abstained
from taking food for whole weeks and lived only on water,]
suppressed all natural requirements, [roused the wonder of the
crowd and] were regarded as moral heroes. Today, however, we
show no respect for such merits any more than we respect a man
for having deprived himself of the ability to love a woman, or
for having crushed his own will to such an extent that he has
become an automaton [who only obeys another's commands]. We
regard all such personalities, and all such behaviour, as a distortion of human nature and a violation of the natural order of things.
We regard it as normal that a man should drink, eat and love a
woman, be conscious of his own personality and strive for free
activity. That being the case, why should we be expected to show
sympathy for a man only because he drinks and eats, or hates
to be restricted? Is that a special merit of his, and not the natural,
inevitable requirement of his organism? A man dislikes being
ordered to do what he does not wish to do, or to do something
not in the way he wishes to do it; what education, what a magnifi-

cent spirit one must possess for this!! Just think of it: he feels
hurt [his arms are being bound], he feels restricted, he wants to
do something that his own reason and will dictates! ... Poor,
noble youth, or man! How can one refrain from shedding tears
of sympathy over his sad fate?

And, indeed, tears were shed; noble youths were depicted in
stories by the dozen, and in spite of their obvious banality, they
engaged the attention of our most talented writers, and were
regarded by public opinion as extremely capable men whom society
needed. It is said that at one time there were reasons for this, but
now we may look upon the matter a little differently. In demanding deeds from people, we can more sternly cross-examine all
the dreamers, no matter how lofty their dreams may be; and the
cross-examination will show that these dreamers are nonentities.

"No, it is not true!" the admirers of the Hamlets of Shchigry
County [and all of their ilk] will exclaim. "If the lofty dreams of
these heroes are so natural and simple, why are they not shared
by the whole world? Why is it that only a few chosen natures
display these strivings, while the majority not only fail to understand them, but even try to oppose them? Is there not some
great merit in the mere fact that these dreamers understand and
have assimilated true human strivings, when everything around
them is distorted, corrupted, given up to falsehood, or completely
indifferent to everything?"

Questions and remarks like these are heard very often, but
they all spring only from a superficial view of the matter. Of
course, one may recognize a certain amount of merit in a man,
even if he has done nothing for society, for having, at least by his
own reflection and independent observations, realized the falsity
of that which everybody around him gives out as the truth. If
among the degenerate members of the human race one person
were found who had so thoroughly preserved his original human
features that no power on earth could obliterate or destroy them,
he would truly be remarkable. It would be worth-while writing
an interesting story about this individual, and the most outstanding
talent in any European country might labour not unfruitfully to
produce, or create, it. But it is not personalities like these that
we see in our literature. We are not shown the inner labours and

spiritual struggle of the man who realizes the falsity of the present order, and who perseveringly and stubbornly strives for the truth; nobody has even thought of depicting for us a new Faust, although we even have a story bearing that title.... No, our noble youths usually acquire their lofty strivings rather simply, and without much trouble: they study in universities and are influenced by the lectures of splendid professors; or even, while still in high school they meet with a young and ardent teacher; or they join a circle organized by some splendid young people who are inspired by the most noble aspirations, sacredly revere Granovsky and admire Mochalov;[101] or, finally, they read good books, *i.e.*, *Otechestvenniye Zapiski* of the 'forties. Very often, all these happy contingencies occur together and supplement each other. Thus, the development of simple human strivings in these good youths takes place without any particularly heroic efforts. They want to eat. On all sides they hear the invitation: come to dinner. And they go. That's all there is to it.

But why don't others go? Why is it that other people who have received the same education and have heard fine lectures turn out to be bribetakers, fops, formalists, petty tyrants, etc., etc.?

The answer to these questions is easy; because they are foolish, or perhaps it would be better to say naive. Finding that the natural inclination for independent, normal activity meets with obstacles on the straight road, all these people try to turn from it a little, in the hope that by going round an obstacle they may come back upon the previous road again. Again it is the same calculation: "I had better go round rather than fight and break through." But here the calculation proves to be a mistaken one, because there is not one obstacle but thousands, and the further a man digresses from the original road the more these obstacles multiply. And now he is compelled, whether he likes it or not, to twist, to dive, to stoop, to leap and trample upon whatever he can along the road, and subject himself to every humiliation, when necessary, in order to continue on his journey somehow. A man in his simplicity thinks to himself: "I will pay for a berth if I can't get one otherwise, but I will be useful in that berth when I get it." It turns out, however, that one payment is not enough, further expenditure must be made later, if not in the form of downright gifts of money, then in the form of dinners, social evenings, favouritism in the service, and so forth. To do this it is found necessary to borrow money with no intention of repaying, to accept gratuities, to take bribes; to take bribes and gratuities one must suppress the prickings of one's conscience in business affairs, and it is necessary to reward scoundrels, to wrong honest people, and so forth. And so a man gets more and more entangled; but at every step he thinks that he is choosing the best way to remove obstacles and to gain scope for his activities.

The noble youths with whom our literature busied itself for so long and so zealously do not get themselves entangled in this way and, therefore, appear to stand much above the crowd. But if you examine them more closely you will find that the only reason why they do not wander from their path is that they do not go anywhere, they stick in one spot. They are not by any means more farsighted than those who went the roundabout way, they do not by any means understand more clearly the extreme importance of preserving their human strivings intact from outside interference: they are simply more slothful. At the beginning of their careers both the first and the second categories equally wish to go straight forward, freely and consciously to the goal of the useful and the good; both are equally faced with enormous obstacles which have to be surmounted at the very first steps. But neither the one nor the other possess sufficient courage and strength to take up the struggle against these obstacles at once: some want to go round them, and thus lose sight of the goal and tumble into the [disgusting] quagmire of falsehood; the others remain in one spot, sit with folded arms, venting their scorn and spleen upon those who have turned aside, and wait in the hope that some Titan will come along and push away the mountain that blocks their path. And what is more amusing, these gentlemen begin to complain not about their own indolence and impotence, and not even about the mountain which blocks their path, but about their comrades who are making a detour. And the inclination for activity common to all men finds expression in them in that they attack the unfortunate wayfarers and try to push them onto the straight road. "We can't go that way. We'll find another road," answer the poor wayfarers. "No, you must come this way!" shout the excited youths; but they make no attempt to advance themselves, they make no

29*

attempt to bore through the mountain, to level it, [to blow it up],
they do not say whether there is a track by which the mountain
could be crossed. They themselves know nothing, they can do
nothing, they are incapable of doing rough work; [their nerves
cannot stand the noise of an explosion;] they cannot help the
wayfarers in any way except by shouting: "Don't go that way, go
this way" ... although it is impossible to go this way without
laying a new road.

"But, after all, they understand that it is wrong to turn aside,
that it is necessary to keep to the straight road; that is why they
cannot possibly tumble into the evil-smelling bog, as the others
do by going the roundabout way: it is for this that they deserve
respect."

Not in the least. If we so freely squander our respect upon
all those who refrain from doing abominable things, we shall
be compelled to agree with all the absurdities expressed by
Mr. Akhsharumov, who, precisely from this point of view, discerns
certain grand patriarchal virtues in Ilya Ilyich Oblomov. There
are very many men in the world who are *proud of the fact that
they are doing no harm*"; but we do not wish even Mr. Akhsharumov to wallow in such pride. Idyllic dreams about blissful solitude,
away from men, are by no means appropriate today. [The social
element has come into its own and] we must regard ourselves as
members of society whose duty it is to do something for it;
otherwise, we shall be doing it harm by the very fact that we are
parasites.

And besides, can the vague, timid half-knowledge which distinguishes the valiant representatives of the finest strivings in our
literature be called true understanding and conviction? In our
opinion, conviction and knowledge can be regarded as true only
when they have penetrated into the depths of a man, have merged
with his feelings and will, are present in him constantly, even
unconsciously, when he is not thinking about them at all. Such
knowledge, if it is practical knowledge, will certainly express
itself in action, and will not cease from troubling a man until it
finds satisfaction. It is a kind of thirst, unquenchable and urgent.
When I am tormented by thirst in a waterless plain and suddenly
see a brook, I rush to it, in spite of the prickly bushes that surround
it and in which snakes are lurking. [The worst I can suffer in these

bushes is death: but I shall die from thirst if I don't get through. Hence, I have nothing to lose. . . .] This is how true, living, complete convictions operate [a man may run the risk of losing his life in trying to realize them; but what does it matter—he would die if he were compelled to suppress his convictions. . . .] Can you find a single one of the good youths of our literature who is filled with such determination and conviction? No, you will not find one.

But even this would not be so bad: we have already said that we do not demand heroism; all we demand is more consciousness and definiteness in the strivings of the good youths. But this we do not find. They are infected with a very high opinion of their own purity and firmness and, therefore, absolutely refuse to look around them and thoroughly appraise their attitude to all that surrounds them. In naiveté and incompetence, they yield nothing to the most simplehearted of those who all their lives have diverged from the straight road, imagining that they will reach the same goal in the end. The first thing we hear from our youths are complaints about their fellow travellers. They want to go by the straight road, but the crowd around them is pushing down a side road and dragging the youths with them; the straightforward youths get excited and loudly upbraid the crowd for turning aside, complain about being jostled by those who run past them, and finally they assert that they cannot go by the straight road because the crowd won't let them. . . . But the well-intentioned, straightforward youths do not even trouble to think seriously over the question as to why their fellow travellers turn aside precisely at this particular spot. Is it just because of caprice, without any reason or necessity? If they were to ask themselves this question they would find that [the reason lies not in the moving crowd, but in the obstacle that blocks the road: that] every one of them would be only too glad to choose the straight road if no exceptional inconvenience were encountered on it, and that the crowd is not at all to blame if the straight road of the ardent youths is becoming hard. It would be enough for them to think a little for all their complaints about the "environment," about its [unpreparedness,] banality and malice, to vanish of their own accord. We admit that the "environment" too deserves no praise: instead of laying a straight road, it makes such big detours that it cannot get back to the road again: this is very foolish and a waste of effort. But the youths too refrain from laying a road and merely huddle in one spot in idleness and perplexity, throwing the blame on others, and not even realizing that the others turn from the straight course for exactly the same reason that they themselves have halted. The valiant youths have little humanity in their hearts, and they seem to treat everything in an official manner, in spite of all their apparent hostility to all formalism; they imagine that a man turns from the straight road, does abominable things, only because he was appointed to do so, because it is part of his official duties; they do not realize that perhaps this man would very much have liked to go along the straight road and not do abominable things, and would have been very glad if somebody had led him along this road, but unfortunately, there was no early prospect of this. For example, the well-intentioned youths fiercely denounce bribetakers, cruel landlords, society fops, and so forth. All this is very fine and noble; but, in the first place, it is futile, and secondly—this denunciation is not even altogether just. Because of the official dryness of their conceptions of people, and carried away by their own pride, these good youths believe that they alone are capable of humane aspirations, while such aspirations are totally alien to everybody else. They imagine that a government official finds exceptional pleasure in making an unjust decision, that nature itself willed that a squire should flog his serfs and overburden them with work, that the society fop lives in the height of bliss in wearing his feet out dancing every night during the whole winter and spending hours over his toilet. These youths simply refuse to understand that all this is done as a consequence of the common human striving to find the best possible place for oneself, to ensure oneself a life of freedom and ease. Make it so that it will be equally to the advantage of the government official to settle matters either honestly or dishonestly—do you think he would still act against his conscience because of some dark, diabolical promptings of his nature? Arrange things so that the "punishment" of serfs should bring the squire nothing but stern justice and retribution—and you will see that these "punishments" will cease. Place any fop you like [, even of the aristocratic breed and of military calling,] in a society where terpsichorean perfection is met with a smile of ridicule, where no attention is paid to toilets, and where more serious things are demanded of a man, and he—even he!—will become serious. We hope that nobody will dispute these propositions: they have been discussed so often and so much [in *Sovremennik*, and today we find these ideas repeated in other publications]. This idea even serves as a basis of a whole story by Mr. Pleshcheyev, namely, *Pashintsev*, which was published in *Russki Vestnik* last year. This Pashintsev is neither one thing nor another, "neither day nor night, nor darkness nor light"; he has good inclinations, he is not a fool and he has a kind heart, but he was badly brought up, and he is very much of a fop. He leaves St. Petersburg for a provincial town and there comes among an ideally good family and seriously sets to work to educate himself; but after being introduced to provincial society and achieving certain success in it, he again becomes submerged in the quagmire of banality. In conclusion, Mr. Zaborsky, the man of common sense in the story, repeats the old song about Pashintsev, that "his environment ruined him." We shall not dispute this; all we demand is that this idea be continued and developed. Pashintsev, like the numerous other heroes of stories of this kind, is not by any means an exceptional phenomenon; the entire environment which ruins him consists of people exactly like himself; all have good inclinations, but they lack initiative, they lack determination to display independent activity. [Now put to each of the members of this "environment" the question which Madame Prostakova puts: the tailor learned his trade from another tailor, and that tailor from a third, and so forth.... That is to say, a man was ruined by his environment, so was another, and a third, but it is these—first, second and third—who constitute the environment; who, or what, made it so ruinous? What is the main cause, the root of it all?] We think that the noble youths who refuse to go along the wrong road, but don't go anywhere, should first of all ponder over this at their leisure and act accordingly; or, at all events, formulate their admonitions to the wayfarers who have turned off the road accordingly.

But these youths do not ponder over this, they vent their anger upon the first comer. In another story by Mr. Pleshcheyev, namely, *Benefaction*, this is shown fairly well. That splendid youth Gorodkov is admitted into the civil service and an important personage becomes his benefactor. Yukontsov, the important personage's office manager, is a scoundrel and takes bribes, this Yukontsov becomes Gorodkov's immediate superior and makes trouble for him. In his simplicity, Gorodkov imagines that the important personage, his benefactor, tolerates a person like Yukontsov as his office manager simply because he does not know the kind of man he is, and so he sets out to *open the eyes* of his benefactor about Yukontsov. What came of this can well be imagined. Later, the benefactor wants Gorodkov to marry his faded mistress, and he makes this proposal to him through this same Yukontsov. Gorodkov rails at Yukontsov and says: "The General can't be so low and shameless; you yourself have deliberately invented this." This, of course, is communicated to the General, after which Gorodkov is dismissed from the service and dies from tuberculosis. The question is: what killed him? His own naiveté. Why did he have to assume that his benefactor was so kind and also so foolish? Why did he have to regard Yukontsov as the obstacle to his honesty, when Yukontsov was not by any means a real independent obstacle but (not now perhaps but he certainly was much earlier) as much an unhappy wayfarer as the rest, compelled—either to halt at the beginning of the journey, or else go by a roundabout way, because the straight road was blocked.

["In that case, must we regard that important personage, Gorodkov's benefactor, as the principal obstacle?..." Good God, what a naive question!... Must we really answer it?... No, no, a thousand times no: Gorodkov's benefactor must also be included in the category of unhappy and unwise wayfarers—and not only he, but also his superior, and his superior's superior, and every man in general, the entire environment....

Who, then, is to blame for all this? Where is the root cause of all these obstacles, jostling and uneasiness?

What is the cause of the jostling we get in the narrow street that leads to some fair ground? Nobody is to blame here: one person pushes and jostles you because somebody pushes him, and that person is pushed by a third. The trouble is that everybody is hastening to the fair, and the street is narrow.... If you want to avoid being pushed while on the way to buy something you need, don't fight unnecessarily with the people who are hastening in the same direction; arrange things so that there shall not be short seasonal fairs but constant trade, and make the street wider. Then there will be no crushing, and the "environment" will cease to burden you.

But to organize such trade capital is necessary, and a fairly large amount of capital at that; but] the bad thing about our youths is that they are so weighted down by stringency and poverty. [The lack of *large* amounts of capital can be remedied; it is not for nothing that joint-stock companies are developing among us nowadays, and everything is being done in partnership and in shares. But unfortunately our poor youths have nothing to go into partnership with: they cannot do anything, they know nothing, they are unfit for anything. If we wait for them, we shall accumulate capital at even a slower rate than Akaki Akakievich saved up money for an overcoat.] Notwithstanding their beautiful aspirations, they are so inert, timid, and their views are so infantile that they can be no more relied upon in practical matters than upon the most empty-headed fop or confirmed bribetaker. Who can be more virtuous than Mr. Pleshcheyev's Kostin, for example? —we are taking our examples only from Mr. Pleshcheyev's stories, but we could quote many others. But recall that story (it was published in *Sovremennik*): what naiveté, what ignorance of life, what indefiniteness as regards means and objects, and how meagre are the resources of this fine, impeccable youth! ... He dies of tuberculosis (Mr. Pleshcheyev's impeccable heroes, like those of Mr. Turgenev and others, die from wasting diseases) without having accomplished anything anywhere; but we do not know what he could have done in the world even if he had not been attacked by consumption, and had not been continuously ruined by his environment. It occurs to us to ask: suppose Kostin had been sent to England, without any funds, of course. What would he have done there? What would he have been fit for? ... In all probability he would have died of hunger, unless he found opportunities for giving Russian lessons. ... And nobody would have pitied him there, because in that country they have long ago ceased to attach any value to people who are gifted with good intentions, but lack character, and the means to put their good intentions into practice.

We admit that we would not have said all this about Mr. Pleshcheyev's stories had we not seen that he was above this worshipping of the good intentions of his heroes. But we have also observed something else about him; a simpler and more correct attitude towards them, an attitude which already reveals a demand for action, and not merely wishes and hopes. If Mr. Pleshcheyev depicts the Kostins and Gorodkovs for us with exaggerated sympathy, it is due to the fact that, so far, no other, more consistently practical types, moving in the same direction, have yet been produced by Russian society. What can be done about it? Recently we saw one of our most talented writers make an attempt to depict a businesslike, practical character, and we saw how little he succeeded in doing so, in spite of the fact that he [took a man who was not a Russian[102] and] gave him an object in life which provided the opportunity to fill his career with the most vigorous activity.... Evidently, the time has not yet arrived to depict active and firm, and at the same time honest, characters in our literature. But that time is drawing near; these very attempts prove this, however unsuccessful they may be. On the other hand, it is also proved by the spread of an ironic attitude about all the "unwanted people" with whom so many sympathized in the past.

We note this ironic attitude in many of Mr. Pleshcheyev's stories too. In general, his heroes may be divided into three categories: some die of tuberculosis—these are the best (see above); others take to drink—these too are not altogether bad; those in the third category arrange their lives somehow, marry rich wives, get promotion in the service, and so forth—these are the utterly vacuous ones. Properly speaking, looking at it from the social point of view, there is little difference between these three categories: all do nothing—not so much because there is nothing to do as because they are indolent and incapable of doing anything; and all ruin themselves and those who love them, not because they are vicious, and not deliberately, but simply because they are so naive and spineless. Pozemtsev (in *His Mission*), who belongs to the last category, marries and wrecks his wife's life by blatantly having an affair with a coquette and hurling shameless reproaches at his wife; Budnev, in the second category, also makes a failure of his marriage and wrecks his wife's life by falling in love with a girl on whom he spends his money, conceals from his wife the reasons for his long absences, and of his sadness, and finally takes to drink. Pashintsev (on whom the author even confers a miserable death) also disturbs his domestic happiness by undertaking to "develop" and by winning the affections of a girl for whom he had no feelings of love whatever, and who was already betrothed to another; the same thing is done by Ivelyev, who belongs to the very last category (in *Frolics*). Granted that Ivelyev does this simply because of his indolence, out of idle curiosity, and that Pashintsev is prompted by a certain amount of sincere conviction that he will benefit the girl; but the results are the same. As you see, if we make a *résumé* of Mr. Pleshcheyev's stories, we shall find that his well-intentioned youths who talk so well cannot even "be proud of the fact that they are doing no harm." True, Kostin, Gorodkov and Zaborsky do not do what the others do; but they too, because of their inability to make their means commensurate with the task that confronts them, are also more capable of harming than benefiting those they love. Kostin, for example, quite innocently becomes the cause of the suffering of the poor woman who fell in love with him, the wife of the squire to whose children he acted as tutor: and the trouble was not that she fell in love with him, but that he could do nothing for her, could not even elope with her, for he had no home to take her to, he had not a kopek to his name, nor any talent to boast of.

Arguing psychologically, of course, we cannot place Kostin on a par with, say, Pozemtsev, or even Pashintsev. Perish the thought! But as regards practical deeds, all, in our opinion, are in the same boat. That is why the author's negative, derisive attitude towards such heroes that we see in *Frolics, The Legacy, His Mission*, etc., pleases us. The only thing is that we think that this attitude should be adopted towards more people.... People with fine dreams and idyllic expectations are of no use to us at all today. We have lived long enough, we have become somewhat more experienced, and most of us already understand that good is good and bad is bad. We do not need mentors for this. Even for the eradication of social injustice we need not so much the words of conviction as practical demonstration. Nobody can find pleasure in dishonesty, deception, cringing, crawling, trampling upon others and being afraid every minute of being trampled upon oneself; and nobody wants to cling to this sort of thing. Hence, there is no need to shout at people: "Don't crawl, walk upright; don't grovel in the mud. Don't eat mouldy bread." Everybody would be glad to stop doing these things without us telling them to do so. What is needed is that the road should be levelled, that fresh provisions should be stocked. If this is not done, the most sincere and well-intentioned shouting will be of no more value than phrases in the guise of philanthropy; and a present-day Kostin will run the risk of being put on a par with Mr. Kokorev: the exhortations of both are equally futile.

There are no grounds for fearing that the practical undertakings of practical people will meet with opposition in the "environment." This environment consists mainly of the good-natured, even-tempered, and partly even, apathetic people who are rather vividly and correctly depicted in many of Mr. Pleshcheyev's stories, even those of a purely anecdotal character. From all the tales, scenes and descriptions of this simple and unpretentious life, one can see that, notwithstanding all the apparent apathy and lack of development of these people, there is among them [something that oppresses them, and which they would like to be rid of] a vague consciousness of the unsatisfactory nature of their position. The very fact that such situations as described in the story *Father and Daughter,* where the chief takes government money from the cashier without giving a receipt for it and then denies that he had taken the money; or such as are depicted in *The Government Official's Wife,* where the appointment of an official depends upon the maid of the wife of a [big] chief—the very fact that such situations are possible should arouse a feeling of positive discontent. There can be no doubt that all these "backward, ignorant people, steeped in routine," etc., etc., as the progressive youths describe them, would gladly accept everything that would give them [firm guarantees in social life and] the opportunity to enjoy its benefits without being dishonest. Only don't rail at them without right or reason; don't demand from them anything which you cannot reward them for. They do not know what self-denial means, they have no initiative: that is their trouble, their sin, if you like. But neither can you boast of initiative, O virtuous and well-intentioned youths who are set up as examples to us in our literature! Your self-denial is also negative, passive if anything, so that we attribute a large part of it to indolence, to Oblomovshchina. True, you do not strive after dishonest gain and honours [high rank, decorations and distinction,] for mansions and serfs: but then, you do not strive after anything. True, Tentetnikov does not, like Chichikov, go about buying up dead souls; but even if he wanted to he could not and would not dare to do it: he did not even display persever-ance on his own estate, but tired of the work at the very outset and gave up all supervision of his serfs. What kind of self-denial is this? The kind of self-denial with which Oblomov moulded his character.

Yes, in perusing Mr. Pleshcheyev's stories we were pleased most of all with that spirit that runs through them, of sympathetic irony at the expense of the Platonic nobility of the people whom some authors have praised to the skies. The original types of shallow little liberals have already been sketched without any sympathy in some of Mr. Turgenev's stories. But in Mr. Turgenev's stories these gentlemen have always been second-rate personages who, as it were, served to set off the principal heroes, who were indeed well-intentioned, and were really "ruined" by the environ-ment. We mean, for example, Panshin by the side of Lavretsky, or Pigassov by the side of Rudin. In Mr. Pleshcheyev's stories, these people are the principal characters, often they constitute the basis and subject of the story; and from the way they are depicted there more and more clearly arises the demand for action, for deeds instead of highfalutin phrases, puerile dreams, impossible hopes and beliefs.

There was a time when hymns were sung in praise of love for a woman; and lady readers shed tears over the sufferings of the Platonic lovers, and male readers sank into melancholy reflection. Later, people began to laugh at Platonic love, and Platonic grief no longer met with any particular sympathy any-where. Owing to some strange circumstance the wind turned in the direction of social problems; and so, for twenty years we have been reading tales and short stories in which the praises are sung of *Platonic love for public activity*, for Platonic liberalism and noble-mindedness. This new Platonic love has also evoked tears and reflections; but it is high time we woke up from this. If Platonic love for a woman is ridiculous, Platonic love for one's country, people, truth, etc., is a thousand times more ridiculous.

We hope that nobody will regard our words as strange [and incomprehensible]: at a time when everything is permeated with a striving towards positivism and realism, one may expect con-currence with the idea that Platonic, inactive, tearful and abstract love for the common cause is of no use whatever. We think that one may also hope that our future talented story-writers will give us heroes with a sounder content and a more active character than those possessed by all the Platonic lovers of liberalism who have appeared in the stories written by the school that has predominated up to now.

FEATURES FOR THE CHARACTERIZATION OF THE RUSSIAN COMMON PEOPLE

STORIES OF THE LIFE OF THE RUSSIAN COMMON PEOPLE
BY MARCO VOVCHOK

Published by K. Soldatenkov and N. Shchepkin

Moscow 1859[103]

LAST YEAR, certain circumstances, which nobody can regret more than we do ourselves, prevented us from discussing in detail Marco Vovchok's Little-Russian* stories, translated by Mr. Turgenev.[104] We were obliged to restrict ourselves to the publication of a short excerpt from the essay which Mr. Kostomarov wrote for *Sovremennik* when *Narodni Opovidannya* (*Popular Stories*) had just appeared in the Little-Russian original. We hope to be more fortunate now with the appearance of another volume of stories by Marco Vovchok, still more interesting for us, because they depict scenes from the life of the Great-Russian people.

It is by no means out of local patriotism that we are more interested in scenes from the life of the Great-Russian people than in those of the Little-Russian people. We are prompted by other reasons, namely, the opinions that have been expressed recently about the Great-Russian peasants to the disadvantage of the Little-Russian peasants. We are bored quite enough with the narrow patriotism, which confines all human interests to one's locality, when we see it among the Germans in, say, the Landgrafschaft of Hessen-Homburg, or the principality of Lichtenstein; we can dispense with it. There is no reason why we should separate ourselves from the Little-Russian people; we cannot understand why, if I come from the Nizhni Novgorod Gubernia and another comes from the Kharkov Gubernia, there should be less in common between us than if that other came from the Pskov Gubernia. If the Little Russians do not altogether trust us, the blame for this rests upon historical circumstances [, in which the administrative section of Russian society is involved,] and not by

---

* *I.e.*, Ukrainian.—*Tr.*

any means upon the people. Incidentally, the mass of the people in Little Russia itself understand this [: there they call the soldiers *Moscals*, in the same way as they call the squires *Pans*. . .].

Marco Vovchok's stories themselves serve as proof that sensible Little Russians know how to appreciate the Russian people, and make no sharp distinction between Little and Great Russia. This new volume of *Popular Stories* reveals the same character and trends that were revealed by the preceding volume, *Narodni Opovi- dannya*. These stories bring to light the great strength that lies hidden among the people, and the different ways it manifests itself under serfdom. The author's staccato, singsong style, the sad and pensive tone of the stories, the pure and fresh poetry in which the second-rate details are described, and the running comment— are all the same as in the preceding stories. Only the names of people and places, the descriptions of the landscape, the games and the songs carry us into Great-Russian life; and the peasants' attitude towards serfdom also has its own peculiar shade here.

It is this peculiar shade that interests us most of all. In the Little-Russian stories we saw how the squires abuse their power, and, not infrequently, abuse it with considerable cruelty. It is said that this even provided a certain well-known Russian critic with a pretext for saying that Marco Vovchok's stories presented *"abominably disgusting pictures,"* and, placing them in the category of accusatory literature, for denying that their author possessed any literary talent. We have not read this stern critic's little screed because our interest in his literary verdicts ceased long ago; nevertheless, we understand the process by which he arrived at his conclusion. He is one of the advocates of the theory of "art for art's sake"; Marco Vovchok's stories have found favour also among advocates of this theory. One can imagine what it is in these stories that found favour in the eyes of these gentlemen. We ourselves have heard two art critics expressing admiration for the extraordinary charm and poetical quality of one passage which, if we remember rightly, reads: "There, there, far in the fields a cross looms over his grave." The stern critic who condemned Marco Vovchok proved to be somewhat more sensible than art critics of this type, for he understood that "there, there, far in the fields" does not mark an exceptionally high pinnacle of art. But that he should have understood nothing else in the *Popular Stories*, is also quite natural, for he would be a very queer fellow indeed who expected any such understanding of him. Were he able to understand anything he would renounce the "art for art's sake" theory; but can he renounce this theory? What would he do without it? What would he be fit for? Without it he would have to vanish from the stage, like Ivan Alexandrovich Chernoknizhnikov[105] and Kuzma Petrovich Prutkov[106] [in the period when great social problems are raised among us].

But it is not a matter of the verdicts pronounced by the art critic: God be with him—after all, nobody takes him seriously, consequently, his artistic amusements are absolutely harmless. We have in mind other comments, other opinions, which we deem it appropriate to discuss now in connection with Marco Vovchok's volume. These opinions are fairly widespread among a certain section of our public which calls itself educated; and yet these people reveal [not only] their failure to understand the subject [, but] also [extreme] frivolity [or the most unreasonable dishonesty]. The opinion we have in mind is the characterization of the Russian peasant and his attitude towards serfdom. Serfdom is coming to an end [and is becoming a matter of history; there is nothing to discuss about it, it has outlived its time]. But the facts [which have been weighing upon the country] for centuries leave their mark, do not pass away without leaving a trace. Precedence, for example, remains a custom two hundred years after it was abolished by law; can we expect all the relationships that arose from serfdom to become transformed at one stroke? No, they will make themselves felt for a long time to come—in books, in drawing-room conversations and in all our everyday relationships. The concepts, not only of the passing generation, not only of the present generation, but also of the generation that is only just preparing to enter the public service, were moulded, if not directly on the basis of the serf [, unfree] system, then, at all events, under its powerful influence. [Until recently it was impossible to protest against these concepts with sufficient directness because their basis—] the serf principle—had the force of law, and was accepted by the state. Now this principle has been rejected, [it is recognized as being abhorrent to the rights of man and has been deprived of the protection of the law,] consequently, the concepts and demands which it engendered and fostered find condemnation in the very thing which had formerly served to protect them. It is now the duty of literature to pursue the remnants of serfdom in public life and deliver the finishing stroke to the concepts it engendered [to get down to their root]. Marco Vovchok, in his simple and truthful stories, is practically the first warrior in this field, and an extremely able one at that. In his latest stories he does not even try, as he did in his preceding ones, to present to us mainly what is usually termed "abuse of the squire's power." What is the use of talking about the abuse of what is in itself an evil [—about the abuse of drunkenness, or of theft, for example]? What is the use of talking about phenomena for which serfdom created the soil, but which did not always necessarily accompany it? No, the author now takes the normal conditions of a peasant who serves a squire who does *not* abuse his power, and depicts these [melancholy, joyless] conditions for us in mild terms, without ire, without bitterness. And from these sketches—in which everyone who has had even a little to do with the Russian people will recognize familiar features—from these sketches arises before us the character of the Russian common people, who have preserved their main features amidst all the oppressing, [deadening] relationships which obliterate personality, to which they have been subjected for several centuries. It is to some of the features of this character that we now wish to draw attention.

It is common knowledge that there are two diametrically opposite opinions about the Russian people. Some are of the opinion that the Russian, by himself, is worthless and is no more than a cipher: that if a [foreign] figure is added to him, something may come of him, but if not, he will remain a complete nonentity. Others, on the contrary, have the same opinion about the Russians that certain common people have about monkeys, namely, that monkeys understand everything and are able to talk, but cunningly conceal their gifts. In our country every muzhik is a genius, you see; we are not educated, but we don't need any education—the Russian muzhik can do more with his axe than the English can do with all their machines; he can do everything, and is capable of doing anything, only—why he does not display his capabilities I cannot say. Many people apply these opinions not only to Great Russia, but also to Little Russia, and White Russia, and to the whole of the Slavonic race. The first opinion, as we know, is now

obsolete: it flourished up to 1812. The Patriotic War* revealed
to us what we are in the world, and we became so puffed up with
the glory of 1812 that, in the end, we made it look ridiculous—to
ourselves and to foreigners. [Thus, in a burlesque history of Russia published in France during the Eastern War, Oleg marches on
Constantinople with the cry: "Let us not disgrace the land of
Russia, let us die for our faith and our fatherland! *We are the
heroes of 1812!*" The same cry is uttered by Igor, Svyatoslav,[107]
etc.]. Indeed, 1812 became for us an inexhaustible source of self-
adulation and the substitute for all virtues. If anybody talks to
us about bribery, we recall 1812, [if anybody points at the Com-
missariat—we point to 1812,] if anybody talks about the progress
of ideas—we at once refer to 1812 and to Pushkin. . . . This was
the case up to 1857, at the end of which year the first official
orders for the emancipation of the serfs were issued. Here the
public looked around and, while continuing to admire Pushkin
and 1812, nevertheless, formulated its opinion more precisely.
It found that 1812, like Pushkin, does not belong to all the people
without exception, that not every poor devil is capable of understanding the charms of *Eugene Onegin*, and that not everybody
can claim even the merit of having frozen the French to death.
It was decided that the progress of ideas and the progress of virtue
in Russia took place among a certain section of the people; and
Moskovski Vestnik has already promised us an article by a celebrated Russian author on the high importance of this section of
the people for the destiny of the whole of Russia precisely in this
respect. We shall wait for the appearance of the promised article
and when it appears, if circumstances permit, we shall attempt to
go into the details of the case presented by the celebrated author;
meanwhile, we shall continue with our explanation of how a somewhat more definite conception of the virtues of the Russian people
has taken shape recently among the educated section of the public.
According to the latest version, these virtues, properly speaking,
are possessed by a "certain section" of society; the masses of the
people, however, while also possessing them, of course, cannot yet
be fully recognized as the possessors of them because they have
not yet begun to live a "conscious life." This opinion was formulat-

---

* The war against the Napoleonic invasion.—*Tr.*

ed so well that it was adopted by everybody—by those who asserted that the Russian was a cipher, as well as by those who let it be
understood that he was a cunning monkey. The former said: "Yes,
of course, when somebody sets to work to show the Russian what
must be done, and how it must be done, he will do it.... This is
exactly what we said—*by himself, without a guide,* he is unfit
for anything." The latter also exclaimed: "Why, of course, we
too have always said that the Russian is capable of doing everything; but it goes without saying that his capabilities must be
directed, he must be properly guided." Thus, everybody agreed
that the Russian is a guidable creature, and urgently needs guidance,
needs a benign, so to speak, paternal tutelage that will concern
itself with his development and direct his hand, his mind and his
will. [The reader will, of course, understand without comment
what this combination of two opposite opinions means, and where
the vital point here lies.... We will add that] it was here that
the idea that the Russians are mainly the Great-Russian peasants
became crystalized. The Slavonic race was called on to the stage
only in conversations of a very highfalutin nature, and then
mainly by people who were fond of talking about the decay of
Europe. As regards general conceptions, the Great-Russian peasant
was clearly distinguished even from his Little-Russian and White-
Russian brothers.

The case of the White-Russian peasant was settled long ago:
he is so utterly downtrodden that he has lost his human capabilities.
We do not know how false this opinion is because we have not
made a special study of the White-Russian region; but it goes without saying that we cannot believe it. [That a whole region should
be utterly downtrodden—it cannot be! One may as well say that
the Italians are utterly downtrodden, enfeebled, that they are no
longer capable of loving their country, of loving freedom! ...
But look at them now! ... At all events, the question of the character of the White Russians must soon be cleared up by the works of
local writers.] We shall yet hear what the White Russians themselves have to say. Incidentally—we have already heard that it is
proposed at the beginning of next year to commence the publication
of the *Byelorusski Vestnik,* the editorship of which has been
undertaken by a Mr. A. Kreitz, a man whose zeal and noble aspirations can be relied upon.

As regards the Little-Russian peasants, far more favourable opinions have been expressed. The educated section of our society has studied history; and it is well known that history records the sanguinary, mortal struggle the Ukraine waged for her nationality. Furthermore, the educated section of our society is distinguished for its taste for the fine arts and poetry; and it is well known that Little Russia is rich in charming songs in praise of Cossack valour and tender love for his family. All this, combined with the fact that serfdom was introduced in Little Russia only very recently (and this we also know from history) has compelled our educated people to exclude the Little Russians somewhat from the wholesale condemnation for the passivity with which they have characterized the Russian. "The Little Russian is lazy and obstinate, but proud and independent; he feels a protest rising within him whenever his rights are encroached upon, and although this protest remains inactive, it nevertheless manifests itself." Such was the opinion about Little Russians that extremely clever people were pleased to express [, even such who have ceased to boast that they only rarely call Little Russians *khokhols** and then only in jest]. It goes without saying that they, nevertheless, add, when expressing this opinion, that the Little Russian too needs guidance, because he too is ignorant and coarse, but, at all events, care must be taken not to provide an excuse for placing him under a tutelage such as is depicted in Marco Vovchok's *Popular Stories.*

The opinions expressed about Great Russians in general were much more stern. Not that people believed that they deserve the treatment that is described in the Little Russian stories, but just like that, you know; the opinion was that the Great Russian would not mind it: he is accustomed to it, and is not so sensitive to such treatment. His fine and delicate feelings have been blunted, he has no sense of dignity and honour, he has no conception of his own rights or of the rights of others and, therefore, many things which [disgust us to the very depths of our souls] fail to rouse in him the slightest indignation, fail to evoke even a feeble protest. More than that: the Russian muzhik cannot even understand any other treatment than severity. It would be useless for you to appeal to his human dignity, to the sacred sense of duty and right: he will

---

* A derisive name for the Ukrainians.—*Tr.*

not understand you, because these feelings are alien to him. He needs stimuli of another kind; the sense of duty must be personified for him in a superior, with stern punishment for every offence against it. That is why it is necessary to retain the practice of corporal punishment in peasant communities for a long time to come, that is why it is dangerous to remove the peasants from the benign, paternal supervision of the squires.

Many wise men argue in this way even in the press. Open any number of *Zhurnal Zemlevladeltsev*, from which was recently reprinted that splendid story *Conversational Evenings* with which our readers are probably familiar from the excerpts published in *Svistok*.[108] Turn also to *Selskoye Blagoustroistvo*—there too you will find the same thing; and if you want to search for it you will find something like it in other magazines too, only in somewhat different forms, of course. We have presented in its crudest, *i.e.*, its simplest form, the opinion that, for whatever reason, the present-day Russian muzhik is of a lower breed than the people who belong to the privileged classes. But this opinion is sometimes expressed in a more involved form. For example: "The Russian is a wonderful creature! What patience, what magnificent self-denial he can display! We howl and make a fuss when somebody hardly puts a finger on us, but the Russian muzhik uncomplainingly bears all possible hardships and burdens and, trusting to the mercy of God, goes on calmly ploughing his lonely furrow, working without respite, and knowing that he will not reap the fruits of his labour. We egoistically calculate every step we take and ask ourselves whether it will profit us or not; but send the common Russian to certain death—he will go without a word, not even asking why he is being sent" ... etc., etc. As you see, in substance, the opinions are alike: the muzhik is coarse and ignorant, and, consequently, has no conception of his rights, has no mind or will of his own. But the latter form is evidently a diplomatic one, and, for that reason, it is usually in such forms that educated people express themselves when they set out to win oratorical triumphs and, in expectation of them, give banquets to distinguished foreigners, before whom they pour out their eloquence.

But are the opinions expressed by these educated and eloquent people correct in substance? Is it true that the essential and distinguishing feature of the common Russian is—"lack of initiative," that he must be prodded from outside? "The muzhik won't cross himself until it thunders," say those who claim to know the Russian people to reinforce their eloquence, and palming off this vulgar aphorism composed by some bookworm as a *Russian popular* saying. But what do they mean by thunder? Surely not the *"applause"* which Shchedrin talks about at the beginning of his *Provincial Sketches*? [109] Surely not that pious word* which convinces the Russian that he must work for another's benefit? Yes, if we [look at it from the legal point of view and] treat the peasant as a chattel, the property of another, then, of course, it follows that he can have no initiative, that it would be a crime for him to display any, and that, since crimes are punished, he does very well not to display initiative. But abandon the feudal point of view, and abandon it not only in a formal way, but utterly, the very substance of it, and try to picture to yourselves the Russian muzhik as an ordinary independent man, as a citizen [enjoying all the rights and privileges provided by a free state]. If you possess enough imagination for this, and if you are in the least bit familiar with the fundamental character and life of the common Russian people, there will at once rise up before you a picture of people who are capable of controlling their actions very wisely and well. To help you to obtain such a picture we take up Marco Vovchok's volume and remind you of several of the Russian characters that are depicted in it.

It must be observed, first of all, that these characters are not portrayed with complete artistic fulness, but are merely sketched in Marco Vovchok's short stories. We cannot expect of him an epic on the life of our people—that would be expecting too much. We may expect such an epic to be written in the future, but at present it is useless even to think about it. The masses of the people are still far from the stage of self-realization when it must find full poetic expression; up to now nearly all the writers among the educated class have dealt with the people as if they were curious playthings and have not thought at all of taking them seriously. We are only just beginning to realize the great role which the masses of the people play in the economy of human society, and side by side with this vague realization serious obser-

---

* *I.e.,* God.—*Tr.*

vations of the life and character of the people are appearing,
prompted by sincerity and love. Among these observations Marco
Vovchok's sketches occupy, perhaps, the most honourable place.
There is much that is scrappy in these sketches, much left unsaid,
sometimes a casual, particular fact is taken and related without
any explanation of its inner or outer causes, is not linked up with
the habitual structure of life as it should be done. But, we repeat,
we cannot yet demand complete finish and all-sidedness in the
stories that are now written about peasant life: that life has not
yet revealed itself to us in all its fulness, and even what is revealed to us we are not always capable of expressing, or do not
know how to express well. We are satisfied even with the fact that
in Marco Vovchok's stories we see a desire and the ability to hearken
to [this still to us remote but in itself loud rumble of] the life of
the people; we sense in them the presence of the Russian spirit,
we meet familiar characters, recognize the logic, the sentiments
[demands and inclinations,] which we ourselves have noted at
some time or another, but allowed to slip our attention. That is
why these stories are precious to us; that is why we esteem their
author so highly. The stories reveal his profound attention and
human sympathy, they reveal his wide understanding of that life
which many of our most educated economists, students of Slavonic culture, lawyers, liberals, novelists, etc., etc., look upon so
lightly, and understand so narrowly and poorly.

Marco Vovchok's volume contains six stories, and every one
of them presents to us female types from the common people.
Side by side with the female personalities are also depicted male
personalities, but in most cases these are somewhat in the shade.
This is mainly to be explained, of course, by the fact that the
author, Marco Vovchok, is a woman. But we see that the choice of
female personages for these stories is justified also by the very
substance of the case. We shall take, first of all, the story *Masha*,
in which this is expressed with exceptional clarity.

We remember when this story first appeared. People who still
believed in the [sacredness and] inviolability of serfdom were
horror-stricken by it [and hurled indignant reproaches at the
liberal censorship which had dared to pass such a story]. The
story revealed the natural and irrepressible development in a peasant girl of love for freedom and hatred of slavery. As you see,

there is nothing criminal about it; but such a story could not but shock those who stand for the maintenance of feudal relationships. It invaded their last refuge, dislodged them from their last position, which they regarded as impregnable. They, you see, being humane and enlightened, agreed that at bottom serfdom [runs counter to the rights of man. They fully realize that for one man to belong to another, a man like himself, is an absurdity,] is incompatible with the achievements of modern education. [All this is true....] But they followed this up by saying that the muzhik was still unripe for real freedom, that he was not even thinking about it and did not want it, that his status was not a burden to him—except, perhaps, that labour rent was too high and stewards were too exacting.... "And besides, how, pray, can the idea of freedom enter the muzhik's head? He doesn't read books [not only prohibited ones but even] of any kind [(and is it not notorious that all this free-thinking comes from nothing else but books?)]; he is not acquainted with writers; he has so much work to do that he has no time to compose utopias.... He lives as his father and grandfather lived before him, and if there is now a wish to emancipate him, it is purely out of charity, out of generosity.... And believe me, the muzhik will not wake up for a long time yet, it will be a long time before he realizes what is being given him, and why.... Many, very many, will yet long for their previous way of life." This is what wise and enlightened [landowners and those like minded] asserted, and believed that it could not be disputed. But suddenly, just imagine—[they are not even opposed, but exposed as liars] the fact on which they based their argument is challenged! They are told of cases which show that love for free labour and an independent life is [possible and] natural even among the serf estate, and that the development of this sentiment does not even need the assistance of writers. The following is the simple case that was related to them.

An old peasant woman is bringing up two orphans: Masha, her niece, and Fedya, her nephew. Fedya—is as a boy ought to be: merry, well-behaved and obedient; but Masha, from her earliest years, displays considerable independence of mind. She is not content with merely obeying a command, but insists on being told the why and the wherefore; she has her ears and eyes wide open to everything, and very early reveals a tendency to form her own opinion. Had this girl had a stern father and mother this nonsense would have been knocked out of her head at once, as is usually done in this country with hundreds and thousands of girls and boys who, in infancy, display excessive inquisitiveness and an inappropriate propensity for premature mental activity. But fortunately, or unfortunately, for Masha, her aunt was a kind and simple woman who not only refrained from punishing her for her inquisitiveness, but even yielded to it herself and felt very embarrassed when she was unable to answer her niece's questions, or prove that she was wrong. Thus, Masha became convinced that she had a right to think, to ask questions and to argue. That in itself was enough. When she was getting on for seven an event occurred to her which gave a peculiar turn to all her thoughts. One day the aunt went to town, taking Fedya with her; Masha stayed to look after the house. She was sitting on the bench outside the house playing with other children when suddenly the squiress passed by, halted, looked at Masha and demanded: "What's the meaning of all this noise? Don't you recognize your mistress? Whose girl are you, eh?" Perhaps Masha was abashed, but whatever the reason, she did not answer, and the lady scolded her and said: "You're a fool. You can't talk." Masha burst into tears. The lady was touched. "Come to me now, you ninny," she said. Masha did not budge. The lady told the other children to lead Masha to her. Masha got up and ran away, and did not return. The aunt and Fedya came back from town and found that Masha was not at home. They went out to look for her. They searched and searched, but could not find her. On the way back home she herself came towards them out of somebody's hemp field. The aunt wanted to take her home, but she would not go. "The lady will take me. I won't go," she said. The aunt managed to soothe Masha somehow and at once began to lecture her saying that she must obey the lady even if she is stern. . . .

"And suppose I don't obey?" enquired Masha.

"Then look out for trouble, my dear," I says.* "Do you think it's good to be punished?. . ."

Even Fedya looked uncomfortable, and stared at his sister with wide open eyes.

"I could run away," says Masha—"run far away. . . . The Trostyanskys ran away last year, do you remember?"

---

* The aunt is telling the story.—*N. D.*

"But they were caught, Masha.... And some died on the road."

"And those who were caught were put in prison and punished very severely," says Fedya.

"They suffered enough, both shame and sorrow, my child," I says; but Masha kept on saying: 'Why are you all sticking up for the mistress?' "

"She's the mistress," we explained to her; "she has rights, she has money.... That's the way things are."

"But tell me," says the girl. "Who stands up for us?"

Fedya and I glanced at each other, wondering what had come over her.

"You've got foolish things in your head, child," I says.

"But who does stand up for us?" she insisted.

"We ourselves, and God stands up for us," I answered her.

And from that time onwards Masha talked about nothing else but the squiress. "Who gave us to her? How? Why? When? The mistress is only one," she says, "but look how many we are! Suppose we all left her and went wherever we liked, what could she do?" The old aunt, of course, could not give Masha a satisfactory answer and the girl had to solve the problem for herself. Soon she had occasion to apply her [radical] ideas. The squiress remembered Masha and ordered the village elder to send her to work in the manor orchard. Masha would not go, however: "I won't," she said, and would not budge. The aunt was sorry for the girl and told the village elder that she was sick. The girl clutched at this excuse: whenever she was ordered to go to work in the manor grounds she pleaded that she was sick. The squiress would summon her and demand: "What ails you?" "All my body aches," answers Masha. The squiress would scold her, threaten to punish and dismiss her. The next time she was ordered to work the same thing happened.

Masha's brother did all he could to persuade her to be more obedient, and her aunt pleaded with her too [for the squiress was angry with her because of her niece] but without avail. Not only did Masha refuse to work, but she behaved as if she had a perfect right to do so, as if she were doing exactly what she ought to do. For example, she refused to ask the squiress to release her from work.

"All she had to do was to go on her knees and beg," says the [simplehearted] aunt, "and the lady herself would have released her; but Masha was not the one to do anything like that. She would stand in front of the lady and refuse to raise her eyes to her face, and her voice was so low you could hardly hear it.... You know what the gentry are: you may be a cheat, a wicked man, but if you go down on your knees, be respectful, beg and pray and say: it is within your power to punish and to forgive, be merciful—you will be forgiven; but if things get so hard that you can't stand any longer and you utter an angry word of protest, even if you are truthful and honest, you will know no mercy, you will be a ruffian! Our lady was supposed to have been kind and merciful, but look how she tormented Masha! 'You wait, I'll teach you all!' she used to threaten. True, she never carried out her threat, but it wasn't a happy time living with those promises hanging over you."

Masha's revulsion for forced labour grew so strong that it drove her to unconscious, reckless heroism. One day her brother reproached her saying that she always pleaded sickness when there was work to do, but she was the first girl in the village in dances and games. "Do you think the mistress will not hear of this?" he asked. "You are bringing her displeasure upon us, and that's not fair." After that Masha kept indoors and would not go out. She was bored, she would stand sadly at the window and see her friends playing outside, tears would roll down her cheeks, but she kept in the house. Her aunt urged her to go out to her friends, her brother pleaded with her to forgive him for having reproached her, but she said: "I am not angry with you, Fedya, but stop pleading with me. It's no use, I won't go." And she did not go out, but she could not sleep at night and wandered about the kitchen garden all alone. She did not tell anybody about this, but one night the aunt chanced to find her in the garden. . . . "God be with you, Masha," she said to her. "Why don't you live as other people do? You could do your share of work and then you wouldn't have to be afraid of anything. . . . But instead of that you wander about at night and in the daytime you dare not show your face outside the gate." "I can't, I can't!" said Masha almost in a whisper. "And I won't, even if you kill me." And so they left her in peace. . . .

Eventually, Masha grew up to be a handsome young woman, ready to be betrothed. The old aunt began to talk to her about marriage and prophesied a happy married life for her. But even this was not to Masha's liking. "What is there in being married," she would say. "What happiness is there in it?" The aunt would tell her that there was not only sorrow in the world, but also happiness. "Yes, I know there is, but not for the likes of us," Masha would answer [with a bitter smile...]. Hearing talk like this, Fedya too would become thoughtful [and sad]. But he had no time for sad reflections; he was doing his quota of forced labour on the squiress' land. Masha, however, stubbornly continued to refuse to do any work. The whole village resented Masha's idleness and began to grumble about it; and one day the squiress became so angry that she ordered Masha to be forcibly brought to her forthwith. This was done. As soon as she appeared the squiress loudly upbraided her, and forcing a sickle into her hand said: "Go and mow the grass in the garden." She stood over her and said sternly: "Go on, mow!" Masha swung the sickle with an angry gesture and struck her own hand with it. Blood spurted from the wound, the squiress got frightened and commanded: "Take her home at once! Here's a handkerchief—tie the hand up!" And there the matter ended. Masha did not even appreciate the squiress' kindness: no sooner did she reach home than she tore the lady's handkerchief from her hand and threw it far away. . . .

Masha's stubborn refusal to perform any job she was called upon to do, her melancholy, and the strange questions she asked had a bad effect on her brother. He too became despondent and began to shirk his work. The old aunt thought it was time for the lad to marry and one day she spoke to him about choosing a bride. "If you cannot find anybody to suit you here," she said, "you could go to Dernovka, there's some nice girls there." "All the Dernovka girls are free," interjected Masha. "Well, suppose they are free," reasoned the aunt. . . . "Don't free girls marry serfs? If only they could take a fancy to our young man." "If I were a free girl," said Masha, trembling as she spoke, "I'd rather put my head on the block than do that! . . ." This remark offended Fedya very much. "You needn't be so hard on serfs, Masha," he said, his face contorted with pain. "They too are God's children, only they are unfortunate." With that he left the house. . . . The aunt, as usual, began to plead with Masha, saying that grief and tears did not ease one's fate, they only cut one's life short. But Masha answered that it was better to die early. "What have I got to live for?" she asked.

And so this poor family lived, suffering from the girl's questions and demands which had arisen so inappropriately and had grown so unlawfully. If this had happened on the estate of a cruel squiress, or of an exacting steward, conduct of this kind could

only have had a very bad ending, of course. But the story depicts
for us a kind and gentle squiress, and one with liberal inclinations
to boot. She decides to grant her serfs permission to purchase
their freedom. One can imagine what effect this news had upon
Masha and Fedya. We cannot refrain from quoting here in full
the two small chapters with which this story by Marco Vovchok
ends.

Fedya became more and more sad and gloomy and Masha, fading
before my very eyes ... fell sick. One day I was sitting next to her—she
was lost in thought; suddenly Fedya came in—bright and cheerful. ...
"Good afternoon," he says. I was so glad. "Good afternoon, good afternoon, my dear!" I says. Masha only glanced at him, as much as to say:
what's he so cheerful about?

"Masha!" says Fedya. "You want to die, but I think you are too
young to die yet."

With that he laughed. But Masha said nothing.

"Wake up, little sister and listen: I've brought you some news."

"God be with you and your news," she answered. "You can be merry
if you like, Fedya, but leave me in peace."

"What news, Fedya, tell me?" I asked.

"Listen, auntie dear," he says flinging his arms around me and kissing
me. "Wake up, Masha!" he went on, taking Masha by the arm and raising
her. "The squiress has told us all: whoever wants to buy his freedom can
do so. . . ."

Masha shrieked and threw herself at her brother's feet! She kissed
and hugged him, while tears streamed from her eyes. She trembled all over
and pleaded in a gasping voice: "Buy me out, my dear, buy me out!
May God bless you! My darling, buy me out! God help us, help us, oh
God. . . ."

Fedya too burst into tears and my heart sank. I stood there gazing at
them.

"Wait a bit. Masha," said Fedya. "Let me collect my thoughts! We
must consider this, think about it very carefully."

"There's no need, Fedya! Buy yourself out at once. ... At once,
brother dear!"

I butted in and said: "There's an obstacle, Masha. We shall have to
sell everything we've got. How shall we be able to live?"

"I'll work. ... Brother, I'll work without rest!" said Masha. "I'll borrow the money. ... I'll bind myself to anybody, only buy me out! Darling,
buy me out. ... I am quite worn out! I have not known a single happy
day, not a single night of peaceful sleep. Pity my youth! My life is nothing
but a torment. ... Oh, buy me out, buy me out! Go to her. . . ."

She helped him on with his coat, urged him to hurry up, meanwhile
sobbing and praying. . . . I barely saw how she got him out of the house. . . .,
And she herself walked up and down the room wringing her hands. ...
And my heart fluttered just as it did when I was a girl—think of what was

happening! It was hard for me to collect my thoughts and still harder
to calm down....

We waited impatiently for Fedya to come back and at last he came.
As soon as Masha set eyes on him she wept bitterly and he shouted even
before he got into the house: "Thank God!" Masha fell down onto the
bunk and went on crying for a long time.... We tried to soothe her. "Let
me cry," she says, "let me alone. I feel happy now, I feel as if I have
been born again! Now give me work. I am healthy ... and strong, if you
only knew how strong I am!"

And so we bought ourselves out. We sold the house, and everything....
I was sorry to leave it, and Fedya was sad too: we had toiled and moiled
to keep it going and now it was goodbye to everything! Only Masha
was bright and cheerful—not a tear did she drop. She looked grand, as if
she had come out of a healing spring—flashing eyes and rosy cheeks, and
it seemed as if every fibre of her being was vibrating with joy.... And she
worked like a fury.... "Take a rest, Masha!" I would say. "Rest? I want
to work!" she would answer with a merry laugh! It was then that I first
learned what a ringing laugh she had! In the old days Masha was looked
upon as a work-shy, but now she was recognized as the best needle woman
and the best worker in the village; and the lads came to court her in
crowds.... And, Oh God, how angry the squiress was! Her neighbours
used to tease her and say: "That silly serf girl of yours deceived you! She
always pretended to be sick.... No doubt you let her go for a song!"
And it's true, the squiress did not demand a high price for Masha....

We moved into a little tumbledown old house in town and started work.
God helped us, and we were able to build ourselves a new house.... Fedya
got married. And so did Masha.... Her mother-in-law thinks the world of
her. "She's a real daughter to me. And what a merry girl she is! And
what a fine worker!" she says. Since then Masha has not been sick once.

After reading this story, practical people with humane views,
but secretly sympathizing with serf relationships, exclaimed:
"A fantasy! And idyll [in the social taste]! Dreams of a
future Golden Age! How could a simple peasant girl develop such
a [love for freedom] consciousness of [the rights of] her personality? If anything like this ever happened it was an [extraordinary]
eccentric case, called forth by some exceptional circumstances.
... The story about Masha does not present us with a picture
of Russian life; it is simply a dream above the clouds [a parable
with a moral, which can apply to Spain, Brazil, as well as to
Russia]. The author did not take an ordinary Russian woman,
but an exceptional case; therefore, his story is false and lacks
artistic merit. Art consists in embodying," etc....

And here the worthy orators launched into discourses on art
and felt entirely in their element.

But [they could argue to their heart's content, the story made an impression upon the public nevertheless] it never entered the heads of disinterested people to deny the possibility and the naturalness of a fact like that related in *Masha*. On the contrary, it seemed [quite] normal [and comprehensible] to everybody who was familiar with peasant life. Indeed, is it possible [even arguing *a priori*] to deny that the peasant possesses what we regard as an essential attribute of human thought in every man? [Consciousness of one's personality inevitably presupposes consciousness of the inviolability and the rights of that personality. And would we dare place the Russian peasants on the level of creatures who are not even conscious of their personality?] That would be going too far. . . .

But put them wherever you please, the facts will prove to you that persons like Masha and Fedya are by no means an exception among the masses of the Russian people. True, one cannot often meet with the spirit of independence that was displayed by Masha, but this proves nothing. The form may be different—that depends upon circumstances—but the substance is the same. [People speak different languages; some are talkative, others are not; some have loud voices, others have feeble voices—there are people who are even quite dumb; but for all that, the fact that man is endowed with the gift of speech remains beyond doubt. Similarly, despite the variety of degree in which the consciousness of their natural rights and the striving to free themselves from forced, serf labour, are displayed by the Russian common people—there can be no doubt that this consciousness and striving exist.] That our serf peasant is in a position in which such strivings usually encounter [almost insurmountable] obstacles is also [beyond doubt and] well known [to all and sundry]. But it is precisely the power of these obstacles that provides us with the criterion with which to gauge the strength of the inner urge of the common people, which preserves its vitality even under [the most unfavourable] conditions. Indeed, if you look at the conditions under which a peasant boy or girl live you will wonder how they are able to preserve their living [human] strivings. The father, the mother and all the relatives, subjected as they are to the power of the feudal squire, having grown accustomed to their position and, perhaps, having learned from their own [bitter] experience [all] the inconveniences

that arise from the independent assertion of one's personality
—all try, for the boy's own good, of course, to teach him from
his early years [implicitly to obey another's commands] to renounce his own reason and will. The child's mental capacities
seem to develop only for the purpose of realizing all the horrors,
all the misfortunes that an inclination to reason, to question and
to demand may call down upon a man's head. [All free] natural
logic is displaced by the rules of everyday life, applied to the
[slavish] position of the child; such are the aunt's admonitions
to Masha when she says: "You know what the gentry are; even
if you are a scoundrel, if you go down on your knees you will
be forgiven; but if you are pure and holy and you say one word
in protest—you are the worst man in the world." The point of
departure of all these arguments is the denial that subordinates
have personality [regarding them as mere creatures, as chattels,
for whom there is no other law of existence than the will of the
one to whom they are subordinated. ...] People acquire these ideas
after a long period of suffering and humiliation, after they have
become convinced of their own impotence against fate; and it is
only in order to save their dear ones from similar suffering and
fruitless effort that they try to imbue them with these ideas. The
child's undeveloped mind and undeveloped will absorb a great
deal; and where such inculcation is reinforced by practical measures, such as kicks and cuffs for every question and every objection,
timid, downtrodden, dull creatures grow up, fit for nothing except
to bend their backs to everybody—to flog or ride on, just as one
pleases.... But this is an exception; taking the mass of people,
it is impossible to distort human nature to such an extent as to
obliterate all traces of natural instincts and common sense. [A celebrated contemporary publicist in Europe[110] recently observed
that if despotism could reign in peace in the world without any
protests being raised against it for only two generations, it could
regard its rule as established forever: two generations are enough
to enable it to twist the mind and conscience of a people in its
favour. But the whole point is that despotism and slavery, being
abhorrent to human nature, can never become *normal*, can never
completely subjugate the mind and conscience of man. Yielding
to force, even compelling himself to compose syllogisms in support of this subordination, man, however, instinctively feels that

31—1241

these syllogisms are conventional and accidental, and that the natural, true and far higher demands of justice are their very antithesis. Hence, the tense, restless, discontented state the masses are always in, even when they appear to submit without complaint to the law of slavery which has been imposed upon them. In the history of all societies where slavery has existed you will see something in the nature of a steel spring: as long as the spring is depressed it remains motionless, but as soon as the pressure is slightly released, or withdrawn altogether, it immediately springs upwards. The law of its construction naturally prompts it to expand, and only an outside force can restrain it. In the same way, the human will and mind can be retained in a state of slavery by outside forces; but however powerful these forces may be, they cannot, without breaking, without destroying the spring, deprive it of its ability to expand, just as they are unable, without exterminating the people, to destroy its inclination towards independent activity and free thought.

Happily, our common people too cannot be robbed of this inclination]. These instincts reveal themselves in a man in his very infancy. [You will not infrequently find the same kind of naive radicals among peasant children as you find among the children of other estates.] In all probability, every one of our readers has on more than one occasion caught children dreaming and building castles in the air, which they make no attempt to conceal. Probably, too, they have entered into arguments with children with the object of reducing these dreams *ad absurdum*. Remember, then, how difficult it is as a rule to achieve this object. Our conventional everyday logic [our proprieties, our positive legislation], does not exist for children. Where it is possible to check an adult with a curt: "It is prohibited, it is not the custom," etc., it is impossible to check a child. Masha cannot possibly understand why everybody stands up for the squiress, and why everybody is afraid of her: "She is only one, but we are many; if all of us left her and went wherever we wanted to—what could she do?..." We very often hear children's arguments of this kind which baffle an adult; they are common to all children [whose development is not stunted at the very beginning]. We hear them from peasant children not less but more often than from children of other estates. The reason for this is clear: speaking generally, peasant children are brought up more freely, the relations between young and old are simpler and more intimate, the child earlier becomes an active member of the family and a participant in its common labours. On the other hand, an important factor is that the natural common sense of the peasant child is less suppressed by the artificial [seemingly satisfactory] replies to questions which the girl or boy among the educated estate receives. We [after all] in our earliest years study numerous sciences, such as mythology and heraldry, and from infancy distort our minds with various casuistic subtleties and sophistries. The peasant child cannot hear anything of the kind in its uneducated family and, therefore, longer remains true to nature [and common sense, until at last it is crushed by the weight of outside forces which are armed with all the implements of up-to-date civilization and rest upon all the syllogisms and maxims that have been invented by enlightened and eloquent people...].

Now this very force [that weighs upon the common people and] checks the normal course of [their] thought, usually leaves women more freedom than men; and that is why we said above that the very nature of the case justifies the choice of a female personage to depict the ardent [free] strivings of thought and will of the peasant estate. A peasant boy [putting on the yoke at an early age] is taught by experience that all his thoughts and dreams are impracticable, and he trains himself regularly to suppress his thoughts [and to subdue his loftier aspirations]. A girl, however, much as she shares the common labour with the men, after all has somewhat more freedom to give herself up to her thoughts. The very nature of many of her occupations favours this: spinning, weaving, sewing and knitting leave much more freedom to think and dream than sowing, ploughing, reaping, threshing, felling trees, and so forth. Moreover, it may be assumed that among the peasants, as is the case among all estates in general, a woman's receptiveness and imagination are more highly developed than those of a man. And indeed, recalling numerous observations we have made of the life of the common people, we find that among them the women are, in general, more inclined to discuss lofty subjects, such as—the soul, future life, the beginning of the world, and so forth. Fortunetelling, healing, collecting herbs and incantations are arts practised mainly by women. Fables, legends [and all sorts of traditions] are preserved in the memory of old women;

31*

and the stories about holy places and foreign lands are also spread
throughout Russia by women pilgrims. One can, within a very
few minutes, start any woman talking about how truth disappeared
from the world and how lawlessness prevails everywhere. True,
the conclusion of the conversation will not be gratifying: "All
this is because of our sins, and no doubt this was determined at
our birth, this is our sad fate, and nothing can be done about it. . . ."
But this is said mainly from habit and from impotence [; if you
continue the conversation and suggest ways of getting out of the
present situation, you will find that the most fatalistic old woman
will not be averse to trying them, only she is afraid and distrusts
you].

Among the men the same apparent fatalism is observed, but
here again it is [not the fatalism of faith but] the fatalism of despair:
that, for example, of the sick man who, convinced of the inevitable
and early approach of death, and having lost confidence in doctors,
refuses to take his medicine. In the same way the muzhik, having
lost all hope of the possibility of extricating himself from his
position, does not even wish to discuss it. But this does not mean
that the patient wants to die, or that the muzhik enjoys his position.
Both would gladly accept any remedy that would bring them real
relief. More than that, medical psychologists say, and one cannot
but believe them, that every patient, even the one most desperately
sick, clings to the very last [decisive] moment to the hope that
such a remedy will be found, and in the depths of his heart continues to wait for it even though he is apparently completely resigned to his fate [and is preparing for death]. It is the same with
people who are living under oppression and have apparently resigned themselves to that condition: [they seem to have despaired
of improving their lot and have reconciled themselves to it, but]
within them there undoubtedly lurks the desire and hope of extricating themselves from this condition. The peasants heard the first
rumours about their forthcoming emancipation with considerable
distrust. More than once did we hear peasants say when this news
was communicated to them: "There has been talk about this for
a long time, but is it likely? We shall go on like this to the end
of our lives." But in spite of his distrust and external indifference,
the same peasant will with the greatest interest ask for details
about the various orders the government has issued in connection

with the emancipation. [And later, when it became clear that this
was not a mere hoax, the question of emancipation came right into
the forefront for our peasants as a most important and vital matter. There is not a corner in any part of Russia where you will
not hear the tale of how, when the emancipation was started, serf
peasants assembled at meetings and elected deputations to go either
to the squire, to the priest, or even to the Zemstvo authorities to
make enquiries about what was intended to be done about them. . . .
Memorable also is the eagerness with which the people of St. Petersburg rushed to the Senate bookstore when, one day, in the
beginning of 1856, the rumour was spread that an edict for the
emancipation of the serfs had been issued and that copies of it were
on sale.]

In addition to these signs there is a fact which serves as mute
but convincing proof that hatred of the serf status [and serf la-
bour] is very strong among the masses. The peasant is unable to
refuse altogether to perform [to protest openly against] serf labour. The possibility of disobeying the squire's orders as Masha
does in Marco Vovchok's story is very rare, and it can be utilized
only by single individuals; it cannot be done collectively, by a
whole crowd. Wherever such an inclination to refuse to perform
serf labour was revealed the consequences [as is known] were
very unpleasant for the peasants. Hence, [willy-nilly] they had
to work. But what do we find? All over Russia, on all estates
employing serf labour, the peasants, without previous agreement
or arrangement, express their protest against forced labour in a
special way: they do the work negligently. In most cases they are
even unable to explain their conduct; but the fact that serf labour
is very inefficient labour is notorious. Except for Professor Gorlov
[and (probably) his zealous students and admirers at the univer-
sity] everybody agrees that free hired labour is ever so much more
efficient and profitable than forced labour.[111] Even many landown-
ers have written to their magazines to this effect. What further
proof do you want? What is this due to, if not to the fact that
every peasant, man and woman, is unconsciously imbued with
the same feeling that Marco Vovchok's Masha so clearly and consciously expressed? The difference lies in its degree of development and the form in which it manifests itself; the substance is
the same.

Yes, we are of the opinion that the case related in *Masha* is not an exception [alien to our way of life and likely to occur to, perhaps, one out of one hundred thousand peasants] as the planters and art critics claim. On the contrary, [we boldly assert that] Masha represents and embodies the [lofty] strivings of the general mass of the Russian people [who are patiently but ceaselessly waiting for the glorious festival of emancipation. We shall never agree with those who even deny that the people are waiting for this, and assert that they have not yet acquired a taste for independent life, for being free in their actions. Thanks to the works on history that have appeared recently, and still more to the latest events in Europe,[112] we are beginning to understand a little the inner meaning of the history of peoples; and today less than ever can we deny the constant striving among all peoples, more or less conscious, but always manifesting itself in facts—to regain their natural rights to moral and material independence of another's will. This striving is not only as strong among the Russian people as it is among other peoples, but, in all probability, it is even stronger. We say this not because we to any degree share the opinion that the Slavonic race is superior to all other races and that its heaven-sent mission is

> To guard for all the world the treasure
> Of high sacrifice and pure deeds,
> To guard the sacred brotherhood of races,
> The life-giving cup of love,
> The wealth of ardent faith,
> And truth, and bloodless justice,[113]

and all the charming things of a similar nature, about which Mr. Khomyakov is able to sing so sonorously. No, leaving aside all subtle views about racial differences, we simply look at preceding events and their results—the present-day conditions of the people. It must be clear to everybody that a very hungry man will eat his dinner with more zest than one who had his lunch before dinner, that one who has no means of livelihood will seek such means more energetically and perseveringly than one who has at least some means of making ends meet. Of all the European peoples, the English are the most conservative and the most devoted to established law and custom, and nothing could be easier to understand. They went through a time of internal unrest, a time during which

they were obliged to purchase the most insignificant rights at a
high price; but after purchasing them they calmed down, if not
completely satisfied, then at all events, with their first and most
urgent requirements met. Once those most urgent requirements were
met, their further strivings automatically became calm and moderate, devoid of all impulsiveness and feverishness. A man who has
taken an umbrella with him may indeed feel some inconvenience
if it rains, but he has some protection and, therefore, does not
have to run for shelter as hurriedly as the one who has no protection at all. ... Now it is with this umbrella, under which a large
section of the peoples of Europe take cover from rain, that our
preceding history was not able to provide us. We are only preparing to take the path which Europe has travelled; it is only recently
that we began to study the route it has taken, and we are scarcely
able as yet to discern the road. That is why we are proceeding so
timidly, haltingly, gropingly as it were; and that is why it seems
as though we lack initiative. But we feel the urge to go, at least
to the first stage; we must not remain in one spot, we must not
halt on the road. Clearly, we must perform the first part of our
journey with greater determination, haste and firmness than other
nations are continuing their journey. Our needs are more urgent,
life is harder without them than without what the European peoples are now striving for. Bright's reform in England, and freedom
of the press for France as demanded by a Favre or Ollivier, are
undoubtedly necessary, and in time will be achieved; but they can
afford to wait a little, they are by no means as essential and urgent
as the legal guarantee of the civil rights and material existence of
millions of people who up to now have suffered, to a greater or
lesser degree, from the crushing effect of tyranny. For these millions
it is not a matter of adding something to rights which they already
possess, but purely a matter of acquiring at least some rights because, under the reign of serfdom they have had no rights whatever,
if not *de jure* then *de facto*. Clearly, the desire for these rights,
once it is felt, must be stronger than any desire to add to already
existing rights; clearly, it is here that the spirit of the people must
reveal itself much more actively than anywhere else, and that is
why this subject deserves the special attention of all those who are
sincerely concerned about the welfare of the people. To this day
many believe that people who have not yet achieved freedom are

unworthy of serious attention because they live and act not according to the dictates of their own will, but as they are ordered. This argument too would be correct if it referred to a mass of people who had entirely lost their personality and lacked all human strivings. But we have already said that we do not even believe in the possibility of a whole people losing their personality in this way, and under no circumstances can this be said of the Russian people.] If the desire to regain the independence of one's personality exists [there is no need for us to know whether it has received official sanction or not; whether it will be officially recognized or not—] it will in any case manifest itself in the facts of national life [emphatically and urgently. Nobody will be able to suppress this desire or divert it into the channel he wishes; it is a river that is forcing its way over all obstacles, and which cannot halt in its progress because this would run counter to its nature].

But what direction can this striving to acquire independence and freedom take in practice? It is common knowledge that these concepts are the most indefinite of all, and there is, perhaps, not another word in the human vocabulary that gives rise to so much controversy as the word "freedom." Scholars and philosophically minded people have been unable to this day to reach final agreement upon a definition of this concept; how will our common people interpret it? Many assert that because of their stupidity and ignorance, the common people will interpret freedom to mean the possibility of doing nothing [refusing to obey anybody], of getting drunk and brawling every day; [our readers already know to what category the people who express this opinion belong. For that reason] we shall [not deal at length with them but] merely say that [these] people who express such opinions about the peasants judge according to their own standards, without taking into consideration the difference in the conditions under which they and the common people have been brought up. To study this difference they should again turn to Marco Vovchok: they will find that he has an instructive story on this subject entitled *Plaything*.

In *Plaything* we get the story of the development of a beautiful child's nature, similar to Masha's, but this time of one who belongs to the gentry. If you compare the two stories you will find that the life of the common people provides immeasurably more guarantees for proper and sound development than the life of a little lady or a little gentleman. Among the former needs are simpler, the goal is nearer and more definite, and the very mode of reasoning is less distorted. The saddest [and most fatal] distortion of the minds of the common people consists in that they lose the clear consciousness [of their human rights,] of their personal independence and of their belonging only to themselves. [In this respect they do, indeed, sink to very great absurdities and forcibly crush their most legitimate natural demands and strivings]. But as natural demands always retain some power over a man, there is always a hope of guiding the poor fellow to the right point of view. And once he adopts this point of view he will put it into practice; it is this practicalness that constitutes the specific feature of the peasant mind [and in it lies its strength]. We usually philosophize as a pastime [sometimes to aid our digestion] and most often about matters which are not our concern [and which we are totally unable to change, and have no intention of changing]. The peasant cannot afford such an intellectual luxury; he must work for his living, and he ponders over what may have a bearing upon his life; and he ponders over it precisely for the purpose of finding in his soul motives for practical activity. Recall what Masha talked about, what she tried to fathom, and what all her reflections brought her to. [We are of the opinion that in her person the author very skilfully brought out the major questions from which the mind of an entire estate must begin to work. The first question, of course, must refer to the inviolability of the person: "What's the meaning of this? I don't want to go, but I am dragged; why—nobody knows; by what right—nobody can understand; this should not be." This simple argument already contains the germ of all possible rights and guarantees. The process of thinking is known: when I want to explain somebody's conduct towards me I put myself in the other's place and try to think what would compel me, if I were in his place, to act in this way; if I fail to find any adequate motive I judge that conduct to be unjust. Therefore,] if a child begins to ponder over the question as to what right others have to encroach upon his personality and ends by finding that there is no such right, this reflection is a guarantee that this child has no inclination to encroach upon another's personality. [Thus, people who protest against violence and tyranny, by that very fact give us some guarantee that they them-

selves will not resort to violence or give scope to their own tyr-
anny]; the desire for the inviolability of their own person will
compel them to respect the persons of others. Of course, people
who act tyrannically and violently must also be supposed to possess
some desire that they should not be treated as they treat others;
but it is permissible to think that owing to their utterly warped
development, even this desire is not very strong, and, moreover, is
subjected to many limitations. [It has been observed that people who are arrogant and despotic towards inferiors are nearly
always despicably obsequious and as meek as lambs before their
superiors. It has also been observed that the most implacable, the
most unbearable stewards of estates are those who have formerly
been lackeys, and that, in general, lackeys are more haughty towards the peasants than their masters. The reader may supplement
these observations with several more examples taken from a wider
sphere, and he will inevitably arrive at the conclusion that the
use of violence against others destroys, or, at all events, considerably weakens, a man's ability to become truly and profoundly indignant when violence is perpetrated against themselves. It is true
that lately we have seen how people who all their lives have known
no other law than tyranny raised a howl against tyranny when
their own interests were affected. But as a rule such people set up
a howl, make a lot of fuss, and then subside: they are unable to
put up a vigorous and active defence of what they regard as their
rights because their consciousness of right in general has become
very faint and obliterated.

Thus, the first thing that is an indefeasible truth for the simple
mind is inviolability of the person.] Side by side with the concept
of the inviolability of the person there [inevitably] arises the
concept of the duty and right to work. "I have no right to restrict
another person because nobody has a right to restrict me; hence,
I cannot count on living at another's expense: for that would mean
robbing others of the fruits of their labour, *i.e.*, violating, enslaving their person. Consequently, I must necessarily secure my own
livelihood, I must work: if I live on the fruits of my own labour
there will be no need for me to rob another; and at the same time,
enjoying material security, I will have means with which constantly
to preserve my own independence." Such are the simplest arguments which lead to the deduction that to work is a duty, a de-

duction that is as clear as daylight to all the common people. And these arguments have not been invented by us theoretically: they are deeply and firmly embedded in the hearts of [every one of the] common people. As a rule, it never enters their heads that it is possible to live without working; so remote are they from this in practical life. Tell any peasant in the busy season to take a rest, to stop working; you will get a simple answer: how shall we get bread then? If I won't work, I won't eat.

You have only to reverse the argument that leads to the deduction that work is a duty and you will come to the rights of those who work. "If I must work for a living because I cannot, and must not, enjoy the fruits of my neighbour's labour, it is evident that my neighbour must also have the same in view. He must work for himself; I have not the least desire, and do not think it fair, to give him what I have earned." And so we come straight to the demands and decisions which Marco Vovchok's Masha arrived at, and which, to a certain degree, are shared by the entire serf population of Russia. "Why should I work for others? Far better that I should do nothing at all"—such is the argument of people who are deprived of the [full] right to the fruits of their labour and [either] refuse to do any work at all where it is possible to avoid it, as Masha [for example] does, or try to exert as little effort and zeal as possible when working for others, as the serf peasants do in general [all over Russia]. Hence, we may draw a simple conclusion about the direction the peasants' efforts will take as soon as they receive the right freely to dispose of their labour: just as Masha, on hearing the first news about the possibility of being freed, exclaimed that she would work hard, was even willing to go into bondage, to earn the money with which to purchase her freedom, so the entire mass, after their liberation, will start working hard and strive to improve their conditions. Now the *whole* of the labour of the emancipated worker will be *his*, will belong to him [inalienably]; hence, the harder he works the more he will get and the better his conditions will be. Under these circumstances, even temporary loss of personal freedom is not so hard to bear. It is worth noting that to acquire freedom Masha is willing to *go into bondage*; hence, it is not the fact that she cannot do what she likes that is her main burden; what is bitter to her is that she must renounce her rights to her labour without any reason,

God knows why. When going into bondage she knows that the terms are binding on both parties; she will be a bondswoman, but she will earn money with which to purchase her freedom. [Thus, here she can see the beginning and the basis of her slavery; and she can also see its end, an end which, after all, is to some degree in conformity with reason; for the period of bondage is determined by the amount of wages to be paid and the value of the labour performed by the bonded person. There was nothing like this in Masha's status in relation to the squiress: here there was neither beginning nor end, neither entrance nor exit, neither sense nor calculation—there was tyranny and nothing else, and, as a consequence, a complete absence of personal guarantees and definite rights; they can do whatever they like with you, without reason, without having to give an account, without being answerable for it. . . . This is the hardest to bear for a man who is even only slightly awakening to the demand for justice, which is natural in all men, but which in many is suppressed by the degradation and suppression of their personalities.]

Thus, assuming that the peasants receive their freedom, we see that it will be followed, as a direct result, by an increase in the quantity and improvement of the quality of their labour. It goes without saying that we would not dare to urge the arguments enunciated above as a binding condition to the government's measures for emancipation, the drafting of which is now being completed by the Drafting Commission. We are only discussing what should be in general, in conformity with the demands of logic and the observations that have been made of peasant life and characters; we have not the slightest desire to touch upon the economic and administrative questions which the Commission is considering, or predict the possible consequences of the measures the government will adopt. Quite naturally, these measures may have a special effect that will be very different from what we can foresee when discussing the matter in general outline and presenting only its logical definition. Our task is merely to point to certain features of the character of the people and not to define the mode of action of peasant committees and commissions with which we are not in the least concerned here. Hence, [having dealt in most general outline with the way every one of our common people should accept and employ his freedom] we shall now return to the parallel which, as we have said, is suggested by the story *Plaything*.

Plaything is [nothing more nor less than] a distortion of the name Agrafena, Grusha, Grushechka* [but a distortion] of a very sad and depressing significance. All her life Grusha, a peasant girl, was actually the plaything of her squiress and the latter's daughter; and the squiress and her daughter, who wrecked Grusha's life, were actually quite innocent, kind creatures, who would never think of tormenting people and wrecking their lives: they could only *play*, amuse themselves with them. The entire life of the gentry as depicted in *Plaything* is so idyllic that one feels ashamed to say anything unkind about these ladies. Not the slightest trace of anything calculated, deliberate, malicious or cunning can be found in their whole lives, in any of their actions, even the worst. How they live and what interests them is best of all told us by "Plaything" herself.

The squire and his lady were young. Her ladyship was considered a beauty. She was tall and graceful, with dark eyebrows and a fair skin—only she was lazy.... Good Lord, how lazy she was! She was born lazy! She even used to look at you with her eyes half closed. All she did was to float from parlour to parlour, her head inclined to one side and rustling her long silk skirts. She would liven up a bit only when guests arrived, the talkative, merry and critical ones. They would make fun of the bonnets some ladies were wearing, gossip about the General's wife from Moscow, sigh for Paris and say nasty things about their county—and then her ladyship would raise her head and be more lively than usual.... The squire was livelier than her ladyship; he was always singing comic songs and whistling. People said that *he didn't have much brains, but he was a nice quiet fellow. He never quarrelled with her ladyship. She too was a very kind lady*; she never punished anybody. *Only rarely did they get angry.* If any of the serfs came to ask for anything, *they didn't mind, they didn't order them to be sent away, except if it was somebody who was bothersome. Then they would order him not to be allowed in, or they would promise to do something, but didn't do it—forgot about it.* And so the squire and his lady lived quite contentedly and merrily, peacefully and quietly. *They would sit in the drawing room; the squire would whistle a tune while her ladyship would allow her eyes to wander about the room.* Suddenly an idea came into her head and she would say to the squire: "My dear, blue wallpaper would be better for this room!" The squire would jump up and say: "What a wonderful idea, my darling! *Why didn't I think of it before?"* And he

---

* Grusha is short for Agrafena. Grushechka is the diminutive of Grusha and in the story is distorted into Igrushechka, which literally means "plaything."—*Tr.*

would stand there stroking his forehead. . . . "Well, a matter like this must not be postponed, I'll send somebody to town at once, and by Sunday everything will be done." "Yes, yes!" her ladyship would say. "Anna Petrovna and Klavdia Ivanovna are coming—won't they be surprised! And Anna Fyodorovna will be so angry that she won't eat anything at dinner. Get it done by Sunday without fail, my dear!" And then there would be a lot of fuss and bother. *What excitement there would be for the next few days:* every minute they would think that a carriage was rolling up and they would exclaim: "Oh, somebody's arrived," and they would look horror-stricken. You see, they wanted to surprise their guests, and here suddenly somebody might arrive and find the walls all bare! *I don't think they had any other cares or worries. I've never seen the squire pondering over anything or her ladyship ever weep—except when they were short of money, or when little missy was sick.* As for being short of money, that often happened. They both liked to live well and to dress luxuriously. Her ladyship wore nothing but silk dresses and fine lace. The squire was also a fine dandy: *he always used to tie his necktie in a dove's wing and sometimes he'd struggle from morning until dinner time trying to get it straight. "What an unlucky day," he would sigh. "I can't get it right anyhow!..."* Her ladyship would go to help him, and they would call Arina Ivanovna, just as if he was dressing for his wedding, *all fussing and worrying about him.... And when he was all dressed up he would look so smart and he would stop in front of every mirror and stroke his cheek.

All this wouldn't have been so bad if they did not change everything, right down to the last rag, several times a year. The money they spent on the house itself! They'd renew everything at Christmas and at Easter too. And how merry the squire was at such times. He would hang the pictures up himself.... *You may think it's funny but I'm telling you the downright truth: he was passionately fond of knocking in nails, and if anybody, wishing to do him a favour, hurried to help him, he used to get angry.... After a time everybody knew that they were not to do anything except get the hammer ready for him. And I must say nobody could knock a nail in as well as he could: he got so skilled at it that he'd just glance at it, give a couple of taps, and the nail would go right in....*

When the squire and her ladyship went to town—what did they not buy! Samovars and dried peas, although the shelves in the storeroom were simply breaking down with the weight of the samovars on them, and the gardeners had stocked enough peas to last a whole year. They bought silk for lining the walls, cans of little fishes that tasted bitter, and snuff boxes which played music.... When the peddlers came around they made an awful lot of money! You know how cunning those merchants are. They would say to the squire. "Don't take this, Your Honour, it's very dear. Take something cheaper." *But the squire would flare up and say: "Show me the dearest thing you have!" And he would buy the very same thing at three times the price. And sometimes he wouldn't take any change.* And he would look at the bearded merchants as much as to say: There, I got the better of you, didn't I! And the merchants would almost sob with joy.... What happened when they celebrated a saint's day, or a birthday, you can hardly imagine. Good Lord—what feasts they had! They would order wines and confectionery, a shawl and a cap for her ladyship, and a necktie and yellow gloves for the squire.... "When you're sending to town," he would say, "order this and that," and one thing and another.... And it amounted to so much that we had to send a cart to the post station to fetch it all.... Although they had lots of fun on these saints' days, they also had lots of trouble and anxiety: they'd get quite worn out before it was over, thinking and worrying what to serve for dinner, what flowers to put on the table, what surprise to give the General's lady, and how to disturb her sleep at night. *They'd get so tired that one would think they had been doing a spell of serf labour.*

This [description of life among the gentry] must be regarded as some of the best pages of Marco Vovchok's latest book. In the amiable [tone in which the tale is told we no longer hear the irritation and anger of the pamphleteer; we hear not passionate struggle, but the calm, unprejudiced, solemn judgment of history on the very substance, the very principle of serfdom. In] this story we see not only the vacuousness and mediocrity of kindhearted gentry who have been brought up under the influence of feudal ideas; the fundamental causes of this vacuousness and mediocrity are clearly discerned in it. You see that these people have been [downtrodden and] robbed of their personality more than any serf; they have been robbed of the sense of their own dignity and duties, they have been deprived of all opportunity of seriously examining themselves, their souls have been extracted and replaced by a few conventional demands and maxims of vulgar civilization. Instead of the behests of common sense they have had it knocked into their heads from infancy, and have grown accustomed to the idea, that they must live [upon the labour of others] without doing anything themselves, that this is [their right] their mission on earth. Their whole upbringing [their whole intellectual and moral development] was made to conform to this mission. That is why they were not taught to do anything, why they are unable to do anything, [have no particular inclination for anything] that is why they do not know how to fill the vacuum of their lives, that is why they are even unable to calculate their expenditures, avoid being short of money and to judge what they ought and what not to buy. [The idea of having to calculate in this way can never enter their minds because they are told: "You possess so and so, and you can enjoy so and so," but it has never been suggested to them that they ought to earn the right to enjoy the blessings of life by their own labour. They are as incapable of grasping the idea that labour is an essential condition of life and the foundation of social morality as they are incapable of grasping the idea that it is necessary to respect every man's natural, inalienable rights.] It never enters their heads to examine themselves seriously, to ask themselves why they are living and what they are in the society from which they demand and receive every kind of benefit and service. It is in regard to them that one may [with every right] say that they have no initiative and that their lives lack all inner meaning. Taken by themselves they are nothing; they live an animal life, almost like automatons, until the resources which came to them by the mercy of fate are exhausted; as soon as these resources have gone, they become the most unhappy and most helpless of creatures. Lacking all means of livelihood, lacking all self-reliance [not even understanding what self-respect means], they are ready to submit to every kind of degradation and meanness if only they can keep themselves alive. Plaything's master and mistress, after squandering their entire estate, go to live with their aunt, an old [prude and] miser, who scolds [and lectures] them all day long. And they are obliged mutely [and humbly] to bear her treatment: they have no other alternative but to live upon another's charity and to submit entirely to the caprices of the one who feeds them. But on the other hand, they retain the privilege of [being parasites and of] doing nothing. . . .

And yet this idleness was inculcated in them artificially! The natural and irrepressible urge for activity does not lose its influence even over them. The only trouble is that owing to their [warped] upbringing they [the squire and the squiress] are not only incapable of putting their hand to anything, but even of thinking of some kind of practical work to put their hand to: so limited are their knowledge and aspirations! And so they devise for themselves special occupations, such as knocking in nails and tying their neckties in dove's wings, make work and trouble for themselves, such as changing the wallpaper and furniture. . . . Did not this gentleman acquire a passion for knocking in nails and even become extremely skilled at this work? Why, then, can he not become a skilled carpenter, shoemaker or paper hanger? Of course, had he been brought up differently, and had he found himself in a different environment, he would have found some useful occupation for himself and would not have been such a parasitic creature [capable only of absorbing other people's lives, of living upon other people's labour]. He would then have been far more self-reliant, firmer, more independent, he would not have known those petty, but for him unbearable, vexations which he feels when he fails to tie his necktie properly, or when the walls of the drawing room are stripped. Then he would naturally have acquired an inclination to calculate and to ponder over his life, and he would not have sunk to the position that is described in *Plaything*:

Feast follows feast—and suddenly they find they have no money. And then they go and sit in the drawing room very despondent. One sits looking out of one window and the other out of another sighing. . . . "Oh, Ah, Oh." And when the trouble is over, after selling or mortgaging another village, money begins to jingle again, and again there are banquets, the house is filled with guests, there's feasting and merrymaking, and they have a very good time (until the money runs out again, of course).

A more ridiculous position cannot be imagined, and it can be borne only if one is trained to it from infancy. But then look how bored they are with life: no wonder they walk up and down the room with drooping eyelids, as if they were sleepy; no wonder they kill time by tying neckties in dove's wings. And they give dinners and suppers only in order to find some occupation and amusement; they are bored to death, but they do not know how to remedy this, and do not realize that a [radical] remedy is needed. . . .

And it is with such parents, amidst such a life, that the vivacious inquisitive nature of the girl, their daughter, has to develop! Needless to say, her strivings are not satisfied and all attempts to satisfy them are absolutely fruitless. But the story of her development, many details of which are familiar to every one of us, proves, on the one hand, how strong and irrepressible are the natural, innate demands of a man's mind and heart, and, on the other hand, what a multitude of obstacles they have to encounter, due to the way of life of the gentry and to our [warped] upbringing.

How, indeed, can the daughter of such parents, seeing around her all that which we have described above, acquire an inclination [to ask the most radical questions] for inquisitive, grave, adult reflection about life and its conditions? How can she cultivate respect for the demands of justice [, contempt for self-degradation and slavery]? Nobody imbues her with anything like it, nothing around her disposes her towards such reflection.... But one thing is enough, namely, that her dear parents should relieve her of their supervision and should cease to care about her moral up-bringing, this one thing is enough to enable her natural human striv-ings to become clearly expressed and gain strength. Only the very slightest contact with a poor girl [with "Plaything," over whom she domineered] was enough to stir up her natural desire for goodness and truth.... But nothing could come of all this: it is natural for a man to breathe, but he cannot breathe without air; it is natural for a seed to vegetate, but it cannot sprout if it is thrown on a bare stone pavement; similarly, the living human organism will fail to develop if it falls into the environment of the heartless, automatic [aristocratic] existence that we see among the gentry to whom Plaything belongs. Here is the story of the girl, which deals mainly with her attitude towards "Plaything."

One day the young lady saw a girl in the village street. "Give me that girl!" she said. They brought the girl to the manor house and told her to play with the young lady. Next day the fam-ily made ready to visit another of their estates and they wanted to send the little village girl home, but the young lady protested and said: "I want to take the girl with me." Every effort was made to persuade her to give up the idea, but the young lady was obdurate, she would not give way and broke into tears. Seeing that nothing could be done, the squiress ordered that the village girl be made ready for the journey. The girl's mother, poor wom-an, came to the house and weeping bitter tears, pleaded: "Give me back my daughter," but the squiress said to her in a kind and reasonable tone:

"I would give her back to you, but our little lady won't let her go, she has taken a great liking to your daughter. *Please don't cry: the little lady will get tired of her soon—children don't keep their playthings long —and then we'll send your daughter back to you at once.*"

And not suspecting how inhuman this kind answer was, the squiress caps it by saying to her housekeeper and hanger-on, Arina Ivanovna:

"*Oh, how sorry I am for this woman—I simply cannot look at her! Go, Arina Ivanovna, be a good soul, and say something to her. Here, give*

*her this money.... * Well, give her one of my things, something already
worn.... Only hurry up about it and let her go away, *I don't want to have
her crying here.*"

You see what a hopeless situation this is: it is as if the squiress
herself is bound to forced labour [exactly like a government
official performing his duty: "In my conscience, as a man, I sympathize with you, but keeping within the exact meaning of the
law I must send you to prison." So it is with her]: she has a kind
heart, she is a mother herself, and she is sorry for the poor woman;
but *noblesse oblige,* and squire's right also *oblige*—she must take
the daughter from her mother, although she does not want to do
so.... And to console the mother she wants to give her a little
money for her daughter [as if she did not get her money from
this very woman and those like her: cheap generosity!]... And
the main object of this generosity is to rid herself of the sight of
the mother's tears and grief, to get her to go away, not to have
her crying *here....*

It goes without saying that in demanding Grusha, who was at
once dubbed "Plaything," the little lady does not even suspect
how immoral her demand is, because she does not yet understand
the legal relationship that exists between her and the peasant girl.
She simply wants to have a playmate and refuses to allow the
girl to whom she has taken a liking to leave her. But in her position she cannot present any ethical demand without suffering for
it: her environment forthwith transforms her simplest wish into
[despotic] violence and [inhuman] tyranny. Here, for example,
is a scene which shows us how a child is corrupted in the most
revolting manner at a very early age.

The young lady is fond of Plaything, but Arina Ivanovna de-
tests her. One day a peasant came to the big house bringing Plaything greetings and a parcel from her mother; Arina Ivanovna
would not let the peasant enter the house. He begged her to let
him in, but she only railed at him. Plaything, who was with the
young lady in the nursery hard by, heard the altercation and
broke into tears. The young lady at once asked her: "Why are
you crying?" The girl told her. Then, notwithstanding Arina Ivanovna's protestations, the young lady imperatively demanded that
the peasant should be allowed to come in and give Plaything the
parcel; she herself even opened the door for the muzhik. The girl

32*

spoke to the peasant and, of course, remembered her mother and her home and began to cry as she examined the contents of the parcel—two chemises, a toy duck made of clay and some honey cakes. Arina Ivanovna made fun of the chemises and wanted to "throw them out of the window," but the young lady would not allow her to do this and ordered her out of the room. Meanwhile, Plaything kept on crying, and the young lady sat beside her deep in thought, casting a sidelong glance at the weeping girl every now and again. God knows what she was thinking about; perhaps she was asking herself why she was causing the poor girl so much suffering by separating her from her mother. But a little later Arina Ivanovna returned to the room. Then the following conversation ensued:

"Why are you so sad, Zinaida Petrovna?" Arina Ivanovna asks the young lady.

The young lady sighed and pointing at me said:

"She is crying all the time for her mother, she wants to go back to her mother."

"Let her want! Why should you disturb yourself about it? If you don't want her to go we shall not let her, my angel, don't you worry!"

"But she's crying!"

"Well, what of it? You took her for your amusement, you are her mistress, my treasure—you may do whatever you wish with her: if you order her to cry, she must cry! If you order her to be merry, she must be merry!"

"But suppose she won't?"

"She won't? We'll teach her such a lesson that she'll be like silk!"

"I'm sorry for Plaything."

"That's the whole trouble! You are sorry for her and in that way you are spoiling her. Stop being sorry for her!"

"I'm so sorry for Plaything, I'm so sorry for Plaything!" the young lady kept repeating.

"I'm telling you, if you stop being sorry for her she will stop crying. Her caprice will pass off at once."

Thus, the young lady's kind and just strivings are killed in the embryo. There is in her not only kindness, which makes her sorry for the weeping girl, but also the elements of respect for human rights and distrust of the [violent] right to tyrannize: when she is told that she can make Plaything do anything she wishes her to, she answers: "But suppose she won't?" This answer already reveals an instinctive realization that every person has a will of his own [and that the violation of another's personality may encounter perfectly legitimate resistance]. But all these germs [of common sense] are at once destroyed by the [slavish] admonitions of the [despicable] housekeeper and hanger-on, and what is most important, the very position in which the young lady finds herself greatly contributes to the suppression of such [healthy] tendencies. While Masha, and those like her, perseveringly go further and further with their thoughts and questions, once they arise, Zinochka, on the contrary, is glad to lull all that which rises from the depths of her mind. This is understandable: Masha is prompted not only by her natural strivings, but also by her vital interest to achieve the theoretical and practical triumph of sound ideas: after all, the warping of the human mind and the reign of tyranny impose upon her all sorts of restrictions [and violations]. The young lady's attitude towards the question is entirely the opposite. Although, at first, it causes her some embarrassment and inconvenience, as everything does which runs counter to the natural demands of one's organism, she, nevertheless, accepts the principle of tyranny [and violence] rather easily, and it soon permeates her being. It destroys her moral fibre, it is poisonous for her, as it is for all those to whom she causes suffering; but it affects her in a way that is very much different from the way it affects the others: it poisons the others like an ordinary poison which causes painful convulsions: upon her it acts like opium, which conjures up charming visions [but by that very fact deadens and slowly saps the strength of her organism]. It is difficult to abandon the use of drugs once one has become an addict to them; it is still more difficult to abandon [the moral poison of] tyranny [and domination] which bring us, although illusory, but [for one who is still at the lower stages of development] extremely attractive advantages. The foundation of respect for another's rights lies, as we have said, primarily in the instinct of self-preservation, in the desire to protect the inviolability of one's own rights; but if repeated examples show a child that it can violate other people's rights with impunity, how can its undeveloped mind find a sufficient bulwark against temptation? Another primary impulse that prompts us to work is the natural necessity to exercise one's strength, and [consequently] the desire to work should be in direct proportion to a man's strength, which in its turn depends a great deal upon exercise. It is natural, therefore, that where there is little strength the wish to work is small too; and if there are no other incentives to work, the child very readily grows accustomed to indolence, as a result of which its strength, receiving no exercise, fails to receive proper development. We see this not only in physical, but also in moral development: when children first go to school they very unwillingly take to lessons in which they have to exercise their brains and achieve results; they prefer to have everything explained to them, and that only passive reception should be demanded of them. Indeed, many parents take care that this is done: a host of teachers, tutors and coaches are hired to masticate all knowledge and put it into the children's mouths; but the result is that these children remain monkeys all their lives, sometimes very learned and, in general, intelligent monkeys, but incapable of rising to the level of independent human thought.

And it is not because of material advantages alone that the young lady's position helps to distort her thoughts and feelings; being unnatural, the very position in which the girl finds herself gives rise to [monstrous] facts which confuse her still more. Take, for example, the continuation of the same scene with Zinochka and Plaything.

Taking the advice of Arina Ivanovna, the young lady orders the girl to be merry, and Arina Ivanovna holds her sides with laughter.

"Be merry, Plaything, be merry," the young lady orders. "Be merry and forget your mother at once. Do you hear what I tell you? Well, have you forgotten your mother?"

"No," I say. "No, I have not forgotten!"

Arina Ivanovna turns to me and says:

"How dare you answer our young lady like this, eh? What? You rude girl! You have been ordered to laugh—laugh at once!"

I laugh in front of her, swallowing my bitter tears.

"There you are, my angel, look, she is laughing!" says Arina Ivanovna to soothe the young lady. *And the young lady looks at me with wondering eyes.*

"Plaything," she says. "How is it, you are crying and laughing? *I wouldn't do it!*"

To this Arina Ivanovna answers: "Whom are you comparing yourself with, my dove? She can do whatever she is ordered to do."

"So that's the kind of girl you are, Plaything!" said the young lady.

As you see, Arina Ivanovna's counsels and assurances are confirmed by facts which create an unpleasant but indelible impression upon the young lady. She *tests* herself and Plaything by ordering her to be merry; she still does not quite believe that this tormenting of a person like herself can be effective. But what happens? The poor child, terrified and helpless, yields; this perplexes and even seems to disappoint the young lady: she feels that there is something wrong here. "I wouldn't do it," she says, passing from this to the thought that Plaything, being a person too, ought not to do it. But here at once the explanation is forthcoming that Plaything is not at all "a person too," but a serf girl, who "can do whatever she is ordered to do. . . ." The fact is obvious: why then not believe this explanation, the more so that it lulls the young lady's instinctive anxiety on this score, relieves her of moral responsibility and flatters her vanity by raising her to the level of a superior being who has the right to dominate the will and personality of other people! . . . Thus, the idea of her kinship with all human beings [and the idea that every man has full rights], the idea of human solidarity, is quickly suppressed in her in the very embryo. There remains only, at first, a feeling of vexation and regret, as if the hopes she had placed in a friend had been disappointed: "So that's the kind of girl you are, Plaything!" the young lady exclaimed in the first moment. But later this passes off: she herself, later on, without any prompting from Arina Ivanovna, says to Plaything threateningly: "Don't mope! You know, I can do anything I like with you. I shall not pamper you," and so forth. . . .

Scenes like these, occurring every day and every hour, are capable of killing [all] common sense [and human feeling], even before they manage to arise. This is what happens to many people. But, as we have said, Zinochka's parents have left her to her fate in the company of Plaything, and nobody, except Arina Ivanovna, teaches her the aristocratic theory. This saves her moral strength and enables it to develop to the stage of, if not real, independent activity, at least to that of eager and persistent desire and enquiry. Some questions trouble her very seriously: she wants to know everything, the how and the why? She questions Plaything about her previous life and about the work the peasants do. The girl tells her about these things. "After I had told her these

things," says Plaything, "she would hug me very tightly and say:
'I would never have learned myself how all this is done, Plaything. Who invented all this in your village, Plaything?' 'I don't
know who invented it, but all of us are able to do things,' I told
her. 'Perhaps it was your mother, Plaything?' 'Perhaps,' I says."
That, of course, ended the explanation she received from Plaything, and it was the best explanation she could receive. When
she talked with her mother and father she could get nothing out
of them. One day, for example, Plaything burst into tears on
hearing that the squire had sold her native village and, consequently, she would never be able to return to it. The young lady
had a talk with her, gazed at her and became pensive. "How
does everything like this happen!" she asked. "How does what
happen?" asked Plaything in her turn. "Well," says Zinochka,
"don't you notice that when some people cry others laugh, that
some say one thing and others say something entirely different?
Now you are crying because Trostino has been sold, but Mama
and Papa are always glad when they get money." And suddenly
she runs up to Plaything and enquires anxiously: "Can't everybody be happy? Is it not possible, Plaything?" "I suppose not,"
she says. "Why not?" "It doesn't happen that way," says the other
girl. "Look at us two, we are always together, and yet we think
differently." "Yes, but why is it like that? Why?" At this juncture
Arina Ivanovna comes into the room and enquires what the girls
are discussing so ardently. But the young lady no longer trusts
her and does not wish to tell her. Then Arina Ivanovna scolds
Plaything, raises the alarm and reports to the parents that Plaything is frightening the young lady and driving her to tears. The
parents come down and start an inquisition. This scene too is very
characteristic and shows what part this good lady and gentleman
who, by the by, are not bereft of the habits of educated society,
take in the upbringing of their daughter. The mother asks:

"Zinochka, what happened? What were you and Plaything talking
about? Come nearer and tell your Mama."
"We said that some people cry while other people are merry...."
"What did you say, my dear?"
The squiress was very much surprised, and the squire stared with wide
open eyes; but the young lady went on:
"That some people laugh while others cry."

The squiress and the squire glanced at each other and then both stared at the young lady.

"Come now, tell me, Mama," pleaded the young lady. "Tell me, why all this is."

She jumped onto her mother's knees, hugged her tightly, looked into her eyes and waited for the answer that she longed for, but the squiress said:

"Clever children never cry, my dear."

"But even clever children feel sad sometimes, Mama. Something hurts and you feel sad...."

But the squiress said: "Clever children are always merry, my dear."

"Oh, God, Mama, how you talk! Well, suppose it's only silly children who are sad and cry, but aren't you in the least bit sorry for them?"

"Silly children are punished, Zinochka, and they soon become clever," said the squire, rubbing his chin.

"Yes, our Zinochka is a clever girl," said the squiress. "She is never sad, she never cries. It's some muzhik who comes to the window who cries, it's not Zinochka. Zinochka is a clever girl."

With that they got up and went out. On reaching the door the squiress says to Arina Ivanovna:

"You frightened me, Arina Ivanovna. I wondered what on earth was the matter, but it turned out to be such nonsense that it is even hard to understand."

And there the matter ended; the young lady only heaved a deep sigh and tears appeared in her eyes....

These are the conditions under which a living soul languishes, thirsting for knowledge, for truth, and trying to solve for itself the riddle of life. When the young lady grew up somewhat they hired a governess for her: a quiet, good-natured German woman, very pedantic, and totally lacking ability. She did everything according to routine and obstinately refused to satisfy the inquisitiveness of her pupil, who was fond of running ahead and also of digressing. They could not get on together, and seeing that things were not going well the little German woman asked to be released. Her place was taken by a frivolous Frenchwoman, and she began to chat and tell stories, and in the beginning completely enchanted Zinochka and took control of the whole house. But even this Frenchwoman failed to satisfy the girl's inquisitiveness: she wanted to know the root and cause of everything, she wanted seriously to analyze and understand every single thing, but for Matilda Yakovlevna everything, of course, was light, pretty, superficial, and—empty. After a little while the young lady herself noticed this and cooled towards the Frenchwoman, stopped asking

her questions and became more and more pensive. Arina Ivanovna ascribed her boredom to the fact that Mademoiselle was
wearying her with lessons, but to this Zinochka answered sadly:
"But I don't know anything, I have not learned anything, how
could she have wearied me?" And she became even more pensive
and ended up, when she was over fourteen, by going out of her
mind. Hers was a sad and quiet lunacy—she was always absorbed
in deep reflection and wept, especially when she saw other people
weeping. Plaything tried to soothe her: "Stop crying," she said,
"you won't have enough strength to cry with everyone." To this
the insane girl answered: "But, Plaything, do you realize how
much a person is in pain when he cries? I do! I know what
pain he must feel!" Shortly afterwards, in this mental state,
she died.

We have purposely dwelt on certain features of this girl's
character and development in order the more clearly to indicate
the difference in the conditions which determine the direction of
thought and will among the educated section of society and among
the lower classes. Everybody will agree that there is little that
is serious in our methods of education, even in the best; they
provide little sustenance for the enquiring mind, they provide far
more unnecessary and unintelligible formalities and abstractions
than answers to the vital questions about the world and people
which rise in the minds of children at a very early age. Consequently, all of us who regard ourselves as educated have been
subjected, more or less, to that moral corruption and to that slow
spiritual strangulation that are [so vividly] depicted for us in
the scenes between Zinochka and Arina Ivanovna and with her
[kind] parents. To this we shall add that the external position
of very many people in the so-called educated section of society
is quite similar to the position of Zinochka: they have no need
to work themselves, they are able to order others about and exploit them for their own caprices [, they have a pretext for regarding themselves in some way superior to this mass of people
who appear to have been created only for the purpose of serving
them]. All this greatly demoralizes and debilitates a man, and
this is the true cause of the universal flabbiness, pettiness and
vacuousness about which serious people in our educated section
of society have been complaining [so much and for so long].

We shall make so bold as to utter a word of truth: whole generations [in this country] have lived to the end of their days without having done anything worth-while and proving only that they were unfit for anything practical precisely because their ideas and habits were always permeated with the ferment of feudal views, and from the very beginning, their whole lives were moulded by the serf system. [While oppressing and crushing only externally, it at the same time still more thoroughly crushed, internally and substantially, also those who wanted to live by oppressing others. It debilitated, vulgarized, corrupted them, made them heartless, and caused them to be far more pitiful, far more insignificant and unfit than those whom they exploited by their tyranny.... It is a good thing that opportunities for such exploitation have now passed away, otherwise, God knows to what it would have led both sides....]

Plaything's sad story continued even after the young lady's death, but we shall not deal with her at length any more—to the end of her days she remained the plaything of fate, and of the kind gentry whom she served. She wanted to arrange her life well and happily: she fell in love with Andrei, the carpenter who worked at the manor house, and he liked her too. They went to ask for the squire's permission to marry just at the time when the latter had sold his last estate, together with Andrei and Plaything. Their appearance only helped to remind the squiress that she was reluctant to part with Plaything, and she went to ask the new owner to allow her to keep the girl. The man consented. Plaything wanted to say that she loved Andrei, but the squiress protested in a pitiful voice: "Oh, oh, Plaything! Aren't you ashamed? Do you really want to leave us? Good God, how is that possible! Everybody is deserting us!" And she burst into tears. They led her to the carriage and put her in it; and they bundled Plaything in too, and they galloped off.... Andrei could only follow the retreating carriage with his eyes, his face as pale as death. The new squire was very cruel, not like the last one. Two months later Plaything learned that in her village "a misfortune happened.... Six men had been sent to the settlements.... Andrei was the sixth man...." And so vanished her last hope of happiness, the possibility of becoming, at last, something more than a "plaything."

In *Plaything* we have before us a person who is absolutely passive: constant sadness and longing—this is the only way in which she can protest against her unhappy fate. It is not surprising: let us remember that she is torn from her kith and kin, forcibly removed from the simple life of the people and hurled [into those still waters] where she is kept as a plaything, forced to be merry, and constantly intimidated and bullied. The simplicity and freshness of the first years of her life, the first impressions of her childhood, must be ascribed to the fact that in this environment she did not become a [despicable and] fawning [menial, talebearer and] troublemaker [like those "noble" hangers-on of the type represented by Vassilisa Peregrinovna in Ostrovsky's *The Ward*].

But in the very humility of the unfortunate ones who are compelled to humble themselves against their will we often see far more determination and energy than in the fussy searchings and tossing from one side to another in which even good people in this country spend their whole lives. To supplement the parallel we drew above, we shall now deal with Marco Vovchok's short story *Sasha*.

The story is a simple one: Sasha was brought from the village to be the squiress' parlourmaid; the squiress' nephew seduced her and later became so attached to her that he wanted to marry her. But as soon as he hinted at this Sasha's tresses were cut off, and she was locked up in a dark room.... The nephew went about weeping and praying, made desperate efforts, and at last secured Sasha's release, after vowing that he would make no attempt to marry her. After that everything pursued its normal course, except that Sasha was so grief-stricken that she began to hate everything around her and begged the squire to permit her to go into a convent where, soon after, she died. And he—"to this day visits her grave and prays there." He did not wish to marry, and always went about looking so sad: "No," he would say, "nobody can gladden my heart as my Sasha did, God rest her soul! May God be the judge of my uncle and aunt!..."

Even from this skeleton of the story we get a glimpse of the difference between these two people. But here are several particular features which depict the two characters even more clearly.

Sasha gave herself to the young man without reserve; she

merged her whole being with him and concentrated all her feelings
and strivings in her love for him. When the news of their love
for each other got abroad and people began to jeer at her for it,
she said:

"Well, if people want to laugh, let them! I love him. I am *his*! Why
should I worry about myself? Let him worry. If he's all right—I'm glad.
If people want to laugh, let them laugh; if it offends him, he'll know what
to do. I shall do as he says, obey his commands."

This argument is in perfect harmony with Sasha's position,
and it shows that she takes a very wise view of her relation to
the young gentleman. Having fallen in love with her, and having
enjoyed her favours, he thereby naturally became her intercessor,
her protector, became bound to her by common interests, and he
should have been the first to understand this had he been a man
of common sense and honour. Sasha regarded him as such, and
placed him on a level which he had not yet managed to reach
with all his education. In his heart he was a good and honest man,
although a thoughtless one. He loved Sasha very much and he
himself confessed to her:

"And yet I intended to deceive you, Sasha, to deceive you and then
abandon you—forgive me! I did not abandon you—I couldn't find the
strength to do it, because I loved you very much."

And indeed, he did not abandon her: he loved her to the end
of her days, and loved her also after she died. But his upbringing
and position were such that they gave him no opportunity seriously
to ponder over his duties and to act in the way that was dictated
by the demands of honesty, or even of his own heart. Sasha was
resigned to her fate; what, indeed, could she do in her position?
It was not her business; she had neither the strength nor the will
to do anything; *he* must arrange everything, and had he possessed
Sasha's heart and mind, he would not have troubled about the
insignificant obstacles that stood in his path, and would not, later,
have complained about his uncle and aunt. But the whole point
is that *such* a mind, *such* a character are not given to people in
his position. Sasha is externally enslaved; lift this yoke from her
and she will be capable of rising to any moral and intellectual
height you like. But the young man she loves lacks all inner independence, has no inner support whatever, and his whole being

is enslaved by the amusing trivialities which society prizes so
highly. He complains that when he was a child his father cowed
and frightened him; be that as it may, the main thing, after all,
is that he is reluctant to forego some of the advantages of his
position, advantages which, though insignificant, are such to which
he is already accustomed and which flatter his vanity. He is educated enough to understand to some extent the insignificance of
these advantages, but he understands this only theoretically, by
cold reasoning, in which the heart takes no part. This explains
why he can neither find the strength to fight nor resign himself
with dignity and firmness. Take, for example, his talk with Sasha:
"Tell me, Sasha, tell me, what shall I do?" he asks tearfully.
"I am suffering and my head is in a whirl.... Oh, Sasha, if
only I could marry you." "*Marry me, then*," says Sasha very
simply, realizing that there is nothing impossible about this. "But
what will people say?" he answers. "Just think, Sasha, what a
fuss everybody will make—my uncle, his wife, who is even worse
than he, all, all the relations! They will peck us to death, Sasha!
I wish I were dead." With that he burst into tears. But Sasha again
answers him simply: "Well, *let's die, if you want to*." She is ready
for anything; if she cannot live with him, she is ready to die with
him—death has no terrors for her.... But he, after weeping a
while, at last decides: "No," he says, "it's a *sin* to die by one's
own hand [(he is struck by a fit of piety!)]; better that I should
marry you, Sasha—*come what may*." And he bravely adds. "What
are they to me? Why should I be afraid of them?..." And, indeed, he has not even any expectations of a legacy from them,
and yet he utters his decision in a tone that would suggest that
he was performing some heroic deed. and that he attaches ever
so much more importance to it than Sasha does to her readiness
to die, which she expressed quite sincerely, and with downright
determination to carry it out. And what is the upshot of his
heroism? The upshot is that he goes to his aunt and uncle to ask
for permission to marry Sasha and says, after all "we are all
equal before God, Auntie," and then looks on tearfully while the
squiress, in his presence, cuts off his beloved's tresses.... It was
here that Sasha realized what he was. and when he came to her
cubbyhole later on she "was not glad and not sorry to see him,
but just felt sadder." On another occasion he went to his aunt to

demand something and strode off with such a bold step that Sasha's
friend was both overjoyed and frightened. But Sasha says to her:
"Don't get excited, my dear: he is not a thundercloud. . . . He has
gone to the squire, and he is brave while he's on the way; but
when he comes face to face with them, all the starch will go out
of him. I know him, believe me." And this is exactly what happened: the upshot of our hero's bravery was that he promised
his aunt that he would abandon all idea of marrying Sasha. . . .
In return for that promise Sasha was given her freedom. Her
friend again expressed the hope that "perhaps later on. . . ." But
by this time Sasha thoroughly understood her position, and understood it in all its details. This is the way she answers her friend:
"Put no hopes in him; he's too timid. It's not every kind of love
that one wants to show to people, my dear! If she's plain and
poorly dressed they keep her at home, in the corner. on the bunk,
and say: 'Sit down, my love, fondle me, but don't go among
people; they will condemn us and make the master ashamed.' "
And in answer to her friend's remark: "But he loves you," she
adds: "Oh, he loves himself more, I tell you." On another occasion, when her friend advises her to "go straight to him, teach
him what to do," Sasha answers: "You couldn't teach him even
if you spent all your life on it, my dear. This subject cannot be
learned." And thus, realizing that she had nothing to wait or
hope for, Sasha indeed did not wait long: she entered a convent,
and even there did not live long: that which had bound her to
life had vanished, and her vital strength vanished too. But *he*—
he still lives and constantly visits her grave. . . . [Why on earth
does he hang around there?. . .]

A similar picture, but with a somewhat different climax on
the male side, unfolds before us in the story *Nadyozha*. After
pondering over this story we understand still more clearly the
difference that distinguishes the feelings and actions of the common man from the feelings and actions of people who have been
corrupted by their unnatural upbringing and position. General
debility, morbidness, incapacity for concentrated and profound
passions, characterize, if not all, then, at all events, the majority
of our "civilized" brothers. That is why they are continuously
darting hither and thither, themselves not knowing what they need
and what it is they are sorry for. Their desire is so strong that

they cannot live without gratifying it, and yet they do nothing
to gratify it: their sufferings are so great that death is preferable
—but they go on living just the same, except that they assume a
melancholy air. This is not the case with the common man: either
he ignores, pays no attention to an object, and certainly does not
talk about his desires; or, if he becomes attached to anything,
if he decides, he does so vigorously, with concentration, and
pursues his object relentlessly. His passion is deep and persevering, and no obstacles daunt him when it is necessary to surmount
them in order to achieve what he passionately desires and has
deeply planned. If the object cannot be achieved, the common
man will not stand by with folded arms; at least he will change
his position, his whole way of life: he will run away, join the
army, enter a monastery: often he simply does not survive failure
to achieve an object which has permeated his whole being and
has become essential to his existence; if his physical constitution
is too strong and can stand more than is necessary for the extreme irritation of the nerves and the imagination—he does not
hesitate to commit suicide. This, too, serves to prove to us that
for the common, healthy man, once he has become conscious of
his personality [and of its rights], the barren, useless life of an
automaton [without principles and strivings] without meaning
and truth, a life like that led, for example, by Plaything's squire
and squiress and many others of the same type, becomes unbearable.

In *Nadyozha* we see a girl who falls in love with a peasant
lad and expects him to sue for her hand. Here we have the same
situation: the other girls in the village jeer at her, tease her about
her sweetheart, because they envy her: her Ivan is the finest lad
in the village—she bears everything and waits until he has settled
the matter. But he goes to another village and there he chums
up with a factory worker—they get him drunk and marry him to
a relative of this factory worker. Later he returns to his own village, wakes up, as it were, and realizes what he has done, but it is
too late. Here commence the sufferings of poor Nadyozha, whom
many jeer at, particularly Ivan's wife, a vivacious and shameless
woman. Bitter is Nadyozha's lot: her love is so great that she
cannot live without her loved one and, moreover, her nature is so
tender, delicate as we say—so the sneers and jeers hurt her pro-

foundly and cause her much suffering. Nor does Ivan find it easy: he ardently loves Nadyozha and, moreover, his conscience pricks him—he feels guilty before the girl whose life he has wrecked. Both suffer, but they suffer inwardly, concentratedly, silently: she does not complain to anybody, nor does he say a word to anybody, and they say nothing to each other, they see each other only at a distance. Once he wanted to stop her and express his grief, but she ran away from him; he watched her from a distance, and he grew thin, his face became waxen, and he became altogether changed. At last he could stand it no longer and one day he went to the house of Nadyozha's aunt and poured out his grief to Nadyozha, but all she could say to him was: "Try and forget that I am alive, don't torment, don't torture me, my love! . . ." At this juncture Ivan's wife, who had been watching her husband, burst into the house and a heated altercation took place; Nadyozha ran out of the house . . . it was a cold and rainy evening; almost out of her wits, Nadyozha stood pressing against the wicker fence until her aunt got the quarrelling couple out of the house and eventually found her. That evening was enough to crush her completely. She took to her bed that very same evening and never rose from it again. Ivan went about as if he were crazy; just before Nadyozha died, when she was lying unconscious, he hastened to her bedside, gazed at her, wept, and then took to his bed himself. "On Thursday Nadyozha was buried and on the following Wednesday Ivan too was carried to the graveyard. . . ."

This more than any other of Marco Vovchok's stories can be suspected of idealization: we are so accustomed to regard the peasant as a coarse creature who is incapable of feeling the *fine* sensation of love, tenderness, shame, etc. But it is doubtful whether we can fully trust our observation on this score; the common people, in general, are not eloquent about their feelings, but we are so accustomed to eloquence that we cannot easily discern the most powerful sentiment if it is not adorned with rhetoric. Moreover, the common people try to conceal from us even the little they would and could express to each other. We would be as justified in judging of the tender feelings of the peasants by their conduct in our presence as we would be in judging of the kindness and compassion of soldiers by their actions on the battlefield. We, unfortunately, must admit the justice of the observation—which, by the by, has long become a commonplace—that [the uniform and] the frock coat does not inspire the peasant with any particular confidence.

As far as one can judge from certain particular cases and negative symptoms, however, we are ready to assert that tender, delicate natures of this kind exist even among the lower class, at least to the same extent that they exist in other classes. It must be observed that, in general, natures of this kind are met with more rarely than we think. We often admire the tender charms of a young lady who is weeping over the death of a pet dog, or who goes into raptures over the art of some particular artist like Pavlov's *Strauss*. But this is not what constitutes true tenderness and delicacy. It must not be sought in vain regrets and rapture, but in genuine sensitiveness to the sufferings and joys of others. Before his mind can determine what conduct is demanded in a certain case, a person of delicacy will, at the first promptings of his heart, try to mould his actions in such a way that they will bring the most benefit and pleasure to other people, or at all events, will not cause anybody unpleasantness. The substance of delicacy lies in that it is a thousand times easier for the person who possesses it to suffer an inconvenience, or even misfortune, than to cause it to others. If he loses something that belongs to you, he will sell his last possessions, will leave himself without a kopek, to compensate you for your loss at all costs. If he has loaned you some money, and sees that you are in need, he will suffer want himself rather than ask for the repayment of the loan. If he himself has borrowed money he will not rest until he has repayed you. His chief thought, his chief concern, is not to hurt anybody, not to be a burden upon anybody. Indeed, such a man may not cause you any particular pleasure (and will certainly not cause you such pleasure if you do not in some way prompt him to do so), but on the other hand, he will cause you no unpleasantness. He is always sensitively watchful that he should not inconvenience you in any way, not bore you, embarrass you by his presence or by his demeanour towards you, etc. In its normal state, *i.e.*, when combined with an energetic character and a properly developed consciousness of one's dignity, such a delicacy is one of the highest virtues of man. It is then a combination of honesty, justice and a practical interest in the fate of one's neighbour.... But as a consequence of falsely directed upbringing [and of the distorted social system in general] the innate delicacy of tender natures, in most cases, receives a wrong development. It is well known that the principle of [blind] obedience to authority predominates in the educational system in this country, a principle which is capable of killing the active strength of the most energetic and proudest natures. But while these are still capable of fighting and, not infrequently, succeed in escaping from the moral yoke that is imposed upon them, the tender and fine natures always bend under this yoke and are very rarely able to rise. They are usually richly endowed by nature; a sensitive perceptiveness enriches them with numerous observations of a diverse kind at a very early age, and this facilitates the wide development of their minds and imaginations and provides sustenance for sincere striving. But nothing is so easy as to *stunt* these natures: reproach is worse for them than stern punishment is for others, ridicule is harder for them to bear than for others to bear abuse; an unsuccessful and severely condemned effort plunges them into despondency and causes them to give up. From childhood they may be told that they are stupid—and they will not argue in the presence of others. And it is not that they believe that they are stupid; no, in their heart of hearts they are convinced that they are more intelligent than many others, perhaps even all those around them, but their natural delicacy prevents them from expressing views which may, and do, seem stupid. "Why should people want to listen to what seems to them to be stupid," they think to themselves, and keep their thoughts to themselves. Later, even when they have entered the field of practical activity, when, in spite of themselves, they have shown what they are capable of, when they have entered another circle in which they meet not with disdain but respect, even then they cannot free themselves from the influence of their former impressions and remain far more taciturn, modest and patient than they ought to be. Their reason compels them to recognize their own worth, but they can rarely find the strength to vanquish their deep-rooted lack of self-confidence, which in many cases becomes transformed into sheer cowardice. They lack enterprise because they are always afraid that they will undertake something beyond their strength; they avoid all managerial work in order that their influence should not restrict others; they even refuse to appraise the results of their own activities properly for fear of elevating themselves too much and thus overshadowing the services of others. Thus, they are in constant conflict and antagonism with their own minds, they are always dissatisfied with themselves, always suffer from self-condemnation and, not infrequently, refuse a role in which they could be more useful than anybody else. Their passion for a thing must be whipped up very much indeed to prompt them to display vigorous and hazardous activity, in which it is necessary not only to give pleasure to others, but also to create unpleasantness for them and meet with considerable opposition. And it must be added, however, that even the passion of people of this type usually assumes a shade of timidity: far from being impulsive, their passion is chronic, prolonged, but quiet and reserved. This may be useful for the work in hand, but even here they get little pleasure out of it; all the time they are afraid that they will discredit themselves and their work and look ridiculous, they regret their lack of energy, mourn over their apathy, etc. Cool reason tells them that they possess both energy and passion to a sufficient degree and that they are by no means apathetic; but—cool reason influences them much less than they themselves think. Lack of self-confidence, which has permeated their natures, compels them also to distrust reason, and sensitive, morbid impressionableness gains the upper hand.

Thus, unfavourable circumstances may have an extremely unfortunate effect upon innate tenderness and delicacy: they can deprive their possessor of energy and drive him to despair. Let us now turn to the peasant world: who will not agree that circumstances that would foster the correct and full development of a kind and tender nature are found there only as rare exceptions? All the conditions of life in that world serve to coarsen and harden the strong nature, while the weak, tender nature is cowed, shrinks, and droops into submissive despair. This often happens, and here, we think, we can find the explanation of the two opposite opinions that are expressed about the Russian people, one—that they are wild beasts, and the other—that they are dumb cattle. And either of these descriptions may fit not only the Russian muzhik, but any man, no matter what class or nation he may belong to. Complete harmony of the feelings which, in psychology, are called sympathetic and egoistic, i.e., the complete and inseparable merging of self-sacrifice with self-preservation, has not yet been achieved in human society. That is why we meet everywhere with two categories of natures: some in which egoism prevails, a striving to impose one's influence upon others, and others' with an excess of devotion which prompts those natures to renounce their own interests for the benefit of others. If unhappily developed, the natures of the first category become hostile to everything that is *not theirs*, they forget about all rights, and become capable of performing every possible deed of violence; but the natures of the second category lose all respect for their own human dignity and permit others to bully them [, actually becoming something in the nature of a tame domestic animal]. . . . It must be admitted, unfortunately, that the two extremes are expressed ever so much more vividly among our peasant estate than among other classes of society. But has this become the nature of the common people? Can we really believe that the [taste for slavery,] habit of carrying somebody on one's back and of being driven has become the muzhik's second nature? And, on the other hand, are there really grounds for fearing that [those] muzhiks [who want freedom will without fail use it like brutes] will run amok as soon as they are left to their own devices? We do not think so, precisely because, all the warping of peasant development notwithstanding, we see among the masses of our people much of that which we have called "delicacy." [We are aware that many will think it strange to apply this word to the peasantry, but we cannot find a better expression. Humility, obedience, patience, self-sacrifice and the other qualities of our people that are praised so highly by Professor Shevyrev, Terti Philippov and other Slavophils of the same breed, are a miserable and ugly travesty of that beautiful quality of delicacy. But, forcibly created, this traversty is constantly sustained by artificial combinations of various kinds. As soon as life takes its natural course, however, the inherent qualities of man will also take their proper direction.] A man will not display brutality if he is not compelled to do so—everybody understands that: people nowadays have ceased to believe even that a snake will, without fail, sting a man for no reason, simply out of hatred for the human race; nevertheless, they believe in the existence of such mythical serpentine natures among men. [Similarly, it is wrong to believe

that there are sheep who regard it as an honour to fall into
the lion's maw, or that there are people who have a natural
fondness for having their noses pulled, or their faces spat into.
If we see that lots of people permit themselves to be subjected
to such experiments, you may take our word for it that they do
so for no other reason than that they are compelled to do so.
Hence, from this aspect, there is nothing to fear: the common
people's "delicacy," warped, stifled and converted into a weapon
against themselves, will take its natural direction at the very first
opportunity.]

But even in the present [warped] state of peasant life and
thought we see traces of the virile, good direction of this delicacy. In this we include, primarily, the consciousness to which
we referred above, and which is immeasurably more developed
among the lower class than among other classes [who are assured
of a constant income]—the consciousness that one must live by
one's own labour and not be a parasite. It is common knowledge
that all over Russia the word *"miroyed"** is one of the most
shameful epithets that one can use, and that it is applied not only
to the village elder, the *zemsky* or the *sotsky*,** but to every
muzhik who battens on the village community. The category of
people to which so many fine, educated young and old gentlemen
in large towns belong—gentlemen who for years and years live
very well by "sponging" with no definite source of income, and
in constant and also indefinite debt, can scarcely be imagined
among the peasant estate. The peasants, as a rule, entertain a
very true and wise opinion of people from their ranks who have
made large fortunes in various shady ways. We ourselves have
had occasion to speak with peasants who remember the careers
of certain well-known wealthy men who came from the ranks of
the common people: we not only failed to see any of that vener-
ation for wealth which is so customary among our enlightened
and "learned" people, but we heard very stern condemnation of
the means by which the millionaires we discussed acquired their
extraordinary wealth. It was evident from what the peasant said
that he was well aware of the means by which these fortunes were

---

* Village shark, a parasite.—*Tr.*
** Rural police.—*Tr.*

made, but that in his heart he loathed them and would not resort to them even if he had an opportunity to do so. It is said that our muzhiks are sly, and that they cheat us in the most outrageous manner to make an extra kopek when opportunity occurs. Yes, that too happens, although not as often as people say, and then it happens mostly in towns and in roadside or trading villages [which have many opportunities for aping the morals of the higher classes of society]. But it must be observed, firstly, what will want not force one to do! And secondly, the peasant resorts to deception and cheating mostly when dealing with members of other classes of society, towards whom he not only feels no kinship or solidarity, but, on the contrary, thinks he has a right to feel distrustful and hostile. As regards their fellow peasants, in their own society, the general opinion is that they are very honest. And this is not surprising: on the one hand, that it is necessary to work for one's livelihood is understood much more vividly, and is practised much more readily, among the common people than among the higher classes of society, the members of which are endowed with a sufficient stock of material comforts even before they are born; we discussed this at considerable length when we analyzed the story *Masha*. On the other hand, respect for the person and rights of others and, consequently, respect for public opinion, is also more developed among the common people [than among those whom fate has placed in a position that fosters indolence and caprice]. The manner in which people in the higher category cultivate disdain for the rights of others and substitute senseless, selfish willfulness for all law we saw in the young lady's upbringing that is described in *Plaything*. How they treat public opinion was shown us by the gentleman who gave up the idea of marrying Sasha out of fear of "what will people say? . . ." This fear can, of course, be ascribed to a good source—respect for public opinion; we see the same principle in operation also in the case of Nadyozha, for example. But if we examine both these cases more closely we shall find a big difference between them. We shall now say a few words [about this difference] to supplement the parallel we have already drawn between the common people and the "educated" people in our society.

Our [educated section of] society, as we know, has no equal for the indifference with which it looks upon public morality.

People notoriously dishonest, exposed and condemned, are received in [good] society as if they had never done anything wrong
in their lives. Hence, on visiting the house of a man who is well
known for his honesty, you cannot be in the least bit sure that
you will not meet people who are very very dishonest. In other
countries, even those which are not particularly famous for civic
heroism, there have been examples of people who, detected in the
embezzlement of state funds, suddenly found that nobody wanted
to dine with them, while others, if only suspected of such action,
became so depressed that they committed suicide. In this country
there is no need for such a drastic measure [and such demonstra-
tions cannot be expected]: public consciousness goes no further
than gossip. When at any ball or a [high society] party, at a
banquet, in any assembly where there is a fair number of people,
enter into conversation with the first chatterbox you come across
about other gentlemen you happen to catch sight of: my God,
what sordid stories [disgusting anecdotes] you will hear, and
what ugly scenes will be described to you about almost half the
company present! . . . This one climbed up in the world by back-
biting [and spying], that one dipped his hands into the state
coffers, that one is kept by a certain old woman who helped him
in his career; one engaged in smuggling [another was a pimp],
a third tyrannized over his peasants, a fourth is a confirmed
bribetaker, a fifth is a cardsharper. . . . Perhaps the chatterbox
you are talking to will exaggerate and lie a great deal: but the
remarkable thing is that all the people assembled in this place
have listened to chatterboxes of this kind on more than one occasion, know all that is said about every one present, and do not
even take the least trouble to find out whether the rumours are
true or false. "They say that all that he now has was stolen;
and indeed, how could he have come into all this wealth without
stealing? But, what business is it of ours? He gives splendid dinners, Prince so-and-so and General so-and-so visit him, and he
is doing well in the service; consequently, we need not turn up
our noses at him [and be ashamed of his acquaintance]." This is
the kind of argument you will often hear among us, and people
shake hands with scoundrels whom in their hearts they are ready
to despise [but dare not]. We do not wish here to enter into an
analysis of the causes of this state of [the educated section of our]

society, we shall put this off for another occasion. Here we shall simply note the fact that if public judgment of the moral worth of people exists amongst us at all, it is only in the form of gossip and talk which is of no practical value; public opinion is stern only in regard to accepted forms and proprieties. Violation of the latter is ruthlessly punished; people who are "not respectable" are given the cold shoulder; people who lack manners are not received in respectable society—unless, of course, they are very rich. . . . Thus, concern for all sorts of niceties fills our whole lives, determines all our actions, from the tying of the necktie and the hour of dinner, from the choosing of polite words in conversation and graceful bows—to the choice of an occupation, an object of friendship and love, and the cultivation of these and those tastes and inclinations. Not the substance, but merely the accepted and conventional form attracts general attention. But by what is the accepted form determined, what is the measure of its worth? [The degree to which it expresses the gentleman, in the bad sense of the term, i.e., tyranny and parasitism.] It is not respectable to be an actor—not because it is a useless occupation, but, you see, because an actor is a hired man, he performs all sorts of antics in public for pay, i.e., a man who, after all, does some kind of work to earn his living. Now that's the bad thing about it: a respectable man ought not to have to work to earn his living, he must be one of the soft white hand type [and a drone]; to work is the plebeian's job. . . . [It is not such an honour to serve in a regiment of the line as in the Guards. Why? Not because the Guards offer more opportunities to benefit the service, but mostly because the uniform is more splendid, and a Guardsman's equipment and maintenance, being more costly, at once reveals the man who can spend a lot of money. It is not respectable to joke with a servant—not out of fear that one's joke may accidentally offend a man who, because of his position, cannot retaliate, but on the contrary, out of fear that the servant may take it into his head to answer our joke with another, and thereby become too familiar with us. . . .] It is wrong to marry a girl from the ranks of the common people, not because she could not satisfy the aspirations of an educated man and understand his interests, but simply because she does not know our customs and would discredit us by her manners and conversation.

This is what all the fear displayed by the gentleman who dared not marry Sasha amounts to, although he loves her, is quite pleased with her, and cannot help seeing that she is more intelligent and purer than he and all his relations and acquaintances whose opinion he fears. . . .

Fear of public censure is different among the common people. It is true that they too have customs which everybody must obey; but failure to obey them does not rouse the whole of society against the offender. For example, a young man may shave off his beard; a poor man may go to work on his plot on Sunday instead of going to church—this will not be followed by persecution on the part of his fellow villagers. But on the other hand, real offences against morals will be very sternly condemned, and if the verdict of public opinion often has no serious practical consequences, the reason for it is that there is absolutely no possibility of putting the public will into action. As you ride into a village your coachman will catch sight of a muzhik whom he will at once start railing at and, in addition, hurl a few unkind epithets after him, calling him among other things Vanka-thief. You ask the coachman what it all means, and he will tell you all about Vanka's exploits, and from his story you will gather that Vanka is really a confirmed and incorrigible thief. "Why then, do you keep him in the village and allow him to remain at large?" you will ask. "What can we do with him?" the peasant will ask in turn. "We wanted to send him to the army, but they said he was unfit and they wouldn't accept him. . . . We have thrashed him more than once, but that didn't help. . . . So what can we do? We can't go to court about him." "But why not go to court?" "Ekh!" the coachman will exclaim and only wave his hand in disgust, not wishing to waste any words on the subject. [His exclamation and gesture will enable you to understand his position and to picture to yourself how much moral purity and firmness he must have not to become utterly corrupted by the different circumstances that oppress him.] It is not surprising that among the peasants too public opinion is often absurd, sometimes dishonest because of insincerity, and sometimes altogether hidden because of cowardice. We do not intend to contest this; we are even prepared to add that in all cases where it is necessary to canvass opinions in order to ascertain the state of the public mind we find far more confusion among the peasant estate than in any other because it is not accustomed to conduct its affairs according to its own wishes. But we assert one thing, namely, that there we will find more regard for human dignity, less indifference to what my neighbour is and what I seem to be to my neighbour. Concern for one's *good name* is met with more often there than among other estates, and in a more normal form. [It is well known that the natural desire to earn the good opinion of people often assumes the form of a morbid quest for a reputation, for the sake of which all sorts of abominable deeds are often committed. But this happens precisely among the members of the "educated" section of society who, having enriched their minds with all sorts of knowledge, see numerous goals and roads before them, but lack the strength to reach these goals; when it comes to taking the road, it turns out that they are very lazy.... Seeing that they cannot achieve the real, they begin to chase after appearances, as much as to say: I may not be rich, but let others say that I am rich— there's something gained at least in that. In ordinary language this hunting for a reputation is called simply deception, hocus-pocus, and cannot possibly be confused with the desire to have a good name. The latter is the direct result of good will towards men and respect for their personality. Developed to the extreme, it is transformed into obsequiousness, timidity, fear of one's own opinion—and this we often see among our peasants, the whole circumstances of whose lives lead to the notorious *meekness* that is lauded by the Slavophils. But at all events, at bottom and in substance] this sensitiveness of the people to public opinion [to a good name—] is one of the proofs of their capability of high [civic] development [on sound and just principles].

We have digressed from the story *Nadyozha*, which prompted our observations on delicacy, respect for another's personality and a good name as the expression of our neighbour's like or dislike for us. But we now revert to this story, and with it we want to demonstrate the difference in the views upon what is shameful and what is not shameful held by the common people and by so-called civilized society. Nadyozha suffers from the insinuations and jeers of her friends. She feels that she has lost her reputation; and yet, as is evident from the story, Ivan did not seduce her, did not do to her what in our common language is called "dis-

honouring" a girl. Ivan too suffers, and all the personages in
this story consider him to be exceedingly blameworthy, although he did not take advantage of the girl's love. Why do
they both suffer and grieve? What is it that is shameful and hard
for them to bear? According to our conceptions of life he has
no obligations towards her, she has in no way disgraced herself
before him, or before other people, for she has not allowed him
to do anything indecent to her.... Yes, but the conceptions of
the common people are different. We know that they show little
concern even for physical purity and so we say that rural morals
are very corrupt. Perhaps. But whatever you might think about
this, you must agree that there is a loftier and purer conception
of the moral aspect of the case in the despair of Nadyozha and
Ivan than in our ordinary judgments and habits. Nadyozha knows
that although she has preserved her physical virginity, her most
sacred, most intimate feelings have been outraged; he too knows
that he has poisoned the girl's inner world, has disturbed her
peace of mind and has desecrated the shrine of her heart by the
mere fact that he has drawn the immodest and jeering attention
of strangers to her secret. Let us now recall and compare with
this delicacy and humaneness the coarseness of an Andrei Kolo-
sov, whom his humane friends regard as being the best among
many!... And, indeed, he is better than others: most of the others
behave in the way Prince N. behaved in *The Unwanted Man*....

But why was Nadyozha ashamed of her feeling if it was so
pure? She was not exactly ashamed; she simply felt embarrassed.
She seemed to be influenced by the thought that all her friends
were angry with her because of the preference Ivan had shown
her, that they thought that she had lured him to herself and were
now laughing at her because her lures had failed.... The morbid
development of her fine and sensitive nature makes her excessively timid and suspicious: she regarded herself as a social outcast. Moreover, her dignity really suffered: suddenly she found
herself in the position of one who, for no reason whatever, is
publicly slapped in the face. Of course, if we examine it coolly
we shall find that this is really nonsense: in discussing the moral
virtues of a man we must enquire whether he deserved to be
slapped or not; whether he was really slapped or not is an entirely
different question, a question of might and not of right. But we ask:

are there many people in the educated section of our society who
could elevate themselves above a slap in the face and remain unem-
barrassed—not only if they themselves are undeservedly slapped,
but even if they have occasion to witness such an incident? ...

Scarcely any class, taken as a whole, can boast of the soundness and common sense of its public opinion. Nor can the common people boast of it: this very story *Nadyozha*, in depicting
the attitude of Nadyozha's friends towards her, demonstrates the
crudeness and fallacy of their judgment. This circumstance has
not escaped our attention, and we do not intend to justify it,
although we must say that false and ignorant concepts of this
kind are more excusable among the peasants than among the higher classes of society which claim to be educated. We have already
referred above to the numerous obstacles the peasant encounters
in his development, and to the amount of inner strength he needs
to guard himself against the complete suppression of his common
sense and clear conscience. And yet, in this situation, we still find
natures in which living human instincts burn, feebly and unevenly, perhaps, but unquenchably, so that if these instincts are insulted, or unsatisfied, the organism itself must die. Persons like
Nadyozha, who at first sight seem to be exceptional, turn out, on
a closer examination of the circumstances and character, to be
by no means as rare among the peasant estate as we are accustomed to think. We repeat, if delicate natures like Nadyozha's are
not more numerous among the common people than among well-
bred young ladies and gentlemen, then at all events they are
equally numerous.

Then there is that passive side, that passive role which such
natures play. Nadyozha is in herself a beautiful personality, but
she needs tender care, and if she gets this, you can expect kindness and tenderness from her. But the moment she finds herself
in adversity, she shrinks and hides, and you will get nothing
from her except bitter tears. ... Among the common people you
will find natures equally tender and kind, but more energetic and
more active. Such natures will also not seem mysterious to those
who do not entirely neglect the study of our common people. We
find one of these personalities in Marco Vovchok's story *Katerina*.

Katerina is also very sensitive to ridicule, reproaches and
even to simple jokes of the most innocent nature. When she was

still a little girl the squiress brought her from Little Russia to a
village in Great Russia; here everything about her seemed strange
—the language she spoke, her embroidered blouse and her lan-
guid and pensive manner. . . . The girls in the village began to
tease and laugh at her. It goes without saying that the little girl
could not clearly and definitely understand the meaning and dignity of everything she did; she could not, like some philosopher,
go on doing what she was doing and disdainfully ignore the jeers
of the mob; she could not but take to heart the teasing of her
friends. If she were a shrew she would have quarrelled with everybody and would have defended herself by force; but her delicacy, her instinctive respect for herself and for others, prevented
her from doing this. Consequently, she simply stopped doing
what seemed strange and comical to others. One day her friends
laughed at the embroidered sleeves of her blouse and she never
wore that blouse again. Another day her friends stole up to a
kurgan,* where she used to go alone, and heard her sing a Ukrainian song. They teased and asked her all sorts of questions—the
result was that she stopped going to the kurgan and never sang
that song again. . . . But in addition to this sensitiveness to every
outside impression, Katerina also possessed an inner strength which
imperatively demanded an outlet, which imperatively had to express itself in some kind of activity. For a long time the circumstances of life ran counter to Katerina's strivings: her mistress
took her to another estate in which she was a stranger; she was
given in marriage to a man whom she could not love. She did
not complain to anybody about her fate, she did not utter a word
about the way she was living, she did not even permit anybody
to pity her in her presence, and she did not quarrel with her
husband; she would "merely stand motionless before him with
downcast eyes, austere and stern. . . ." She wanted to find some
occupation, but there was nothing for her to do. She learned to
sing so well that one's heart was torn with yearning listening to
her. She was the first to be invited to weddings, at which she
sang sad songs and thus gave vent to her feelings. But this was
not enough: she found life so unbearable that she even took to drink.
One day her friend said to her: "Katerina, darling, don't drink

* Ancient burial mound.—*Tr.*

much! There are strangers here, and they will condemn you. Better sing to us!" And this is what she answered: "Oh, you people have no pity! You keep on telling me to sing, to sing; you don't give me a moment's rest! Let me rest! Let me drink and forget!" Evidently she found it hard to live without doing something, without being of some use. And so she would probably have ruined herself had she not, happily, found something to do: she heard of a witch doctor who lived near the village and she decided to ask her to teach her to cure sickness; even as a child she had been fond of examining and learning to recognize all sorts of flowers and herbs. This is the way the witch doctor herself describes Katerina's visit to her:

"She came to me and asked: 'How shall I live?' and she stared at me so hard that she positively frightened me. 'Live as all people live, my dear,' I said. 'No, you tell me how I should live!' 'Sit down,' I said, 'cross yourself and say a prayer: somebody's cast a spell over you.' She sat down, crossed herself and broke into tears. I had herbs hanging on the walls, and also on the windowsill, drying in the sun. 'What do you want all these herbs for?' she asked me. 'To cure people,' I said. 'Then cure me, my dear!' 'But what is the matter with you? Tell me.' 'My heart aches!' she said softly, and the tears rolled down her cheeks. 'And doesn't your head ache?' 'Yes, my head aches too; everything aches!' So I gave her some herbs; she bowed and went away. I took a nap, but in my sleep I heard a knock at the door again. It was she. She had come back. 'What do you want?' I asked. 'Tell me, my dear, what portions do you use for cures?' I got angry and told her to go, but she burst into tears, worse than before. 'If you won't tell me then kill me right here! I shall die anyhow.... Look,' she said, 'how much I am suffering—my life is so empty, I bring no joy to others, and nothing rejoices me, and there is nothing to do that I really like.' She's mad, I thought to myself, and I felt sorry for her. And so I told her a thing or two, more to soothe her than anything. She won't remember all this, I thought to myself! But she did remember everything, and later I heard that she had begun to treat patients. I was vexed and offended at the thought that she was robbing me of my livelihood. One day she came to me with her arms full of herbs. I did not welcome her at all kindly, but she pretended not to notice it. 'Do you know these herbs, Granny?' she asked. 'No, and I don't want to,' I says. 'But take them, I brought them for you,' she says. 'They are useful herbs, good for healing!' 'What have you tried them on? How do you know what they are good for?' 'I tried them on myself, Granny.' 'On yourself! What do you mean?' 'Oh, just like that,' she answers. 'I always try them on myself first, and if they do me no harm I give them to others.' That girl astonished me, it's God's truth! But she spoke in such a way that I couldn't help believing her.... And since then she has been bringing me all sorts of herbs. And I am grateful to her for rewarding me for having taught her."

And as soon as Katerina found "something to do that she really liked" she stopped drinking and became cheerful and kind. She became calm about herself, but other people's sorrows made her sad and gave her no rest. The first thing she asked her patients was whether they were in trouble. One sick woman said to her: "What is there to tell? Nobody can understand another's troubles." "What! I can't understand?" exclaimed Katerina. "Is my life not bitter enough? There is no trouble in the world that is not my trouble—all grief is my grief. If you lived as I lived, you would understand!" The sick woman was surprised to hear this, but remembering Katerina's husband, whom she refused to **fondle** and **love** no matter how much he loved her, she said by way of an answer: "But what about your husband?" This did not annoy Katerina. She merely thought for a moment and said: "And his grief is my grief too, but it is not my business to help him!... It was not my fault that I was thrust upon him; he acted unwisely." How vividly these simple words express the conscious, independent energy of Katerina's character!... She stands far higher than Plaything or Sasha, for example: she will not allow her heart to be dominated by others, she will not surrender herself to the one with whom fate had bound her against her will; she wants to love everybody, to see everybody happy, but she seeks free scope for her activity and her love. If she were taken forcibly and told: "Make this one happy, but not that one." her whole nature would revolt against this violence and, in spite of the abundance of love that fills her, she would not find the strength to obey this command. Her kind and tender nature urges her to devote herself to the welfare of her neighbours; but this voluntary service has nothing in common with renunciation of one's personality, with permitting oneself to become the plaything of another's caprice. No, her consciousness of her dignity, of her independence. is as strong as her consciousness of her kinship with people and of the duty of people to help each other in the common labours and cares of life. [All that she lacks to enable her to occupy a high place in the ranks of the finest personalities, whose memory is preserved in history and popular tradition, are favourable conditions for development and wider scope for activity.]

It is rare to find a person who has remained so free from the two opposite extremes—carrying generosity to the point of losing one's own freedom, and the egoistical exaltation of one's own personality to the point of forgetting the rights of others. It must be observed, however, that it is not only among the common people that such persons are rare; unfortunately, we see in all classes of society kind men who carry their kindness to the point of allowing everybody to order them about, and men who carry their self-esteem to the point of tyrannizing others as much as they possibly can. Under these circumstances, we often wonder at the moral qualities of some people only because they do not fawn upon or tyrannize others as much as they might do in the positions they occupy. Thus, we praise the good squire who does not exact an excessive quit rent from his peasants, the honest tavern licensee who sells tolerable vodka [the government official who, although he acts against his conscience by order of his superiors, manages to behave not too much like a flunkey] etc., etc. Compelled as we are to use this measure to appraise the moral virtues of people in our society, we ought to be very pleased when we see at least the possibility of the appearance of personalities like Katerina among the peasant estate. If the majority of people were like her, history, of course, not only ours but of the whole of mankind, would be entirely different from what it is. But important for us is the mere fact that beneath the heap of rubbish that has been blown upon our common people from different sides, we still find that they have sufficient vital strength to preserve the good human instincts and sound common sense and to force them to the surface. Often the shoots of innate strength are feeble, scarcely visible, and often wither before they push their way into the light of day, rarely are they able to withstand misfortune with the fortitude we saw in the case of Masha and Katerina. But the fact that the elements which are so vividly expressed in these two women can be observed among the people even if only to a slight degree is already of great importance. That we will see them if we study the life of the common people with attention and love —we can safely guarantee. Then it will no longer be difficult for us to understand why, in most cases, the development of these elements among the people stops so early and is often quite stifled; nor will it be difficult to understand to what extent the common people themselves are to blame for the incompleteness, or total cessation, of their development, and to what extent all we who count ourselves among the educated are to blame for it. If we do take the trouble to ponder over this, we shall inevitably arrive at the question: what must we do to remove as much as possible that which so frightfully hinders the development of the good qualities of the people?

We shall not stop to answer this question here; it is immeasurably easier to deduce this answer for oneself than to formulate it intelligently [in a Russian book: that may lead to no end of trouble!]. But we can here turn the readers' attention once again to the idea, the development of which is the main object of this essay—the idea that the common people are as capable of displaying all sorts of lofty sentiments and actions as the people of any other estate [if not even more], and that a strict distinction must be drawn between the consequences of the external oppression they have to bear, and their inner and natural strivings, which have by no means been stifled, as many think. Whoever sincerely accepts this idea will feel more confidence in the common people, will be more eager to come closer to them in the full hope that they will understand wherein their welfare lies, and will not renounce it out of laziness or cowardice. Imbued with this confidence in the strength of the people and hope for their good will, one can influence them straightforwardly and directly [in order to rouse strong fresh forces for real action and to protect them from the distortion to which they are so often subjected under the present order of things.

This distortion causes much suffering to the unfortunate ones but in most cases it benefits those who have been placed over them, those who own them]. But [it must not be forgotten that sometimes things turn in the opposite direction:] not all natures are soft and yielding like those of Sasha or Nadyozha, not all are as firm and sensible as Katerina, not all are stubbornly opposed to evil like Masha; we meet with other natures, stern and ruthless, whose inner reaction towards every encroachment upon their personality develops to truly formidable dimensions and assumes an aggressive character. We were prompted to think of this circumstance (which, incidentally, must on no account be lost sight of) by the character of Yefim in Marco

Vovchok's story *A Merchant's Daughter*. We have not yet said anything about this story; we shall deal with it now and finish our essay which, to our own surprise, has grown to such an incredible length.

Yefim is a muzhik, the squire's coachman, a tall, dark, bearded fellow with rosy cheeks, flashing eyes, a fine proud face and a merry but ironic smile. The squiress hires a parlourmaid, Anna Akimovna, a poor merchant's daughter. Yefim takes a fancy to Anna Akimovna the very first time he sets eyes on her, and at that very first encounter she offends him: she walks past without even glancing at him, and barely mumbles a word in answer to his first question. Her haughtiness touches him on the raw, and he begins persistently to persecute her, determined at all costs to subdue and possess her. He causes her a great deal of unpleasantness in numerous ways; they constantly quarrel, and yet they take an increasing interest in each other. A year went by; the other servants in the house noticed that Anna Akimovna was always turning the conversation on Yefim. It was always: "Yefim has gone to get the horses shod; Yefim sings well; it's time Yefim got married, I wonder whom God will send him for a bride?" This is what the servants said in the presence of Anna Akimovna, but she said nothing, she merely listened and did slyly try to turn the conversation in that direction. Misha, the cook's boy, saw through Anna Akimovna's cunning and told Yefim about it. Anna Akimovna guessed that Yefim knew something and they had a real quarrel. Anna Akimovna threw up in Yefim's face that he was a muzhik.

"You've grown too conceited, too conceited!" Anna Akimovna burst out at him. "Let you sit at a table. . . You've forgotten who you are. . . . A fine lord, to be sure! . . . What do you think you are?"

Yefim stood in front of her shaking his head:

"What princely family do you come from?"

"How dare you compare yourself with me? You've got no shame! My father was a merchant, he had his own business. . . ."

"Ye-e-e-s, ye-e-e-s! We know all about that! Suppose you are merchants. You only know how to cheat. Why, only yesterday I bought a kerchief. How that wicked kinsman of yours swore that it would never wear out. But look at it, it's full of holes!"

And saying this he calmly unfolded the kerchief; she stood there pale and trembling.

33*

"I'll complain to the mistress about you!" she screamed. "Don't dare mock at me, you stupid muzhik!"

"Here, what do you mean!" exclaimed Yefim in feigned astonishment.

"Yes—you're a stupid muzhik!" screamed Anna Akimovna.

Yefim looked as if somebody had stroked him the wrong way; he tossed his curly hair and stroked his beard.

"Wait a minute, wait a minute," he began, restraining his vibrant voice. "You say I'm a muzhik. . . . Well, I admit it. I am a muzhik. And it's not long since I came from the village. I admit that too. I ploughed and sowed, provided for my own needs and had enough to sell, and dealt honestly with people, kept friendly with them. I'm good-tempered. But you. Anna Akimovna, a merchant's daughter, what have you got to boast about? What if you have a pretty face? That's not worth anything. The important thing is your heart, your temper. You are quarrelsome; too much of a shrew. . . ."

"How dare you?" she squealed. But he kept on:

"You are no longer young, but nobody shows you any respect. . . . No matter what you may call yourself, no matter how much you show off, people pass you by and don't even ask: who is this Anna Akimovna?. . . My father tilled the soil and everybody will say: 'He was a good muzhik, was the old man!' But nobody has a good word to say about your father even if he did wear coats lined with fox fur."

They quarrelled very seriously and stopped talking to each other, except that they teased each other at mealtime. Meanwhile. both grew thin and pale, and were sad and pensive when alone. At last Yefim decided to do something about it. One day, after Anna Akimovna had been making fun of muzhiks and muzhik ways for a long time, Yefim exclaimed: "Ekh, little mother. Anna Akimovna! And yet, I a muzhik, wanted to sue for your hand. I thinks to myself: although she's not over clever, she's stuck up and a shrew, still, she can trail behind the baggage cart." Anna Akimovna flared up and trembled with passion, but he went on: "Take care, little mother, don't get so excited, something might happen to you. You needn't be afraid about my proposing to you now. It was just a silly idea that had entered my head, but it's gone now. Every man should know his place. I shall find somebody who's my equal." And, indeed, after that Yefim would dress in his best clothes and leave the house every day; and he would come back singing in a very merry mood. Anna Akimovna calmed down and waited to see what would happen. One evening Yefim came into the servants' room and announced that he was going to the squiress to ask her permission to marry. He then turned to the merchant's daughter and said: "And you, Anna Akimovna,

I hope you will let bygones be bygones and be kind to my intended wife. She's a nice girl!" Anna Akimovna's face paled and her
lips trembled. She left the room, hid herself in a nook on the
staircase and wept bitterly; she wept for a long time and did not go
down to supper.... When Yefim was told about this he rushed
to her, took her in his strong arms and kissed her.... She gasped
with astonishment, glanced at and recognized him, and then threw
her arms round his neck and wept and wept....

He picked her up and carried her out of that nook. She struggled
to get out of his arms, but he would not let her go; he put her down in
the moonlight:

"Aha, merchant's daughter, Anna Akimovna!" he said. "Now you are
mine!"

And he said it in a tone that sounded as if he had vanquished his
bitter enemy; meanwhile, two tears rolled down his cheeks and there was
such a malicious smile on his lips! It was terrible and amazing to look at
him then.

They got married. From the very first day of the marriage
celebrations Yefim began to play pranks on his wife to tame her.
He urged her to invite her friends and distant relatives—merchants'
wives and daughters—to her spinster's party and to the wedding.
She did so. He did not invite any of his relatives to this party,
and Anna Akimovna was very glad; she was very much afraid
of uncouth guests, and every time the door opened she turned
pale, but no uncouth guests came; merchants' daughters alone
sat round the table cracking nuts. Next day, however, on returning from the altar, the young couple was met with bread and
salt by a little muzhik in bast shoes and a threadbare peasant coat.
When they opened the door they found their house full of muzhiks
in bast shoes. Anna Akimovna staggered and she could only
whisper: "Villain!" The merchants' daughters shrank back and
pouted their lips; Yefim told them not to be haughty and sit down
to enjoy the wedding feast, but they turned their backs on him
and faced the wall, whereupon Yefim flung the door wide open
as a hint for them to go.... Anna Akimovna was so overcome
by this incident that next day she fell seriously ill. Yefim became
sad and despondent and sat at her bedside for whole nights gazing
at her; but even then he was stern with her, and only once did
he tenderly urge her to take a cure. She only turned her back on
him. After that he became still more stern; and when she recov-

ered he made her life a misery, paying her out for her former pride. "Yes, Anna Akimovna," he would say, "you ceased to be a princess when you married me! What a terrible mistake you made—simply awful!" She never uttered a word; he would glare at her as if she were his fiercest enemy, and sometimes he would say with an ironic smile: "Nettles grow with stings, but even they can be boiled soft!" She withered and pined away under his torments, but he himself suffered too: he aged, his face became wrinkled, all his merriment left him, his smile became sardonic and his conversation bitter and caustic. . . . Anna Akimovna did not hold out long; she died in the autumn, quietly and without pain. Yefim was not at home at the time: the squiress had sent him on some errand. When he returned he found her laid out on the table—he stood stock-still without uttering a word, and "he stood there all night; he didn't move, didn't utter a sigh. Next morning he went to buy a coffin, went to the priest to arrange for the funeral service and dug his wife's grave with his own hands. Guests were invited to the funeral. The man seemed to be quite calm, but there was something menacing in the air; your heart felt, told you, that something terrible was going to happen. . . ." And indeed, something terrible did happen.

They carried Anna Akimovna to the graveyard and buried her in the cold damp earth. The people returned from the graveyard; a commemoration dinner was given and Yefim himself saw to all the arrangements. When all the guests had left he took the horses to be watered. As he went out he said to Misha:

"Listen, Misha, and remember! In case I die, I leave all my property to my wife's aunt; let them give her everything. Did you hear what I said?"

Misha was scared to death.

"Yes, I heard," he said.

"Well, don't forget!. . ." And he galloped off.

Misha ran into the servants' room trembling all over.

"Yefim wants to do away with himself!"

Everybody was startled: they ran to the river. They found all the horses tethered to the willow trees at the foot of the bank, but of Yefim there was not a sign. . . . They called and searched for him and at last they found his cap near an old, disused well. . . . A long time ago a girl was drowned in this well—there was no bottom to it. Near that well they found his cap. They called men with boat hooks, and amidst a lot of shouting and talking they fished Yefim out. He was dead.

Everybody will doubtless discern in Yefim the features of the purely Russian character, and moreover, a character not ironed out by education, i.e., the character that one usually finds precisely among the common people. This stubbornness, this inability peacefully to forget and forgive, this senseless urge to nag a person continuously and without respite, while at the same time feeling a strong attachment to him—all these are features which the host of his detractors and the party of his quasi defenders readily ascribe to the Russian. His quasi defenders will, of course, discern in this a magnificent spirit, will find the prototypes of characters like these in Ivan Grozny and Peter the Great, and sometimes, in order to draw parallels, will even disturb the repose of the austere and virtuous Spartans and ancient Romans. We confess that the worthy defenders of the Russian people go a little too far. It is rather difficult for a man who is not heartless to admire a character like Yefim's. But there is one thing that cannot be denied him, namely, strength; and there is one thing that cannot but be admitted, namely, that it is dangerous to play pranks with this strength.

Indeed, see how frightfully he avenged himself upon Anna Akimovna for offending his pride ! And how fatal and inexorable was this vengeance! If he had simply planned, and had coolly carried out his plan—to induce the girl to marry him—it would have been a miserable intrigue, testifying only to his heartlessness and malice. But this was not the case: he actually loved the girl, and that is why her disdain offended him so deeply; in striving to win her love he responded to the promptings of his heart rather than to the voice of vengeance; he could not have wanted to ruin her— this is proved by the fact that he could not survive her death. But some power drove him to go on cruelly insulting her. This power was savage, unreasoning, fatal to himself; but he was not strong enough to resist it because hostile circumstances prevented the humane and reasonable demands of nature from developing in him sufficiently. Victory over the proud woman gave him twofold pleasure—the satisfaction of his pride and the winning of her love, for which he had been striving. But his malice was stronger than love, he was too proud and self-confident to set too high a value to the woman's love he had won. But the insults she had inflicted upon him had sunk deeply into his heart, and he could neither forget nor forgive them. No submission, no sacrifice could placate him; he himself suffered, some kind of longing oppressed him and he became more and more gloomy as he wreaked his vengeance upon his beloved wife; but he could not stop. A sort of insatiable, infinite desire to humiliate her was roused in him, a desire to make her suffer for what he himself had suffered, to trample upon her as if desiring in this way to restore his own rights which had been trampled upon, his own dignity which had been degraded and despised. His whole conduct is explained by that general law of reaction by which one extreme always calls forth another. For many years Yefim went on living without giving a thought to his [human] dignity and bearing the numerous humiliations connected with his position. But one day his dignity received a particularly painful blow in collision with a woman he had taken a liking to and whose position he regarded as being equal to his own; the bitterness of the insult roused his consciousness; and once having pondered over his humiliation, having felt it, he strove to raise his own dignity with all the energy inherent in his nature. His marriage to Anna Akimovna was not enough for him; he could not clearly grasp the significance of the step which the "merchant's daughter" took in marrying him, a muzhik; in order fully to feel his victory he had constantly to remind her of it, he had constantly to exercise the rights of the victor over his victim. However much he insulted her, however much he cowed her, however much he tormented her, it all seemed to him inadequate. She humbly and tacitly confessed her impotence, admitted his right over her, but it still seemed to him that he had not yet sufficiently proved his dignity to her and restored it in her eyes. That is why his vengeance was senseless, instinctive, painful to himself, and unable to find satisfaction, became a condition of his life. While he was dying he was probably thinking that he had not yet sufficiently asserted himself, and if his wife were resurrected he, no doubt, would start all over again, at the very first opportunity. After all, reason was beginning to awaken in him during her illness—he tenderly urged her to take a cure; but she turned her back on him, and he became still more stern and merciless.

There is little of the greatness of spirit here, of course; but it cannot be denied that a nature which acts in this manner possesses a strength which, if cultivated and directed differently, could have assumed a more rational human character. To this we shall add that this strength is by no means the exclusive possession of a few natures; it is fairly widespread among our common people. Circumstances do not favour its correct development and exercise; that is why it manifests itself mostly in monstrous, lawless and even criminal actions. This cannot be praised, but it is possible, after all, to draw a distinction between what in these shortcomings and crimes is produced by the external pressure of circumstances and what by a man's very nature. What results from the outside circumstances which surround our common people? What character must their position communicate to all their inclinations? Hardly anybody [among the most ardent champions of the plantation system] will assert that the conditions under which our peasants live can facilitate the development of straightforwardness, strength [civic courage], etc., among them. It is a fact that needs no proof, that the entire environment and upbringing of our common people has led, to a greater or lesser degree, to the development of the vices and weaknesses which [inevitably] accompanies [slavish, or feudal in general] oppression—flattery, deception, obsequiousness, corruption, indolence, theft, etc., in general, all those vices in practising which one must act clandestinely, stealthily, but not openly to employ strength, not go straight forward and look danger in the face. . . . And yet, in spite of all this, see how much of this element of energy and courage has been preserved among the people! We shall not here point to the valiant deeds performed by our peasants in saving those who are perishing in fire or water, we shall not remind the reader of their courage during bear hunts, or, say, during the last war. Whatever all facts of this nature may prove, we shall leave them aside; we have referred to vices and crimes and, therefore, without leaving this groove, we shall point only to the statistics of crime among the lower classes of our people. Read at least the reports on this subject in the now defunct *Russki Dnevnik*, or in the present *Severnaya Pchela* and try to visualize what the predominating character of these crimes is. You will be amazed if you are accustomed to regard the Russian people as being only rascally, and in all other things—weak and apathetic: you will meet with southern passions at every step, bloody scenes caused by love and jealousy, poisoning, throat-cutting and arson; cases of vengeance of the most brutal kind will continuously meet your eye in these reports [; and we know how much they like to report things in our country, and how much, as a consequence, fails to reach the public about what goes on]. . . .

What is the conclusion to be drawn from this? We think it is possible to draw only one conclusion: the people are not stagnating, have not become degraded, the source of life has not dried up among them; but the strength which lives in them, finding no free and proper outlet, is compelled to force an unnatural way for itself and manifest itself instinctively, noisily, overwhelmingly, often in a way fatal to itself. Needless to say, this is bad; how desirable it is that the strength of the people should be better directed and be beneficial and not harmful to themselves—this too requires no explanation. But, unfortunately, it is still necessary to convince many that the people possess this strength, and that the bad or good direction it takes depends upon the circumstances of the people's lives and not upon the alleged fact that the masses of our people belong to some special breed which is capable only of apathy or of brutality. There are still no few gentlemen in the educated section of society who think nothing of accusing a whole people of being unfit for [civic life and] independent government, just as there are no few who are ready to defend the people so vigorously and to ascribe to them such lofty sentiments that, listening to them, one can only bewail the destruction of our national virtues. We think that it would be extremely useful for both these categories of gentlemen to ponder deeply over Marco Vovchok's book of stories. It was to help them in this difficult process that we have attempted in this essay to analyze some, the most interesting, of the features of the life of the people which are very clearly and vividly depicted in *Popular Stories* but, if read hastily and superficially, may not have roused the reader's attention to the degree that they deserve. In order to widen the scope for judging the qualities of our people, we have also tried to draw several parallels between the people of lower calling and those of the society which calls itself educated on the grounds that, having mastered five or six brain-racking sciences within the scope of German high-school courses, and even then only barely mastering them, and having plunged into an immature cosmopolitanism, they have broken off connection with the people and have lost the ability even to understand the main features of their character. We have not found much that is superior in this society as regards moral virtues; we have not found much that would entitle it to elevate itself particularly above the common people. Without going too far, only by analyzing in greater detail a few of Marco Vovchok's stories which are so true to Russian life, we found that the unnatural feudal relationships between the people and the higher classes which have existed up till now, while being materially and morally harmful for the peasants, have been even more fatal for the serfowners themselves. To people in the position of Plaything's master and mistress they have evidently brought some external benefit. But, because of this, they, in all their absurdity and inhumanity, contaminated the souls of these ladies and gentlemen, became the foundation of their morality, expelled sound ideas from their minds and made them totally unfit for anything— whereas the same relationships affected Masha, Katerina, Nadyozha and all those in their position, more externally, did not penetrate them inwardly, precisely because they have always been so hard and unpleasant. True, among this class of people too the serf system has caused a considerable distortion of concepts and strivings: in the case of Nadyozha and her friend, of downtrodden Plaything, and of cruel Yefim we have seen how the development of the finest elements, of the most natural requirements, often take a wrong direction. But at all events this effect is not direct but indirect, not positive but negative, and mainly, this wrong development of the natural elements brings the poor no benefits whatever, not even external. They may be compared with people who are compelled to eat bread mixed with chaff: the consumption of such food for a long time, of course, affects the organism and ruins its health; but hardly anybody will assert that because a man has eaten bread adulterated with chaff for many years he becomes incapable of eating pure bread. [On the contrary, those who benefited by the former serf system, and from all the social relationships which resulted from it, may be compared with gourmets whose stomachs have been weakened and made tender by the subtle inventions of the culinary art: it is clear, firstly, that they will cling to their choice dishes much more tenaciously than the poor man will cling to his chaff; and secondly, if they are compelled to eat coarser food, they are more likely to perish from it than the poor man who changes from chaff bread to pure bread....]

After reading our fragmentary and disjointed observations [(which will appear to be even more disjointed in print than they do in the manuscript)] some people will, of course, say that there is nothing new about them and that they need not have been written, while others will say that what we have written is unfounded, exaggerated and improbable. The majority of people who are fond of literature will say that there is no *criticism* whatever of Marco Vovchok in the essay. We are accustomed to hear remarks of this kind and, we think, we have on more than one occasion already explained what we regard as the task of the critics of Russian literature. But it will be appropriate here to say another few words on this subject in concluding this essay.

We said in the beginning that Marco Vovchok has not given us a poem on the life of the people, that in his stories we get only hints, sketches and not complete, finished pictures. Consequently, there was no need for us to attempt to determine the absolute-aesthetical merits of the *Stories*. It was necessary to show how clear, vivid and truthful these sketches are, and the degree of importance of the phenomena of life with which they deal. This is exactly what we set out to do: we have analyzed the characters which Marco Vovchok portrayed, described the circumstances which determine their proper or false development, recalled the real state of affairs in Russia, and have stated to what extent, in our opinion, the author has portrayed the Russian characters truthfully and vividly, and how great is the significance of the phenomena with which he dealt. The conclusion we arrived at was that Marco Vovchok's book truthfully portrays the realities of Russian life, that his stories deal with extremely important aspects of the life of the people, and that in his slight sketches we discern strokes which reveal the hand of the skilled artist and a profound and serious study of the subject. To confirm these conclusions we entered into a rather lengthy discussion of the qualities of our common people and of the various conditions of our public life. We now leave it to the reader to decide whether, firstly, we have correctly interpreted the meaning of Marco Vovchok's stories, and secondly, whether our observations concerning the Russian people are just, and to what extent they are just. By deciding these two questions the reader will at the same time also decide for himself the question of the merits of Marco Vovchok's book. If we have distorted its meaning, or have said what is untrue about the life of the people, *i.e.*, if the scenes and persons described by Vovchok do not portray the Russian people as we have tried to prove, but simply relate exceptional and curious cases of no importance at all, it is evident that the literary merit of *Popular Stories* is absolutely insignificant too. If, however, the reader agrees with the opinion we have expressed about the book under review, if he admits that the features that we have pointed to in Marco Vovchok's book are general, and of great importance, then it goes without saying that he cannot help admitting the high merits of the literary production which so many-sidedly, vividly and truthfully portrays the life of the people, and which peers so deeply into the soul of the people. Thus, our literary-critical object will be achieved without the aid of aesthetical fog, which is always very boring and barren.

As regards the other object which we had in mind in this es- say—it too is not alien to literature. It was with the aid of Marco Vovchok's book that we wished to attract the attention of the people who write about the external conditions and inner qualities of the people [who are now ready to enter the new period of their lives]. Up to now we have heard the most contradictory opin- ions about our common people and—it is no use hiding it—it was the [most] ignorant and hostile opinions that were expressed loud- est of all. Literature, however, which by its very nature should be the vehicle of enlightened and not of ignorant ideas, has done very little on the question which is now immeasurably more im- portant for us than not only poetical descriptions of various spe- cies of roses, or lectures on the Sanskrit epic, but even of all the merits of Madame Svechina.[114] Our literature can boast of names like that of State Councillor Grigori Blank, Master of Arts Nikolai Bezobrazov, Count N. Tolstoy, Orlov-Davydov, and so forth, and we can recall opinions such as that education spoils the muzhik, that the rod is needed to maintain order among the people, etc. But we shall find few people who have with love and knowledge tried to portray for the public the virtues of the people and to champion their [full] right to share in all the benefits of civic life. Many have protested against obscurantism and the rod; but even here the most brilliant essays have been written from the point of view of the abstract right and the general demands of civilization [and there has been scarcely a single essay which has intelligently discussed the question as to what extent, and under what conditions, *our people* can dispense with the rod and suffer no harm from education]. It is evident, unfortunately, that our literature has yet little in common with the people. The fate of Marco Vovchok's stories is additional proof of this; they have been known to the public for nearly two years since their appearance in *Russki Vestnik*; at the beginning of this year they were published in book form, but to this day our magazines have barely said "a few cordial words" about them owing to magazine routine. But during this time the magazines have been filled with profound arguments about first love, the artistic merits of Mr. Nikitin, the morality of Helena in *On the Eve*, and similar stuff. One critic did start out to say something about Marco Vovchok, but he only succeeded in proving his utter inability to discuss a subject so far beyond his intellect.... [Is our literature really doomed to remain forever in the narrow little sphere of a banal society which is stirred by the petty passions of the card table, love for official decorations, and fear to wish for anything passionately and strongly?] Is it only this cheap "education," which transforms a man into a trained parrot and palms off on him the routine maxims of [out-of-date] authorities of every kind in place of the living demands of nature—is it only this education that will always pose before us in the best productions of our literature and engage the attention of our talented publicists, critics and poets? Is it not high time that we turned away from these withered and emaciated products of a civilization which has proved a failure to the fresh, sound shoots of life among the people, to assist their correct and successful growth and blossoming, and to guard their splendid and abundant fruits so that they shall not be spoilt? [Events are calling upon us to do this,] the murmur of life among the people is reaching our ears, and we must not miss a single opportunity to pay heed to this murmur.

Readers who admit the truth of these observations will—we hope—[understand and] forgive the length of our essay.

A RAY OF LIGHT IN THE REALM OF DARKNESS*

THE THUNDERSTORM A DRAMA IN FIVE ACTS
BY A. N. OSTROVSKY,
St. Petersburg 1860[115]

SHORTLY before *The Thunderstorm* appeared on the stage we reviewed in great detail all of Ostrovsky's works. In our endeavour to appraise the author's talent, we at that time drew attention to certain phenomena in Russian life which are reproduced in his plays, tried to grasp their general character, and ascertain whether the meaning they convey to us in the works of our dramatist holds good in real life. Our readers will perhaps remember that we then arrived at the conclusion that Ostrovsky possesses a profound understanding of Russian life and great skill in depicting sharply and vividly its most important aspects. Soon after *The Thunderstorm* served as fresh proof of the correctness of our conclusion. We were prompted to discuss this play immediately after it appeared, but we realized that we would have to repeat a great deal of what we had already said, and so we decided to say nothing and to leave it to our readers who were interested in our opinion to take the play as a test of the correctness of the general observations about Ostrovsky that we had given utterance to several months before it appeared. We were strengthened in our decision when a whole series of long and short reviews of *The Thunderstorm* appeared in all the magazines and newspapers, commenting upon the play from the most diverse points of view. We thought that these numerous comments would at last contain something more about Ostrovsky and the importance of his plays than we had seen in the reviews we mentioned in the beginning of our first essay on "The Realm of Darkness."** Hoping that this would be the case, and believing that we had expressed

---

* *See* Essays on "The Realm of Darkness" in *Sovremennik* Nos. 7 and 9, 1859.—*N. D.*
** *See Sovremennik* No. 7, 1859.—*N. D.*

our own opinion on the meaning and character of Ostrovsky's productions fairly definitely, we thought it best to refrain from making any comment on *The Thunderstorm*.

Now, however, meeting with Ostrovsky's play in a separate edition, and recalling all that had been written about it, we think it would be by no means out of place for us to say a few words about it. It provides us with the occasion to add something to our comments on "The Realm of Darkness," to amplify some of the ideas we then gave utterance to and, incidentally, briefly settle accounts with certain critics who, directly or indirectly, had subjected us to abuse.

We must give some of these critics credit for understanding the differences between us. They reproach us for adopting what they think is a bad method of reviewing an author's production and then relating what it contains and the nature of its contents on the basis of that review. They employ an altogether different method. They first of all tell themselves what the production *should* contain (in their opinion, of course) and then determine to what extent it actually contains (again in their opinion) what it *should* contain. Naturally, with this difference in our points of view, they express indignation at our reviews, which one of them describes as "looking for the moral of the fable." But we are very glad that the difference between us has at last been discovered, and we are willing to stand any comparison. Yes, if you will, our method of criticism is something like looking for the moral of the fable: it will differ in its application to Ostrovsky's comedies, for example, only to the extent that comedies differ from fables, and to the extent that the human life depicted in those comedies is more important and nearer to us than the lives of the asses, foxes, reeds and other personages that figure in fables. At all events it is far better, in our opinion, to analyze a fable and say: "This is its moral, and this moral seems to us to be good, or bad, and for the following reason," than to decide at the very outset that the fable should contain such and such moral (respect for parents, for example), and this is how it should be expressed (for example, in the form of a young bird which disobeys its mother and falls out of its nest); and then go on to argue that this condition is not adhered to, it contains a different moral (for example, parents' neglect of their children), or else it is not properly expressed (for example, in the form of a cuckoo which lays its eggs in another bird's nest), and this proves that the fable is no good. We have seen this form of criticism applied to Ostrovsky more than once, although, of course, nobody is willing to admit this; and on top of this, these critics, blaming others for their own sins, accuse us of proceeding to analyze literary productions with preconceived ideas and demands. But what could be clearer? Have not the Slavophils said that the Russian must be depicted as a virtuous man and that the root of all virtue lies in the old way of life? Ostrovsky, they argued, did not do this in his early plays, and therefore, *A Family Picture* and *Our Own Folks*, in their opinion, are unworthy of him, and his writing them can be explained only by the fact that he then imitated Gogol. And did not the Westerners shout that comedies should be a means of preaching the harmfulness of superstition, and that Ostrovsky saves one of his heroes with the aid of the ringing of church bells? It must be impressed upon everyone, they argued, that true virtue lies in education, and yet Ostrovsky in his comedy makes educated Vikhorev look ridiculous compared with the ignoramus Borodkin. Clearly, therefore, they argued, *Don't Get Into Another's Sleigh* and *You Can't Live As You Like* are bad plays. [And did not the champions of art proclaim that art must serve the eternal and universal demands of aesthetics, whereas Ostrovsky in *A Lucrative Post* degraded art to the service of the petty interests of the day, and therefore, *A Lucrative Post* is unworthy of the name of art and should be placed in the category of accusatory literature?...] And did not Mr. Nekrasov of Moscow[116] assert that Bolshov is not worthy of our sympathy, and yet the fourth act in *Our Own Folks* was written with the object of rousing our sympathy for Bolshov, and consequently, the fourth act is superfluous? ... And did not Mr. Pavlov (N. F.) wriggle and twist to bring forth the following argument: Russian national life can provide materials only for plays to be performed at country fairs, it contains no elements from which to build anything that conforms to the "eternal" requirements of art; obviously, therefore, Ostrovsky, who takes his subjects from the life of the common people, is nothing more than a writer of plays for country fairs...? And did not still another Moscow critic arrive at the following conclusion: drama should present us with a hero who is imbued with lofty ideas; the heroine in *The Thunderstorm*, however, is imbued with mysticism. Consequently, she is unsuitable for drama, because she cannot rouse our sympathy; consequently, *The Thunderstorm* is only a piece of satire, and rather feeble satire at that, and so on and so forth...?

Those who have followed what has been written about *The Thunderstorm* in this country will very easily recall several more criticisms of this type. It cannot be said that all these criticisms were written by men [completely] destitute of intelligence. How then are we to explain the absence of a straightforward view of things which the unbiassed reader is astonished to observe among all of them? This, without the slightest doubt, must be attributed to the old critical routine which has survived in the minds of many as a result of the scholastic conceptions of art they imbibed from the textbooks of Koshansky, [Ivan Davydov,][117] Chistyakov and Zelenetsky. It is well known that in the opinion of these esteemed theoreticians, criticism is the application to a given production of the general laws which are enunciated in the textbooks these very theoreticians have written. If the criticism fits in with those laws it is good, if it does not, it is bad. Not a bad scheme, as you see, for these ancients who are living their last days. As long as this principle remains alive in criticism they can feel sure that they will not be regarded as altogether antiquated, no matter what happens in the literary world. They firmly established these laws in their textbooks on the basis of those productions which they believe are beautiful. As long as everything new is judged according to the laws which they have established, only that which conforms to those laws will be regarded as artistic, nothing new will be able to assert its rights. These ancients will be right in believing in Karamzin and in refusing to recognize Gogol, in the same way as those estimable gentlemen claimed to be right who admired the imitators of Racine and, following Voltaire, abused Shakespeare as a drunken savage, or who worshipped *Messiada* and on those grounds rejected *Faust*. Men of routine, even the most mediocre, need not fear criticism which serves as a passive test of the rigid rules of stupid Schoolmen; and at the same time, the most gifted author has nothing to hope for from it if he introduces something new and original in art. Such authors must brave all the reproaches of "correct" criticism, establish their fame in spite of it, establish a school in defiance of it, and induce some new theoretician to consult with them in drawing up a new code of art. The critics will then humbly recognize their merits [; but until then they must remain in the position the unhappy Neapolitans found themselves at the beginning of this September, namely: while knowing that Garibaldi will come any day, they were nevertheless forced to recognize Francis as their king until His Royal Majesty is pleased to leave his capital].

We are surprised that such estimable men should reduce criticism to such an insignificant, to such a degrading role. By limiting its functions to that of applying the "eternal and universal" laws of art to particular and transient phenomena, they condemn art to immobility, and invest criticism with exclusively official and police functions. Many do this with perfect sincerity! An author, concerning whom we expressed ourselves somewhat disrespectfully, reminded us that a judge who is disrespectful to a person he is trying commits a crime. Oh naive author! How fully imbued he is with the theories of Koshansky [and Davydov]! He really takes in its literal sense the banal metaphor that criticism is a tribunal before which authors stand like defendants! Probably he also takes at its face value the opinion that bad verse is a sin against Apollo and that bad authors are punished by being drowned in the river Lethe! ... How otherwise can they fail to see the difference between criticism and a police court? Men are haled before a court on suspicion of having committed a misdemeanour, or a crime, and it is the function of the judge to decide whether the accused is innocent or guilty. But is an author accused of anything when he is criticized? One would have thought that the time when the writing of books was regarded as heresy and a crime had passed away long ago. A critic expresses his opinion and says whether he likes a certain work or not; and as it is assumed that he is not a mere windbag but a man of judgment, he endeavours to give reasons as to why he regards one thing good and another thing bad. He does not regard his opinion as a definite verdict, binding upon all. If we are to draw an analogy with the sphere of law, we would say that the critic is an advocate rather than a judge. Having adopted a certain point of view, which he thinks is the most correct, he explains the details of the case to his readers in the way he understands it, and tries to swing his readers for or against the author he is discussing, as the case may be. It goes without saying that

35*

in the course of this he may resort to every means he thinks fit, provided, however, he does not distort the facts. He may rouse either our horror or our sympathy, cause us to laugh or to weep, compel the author to make admissions against himself or force him into a position where he can make no reply. [Criticism exercised in such a way may produce the following result: the theoreticians, consulting their textbooks, may, after all, ascertain whether the work under discussion conforms to their rigid laws and, performing the function of a judge, they may decide that the author is guilty or not guilty. It is well known, however, that it not infrequently happens at public trials that the public present in the court do not by a long way agree with the verdict pronounced by a judge in conformity with such and such an article of the Legal Code. In such cases the public conscience reveals total disagreement with the articles of the law. The same may happen even more often during the discussion of literary productions:] when the critic-advocate has presented the case properly, has grouped all the facts and has thrown upon them the light of certain convictions, public opinion, ignoring the laws of poetics, will know what side to take.

If we examine closely the definition of criticism as a "trial" of an author, we shall find that it closely resembles the conception which is associated with the word *"criticism"* by our provincial young ladies and their mothers at whose expense our novelists used to exercise their wit. Even today it is not rare to find families which look upon an author with a certain amount of fear because he "may write criticism" about them. The unhappy provincials who have allowed this idea to get into their heads do really present the pitiful spectacle of defendants at the bar, whose fate depends upon the pen of an author. They look pleadingly into his eyes, embarrassed and apologetic, and try to justify themselves, as if indeed they were guilty and were expecting either execution or reprieve. It must be said, however, that naive people like these are becoming very rare even in the remotest corners of our land. To the degree that the right "to dare to have one's own opinion" [is ceasing to be the possession of only a certain rank or station and] is becoming available to all and sundry, people in their private life are displaying more self-confidence and independence, less fear of the judgment of others. Today people are already expressing their opinion simply because it is better to express than to conceal it, because they think that an exchange of opinion is useful, because they recognize the right of everybody to hold views and make demands, and lastly, because they even think it is the duty of everyone to take part in the general movement and to contribute his observations and opinions to the best of his ability. This is very far from the role of a judge. If I tell you that you have dropped a handkerchief, or that you are going in the wrong direction, etc., it does not mean that I am a judge and you are a defendant. Nor will I be a defendant before you if you describe me to your friends in order to give them an idea of what I am like. On entering a particular company for the first time I know perfectly well that people will watch me and form an opinion about me, but does that give me any ground for thinking that I am standing before some areopagus and trembling in anticipation of the verdict? There can be no doubt that comments about me will be made: one will find that my nose is too long, another that my beard is red, a third that my bow is not tied properly, a fourth that I am morose, and so forth. Well, let them make their comments. Why should that disturb me? It is no crime to have a red beard, and nobody has a right to call me to book for having a long nose. Hence, I have nothing to worry about. Whether people like my face or not is a matter of taste, and I cannot forbid anyone to express an opinion about it. On the other hand, I shall lose nothing if my moroseness is observed, if I am really not talkative. Thus, the first function of criticism (in our sense of the term)—to note and to point to facts—is performed quite freely, and without offence to anybody. The next function—to judge on the basis of the facts— also continues to hold the scales equally for both the judge and the one who is being judged. This is because, in expressing the conclusions he draws from certain data, a man always subjects himself to the judgment and test of others as regards the fairness and the soundness of his opinions. If, for example, somebody decides that I have been badly brought up merely on the grounds that my bow is not tied quite elegantly, such a judge runs the risk of those around him forming a low opinion of his logic. Similarly, if a critic reproaches Ostrovsky for having presented Katerina in *The Thunderstorm* as a disgusting and immoral woman, he does not inspire exceptional confidence in the purity of his own moral sentiments.[118] Thus, as long as a critic points to the facts, analyzes them and draws his conclusions, the author stands in no danger, and the case against him is not serious. A protest can be raised only if the critic distorts the facts, if he tells lies. If, however, he presents the case fairly, then no matter what tone he speaks in, or what conclusions he arrives at, his criticism will always, like all free argument backed by facts, do more good than harm—for the author, if he is a good writer, and at all events for literature, even if the author turns out to be a poor writer. Criticism—not as a court trial, but ordinary criticism as we understand it—is beneficial by the mere fact that it gives people who are unaccustomed to concentrate their thoughts on literature an extract, so to speak, of the author, and thereby enables them to understand the character and importance of his productions. Once the author is properly understood, an opinion about him will soon be formed, and justice will be done without the sanction of esteemed compilers of codes.

True, in explaining the character of a certain author or production the critic may claim to have found in that production something that is really not there; but in such cases the critic always betrays himself. If he takes it into his head to attribute to a work he is reviewing a livelier and wider idea than that which the author has put into it, he will obviously be unable adequately to confirm his opinion by references to the work itself. Consequently, the critic who points out what the work under review might have been thereby only more vividly reveals the paucity of its idea and inadequacy of its execution. As an example of this sort of criticism we may point to Belinsky's review of *Tarantas*,[119] which he wrote in a strain of most biting and subtle satire. Many accepted this review at its face value, but even these found that although the idea which Belinsky ascribed to *Tarantas* was well brought out in his criticism, it did not harmonize with Count Sollogub's story. Critical travesties of this kind, however, are met with very rarely. Far more often we meet with cases when a critic really fails to understand the author he is discussing and draws entirely wrong conclusions from his works. But even here no great harm is done; the critic's line of reasoning at once reveals to the reader the kind of critic he is dealing with, and if only the facts are given in the criticism, the false reasoning will not deceive the reader. For example, a certain Mr. P., in reviewing *The Thunderstorm*, decided to adopt the same method that we adopted in our essays on "The

Realm of Darkness," and after relating the contents of the play he set to work to draw conclusions. It turned out that in his opinion Ostrovsky made a laughing stock of Katerina, as he wished, in her person, to ridicule Russian mysticism. On reading such a conclusion one, of course, sees at once what category of mind Mr. P. belongs to, and whether his judgment can be relied upon. Such criticism will mislead nobody, it is not dangerous to anyone....[120]

It is quite another matter when a critic approaches an author in the same way as recruiting officers approach peasants who have been brought to the recruiting office—with a rule to measure them and with the exclamation of "fit!" or "unfit!" according to whether the recruit comes up to the standard or not. Here the author gets short shrift, and if you believe in the eternal laws of art that are enunciated in the textbooks, you will not be able to get rid of such a critic. He will prove to you point by point that the things you admire are no good and that the things that send you to sleep, make you yawn or give you a nervous headache are the real treasures of art. Take *The Thunderstorm*, for example. What is it? An outrageous insult to art and nothing more! This can be easily proved. Open *Readings in Literature* [by Merited Professor and Academician Ivan Davydov] compiled [by him] with the aid of a translation of Blair's lectures; or glance at Mr. Plaksin's[121] textbook on literature [for Cadet Schools]; there you will find a careful enumeration of the points that go to make exemplary drama. The subject of a drama must without fail be an event in which we see the struggle between passions and duty, with either an unhappy ending in the case of the triumph of passion, or with a happy ending if duty triumphs. The development of the drama must be marked by strict unity and consecutiveness; the climax must naturally and necessarily emerge from the plot; every scene must without fail contribute to the development of the action and push it to its climax; hence, there must not be a single personage in the play who does not take a direct and necessary part in the development of the drama, and there must not be a single dialogue that is not directly connected with the substance of the play. The characters of the personages must be clearly depicted, and they must necessarily reveal themselves gradually, as the action develops. The language must suit the station in life of every personage concerned, but must not depart from the pure language of literature and sink into vulgarity.

These, we think, are the principal rules of the drama. Let us apply them to *The Thunderstorm*.

"The subject of the drama is, indeed, the struggle that goes on within Katerina between her sense of duty as a wife and her passion for young Boris Grigoryevich. Thus, the first requirement is adhered to. But starting out from this requirement we find that all the other rules for exemplary drama are violated in the most outrageous manner in *The Thunderstorm*.

"Firstly, *The Thunderstorm* fails to meet the most important inner object of the drama, namely, to inculcate respect for moral duty and to show the fatal consequences of yielding to passion. Katerina, that immoral, shameless (to use N. F. Pavlov's apt expression) woman who goes out at night to meet her lover as soon as her husband leaves the house, this criminal is presented to us in the drama not [only in an insufficiently gloomy light, but actually with the halo of martyrdom around her head]. She speaks so beautifully, she suffers so pitifully, and everything around her is so bad that no feeling of indignation against her arises in your breast; you pity her, you take up arms against her oppressors [and thus in her person you justify vice]. Consequently, this drama does not fulfil its lofty mission and becomes, if not a bad example, at all events a useless plaything.

"Further, from the purely artistic point of view, we find flaws of a most important nature. The development of passion is inadequately presented: we do not see how Katerina's love for Boris began and grew, and what motivated it; hence, the very struggle between passion and duty is not brought out clearly and strongly enough.

"Nor is the unity of impression maintained; it is disturbed by the intrusion of an extraneous element—the relations between Katerina and her mother-in-law. The mother-in-law's intervention constantly prevents us from concentrating our attention upon the inner struggle that must be going on in Katerina's soul.

"Moreover, we find in Ostrovsky's play a blunder against the first and fundamental rules of every poetical production that would be unpardonable even for a novice. In drama this blunder bears the special name of 'double intrigue'; here we see not one love but two—Katerina's love for Boris and Varvara's love for Kudryash. This is all very well only in light French vaudeville, but it is out of place in serious drama, where the spectator's attention must on no account be distracted.

"The opening and the climax also transgress against the requirements of art. The plot opens with a simple incident—the husband's departure; the climax is also quite casual and arbitrary—a thunderstorm, which frightens Katerina and compels her to confess to her husband. This is nothing but a *deus ex machina*, quite on a par with the vaudeville uncle from America.

"The entire action is listless and slow because it is overburdened with entirely superfluous scenes and personages. Kudryash and Shapkin, Kuligin, Feklusha, the old lady and her two flunkeys, and Dikoi himself, are all personages who have no direct connection with the plot. Superfluous persons continuously come on to the stage, say things that have nothing to do with the story, and go off again, nobody knows why, or where to. All Kuligin's declamations, all the sallies of Kudryash and Dikoi, not to speak of the half-insane lady and the chatter of the townspeople during the thunderstorm, could have been left out without any harm to the plot.

"We find scarcely any strictly defined and finished characters in this crowd of superfluous people, and as for the gradual revelation of these characters, there is no sign of it. They appear before us *ex abrupto* with labels stuck on them. The curtain rises and we hear Kudryash and Kuligin saying to each other what an abusive fellow Dikoi is and then Dikoi himself appears, but you can hear him swearing while he is still in the wings. . . . The same applies to Kabanova. Kudryash too lets you know from the very first words he utters that he is 'fond of the girls'; and Kuligin, the moment he comes onto the stage, is introduced as a self-trained mechanic and an admirer of nature. And so they remain right to the end: Dikoi swears, Kabanova grumbles and Kudryash gallivants at night with Varvara. . . . But throughout the play we fail to see the complete development of their characters. The portrayal of the heroine is very feeble; evidently the author himself had no definite idea of what her character is like, for, while not presenting her as a hypocrite, he nevertheless compels her to utter emotional monologues and at the same time act as a shameless woman who is prompted solely by her sensuousness. Of the hero it is needless to speak, he is so colourless Dikoi and Kabanova, characters which come most within Mr. Ostrovsky's genre, represent (according to the apt remark of Mr. Akhsharumov, or it may have been somebody else) deliberate caricatures, almost lampoons; they are not living persons but 'the quintessence of the monstrosities' of Russian life.

"Lastly, the very language in which the personages in the play speak tries the patience of well-bred people to breaking point. It goes without saying that merchants and townspeople cannot speak in the elegant language of literature, but we cannot agree that a playwright should, for the sake of reality, introduce into literature all the vulgar expressions with which the language of the Russian people is so replete. The language of dramatic personages, whoever they may be, may be simple, but it should always be noble and should not offend educated taste. In *The Thunderstorm*, however, we hear the personages say: 'Impudence! What are you shoving your mug into it for!' 'It sets all my innards afire!' 'The women can't get any flesh on nohow!!. . .' What phrases are these, what words? Involuntarily one repeats the words of Lermontov:

> Whose portraits are they painting?
> Where do they such conversation hear?
> Even if they see and hear them
> We do not wish to know them.[122]

Perhaps there are people 'in the town of Kalinov, on the bank of the Volga' who speak like this, but what has that to do with us?"

The reader will understand that we made no special effort to make this sort of criticism sound convincing and so it will be easy to pick out the flaws in it. But we assure them that it can be made extremely convincing and overwhelming; with it you can crush an author once you take the stand of the [school] textbooks. And if the reader granted us the right to approach a play with ready-made demands concerning what it *should* be, we would need nothing more; we would be able to destroy everything that did not fit in with our accepted rules. The excerpts which we would carefully choose from the comedy would strongly prove the correctness of our arguments; quotations from various learned books, beginning with Aristotle and ending with Vischer[123] who, as is known, has uttered the last and final word on the theory of aesthetics, would prove the soundness of our education; facile exposition and wit would help us to captivate your attention and without realizing it you would agree with us. But do not for a moment allow any doubt to creep into your mind about our absolute right to claim that the author has certain duties and then *to judge* whether he has performed these duties or has failed to perform them. . . .

But the whole trouble is that nowadays not a single reader is safe from such doubt. The contemptible mob which formerly listened to our admonitions with open-mouthed awe now presents a spectacle—deplorable and dangerous to our authority—of the masses armed, as Mr. Turgenev has so splendidly expressed it, "with the two-edged sword of analysis." Everybody who reads our thunderous criticism says: "You are giving us your own 'storm' when you assert that everything that is to be found in *The Thunderstorm* is superfluous and that it does not contain what is needed. But in all probability the author of *The Thunderstorm* thinks the very opposite; allow us to analyze you. Please analyze the play for us, present it to us as it really is and give us your opinion about it based on what it really is and not on obsolete ideas which are totally superfluous and extraneous. In your opinion this or that should have been left out; but perhaps it fits in very well in the play, in that case why should it have been left out?" Every reader will dare to argue like this today, and this unpleasant fact explains why the magnificent exercises in criticism indulged in by N. F. Pavlov, for example, in reviewing *The Thunderstorm*, suffered such an utter fiasco. Indeed, everybody, authors as well as the general public, protested against the criticism of *The Thunderstorm* that was published in *Nashe Vremya*, and this protest was roused not because the critic dared to show lack of respect for Ostrovsky, but because he, in his criticism, showed disrespect for the common sense and the good will of the Russian public. Everybody has realized for a long time that Ostrovsky has in many ways departed from the old stage routine, and that in the very meaning of every one of his plays there are factors which necessarily carry him beyond the limits of the well-known theory to which we made reference above. The critics who dislike these departures from the old stage routine should start by pointing to them, analyzing and generalizing them, and then openly and frankly contrast them with the old theory. This is the critic's duty not only towards the author he is discussing, but also, and still more so, to the public which so consistently approves of Ostrovsky, in spite of all the liberties he takes and the departures he makes, and becomes more and more attached to him with every new play he writes. If the critic is of the opinion that the public errs in its sympathies towards an author who is committing a crime against the critic's theory, he should start by defending that theory and presenting solid proof that departure from it cannot be good. If he did that he, perhaps, would succeed in convincing some, and even many; for it cannot be denied that N. F. Pavlov wields a facile pen. But what did he do? He completely ignored the fact that the old laws of art [which continue to exist in the textbooks and are taught in high schools and universities] have long lost the odour of sanctity in literature and among the public. He valiantly set to work to annihilate Ostrovsky, point by point, according to his theory and tried to compel the reader to regard it as inviolable. He deemed it fit to wax ironic about a gentleman who, being his "neighbour and brother" in that he sat in the first row of the stalls and wore "fresh" gloves, nevertheless dared to express admiration for the play which he, N. F. Pavlov, so utterly disliked. This contemptuous treatment of the public, and of the very issue which the critic set out to settle, naturally roused the majority of his readers against him rather than for him. The readers pointed out to the critic that he was running around with his theory like a squirrel in a cage, and they demanded that he should leave his cage and come out on to the straight road. They found that well-rounded phrases and subtle syllogisms

were not enough; they demanded solid proof of the premises from
which Mr. Pavlov drew his deductions and which he presented as
axioms. He said: the play is bad because there are many personages in it who do not facilitate the direct development of its action.
To this the public stubbornly retorted: but why should there not
be persons in the play who take no direct part in the development
of the plot? [The critic asserted that the drama lacked importance
if only for the one reason that the heroine is an immoral woman,
but the readers cut him short and asked him: why do you think
she is immoral? And what are your conceptions of morality based
upon?] The critic expressed the opinion that nocturnal tryst,
Kudryash's audacious whistling, and the scene where Katerina
confesses to her husband, were vulgar and obscene, unworthy of
art; but again he was asked why he regarded this as vulgar and
why high society intrigues and [aristocratic] passions are more
worthy of art than the infatuations of plain townspeople? Why is
the whistling of a young lad more vulgar than the earsplitting
rendering of Italian arias by [some] high society youth? To cap
his arguments N. F. Pavlov superciliously decided that plays like
The Thunderstorm are not drama, but fit only for country fairs.
In answer to this he was asked: but why are you so contemptuous
towards country fair plays? Whether every well-groomed drama,
even if it conforms to all the three unities, is better than any
country fair play is still an open question. We shall yet debate
with you the question of the place the country fair play holds in
the history of the theatre and in national development. The last
objection was dealt with in fairly great detail in the press.
But where was it raised? It would have been understandable had
it been raised in *Sovremennik*, which, as everybody knows, has a
"whistle" of its own* and, consequently, cannot be horrified by
Kudryash's whistling, and ought to be well-disposed to country
fairs in general. But no, the ideas about country fair plays were
expressed in *Biblioteka dlya Chteniya*, the well-known champion
of all the rights of "art," by Mr. Annenkov, whom nobody will
accuse of an excessive attachment to "vulgarity."124 If we have
understood Mr. Annenkov aright [(which, of course, nobody can

---

* An allusion to the satirical supplement published by *Sovremennik*
entitled *Svistok*—literally "the whistle."—*Tr.*

guarantee)], he is of the opinion that the theory of modern drama has departed from living truth and beauty more than the original country fair play did, and that in order to revive the theatre it is necessary first of all to return to the country fair theatre and commence the development of the drama from the beginning. Such were the opinions which Mr. Pavlov encountered even on the part of esteemed representatives of Russian criticism, not to speak of those who are accused (by respectable-minded people) of displaying contempt for science and of repudiating everything that is lofty! Naturally, here the critic could no longer brush objection aside with more or less brilliant repartee; he was obliged seriously to examine the grounds on which he arrived at his verdict. But as soon as the question was shifted to this ground the critic in *Nashe Vremya* proved to be utterly bankrupt and was obliged to cease his critical harangues.

It is obvious that a critic who becomes the ally of the pedant and sits down to review literary productions according to the paragraphs in his textbook must often find himself in a ridiculous position. Becoming a slave to the reigning theory, he at the same time dooms himself to fruitless opposition to all progress, to everything that is new and original in literature. And the stronger the new movement in literature, the more fiercely he opposes it, and the more clearly he exposes his toothless impotence. Hunting out some lifeless perfection, exhibiting to us obsolete ideals to which we are indifferent, and hurling at us fragments torn from a beautiful whole, critics of this kind always remain aloof from the living movement, shut their eyes to the new living beauty and refuse to understand the new truth which springs from the new course of life. They look down with disdain upon everything, pronounce stern verdicts, are ready to denounce every author who fails to come up to the level of their *chefs-d'œuvre* and arrogantly spurn the living relations between an author and his public and his epoch. All this, you see, are "interests of the day," and can serious critics compromise art by allowing themselves to be carried away by such interests? Poor, soulless people! How miserable they look to a man who cherishes the cause of life, its work and its blessings! An ordinary man, a man of common sense, takes what life gives him and gives it what he can; but pedants always look down with disdain upon everything and paralyze life with lifeless ideals and abstractions. What would one think of a man who, on seeing a beautiful woman, begins to argue that her figure is not like that of Venus of Milo, that her mouth is not as well shaped as that of Venus de' Medici, that her eyes are not as expressive as those of Raphael's Madonna, and so on and so forth. All this gentleman's arguments and comparisons may be extremely correct and witty, but what can they lead to? Do they prove that the woman we are discussing is not beautiful? Are they able even to convince us that the woman is less beautiful than this or that Venus? Of course not, for beauty lies not in individual features and lines, but in the general expression of the face, in the living meaning it expresses. When this expression is attractive to me, when I can grasp the meaning and it satisfies me, I simply yield to that beauty with all my heart and mind, without making any lifeless comparisons, without claiming that they are sanctified by the traditions of art. If you wish to impress me with a living image, if you wish to make me love beauty, then have the skill to grasp and depict that general meaning, that breath of life; have the skill to point to it and explain it to me. Only if you do that will you achieve your object. The same applies to truth. You do not arrive at truth by means of subtle dialectics, or by correctly formulated syllogisms, but by bringing out the living truth of what you are discussing. Help me to understand the character of a phenomenon, its place among the rest, its meaning and importance in the general course of life, and I assure you that in this way you will help me to form a far more correct opinion about the matter in hand than you will with all the syllogisms you may choose to prove your case. If ignorance and credulity are still strong among people it is because they are fostered by the kind of critical arguments that we are attacking. Everywhere, and in all things, the synthesis reigns; people say that a certain thing is useful and then they go hunting around for arguments to prove that it is useful; they stun us with a maxim [: this is what morality must be] and then they condemn [as immoral] everything that does not comply with that maxim. In this way human thought is constantly being distorted, and we lose the desire and the ability to think for ourselves. It would be entirely different if people learned to think analytically: such is the case, such are its consequences, such are its advantages and disadvantages; weigh it up and judge to what extent it will be useful. People

would then always have the facts before them, they would base
their judgments on these facts, they would not grope in a synthet-
ical fog and would not bind themselves with abstract theories and
ideals [by whom composed, and when, nobody knows]. To achieve
this all people must be willing to think for themselves [and not
allow others to think for them]. This, of course, mankind will not
achieve soon. But the existence of that small section of mankind
which we call the "reading public" gives us grounds for thinking
that this desire for independent intellectual life has already awakened among it. That is why we think that it is most unseemly
to look down upon it superciliously and disdainfully throw at it
maxims and verdicts based on God knows what kind of theories.
The best mode of criticism, in our opinion, is that which explains
a situation in such a way that the reader himself may draw his
own conclusions on the basis of the facts presented to him. We
group the facts, discuss the general meaning of the production we
are reviewing, point out its relation to the realities of our life,
draw our conclusions and endeavour to prove them to the best of
our ability; but we try to do this in such a way that the reader
himself may be able fully to judge between us and the author.
More than once we have been reproached for writing our reviews
with a touch of irony. "From the passages you quote, and from
your summary of the contents, it is evident that the author is bad
or harmful, and yet you praise him. Are you not ashamed of yourself?"—we have been told. We confess that reproaches of this
kind have left us quite cold; true, the reader formed a none too
flattering opinion about our critical faculties, but we achieved our
aim—a bad book [(which, sometimes, we could not openly condemn)] was shown to the reader to be bad by means of the facts
that were presented to him. We have always been of the opinion
that only factual, real criticism can have any meaning for a reader. If there is anything in a work, show us what it is; this is far
better than indulging in speculation about what it does not contain
and what it ought to have contained.

It goes without saying that there are general concepts and
laws which every man invariably has in mind when discussing a
subject, no matter what it may be; but one must distinguish between the natural laws which follow from the very nature of the
case and propositions and rules which have been laid down in

some system or other. There are certain axioms without which it
is impossible to think at all, and every author assumes that his
readers adhere to them, just as we assume that everybody we discuss things with adheres to them. It is sufficient to say that a man
is a hunchback, or is cross-eyed, for everybody to recognize this
as a defect and not an ornament to his general make-up. Similarly,
it is sufficient to note that a certain literary production is illiterate
or full of falsehood, and nobody will regard it as one of the merits of this production. But if you say that a man wears a peak
cap and not a hat, it is not sufficient to cause people to form a bad
opinion about him, even though, in a certain circle, it is deemed
improper for a respectable man to wear a cap. Similarly, in a
literary production, if you find that certain unities have not been
adhered to, or that there are personages in it who are not essential for the development of the plot, it means nothing to a reader
who is not prejudiced in favour of your theory. On the other hand,
I need not denounce what must appear to every reader as a violation of the natural order of things and an insult to plain common sense, for I can assume that the mere statement of the facts
will evoke condemnation in the reader's mind. But one must not
carry this assumption too far. Critics like N. F. Pavlov, Mr. Nekrasov of Moscow, Mr. Palkhovsky and others err especially in
that they assume that public opinion agrees with them on a far
larger number of points than is actually the case. In other words,
they regard as indefeasible axioms obvious to all, many opinions
which they alone regard as absolute truths, but which most people
even regard as running counter to certain generally accepted ideas.
For example, it is clear to everybody that an author who wishes
to do anything worth-while, must not distort reality; both the
theoreticians and public opinion will agree on that. But the theoreticians demand, and advance as an axiom, that an author must
improve upon reality by eliminating all that is superfluous from
it and by choosing only that which is specifically necessary for the
development of the plot and the climax of the play. In conformity with this second demand, Ostrovsky has been very furiously
attacked many times. But far from this being an axiom it obviously contradicts the demand for a truthful picture of real life,
which everybody admits is essential. How, indeed, can you make
me believe that in a matter of half an hour ten persons, precisely

those who are needed, will follow each other into a room, or a public square, precisely at the moment they are needed, that they will meet the persons they need, will *ex abrupto* begin to talk about what is needed, go off and do what is needed, and re-appear when they are needed again? Is this what happens in real life? Has this any resemblance to the truth? Who does not know that it is the most difficult thing in real life to fit one favourable circumstance to another, to arrange the course of affairs in accordance with logical necessity? Usually, a man knows what he ought to do, but he cannot arrange things so that he can employ for his affairs all the means which an author has at his command. The people he needs fail to appear, letters fail to arrive, discussions do not proceed in a way that will promote affairs. In real life everybody has numerous affairs of his own, and rarely does any one work like a machine, as they do in dramas, which the author sets in motion in a way most suitable for the action of his play. The same thing must be said about the opening and climax. Do we see many cases in real life where the end is the purely logical result of the beginning? We may see this in history in the course of centuries, but not in private life. True, the same historical laws operate here, but there is a difference in space and dimensions. Speaking absolutely, and taking into consideration the infinitely small, we shall, of course, find that a sphere is also a polyhedron; but try to play billiards with polyhedrons—nothing will come of it. Similarly, the historical laws of logical development [and of inevitable retribution] never manifest themselves as clearly and fully in the events of private life as in the history of nations. Deliberately to lend them this clarity means violating and distorting actual reality. Does every crime really carry within itself its own punishment? Is crime always accompanied by the prickings of conscience, if not by external punishment? Does thrift always lead to wealth, is honesty always rewarded by universal esteem, do all doubts find their solution, and does virtue always provide inner satisfaction? [Is not the opposite more often the case, although, on the other hand, even the opposite cannot be asserted as a general rule. . . . It cannot be said that people are wicked by nature, and for that reason we cannot accept for literary productions principles such as, for example, that vice always triumphs and virtue is always punished. But it has become impossible, even ridiculous, to build drama on the idea that virtue must triumph.] The point is that human relationships are rarely based on rational calculation; for the most part they arise fortuitously, and moreover, the behaviour of some towards others is in most cases quite unconscious, as it were, it is dictated by routine, by one's disposition at the given moment, by the influence of numerous extraneous causes. The author who ventures to brush aside all these fortuities for the sake of the logical development of his plot usually loses his sense of the average and becomes like the man who measures everything by the maximum. He finds, for example, that a man can work fifteen hours a day without any direct effect upon his health and on this he bases his demands upon the people he employs. It goes without saying that this calculation, while valid in extraordinary cases, for two or three days say, turns out to be absolutely absurd as a standard of continuous work. Such, very often, proves to be the logical development of the human relationships which theory demands from drama.

We shall be told that we are revealing a tendency to deny all artistic creativeness and that we recognize art only in the form of a daguerreotype. Nay more, we shall be asked to carry our view to the extreme and argue that a dramatist has no right to exclude anything, or to adapt his play to his object, and therefore, must simply record all the irrelevant conversations of the persons met with, so that, if an action lasts a week, the same time will be required to present it in the theatre, and that for some episodes the presence of all the thousands of people who stroll along the Nevsky Prospect or the English Embankment will be required. Yes, this will indeed be the case if the theory, the postulates of which we have just challenged, remains the supreme criterion in literature. But we are not turning in that direction in the least. It is not our wish to correct two or three points of this theory; such corrections will only worsen it, will make it more confused and contradictory. We reject it altogether. We have other criteria for judging the merits of authors and their productions, and by adhering to these criteria we hope to avoid arriving at any absurdities, and avoid disagreeing with the common sense of the wide public. We have already discussed these grounds in our first essays on Ostrovsky, but perhaps it is necessary briefly to sum them up again.

The criterion we apply to an author, or to a literary production, is the extent to which it serves to express the [natural] strivings of a given period and nation. [The natural strivings of mankind, reduced to a simple denominator, may be expressed in the following few words: "that all should live well." Clearly, in striving towards this goal. men, by the very nature of the case, at first, actually departed from it; each individual wanted to live well, and in arranging for his own welfare he hindered others; people had not yet learned how to arrange their own affairs in such a way as not to hinder others. Similarly. inexperienced dancers are unable to control their movements and continuously collide with other couples even in a fairly spacious ballroom. Later, having become more skilled in the art, they are able to avoid colliding with other dancers even in a smaller ballroom, and with a larger number of dancers. But until they have acquired this skill, it is impossible to allow a large number of couples to go waltzing around the room; to avoid constant collisions some of the dancers must wait, and the least skilled may even have to give up the idea of dancing altogether and instead take a hand at cards, and perhaps lose. even a large sum. . . . Such has been the case in the arrangement of life: the more skilled continue in the pursuit of their happiness, while others have been obliged to stand aside, engage in matters they should not have engaged in, and lose. The general festival of life was disturbed at the very beginning; many ceased to come for merriment, many became convinced that merriment is only for those who can dance skilfully. And the skilful dancers, having arranged their affairs well, continued to indulge in their natural inclinations, seized more and more space, more and more means of merriment for themselves. At last, they lost all sense of proportion; the rest found themselves pushed into a corner, and they jumped from their seats and hopped about, not because they wanted to dance so much, but simply because it became extremely inconvenient for them even to sit. Amidst this hopping and jumping some of these people found that they were fairly light on their feet, and these attempted to mingle with the merry throng. The original dancers, the privileged ones, however, looked upon them with a very unfriendly eye, they regarded them as uninvited guests and refused them admission into their circle. A struggle ensued, a long struggle which assumed diverse forms, mostly to the disadvantage of the newcomers. They were ridiculed, pushed aside, compelled to pay the cost of the festival, the gentle-

36*

men were deprived of their partners and the ladies of theirs, and in the end they were driven away from the festival altogether. But the worse things become for people, the more strongly they feel the need for things to be good. Demands cannot be checked by privation, it only stimulates them the more. Hunger can be appeased only by taking food. Hence, the struggle goes on to this day; the natural strivings, now appearing to be subdued and now manifesting themselves with greater force, are still seeking satisfaction. Herein lies the essence of history.]

In all times, and in every field of human activity, men have appeared, so sound and so endowed by nature, that they expressed the natural strivings very strongly and irrepressibly. In their particular activity they [often became martyrs to their strivings, but] never passed away without leaving a trace, they never remained alone; in public activities they formed a party, in pure science they made discoveries, in art, in literature, they formed schools. We shall not speak of those active in public affairs [whose role in history everybody should now understand after what we have said on the preceding page], but we shall observe that in science and in literature the great personalities have always displayed the character which we have described above as the power of natural, living strivings. When these strivings were distorted, absurd conceptions of the world and man arose among the masses; and these conceptions, in their turn, hindered the common good. [Not to go too far, we shall merely mention the evil which has been caused mankind by the absurdities of fetishism and all sorts of cosmogonical ravings and astrological and cabalistic mysteries of various kinds.] Men of pure science who made discoveries in astronomy and physics, or who established new philosophical principles, were able to heed the natural and sound demands of the mind and to help mankind to rid itself of the artificial combinations which hindered the arrangement of the common good. With every one of these men mankind took another step in forming correct, natural concepts, and it is by the importance of these steps that we can gauge the personal merits of each of these men. The same applies to men of applied science, technicians, mechanics, agronomists, physicians, and so forth. We see the same also in the sphere of art and in literature.

Up till now literature has been assigned a minor role in this progress of mankind towards natural principles [from which it had digressed]. By its very nature, literature is not an active factor; it either only assumes what should be done, or depicts what is being, or has been, done. In the first case, that is to say, in its assumptions of what should be done in the future, it takes its materials and its grounds from pure science; in the second case it takes them from the facts of life. Thus, speaking generally, literature is an auxiliary force [, the importance of which lies in propaganda, and the merit of which is determined by what it propagates, and how it propagates it]. Incidentally, only a few men have appeared in literature so far, who [in their propaganda] stand so high that they are unexcelled either by the practical workers [for the good of mankind] or by the men of pure science. These authors have been so richly endowed by nature that they have been able, instinctively, as it were, to approach closely to the natural conceptions and strivings which their contemporary philosophers were only seeking with the aid of pure science. More than that, the truths which the philosophers only divined in theory were grasped in real life by the authors of genius and depicted in action. Thus, most fully representing a higher stage of human consciousness in a certain epoch, and scanning the life of men and nature from this elevation and depicting it for us, they rose above the auxiliary role of literature and entered the ranks of the historical leaders who have helped mankind to become most clearly conscious of its vital strength and natural inclinations. Such a one was Shakespeare. Many of his plays may be described as discoveries in the sphere of the human heart; his literary activities raised the general consciousness of men several stages, to which nobody had raised it before him, and which a few philosophers had only pointed to from a distance. That is why Shakespeare is of such universal importance; he symbolizes several new stages of human development. But then Shakespeare stands outside the ranks of ordinary authors. The names of Dante, Goethe and Byron are often placed on a par with his, but one can hardly say that any of these so fully symbolize an entire new phase of human development as Shakespeare does. As for the ordinary talents, to them remains the auxiliary role to which we have referred. Failing to present the world with anything new and hitherto unknown, failing to indicate new paths of development for the whole of mankind, not even pushing it forward along the

accepted path, they must confine themselves to more particular
and special services; they awaken the consciousness of the masses
to what the advanced leaders of mankind have discovered; they
reveal and explain to people what, as yet, lives in them vaguely
and indefinitely. But the author does not as a rule borrow his ideas
from the philosopher and introduce them in his productions. No,
the philosopher and author work independently, both proceed from
the same starting point, namely, real life, [only each sets to work
in a different way. The thinker, noticing, for example, that people
are discontented with their present position, analyzes all the facts
and tries to discover new principles that might satisfy the demands
that arise. The author-poet, however, noticing the same discontent,
paints such a vivid picture of it, that it attracts universal attention,
and of itself suggests to people what it is they need. The result in
either case is the same, and the significance of the two types of
men would also be the same;] but the history of literature tells
us that, apart from a few exceptions, the author is usually belated.
While thinkers, taking up the faintest symptom and relentlessly
pursuing an idea down to its very last foundations, not infrequently note a phenomenon in its very embryo, most authors are less
sensitive; they note and depict [a rising movement] only when it
is already fairly evident and strong. On the other hand, the masses
understand them better, and they meet with better success among
them [: they are like a barometer, which anybody can handle,
whereas nobody wants to bother with meteorological and astronom-
ical calculations and forecasts]. Thus, we think that the principal
function of literature is to explain the phenomena of life, and that
is why we demand that it should possess a quality, without which
it can have no merit whatever. This quality is *truth*. The facts from
which the author proceeds, and which he presents to us, must be
presented truthfully. If he fails to do that, his literary production
loses all significance; in fact it becomes harmful, because it serves
not to enlighten the human mind, but, on the contrary, still further
to obscure it. In such a case, it would be useless for us to seek
for any talent in the author, except that of a liar. In productions
of a historical character truth must be factual; in fiction, where
the events are imaginary, factual truth is replaced by logical
truth, that is to say, by reasonable probability and conformity
with the actual course of things.

But while truth is a necessary condition for a literary production it does not yet constitute its merit. We judge its merit by
the breadth of the author's views, the correctness of his understanding, and the vividness with which he depicts the phenomena
with which he deals. [And primarily, in conformity with our criterion, we draw a distinction between authors who come out as
representatives of the natural and true strivings of the people,
and those who serve as the mouthpieces of various artificial trends
and demands. We have already seen that artificial social combinations, being the result of men's original inability to arrange their
welfare, have extinguished in many the consciousness of natural
requirements]. Among all nations we find numerous authors who
devote themselves entirely to artificial interests and are not in the
least concerned about the normal [demands] of human nature.
These authors may not be liars; nevertheless, their productions
are no less false for that; and we can recognize no merit in them
except, perhaps, as regards form. For example, all those who sing
the praises of illuminations [, military triumphs, massacre and
plunder by command of some ambitious ruler, the writers of flattering dithyrambs, inscriptions and madrigals] can have no importance in our eyes, because they are extremely remote from
natural strivings [and requirements of the people]. In literature
they stand in the same relation to true authors as astrologers and
alchemists stand to the true naturalists in science, as a Book of
Dreams stands to a textbook on physiology, and as a book on fortunetelling stands to the theory of probability. Among authors who
do not depart from natural concepts we discern men who are more
or less profoundly imbued with the urgent [requirements] of the
epoch, [who are more or less widely cognizant of the movement
that is taking place in human society], and who more or less
strongly sympathize with it. The degrees here may be infinite.
One author may deal exhaustively with one problem, another with
ten, a third may reduce them all to one higher problem [and take
it up for solution], a fourth may point to problems which arise
after this higher problem has been solved, and so forth. One may
deal with the facts in a cool and epic manner, while another may
attack falsehood and sing the praises of virtue and truth with
lyrical power. One may deal with a question superficially [and
urge the necessity of external and partial improvements], while

another may delve down to the roots [and bring to light the intrinsic ugliness and unsoundness of the object, or the intrinsic strength and beauty of the new edifice that is being erected as mankind progresses. According to their breadth of views and strength of feeling, authors will differ in their method of depicting objects and in the very manner in which each depicts them. It is not a difficult matter to analyze this relation between external form and inner strength; the main task of the critic is to determine whether the author stands on a level with the natural strivings which have already awakened among the people, or should be awakened soon by the demands of the present order of things, and also to what extent he has understood and expressed these strivings, whether he has grasped their substance, their roots, or only their externals, or whether he has embraced the object as a whole, or only some of its aspects].

We deem it unnecessary to dilate on the fact that we have in mind here not a theoretical discussion, but the poetical presentation of the facts of life. We have sufficiently discussed the difference between abstract thinking and the artistic method of presentation in our preceding essays on Ostrovsky. Here we shall repeat only one observation in order to avoid being accused once again by the champions of pure art of thrusting "utilitarian themes" upon the artist. We do not in the least think that every author should produce his works under the influence of a certain theory; he may hold any opinions he pleases, as long as his talent is sensitive to the truth of life. An artistic production may express a certain idea not because the author set out to propagate this idea in his work, but because he was struck by certain facts of real life from which this idea logically arises. Thus, for example, in relation to the religious doctrines of the Greeks, the philosophy of Socrates and the comedies of Aristophanes served to express the same common idea, namely, the unsoundness of the ancient faiths; but this does not in the least imply that Aristophanes set himself this object in writing his comedies; it follows logically from the picture that he paints of Greek morals in his time. From his comedies we gain the firm conviction that at the time he wrote them the [reign] of Greek mythology was already over, that is to say, he brings us, in practice, to what Socrates and Plato proved in philosophy. Such, in general, is the difference in the mode of operation of poetical works and theoretical works proper. It conforms to the difference in the very modes of thinking of the artist and the thinker; one thinks concretely, he never loses sight of particular phenomena and images; the other strives to generalize everything, to merge particular symptoms in a general formula. But there can be no material difference between true knowledge and true poetry; talent is an attribute of human nature and, therefore, it undoubtedly guarantees for us a certain strength and breadth of the natural strivings of the one whose talent we recognize. Hence, his works must be produced under the influence of these natural and true requirements of nature; his consciousness [of what the normal state of affairs should be] must be clear and vivid; his ideals must be simple and rational, and he will refuse to serve falsehood and nonsense not because he does not wish to, but simply because he cannot—nothing will come of it even if he took it into his head to violate his talent. [Like Balaam, even if he wanted to curse Israel, blessings and not curses would fall from his lips at the solemn moment of inspiration. And even if he succeeded in uttering a curse it would lack internal passion, it would be feeble and incoherent. We need not go far for examples; our literature teems with them more than any other, perhaps. Take Pushkin and Gogol, for example. What poor jingle are the verses that Pushkin wrote to order; how miserable Gogol's ascetic efforts are in literature! They abound in good will, but their imaginations and sentiments failed to provide them with sufficient material with which to create truly poetical productions on artificial themes written to order]. This is not surprising. The reality from which the poet takes his materials and his inspiration has its natural meaning; if this is distorted the life of the object is destroyed and only its dead skeleton remains. It is with this skeleton that an author has always remained when he attributed to phenomena not their natural meaning, but one that was contrary to their substance.

As we have already said, however, the natural strivings of man and sound simple conceptions of things are sometimes distorted in many people. Owing to defective development, people often regard as quite normal and natural that which in substance is really a [most absurd] violation of nature. As time passes mankind rids itself more and more of artificial distortions and comes nearer to natural demands and views. We no longer see mysterious forces in every forest and lake, in thunder and lightning, in the sun and the stars; [we no longer have castes and pariahs in civilized countries]; we no longer mix up the relations of the two sexes as the peoples of the Orient do; [we no longer recognize a slave class as an essential attribute of the state, as was the case among the Greeks and Romans;] we repudiate the principles of the Inquisition which reigned in mediaeval Europe. Even if we do meet all these things in places it is only by way of an exception; the general situation has changed [for the better]. Nevertheless, even today people are still a long way from clearly understanding all natural requirements, and they cannot even agree, as yet, upon what is natural for man and what is not. The general formula—that man naturally strives for something better—everybody accepts, but differences arise over what should be regarded as good for mankind. We think, for example, that good lies in work and, therefore, we think that work is natural for man; but *Ekonomicheski Ukazatel* assures us that people are naturally lazy, for good lies in employing capital. We think that stealing is [an artificial] form of appropriation to which a man is sometimes driven by need, but Krylov says that stealing is a natural quality of some men and that

> Even if you give a thief a million
> He will never cease from stealing. [125]

And yet Krylov is the famous fabulist, and *Economicheski Ukazatel* is published by Mr. Vernadsky [Doctor and State Councillor]; their opinions cannot possibly be ignored. What is to be done here, what can we decide? We think that nobody can undertake to make a definite decision here; everybody may regard his own opinion as the most correct; in this case more than in any other the decision must be left to the public. This is a matter that concerns it, and only in its name can we advance our propositions. We say to the public: "We think that you [are capable of this], that this is what you feel, [this is what you are discontented with, this is what you wish"]. It is for the public to say whether we are mistaken or not. All the more, therefore, can we rely on the public verdict in a matter like a review of Ostrovsky's comedies. We say: "This is what the author has depicted; this is what the images he has reproduced signify in our opinion; this is their

origin, this is their meaning; we think that it all has a living relation to your life and morals [and explains such and such requirements, the satisfaction of which is necessary for your welfare"].
Who else is to decide whether we are right or wrong if not the
very public which is being discussed. and which is being addressed?
Its verdict should be equally important and final for us, as
well as for the author whom we are discussing.

Our author is very well received by the public; hence, half
of our question is answered in the affirmative; the public admits
that he correctly understands and depicts it. There remains the
other question, namely, do we understand Ostrovsky correctly
when we ascribe a certain meaning to his productions? Some hope
of a favourable answer to this question is provided, firstly, by the
fact that the critics who hold views opposite to our own did not
meet with particular approval among the public, and secondly,
by the fact that the author himself appears to agree with us, for
in *The Thunderstorm* we find new confirmation of many of the
thoughts we have expressed concerning Ostrovsky's talent and
the significance of his productions. Incidentally, we say once
again that our essays, and the grounds upon which we base our
judgment, are before everybody's eyes; whoever does not wish
to agree with us may read our essays, test them by his own
observations and draw his own conclusions. We shall be content
with that.

Having explained the basis of our criticism [we beg our readers to pardon us for the length of this explanation. It may, of
course, have been given on two or three pages, but those pages
would not have seen the light for a long time. The length is due
to the fact that often we are obliged to explain by endless paraphrasing what could be explained simply in a few words. The
trouble is, however, that these words, quite ordinary in other
European languages, usually lend a Russian essay a form in which
it cannot appear before the public, and so, willy-nilly, one is
obliged to twist and turn one's phrases in order somehow to convey the substance of his idea to the reader.

But] let us turn to the actual subject of our essay—to the
author of *The Thunderstorm*.

Readers of *Sovremennik* will perhaps remember that we appraised Ostrovsky very highly, and expressed the opinion that he has succeeded in depicting very fully and exhaustively the essential aspects and requirements of Russian life. We shall not speak of those authors who have taken particular phenomena, the transitory and external demands of society, and have depicted them with greater or lesser success [as, for example, the demand for justice, religious tolerance, sound administration, the abolition of tavern licenses, the abolition of serfdom, etc.]. But even those authors who have taken more the inner aspect of life have confined themselves to a very narrow circle and have noted phenomena that are far from being of national importance. Such, for example, are the descriptions in innumerable stories of men who stand above their environment in development, but, lacking energy and will, perish in inaction. [These stories were of importance because they clearly revealed the vicious environment which hindered useful activity and expressed the demand, although vaguely conceived, for the energetic application in practice of the principles which we accept as true in theory.] Even such stories were of greater or lesser importance, according to the talent of the author; all, however, suffered from the defect that they dealt with only a (relatively) small section of society and had scarcely any relation whatever to the majority. Not to speak of the masses of the people, even among the middle classes of our society we see far more people who still have to acquire and understand correct concepts than such who have acquired ideas but do not know what to do with them. Hence, the importance of the stories and novels referred to above remains very special, and is appreciated by a certain close circle rather than by the majority. It cannot be denied that Ostrovsky's work is far more fruitful. He has taken up those general strivings and requirements with which the whole of Russian society is imbued, the voices of which are heard in all the phenomena of our life, and the satisfaction of which is an essential condition for our further development. We shall not repeat here what we have said at considerable length in our first essays, but, in passing, we shall mention the strange perplexity concerning our essays that overcame one of the critics of *The Thunderstorm*, we mean Mr. Apollon Grigoryev. It should be mentioned that Mr. A. Grigoryev is an enthusiastic admirer of Ostrovsky's talent, but he never succeeds—probably because of overenthusiasm—in explaining with any clarity what it is he appreciates in Ostrovsky. We, the readers of his articles, have never been able to understand him. And yet, in reviewing *The Thunderstorm*, Mr. Grigoryev devotes several pages to us, and accuses us of having attached labels to the personages in Ostrovsky's comedies, of having divided them into two categories, *tyrants and downtrodden personalities*, and of having reduced the entire work of our comedy writer to a description of the relations between these categories which are customary in the life of the merchant class. After making this accusation Mr. Grigoryev exclaims: No! This is not what constitutes Ostrovsky's originality and merit; it is *nationality*! But Mr. Grigoryev failed to tell us what nationality is, and, consequently, his retort seemed to us to be very amusing. As if we refuse to admit the quality of nationality in Ostrovsky's works! Actually, we started with that, continued and ended with it. We tried to ascertain how, and to what extent, Ostrovsky's productions express national life, national strivings; what is this if not nationality? But we did not shout about it with exclamation marks in every second line; we tried to define its content, which Mr. Grigoryev has never taken the trouble to do. Had he tried to do so, perhaps he would have arrived at the very same conclusion he censures us for, and would not have unjustly accused us of believing that Ostrovsky's merit lies in his correct descriptions of the domestic relations of merchants who adhere to the old way of life. [Everybody who read our essays was able to see that we had not only the merchants in mind when we pointed to the main features of the relationships prevailing in our social life, so well reproduced in Ostrovsky's comedies. The present-day strivings of Russian life are depicted in their widest dimensions in the works of Ostrovsky as a comedy writer in their negative aspect. By painting for us a vivid picture of false relationships, with all their consequences, he himself echoes the demand for a better arrangement of society. Tyranny, on the one hand, and lack of consciousness of the rights of one's own personality on the other—such is the basis of all the outrageous relationships that are depicted in most of Ostrovsky's comedies. The demand for right, for law, for respect for the human being—this is what every attentive reader hears from the depths of this outrageous state of affairs. What, will you deny the great importance of these demands in Russian life? Will you not admit that this background of the comedies conforms to the condition of Russian society more than of any other in Europe? Take history, recall your own lives, look around you—everywhere you will find confirmation of this. This is not the occasion to launch into historical researches; it is sufficient to observe that our history up to modern times has not facilitated the development of a respect for law (with which even Mr. Pirogov agrees, see: *Penal Regulations for the Kiev Area*), it has not created firm guarantees for the individual, but it has created a wide field for tyranny. This historical development, of course, resulted in deterioration of public morality; respect for one's own dignity was lost, belief in right and, consequently, the sense of duty declined; tyranny trampled upon right; cunning undermined the reign of tyranny.] Some writers, [lacking the sense of normal requirements and] misled by artificial combinations, while admitting certain facts of our present way of life, wanted to give them the force of law, to praise them as a normal standard of life instead of condemning them as a distortion of natural strivings brought about by an unfavourable historical development. Thus, for example, they wanted to describe tyranny as a special, natural quality of the Russian's nature, which they called "the expansive nature"; they also wanted to legalize roguery and cunning among the Russian people by calling it sagacity and shrewdness. Some critics even wanted to regard Ostrovsky as the bard of the expansive Russian nature. This explains the hubbub that was once raised about Lyubim Tortsov, who was proclaimed as the highest type our author had produced. But Ostrovsky, being a man of strong talent and, consequently, possessing a sense of truth, an instinctive inclination for natural and sound demands, could not yield to temptation, and so tyranny, even the most expansive, always appeared in his productions as it appears in reality—brutal, ugly and lawless—and the idea of his plays has always been a protest against this tyranny. He has proved that he is able to discern the meaning of this expansive nature and branded [denounced] it by depicting several types of it and by calling it tyranny.

But he did not invent these types, any more than he invented the word "tyrant." He took both from life itself. Clearly, life, which provides the materials for the comical situations in which Ostrovsky's tyrants are often placed, life, which gives them a fitting name, is no longer entirely under their influence, but contains within itself the seeds of a more rational, [lawful] and proper order of things. And indeed, after each of Ostrovsky's plays appears everybody feels inwardly conscious of this himself, and on looking round he observes the same in others. If you study this idea closely, if you examine it longer and more deeply, you will note that this striving for a [new] more natural system of relationships contains the substance of all that which we call progress, that it constitutes the direct goal of our development [, absorbs all the work of the new generations]. No matter where you look, everywhere you will find an awakening of personality, [a claim for its legitimate rights,] a protest against violence and tyranny [in most cases still timid. indefinite, ready to hide, but for all that] already making its existence felt. [Take, for example, the legislative and administrative side, which, although always fortuitous in its particular manifestations, serves, in general, as an index of the conditions of the people. This index is particularly true when legislative measures bear the impress of reliefs. concessions and extension of rights. Burdensome measures, measures which restrict the people's rights. may be called forth despite the demands of national life, simply by arbitrary action, for the benefit of the privileged minority, which gains from the restrictions imposed upon the rest. Measures which reduce privileges and enlarge common rights cannot, however, spring from anything else than the direct and persistent demands of national life. which irresistibly affect the privileged minority even when it is against their direct personal advantage. See what is going on in this country in this respect: serfs are being liberated. and the very squires who had formerly argued that it was too early to liberate the serfs are now becoming convinced. and admit that it is time to settle this question, that it has really matured in the mind of the people.... What else lies at the bottom of this question if not the decline of tyranny and the elevation of the rights of human personality? The same applies to all other reforms and improvements. How has public opinion regarded the financial reforms, all the commissions and committees which discussed banks, taxes and so forth? What did public opinion expect of them if not the formulation of a more correct and efficient system of financial admin-

istration and, consequently, the enthronement of law in place
of arbitrary actions of every kind? What compelled the authorities to grant certain rights of publicity, which they had feared
so much before, if not realization of the strength of the protest
against lack of rights and tyranny which has been growing among
the public for so many years, and which, at last, they were no
longer able to repress? What were the police and administrative
reforms, that concern for justice, the projects for introducing public trials, milder measures against the Dissenters and the abolition
of tavern licensing due to? ... We are not speaking of the practical importance of all these measures; we only assert that the
very attempt to proceed with them proves how strongly developed
is the general idea to which we have pointed. Even if they all
collapsed, or proved unsuccessful, it would only show that the
means adopted for their execution were inadequate, or wrong;
it would not be an argument against the conditions which called
them forth.] That these [demands] exist is so evident that they
have been even expressed in our literature [forthwith, as soon as
it became actually possible for them to manifest themselves.]
They were expressed in Ostrovsky's comedies with a fulness and
power that we found in few other authors. But it is not only the
degree of power that constitutes the merit of his comedies; what
is equally important for us is that he discovered the substance of
the general [demands] of life when they were still hidden, were
expressed by a very few, and very faintly expressed at that.
Ostrovsky's first play appeared in 1847; [it is well known that
since then, until recent years, even the best of our authors have
almost lost the trail of the natural demands of the people and
have even begun to doubt their existence. If they have felt their
breath sometimes, it has been very faintly, indefinitely, only in
some particular cases and, with few exceptions, they have never
been able to find a true and appropriate expression for them.
This general situation] of course partly affected Ostrovsky too;
this, perhaps, largely explains that indefiniteness which we observe to some extent in some of his subsequent plays, and which
provided the pretext for the attacks that were made upon him in
the beginning of the 'fifties. But today, carefully reviewing the
sum total of his productions, we find that his feeling for the true
[requirements and] strivings of Russian life had never left him;

sometimes it did not reveal itself at first sight, but it was always at the root of his productions. Those who wanted impartially to delve to the roots of their meaning could always find that their action was presented not superficially, but from the very root. It is this feature that establishes Ostrovsky's productions on their high level even today, when everybody is trying to express [the same striving that] we find in his plays. To avoid dealing with this at too great length we shall note only one thing: you will find [the demand for rights], respect for the individual and the protest against violence and tyranny in many of our literary productions of recent years, but in most of them the case is not presented in a living practical manner; [the abstract philosophical aspect of the question is felt, and from this everything is deduced; *right* is indicated, but real *possibility* is ignored.] This is not the case with Ostrovsky. In his productions you will find not only the moral, but the everyday, economic aspect of the problem; and this is the very essence of the matter. In his productions you clearly see that tyranny rests on fat purses [which are called "God's blessing" and] that people's dumb submission [to tyrants] is due to their material dependence [upon them]. More than that, you see that in all everyday relationships this material side predominates over the abstract side, that people who lack material security attach little importance to abstract rights and even lose a clear conception of what they are. Indeed, a well-fed man can coolly and intelligently discuss whether it is advisable for him to eat a certain dish or not; but a hungry man rushes for food wherever he sees it, and whatever kind it may be. This phenomenon, occurring in all spheres of social life, is well noted and understood by Ostrovsky, and his plays reveal to the attentive reader better than any arguments how the system of oppression and crude, petty selfishness that is established by the tyrants corrupts even those who suffer from it; how the latter, if they have retained even the slightest remnants of energy, try to take advantage of it in order to gain the opportunity to live independently, and how in the process they lose all scruples about both means and rights. We have discussed this subject in too great detail in our earlier essays to justify our returning to it here; besides, having recalled the aspects of Ostrovsky's talent which are revealed in *The Thunderstorm,* as well as in his previous productions, we ought after all, briefly review the play itself and show how we understand it.

Actually this ought not to have been necessary; but what the critics have written about *The Thunderstorm* up to now shows that our remarks will not be *superfluous*.

We have already observed in the case of Ostrovsky's previous plays that they are not comedies of intrigue, and not even character comedies in the strict sense of the term, but something new, which we would call "plays of life" if that term were not too wide and, therefore, not quite definite. What we want to say is that in the foreground of his plays we always find the, general conditions of life which are not dependent upon any of the personages in the play. He punishes neither the villain nor his victim; both look pitiful to you, not infrequently both are comical, but they are not the direct objects of the sentiments which the play rouses in you. You see that their conditions dominate over them, and you blame them only for failing to display sufficient energy to extricate themselves from them. The very tyrants who should naturally rouse your indignation turn out, on closer examination, to be deserving of pity rather than anger; they are virtuous and even intelligent in their own way, within the limits prescribed for them by routine and maintained by their position; [but this position is such that it makes a full, healthy, human development impossible]. We saw this particularly when analyzing the character of Rusakov.

Thus, the struggle which theory demands from the drama takes place in Ostrovsky's plays not in the monologues of the personages, but in the facts which dominate their actions. Often. the personages in the comedies themselves have no clear conception, or no conception at all, of the meaning of their position and of their struggle; on the other hand, this struggle takes place very distinctly and consciously in the heart of the spectator who [involuntarily] protests against [the conditions] which give rise to such facts. That is why we cannot bring ourselves to regard as unnecessary and superfluous those personages in Ostrovsky's plays who take no direct part in the plot. In our opinion, these personages are as necessary for the play as the principal personages; they reveal to us the environment in which the action takes place, they depict the situation which determines the actions of the prin-

cipal personages. To ascertain the characteristics of the life of a
plant we must study it on the soil on which that plant grows;
torn from that soil, you will have the form of the plant, but you
will never fully learn its life. Similarly, you will never learn the
life of society if you examine it only in the direct relationships of
a few persons who, for some reason, come into collision with each
other. You will see only the business, official side of life, whereas
what we want is its everyday surroundings. The outside, inactive
participants in the drama of life, each apparently engaged only
in his own affairs, often, by the mere fact of their existence, exercise an influence upon the course of affairs that cannot possibly
be resisted. How many enthusiastic ideas, how many far-reaching
plans, how many enthusiastic impulses collapse at a mere glance
at the indifferent prosaic crowd which passes us with contemptuous
unconcern! How many pure and virtuous sentiments die within
you out of fear of being ridiculed and scorned by this crowd!
On the other hand, how many crimes, how many acts of tyranny
and violence are halted by the decision of this crowd, which always seems to be so indifferent and complaisant, but which is
actually very firm on something it has once recognized. Hence,
it is extremely important for us to know what conception this
crowd has of good and evil, what it regards as truth and what as
falsehood. This determines our view of the situation in which the
principal personages of a play find themselves and, consequently,
the degree of our sympathy towards them.

In *The Thunderstorm* we see with exceptional clarity the need
for the so-called "superfluous" personages; without them we would
be unable to understand the personality of the heroine, and we
would easily misinterpret the meaning of the whole play, as most
of the critics did. Perhaps we shall be told that, after all, the
author himself is to blame, if he is so easily misunderstood; but
to this we would answer that an author writes for the public, and
the public, even if it does not at once grasp the whole meaning
of his plays, will not distort it. As for the point that some of the
details could have been worked out better, we shall not attempt
to deny it. No doubt the gravediggers in *Hamlet* are more in place
and more closely connected with the action of the play than, for
example, the half-insane lady in *The Thunderstorm*; but we are
not arguing that our author is a Shakespeare; all we are urging

37*

is that there is reason for the appearance of his outsiders, and even that they are needed for the completeness of the play we are reviewing just as it is, and not in the sense of absolute perfection.

The Thunderstorm, as you know, presents us with an idyll in the "realm of darkness" which Ostrovsky, with his talent, gradually reveals to us. The people you see here live in idyllic surroundings: the town, all in green, is situated on the steep bank of the Volga, from which an extensive view of spreading cornfields dotted with villages is obtained. The beautiful summer's day tempts everybody to the river bank, into the air, under the open sky, to breathe the soft zephyrs that blow from the Volga.... And indeed, the townsfolk do sometimes take a stroll along the boulevard that overlooks the river, although they are accustomed to the beauties of the Volga scene. In the evenings they sit at the gates of their houses and engage in pious conversation. But they spend most of their time in their homes, busy with their domestic affairs, eat and sleep—and they go to sleep very early, so that one who is unaccustomed to this habit finds it hard to stand the long sleepy nights that they indulge in. But what else can they do but sleep when they are sated? Their lives pass so smoothly and evenly, no world interests disturb them, because these interests never reach them: kingdoms may collapse, new countries may be discovered, the face of the earth may change as it pleases, the world may start a new life on the basis of new principles, but the inhabitants of the township of Kalinov will remain in complete ignorance about the rest of the world. On rare occasions a vague rumour will reach them to the effect that Napoleon of twenty tongues* is rising again [or that the antichrist has been born], but they accept even this as a curious joke, similar to the news that there is a country which is inhabited by people with dogs' heads. They will shake their heads, express astonishment at the wonders of nature, and then go home to take a bite.... When young, they display a certain amount of interest in things, but this soon dies for want of nourishment. News reaches them as it did in ancient Rūs at the time of Daniel the Pilgrim, only from pilgrims, and even of these there are few real ones left today. They have to be satisfied with such who "themselves, being so weak,

* So called because of the numerous nationalities represented in Napoleon's army.—*Tr.*

have not been far, but have heard a great deal," as is the case
with Feklusha in *The Thunderstorm*. Only from them do the inhabitants of Kalinov learn what is going on in the world. If it
were not for them, they would think that the whole world is like
their own township [and that it is quite impossible to live differently from the way they are living]. But even the information
communicated to them by Feklusha is of a nature not calculated
to imbue them with a strong desire [to change their way of life
for a different one]. Feklusha [belongs to the patriotic and extremely conservative party, she] lives in clover among the [pious
and naive] Kalinovites. She is respected, entertained and supplied
with all she needs; with a most serious air she [assures you that
her very sins are due to the fact that she is superior to other
mortals]. "Ordinary people," she says, "are tempted by one adversary, but we pilgrims, some of us have six and some twelve,
and we have to contend against them all." And the Kalinovites
believe her. [Clearly, the mere instinct of self-preservation must
prevent her from saying a good word about what is going on in
other countries. And indeed, listening to the conversations of the
merchants, the townsfolk and the petty officials in a remote country
town, what amazing information one hears about heathen and
pagan countries, how many tales one hears about the time when
people were burned and tortured, when robbers sacked towns, and
so forth, and how little information one hears about life in Europe,
about a better arrangement of society. Even in the so-called educated section of society, among the people who have become
Europeanized, will you not find, together with numerous enthusiasts who go into raptures over the new Paris streets and furniture, an almost equal number of grave critics who terrify their
listeners by telling them that there is no order in any part of
Europe except Austria, and that justice cannot be found anywhere! . . .] All this leads to a situation where Feklusha expresses
herself so positively in terms like the following: "What magnifishence, my dear, what magnifishence, what wonderful beauty!
Why, you are living in the Promised Land!" And this is undoubtedly the case [when you think of what is going on in other countries.] Listen to Feklusha:

"They say, my dear, that there are countries where there are no
Christian kings, and Sultans rule the land. In one country the Turkish

Sultan Mahnut sits on the throne, in another the Persian Sultan Mahnut sits on the throne, and, my dear, they sit in judgment over all men, and they judge unjustly. They cannot do a single thing righteously, my dear. That's their faith, they can't help it. Our laws are righteous laws, my dear, theirs are unrighteous. What is right according to our laws is wrong according to theirs. And all the judges in those countries are unrighteous too. In fact, my dear, in their petitions they write: 'Judge me, unrighteous Judge!' And there is also a country where all the people have dogs' heads."

"But why with dogs' heads?" Glasha enquires. "Because they are heathens," answers Feklusha curtly, regarding all further explanation superfluous. But Glasha is satisfied even with that. In the boring monotony of her life and thoughts she is pleased to hear anything that is in the least new and original. In her mind the vague thought is already awakening that "after all there are people who live differently from the way we live. Of course our way is better; but then, who knows! Things are bad even here, but we don't know very much about those other countries, we only hear something now and again from good people...." And a wish to know more, and in greater detail, steals into her heart. This is evident to us from what Glasha says when the pilgrim woman goes away: "So that's the kind of countries there are! What wonders there are in the world! But we are stuck here and know nothing about them. It's a good thing that there are good people about. After all, we do hear about what is going on in the world now and again. If it were not for them we'd remain ignorant to the end of our days." As you see, the unrighteousness and heathenism in other countries rouse no horror or indignation in Glasha's heart; what interests her is the new information she receives, and which conjures up in her mind something mysterious, "wonders" as she puts it. As you see, she is not satisfied with Feklusha's explanations, which only rouse in her regret about her ignorance. Evidently she is halfway on the road towards scepticism. But how is she to preserve her incredulity when it is being constantly shaken by stories like those told by Feklusha? How is she to acquire correct conceptions, or even reach the stage when she can put intelligent questions to herself, when her desire for knowledge is hemmed in by the ring which is drawn around her in the town of Kalinov? But this is not all. How can she dare not to believe and to press her questions when her elders and betters are so positively calm in the conviction that their conceptions and mode of life are the best in the world, and that everything new comes from the Evil One? It is frightful and hard for every novice to attempt to go against the demands and convictions of this ignorant mass, which is terrible in its naiveté and sincerity. It will curse us, it will shun us like the plague, not in anger, not deliberately, but from the profound conviction that we are related to the antichrist. We shall be lucky if it only regards us as semi-imbeciles and merely makes a laughingstock of us. ... It seeks knowledge, it loves discussions, but only within the definite limits that are prescribed by its fundamental concepts, which befog the mind. You may impart to the inhabitants of Kalinov a certain amount of knowledge of geography, but don't attempt to tell them that the earth is not supported by three whales [or that Jerusalem is not the hub of the world], they will not agree with you the least little bit, although they have as much idea about [the hub of the world] as the people in *The Thunderstorm* have about Lithuania. "And what is this, neighbour?" a peaceful citizen asks another, pointing to a picture. "Ah, that's the devastation of Lithuania," the other answers. "You see, it's a battle! That was when our country was fighting Lithuania." "What's this Lithuania?" "Oh, Lithuania, just Lithuania," answers the one who is explaining. "They say, neighbour, that it dropped down upon us from the sky," continues the first citizen. But his neighbour is very little concerned about that. "From the sky? All right, let it be from the sky," he answers. ... Here a woman joins in the conversation. "Don't argue!" she says. "Everybody knows it dropped from the sky. And where the battle took place big mounds have been piled up as a monument." "Why, that's absolutely true, neighbour!" exclaims the first speaker, now fully satisfied. Ask him what he thinks about Lithuania after that! This is the upshot of all questions put by the people here who have a natural inclination for knowledge. And this is not because these people are more stupid and ignorant than many others we meet in academies and scientific societies. No, it is all due to the fact that they [have been trained by their conditions, by their life under the yoke of tyranny, to accept the irrational and senseless, and so they] deem it improper [and even presumptuous] to dig perseveringly to the rational foundations of anything. They have

spirit enough to ask a question, but if the answer is in the nature
of "a cannon is one thing and a mortar another," they will not
dare to enquire further and humbly rest content with the explanation given them. The secret of this indifference to logic lies primarily in the absence of [all] logic in the relationships of everyday
life. The key to this secret is provided for us, for example, by the
following retort made by Dikoi in *The Thunderstorm*. In answer
to his rudeness Kuligin says: "Why, Sir, Savel Prokofich, do you
insult me, an honest man?" To this Dikoi replies as follows:

"What! Have I got to answer to you for what I say? I don't have
to answer to anybody, even to people more important than you. If I want
to think of you in a certain way, I think it! You may be an honest man
to others, but I think you are a rascal, and that's all there is to it. Did
you want to hear that from me? Well, hear it! I say you are a rascal,
and there's an end to it! Do you think of taking me to court? Well,
remember, you are a worm. If I want to I'll spare you, and if I want to
I'll crush you."

[What theoretical reflections can survive where life is based
on principles such as these? Absence of law and logic—such is
the law and logic of this life. It is not anarchy, it is something
far worse (although the educated European cannot imagine anything worse than anarchy). We know that there is no principle
in anarchy; everybody does as he pleases, nobody commands
others, and if anybody attempts to command, the one who is
commanded may answer that he refuses to recognize the other, and
so everybody misbehaves and no agreement can be reached. The
situation in a society in which such anarchy prevails (if it is at
all possible) is awful indeed. But imagine that such an anarchic
society is divided into two sections and that one section claims
the right to misbehave and to recognize no law, while the other
is compelled to recognize all the claims of the first as the law, and
uncomplainingly put up with all its whims and all its outrages. . . .
This would be more awful, would it not? The anarchy would be
the same, because society would still not be based on any rational
principles, misbehaviour would continue, but half the members
of that society would be compelled to suffer from this misbehaviour and constantly encourage it by their own humility and submissiveness. Clearly, under such circumstances, misbehaviour and
lawlessness would assume dimensions which they could never
assume under universal anarchy. Indeed, whatever you may say,

one man left to himself cannot do much mischief in society and would very soon feel the necessity of agreeing and coming to some arrangement with the other members of society for the common good. But a man will never feel this necessity if he finds in many others like him a wide field for the exercise of his whims, and if in their dependent and degraded conditions he finds constant encouragement for his tyranny. Thus, having this in common with anarchy that there is an absence of all law and right obligatory for all, in substance, tyranny is far more awful than anarchy, because it provides more means and scope for misbehaviour, it compels a larger number of people to suffer, and it is more dangerous because it can last far longer. Anarchy (if it is at all possible, we repeat) can be only a transient condition, which must of its own accord, and at every step, bring people to their senses and lead to something more sound. Tyranny, however, tries to establish itself as the law, as a permanent system. That is why, while having such a broad conception of its own freedom, it tries to adopt every possible measure to retain this freedom entirely for itself forever and to safeguard itself against all audacious encroachments. To achieve this object it ostensibly recognizes certain higher demands, and although it itself violates these demands it strongly champions them in face of others.] A few minutes after he so emphatically rejected, in favour of his own whim, all moral and logical grounds for judging a man, Dikoi fiercely attacks Kuligin when the latter, in explaining the cause of the thunderstorm, utters the word electricity. "Well, aren't you a rascal after that?" he bawls. "Thunderstorms are sent us as a punishment, to make us feel. But you want to protect yourself with pikes and spears, God forgive me. What are you, a Tatar? Are you a Tatar? Tell me, are you a Tatar!" Kuligin, however, dares not answer: "I want to think that way and so I do, and nobody can command me." How can he? He cannot even present his explanation; it is met with abuse, he is not even allowed to speak. [You will stop arguing whether you like it or not when every argument is answered with the fist; and when, in the long run, the fist always remains in the right. . . .]

But wonderful to relate, in their unchallenged, irresponsible reign of ignorance, giving free rein to their whims, disregarding all law and logic, the tyrants in Russian life, however, are beginning vaguely to feel a sort of discontent and fear, although they do not know of what, or why. Everything seems to be running as smoothly as before: Dikoi hurls his abuse at everybody he pleases. When he is asked: "How is it nobody in the whole house can please you?" he smugly answers: "Just imagine!" Kabanova still keeps her children in fear and trembling, still compels her daughter-in-law to adhere to the etiquette of the old way of life and eats her heart out as rust eats iron, she still regards herself as absolutely infallible [and is flattered by all sorts of Feklushas]. And yet something disturbs them, they are haunted by misgiving. Independently of them, and without their permission, a different life has sprung up, a life based on different principles; and although it is still remote and not yet visible, it is nevertheless making itself felt [and is giving the tyrants bad dreams in their realm of darkness. The tyrants are fiercely hunting for their enemy, they are ready to hurl themselves upon the most innocent, upon a Kuligin, for example, but there is no enemy, no guilty one whom they can destroy. The law of the times, the law of nature and history, is coming into its own, and the old Kabanovs are gasping for breath; they feel that there is a power stronger than they, a power which they cannot overcome, and which they do not even know how to contend against. They do not wish to yield (and so far nobody is calling upon them to yield), but they shrink and cower. Formerly, they wanted to establish their system of life for ages to come, and they advocate the same thing now, but their hopes are fading, and they are really disturbed at the prospect of their system not even lasting their own lifetime. . . .] Kabanova says "the end of the world is coming," and when Feklusha tells her about all the horrors that are going on at the present time—the railways that are being built, and so forth—she [prophetically] observes: "And worse than that will happen." "I hope we don't live to see it," says Feklusha with a sigh. "Perhaps we shall," answers Kabanova fatalistically, thereby betraying her doubts and misgivings. But why is she alarmed? Suppose people are travelling by railway, what has it to do with her? But you see: although she herself would never travel by this invention of the devil "not even if you gave her her weight in gold," more and more people are travelling by railway, completely ignoring her imprecations. Is not that sad? Is not this proof of her impotence? People have

learned about electricity, but why should this offend [the Dikois
and Kabanovas]? Well, you see, Dikoi says that "thunderstorms
are sent to punish us, to make us feel," but Kuligin does not feel,
or feels something entirely different, and talks about electricity.
Is this not license, is this not disrespect for the [power and] importance of Dikoi? The people do not wish to believe in what he
believes; this means that they do not believe in him, that they
think they are cleverer than he. Think of what this will lead to!
It is not surprising that Kabanova says with reference to Kuligin:
"How times have changed! What new teachers have appeared!
If an old man talks like that, what can you expect of the young
one?" And Kabanova is very seriously disturbed about the future
of the old order, to which she has been accustomed all her life.
She foresees its end, strives to keep it in being; but she feels that
the former respect for the order has gone [that it is being maintained unwillingly, only by compulsion, and that it will be cast
aside at the first opportunity]. She herself has lost some of her
[chivalrous] ardour, she no longer observes the old customs with
her former zeal, and many of them she has abandoned [has resigned
herself to the fact that it is impossible to stem the tide] and
can only watch in despair how [it] is gradually washing away the
colourful garden of her whimsical superstitions. Like the last of
the heathens before the power of Christianity, the generation of
tyrants, caught in the current of the new life, are yielding, and
are being washed away. They even lack the determination to enter
into an open struggle against it; they are trying only to cheat
time, as it were, and indulge in fruitless complaints against the
new movement. These complaints have always been heard from
the old generation, because new generations have always introduced something new into life, opposed to the old order; but
today the complaints of the tyrants assume an exceptionally gloomy
[funereal] tone. The only consolation Kabanova can find is that,
somehow, with her assistance, the old order may last until her
death; after that, what will be will be, she will not see it. When
her son starts out on his journey and everybody comes out on the
porch to bid him farewell, she complains that nothing is done
in the way she thinks it should be done: her son does not bow
low to her, she has to order him to do so, he does not think of
it himself; he does not "command" his wife to behave properly

during his absence, he does not even know how to command, and in taking leave of his wife he does not order her to bow low before him; and the daughter-in-law, in saying farewell to her husband, does not wail and lie down on the porch to demonstrate her love. Kabanova tries to maintain the old customs to the best of her ability, but she already feels that it is impossible to carry on in the old way. For example, as regards wailing on the porch, she only offers remarks to her daughter-in-law by way of advice, she no longer dares imperatively to demand this.... But the whole ceremony of leave-taking of her son arouses sad reflections in her:

"Youth tells! It's funny even to look at them! If they were not my children I'd laugh until my sides ached. They don't know anything. They don't know how things ought to be done. They can't even bid each other farewell properly. *It's a good thing there are still old people in the house.* It's they who keep the home going, while they are still alive. *The stupid fools! They want their freedom.* But when they get their freedom they mix everything up disgracefully, enough to make good people laugh. Some will pity us, of course, but most people will laugh. And how can they not laugh? When they invite guests they don't know how to seat them, and if you're not careful they might even forget some of the relations. Isn't that enough to make you laugh? *And that's how the old ways are passing away.* You feel you don't want to visit other people's houses. When you do, you're so disgusted you want to get out again as quickly as you can. *What's going to happen when we old folks die? How the world will go on, I really don't know. There's one consolation, I won't live to see it."*

By the time the old folks die the young folks will have grown old—the old lady need not worry. But you see, the important thing for her is not so much that there should be somebody to look after things and to teach the inexperienced, as that the old order should remain undisturbed, that the concepts which she regards as correct should remain inviolate. [Her crude and narrow selfishness prevents her from rising even to the height of resigning herself to the triumph of a principle even at the sacrifice of existing forms; nor can this be expected of her, for actually she has no principle, no general convictions to govern her life. In this respect she is far lower in the scale than the people who are called enlightened conservatives. The latter have, to some extent, widened their selfishness, have combined it with demands of a general character, so that they are even capable of sacrificing certain personal tastes and advantages for the sake of preserving the old order. If they were in Kabanova's place they, for example, would not insist on the monstrous and degrading demand for low bows, and for insulting "commands" from the husband to the wife, they would merely take care that the general idea was preserved, namely, that the wife should fear her husband and be obedient to her mother-in-law. Then the daughter-in-law would not have gone through such painful scenes, although she would have remained just as completely dependent upon the old woman. The result would have been that, hard as it may have gone with the young woman, her patience would have lasted ever so much longer, for it would have been subjected to a slow and even pressure instead of sharp and severe blows. Hence, it is clear, that it would be much more profitable for Kabanova herself, and for the old way of life which she defends, to forego some of the empty forms and make partial concessions in order to retain the substance. But people of the Kabanova breed fail to understand this; they have not reached the stage of conceiving of, or defending, any principle outside of themselves—they are a principle in themselves and, therefore, regard everything that concerns them as being of absolute importance. They not only demand respect for themselves, they also demand that this respect should be expressed in definite forms. This is the stage they are still in! That is why, of course, the external aspect of everything over which their influence extends preserves more of the old way of life and seems to be more fixed than it is in those places where people have abandoned tyranny and try only to preserve the substance of their interests and importance. Actually, however, the inner importance of the tyrants is much nearer to its end than the influence of people who are able to maintain themselves and their principles by means of outward concessions]. This is what makes Kabanova so sad and Dikoi so mad; they refuse to put a curb on their arrogance until the very last moment [and so they are now in the position of a rich merchant on the eve of bankruptcy]. This rich merchant goes on living as before [he is giving a banquet today; this morning he arranged a deal running into a million, his credit is still good, but already dark rumours are afloat to the effect that he has no available capital, that his business is shaky, and that several creditors intend to put in their claims tomorrow; he has no money, he will get no postponement, and tomorrow the whole edifice of chicanery and phantom wealth will collapse. He is in a tight fix....

It goes without saying that in this situation the merchant will concentrate all his efforts on an attempt to fool his creditors and induce them to believe that he is rich. Similarly, the Kabanovas and Dikois are now concerned only with making people continue to believe in their power. They no longer hope to improve their affairs, but they know that there will be plenty of scope for their tyranny as long as people tremble before them. That is why they are so stubborn, so arrogant, so menacing even in their last moments, of which only a few are left, as they themselves feel. The more they feel their real strength ebbing away, the more they are affected by the influence of free common sense which proves to them that they have no rational support, the more insolently and furiously do they reject all demands of reason and substitute themselves and their tyranny for them.] The naiveté with which Dikoi says to Kuligin: "I want to think you are a rascal and so I think so, I don't care whether you are an honest man or not, and I don't have to tell anybody why I think so,"—this naiveté could not have been expressed in all its [tyrannical] absurdity had not Kuligin called it forth by the humble question: "Why do you insult an honest man?" [You see, Dikoi wanted to scotch at once any attempt to demand an account from him, he wanted to show that he was not only above responsibility to anybody, but even above ordinary human logic. He thinks that if he admits that the laws of common sense which are common to all people have any power over him, his importance will suffer greatly. Indeed, in most cases, this is actually so, for his claims are opposed to common sense.] This is why constant dissatisfaction and irritation develop in him. He himself explains his attitude when he tells us how hard it is for him to part with money.

"What can I do when my heart is what it is? I know perfectly well that I must pay, but my heart won't let me. You are my friend and I ought to repay you, but if you come and ask me for money I shall swear at you. I'll repay all right, but I'll swear at you just the same; because the moment you mention money to me all my innards seem to catch fire; all my innards burn, and that's a fact.... Well, when I'm in that state I can't help swearing at people."

Parting with money, which is a material and demonstrable fact, awakens reflections even in Dikoi's mind. He realizes how absurd he is, but he puts the cause down to the fact that his "heart

is what it is"! In other cases he does not even fully realize his
own absurdity, but by his very nature he must feel the same irritation at the triumph of common sense as when he is obliged to
part with money. He finds it hard to pay his debts because, owing
to his natural selfishness, he wants to be comfortable, and everything around him convinces him that this comfort can be purchased
with money. Hence his strong attachment to money. But here his
development stops, his selfishness remains within the limits of an
individual and refuses to recognize his relation to society, to his
neighbours. He needs a lot of money, this he knows and, therefore,
he wishes only to acquire money, not to part with it. When, however, by the natural course of events, it comes to parting with
money, he gets angry and swears, he regards it as a misfortune,
as a punishment, like a fire, a flood, or a fine, and not as the due
and lawful payment for services others have rendered him. So it
is in all things: wishing himself well, he wants room, independence,
but he refuses to recognize the law which determines the mode of
acquiring and enjoying all rights in society. [He only wants
more rights, as many rights as possible, for himself; when, however, it is necessary to recognize the rights of others, he regards
it as an encroachment upon his personal dignity, he gets angry,
procrastinates and tries to prevent it in every possible way. Even
when he knows that he must and will yield in the end, he tries
to do mischief. "I'll repay all right, but I'll swear at you just
the same!" And we must suppose that the larger the sum he has
to part with, and the more imperative the necessity of paying it,
the stronger is the language he uses. . . . From this it follows firstly,
that his vituperation and abuse, although unpleasant, are not particularly frightful, and whoever is intimidated by them, stops
asking for his money and gives it up for lost, acts very foolishly.
Secondly, it would be hopeless to try to reform Dikoi by reasoning
with him; his habit of bullying is so strong that he yields to it
even in spite of the voice of his own common sense. Clearly, no
appeals to reason will stop him until reason is combined with
some tangible external force. He swears at Kuligin and will not
listen to reason, but when, while crossing the Volga one day, a
Hussar officer swore at him, he dared not talk back. He gave vent
to his anger when he got home; for two weeks after that his domestics hid from him in the attic and in the pantry. . . .

All such relationships] make us feel that the position of the Dikois, Kabanovas and all [tyrants] like them is far from being as safe and secure as it was in times gone by, in the blessed days of patriarchal customs. Then, if we are to believe what the old folks say [, Dikoi could indulge in his arrogant whims not merely by virtue of his power, but by universal consent. He raved and swore because he did not anticipate any opposition, nor did he meet with any; all those around him were imbued with but one thought, with one desire, namely, to please him; nobody could conceive of any other aim in life except that of pandering to his whims]. The more truculently some parasite acted [the more arrogantly he trampled upon human rights], the more pleased were those [who by their labour fed him and] whom he made the victims of his fantasies. The stories old footmen told with awe about how their [aristocratic] masters humiliated the small squires [seduced other people's wives and innocent girls, had officials who were sent to investigate flogged in their stables] and so forth—[the stories the historians of war tell us about the greatness of a Napoleon who fearlessly sacrificed hundreds of thousands of men to exercise his genius] the recollections of ancient gallants about a certain Don Juan of the days of their prime who "never let anybody out of his clutches and was able [to seduce any girl and] set any family at loggerheads—all stories of this kind prove that these patriarchial times have not yet receded very far from us. [But, to the extreme disappointment of the tyrannical parasites, they are now receding fast, and the position of the Dikois and the Kabanovas is far from being so pleasant. They must now take steps to reinforce their position and to safeguard themselves, because everywhere demands are arising hostile to their tyranny, and holding out for them the menacing prospect of having to fight the awakening common sense of the overwhelming majority of mankind. Hence the constant suspicion, the sensitiveness and quarrelsomeness of the tyrants. Inwardly realizing that they are not worthy of respect, but refusing to admit this even to themselves, they reveal their lack of self-confidence by the pettiness of their demands, and by constantly reminding and exhorting everybody. in season and out of season, that they must be respected. This feature is very vividly expressed in *The Thunderstorm* in the scene with Kabanova and the children, where, in answer to her

son's humble remark: "Would I dare to disobey you, Mama?"
she says: "Elders are not very much respected nowadays!" And
then she begins to nag her son and daughter-in-law in such a way
as to make even the spectator squirm].

K a b a n o v: I would not do a thing without your permission, Mama,
you know that.

K a b a n o v a: Yes, I'd believe you, my dear, if I did not see with
my own eyes and hear with my own ears how children respect their parents
nowadays! If only they would remember how much pain mothers have to
endure for their children's sake.

K a b a n o v: I, Mama. . . .

K a b a n o v a: Even if a mother is harsh sometimes and offends your
pride, I think you ought to bear it! What do you think?

K a b a n o v: But Mama, when have I ever protested against what
you have said?

K a b an o v a: Mothers are old and foolish; you young people are
clever and should not expect too much from fools like us.

K a b a n o v (aside—with a sigh): Oh Lord! (*To his mother*): Would
I ever dare, Mama!

K a b a n o v a: After all, it is out of love that parents are strict with
you, it is out of love that they scold you, it's because they want to teach you
to be good. But children don't like this nowadays, and they go among
people and say that their mothers are always grumbling and nag them to
death. . . . And God save us if we say anything that displeases our daugh-
ters-in-law! Then there is no end of talk about mothers-in-law being unbearable.

K a b a n o v: Does anyone say anything like that about you, Mama?

K a b a n o v a: *I've not heard it, my dear, I've not heard it, I won't
tell a lie. Had I heard it, I should have talked to you quite differently,
my dear.*

And after this admission, the old woman continues to nag her
son for the space of two whole pages. She has no grounds whatever for doing so, but her heart is disturbed. Her heart is her prophet, and it is warning her that something is wrong, that the internal, living connection between her and the younger members
of her household has [long ago] collapsed, that they are now
bound to her only mechanically, and would be glad of any opportunity to break away from her.

We have dealt at this great length with the leading personages
in *The Thunderstorm* because, in our opinion, Katerina's tragedy
is due entirely to the position that is inevitably hers among these
personages, to the way of life that was established under their
influence. *The Thunderstorm* is undoubtedly Ostrovsky's most out-

spoken play. In it the relations between tyranny and weakness are carried to their most tragic consequences; and yet, most of those who have read and have seen the play agree that it creates a less oppressive and mournful impression than Ostrovsky's other plays (not to speak, of course, of his purely comical studies). There is even something refreshing and encouraging in *The Thunderstorm*. That "something," in our opinion, is the background of the play which we have indicated, and which reveals the precariousness of the position [and approaching end] of tyranny. Furthermore, the very character of Katerina, which is depicted against this background, also breathes of the new life that her death opens for us.

The point is that, as portrayed in *The Thunderstorm*, Katerina's character marks a step forward not only in Ostrovsky's dramatic activities, but also in the whole of our literature. It corresponds to the new phase of our [national] life, it has long demanded portrayal in literature, our best writers have toyed with it, but they were only able to appreciate its necessity, they were unable mentally to grasp and to feel its substance. Ostrovsky was able to do that. Not a single critic of *The Thunderstorm* has wished, or has been able, to write a correct appreciation of this character, and for this reason we take the liberty to continue our essay a little longer in order to explain rather fully how we understand Katerina's character [and why we think its creation is so important for our literature].

[Russian life has at last reached the stage where virtuous and esteemed, but weak and spineless individuals no longer satisfy the public conscience and are regarded as totally useless. An urgent need is now felt for men who, if less beautiful in character, are more active and energetic. Nor can it be otherwise]. As soon as the consciousness of truth [and right], as soon as common sense awoke in the minds of men, it imperatively demanded not only agreement with it in the abstract [(in which the virtuous heroes of the past were always so brilliant)] but its application to life, to activity. But before it can be applied to life, many obstacles [raised by the Dikois, Kabanovas and their ilk] have to be overcome, and to overcome these obstacles [enterprising] determined and persevering characters are required. These must personify, merge themselves with the [general] demand for truth [and right] which has [at last] awakened [in men] and is breaking through all the barriers [erected by the Dikoi tyrants]. The great problem now is, how should the character which the new phase of social life [in this country] is calling for be formed and manifest itself? Our authors have tried to solve this problem, but their efforts have always been more or less unsuccessful. We think that their failure has been due to the fact that, after arriving at the conclusion—by a purely logical process—that Russian life was searching for such a character, they set to work to mould this character in conformity with their own conception of what valour in general, and Russian valour in particular, demands. In this way there appeared, for example, Kalinovich, who nearly pulled a merchant's beard to compel him to contribute 10,000 rubles for a public purpose, and who tortured in prison an old prince, whose mistress he married in order to make a career. In this way also appeared Stolz, the excellent steward [who managed estates so well and was able promptly to destroy forged promissory notes with the aid of a charitable official]. There appeared Insarov [who threw the German into the water] refused to live as a non-paying guest at his friend's country house, and even dared to marry the girl he loved [! !]. There appeared also Princess Zinaida, who was something between a Pechorin and Nozdrev in a petticoat. . . . All these were acclaimed as strong and integral characters. But above them all, last year, towered Anani Yakovlev, concerning whom Mr. Apollon Maikov of Moscow [126] published such an amazing comment in the *Sankt Peterburgskiye Vedomosti* that I cannot understand how it is that Kuzma Prutkov has not yet composed a new series of aphorisms out of it. You are probably aware that Anani Yakovlev flies into a rage on learning that his wife had had a child with the local squire during his absence; but although he is very respectful to the squire when he goes to him to demand an explanation, he is extremely rude to the squire's steward, beats his wife and finally, losing all self-control, he dashes the infant's head against the corner of a wall. He then runs away into the woods, but driven by hunger, he gives himself up into the hands of justice. Obviously, this is a strong person, but in the physical rather than in the moral and literary sense. It is not this strength that is pushing to the surface out of the hidden recesses of Russian life [and this is not the way it should manifest itself.] That is why

38*

we totally fail to understand how it is possible to appraise *A Bitter Fate* higher than the innumerable novels, comedies and dramas which expose the evils of serfdom [, the stupidity of government officials] and the coarseness of the Russian muzhik. If you offer it to us as a play without any exceptional claims, merely as a melodramatic episode after the type of the gruesome production of Eugene Sue, we shall raise no protest; in fact we shall even be pleased. After all, it is better than, for example, the [sentimental] scenes presented by Mr. N. Lvov and Count Sollogub [which amaze us for their utter distortion of the concepts of duty and honour]. But if you claim some higher and more general significance for this play, then we cannot possibly agree with you. It seems to us that Anani Yakovlev, taken [not as a timid exception but] as a type, is a travesty of the Russian character [and of Russian life, which is incapable of producing characters like Anani and squires like Cheglov]. Either one thing or the other: if Anani is really a strong character, as the author claims he is, then he [should have vented his rage upon the direct cause of his unhappiness] or else, guided by the consideration that nobody was to blame, he should have kept his anger under control. We constantly see such climaxes in Russian life when strong characters come into collision with hostile circumstances. If, however, he is simply a cowardly and senseless bully, as he actually appears to be in the play, then it must be admitted that the position created for him in the play is totally unsuitable to this type, and it is not in the least developed in such a way as clearly to reveal his essential features. But let us not bother any more with this play, it is already forgotten, as is Prince Lupovitsky,[127] and other well-intentioned but false productions that claimed to present characteristic national types. We dwelt on it for a moment only because many people took Anani for a purely Russian type, whereas to us it seemed that we were simply being offered a travesty of what some authors describe as "the expansive Russian nature." In our opinion, the author of *A Bitter Fate* unintentionally achieved a result similar to that achieved by the comedies that were written by command of Peter the Great against the Dissenters. Everybody knows that in these comedies the Dissenters were always presented as wild and senseless monsters, as much as to say: "Look what they are like! Can their doctrine be trusted, and can their de-

mands be conceded?" Similarly, *A Bitter Fate* says to us through
the character of Anani Yakovlev as depicted in it: "This is what
the Russian is like when he [becomes slightly conscious of his
personal dignity and, as a consequence] runs amok!" And the
critics who attribute general significance to *A Bitter Fate* and regard Anani as a type become accomplices in this slander which,
of course, the author indulges in unintentionally.

This is not how the strong Russian character is understood and
expressed in *The Thunderstorm*. What strikes us first of all is the
antithesis it presents to all tyrannical principles. It does not reveal
any inclination for violent outbursts [and destruction]; nor practical adroitness in arranging [for lofty objects] its private affairs.
It does not display senseless and highfalutin pathos, nor diplo-
matic-pedantic calculation. No, it is concentrated and resolute,
undeviatingly loyal to the sense of [natural] truth, imbued with
faith in [new ideals] and is self-sacrificing [in the sense that it
prefers to die rather than live under a system which it detests].
It is guided not by abstract principles, not by practical considerations, and not by fleeting pathos, but simply by its *nature*,
by its whole being. The integrity and harmony of this character
constitute its strength [and make it absolutely essential at a time
when the old savage relationships, although having lost all their
inner strength, continue to survive only because of their external
mechanical bonds]. A man who understands the absurdity of the
tyranny of the Dikois and Kabanovas only from the force of logic
will do nothing against them, for the simple reason that before
them all logic disappears; [no syllogisms will help you to convince the chains to slip off the arms and legs of a captive, nor
induce a fist to inflict no pain upon the one it strikes. Similarly
you will fail to convince Dikoi to behave more sensibly, and you
will not convince the members of his household that they must
refuse to obey his whims. He will simply thrash them all, and
what can you do about it!] Obviously, characters which are strong
only on the logical side must develop very feebly and exercise
extremely feeble influence on life, where all life is governed not
by logic but by [sheer] tyranny. Nor is the rule of the Dikois
favourable for the development of men who possess strong, so-
called practical minds. Whatever you may say about these minds,
in substance, they are nothing more than the ability to take ad-

vantage of circumstances and to turn them in your favour. Hence, a practical mind can lead a man to straightforward and honest activity only when circumstances harmonize with sound logic and, consequently, with the natural demands of human ethics. But where everything depends upon [brute] force, where the unreasonable whims of a few Dikois, or the superstitious obstinacy of a Kabanova, wreck the most correct logical calculations and arrogantly trample upon the very first principles of mutual rights, the ability to take advantage of circumstances will obviously become transformed into the ability to adjust oneself to all the whims of the tyrants and to pander to all their absurdities in order to pave the way to a lucrative position. The Podkhalyuzins and Chichikhovs are the strong practical characters [in the "realm of darkness"]; others do not develop among men of a purely practical mould under the rule of the Dikois. The best that we can hope for as regards these practical men is that they should resemble Stolz, that is to say, be able to make a clean job of all their affairs without sinking to roguery; they cannot, however, become virile [public] leaders. [No greater hopes can be placed upon the] characters which are given to pathos, which are moved by fleeting impulses. Their impulses are fortuitous and of short duration [; their practical significance is determined by luck]. As long as things are proceeding in conformity with their hopes they are vigorous and enterprising; but as soon as they meet with strong opposition they lose heart, their ardour cools, they abandon the cause and confine themselves to fruitless although vociferous exclamations. [As, however, Dikoi and his ilk cannot possibly surrender their importance and strength without resistance, and as their influence has already left deep traces upon our way of life and, therefore, cannot be destroyed at one stroke, it is useless regarding the men of pathos in any way as serious factors. Even under the most favourable circumstances, apparent success encourages them; that is to say, if the tyrants realized how precarious their position is and began to make concessions, the men of pathos would not be able to do very much! Their distinguishing feature is that], absorbed by externals [and by the immediate consequences of their actions], they are never able to peer into the depths, into the very substance of a case. [That is why they are very easily satisfied, deceived by the partial, insignificant

symptoms of success of their principles]. When [however] their
mistake becomes obvious to themselves, they are discouraged, become apathetic and do nothing. [Dikoi and Kabanova continue to
reign supreme.]

Thus, in analyzing the various types that have appeared in our
life and have been reproduced in literature, we always arrive at
the conclusion that they cannot serve as representatives [of the
public movement that we are feeling in this country today, and
with which we dealt in the fullest possible detail above]. In view
of this, we asked ourselves: how then will [the new strivings of
individuals reveal themselves? What features must the character
possess which resolutely breaks with the old absurd and violent
relationships of life?] In the real life of [awakening] society we
have seen only hints of the solution of our problem, and in literature we have seen only faint echoes of these hints. In *The
Thunderstorm,* however, these hints constitute a whole, already
having fairly distinct outlines. Here we have before us a character
taken straight from life, but clarified in the mind of the artist and
placed in situations which enable it to reveal itself more fully
and resolutely than in most cases in ordinary life. Thus we see
here not daguerreotype exactitude, which some critics accuse
Ostrovsky of producing; what we have is the artistic combination
of similar features which manifest themselves in various situations
in Russian life, but serve as the expression of a single idea.

In Ostrovsky's play, the resolute and integral Russian character [acting in the environment of the Dikois and Kabanovas] appears in feminine form, and this is of weighty importance. It is
well known that extremes beget extremes, and that the strongest
protest is the one that rises, at last, from the breast of the weakest
and most patient. The field in which Ostrovsky observes Russian
life and presents it to us [does not include purely public and state
relationships, it] is confined to the family. Who, in the family,
has to bear the brunt of the tyrant's oppression if not the woman? Which of Dikoi's shop assistants, workmen or servants can
be so oppressed, so downtrodden and robbed of personality as his
wife is? In whose breast can more suffering and indignation accumulate against the tyrant's absurd whims? At the same time,
who has fewer opportunities to express discontent, to refuse to do
what is abhorrent? The servants and shop assistants are bound

to the tyrant only by material bonds; they can leave him as soon as they find another situation. His wife [according to prevailing ideas] is bound to him inseverably, spiritually, by sacrament; she must obey her husband in all things and share his [senseless] life with him. Even if she could leave him, where can she go, what can she do? Kudryash says: "Dikoi needs me, and so I am not afraid of him. I will not allow him to take liberties with me." Things are easy for a man who realizes that he is really needed by others, but what about a woman, a wife? What is she needed for? Does she not, on the contrary, take everything she needs from her husband? Her husband gives her shelter, food and clothing; he protects her and gives her a position in society.... Is she not usually regarded as a burden upon her husband? [Do not sensible people say in urging young men not to marry: "A wife is not a slipper, you can't kick her off your foot"? And in the general opinion, the biggest difference between a wife and a slipper is that a wife brings with her a cartload of trouble which the husband cannot get rid of, whereas a slipper is only a convenience, and if it is irksome, it can easily be kicked off....] Being in such a situation, the woman, of course, must forget that she is as human [and has the same rights] as the man. She can only become de-moralized, and if she has a strong character she may develop an inclination for the same tyranny that she herself has suffered so much from. We see this, for example, in the case of Kabanova, as we saw it also in the case of Ulanbekova. Her tyranny is only of a more petty nature compared with male tyranny and is, for that reason, perhaps, still more senseless. It is smaller in scope, but within its limits it is more intolerable for those who come under its yoke. Dikoi swears, Kabanova grumbles; Dikoi will give his victim a thrashing and be done with it, but Kabanova will nag her victim, long and relentlessly; Dikoi raves and storms when the fancy takes him, but he cares very little how you behave as long as your behaviour does not affect him in any way. Kaba-nova, however, has created for herself a little world of special rules and [superstitious] customs for which she stands up with all the obtuseness of a tyrant. In general, even a woman who has reached a position of independence and exercises her tyranny *con amore* always reveals her comparative impotence, the outcome of the age-long oppression she has suffered; she is more difficult to get on with, more suspicious and more heartless in her demands; she refuses to yield to reason not because she despises it, but rather because she is afraid she will be unable to contend against it. "If you begin to argue," she says, "you don't know what will come of it. They're sure to get the better of you." As a consequence, she adheres strictly to the ancient customs and to various maxims like those imparted to her by a woman of the type of Feklusha....

It is clear from this that when a woman decides to free herself from this situation she will act in earnest and with determination. It is nothing for a man like Kudryash to have a quarrel with Dikoi: both need each other, and therefore it requires no exceptional heroism on Kudryash's part to present his demands. But then his conduct will not lead to anything serious; he will swear, Dikoi will threaten [to get Kudryash called up for the army, but will not do so], Kudryash will be pleased with having given Dikoi a bit of his mind, and things will go on as before. But not so with a woman; she must be of strong character to be able to express her discontent and present her demands. At the very first attempt she will be made to feel that she is nothing [that she may be crushed]. She knows that this is so and must be resigned, otherwise the threat will be put into execution—she will be beaten, locked up [put on bread and water until she repents], deprived of the light of day; all the methods of domestic correction employed in the good old days will be applied to her and, at last, she will be brought to submission. A woman who wants to go to the end in her protest against the oppression and tyranny of elders in the Russian family must be imbued with the heroic spirit of self-sacrifice, she must dare to do everything, and be prepared for everything. How can she sustain herself? How is she to acquire such strength of character? [The only answer to this question is that it is impossible completely to crush the natural strivings of human nature. It is possible to divert them, to hem them in, to restrict them, but only to a certain degree. The triumph of false situations only proves how flexible human nature can be; but the more unnatural a situation is, the more urgent is the necessity to find a way out, and the nearer is that way out. And a situation must be very unnatural indeed if even the most flexible natures, even those which submit most to the forces which create such situations, can no longer bear them. If the flexible body of a child cannot perform a certain gymnastic trick, it is obviously impossible for an adult, whose limbs are stiffer, to perform it. Adults, of course, would not attempt such gymnastic tricks, but they might easily try them on children]. How is a child to acquire the strength of character to resist all these forces even when resistance threatens to entail the severest punishment? There is only one answer to this question, namely, that it is unable to do what the adult is trying to compel it to do. The same must be said about the weak woman who decides to plunge into the struggle for her rights. Things have reached such a pitch that even she is no longer able to stand her degradation, and so she tears herself out of it not because she calculates what is better or what is worse, but only because she strives intuitively towards what is bearable and possible. Here *nature* takes the place of the dictates of reason and the demands of feeling and imagination; all this merges in the general feeling of the organism, which is demanding air [sustenance, freedom]. Herein lies the secret of the integrity of the characters which appear in circumstances like those we see in *The Thunderstorm*, in the environment in which Katerina finds herself.

Thus, the rise of energetic feminine characters is quite logical at the stage which tyranny has reached in Ostrovsky's drama. It has reached the extreme, the negation of all common sense; it is more than ever hostile to the natural demands of mankind, and is more fiercely than ever striving to check their development, for in their triumph it sees its inevitable doom. As a consequence, it rouses still more discontent and protest even among the weakest. [At the same time, as we have seen, tyranny has lost its self-confidence, has lost also its firmness in action, has lost a considerable part of its strength, which consisted in its ability to inspire fear in all. Hence, the protest against it is no longer crushed at its birth; it can develop into a stubborn struggle. Those who still find life tolerable do not wish to take the risk of entering into such a struggle, hoping that in any case tyranny has not long to live.] Although Katerina's husband, young Kabanov, suffers a great deal from old Kabanova, he is, after all, more independent. He can go to Savel Prokofich and have a drink with him. He can leave his mother for a while; he can go to Moscow and have a good time there. If the old woman becomes too unbearable, he has

somebody upon whom to vent his feelings—he can bully his
wife. . . . And so he lives and moulds his character, useless for
anything [always secretly hoping that he will be able to free
himself somehow.] His wife, however, has no hope, no consolation, she has no respite; let her live without breathing if she can,
[forget that there is such a thing as the free air], let her renounce
her own nature and merge herself with the capricious whims [and
despotism] of old Kabanova. But [free] air and light do force
their way into Katerina's cell [in spite of all the precautions taken
by dying tyranny]. She feels it possible to satisfy the [natural]
thirst of her soul and can no longer remain inert; she struggles
towards the new way of life even if she has to die in the effort.
[What is death to her? In any case she does not regard as life
the wretched existence that has fallen to her lot in the Kabanov
family.]

Such is the basis of all the actions of the character that is
depicted in *The Thunderstorm*. [This basis is more reliable than
all possible theories and pathos, because it forms the very substance of the given situation, it irresistibly draws a man into
action, it is not dependent upon any particular capability or impression; it rests upon the entire complex of demands of the organism, upon the way the entire nature of man is moulded.] It will
be interesting now to see how such a character develops and manifests itself in particular cases. We can trace this development in
the personality of Katerina.

The first thing that strikes you is the extraordinary originality
of this character. There is nothing superficial or borrowed in it,
everything seems to emerge from within it; every impression undergoes a process in it and then organically merges with it. We
see this, for example, in the simple story Katerina tells about her
childhood, and about her life at home with her mother. It appears that she gained nothing from her upbringing and youth;
her life in her mother's home was the same as that in the Kabanov's
home—they went to church, did embroidery with gold thread on
velvet, listened to the tales told by pilgrim women, dined, took a
stroll in the garden, again chatted with the pilgrims and after
that they said their prayers. . . . On hearing Katerina's story Varvara, her husband's sister, observes with astonishment: "Why, it's
the same with us here!" But Katerina promptly defines the differ-

ence in a few words: "Yes, but here everything seems to be done by compulsion!" And the subsequent conversation shows that Katerina could see a special meaning in all the externals that are so customary among us everywhere, she was able to apply this meaning to her own requirements and strivings until the heavy hand of Kabanova was laid upon her. Katerina is not by any means one of those turbulent characters who are never satisfied and who are fond of [destruction at all costs]. On the contrary, hers is mainly a [constructive,] loving, ideal character. That is why she always tries in her imagination to give meaning to and idealize everything; the mood in which, as the poet expresses it,

> The whole world is by a noble dream
> Cleansed and purified before him,[128]

this mood remains with Katerina to the very last. She tries to harmonize every external discord with the harmony of her soul, to compensate for every defect with the fulness of her own inner strength. In her mind the crude superstitious tales [and senseless ravings] of the women pilgrims are transmuted into golden, poetical dreams of the imagination, not terrifying, but serene and good. Her images are pale because the materials with which reality provides her are so monotonously uniform; but her imagination works tirelessly even with these poor materials and carries her into a new world, bright and serene. [In church it is not the religious ceremonies that engage her mind; she does not hear the prayers and hymns, her soul is filled with different music, with different visions, for her the service ends before she is aware of it, in the space of a second, as it were.] She gazes at the trees so queerly depicted [on the icons] and she pictures to herself an entire country of gardens, where all the trees are like that, all in bloom and fragrant, and the air is full of celestial music. Or one fine sunny day she sees "a beam of light descending from the bright dome, and in this beam smoke is twirling like a cloud," and it looks to her ' as if angels are flying and singing in this beam." Sometimes she asks herself why she too should not fly, and when she stands on top of a hill she feels an irrepressible desire to do so—to take a run, spread out her arms and fly. In the opinion of those around her, she is queer and crazy, that is because she cannot accept their views and inclinations. She takes materials from

them because she has no other source, but she does not take their
conclusions; she seeks her own, and often arrives at something
entirely different from what they are content with. We find a
similar attitude towards external impressions in another sphere,
among people who by their upbringing are accustomed to abstract
reflections and are able to analyze their feelings. The only difference is that, in the case of Katerina, who is frank and vivacious,
everything is done by the promptings of her nature, without a
distinct consciousness, whereas among people trained to think
theoretically and possessing strong minds, logic and analysis play
the principal role. What distinguishes the strong mind is precisely
the inner strength that enables it to resist the influence of ready-
made views and systems and to create its own views and conclusions on the basis of vivid impressions. It does not reject anything at the outset, nor does it accept anything; it merely takes note
of things and interprets them in its own way. We see similar results in the case of Katerina, although she does not reason and
does not even understand her own sensations, but is directly guided
by her nature. From the dry monotonous life of her girlhood,
and from the crude and superstitious conceptions of her environment, she is always able to take that which harmonizes with her
natural striving for beauty, harmony, contentment and happiness.
In the tales of the pilgrim women, in the bowing and chanting
she sees [not a lifeless form, but something] different, towards
which her heart has always striven. On their basis she has built
her own ideal world, a world without passion, without want, without sorrow, a world entirely devoted to virtue and happiness. But
she is unable to define for herself what real virtue and true human happiness are. This explains the sudden impulses, the vague
and inexplicable strivings which she recalls:

"Sometimes I'd go into the garden early in the morning, just as the
sun rose, and fall on my knees and pray and weep, not knowing myself
what I was praying for and why I was weeping. There they would find me.
I don't know what I prayed for, what I asked for; I did not need anything,
I had enough of everything."

Poor girl, not having received a wide theoretical education,
not knowing what was going on in the world, not even fully understanding her own requirements, she could not, of course, understand what she needed. As long as she was living with her

mother in full freedom, free from mundane cares, while the requirements and the passions of the adult were still dormant in her, she could not even distinguish her own dreams, her own inner world, from external impressions. Absorbed [among the worshippers] in her own radiant thoughts and roaming in her own beautiful kingdom, she [thinks that her contentment comes from those worshippers, from the lamps in front of the icons hanging in all the corners of the house, from the chanting she hears around her;] with her feelings, [she] puts life into the lifeless environment in which she is living and merges the inner world of her soul with it. This is the period of childhood which, with many, drags on for a long, a very long time, but at last comes to an end. If the end comes very late, when a man begins to understand what he needs only when the greater part of his life has passed, almost nothing else remains for him than regret that he had for so long taken his own dreams for reality. He then finds himself in the sad position of the man who, in his imagination, had ascribed every possible perfection to the woman of his heart and, after binding his life with hers, suddenly discovers that all these perfections existed only in his imagination and that she herself bears not a trace of them. But strong characters rarely commit such a grave blunder; the demand for clarity and reality is strongly developed in them, and that is why they are not content with indefiniteness, but strive to get out of it at all costs. Becoming conscious of their inner discontent, they first try to drive it away, but on finding that it will not go, they end up by giving full freedom of expression to the [new] demands which arise in their souls and then do not rest content until those demands are satisfied. Here life itself comes to their aid—for some favourably, by expanding the circle of their impressions, and for others hard and bitter, bringing restrictions and cares which destroy the harmony of their youthful dreams. It was the latter that fell to the lot of Katerina [as it falls to the lot of most people in the "realm of darkness" of the Dikois and Kabanovas].

Amidst the sombre surroundings of her new home, Katerina begins to feel the inadequacy of the externals with which she was content before. Under the heavy hand of the heartless Kabanova there is no room for bright visions, as there is no freedom for her feelings. In a fit of tenderness for her husband she wants to embrace him, but the old woman shouts at her: "What are you hanging on his neck for, you shameless hussy? Bow low to him!" She wants to remain alone and grieve quietly as she used to do, but her mother-in-law says: "Why don't you wail?" She seeks light and air, she wants to dream and to gambol, to water her flowers, to look at the sun and at the Volga, to greet all living things—but she is kept in captivity, she is constantly suspected of harbouring impure and dissolute thoughts. She seeks refuge, as before [in religious exercises, in going to church,] in pious conversation, but here too she fails to find her previous impressions. Crushed by her daily drudgery and constant captivity, she can no longer as vividly as she did before [dream of angels singing in the dusty beam of sunlight, she cannot] picture to herself celestial gardens with their undisturbed tranquility and joy. Everything is cold, gloomy and frightful around her, some irresistible danger seems to hover everywhere; [the faces of the saints are so stern, the chanting of the prayers so sinister, and the tales of the pilgrims so monstrous. . . . Actually they have not changed in the least, she herself has changed;] she has lost the desire to conjure up fantastic visions, and the vague pictures of bliss that she enjoyed before no longer satisfy her. She has matured, other desires, more real, have awakened in her; knowing no other field except the family, no other world except that which grew up around her in the society of her town, she, naturally, of all human strivings, begins to become conscious of that which is most inevitable and nearest to her—the striving for love and devotion. Before, her heart had been too full of dreams, she had paid no attention to the young men who made eyes at her, she merely laughed. She did not love Tikhon Kabanov when she married him, she did not yet know what love is. She was told that every young woman must marry; Tikhon was introduced to her as her future husband and so she married him with a feeling of absolute indifference. Here too, the specific feature of her character reveals itself. According to our commonly accepted notions, she should have protested if she really had a resolute character; but she did not protest because she had not sufficient grounds for this. She was not particularly eager to marry, but marriage was not repugnant to her; she did not love Tikhon, but she did not love anybody else. It was all the same to her [for the time being], and that is why she allowed them to do what they liked with her. This was not a sign of impotence, or of apathy; it may be regarded only as lack of experience, and also as a too great readiness to do everything for others without consideration for oneself. She possessed little knowledge, but she was very trustful, that is why she [for a time] offered no opposition to those around her and decided to suffer rather than do anything to spite them.

But [when she understands what she needs and wants to achieve something, she will achieve it at all costs; here the full strength of her character, unwasted on petty efforts, will reveal itself. At first, owing to the innate goodness and nobility of her soul, she will make every possible effort not to violate the peace and the rights of others. She will endeavour to obtain what she wishes while obeying as far as possible all the demands made upon her by people who are in any way connected with her. If they are able to take advantage of this initial mood of hers and dare to give it full satisfaction, it will be good for her and for them. But if they do not, nothing will restrain her—neither law, kinship, customs, the judgment of people, nor the rules of common sense; everything will be swept away by the power of her inner passion, she will not spare herself nor think of others. This was the way out that presented itself to Katerina. No other could be expected in the environment in which she lived.]

Her love for a man, her desire to find a kindred echo in another heart, and the desire for tender embraces awoke naturally in the young woman and changed her former, indefinite and incorporeal dreams. She says to Varya:

"I can't sleep at night. It seems to me I can hear somebody whispering, somebody speaking tenderly to me, like the cooing of a dove. I no longer dream, as I did before, about trees and mountains in paradise; I feel as if somebody is passionately embracing me, oh, so passionately, and leading me somewhere, and I follow him, follow him. . . ."

She became conscious of and understood these dreams rather late, but, of course, they pursued and tormented her long before she understood them. When they first appeared she immediately turned her affections upon the one who was nearest to her—upon her husband. For a long time she tried to merge her soul with his, to assure herself that with him she wanted nothing, that in him she could find the bliss which she was so anxiously seeking.

It was with fear and perplexity that she considered the possibility of seeking mutual love with somebody else. In the play, which opens with Katerina on the threshold of love for Boris Grigorich, we still see the traces of Katerina's last desperate efforts to force herself to love her husband. The farewell scene makes us feel that all is not yet lost for Tikhon, that he can still preserve his right to this woman's love; but this very same scene gives us, in brief but clear-cut outline, the whole story of the torments Katerina endured, which killed her first feelings towards her husband. Tikhon appears here as a simplehearted, banal, not altogether bad, but an extremely characterless individual who is unable to do anything in disobedience to his mother. And the mother is a heartless brutal woman who converts love, [religion] and morality into Chinese ceremonies. [Between her and his wife Tikhon represents one of those innumerable wretched types who are usually described as harmless, although, in general, they are as harmful as the tyrants, because they serve as the latter's devoted assistants.] Tikhon really loves his wife and is ready to do everything for her, but the oppression under which he grew up warped his character to such a degree that no strong sentiment, no determined strivings could develop in him. He has a conscience, he has a desire to do good, but he is always acting against himself, and serves as his mother's obedient tool even in his relations with his wife. We see what position Katerina occupies between her husband and her mother-in-law in the very first scene, where the Kabanov family appears in the boulevard. Kabanova scolds her son and reproaches him with the fact that his wife does not fear him. He dares to object and says: "Why should she fear me? I am quite satisfied with the fact that she loves me." But the old woman at once retorts fiercely:

"What do you mean, why should she fear you? What do you mean, why should she fear you? Have you taken leave of your senses? *If she does not fear you, she will certainly not fear me,* and what order will there be in the house then? You are living in lawful wedlock with her, are you not? Or perhaps the law doesn't mean anything to you!"

With such principles prevailing, Katerina's love for her husband naturally finds no outlet, it hides within her, revealing itself only at times in convulsive outbursts. But Tikhon does not know how to take advantage of these outbursts; he is too downtrodden to understand the power of her passionate longing. "I can't understand you, Katya," he says to her. "I can't get a word let alone a kiss out of you sometimes, but at other times you yourself come begging to be petted." This is the way commonplace and warped natures usually judge strong and fresh natures; judging by themselves, they do not understand the feelings that lie buried in the depths of the soul and regard all introspection as apathy. When, at last, unable to conceal itself any longer, the inner strength bursts from the soul in a broad and rapid flood, they are amazed and think it is a conjuring trick, a whim, like those which sometimes enter their own heads—to indulge in pathos, or to go on the spree. And yet these impulses are a necessity for strong natures, and they are the more powerful the longer they are repressed. They are not deliberate, not calculated, they are called forth by natural necessity. The strength of a nature which has no opportunity to develop itself actively also expresses itself passively, by patience and restraint. But do not confuse *this* patience with that of a feebly-developed personality, which ends in that individual becoming accustomed to insult and to burdens of every kind. No, Katerina will never grow accustomed to this; she does not yet know what she will dare do or how she will do it; she does not violate her obligations to her mother-in-law, she does all in her power to get on with her husband, but everything goes to show that she is conscious of her position and that she is longing to extricate herself from it. She never complains, she is never disrespectful to her mother-in-law, the old woman herself cannot accuse her of that; nevertheless, the mother-in-law feels that Katerina is somehow at variance with, hostile to her. Tikhon, who fears his mother like the very devil, and at the same time is not distinguished for any particular delicacy or tenderness, nevertheless feels conscience-stricken before his wife when, at his mother's command, he must tell her "not to go gazing out of the window" and "not to make eyes at young men" while he is away. He realizes that such admonition would be painfully offensive to her, although he does not fully understand her state of mind. When his mother leaves the room he consoles his wife in the following way:

"Don't take it all to heart, otherwise you may soon get consumption. What's the use of listening to her! She's got to say something. Well, let her talk, but don't pay any attention to what she says."

[It is this indifference that is bad and hopeless, but] Katerina can never reach this state. Although, to look at her, one would think that she is less hurt than Tikhon, although she complains less, actually she suffers far more than he does. Tikhon too feels that he lacks something that he needs, he too is discontented [but his discontent is at a stage which may, for example, be compared with the passion which a ten-year-old boy with a perverted mind entertains for an adult woman]. He cannot resolutely strive for independence [and his rights] for the simple reason that he does not know what to do with them; his desires are more of a [mental] superficial character [but his own nature, suppressed by his upbringing, has remained almost dead to natural strivings]. Hence, his very quest [for freedom] assumes a perverted form [and becomes repulsive, as repulsive as the cynicism of a ten-year-old boy who senselessly, and without any inner promptings, repeats the loathsome things he hears from grownups]. You see, Tikhon heard from somebody that "he too is a man" and therefore ought to enjoy a certain share of power and importance in the family; consequently, he considers himself to be far superior to his wife, and although he believes that God himself has commanded her to be patient and resigned, he looks upon his own position under the tutelage of his mother as bitter and humiliating. Moreover, he is fond of pleasure and mainly regards this as freedom; [like the boy we referred to above who is unable to understand what makes the love of woman so sweet and who knows only the external aspect of love, which for him is transformed into obscenity, Tikhon], when preparing for his journey, says with shameless cynicism to his wife, who begs him to take her with him:

"From a captivity like this one would run away even from the most beautiful wife! Just think: *whatever kind of man I may be, I am a man for all that.* When one has to live all one's life like this, as you see, one would run away even from one's wife. As it is, I know that I shall have no fury over me, no chains to my feet, for at least a couple of weeks. What do I need a wife for under those circumstances?"

All that Katerina can say in reply is: "How can I love you when you say such things to me?" But Tikhon does not understand the implication of this stern and emphatic reproach; like a man who has taken leave of his senses he answers carelessly: "What things? What else should I say to you?" and hastens to

39*

get out of his wife's sight. But why? What does he want to do?
How does he want to relieve his feelings when he gains his temporary freedom? He himself tells this later to Kuligin.

"When I was about to leave, Mama read me a long lecture; but as
soon as I got away I let myself go," he says. "*I was so glad to get free.*
I drank all the way, and I drank all the time I was in Moscow. I had a
grand time. *I had a spree that will last me for a whole year!...*"

And that is all! It must be said that in former times, when
the sense of personality [and of its rights] had not yet awakened
in the majority of people, they did almost nothing more than this
[in the way of protesting against the yoke of tyranny. And even
today one can still meet with Tikhons who intoxicate themselves,
if not with wine, then with all kinds of arguments and speeches,
and relieve their feelings in noisy orgies of verbosity. These are
the people who are constantly complaining about the restrictions
they have to put up with, and yet are infected with the proud
thought of their privileges and superiority over others: "Whatever
kind of man I may be, I am a man for all that—so how can I
put up with it." In other words: "You put up with it because you
are a woman, and consequently, mere trash, but I must have freedom, not because it is a human, natural requirement, but because
it is the right of my privileged person." ... Clearly, nothing could
come, or ever will come from such people with such habits.

But there is no resemblance between them and the new movement in the life of the people to which we referred above, and
the reflection of which we have found in Katerina's character. In
this personality] we see [an already mature] demand, which
springs from the depths of the entire organism, for [rights and]
living space. [Here it is no longer imagination, no longer hear-
say, or an artificially excited impulse, but a vital natural requirement.] Katerina is not capricious, she does not flaunt her discontent and anger, it is not in her nature to do so; she does not
want to impress others, to pose and boast. On the contrary, she
lives very peacefully and is ready to submit to everything that is
not abhorrent to her nature; her principle, if she could grasp and
define it, would be: to thrust her personality upon others [and to
disturb the general course of things] as little as possible. On the
other hand, recognizing and respecting [the strivings of] others,
she demands the same respect for herself, and violence and re-

striction in every shape and form rouse her intense indignation. If she could she would drive far away from herself all who live unrighteously and harm others; but being unable to do this, she does the opposite; she runs away from tyrants and evildoers. Only not to submit to their ways, which are abhorrent to her nature, only not to resign herself to their [unnatural] demands— what comes after, a better lot for herself or death, she does not care [in either case, she obtains her freedom...]. Katerina tells Varya about one feature of her character that revealed itself when she was still a child. "I was born such a hothead!" she says. "I was only six years old, but what do you think I did? Somebody in the house offended me, it was in the evening, and already dark. I ran to the Volga, got into a boat and pushed away from the bank. They found me next morning about ten versts away...." Katerina retained this childish hotheadedness, except that on attaining maturity she acquired the strength to withstand impressions and to keep them under control. Katerina, the grown-up woman, faced with the necessity of suffering wrongs, finds the strength to bear them for a long time without [vain] complaints, [semi]-resistance and noisy outburst. She bears them until some interest that is particularly close to her heart [and lawful in her eyes] begins to speak in her, until such a demand of her nature is roused that gives her no rest until it is satisfied. When that happens, she gives no consideration to anything. She does not resort to diplomatic tricks, to deception and rascality, she is not that kind. If it is absolutely essential to deceive, she prefers to suppress her impulse. Varya advises her to conceal her love for Boris, but she says: "But I cannot deceive, I cannot conceal anything," and after that she makes an effort to steel her heart and says to Varya: "Don't talk to me about him. Do me a favour and don't talk to me about him! I don't want to know him! *I will love my husband. Tikhon, my dove, I'll not give you up for anyone!*" But this effort was more than her strength could stand; a moment later she feels that she cannot kill her awakening love. "I don't want to think about him," she says. "But what can I do when I cannot get him out of my mind?" These simple words very clearly reveal how the strength [of her natural strivings], imperceptible to Katerina herself, gains the upper hand within her over all the [external] demands [prejudices and artifical combinations in which her life is entangled]. We shall observe that Katerina cannot reject any one of these demands theoretically [she cannot free herself from any obsolete opinions;] she goes against all of them only with the strength of her feeling, with the instinctive [consciousness of her direct and inalienable right to life, happiness and love....] She does not reason in the least, but she settles all the difficulties of her position with astonishing ease. This is her conversation with Varvara:

> *Varvara*: You've got such queer ideas, bless you! In my opinion, one should do as one likes, as long as you can keep it dark.
> *Katerina*: I don't want to do anything like that. Besides, what's the good? *No, I'd better bear it, as long as I can.*
> *Varvara*: And when you can't bear it any longer, what will you do?
> *Katerina*: What will I do?
> *Varvara*: Yes, what will you do?
> *Katerina*: *I'll do exactly as I like.*
> *Varvara*: You try! They'll make your life a misery.
> *Katerina*: What do I care! I'll go away, and that's all.
> *Varvara*: Where will you go? You are a married woman.
> *Katerina*: Ekh, Varvara, you don't know my character! *God grant that it does not happen, but if it gets too bad for me here, no power on earth will keep me here. I'll jump out of the window. I'll throw myself into the Volga. If I won't want to live here I won't, even if they cut me up into pieces.*

This is [the true] strength [of character that one can really rely upon! This is the height] to which [our] national life is rising in its development, but to which in our literature very few could rise, and on which nobody has kept so well as Ostrovsky. He realized that [not abstract faith but] the facts of life govern the conduct of men, that not a mode of thought [not principles] but nature is needed to form and reveal a strong character, and he was able to create a person who [serves as a representative of a great national idea], and without carrying [great] ideas either on her tongue or in her head, self-sacrificingly fights on to the end in an unequal struggle and dies without dooming herself to [lofty] self-abnegation. Her conduct is in harmony with her nature, for her it is natural and necessary, she cannot renounce it even if it leads to the most fatal consequences. The [ostensibly] strong characters in other of our literary productions are like little fountains which play rather beautifully and briskly, but depend for their display upon the outside mechanisms which are

attached to them. Katerina, however, may be compared with a full
and flowing river; it flows according to the dictates of its nature,
its current changes in conformity with the locality through which
it passes, but it never stops; if its bed is level, it flows smoothly, if
it encounters boulders it sweeps over them, if it reaches a preci-
pice it falls in a cascade, and if it is dammed up, it will storm
and rage and break through in another place. [It is turbulent not
because its waters suddenly want to make a noise, or because they
are enraged against the obstacles, but simply] because it must be
so in order to carry out its natural requirements, so that it may
flow on further. [So it is with the character which Ostrovsky
portrays for us. We know that it will sustain itself in spite of all
obstacles, and if its strength gives out it will perish, but remain
true to itself. The high spokesmen for truth with claims to "self-
abnegation for the sake of a great idea" very often end by giving
up their service on the plea that the struggle against evil is still
hopeless, that it will lead only to needless sacrifice of life, and so
forth. They are right, and they cannot be accused of fainthearted-
ness; but one cannot fail to see that the "idea" which they want
to serve is for them something external, which they can very well
dispense with, and which they can very well separate from their
direct personal needs. Clearly, no matter how great their ardour
for an idea, it will always be much weaker and lower than that
simple, instinctive, irresistible passion which governs the actions
of personalities like Katerina, who do not think at all about any
lofty "ideas."]

In the position in which Katerina finds herself we see [on
the contrary] that all the "ideas" with which she has been imbued
since childhood, all the principles that prevail in her environment,
rise against her [natural strivings and] behaviour. The frightful
struggle which the young woman is condemned to wage is reflected
in every word, in every action in the drama, and here is revealed
the importance of the subsidiary personages for which Ostrovsky
has been so severely criticized. Look closely: you will see that
Katerina was brought up in the conceptions that prevail in the
environment in which she is living, and that she cannot renounce
them as she has had no theoretical education. Although she interprets the tales of the pilgrim women and the admonitions of the
other members of the household in her own way, they, nevertheless,

cannot but leave [ugly] traces on her soul. And, indeed, we see in
the play that although Katerina has lost her beautiful dreams,
ideals and noble strivings, she has retained from her upbringing
[one] strong feeling, namely [*fear* of certain dark forces] of
something unknown, which she can neither explain to herself
properly nor thrust aside. [Every thought of her own terrifies her;
she expects to be punished for the slightest emotion that she feels;
she thinks that the thunderstorm will kill her because she is a
sinner, and the pictures of the fiery Gehenna on the church walls
seemed to her to be the harbinger of eternal torment for herself....
And] all those around her foster and develop [this fear] in her.
Feklushas come to Kabanova to talk about the approaching end
of the world; Dikoi asserts that thunderstorms are sent as a punishment to make us feel, [the insane lady who terrifies the whole
town turns up several times to shout at Katerina in a sinister voice:
"You will all burn in unquenchable fire"]. Everybody around her
is full of [superstitious] fear, and everybody around her, in conformity with Katerina's own conceptions, must regard her feelings
for Boris as a heinous crime. Even gallant Kudryash [the *esprit-
fort* of this environment,] is of the opinion that lassies may gal-
livant with lads as much as they please, there is nothing wrong
in that, but married women should be kept locked up. So strongly
is he imbued with this conviction that on learning that Boris is
in love with Katerina, he, in spite of his gallantry and his being
somewhat of a daredevil, he says that Boris "ought to chuck that
business." Everything is against Katerina, even her own conceptions of good and evil; everything must either compel her to suppress her impulse and wilt in the cold and sombre formalism of
domestic resignation and submission, [without any living striv-
ings], without a will and without love, or to learn to deceive
people and her own conscience. [But have no fears about her,
have no fear even when she speaks against herself; she may, for
a time, appear to be resigned, or even resort to deception, as a
rivulet may run under ground, or turn from its course, but the
flowing water will neither be halted nor turned back, it will go
on to its destination, to the place where it can merge with other
waters, and with them flow to the waters of the ocean]. The environment in which Katerina lives demands that she should lie and
cheat,

"You can't get on without that," Varvara says to her. "Remember where you are living. Our whole house rests upon that. I was never a deceiver before, but I learnt to deceive when it became necessary."

Katerina yields to her situation, goes out to meet Boris at night and conceals her feelings from her mother-in-law for ten days. . . . One might think: [here is another] woman [who has left the path of virtue], has learnt to deceive the members of her household, and will now live in secret debauchery, while hypocritically caressing her husband and wearing the [disgusting] mask of resignation! [She would not deserve stern condemnation for this, her position is so hard!] But then, she would have been one of those ordinary personages of the type that has become threadbare in novels [showing how "environment ruins good people"]. But Katerina is not of that kind. The climax of her love in the domestic environment in which she lives can already be foreseen when that love only commences. She does not indulge in psychological analyses and, therefore, cannot express subtle observations concerning herself; what she does say about herself is something that affects her very strongly. At Varvara's very first suggestion that she should meet Boris she exclaims:

"No, no, that must not be! What are you talking about! *God forbid!* *If I meet him only once I shall run away from home, I shall not go back, not for anything in the world!*"

[This is not wise precaution speaking within her, it is passion, and] it is evident that, strong as may be the restraint which she puts upon herself, passion is stronger than she is, stronger than all [her prejudices and fears, stronger than all] the admonitions she has heard since childhood. That passion constitutes her whole life; all the strength of her nature, all her living strivings merge in it. She is drawn to Boris not only because she likes him, because both in appearance and in his speech he is unlike the rest of the people around her; she is also drawn to him by her desire for love, which found no echo in her husband, by her outraged feelings as a wife and a woman, by the deadening boredom of her monotonous life, and by her desire for freedom and space, [for ardent, unconstrained] freedom. All the time she is dreaming of "flying invisibly wherever she wants to"; and sometimes the following idea enters her head: "If I had my way I would go for a row on the Volga, in a boat, and sing songs, or for a ride in a fine troika,* with our arms around each other...." "Only not with your husband," says Varya, prompting her. Katerina cannot conceal her feelings and at once betrays them by asking: "How do you know?" Evidently Varvara's remark explains a great deal to her: when relating her dreams so naively she does not herself fully understand their significance. But a single word is sufficient to lend her thoughts that definiteness which she herself is afraid to give them. Up to now she could only doubt as to whether this new feeling was really the bliss that she had been longing for. But once having pronounced the secret word she does not retreat from it even in her thoughts. Fear, doubt, the idea of sin and of people's censure all enter her head, but they no longer have any power over her [; they are only formalities to soothe her conscience]. In the monologue with the gate key (the last in the second act) we see a woman who, in her heart, has already taken a decisive step but only wants, in some way, to "persuade" herself. She tries to get out of herself, as it were, and to judge the act which she has decided to commit as if it was somebody else's, but all her thoughts are bent on justifying this act. She says: "It doesn't take long to die.... Who can be happy in captivity.... Take myself, now, I live in torment, I see no ray of light before me.... My mother-in-law has crushed me"... and so forth—all pleas of justification. And then come mitigating circumstances: "Evidently fate wants it so.... What sin can it be if I just take one look at him.... Even if I talk to him no harm will be done. I may not have another chance like this for the rest of my life...." This monologue prompted some critics to wax ironic at Katerina's expense and accuse her of being a shameless hypocrite; but can we [conceive of anything more shameless than to] assert that we [and some of our ideal friends] have never made such bargains with our consciences?... [It is not the individuals who are to blame for striking these bargains, but the concepts that were knocked into their heads in childhood, and which so often run counter to the natural course of the living strivings of the soul. Until such concepts are driven out of society, until the complete harmony of the ideas and requirements of nature is restored in the human being, such

---

* A carriage drawn by three horses abreast.—Tr.

bargains will be inevitable. We must be thankful that in striking these bargains we arrive at what is natural and conforms to common sense, and that we are not crushed by the conventional admonitions of artificial morality. It is precisely for this that Katerina finds strength, and the more powerfully nature speaks in her, the more calmly she looks into the face of the childish bogeys which those around her have taught her to fear.] For this reason we think that [even] the actress who plays the part of Katerina on the St. Petersburg stage makes a slight mistake in rendering the monologue to which we have referred in a too passionate and tragic tone. Evidently she wants to give expression to the struggle that is taking place in Katerina's soul, and from this point of view she delivers this difficult monologue splendidly. But it seems to us that it would be more in conformity with Katerina's character and situation in this case to lend her words a calmer and lighter tone. Actually, the struggle is over, only brief reflection remains [, the old rags still cover Katerina, but little by little she is casting them off. . . .] The conclusion of the monologue reveals the state of her heart: "What will be will be, I shall see Boris," she says, and full of longing and anticipation she exclaims: "Oh, I wish night would come soon!"

Such love, such feeling, cannot live side by side with pretence and deception within the walls of the Kabanovs' house. She decides to go to a clandestine tryst, nevertheless, on the very first occasion, in an outburst of love, she says to Boris who assures her that nobody will find out:

"I don't deserve any pity, nobody is to blame—I did this of my own accord. Ruin me without pity! Let everybody know, let everybody see what I am doing. . . . If I do not fear to sin with you, do you think I will be afraid of what people say?"

And indeed she fears nothing, except the danger of losing the opportunity of meeting her lover, of speaking to him, of enjoying those summer nights with him, enjoying those, for her, new emotions. Her husband returns and her life becomes a living death. She is obliged to be secretive and sly, and this she cannot and does not wish to be; she is obliged to go back to the old hard life of boredom, which seems to her to be more bitter than ever before. In addition to all this she has to keep watch over herself every moment, to be guarded in every word [particularly in the presence of her mother-in-law, and she has also to fear some frightful punishment for her soul. . . .] Such a situation is intolerable for Katerina; she broods and broods night and day, suffers, spurs on her already inflamed imagination and in the end she can hold out no longer, and in the presence of the crowd that has gathered in the gallery of the ancient church, she confesses everything to her husband. His first reaction is that of fear of what his mother will say. "Don't! Don't talk. Mother is here," he whispers to her in embarrassment. But the mother has already heard and demands a full confession, and when it is over she draws [her moral]: "There you are, my son, you see what freedom leads to!"

[There cannot, of course, be a greater mockery of common sense than that contained in Kabanova's exclamation; but common sense counts for nothing in the "realm of darkness"; against the "criminal"] measures are taken [quite abhorrent to common sense but] common in that environment: at his mother's command the husband thrashes his wife, the mother-in-law keeps her under lock and key and nags and nags her. . . . Freedom and repose come to an end [for the poor woman]. Before they had nothing to reproach her with and she could at least feel that she was [fully] righteous in the eyes of these people; but now, whichever way you look at it, she is guilty before them, she has violated her obligations to them and has brought sorrow and shame upon the family. Now the cruelest treatment has its reason and justification. What can she do? All she can do is mourn over her failure to gain her freedom and abandon her dreams of love and happiness, as she had abandoned her joyous dreams of wonderful gardens and celestial music; resign herself to her fate, renounce the idea of leading an independent life, obey her mother-in-law and do every-thing to please her, become the humble slave of her husband and never again dare attempt to reveal her [demands]. . . . But no! Such is not Katerina's character [; the new type which Russian life has created was not reflected in her merely to become a fruitless attempt and to perish after the first failure]. No! She will not return to the old life; if she cannot satisfy her emotions, enjoy her freedom [quite legitimately and sacredly] in the light of day, in sight of all, if what she has found, and what is so precious to her, is torn out of her hands, then she wants nothing of life, she does not want even life itself. The fifth act in *The Thunderstorm* constitutes the apotheosis of this character, which is so simple, so profound [and is so close to the position and to the heart of every decent person in our society.] The artist did not place his heroine on a pedestal, he did not even make her heroic; he allowed her to remain the simple, naive woman that she was when she appeared to us before she had committed her "sin." In the fifth act she has only two monologues and a dialogue with Boris, but, brief though they are, they are filled with such strength, with such significant revelations, that in touching upon them we fear that we have enough comment to make upon them for another whole essay. We shall try to limit ourselves to a few words.

It is evident from Katerina's monologues that even now she has nothing in the way of definite formulae; right to the end she is guided by her nature and not by given decisions, because for decisions she needs firm logical ground, whereas the principles which she possesses for theoretical argument are totally abhorrent to her natural strivings. Hence, far from assuming a heroic pose and giving utterance to speeches that would prove the firmness of her character, she comes before us as a weak woman, unable to resist her passion, and tries to justify the heroism that reveals itself in her actions. She decides to commit suicide, but she is terrified by the thought that this is a sin, and it seems as though she is trying to prove to us, and to herself, that she might be forgiven because her life is so very hard. She wants to enjoy life and love, but she knows that this is a crime, and therefore she says in her own justification: "What does it matter now, my soul is already damned!" She makes no complaint against anybody, she blames nobody, she does not even think of doing so; on the contrary, she feels that she has sinned against everybody. She even asks Boris whether he is angry with her, whether he is cursing her. . . . She feels neither anger, nor contempt, nor any of the things with which disappointed heroes who voluntarily abandon the world usually ornament themselves. But she cannot live any longer, she cannot, and that is all there is to it; from the bottom of her heart she says:

"Oh, how weary I am. . . . How much longer will I be tortured like this? What is life to me now, what is the use of living? I don't need anything, I hate everything, I hate the light of day—but death won't come!

[I call it, but it does not come]. Whatever I see, whatever I hear, only gives me a pain here" (*pointing to her heart*).

She finds some relief in thinking of the grave—serenity seems to fill her soul.

"It is so quiet, so good. . . . I don't want to think of life. . . . What, live again? . . . No, no, I don't want to. . . . It's horrible. I hate the people, I hate the house, the very walls are hateful to me! No, I won't go there! I won't! I won't! If I go back—they will walk and talk—what do I want that for. . . ."

And the thought of the bitter life she would have to bear torments Katerina's soul so much that it throws her into a fever. At the last moment all the horrors of her life at home flash through her mind with exceptional vividness. She exclaims: "If they catch me they will drag me home by force! . . . Quick, quick. . . ." And all is over. She will no longer be the victim of her [heartless] mother-in-law, she will no longer languish in captivity with her spineless and hateful husband. [She is free! . . .]

Sad and bitter is such a deliverance, but what is one to do when there is no other way out. [It is a good thing the poor woman possessed the determination to make at least this frightful exit. Herein lies the strength of her character; that is why *The Thunderstorm* makes such a refreshing impression upon us, as we said above.] Undoubtedly, it would have been better if Katerina could have liberated herself in some other way [from her torturers], or if those [torturers] around her had changed and had reconciled her with themselves and with life. But neither the one nor the other fits in with the order of things. Kabanova could not have abandoned what she had been brought up with, and with which she had lived all her life; her spineless son could not suddenly, without any cause, have acquired sufficient firmness and independence to have renounced all the absurdities which the old woman was teaching him; everything around could not suddenly have changed in such a way as to make the young woman's life sweet for her. The most they could have done was to forgive her [, to alleviate somewhat the burden of her domestic captivity, to say a few kind words to her, perhaps grant her the right to a voice in the affairs of the household when her opinion was asked for.] Perhaps this would have been sufficient for another woman, a woman downtrodden and weak, [and for another time, when the tyranny of the Kabanovs rested on general dumb submission and they did not have so many occasions to flaunt their insolent contempt for common sense and all rights.] But we see that Katerina did not kill the human nature in her, and that only externally, owing to her position, did she bear the burden of life under the yoke of tyranny; inwardly, however, in her heart [and mind] she realized how utterly absurd it was [and the absurdity of it was enhanced by the fact that the Dikois and Kabanovas, meeting with opposition and not being strong enough to vanquish it, but still wishing to have their own way, openly set themselves against logic, that is to say, made fools of themselves in the eyes of the majority of people]. It goes without saying that under such circumstances, Katerina could not be satisfied with the generous forgiveness [of the tyrants and restitution of her rights in the family]; she knew what Kabanova's charity was like, and what the position of a daughter-in-law must be under such a mother-in-law. . . . [No, it was not concessions or mere alleviation of her position that she needed, but that her mother-in-law, her husband and all those around her should become capable of satisfying the living strivings with which she was imbued, of recognizing the legitimacy of her natural demands, of renouncing all rights of compulsion over her and of becoming regenerated to such an extent as to be worthy of her love and confidence. Needless to say, it was impossible for them to undergo such a regeneration. . . .]

Less impossible would have been another solution, namely, to elope with Boris, to flee from the tyranny and violence of the household. [Notwithstanding the strictness of the formal law, notwithstanding the cruelty of crude tyranny,] such a step would not have been impossible in itself, especially for a character like Katerina. And she did not ignore this way out because she was not an abstract heroine who sought death on principle. When running from the house to meet Boris, and already thinking of death, she was by no means averse to flight. On hearing that Boris is going far away, to Siberia, she says to him very simply: "Take me with you away from here." But here we get a glimpse of the weight which keeps people [in the depths of the slough which we call the "realm of darkness."] That weight is material dependence. Boris is penniless and is wholly dependent on his uncle, Dikoi.

Dikoi and the Kabanovs arrange to send him to Kyakhta and, of course, they would not allow him to take Katerina with him. That is why he answers her: "It can't be done, Katya. I am not going because I want to. My uncle is sending me, and the carriage is ready," and so forth. Boris is not a hero, he is far from being worthy of Katerina. She fell in love with him mainly because she had nobody better to fall in love with. He managed to get some "education" and cannot possibly cope with the old way of life, neither with his heart nor with common sense, and he wanders around like a lost soul. He lives with his uncle because the latter is holding in trust for him and his sister a part of their grandmother's legacy, which will pass to them "if they are respectful to him." Boris knows perfectly well that Dikoi will never admit that he is respectful and, therefore, will not give him anything. Nor is this all. Boris tells us the following: "No, first he will tyrannize and bully us to his heart's content, and in the end he will give us nothing, or perhaps he will give us a tiny share and say that he did so out of charity, and that he need not have given us anything at all." Nevertheless, he lives with his uncle and puts up with his bullying—why, nobody can tell. At his first meeting with Katerina, when she tells him what awaits her for having met him, Boris interrupts her and says: "Let's not think about it, as long as we are happy now." And at the last meeting he whines: "Who could tell that you and I would suffer so for our love? It would have been better had I gone away from here!" In short, he is one of those by no means rare individuals who cannot do what they understand, and do not understand what they do. That type has been frequently depicted in our literature, sometimes with exaggerated sympathy and sometimes with excessive severity. Ostrovsky presents it to us as it really is, and with the exceptional skill characteristic of him, he, in two or three strokes, depicts its utter insignificance, although not without a certain spiritual nobility. There is no need to deal at length with Boris. Strictly speaking, he too is part of the *environment* in which the heroine of the play is placed. He is one of the factors which makes the fatal ending necessary. If he were another man, and in a different position, it would not have been necessary for her to have thrown herself into the river. [But the whole point is that the environment that is subject to the power of the Dikois and

Kabanovas usually produces Tikhons and Borises, who are incapable of asserting their human nature even when faced by a character like Katerina.] We said a few words about Tikhon above.
Strictly speaking Boris is of the same type, only he is "educated."
Education deprived him of the power to do mischief, but it did
not give him the power to oppose the mischief that others did;
it did not even develop in him the ability to conduct himself in
such a way as to remain alien to the abominations which seethe
around him. Not only does he fail to oppose the abominable
things others do, but he submits to them, willy-nilly participates
in them and must accept all their consequences. But he understands the position he is in, he discusses it and, not infrequently,
he at first deceives truly virile and strong natures who, judging
others by their own standards, believe that if a man thinks and
understands things in a certain way he ought to act in that way.
[Looking at things from their own point of view, such natures
find no difficulty in saying to the "educated" martyrs who are
fleeing from the bitter circumstance of life: "Take me with you.
Wherever you go I will go." But here the impotence of these
martyrs is revealed; it turns out that they had not foreseen, they
curse themselves, they would be glad to do something, but it is
impossible, they are not free, and above all they are penniless,
and to keep themselves alive they must serve the very Dikoi whom
they, and we, want to get rid of....]

These people are worthy of neither praise nor blame [but
attention must be turned upon the practical ground to which the
question is being shifted;] it must be admitted that it is hard for
a man who expects a legacy from his uncle to throw off his dependence upon that uncle; [but then, it is necessary to abandon vain
hopes in nephews who expect legacies no matter how highly they
are "educated"; if we look for the guilty party we shall find
that it is not so much the nephews as the uncles, or rather, their
legacies.]

Incidentally, we discussed the importance of material dependence [as the mainstay of the whole power of the tyrants in the
"realm of darkness"] at great length in our previous essays.
[Hence] we shall revert to it here merely to point out that the
fatal end that Katerina meets with in *The Thunderstorm* was ab-

solutely inevitable, and, consequently, that the appearance of a character that would, in the given situation, be prepared for such an end was also inevitable.

[We have already said that in our opinion this end is encouraging; it is easy to understand why. It is a terrific challenge to the power of tyranny; it tells tyranny that it cannot go on any longer, that it is impossible to live any longer with its violent and deadening principles]. In Katerina we see a protest against the Kabanov conceptions of morality, a protest carried to its logical extreme, proclaimed under domestic torture and over the chasm into which the poor woman threw herself. She refuses to resign herself to her lot, she refuses to drag out the miserable existence which she is offered in exchange for her living soul. [Her death is the realized song of the Babylonian captive. "Play and sing the songs of Zion to us," the conquerors said to the Judeans. But the mournful prophet answered that the sacred songs of homeland cannot be sung in slavery, that it were better that their tongues should stick to the roofs of their mouths and their hands wither rather than that they should strike the harp and sing the songs of Zion for the entertainment of their captors. Notwithstanding the desperation with which this song is permeated, it is gratifying and encouraging; one feels that the Hebrew nation would never have perished had the whole nation always been imbued with such sentiments. . . .]

But even without any lofty considerations, simply in a human way, we are glad to see [the deliverance of] Katerina [even by death if it was impossible in any other way. As far as that goes, the drama itself gives us frightful evidence of the fact that life in the "realm of darkness" was worse than death]. Tikhon, throwing himself upon his wife's corpse when it is dragged out of the water, cries out in despair: "You are all right now, Katya! But why have I remained alive to live in torment?" With this exclamation the play ends, and in our opinion no more powerful and truthful end could have been found for it. Tikhon's words provide the clue to the play even for those who had not understood its substance earlier; they compel the spectator to think not of the love intrigue, but of this entire life [in which the living envy the dead, and what kind of dead—suicides!] Strictly speaking, Tikhon's exclamation is silly. The Volga is quite close. What prevents him from jumping into it if he is tired of life? But the whole trouble is that he finds life so hard because he is absolutely incapable of doing anything [even that upon which, as he himself realizes, his happiness and salvation depends. This moral depravity, this annihilation of a man, makes a more horrible impression upon us than any, even the most tragic event. In the latter we see sudden death, and end of suffering, relief from the necessity of serving as a miserable instrument in some abomination; but here there is constant, oppressive pain, enervation, a semi-corpse which has been rotting alive for many years. . . . To think that this living corpse is not unique, not an exception, that there is a vast mass of people who are subject to the corrupting influence of the Dikois and Kabanovas! To feel that there is no deliverance for them—is that not horrible? On the other hand, what a joyous, fresh life breathes for us from the healthy personality which finds the resolution to put an end to this decaying life at all cost!...]

With this we shall end. There is much that we have not discussed—the scene where Katerina and Boris meet at night, Kuligin's personality, which is also not without importance in the play, Varvara and Kudryash, Dikoi's conversation with Kabanova, and so on and so forth. This is because our aim has been to point to the general meaning of the play and, absorbed in the general, we could not enter sufficiently into an analysis of all the details. The literary judges will again be displeased; the artistic merit of the play has not been gauged and explained sufficiently, the best passages have not been indicated, a sharp line of demarcation has not been drawn between the secondary and the principal characters [and above all—art has again been made an instrument of a certain extraneous idea! ...] We are aware of all this, and we have only one answer to make: [let the readers judge for themselves (we assume that all have read or seen *The Thunderstorm*), *whether the idea we have pointed to is entirely extraneous to "The Thunderstorm,"* whether we have forced it upon the play *or whether it emerges logically from it,* whether it constitutes its substance and defines its direct meaning. . . . Whoever argues that we are wrong let him prove it, let him give another, more suitable meaning to the play. . . . If, however, our views are in keeping with the play, we ask for an answer to another question, namely: *does the living Russian nature really find expression in Katerina; are Russian conditions really reflected in everything that surrounds her, and are the demands of the nascent movement in Russian life truly reflected in the meaning of the play as we understand it?* If "not," if the reader does not recognize in it anything that is familiar, dear to his heart, close to his urgent requirements, then, of course, our labour has been wasted. But if "yes,"] if our readers, after pondering over our observations find that in *The Thunderstorm* the artist has indeed challenged Russian life and Russian strength to take determined action, and if they feel that such action is legitimate and important, then we shall be satisfied, no matter what our scholars and literary judges may say.

RUSSIAN CIVILIZATION AS CONCOCTED BY MR. ZHEREBTSOV[129]

ESSAI SUR L'HISTOIRE DE LA CIVILISATION
EN RUSSIE, par NICOLAS DE GEREBTZOFF.
Paris 1858, Two Volumes

> The moon is usually made in Hamburg,
> and it is made very badly.
> *Gogol (The Memoirs of a Lunatic)*

PATRIOTISM in the pure sense of the term, as a specific manifestation of a man's love for mankind, is quite natural and legitimate. As a vague and unconscious sentiment it appears with
the first development of a child's conceptions, as soon as it begins to distinguish between itself and objects around it. It is not
worth while, of course, speaking of this infantile patriotism as
of something lofty and important, but its importance during the
period of a man's childhood and adolescence cannot be denied.
During the first years of his life, a man is not yet able to conceive of abstract objects; still less can he understand the general
principles and the eternal laws of universal life. He possesses an
egoism which prompts him to seek for the best, and like all animals
of the gregarious species, he possesses a vague instinct which tells
him that the best can be found not in isolation, not in himself,
but in the society of others. The child's subsequent experience of
life day after day confirms and clarifies this dark surmise, and it
already begins to understand the connection that exists between its
own welfare and the welfare of others. At first it yields to the
desire to use the welfare of others for itself; it finds pleasure in
this, and this pleasure continues for a more or less lengthy period,
depending upon the extent to which its environment favours the
development in it of rapacious instincts. If the child develops normally, however, its egoism does not for long impel it to oppress
the personality and encroach upon the property of others for its
own benefit. Soon it begins to feel that by battening upon others
it again becomes isolated, alien to all, and seemingly the only
member of a separate species, the special function of which is to

devour everything around it. The realization that it is in such a
position becomes painful, because it runs counter to the natural
instincts of man and even of animals in general. This explains
why, as pedagogues have observed, the egoism of children remains
in that crude form which demands only the satisfaction of personal, exclusively animal requirements, only for a very short time.
As soon as thought awakens in the child and its mind begins to
work, its very egoism takes a different turn: its satisfaction calls
for sympathy towards others. And this is still further fostered by
the limitless services and assistance of every kind which elders
necessarily render a child. It is upon them that the child first
of all devotes that feeling of love which is natural in every man,
and which, in its subsequent development, must embrace the whole
of mankind. From this only a small step is needed to extend this
love to the objects, to the habits, to the ideas, etc., of the persons
who are loved. This is the origin of the charm, which many feel
to the end of their lives,

> Of native fields and hills,
> Native sky of enchanting hue,
> Familiar streams,
> The pleasant games of early years,
> And the first years at school.[130]

This sentiment cannot be condemned even in an adult, as long
as it remains a sentiment and the adult does not begin to mor-
alize about it. Nobody has a right to encroach upon my subjective
life. Who can reproach me if the sight of a table covered with a
Yaroslavl print tablecloth on which stands a steaming samovar,
or the strains of the sentimental song "When I Go Down to the
Brook" accompanied by a guitar, awaken in me bright recollections of my childhood? I may appear ridiculous to you by allowing these objects to create a stronger impression upon me than
you think they should; but even your ridicule will be inhumane
if, in yielding modestly to my subjective mood, I do not inconvenience others. It is another matter if I begin to thrust my sentiments upon others and insist that all those around me should share
them. In such a case, everybody has a perfect right to condemn
me and make fun of my fantasy, because it then assumes an
objective significance which becomes liable to the judgment of
others. When I demand that others should feel what I feel, I

thereby consider that the object which rouses a particular sentiment in me is capable of rousing that sentiment of itself and not
because of accidental relationships of significance to me alone.
And in taking this stand I am already expressing an opinion with
which others may not agree, and for which they may regard me
as an idiot. If, for example, I insist that others should admire a
silly song which is pleasant to me because it rouses in me recollections of my childhood, I thereby show that I do not think it
is silly but see real virtues in it. It is for this, of course, that
I will be regarded as a man who lacks aesthetic taste—but this
cannot be said of me merely on the grounds that I personally
feel pleasure on hearing this song. Every man, no matter what
his level of development may be, always retains certain habits,
predilections and memories, of which his heart cannot completely
rid itself even though his mind tells him that they are absurd.
This slight disharmony within a man is inevitable owing to the
weakness of human nature, and it should not be judged too sternly
as long as it does not find expression in a man's outward activities. But when it does, and a man demands that his childish dreams
should be accepted by others as truth, then he must be exposed
and attacked. And in exposing him we already have a perfect right
to say, without mincing words, that the gentleman who makes
such demands is stupid, and that the very demands that he makes
are pernicious, because they represent an attempt to thrust one's
own stupidity upon others.

Turning now to what, among us, is usually called patriotism,
we can apply to it much of what we have said about the impressions of childhood in general. In its first manifestation, patriotism
does not even assume any form other than that of a partiality for
native fields and hills, the pleasant games of early years, and
so forth. But fairly soon it assumes a more definite shape and
contains all the historical and civil concepts that the child has
managed to acquire. Up to a certain time, this patriotism is distinguished for complete and boundless devotion to *everything that
is one's own*—good or bad. The reason for this lack of discrimi-
nation is that the child does not yet properly understand the difference between bad and good, for it has few objects, or no objects
at all, for comparison. Not knowing that other towns exist, how
can a child express displeasure with the arrangement of its own

town? Living an unsophisticated life, guided in all things only by the desire to extend as much as possible the limits of its own egoism and to link it with the egoism of others, the child admires everything which, in whatever sense, it can call *its own*. In its subsequent development, when the acquisition of new concepts broadens its outlook, it begins to discern the good and bad sides of an object which had formerly appeared to it to be quite perfect. Thus, gradually passing from one thing to another, a man casts off his indiscriminate partiality and acquires a correct opinion first about his own family, his own village and his own county, and then about his province, another province and a third, the capital, and so forth. In the end he finally casts off local prejudices and admires only what constitute national or state features. But a man who develops normally cannot halt even at this stage of patriotism. He realizes that his feelings for his own country, strong and virile though they are, still lack that intelligent clarity which comes only from a study of a subject in conjunction with all analogous phenomena. Thus, a man whose development is not checked studies other nationalities and thereby rises from the idea of his own nation and state to the idea of nation and state in general; finally he grasps the abstract idea of mankind, so that he sees in every man he meets primarily a man and not a German, a Pole, a Jew, a Russian, and so forth. At this stage of development, what had been childish and dreamy in his patriotism, what had only roused childish fantasies unrelated to reality and common sense, must necessarily disappear. All the exclusive predilections, all the utopian dreams about the divine preordination of one nation for one thing and of another nation for another thing, all the disputes among nations about superiority, disappear from the mind of a man who is properly and fully developed. For him there no longer exist such questions as: boastful Pole or faithful Rūs? etc.; will the German or the Slavonic race be superior in coming centuries? etc. He already regards such discussions as phrasemongering, and they amuse him just as we are amused, for example, by the recrimination between Moscow and St. Petersburg which breaks out from time to time in our immature literature. But this theoretical indifference and indiscrimination towards nationalities must not lead to the deduction that a man's higher development has made him incapable of being patriotic. On the contrary, only this can make a man a real, genuine patriot—and for this reason.

When an educated man acquires a conception of the general, *i.e.*, of the permanent laws which govern the history of nations, when his world outlook is broadened to the degree of understanding the common needs and requirements of mankind, he feels a powerful urge to carry his theoretical views and convictions into the sphere of practical activity. But the sphere of a man's activities, or his strength and very wishes, cannot evenly cover the whole world and, therefore, he must choose some particular, limited sphere in which to apply his general convictions. This sphere will most likely, and most naturally, be his own country. We feel a closer kinship with our own country, we know it better and, consequently, our feelings for it are stronger. And these feelings do not in any way prejudice our love and respect for other nations; no, they are simply the outcome of our closer familiarity with one than with another. We can remain calm when we read in the newspaper that so many and so many people were killed in a collision; but the same news will affect us very profoundly if we read in the list of killed the names of people whom we know; it may plunge us into profound grief if our best friend is among the killed. But in grieving over him we do not think that the others were inferior to him and undeserving of our grief. Had we met them previously, perhaps we would grieve over them even more than we grieve over our friend, but fate did not bring us together, and we cannot grieve over all those who are killed. It is the same with patriotism: we feel more strongly for our own country because we know its needs better, we are better able to judge its position, we are more closely bound with it by our recollection of common interests and strivings, and lastly, we feel that we can be more useful to it than to any other country. Thus, in a decent man, patriotism is nothing more nor less than a desire to work for the benefit of one's country, and it springs from nothing else than a desire to do good—as much as possible and as well as possible. Hence, nobody can cast reproach at splendid workers if they transfer their activities from one country to another in the belief that they can be more useful there than in their own country. John Law applied his theories of finance in France. Lafayette took part in the American War of Independence, Byron fought on behalf of the Greeks: who, because of this, will accuse them of lacking patriotism? Quite naturally, one sought a sphere where he could more easily put his plans into operation, others hastened to the area where danger was greatest. The distinguishing feature of virile, active patriotism is precisely the fact that it precludes all international enmity, and a man who is inspired by such patriotism is ready to work for the whole of mankind, if only he can be useful to it. If he confines his activities to his own country, it is because he feels that this is his proper place, that this is where he can be most useful. This explains why the real patriot cannot bear to hear boastful and rapturous outcries about his own people; this explains why he looks with disdain upon those who try to draw lines of demarcation between races. Real patriotism, being a specific manifestation of love for mankind, is incompatible with dislike for individual nations; and as a virile and active phenomenon it cannot tolerate the least rhetoric which in any way reminds one of graveside speeches over a corpse. If we interpret patriotism in this way we will understand why it is developing with exceptional power in those countries where every individual is given considerable opportunity consciously to work for the benefit of society and to participate in its undertakings. . . .

. . . Of course, the struggle between aristocracy and democracy forms the entire content of history; but we would have a very poor understanding of history if we took it into our heads to limit it merely to genealogical interests. Behind this struggle there was always concealed another circumstance, far more important than abstract theories about breed and hereditary difference of blood between people of noble and people of low birth. The masses of the people have always felt, though vaguely and instinctively, as it were, what is now in the minds of educated and respectable people. In the eyes of the truly educated man there are no aristocrats and democrats, no lords and villeins, Brahmins and pariahs, there are only *working people* and *parasites*. To destroy the parasites and to raise labour to a higher status—such is the constant trend of history. It is by the degree to which labour is respected and appraised in accordance with its true value that we can tell the degree of a nation's civilization. The degree to which parasitism is possible and widespread among a nation can serve as an infallible index of whether its civilization is adequate or not. From this point of view it is not genealogical traditions, or the external harmony of the state organization, that should occupy the attention of the historian of a nation's education. Far more worthy of his attention are, on the one hand, the rights of the working classes, and on the other hand—parasitism in all its forms—whether in the deplorable *taboos* of savages in the Pacific Isles, Indian Brahminism, Persian satrapism, Roman patricianism, the tithes and feudalism of the Middle Ages, or in present-day tavern licensing, bribery, embezzlement of state funds, sponging, idling in government service, serfdom, mercenary marriages, ladies with camellias, and similar phenomena, which even the satirist has not yet dealt with. A study of all this will show the degree to which knowledge is disseminated among the people and the degree of their moral strength. Nowhere has parasitism, vanished, but everywhere it is gradually diminishing with the progress of education. Labour is despised by ignorant nations among whom robbery is regarded as a more honourable means of acquisition than work. Labour did not receive proper recognition throughout the entire world of antiquity, which only reached the stage of recognizing *some kinds* of work as being fit for the better classes of society, while leaving all other kinds to the slaves. Plato himself, in his republic, deemed it necessary to have a slave class to perform the manual labour necessary to supply the higher classes—governmental and military—with all their needs. In the Middle Ages—not to speak of feudalism—the best people were engrossed in the *artes liberales, i.e.*, only intellectual pursuits were regarded as being fit for free people; all other work was despised. In modern history, all work has received recognition; but no country to this day has reached the stage of being able properly to appraise labour fully in accord with its utility. Often, entirely unproductive occupations enjoy respect, while highly useful work is treated with disdain. True, parasitism today hides under the cloak of capital and of various commercial enterprises; nevertheless it exists everywhere, exploiting and oppressing the poor toilers whose labour is not fairly appraised. Clearly, all this is due to the fact that the amount of knowledge that is disseminated among the masses is still too insignificant to enable them to understand the relative values of things and the different relations between them. That is why, having renounced and condemned robbery under its real name, modern nations are still unable to discern this same robbery when the parasites disguise it under different fictitious names. True, the scale upon which robbery goes on now is not the same as it was before; the modern Luculluses and Vitelliuses are pygmies compared with those of ancient times. But still, there are little Luculluses, and there can be no doubt that they exploit very many people. From this standpoint, luxury is, indeed, one of the principal manifestations of social immorality, but not by any means because it softens and debilitates a man, diverts his thoughts from exalted ideas to material pleasures, etc. No, not at all—it is an indication of social immorality because it points to the deplorable state of society in which the blood and sweat of many toilers must be spent to maintain a single parasite. . . .

EXPLANATORY NOTES*

A LETTER TO V. V. LAVRSKY

1 Published in N. G. Chernyshevsky's *Materials for a Biography of N. A. Dobrolyubov, Collected in 1861-1862*, Vol. I, Moscow, 1890.

2 Variation of a passage from Lermontov's poem "Angel."

3 *Andrei Yegorovich* 'Vostokov, a teacher at the Seminary at Nizhni Novgorod.

4 *Orthodoxy, autocracy and nationality*—the motto proclaimed by S. S. Uvarov, a reactionary cabinet minister in the thirties and forties of the 19th century. By "nationality" he meant serfdom.

5 For reasons of the censorship Chernyshevsky omitted several words here, but put in a footnote: "Then follow examples of the subjects dealt with in the academies," meaning Theological Academies.

6 *Pravoslavny Sobesednik*, a theological magazine published in Kazan from 1885 onwards.

7 The references to the "corrupting breath of the turbulent West," "pernicious convictions," Herzen, etc., are, of course, ironical.

8 *Father Paissi*, a priest, an inspector of the Seminary in Nizhni Novgorod which Dobrolyubov attended. The Most Reverend *Jeremiah*, Bishop of Nizhni Novgorod.

THE IMPORTANCE OF AUTHORITY IN EDUCATION

9 This essay, first published in *Sovremennik* No. 5, 1857, was one of Dobrolyubov's first extensive expositions of his views on education. It was written as a review of an article entitled "Problems of Life," which caused considerable stir in Russia after the Crimean War, written by the celebrated Russian surgeon N. I. Pirogov and published in *Morskoi Sbornik*, No. 9, 1856. After the Crimean War Pirogov became one of the most popular public figures in Russia. The article referred to drew public attention because of the originality and boldness with which the author expressed views that were extremely progressive for that time. An enormous literature

---

* Words and phrases that had remained unfinished in the MSS. or in previous editions of Dobrolyubov's essays have been restored in this volume, but indicated by square brackets.

sprang up around that article, and it was translated into many European languages.

[10] In an article entitled "Domestic and Public Education," written in criticism of Pirogov's article.

[11] *Molchalin*, the hero in Griboyedov's comedy *Wit Works Woe*, a fawning and obsequious government official.

PROVINCIAL SKETCHES

[12] This essay was published in *Sovremennik*, No. 12, 1857.

[13] Shchedrin's "Provincial Sketches" began to appear in No. 8 of *Russki Vestnik*, 1856, when that magazine followed a moderate liberal trend and the editor, M. N. Katkov was not yet openly preaching the ideology of the autocracy and the serf owners.

[14] From Lermontov's poem "Thought."

[15] *Ilya Murom*, a hero of ancient Russian legend.

[16] From Lermontov's poem "Believe not Thyself."

[17] From Pushkin's poem "To the Slanderers of Russia."

[18] From Shcherbina's poem "To the Poet," (1855).

[19] *Nadimov*, the hero in Sollogub's comedy *The Government Official*.

[20] *The Alexandrinsky Theatre*, one of the oldest Russian theatres built in St. Petersburg in 1832.

[21] The words of the first comic in the finale of Gogol's *Inspector General*.

[22] From Zhukovsky's poem "Life."

[23] From Koltsov's poem "The Forest."

[24] From Koltsov's poem "Husbandman, Why Do You Sleep?"

[25] From Lermontov's poem "Thought."

[26] *Pechorin*, the principal character in Lermontov's *A Hero of Our Time*.

[27] *Rudin*, the hero in Turgenev's novel *Rudin*.

[28] A reference to Kapnist's comedy *The Talebearer*.

[29] A reference to Shchedrin's series of stories *Past Times* in his *Provincial Sketches*.

[30] From Karamzin's poem "Ilya of Murom."

[31] From Heine's poem "Zu fragmentarisch ist Welt und Leben."

A COMPARATIVE PHYSIOLOGICO-PSYCHOLOGICAL VIEW OF THE BEGINNING AND END OF LIFE

[32] This essay, published in *Sovremennik*, No. 3, 1858, was written in connection with the refusal of the students of the Kazan University to attend the lectures of Prof. Bervi. The work reviewed in this essay was

published in *The Scientific Papers of the Kazan University*, 1858. Its author, on graduating from the Medico-Surgical Academy, served as a ship's surgeon and later practised as an accoucheur. On the recommendation of the Minister for Education he was appointed to the Chair of Physiology at the Kazan University. Owing to the growth of the experimental materialist trend in the field of physiology, the idealistic views that were expounded by Prof. Bervi evoked the collective protest of his students and they refused to attend his lectures. As a result the professor was obliged to resign. The student "culprits," however, were threatened with dire punishment, but Dobrolyubov's essay helped them to escape the wrath of the authorities.

33 A variation on the lines in Derzhavin's ode "God."

34 A reference to the left-wing Hegelians: Strauss, Feuerbach, and others.

35 *Kifa Mokiyevich*, an anecdotal character in Gogol's *Dead Souls.*

36 Kurganov's *Epistolary*, a compilation of grammatical rules, stories, verses and anecdotes in circulation in Russia in the 18th and beginning of the 19th century.

THE ORGANIC DEVELOPMENT OF MAN IN CONNECTION WITH HIS MENTAL AND SPIRITUAL ACTIVITIES

37 This essay was published in *Sovremennik* No. 5, 1858.

38 *Prostakova* and *Skotinin*, characters in Fon-Vizin's comedy *Infant.*

39 *Pan Khalyavsky*, a historical novel by the Ukrainian author Kvitko-Osnovyanenko.

40 *Mitrofanushka*, a pampered little boy, the principal character in Fon-Vizin's comedy *Infant.*

41 Actually, Beethoven produced his finest works in the last years of his life when he was stone deaf.

42 From Pushkin's poem "To Kozlov," the blind poet.

THE FIRST YEARS OF THE REIGN OF PETER THE GREAT

43 These essays were published in *Sovremennik*, Nos. 6-8, 1858, (*Collected Works*, Vol. III). Only the "Third and Last Essay" is given in this edition as the most interesting exposition of Dobrolyubov's views on the philosophy of history.

44 Excerpt from V. G. Belinsky's review of Ustryalov's three volume *History of the Reign of Peter the Great.*

45 *The May Rebellion, i.e.*, the mutiny of the Streltzi or Musketeers, on May 15, 1682.

46 The Dissenter movement in 1682, led by the Suzdal priest *Nikita Pustosvyat.*

THE WORKS OF V. BELINSKY

[47] This comment was published in *Sovremennik*, No. 4, 1859, on the announcement of the publication of the first volumes of the works of V. G. Belinsky after an eight years' ban not only on the works of the great critic but also on his name.

[48] The editorial staff of *Sovremennik* at that time consisted of Chernyshevsky, Nekrasov and Panayev. The two latter joined the staff with Belinsky in 1847.

[49] A reference to Chernyshevsky's essays on "The Gogol Period of Russian Literature," which dealt with Belinsky's work as a revolutionary critic and were published in *Sovremennik* in 1855-1856. Dobrolyubov himself wrote about Belinsky in his essay "When Will the Day Come," in this volume.

WHAT IS OBLOMOVSHCHINA?

[50] This essay was published in *Sovremennik*, No. 5, 1859. The epigraph, slightly misguided, is from Vol. II of Gogol's *Dead Souls*. Goncharov's novel was published in *Otechestvenniye Zapiski*, Nos. 1-4, 1859. Hence, Dobrolyubov reviewed it immediately on its appearance.

[51] In addition to its theoretical content, this essay was of exceptional importance for a literary-historical biography of Goncharov, for it revealed to wide circles of readers that the author of *Oblomov* was one of the greatest Russian novelists.

[52] In 1849 *Literaturny Sbornik* published an excerpt from Goncharov's novel entitled *Oblomov's Dream*.

[53] A variation of a passage from Tyutchev's poem "Silentium."

[54] *A Hero of Our Time*, a novel by Lermontov; *Who Is to Blame?* a novel by I. Herzen; *Rudin*, a novel by Turgenev; *Unwanted* (full title: *The Diary of an Unwanted Man*) a novel by Turgenev; *Hamlet from Shchigry County*, a story by Turgenev.

[55] *Tentetnikov*, one of the characters in Gogol's *Dead Souls*, Vol. II, Beltov, the principal character in Herzen's novel *Who Is to Blame?*

[56] From Pushkin's *Eugene Onegin*.

[57] From Chap. 4 of Nekrasov's poem "Sasha." The two lines lower down are also from the same source.

[58] From Pushkin's *Eugene Onegin*.

[59] From Pushkin's *Eugene Onegin*.

[60] From Pushkin's *Eugene Onegin*.

[61] From Benedictov's poem "A Modern Prayer."

[62] Murazov and Konstanzhoglo, characters in Gogol's *Dead Souls*, Vol. II.

REALM OF DARKNESS

63 This essay was published in *Sovremennik* No. 7, 1859. As the historians of Russian literature observe, none of Ostrovsky's closest friends on the staff of the Slavophile magazine *Moskvityanin* who praised the playwright in poetry and prose succeeded in making such a profound analysis of his plays as Dobrolyubov did in this essay.

64 Ostrovsky's play *Our Own Folks—We'll Settle It Among Ourselves*, was published in *Moskvityanin* No. 6, 1850. It was appraised by literary circles as an outstanding Russian play even before it appeared. The "accident" referred to in the next line was the persecution of the police censorship. The authorities summoned him with the object of "bringing him to his senses," he was put under police surveillance and the tsar forbade its performance on the stage.

65 Here and further on Dobrolyubov quotes from Apollon Grigoryev's poem "Art and Truth." *Apollon Grigoryev* (1822-1864) was a poet and critic who in his essays advocated the theory of "pure art."

66 *D. V. Grigorovich* (1822-1899), author of *Anton Goremyka, The Village, Migrants* and other novels, a member of the staff of *Sovremennik*.

67 *Eugenie Tour* (1815-1892), the pen name of Countess Salias de Tournemir, authoress of numerous novels, short stories and essays.

68 From Pushkin's *Eugene Onegin*.

69 *A. F. Veltman* (1800-1870), poet, author and archeologist.

70 *Lugansky, Lugansky the Cossack*, the pen name of V. I. Dahl (1801-1872), author, ethnographist and compiler of the *Dictionary of the Living Great-Russian Language*.

71 *I. T. Pososhkov* (1652-1726), a prominent publicist and economist in the reign of Peter I, author of a treatise on "Scarcity and Riches."

72 *T. I. Philippov* (1825-1899), Slavophile publicist.

73 *N. D. Akhsharumov* (1819-1893), author and critic, a contributor to *Otechestvenniye Zapiski, Russki Vestnik, Epokha,* and other magazines.

74 These and other quotations in this essay are slightly amended excerpts or combination of excerpts from the articles mentioned.

75 *B. P. Almazov*, (1827-1876) a contributor to *Moskvityanin*.

76 *V. A. Sollogub* (1814-1882), author of the tale *Tarantas* and the comedy *The Government Official*.

N. M. Lvov (1821-1872), author of the comedy *There Are Good People in the World*, and others, and editor of the satirical journal *Veselchak*.

77 *Oryel*, a reactionary magazine of which only four numbers were issued in 1859.

78 By referring to the first edition of *Our Own Folks*, Dobrolyubov is hinting at the revisions Ostrovsky made for the second edition on the insistence of the censor.

⁷⁹ *M. P. Rosenheim* (1820-1887), poet, contributor to *Otechestvenniye Zapiski* and *Russki Vestnik.*

⁸⁰ A reference to Gogol's *Selected Passages From Correspondence With Friends,* the reactionary feudal trend of which evoked a sharp protest from Belinsky, expressed in the latter's "A Letter to Gogol."

⁸¹ *A. A. Potekhin* (1829-1908), a playwright of the Ostrovsky school.

⁸² From Lermontov's poem "Three Palms."

⁸³ Variation of the concluding lines from Lomonosov's *Ode Chosen From Job.*

CHENSKY'S COURTSHIP OR MATERIALISM AND IDEALISM. THE INEVITABILITY OF IDEALISM IN MATERIALISM

⁸⁴ This essay was published in *Sovremennik* No. 8, 1859. By reviewing two such totally different productions in one essay Dobrolyubov wished to emphasize the mediocrity of both.

⁸⁵ From Ostrovsky's play *A Holiday Dream Before Dinner.*

⁸⁶ *N. F. Koshansky* (1781-1831), professor of literature at the Lyceum in Tsarskoe Selo. Author of two textbooks on rhetoric.

⁸⁷ A reference to a reactionary book by Barkov and Kulzhinsky. *Modern Ideas* ... which Dobrolyubov reviewed in an essay entitled "The Voice of the Ancient Church of Russia."

⁸⁸ *E. Dimman,* author of *The Science of Life or How a Young Man Should Live. M. Miller-Krasovsky,* author of *The Fundamental Laws of Education.* Both books were published in 1859, and were expositions of the author's reactionary views on the upbringing of the young generation.

WHEN WILL THE DAY COME?

⁸⁹ This essay was published in *Sovremennik* No. 3, 1860. The revolutionary ideas expressed in this essay roused indignation among the liberals and gave rise to a vociferous controversy in literary circles.

⁹⁰ *A Thousand Souls,* a novel by A. F. Pisemsky.

⁹¹ *Fet* (Shenshin) *A. A.* (1820-1892). A Russian lyrical poet.

⁹² *Timofei Nikolayevich* Granovsky (1813-1855), professor of history at the Moscow University.

⁹³ *S. M. Solovyov* (1820-1879) Russian historian. Professor at the Moscow University.

⁹⁴ From Tyutchev's poem "To the Russian Woman," first published in 1850 under the title "To My Countrywoman." *F. I. Tyutchev* (1803-1873), Russian lyrical poet.

GOOD INTENTIONS AND ACTION
TALES AND SHORT STORIES BY A. PLESHCHEYEV

95 This essay was published in *Sovremennik* No. 7, 1860. *A. N. Ple-shcheyev* (1825-1893), Russian author and member of a revolutionary circle formed in St. Petersburg in the 1840's by the utopian socialist M. V. Petrashevsky. Denounced by a provocateur, the members of this circle were arrested. Many of them were sentenced to death, but the sentences were commuted to penal servitude and exile to Siberia. Among literary men who were members of this circle were Dostoevsky, Saltykov-Shchedrin, Pleshcheyev and Maikov.

96 Madame *Kokhanovskaya*, the pen name of N. S. Sokhanskaya (1825-1884), an authoress, the keynote of whose writings was "submission."

97 *P. P. Kamensky*, author (died in the seventies of the 19th century). *M. I. Voskresensky*, novelist of the 1830's-1850's, died in 1867. *V. A. Vonlyar-lyarsky* (1814-1852), author of numerous novels and short stories.

98 A reference to Grigorovich's *Anton Goremyka* (*Poor Anton*), Dostoevsky's *Poor Folks*, Butkov's *The Pinnacles of St. Petersburg* and Nekrasov's *The Nooks of St. Petersburg*.

99 Long silence owing to his exile in connection with the Petrashevsky circle case and to the long period he lived in the provinces.

100 *Frederika Bremer* (1801-1865), a Swedish authoress.

101 *P. S. Mochalov* (1800-1848), a celebrated Russian tragedian.

102 A reference to the Bulgarian Insarov in Turgenev's *On the Eve*.

FEATURES FOR THE CHARACTERIZATION OF THE
RUSSIAN COMMON PEOPLE

103 This essay was published in *Sovremennik* No. 8, 1860. *Marco Vovchok* (the pen name of M. A. Markovich) (1834-1907), a Ukrainian authoress.

104 A reference to Marco Vovchok's *Ukrainian Popular Stories*, translated into Russian and with a preface by Turgenev.

105 A reference to *A. V. Druzhinin* (1824-1864), who, under the pen name of I. Chernoknizhnikov, wrote banal feuilletons.

106 *Kuzma Prutkov*, the joint pen name of the brothers Zhemchuzhnikov, Alexander, Alexei and Vladimir, and Count K. Tolstoy, who wrote a book of satire containing the banal utterances of the fictitious author "Kuzma Prutkov." It is considered a classic of Russian humorous literature of the 19th century. Many of Prutkov's sayings have gone into the language as illustrations of banal wit and wisdom.

107 *Oleg* (approx. 879-912) Prince of Novgorod, captured Kiev, became Prince of the United Novgorod-Kiev State. *Igor* (912-945), Grand Prince of Kiev. *Svyatoslav* (957-972), one of the outstanding Princes of Kiev Rūs

[108] Dobrolyubov here refers to his humorous verses entitled *A Friendly Correspondence Between Moscow and St. Petersburg* in No. 4 of *Svistok*, the satirical supplement to *Sovremennik*.

[109] In his *Introduction* to *Provincial Sketches* Saltykov-Shchedrin describes how a police inspector interrogates a peasant with the aid of "applause," *i.e.*, slaps in the face.

[110] A reference to the celebrated publicist Proudhon.

[111] *I. Y. Gorlov* (1814-1890), professor of political economy and statistician. In his *Principles of Political Economy* Prof. Gorlov wrote that the emancipation of the slaves caused a decline in the production of sugar in the West Indies.

[112] A reference to the revolutionary movement in Europe in 1848-1849.

[113] From Khomyakov's poem, "Russia." *A. S. Khomyakov* (1804-1860), Russian author and poet.

[114] *S. P. Svechina* (1782-1850), a Russian authoress of a religious and mystical trend.

A RAY OF LIGHT IN THE REALM OF DARKNESS

[115] This essay was published in *Sovremennik* No. 10, 1860.

[116] *N. P. Nekrasov* (1828-1913), literary critic, a contributor to *Atenei*.

[117] *I. I. Davydov*, Principal of the Central Pedagogical Institute. *M. B. Chistyakov* (1809-1885), pedagogue and author of books for children. *K. L. Zelenetsky* (1812-1858), a professor at the Lyceum in Odessa and author of textbooks on Russian literature.

[118] A reference to the author N. F. Pavlov (1805-1864), who in a review on *The Thunderstorm* wrote that the "play is immoral."

[119] In his review of Sollogub's *Tarantas* Belinsky ridiculed the author's reactionary Slavophilism.

[120] *Mr. P.*—A. Palkhovsky, literary critic and contributor to *Moskovskiye Vedomosti*.

[121] *V. G. Plaksin*, a teacher of literature at the St. Petersburg Cadet School.

[122] The Reader's Words in Lermontov's poem "The Journalist, the Reader and the Author."

[123] *Friedrich Theodor Fischer* (1807-1887), a German philosopher of the Hegelian school.

[124] *P. V. Annenkov* (1812-1887), a writer on the history of literature, wrote a review of *The Thunderstorm* in which he criticized the review of that play written by Pavlov.

[125] *I. A. Krylov* (1766-1844), the celebrated Russian fabulist. The lines are from his fable "The Peasant and the Fox."

126 *Maikov of Moscow*, A. A. Maikov, a Slavophile. Wrote a review of Pisemsky's *A Bitter Fate* for 'Sankt Peterburgskiye Vedomosti*, 1860.

127 *Prince Lupovitsky, or a Visit to the Country*, a play by K. S. Aksakov, playwright and publicist (1817-1860).

128 A variation of the author's reply in Lermontov's poem "The Journalist, the Reader and the Author."

RUSSIAN CIVILIZATION AS CONCOCTED BY Mr. ZHEREBTSOV

129 This essay was published in *Sovremennik* Nos. 10 and 11, 1858. *N. A. Zherebtsov*, the author of the work reviewed in this essay, was born in 1807 and died in 1868. Only two excerpts from this essay are given in this volume.

130 A variation of Zhukovsky's Russian translation of Schiller *The Maid of Orleans*.

NAME INDEX

A

Adrian — 113, 168
Aeschines — 58
Afanasi, Archbishop — 119
Akhsharumov — 225, 234, 452, 553
Alexander of Macedon — 86, 144
Alexei Mikhailovich, Tsar — 146-150, 167
Alexei Petrovich, Tsarevich — 113, 149
Almazov — 234
Annenkov — 556
Apraksin, F. M. — 119, 123, 124, 132
Aristophanes — 58, 232, 568
Aristotle — 78, 554
Augustus — 142

B

Bacon — 63
Balashevich — 275
Ban — 127
Bauer, Bruno — 4
Barkov — 381, 382
Beethoven — 75, 84
Belinsky — 4, 172, 173, 291, 394, 395, 550
Benedictov — 212
Bervi, Wilhelm — 62-71, 100
Bezobrazov, Nikolai — 541
Bibro — 89
Blair — 551
Blank, Grigori — 541
Blumenbach — 63
Bock, K. E. — 72, 87, 92-98, 103
Böhm — 6
Böhmer, F. — 72

Bonaparte — 267
Bougainville — 63
Brandt, Carsten — 111, 113, 157
Bremer, Frederika — 444
Bright — 487
Buturlin — 120
Byron — 75, 440, 565, 633

C

Caesar, Julius — 86
Cherkassky — 166
Chernoknizhnikov, Ivan Alexandrovich — 465
Chistyakov — 546
Cicero — 63
Cleon — 58
Cocles, Horatius — 86
Corneuille — 440
Cushke — 90
Cuvier — 90

D

Dalberg — 142, 143
Daniel, the Pilgrim — 580
Dante — 439, 565
David — 116
Davydov, Ivan — 546, 547, 551
Demosthenes — 58
Derzhavin — 10
Dimman — 382
Diogenes — 144
Dobrolyubov, N. — 5
Dolgorukys — 112
Du Bois-Reymond — 63

E

Eschenmayer — 63

F

Favre — 487
Fet — 242, 392
Feuerbach — 4, 409
Fichte — 64
Fletcher — 147
Flourens — 191
Francis — 547
Frederick William — 142
Fyodor, Tsar — 147-149

G

Garibaldi — 547
Godunov, Boris — 147, 148
Goethe — 70, 440, 565
Gogol — 22, 34, 173, 174, 210,
218, 227, 232, 233, 291, 545,
546, 569, 629
Golitsyn — 149-151
Golitsyn, Boris Alexeyevich — 116,
122
Golitsyns — 112
Goncharov I. A. — 174-182, 204,
205, 210-214
Gordon, Patrick — 111, 113, 117,
119, 124-128, 134, 157, 161
Gorlov — 485
Grames, John — 120
Granovsky — 450
Grigorovich — 221
Grigoryev, Apollon — 572, 573

H

Hauser, Kaspar — 94
Hegel — 64
Heine — 57, 388
Herzen — 4
Hohenstaufen — 407
Homer — 76, 84, 439, 440
Hulst — 111

I

Igor, Prince — 467
Ivan Grozny — 147, 535

J

Jeremiah — 5
Joachim, Patriarch — 113

K

Kalam — 84
Kamensky — 441
Kapnist — 55
Karamzin — 147, 148, 159, 170,
447, 546
Karlowicz — 153-156
Khalyavsky — 72
Khomyakov — 486
Kikodze, Archimandrite Gavriil —
374
Kokhanovskaya — 439
Kokorev — 165
Kort — 111
Koshansky — 546, 547
Koshikhin — 147, 151-153, 295
Kostomarov — 463
Kotsebu — 227
Kreitz, A. — 468
Krevst — 111
Kreyss — 163
Krylov — 570
Kuhlmann — 112
Kulzhinsky — 381
Kurbatov — 163
Kurganov — 68

L

Lafayette — 633
Lavoisier — 63, 64
Lavrsky, V. V. — 3
Lebedev, P. S. — 382
Lefort — 109-111, 113-114, 116, 117
119, 124, 125, 127, 128, 135,
157
Leonidas of Sparta — 86
Lermontov, M. Y. — 3, 204, 287,
440, 553
Liebig — 63
Lomonosov — 108, 328
Lopukhins — 112
Louis XIV — 70, 112
Loyola, Ignatius — 76, 81
Lucullus — 636
Lugansky — 223
Lvov, N. — 240, 596

M

Maikov — 439, 595
Markell — 113

Megden — 111
Menshikov, Alexander — 159
Mikhail Fyodorovich, Tsar — 146
Miller-Krasovsky — 382
Miloslavsky, Ivan Mikhailovich — 150, 160
Miltiades — 58
Milton — 76
Mochalov — 450
Mohammed — 76
Moleschott — 63, 89
Molière — 232
Morozov — 150

N

Nadimov — 34
Napoleon — 70, 86, 142, 186, 580 592
Naryshkin, Lev Kirillovich — 116, 122
Naryshkins — 112
Natalya Kirillovna, Tsarina — 113, 118
Nefimonov, Kuzma — 152, 155
Nekrasov, N. P. — 230, 274, 275, 545, 560
Nero — 446
Newton — 70
Nikitin, Ivan — 542

O

Oken — 64
Oleg, a Prince of ancient Russia — 467
Ollivier — 487
Osnovyanenko — 72
Ostrovsky — 218, 219, 221-234, 238-240, 242 244, 247-250, 254, 256, 261, 264, 268, 269, 271, 273-275, 277, 278, 285-287, 289-291, 293-296, 303, 304, 307-309, 312, 318, 328, 335, 339, 342, 346, 347, 353, 355-357, 361, 363, 364, 366-369, 371, 374, 440, 508, 543-545, 549, 551, 552, 553, 555, 560, 562, 568, 570-578, 580, 594, 599, 602, 614, 615, 624
Orlov-Davydov — 541

P

P. (Palkhovsky) — 550, 551, 560
Paissi, Father — 5
Patkul — 156, 163
Pavlov, N. F. — 514, 545, 552, 554, 555-557, 560
Pell, P. A. — 63
Perry — 140
Pestallozzi — 28
Peter the Great — 86, 104, 108-126, 129-171, 222, 535, 596
Philip of Macedon — 58
Philippov, Terti — 223, 517
Pirogov — 6-8, 27, 574
Pisemsky — 439
Plato — 64, 568, 635
Pleshcheyev — 439-443, 445, 446, 455, 457-461
Pleyer — 128
Plinius — 63
Pososhkov — 223
Potekhin — 299
Poulsen, J. — 72
Protasyev — 140, 152
Prutkov, Kuzma Petrovich — 465, 595
Pushkin — 10, 56, 76, 204, 467, 569
Pustosvyat, Nikita — 151

R

Rachel — 220
Racine — 546
Raphael — 84, 508
Razin, Stepan — 148, 149
Regulus — 70, 162
Richelieu — 142
Romodanovsky — 115, 116, 161, 165, 166
Romodanovskys — 112
Rosenheim — 291

S

Sand, George — 49, 444
Savich, Y. — 373, 374, 376-378, 380-387
Say — 191
Scaevola, Mucius — 86, 162
Schelling — 64, 434
Schiller — 3

Schnell, K. F.—72, 88, 100, 102, 103
Schubert, Anthropologist — 63
Scipio — 70
Scott, Walter — 440
Sederholm — 13, 17, 18
Seneca — 63
Schafirov — 137, 138, 159
Shakespeare — 84, 219, 232, 233, 271, 439, 440, 546, 565, 579
Shchedrin — 30, 35-37, 40, 42, 45, 49, 50, 55, 58-60, 442, 471
Shchepkin — 173, 463
Shein — 166
Sheremetev — 129
Sheremetev, Boris Petrovich — 122
Sheremetev, Peter Vassilyevich — 117
Shevyrev — 517
Socrates — 68, 568
Sokovnin — 160
Soldatenkov, K. — 173, 463
Sollogub — 240, 290, 550, 596
Solomon — 116, 213, 344, 366
Solovyov — 421
Sophia, Tsarina — 110, 112, 147, 149, 150, 153, 162
Staël, Mme. de — 29
Strauss — 4
Streshnev — 115, 166
Streshnev, Tikhon Nikitich — 119
Streshnevs — 112
Sue, Eugene — 596
Sumarokov — 55
Suvorov — 86
Svechina — 541
Svyatoslav, Prince — 467
Swert — 128

T

Themistocles — 58
Tiedeman — 90
Timmerman — 111, 113, 150, 157
Tolstoy, N. — 541
Tour, Eugenie — 221
Tsikler — 160

Turgenev — 176, 204, 388, 389, 391-393, 395-399, 402, 403, 412, 414, 415, 419, 439, 442, 457, 461, 463, 554
Tyutchev — 242

U

Ukraintsev Emelyan — 152, 155, 159
Ustryalov — 104, 108, 110, 111, 113, 115-117, 119, 120, 122, 133, 136, 138, 142, 143, 145, 146, 151, 152, 160-162, 164, 166, 169-171.

V

Valentine — 91
Veltman — 223
Verdi — 84
Vernadsky — 570
Vikula, Priest — 165
Vinius — 111, 121, 139, 155
Vischer — 554
Vitellius — 636
Vladimir, Grand Prince — 135
Vogt — 63, 90
Voltaire — 20, 70, 546
Vonlyarlyarsky — 441
Voskresensky — 441
Vostokov, Andrei Yegorovich — 4.
Vovchok, Marco — 463-466, 469, 471, 472, 478, 485, 488, 491, 495, 508, 513, 525, 531, 538-542

W

Weide, Adam — 127

Z

Zelenetsky — 546
Zeno — 44
Zhelyabuzhski — 152
Zherebtsov — 629
Zotov, Nikita Moiseyevich — 117